Götz-Dietrich Opitz

Haitian Refugees Forced to Return

Nordamerikastudien

Münchener Beiträge zur Kultur und Gesellschaft
der USA, Kanadas und der Karibik

herausgegeben von

Prof. Dr. Berndt Ostendorf

(Amerika Institut)
(Universität München)

Band 2

LIT

Götz-Dietrich Opitz

Haitian Refugees Forced to Return
Transnationalism and State Politics, 1991 – 1994

LIT

Cover Picture: Krome Detention Center in Miami where Haitians are held, June 1991 (courtesy Maggie Steber)

Umschlaggestaltung: Marion Aichele, München

Bibliographic information published by Die Deutsche Bibliothek
Die Deutsche Bibliothek lists this publication in the Deutsche Nationalbibliografie; detailed bibliographic data are available in the Internet at http://dnb.ddb.de.

ISBN 3-8258-4544-3

Zugl.: München, Univ., Diss., 1999

© LIT VERLAG Münster 2004
Grevener Str./Fresnostr. 2   48159 Münster
Tel. 0251-23 50 91   Fax 0251-23 19 72
e-Mail: lit@lit-verlag.de   http://www.lit-verlag.de

Distributed in North America by:

Transaction Publishers
New Brunswick (U.S.A.) and London (U.K.)

Transaction Publishers
Rutgers University
35 Berrue Circle
Piscataway, NJ 08854

Tel.: (732) 445 - 2280
Fax: (732) 445 - 3138
for orders (U. S. only):
toll free (888) 999 - 6778

Acknowledgments

This study was accepted as a doctoral thesis at the University of Munich in the summer semester 1998. A longer version was published in 1999 as a microedition by Tectum in Marburg. This book is in many ways the product of a collaborative effort. It would have not been possible without the assistance and support of many people. First of all, I am appreciative of the help given throughout the process by my doctoral advisor Prof. Dr. Berndt Ostendorf at the Amerika Institut. I am indebted to the *German Marshall Fund of the United States* for its generous financial support. It made possible for me to work as a Congressional Fellow for the Hon. Charles B. Rangel in 1992 and to conduct ethnographic field work in New York City from 1994-1995. I have benefited immensely from Mr. Rangel´s sustained support. His legislative director, Emile Milne, first aroused my interest in Haitian affairs when I assisted him on Capitol Hill.

I am especially indebted to my dear friend Jennifer Trice who gave me the emotional support needed during my research stay. So did my hosts in Brooklyn, the Haitian family I lived with in 1994-1995. I owe, of course, special thanks to the many Haitian as well as American informants whom I met and talked to in the course of my stay. Jocelyn McCalla, executive director of NCHR, was especially helpful in granting me so much interviewing time. Carolle Charles, anthropologist at Baruch College in New York City, was of invaluable assistance in working through problems and concepts. The University of Munich granted me a post-graduate fellowship upon my return to write up my thesis. I am also very grateful to Maggie Steber, American Pulitzer-prize-winning photographer, for giving me permission to reprint some of her pictures. Last not least many thanks to Betsy Wentzel, who read parts of an earlier draft, and to David Mullinger for reading the entire manuscript and for offering constructive criticism for the final form of this study.

To My Son Levin Elias

Abbreviations (124)

10e of New York:	10th Department Organization of New York
AAHP:	American Association of Haitian Physicians
ABA:	American Bar Association
ACT UP:	AIDS Coalition to Unleash Power
ACTWU:	Amalgamated Clothing & Textile Workers Union
ADH:	Artists for Democracy in Haiti
AEH:	Alliance des Émigrés Haitiens/Wilson Désir's Office
AfA:	Americans for Aristide
AFL-CIO:	American Federation of Labor/Congress of Industrial Organizations
AIFLD:	American Institute for Free Labor Development
AJC:	American Jewish Committee
APN:	Assemblée Populaire Nationale
BfA:	Brooklyn for Aristide
CABP:	Counseil d'Administration du Barreau de Philadelphie
CARICOM:	Caribbean Community and Common Market
CATH:	Central Autonome des Travailleurs Haitiens
CAU:	Comité d'Action Unitaire
CBC:	Congressional Black Caucus
CBI:	Caribbean Basin Initiative
CCR:	Center for Constitutional Rights
CCRH:	Comité Contre la Répression en Haiti
CDC:	Centers for Disease Control
CEH:	Conféderation des Étudiants Haitiens
CEIP:	Carnegie Endowment for International Peace
CGT:	Centrale Générale des Travailleurs/Central of Haitian Workers
CHADEL:	Haitian Human Rights Center
CHC:	Coalition for Haitian Concerns
CHRCL:	Center for Human Rights and Constitutional Law
CIP:	Center for International Policy
CIRR:	International Congress of Resistance and Return
CJP:	Haitian Commission Justice et Paix/Justice and Peace Commission
CLAA:	Caribbean Latin American Action
CNG:	Gonseil National Gouvernement
CODH:	Centre Oecuménique pour les Droits Humains
CPL:	Coalition Patrice Lumumba
CRP:	Crowing Rooster Productions

CTH:	Confédération des Travailleurs Haitiens
CWS:	Church World Service
CWS/IRP:	CWS's Immigration and Refugee Program
ECHR:	Emergency Coalition for Haitian Refugees
EMM:	Episcopal Migration Ministries
FAIR:	Federation for American Immigration Reform
FDA:	Food and Drug Administration
FNCD:	National Front for Change and Democracy
FONDEM:	Fondation Développement et Démocratie
FRAPH:	Front pour l'Avancement et le Progrès d'Haiti/Haitian Front for Adv. and Progress
GE:	Global Exchange
GIA:	Governors Island Agreement of July 3, 1993
HACSO:	Haitian American Cultural and Social Organization
HAIC:	Comité Contre l'Intervention en Haiti/Haiti Anti-Intervention Committee
Haiti Commission	Commission Indépendente d'Enquête sur le Coup d'Etat du 29 Septembre
HAUP:	Haitian Americans United for Progress
HCA:	Haitian Community Association
HCAIDS:	Haitian Coalition on AIDS
HCC:	Haitian Centers Council
HEAR:	Haitian Enforcement Against Racism
HM:	Haiti en Marche
HNSC:	Haitian Neighborhood Service Center
HO:	Haiti Observateur
HoC:	Home of Champions
HP:	Haiti Progrès
HRC:	Haitian Refugee Center
HRW/A:	Human Rights Watch/Americas
HSN:	Haitian Solidarity Network
HWHR:	Haitian Women for Haitian Refugees
HWP:	Haitian Women Program
IACHR:	Inter-American Commission for Human Rights
ICB:	Inner City Broadcasting
ICP:	In-Country Processing of refugee claims:
ILGWU:	International Ladies Garment Workers Union
INS:	Immigration and Naturalization Service
IPS:	Inter Press Service
JCRC:	Jewish Community Relations Council
JLC:	Jewish Labor Committee

JRS:	Jesuit Refugee Service/USA
KOZA:	Komite Pou Zafè Ayisyen/Haitian Affairs Committee
LIRS:	Lutheran Immigration and Refugee Service
MPP:	Movement Paysan de Papaye
NAACP:	National Association for the Advancement of Colored People
NACLA:	North American Congress on Latin America
NCCB:	National Conference of Catholic Bishops
NCHR:	National Coalition for Haitian Refugees
ND:	Newsday
NED:	National Endowment for Democracy
NGO:	Non-Governmental Organization
NIF:	National Immigration Forum
NLC:	National Labor Committee
NSC:	National Security Council
NYAN:	New York Amsterdam News
NYANA:	New York Association For New Americans
NYPD:	New York Police Department
NYT:	New York Times
OAS:	Organization of American States
ORR:	Office of Refugee Resettlement
PLANOP:	Plateforme des Organisations Populaire
Platform	Plate-forme des Organismes Haitien de Défense des Droit Humains
Prominex:	Center for the Promotion of Investment and Export
QC/QP:	Quixote Center/Quest for Peace
SCLC:	Southern Christian Leadership Conference
SIN:	National Intelligence Service
TNC:	Transnational Corporation
TPS:	Temporary Protected Status
UN:	United Nations
UN/OAS-ICM:	UN/OAS International Civilian Mission
UNGA:	General Assembly of the UN
UNSC:	UN Security Council
US:	United States
USAID:	United States Agency for International Development
USCC:	United States Catholic Conference
USCC/MRS:	USCC´s Migration and Refugee Services
USCG:	US Coast Guard
USCR:	United States Committee for Refugees

USHIA:	US-Haitian Interdiction Agreement of 1981
USJD:	US Justice Department
USSC:	US Supreme Court
USSD:	US State Department
USTD:	US Treasury Department
VoA:	Voice of America
VOAM:	Voye Ayiti Monte
volag:	voluntary agency
WOH:	Washington Office on Haiti
WP:	Washington Post

Table of Contents

1 Introduction _____ 13
1.1 Autobiographical Information and Course of Examination _____ 15
1.2 Research Methods and Sources of Information _____ 20
1.3 Structure of Study and Mode of Presentation _____ 25
2 Brief Review of Literature _____ 29
2.1 Globalization and Transnationalism _____ 29
2.2 Refugee Studies and Haitian Community Studies _____ 34
2.3 A Relational Theory of Transnationalism _____ 38
    2.3.1 "Nationalistic" and "Ethnic" Organizing in the Context of Refugee Flows _ 45
3 Methodological Considerations Regarding the First Level of Analysis _____ 51
3.1 The New York Times as a Newspaper Relying on Governmental Sources _ 51
3.2 The New York Times as a Repository of American Cultural Values _____ 53
3.3 The New York Times as a Newspaper Possibly Affecting Haitians´ Views _ 55
4 The Haitian Crisis in the Context of International State Relations _____ 60
4.1 The New York Times´ Folk Model: Representing the Haitian Crisis _____ 60
5 Nationalistic and Ethnic Organizing: Responding to the Haitian Crisis _____ 65
5.1 Responses to the US Mainstream Media´s Coverage of the Haitian Crisis _ 68
5.2 Fighting the Cause I: Working for Aristide´s Return from Within Through Resistance and Mobilization (Direct Transnational Relations) _____ 73
    5.2.1 Starting to Get Organized: Street Rallies as Emotional and Moral Support _ 73
    5.2.2 Broadening the Effort: Outside Help in Denouncing the Military Junta _____ 78
    5.2.3 Showing Monied Muscle: Material Support for the Victims of Repression _ 86
    5.2.4 NCHR´s First Post-Coup Reports: Human Rights Before, After the Coup _ 94
    5.2.5 The Role of Haiti´s Free Press and the *Macoute* Onslaught in the US _____ 100
    5.2.6 The Aid of Moving Pictures: Documenting the Repression in Haiti on Film 106
    5.2.7 The Haitian Diaspora and US-Haitian Economic Societal Transnationalism 110
    5.2.8 NCHR´s Further Post-Coup Reports: Repression and Dislocation in Haiti _ 115

5.3 Fighting the Cause II: Working for Aristide´s Return from Without by Means of Sanctions and World Opinion (Indirect Transnational Relations) ___ 119
    5.3.1   From Initial Euphoria over Successes to First Signs of Skepticism_____ 119
    5.3.2   NCHR´s Role in US Foreign Policy, Toward International Organizations _ 122
    5.3.3   Exposing a Hypocritical US at the Bar of Public World Opinion _____ 127
    5.3.4   Growing Mistrust of International Organizations Seen as US-Dominated __ 132

5.4 Fighting the Effect: Solidarity with Haitian Refugees Detained at Guantanamo, Repatriated to Haiti, or Processed in Haiti (Extra-territorial Ethnic Organizing) _____ 138
    5.4.1   Initial Responses to the Refugee Crisis: Demarcating the Policy Arena___ 141
    5.4.2   NCHR´s Initial Steps in its Refugee-oriented Strategy: Targeting Congress 148
    5.4.3   Isolated Initiatives from Haitians in the US: Guantanamo and Litigation__ 155
    5.4.4   NCHR´s Lobbying with Haitian Refugees Until the Transition to Clinton _ 164
    5.4.5   The Role of "Our Guantanamo Contacts" in "Client Services"_____ 173
    5.4.6   "Shut Down Guantanamo": ECHR´s Limited Success in Mobilizing_____ 178
    5.4.7   Clinton´s Reversal and NCHR´s Activism: Guantanamo, Repatriation, ICP 185
    5.4.8   Mounting Pressure: From the Miami Conference to Robinson´s Fast _____ 192

5.5 The Primacy of History: US Responsibility and Liability _____ 202
    5.5.1   The Haitian Diaspora as the Modern Version of *Maroon* Societies _____ 203
    5.5.2   The External Enemy: From the French Empire to the "American Plan"___ 205
    5.5.3   Focusing on the Cause: Unmasking the US as Coup-Instigator _____ 210

5.6 The Imminent Danger for Haiti´s Self-Determination: US Military Power 218
    5.6.1   The Linkage between the Refugee Issue and the Issue of US Invasion ____ 222
    5.6.2   Military Intervention After Governors Island: From Tactics to Reality____ 228

5.7 The Eternal Probation: Haitian Pride of Capable Self-Government _____ 234

5.8 Haiti´s Messiah: Aristide´s Popularity with the Haitian People _____ 244

5.9 Negotiation and Compromise?: The Exile Government´s Strategy _____ 250

5.10 Socio-economic Class Differences in the Haitian Transnation _____ 258

5.11 Getting Ahead in the US: The Stigmatization of Haitians with AIDS ____ 270

5.12 Who Gets Used?: Varying Assumptions in US Presidential Elections ___ 277

5.13 Representation and Resettlement: The Lack of Resources _____ 282

6 Summary and Conclusions _____ 292

7 Bibliography (Primary and Secondary Sources) _____ 300

8 Appendix _____ 353

1 Introduction

On September 30, 1991, Haiti´s democratically elected President, Jean-Bertrand Aristide, was overthrown by a coup d´etat headed by Lieutenant-General Raoul Cédras and driven into exile in the United States (US). The Haitian political crisis triggered a stream of refugees bound foremost for the US. Initial responses to the political crisis and to the worsening human rights situation in Haiti were marked by intense and unprecedented international pressure for political negotiation comprising an economic embargo on Haiti under the aegis of the *Organization of American States* (OAS). In the fall of 1991, the US Coast Guard (USCG) began detaining interdicted Haitians at the US naval base at Guantanamo Bay, Cuba, as well as forcibly returning a certain number to the Haitian capital, Port-au-Prince, pursuant to the US-Haitian Interdiction Agreement of 1981 (USHIA). Many of the detained Haitians, who tested HIV-positive, were prevented from entering the US. Advocates for the Haitian boat people claimed that the repatriation procedure violates the *nonrefoulement* principle of international refugee law and responded with a legal challenge. President George Bush issued an executive order in May 1992, directing the USCG to forcibly return all interdicted Haitians to Haiti, without first allowing them to be interviewed for plausible asylum claims.

After the US presidential elections of 1992, President-elect Bill Clinton reversed his opposition to the Bush Administration´s policy on Haitian refugees and continued the forced repatriations. At the same time, however, the Clinton Administration pledged to increase diplomatic efforts in the international arena to reach a political solution in Haiti, to which the Haitian military junta had remained opposed. Negotiations under the aegis of the *United Nations* (UN) resulted in the Governors Island Agreement (GIA) of July 3, 1993, stipulating the reinstatement of the legitimate government of Haiti under President Aristide. After the collapse of the Governors Island process in the fall of 1993, Aristide convened the Miami conference in January 1994, originally designed to focus on the refugee issue, and abrogated the USHIA in April. Increasing political pressure from a variety of groups within the US, including *Trans-Africa* and the *Congressional Black Caucus* (CBC), further contributed to a reversal of US policy vis-a-vis Haitian refugees. It culminated in the passing of resolution 940 by the UN Security Council (UNSC), the US-led multinational military intervention of September 19, and Aristide´s return to Haiti on October 15, 1994.

This is, in short, the story of the thirty-seven-month-long Haitian political and refugee crises between September 1991 and October 1994. The synopsis of these crises reveals a range of actors that played significant roles during the time period under investigation: Aristide and the Haitian military junta under Cedras; the OAS and the UN; the Bush and Clinton Administrations, the CBC and US authorities such as the USCG; refugee advocates, pressure groups such as *TransAfrica*, and, last but not least, the refugees themselves. Furthermore, the synopsis reveals the major issues, around which the Haitian crisis centered: the coup d´etat, international negotiations, and economic sanctions for the return of Aristide (return issue); human rights in Haiti, interdiction and repatriation, and Guantanamo-based HIV-tests of Haitian refugees (refugee issue); US presidential elections, foreign intervention, and the US invasion. There have been a certain number of studies dealing with those actors and issues focusing, most of all, on the return issue as it unfolded on the international level.[1] But what was the role played by the Haitian diaspora in the US? How did Haitian immigrants respond to the refugee crisis in relation to the spectrum of actors and issues involved? How did they assess in strategical terms the "refugee issue" vis-a-vis the "return issue"? What were their particular contributions?

In general terms, this study examines the Haitian refugee crisis between 1991 and 1994 as a process, which linked together Haiti and the US. The large-scale outpouring of Haitian refugees is to be studied as an example of how, and to what extent, events which took place in Haiti impacted on the Haitian community in New York City, and vice versa. The title of this study reflects an interdisciplinary approach designed at exploring the Haitian refugee crisis on three different levels of analysis:

- first, the level of bilateral relations between Haiti and the US, embedded, as they are, in an international context;
- second, the level of nationalistic organizing by Haitian immigrants in New York City, mainly oriented toward the country of origin; and,
- third, the level of ethnic organizing, predominantly directed toward the host country.

In this view, the Haitian refugee crisis represents a social field of bi-directional and reciprocal patterns of stimuli and responses, which was affected by both international actors and transnational formations. Hence, the study is confined to mechanisms of political mobilization of Haitian organizations at a given place and time: the multicultural urban environment of New York City between 1991-94.

Finally, this study evaluates whether or not the Haitian refugee crisis has had a unifying effect on the Haitian community in New York City regarding both the objectives pursued and the means employed to reach these objectives, and how this process was shaped, internally and externally, by constellations of socially constructed categories such as nation, race, ethnicity, and class. Were Haitian organizing efforts based on a specific national concept, or were they rather informed by a racial consciousness? Were they shaped by a specific ethnic identity, or were they the result of a perceived class status? Can this be seen from various alliances and coalitions Haitians in New York City forged - or rather refused to forge - with other groups both in the US and in Haiti? This study is a contribution to the examination of the problem of refugee and migratory flows from ever new perspectives, encouraged by Sadako Ogata, the former *United Nations High Commissioner for Refugees* (UNHCR) (1997:9).

---

[1] See, for example, Clifford E. Griffin´s "Haiti's Democratic Challenge" (1992:663-673), Pamela Constable´s "Dateline Haiti: Caribbean Stalemate" (1992/93:175-190), Ian Martin´s "Haiti: Mangled Multilateralism" (1994:72-89), "Haiti" in *Political Handbook of the World* (1995:393-394), or David Malone´s "Haiti and the International Community: A Case Study" (1997:126-134).

1.1 Autobiographical Information and Course of Examination

My interest in the Haitian refugee crisis resulted from working for the Hon. Charles B. Rangel[2] on Capitol Hill in 1992 as a Congressional Fellow of the *American Political Science Association* (APSA) from the University of Munich, Germany. In this capacity, I assisted in guiding House Concurrent Resolution 220, which contained the provision of Temporary Protected Status (TPS) for Haitian refugees, through the legislative process by providing a variety of services ranging from conducting research to organizing staff briefings. Since Mr. Rangel´s office on Capitol Hill became one of the most important Congressional hubs for political information and political initiatives concerning the Haitian crisis, my internship offered me the first opportunity for participant observation from a unique Congressional point of view.[3]

I was well aware of the immense task ahead of me in terms of the scope and magnitude of my research project as outlined in my Dissertation Research Proposal of March 1994. This was true in particular with regard to the second and third levels of analysis, in which I set out to explore a complex international situation as a German national, foreign to Haitian culture.[4] Given the limited amount of time at my disposal, I was well advised by what anthropologist James P. Spradley (1979) recommends to his colleagues. He reminds us that a complete ethnography, even for a rather limited cultural scene, would take years of intensive research. All ethnographers must limit their investigation in some way, he cautioned, and some aspects of the culture will have to be studied more exhaustively than others. At some point in time, the ethnographer faces a choice regarding further research. He or she can either carry out a "surface analysis" of as many domains as possible or conduct an "in-depth analysis" of a limited number of domains. But, Spradley continues, because time and resources are limited, most ethnographers agree that an exhaustive study of an entire culture will never be accomplished. In actual practice, most ethnographers adopt a compromise: They study a few, selected domains in depth while still attempting to gain a surface understanding of a culture or cultural scene as a whole (Spradley 1979:132-134).

Translated into the requirements of my research project, there were two basic options available to me in order to manage the work load inherent in the structure of my study and its general research objectives. The first option was to reduce the empirical basis of my study by concentrating on a carefully chosen number of Haitian com-

---

[2] Mr. Rangel at that time was the chairman of the powerful Ways & Means Committee´s Select Revenue Measures Subcommittee and of the Select Committee on Narcotics Abuse & Control.

[3] In late 1993, I decided to focus my dissertation on the Haitian refugee crisis. The *German Marshall Fund of the United States* awarded me a research grant in 1994 (grant # A-0172-25) that enabled me to conduct ethnographic field work in New York City with the "full cooperation and support" of Mr. Rangel, ascertained in a support letter.

[4] On the subject of the "personal equation of the observer", as Malinowski called it in 1922, theorists of ethnoscience like Werner Oswald and G. Mark Schoepfle propose that the ethnographer not only keep a separate journal containing personal reactions to the surrounding culture as a "retrospective record of his or her learning process", since "what and whom we study is rarely accidental". They also suggest to take "one´s own detailed life history", which may be equally illuminating as to the "degree to which we influence the fieldwork situation". This "autobiography" should give the reader a "thorough view of the writer´s formative experiences, personal accomplishments, biases, and (at least indirectly) his or her blind spots" (1987a:165-176;1987b:313-314). I included a few remarks to this effect in the microedition of my dissertation (Opitz 1999).

munity organizations instead of futilely trying to cover the totality of the organizational infrastructure. The second option was to fine-tune the set of goals of my research to a manageable degree rather than ask all the questions in the context of the general research objectives.

The second option was my first concern: While it is true, as I stressed in my Research Proposal, that it is "impossible to dissociate the refugee crisis from the political crisis in Haiti", I still felt constrained, for economic reasons, to neglect certain questions for the sake of bringing clearly refugee-related themes to the foreground of my research (refugee issue). This fine-tuning process had implications for the first option. After completing what Spradley calls "surface analysis" during the first half of my stay, I decided to concentrate my research primarily on the associations *Brooklyn for Aristide* and the *National Coalition for Haitian Refugees* and their most important members, respectively, as well as *Wilson Désir´s Office*. However, in the course of time and for a number of reasons, I decided to slightly change the sample of organizations under scrutiny by both omitting and, above all, adding certain groups while devoting much of my research time to the most important ones. Generally speaking, I first decided to omit organizations that seemed to be too political or partisan in terms of their overall strategy of concentrating on the return issue at the expense of dealing with the refugee crisis. Accordingly, I added organizations that concentrated their energies more clearly on the refugee issue.

The first half of my research stay in the US, which lasted about eleven months (September 1994 - July 1995),[5] required an inventory of the organizational infrastructure of the Haitian community in New York City. One article confirming Spradley´s recommendation appeared in the *Big Red News* entitled "Grassroots Groundswell Demands Democracy in Haiti" (BRN 1992:4). It states that 3,500 individuals and organizations representing hundreds of thousands of US citizens, among them presumably many Haitians, signed a full-page ad in the *New York Times* (NYT) of Monday, March 16, 1992. A meaningful selection was, therefore, even more urgent and imperative. A variety of independent sources and my own research findings revealed the preliminary number of approximately 20 organizations in New York City, which could be dubbed as generic Haitian community organizations in terms of their authenticity and originality. One of these sources was a copy of the *Directory of Organizations*.[6] The directory lists 156 Haitian organizations of various kinds in the New York metropolitan area (Glick Schiller, Brutus 1986), in which about 500,000 people of Haitian descent live,

---

[5] In spite of Mr. Rangel´s support letter, it was not easy to get access to Haitian organizers. Consequently, it took about seven months for the plurality of research interviews to be conducted (see the "Chronology and Interview Statistics" in the microedition). This is, however, not only due to the distrust often observed with Haitians (Weinstein,Segal 1992:7), even though some Haitian anthropologists themselves felt they had to pass an initial test of establishing their Haitian identity and "credentials", as Rose-Marie Cassagnol Chierici notes with regard to her own field work in Rochester: "Although I was accepted as a fellow Haitian, there were still questions about the reasons for my presence in the camps" (1991:45-47). Nevertheless, I was often under the impression that my "outsider role", including my ability with French and my upbringing next to the French border, occasioned positive responses from my informants. The delay in getting access was also caused by completing the surface analysis and by the necessity to gradually familiarize myself with my new surroundings. My kind Haitian host family helped a lot in this sometimes frustrating process of adaptation, for which I am very grateful.

[6] The *Directory* was provided by Ms. Carolle Charles, the Haitian-American anthropologist of Baruch College, whom I met three times in the course of my stay in order to discuss my research project.

according to one estimate (Dreyfuss 1993:20-21).[7] Far from covering the totality of the organizational infrastructure of the Haitian community in New York City, I supplemented my own list of organizations, which then came to total 25 groups.[8] They were relevant to my research on account of either their handling of immigration and refugee issues in general or their activities in the wake of the Haitian political and refugee crises.

These 25 groups represent a pool of organizations, out of which I selected 10 groups for further examination during my research stay. These organizations are, in alphabetical order:

1) *Brooklyn for Aristide* (BfA)
2) *Emergency Coalition for Haitian Refugees* (ECHR)
3) *Haitian Americans United for Progress* (HAUP)
4) *Haitian Centers Council* (HCC)
5) *Haitian Enforcement Against Racism* (HEAR)
6) *Haitian Women for Haitian Refugees* (HWHR)
7) *Haitian Women Program* (HWP)
8) *National Coalition for Haitian Refugees* (NCHR)
9) *St. Jerome's Roman Catholic Church* (Haitian Apostolate Sansaricq) and the
10) *Haitian Consulate* (Wilson Désir).

After returning to Munich, I decided to add the

11) *10th Department Organization of New York* (10e of New York), the
12) *Episcopal Migration Ministries* (EMM), and the
13) *Haitian Coalition on AIDS* (HCAIDS).

Analyzing a host of articles published in the Brooklyn-based Haitian weekly *Haiti Progrès* (HP), I became aware of a multitude of additional Haitian community organizations, which will be mentioned in this study.

NCHR along with BfA served as the starting points, from which I began to study the Haitian community in depth. Two common characteristics of both organizations are the reason for using them as a starting point: Both are coalition-type organizations and both operate at the intersection between the Haitian community, on the one hand, and, on the other, US society at large, as well as the legislative branch of the US government. HCC, HAUP, and *St. Jerome* (Haitian Apostolate) were chosen as another important research focus simply by virtue of their being members of NCHR. At a later point in the research process, I learned of the importance of HWHR, HWP as well as ECHR and thus included them into the sample. The *Haitian Consulate* and later HEAR were selected as two more politically oriented organizations to be juxta-

---

[7] There were about 290,000 people who claimed Haitian ancestry in the 1990 census. Laguerre estimates, however, that as many as 1.2 million people in the US are of Haitian origin, when including the tens of thousands who are in the country illegally, as well as second- and third-generation Haitian-Americans, who simply identify themselves as black. The next largest Haitian community after the New York metropolitan area (500,000) is in southern Florida (300,000), with smaller communities in Boston and Chicago (Dreyfuss 1993:20-21).

[8] See the list of 25 Haitian-(American) organizations in New York in the appendix.

posed with the other service-providing and refugee-related organizations in the pool. The *10e of New York*, according to its president, Guy Victor, the largest Haitian organizer in New York during the crisis (Victor 1996),[9] served the same purpose. Having selected these three organizations, I did not concentrate on *Wilson Désir's Office*, and, anyway, the group did not seem to be willing to cooperate.

The transition from what Spradley calls "surface analysis" during the first half of my stay to an "in-depth analysis" during the second half, which began in early February 1995, required many investigative steps. They gradually and continuously led me from the wide angle and the perspective of the neutral observer overlooking a host of actors and issues associated with the Haitian crisis ("surface analysis") to the narrower focus and the perspective of the uniquely positioned insider ("in-depth analysis"). In other words, after advancing from the first level of analysis as outlined in my Proposal, i.e. the "bilateral relations between Haiti and the US, embedded, as they are, in an international context", to the second and third levels of analysis, i.e. "nationalistic and ethnic organizing by Haitian immigrants", I ended up looking back from these two levels of analysis to the first level - in order to, as Malinowski put it in 1922, "grasp the native's point of view" (Spradley 1979:3), in order "to obtain the cultural knowledge of the natives" (Oswald,Schoepfle 1987:23). After leaving the field and while analyzing my findings, I synthesized the "top-down" and the "bottom-up" perspectives into an organic whole. I assessed how all levels were interrelated while also taking into account the historical dimension of the subject matter. I therein followed the definition of culture as a "system of meaningful symbols" suggested by Spradley: "the acquired knowledge that people use to interpret experience and generate social behavior" (1979:5). In addition, I based my analysis on the "idea of a basic permeability" of all cultures (Ostendorf 1992:6).

---

[9] For a listing of all interviews made during the research stay, see the "Chronology and Interview Statitsics: November 1994 - January 1997" in the appendix.

Offices of Haiti Progrès in Brooklyn (by Götz-Dietrich Opitz)

Haitian cab driver at Haitian cafe, New York City (courtesy Maggie Steber)

1.2 Research Methods and Sources of Information

The surface analysis of my study required obtaining many Haiti-related documents.[10] In addition, as stated in my Dissertation Research Proposal, the data concerning the second and third levels of analysis would have to be collected during field work in Haitian neighborhoods, which can be found in Brooklyn, Queens, and Manhattan (Laguerre 1984:50). Since ethnography as a way of learning from people, rather than studying people, requires making cultural inferences from what people say, from the way people act, and from the artifacts people use (Spradley 1979:3,8), I decided to apply qualitative methodological procedures such as participant observation in a variety of events and unstructured interviewing with the leaders of Haitian organizations. These research strategies allow one to obtain first-hand knowledge about the empirical social world in question. These also advocate an approach requiring one to interpret the real world from the perspective of the subjects of the investigation (Filstead 1970:6-7). Both methods must be seen as complimentary in the sense that the accuracy of interviewing can be improved by taking into account suggestions made from the perspective of participant observation providing situations, in which the meanings of words used in interviews can be learned through study of their use in context (Becker 1970:134-135;Whyte 1984:96).[11]

---

[10] I obtained those in the *OAS Columbia Memorial Library* and in the *UN Information Center* in Washington, D.C., where I did research at a variety of places. One of the most important of these was the Newspaper and Current Periodical Room in the *Library of Congress*, which offers access to, for example, full-text articles of the US ethnic press from the computer-assisted database *Ethnic News Watch* as well as NYT-abstracts from the database *Proquest*. In the Jefferson Reading Room and the Adams Reading Room, I surveyed refugee-related literature as well as literature on the issue of ethnic lobbyism in the field of foreign policy and on other related issues. I drew up excerpts from a limited number of these texts containing background knowledge, which I incorporated into the standardized questionnaire to be used for and adapted to the various interviews yet to be conducted. In October 1993, I was already at the *Library of Congress* as well as the *OAS Columbia Memorial Library* and the *UN Information Center*. In addition, I conducted research at the *Henry L. Stimson Center*, the *U.S. Committee for Refugees* (USCR), and at *Global Exchange*. In December 1993, I went to the *Congressional Research Service* (CRS), the Statistical Division of the *Immigration and Naturalization Service* (INS), to the *U.S. Coast Guard Headquarters*, and to the *Urban Institute*. I also conducted an interview with Ms. Ellen Angeles, staff member of the *State Department´s* Haitian Working Group. In April 1994, I returned to the US and participated in a meeting in Washington on April 20, initiated by *InterAction* to form a special Task Force on Haiti, where I met representatives of the *Refugee Policy Group*, of *Americas Watch*, of *World Vision*, of *Church World Service* (CWS), and of the *Episcopal Migration Ministries* (EMM). During my research stay, I conducted further research in Washington at the *US General Accounting Office*, the office of *Caribbean/Latin American Action* (CLAA), the *Embassy of Haiti*, the *National Democratic Headquarters*, the Arthur R. Ashe, Jr. Foreign Policy Library in the headquarters of *TransAfrica*, the headquarters of the *National Rainbow Coalition*, the *Office of Refugee Resettlement* (ORR), and Mr. Rangel´s as well as Congressman Major R. Owens´ office on Capitol Hill. Additional information was gathered by conducting research at a variety of places in New York such as the library of the *Brooklyn College*, the *Brooklyn Public Library*, the *Schomburg Library* in Harlem as well as the *North American Congress on Latin America* (NACLA) to do research on HP, the *Foundation Center*, the headquarters of *Human Rights Watch/Americas*, the *Church Avenue Merchants Block Association* (CAMBA), the headquarters of CWS, and *Catholic Charities* in Brooklyn.

[11] Among the theoretical literature on anthropology, ethnoscience and ethnographic field work that I utilized the most to harness my research in the US are Spradley´s two works *The Ethnographic Interview* (1979) and *Participant Observation* (1980). To a lesser extent, I drew upon Oswald´s and Schoep-

The stated goal was to explore the subjective dimensions of meanings behind various constructs such as nation, race, ethnicity, class and other identities as an expression of social (transnational) relations and praxis at the level of objective reality. Empirical data gathered this way would allow for the qualitative as well as the quantitative analysis of that material (Brenner 1985:150). Access to "gatekeepers", with whom social acceptance in community-based studies must be negotiated (Whyte 1984:62), was to be provided by Mr. Rangel (support letter). The utilization of the "outsider role", which I would inevitably have to assume as a "white" individual from Germany, promised to offer the advantage of maintaining neutrality relative to internal group differences. It was also likely to stimulate more uninhibited response from informants as data-bearers and to maintain utmost objectivity (Trice 1970:80-81).

While gradually and continuously proceeding from the "surface analysis" to the "in-depth analysis", I applied these two basic qualitative methodological procedures of ethnographic field work, with a stronger reliance on interviews. A statistical analysis of the interviews I conducted during my research yielded a group of 22 interviewees, who are either representatives of the 10 organizations under investigation or representatives of other organizations that are part of the same network. After my research stay, I also conducted two telephone interviews as well as two interviews in person, thereby supplementing the group of interviewees to a total of 26. As to national origin and "race", 15 of these 26 interviewees are Haitian and "Black", 9 are American and "White", and two are American and "Black".[12] The non-Haitian informants were interviewed in order to acquire accounts from an outsider's point of view. With these interviewees, I conducted a total of 38 interviews of varying length resulting in 49 hours of interviewing time.[13] I used a standardized questionnaire adapted to the various interviews.

The questionnaire was broken down into six major fields of inquiry, with questions pertaining to the particulars of the person interviewed, questions pertaining to the organization under scrutiny (its history, staff and organizational structure), questions pertaining to coalition-building, questions pertaining to lobbying/advocacy work, and questions pertaining to political issues as well as concepts such as nation, race, and ethnicity.[14] In the course of my research, I incorporated additional questions, which included knowledge obtained as a result of preceding interviews. More often than not, this knowledge contained reservations voiced by my informants towards organizing on the refugee issue. Questions of this sort were to elicit evidence, which is sometimes referred to as "respondent validation" (Hammersley 1990:83). The variety of questions used can be categorized as "descriptive", "structural", and "contrast" questions (Spradley 1979:60). I did not follow the order of questions strictly, but allowed for a certain amount of leeway in asking questions, necessary to adapt to the nature of the subject under discussion, the interviewing situation as well as interview time at my disposal, and the personality of the interviewee. In addition to the more structured interviews, I conducted a certain number of short telephone interviews during my research stay.

---

fle's *Systematic Fieldwork: Foundations of Ethnography and Interviewing* (1987) and Martyn Hammersley's *Reading Ethnographic Research: A Critical Guide* (1990).

[12] I put "race" in quotation marks in order to indicate that I do not believe in the so-called "one-drop-rule" that informs race relations in US society.

[13] See the chart "Chronology and Interview Statistics: November 1994-January 1997" in the appendix.

[14] A copy of two versions of the questionnaire is included in the appendix.

I used the technique of participant observation complimentary to the method of interviewing. In general, participant observation provided for contacts with Haitians in natural settings that conveyed a "feeling" for Haitian culture. A statistical analysis of participant observation during my research yielded the number of 21 different events, including three social situations under long-term observation. The living arrangements during my research stay in Flatbush, Brooklyn, constitute one of these social situations.[15] During these events, which cover the time period of approximately 70 hours of investigation, a multitude of informal and, in part, anonymous informants could be used. 7 of these events were tape-recorded resulting in about 15 hours of observing time.[16] Tape recorded interviewing time and observing time combined for a total of about 64 hours of recording time.

The interview of March 29 with the Haitian-born executive director of NCHR, Jocelyn McCalla, who does not hold US citizenship, marked both a low and turning point in my research process. Not only did I learn that one of the weaknesses of NCHR, in its capacity as an American organization,[17] is its not being deeply rooted in the Haitian community, but Mr. McCalla also made the surprising, categorical statement that the Haitian refugee crisis "was not an issue" for the Haitian diaspora: "For the Haitian community, the issue was that Aristide has been kicked out of office. So the refugees were not the issue ... [I]f you go back and look at any number of videotapes on demonstrations held by Haitians in New York City, ... if you look at anything written in terms of the demands by Haitians, there is no way you are going to find demands for refugees, except indirectly" (McCalla 1995). At this point, I might as well have packed my suitcase. Instead, I decided to test Mr. McCalla´s statement against my perception of reality by following up on two questions:

1) Is McCalla´s assessment of the Haitian community correct, despite NCHR´s weakness of not being deeply rooted in the Haitian community? Or is Nina Glick Schiller,

---

[15] In early October 1994, I moved into a little room on the second floor of a small row house on Nostrand Avenue, where most Haitians in Brooklyn live. Haitians were shown to have an "affinity for residential proximity to English-speaking immigrants" in New York City, especially in Brooklyn and South Queens, rather than exhibiting a separate residential pattern (Conway,Bigby 1987:74-83). My landlords, whom I shall call Loueurs, a married couple, who live on the first floor along with their four children and their grandmother, are both Haitian-born and have lived in the US since the late 1970s. Living in this environment allowed intimate insights into the culture of a Haitian immigrant family and provided some feedback on political developments related to both the US and Haiti. One of my four room mates on the second floor is Haitian-born, too. Another came from Jamaica, another from Trinidad, and the third was African-American.
[16] See the chart "Chronology and Events Statistics: September 1994-July 1995" in the appendix.
[17] In contrast, Felix Eme Unaeze and Richard E. Perrin erroneously implied in the *Gale Encyclopedia of Multicultural America* that NCHR is an organization in and of the Haitian community in New York City (1995:652). The chapter on "Haitian Americans" is, however, a valuable overview of Haitian life in the US. I received permission from Mr. McCalla to do research in NCHR´s archives. This kind of openness is indicative of the fact that NCHR, in contrast to other groups in my sample, which were more arcane, is not an authentic Haitian community organization, but an American coalition that merely includes a limited number of Haitian-American organizations. In NCHR´s archives, I copied about 320 pages of material included in the so-called yearbooks of the organization, covering the time period of Aristide´s exile.

anthropologist at the University of New Hampshire, correct.[18] She observes in *Nations Unbound* that "[t]he Haitian boat people of the 1990s, who fled the political repression and economic deterioration that accompanied the ousting of Aristide, received a dramatically different reception from the Haitian diaspora. The 10th Department *embraced* these refugees" (Basch et al. 1994:220; author´s italics).[19]

2) If McCalla is correct, what are all the reasons why the Haitian refugee crisis was "not an issue" for the Haitian community? Why were the Haitian boat people *not* "embraced" by the Haitian diaspora?

Further field work in the Haitian community was needed and designed to find the right answers. Nevertheless, since I started to dive into a politically sensitive area, I was occasionally going to get the "run around". Before establishing contact with representatives of the *Haitian Consulate*, ECHR, HWP, HWHR, and HEAR, I had to assume that McCalla´s assessment that the Haitian refugee crisis was "not an issue" for the Haitian community was basically correct. At this point, the Haitian community in New York City seemed, by and large, to have lacked interest in or support for the Haitian refugees. While political Haitian groups with a large following preferred to concentrate on the "return issue", a small group of service-providing Haitian organizations stressed the "refugee issue". While also sensing some tensions between Haitians and African-Americans based on differing concepts of race, my preliminary conclusion was thus that a set of interconnected reasons must have been responsible for that. These reasons are the following:

1) The AIDS-stigma, which Haitians try to get rid of, in conjunction with the discriminatory HIV-testing of Haitian refugees on Guantanamo
2) Socio-economic class differences both in Haiti and in the Haitian community, alienating the political elite in the Haitian diaspora from the refugees
3) The exile government´s strategic-tactical considerations preferring international negotiation and compromise with the military junta in Haiti
4) President Aristide´s overwhelming popularity with the Haitian people, who followed him, according to one informant, "like sheep"
5) A lack of resources within the Haitian community and the "monopoly" of the *Catholic Charities*, aggravating effective community-based refugee assistance
6) The complexity of refugee law.

After focusing on the *Haitian Consulate*, ECHR, HWP, HWHR, and HEAR, I had to revise my preliminary conclusion slightly. In addition, I cautioned in my Final Research Report of August 1995 that "further analysis is needed" to fully comprehend

---

[18] I had the pleasure to briefly discuss my research topic with Ms. Glick Schiller over the phone a few times during my research stay.
[19] In the same vein, Unaeze and Perrin observed that in the Haitian community in New York City "an increasing amount of political activity has [currently] involved attempts to help `boot people'" (1995:652). The phrase "10th department" refers to all Haitians living abroad. As used in this book, the term especially refers to those living in the US, but it embraces the whole Haitian diaspora. The Haitian state consists of 9 departments (Jean-Pierre 1995, Richman 1992).

nationalistic and ethnic organizing by Haitian immigrants in New York City. Studying, for example, articles published in HP during the time period under investigation would be necessary in order to compare the information contained therein with the various statements made in the interviews. Since I could not find a single library in New York that carries copies of *Haiti Observateur* (HO), the Brooklyn-based conservative Haitian weekly, or *Haiti en Marche* (HM), the moderate Haitian weekly published in Miami, I had to rely solely on HP as one of the three "Haitian `think tanks`". But this left-of-center Haitian newspaper, published in Brooklyn and distributed in both the US and Haiti, promised to be a comparatively suitable source of information by virtue of the fact that it was both ideologically linked to the populist movement in Haiti and later critical of Aristide during the time period under study (Jean-Pierre 1995:200).

HP-based data had four more advantages: First, it contained information on concrete events in the Haitian community, which my informants could not remember any more in detail; second, it added the dimension of time, making it possible to discern various stages of organizing that presented the crisis as a progressing evolution. In contrast, my informants evaluated in hindsight organizing activities as an aggregate that lumps together all groups regardless of time; third, HP quoted verbatim participants in these events, who voiced their opinions on the crisis *in situ*; fourth, a transnational actor in its own right, HP commented on the participants in these events, thereby virtually assuming the role of yet another evaluating informant. Along with the research interviews providing the Haitians´ view and the scientific literature providing the historical and anthropological dimension, HP-articles constitute one of the three major sources of information, upon which this study relies. The very time-consuming analysis of about 330 French-language articles in HP[20] after my research stay in the US - most of them appeared in the section "Dans Le Dixième Département" - revealed four more factors that seem to have restrained organizing on the refugee issue. Yet, this source of information also deepened my understanding of what lacking "interest or support" for Haitian refugees in the context of the crisis really meant. It demonstrated that it is not enough to concentrate only on clearly refugee-related themes, as I did at the outset of my research, since Haitian organizing against the backdrop of the refugee crisis was shaped by all the major issues mentioned in the synopsis above. The factors are the following:

7) A different concept of race, generating frictions with African-Americans
8) A markedly historical interpretation of events before and after September 1991
9) The fear of US military intervention of Haiti as an imminent danger
10) Haitian pride of Haiti´s capacity for self-government
11) Partial suspicion of being instrumentalized in US electoral politics

---

[20] Though it contains about 330 articles, my record of HP-publications for the time period under investigation is not complete (see chart in the appendix). A total of 41 issues are missing, with the longest gap being the 7 months from May to November 1993. I filled the void with articles from other newspapers.

1.3 Structure of Study and Mode of Presentation

Nine of the eleven inhibitory factors, which helped curb nationalistic and ethnic organizing on the refugee issue, constitute the headings for several subchapters in Chapter 5 of this study. They are preceded by three subchapters arranged in hierarchical order, which present the thrust of organizing strategies prioritized by the majority of Haitian community organizations. These are direct transnational relations centering around "resistance" and "mobilization" by Haitians inside Haiti and Haitians outside their home country, respectively; indirect transnational relations centering around "world opinion" and "sanctions" emanating from the international community; and extra-territorial ethnic organizing efforts centering around solidarity with Haitian refugees detained at Guantanamo, repatriated to Haiti, or processed in Haiti. The first and the latter subchapters delineate the differing race concepts, while the latter also exemplifies the complexity of refugee law. Intra-territorial ethnic organizing is covered in the chapter on "resettlement". The technical terms relating to transnationalism and Haitian organizing used above will be explained in the following chapter.

The chapters on nationalistic and ethnic organizing (chapters 5.3-5.5) present the empirical data in an *issue-centered* fashion as the supreme criterion of order. In other words, it structures all relevant information on the factors inhibiting nationalistic and ethnic organizing in terms of a taxonomy illuminating the logical links among these factors. Since this part is partially structured along both citizen-to-citizen and citizen-to-state relations, it is also arranged in a *relation-centered* fashion. Another mode of presentation would have been to select the various groups under investigation as units of analysis. This *organization-centered* approach depicts the empirical data according to the activities carried out by each group. I applied it in my Final Research Report, but it is not suitable for this study because of the high number of organizations mentioned. Yet another mode of presentation would have been to exhibit the empirical data, relevant to all three levels of analysis, according to the investigative steps taken during my research stay in the US. This type of ethnographic writing, in which the "inside story" of the research itself is told, has been referred to as the "confessional mode" and has become common among ethnographers in recent years (Hammersley 1990:21). But it had to be discarded in this study by virtue of the complexity of the subject matter under investigation. Evidently, I partially utilized this *research-centered* mode of presentation in this introduction (chapters 1.1-1.2).

The issue-centered and relation-centered approaches chosen as mode of presentation for this study are intended to provide an analytic, theoretical or, as Clifford Geertz calls it, "thick" description of the subject matter in contrast to the relatively concrete sort of ethnographic accounts referred to as ethnographic "realism" or "naturalism". The mode of presentation chosen here, which Hammersley calls "legitimatory" ethnographic writing, theoretical hypotheses, interpretations, and conclusions are woven into the account as part of the description (1990:18-20). What will be equally woven into my account, where necessary, is organization-centered as well as research-centered information. Each of the subchapters on nationalistic and ethnic Haitian organizing presents its proper data in chronological order following the information given in the process analysis of the Haitian crisis in the context of international state relations as covered by the NYT.

This kind of arrangement reflects the central concern of this study: It tries to give an explanatory description of the ways Haitian immigrants in New York City as transnational actors responded to the Haitian crisis in their own right. It equally strives to give an explanatory description of the ways they *responded to the responses* to the Haitian crisis, prioritized by powerful actors in the international state arena. Finally, it tries to give an explanatory description of the ways they *responded to the responses* to the Haitian crisis, preferred by other transnational actors. For all three social fields, i.e. the Haitian diaspora, the governmental spheres, and a score of transnational realms, are interconnected and influence each other in varying degrees. Haitian migrants in New York responded by way of establishing relations, to which they ascribed varying cultural meanings. In this sense, the structure of chapter 5 constitutes a taxonomy of what Spradley calls cultural "domains" defined as the "larger units of cultural knowledge" (1979:94). According to Spradley, in writing an ethnography as a translation process communicating the meanings of the investigated culture to the readers unfamiliar with that culture, "the concern with the particular is incidental to an understanding of the general" and "the concern with the general is incidental to an understanding of the particular".[21]

The structure of this study is inherent in its title "transnationalism and the interest of the state". "Transnationalism" refers to both nationalistic and ethnic organizing by Haitian immigrants in New York City and its links to organizing activities by other transnational actors rooted in civil society. The "interest of the state" refers to the measures selected by the US government (Bush, Clinton, Congress, and the US Supreme Court [USSC]) unilaterally (or multilaterally on the international level) in response to the Haitian (refugee) crisis as a foreign policy problem of the US. But "interest of the state" also refers to the strategies pursued by both the Haitian military junta and, most of all, by Aristide´s exile government. Since various transnationalisms under specific consideration of Haitian organizing are to be contrasted with the international state sphere, it is recommendable to juxtapose the facts on the first level of analysis with the empirical data on the second and third levels of analysis. The first level of analysis treats the *governmental* domain, as opposed to the second and third levels of analysis, which treat the *non-governmental* domain. This contrast is to discern consistencies or inconsistencies of interest between distinct actors differentiated by whether or not they are endowed with the characteristic of statehood.

But what constitutes "statehood"? Max Weber´s well-known definition of a state can serve as a valuable starting point when it comes to establishing an operational definition for the purpose of this study. He characterized a state as "a human community which successfully claims within a given territory the monopoly of the legitimate use of physical force" (Smith 1983:178).[22] Even if this definition does not take into

---

[21] With at least six levels of ethnographic writing possible as identified by Spradley, the levels intrinsic to chapter 5 of this study range from "cross-cultural descriptive statements" (level 2), over "general statements about a society or cultural group" (level 3), "general statements about a specific cultural scene" (level 4), and "specific statements about a cultural domain" (level 5), even to "specific incident statements" (level 6) (1979:205-210). The language used for this ethnographic account can therefore be called an "epic prose" designed to convey an immediacy of what is described.

[22] An exhaustive definition of the "state" is, of course, a painstaking undertaking. *The Blackwell Encyclopedia of Political Institutions* distinguishes between three conceptions of the state: the "state as might" (*Machtstaat*); the "state as law" (*Staatsrecht*); and the "state as legitimacy" (*Rechtsstaat*). It

consideration the existence of human communities successfully claiming and executing, first, the *illegitimate* use of physical force, which can be projected, second, *beyond* its territory, it is illuminating in that it stresses the exclusive coerciveness of state power (*Gewaltmonopol*). The modern "state" as a territorial compulsory association exercising disciplinary-regulatory centralized power is a pre-national and pre-ethnic creation of European culture at the time of the renaissance, taking the form of an absolutist monarchy during the first phase of its existence (Kimminich 1994:182-184).[23] The human community constituting the present-day state institutes a government as representation of its state, exercising authoritative power over its territory and people, who belong to this community. The phenomenon of refugees, in Joseph H. Carens words the "orphans of the state system" (1991:23), testifies to serious abuse of illegitimate state power. These extreme cases illustrate the potential inconsistencies between the state and the norms of civil society, inherited from the Enlightenment, such as individual rights, privacy, voluntary association, formal legality, plurality, publicity, and free enterprise, which in theory the state should protect by law.

To further develop an operational definition of a state, it is useful to contrast the traits of statehood with the concept of civil society. Cohen and Arato suggest a three-part model distinguishing civil society from both state and economy. This model is to underwrite the "dramatic oppositional role" of the concept of civil society under authoritarian regimes as well as to renew its critical potential under liberal democracies. Cohen and Arato understand "civil society" to be a sphere of "social interaction between economy and state", composed above all of the intimate sphere (especially family), the sphere of associations (especially voluntary associations), social movements and forms of public communication. They distinguish civil society from both a political society of parties, political organizations, and political publics (in particular parliaments) and an economic society composed of organizations of production and distribution, usually firms, cooperatives, and partnerships, since the actors of political and economic society are directly involved with state power and economic production. On the other hand, political and economic societies also refer to mediating spheres, through which civil society can gain influence over political-administrative and economic processes (1992:ix-x,chapter 1).

Antonio Gramsci simplifies the relationship between the three spheres by stating that "between the economic structure and the state with its legislation and coercion stands civil society" (1971:209). In reality, however, all three realms interpenetrate in many ways. This study is mainly interested in the so-called "third sector" as one part of civil society, distinct from both the public and the private sectors. It designates "all organizations, which are neither profit-oriented businesses nor governmental agencies or bureaucracies" (Anheier,Seibel 1990a:7). Civil law countries such as Germany,

---

distinguishes further historically by reference to the different social and economic experiences that theories of the state reflect: the "state as reflection of a hierarchical social order"; the "state as reflection of an individualistic social order"; the "state as the embodiment of community in society" (Bogdanor 1987:590-593). *The Hutchinson Dictionary of Ideas* describes the state with reference to the "classic definition" by R.M. MacIver (The Modern State 1926): "An association which, acting through law as promulgated by a government endowed to this end with coercive power, maintains within a community territorially demarcated the universal external conditions of social order" (Norton 1994:488).

[23] For Hannah Arendt´s and Michel Foucault´s conception of the "state", see Cohen/Arato (1992:194-195,282-286).

Austria, Italy, and France developed a "state-oriented third sector", whereas a more "market-oriented" third sector evolved in common law countries such as the United Kingdom and the US (Anheier,Seibel 1990b:384). Not surprisingly, associational voluntarism in democratic US society developed faster under the constitutional protection of the First Amendment (free exercise clause) in comparison to Haiti with its long succession of authoritarian regimes.[24] These cross-cultural variations must be taken into consideration in this study, which therefore actually deals with two sets of the three sectors: one situated in Haiti, the other in the US.

An operational definition of the "state" for the purpose of this study reduces it to an entity, which exercises the use of *legitimate* or *illegitimate* power within or beyond its own territorial boundaries through *governmental* agents, which claim to act on behalf of *one nation* on a *variety* of issues. It is distinguished from, albeit may overlap with, "civil society" defined as the sociocultural space of conscious association, *self-organization* and organized communication, in which *non-governmental* agents, claiming to act on behalf of a *separate group* of people, operate *within* or *across* national borders on one *special issue* in accordance with or in opposition to a state, which protects or infringes the law guaranteeing *voluntary action*.

---

[24] Alexis de Tocqueville wrote about US society: "In no country of the world has the principle of association been more successfully used or applied to a greater multitude of objects than in America. ... Americans of all ages, all conditions and all dispositions constantly form associations. ... [T]he Americans form associations for the smallest undertakings. ... Citizens who are individually powerless do not very clearly anticipate the strength that they may acquire by uniting together" (1945:189/vol.1,115,123/vol. 2). In contrast, Marian McClure observes: "Rural Haiti is organized around the avoidance of social organization beyond the level of kinship. There is a lack of organizations at the intermediate level between kin and the state" (1986:25). On the other hand, an anthropologist like Nina Glick Schiller points out that hundreds of projects in Haiti, begun by international organizations in the 1970s, promoted the "participation of peasants in grassroots development", which came to be used in turn by Haitian Catholic priests "to build a ti legliz (little church) movement that addressed both the needs and aspirations of the poor" (Basch et al. 1994:197). Other observers state, however, that "Haiti lacks an active civil society" (Weinstein,Segal 1992:163).

2 Brief Review of Literature

The following brief review of literature links phenomena such as globalization and transnationalism to Haitian community studies and refugee studies. It introduces a relational theory of transnationalism, which serves as the epistemological framework for the analysis of nationalistic and ethnic organizing by Haitian immigrants in New York City against the backdrop of Haitian refugee flows from Haiti during the political crisis between 1991 and 1994.

2.1 Globalization and Transnationalism

In 1993, Michael Walzer prognosticated that the interest of political theory over the next decade will lie in transnational formations of different sorts "above and below the level of nation-states", embedded in civil society of the respective countries, and linked by border-spanning arrangements. Walzer defines civil society as "a realm of fragmentation made up of churches, ethnic groups, social movements, unions, professional associations, organisations for mutual aid and defence" that constitute the "third sector". They are external to both the market and the state while, at the same time, depending on both private and tax money for survival. The increasing number of these groups, the work of which necessarily carries them beyond the borders of their own state, makes up "this nascent international civil society". The regular appearance of the groups in the political arena, Walzer augurs, may well mean that democratic government will be more difficult to manage. While there will be more sovereign states, they will have in fact less power than statehood once implied, as their independence will be compromised in new ways (1993:51-54).

Corroborating Walzer´s thesis of a "nascent international civil society", Lester M. Salamon (1994:109-118) observes that "we are in the midst of a global `associational revolution´" that manifests itself in a striking upsurge in organized voluntary activity and the creation of private, non-profit or non-governmental organizations around the world. While a significant expansion of citizen activism in the developed countries had been evident for several decades, the situation in the developing world was even more dramatic: A 1982 survey of non-profit human service associations in 16 US-American communities showed that 65% had been created since 1960. Some 4,600 Western voluntary organizations were active in the South, providing support to approximately 20,000 indigenous non-governmental organizations. The emergence of this "global third sector", Salamon explains, had been brought about by the perceived crisis of the modern welfare state, a crisis of development, a global environmental crisis, the crisis of state socialism, and was facilitated by a dramatic revolution in communications and considerable global economic growth during the 1960s and early 1970s. He predicts that the proliferation of these groups may "alter permanently the relationship between states and citizens" and may prove to be "as significant to the latter twentieth century as the rise of the nation-state was to the latter nineteenth".

From a US perspective, Walzer´s and Salamon´s prognosis become a diagnosis in Michael Clough´s 1994 analysis of what he perceives as the "current crisis in American foreign policy", the roots of which run to the "collapse of America´s postwar policy making system" put in place during the Cold War. Technological and demographic transformations, increased mobility, and higher levels of immigration have integrated Americans with each other as well as with the rest of the world to an unparalleled degree and led to a "fresh constellation of domestic forces" creating its own global policy and rendering the idea of a separation between domestic and foreign affairs untenable. He concludes that making sense of US foreign policy requires a fuller understanding of these pressures, the foremost of which he dubbed the "regionalization of global policy making" by a variety of actors, the "impact of ethnicity" in an ethnically more diversified America, and the "rise of powerful global issue groups" organized around individual issues. These "new domestic forces" could well lead to the "balkanization of the foreign policy making process" (1994:2-7). Single-issue-lobbying, which can involve foreign governments, is reflected in an increasingly fragmented US Congress, as Roger H. Davidson and Walter J. Oleszek show (1990:281-304).

The recent rediscovery of "civil society", the modern concept of which was revived in the struggles of the democratic oppositions in Eastern Europe against authoritarian socialist party-states (Cohen,Arato 1992:15-18), coincides with a heightened interest in transnationalism. In contrast to "transnationalism", the term "civil society" can be found in many contemporary dictionaries of political theory, such as *The Blackwell Encyclopedia of Political Thought* (Miller 1987:77), the *Oxford Illustrated Encyclopedia* (Hoggart 1993:52), or *The Hutchinson Dictionary of Ideas* (Norton 1994:100). For a detailed definition of the term "transnational", however, one has to go back in time and consult, for example, *The Harper Dictionary of Modern Thought* (Bullock,Stallybrass 1977:644). There we learn that "transnational relations" and "transnational society" are terms that were coined by Raymond Aron in his book *Paix et Guerre entre les Nations* of 1962 to "describe the variety of relationships, activities, and organizations which operate across national frontiers".[25] Aron suggests that such activities flourished in Europe before 1914, when economic enterprises, labor parties, sporting organizations (Olympic Games), Christian Churches and citizens, for example, in Germany and France created a "transnational society" that "reveals itself by commercial exchange, migration of persons, common beliefs, organizations that cross frontiers and, lastly, ceremonies or competitions open to the members of all these units". He contrasts this time period with that between 1946 and 1953, when the Cold War was at its height, leading to "this total rupture of transnational society". Communication between Western and Soviet Europe was reduced to a minimum and conducted solely through governmental channels (1966:104-106).

The *Harper Dictionary of Modern Thought* also refers to the study *Transnational Relations and World Politics*, edited by Robert O. Keohane and Joseph S. Nye in 1972. Arguing with Aron's observation of the impact of the Cold War, it is maybe no coincidence that this important work was published at a time when the bipolar world of East-West antagonisms, dominated by militarily opposed state alliances, experienced a period of détente that allowed to question the legitimacy of a "state-centric view of world affairs" and to sharpen the sight for other modes of "intersocietal inter-

---

[25] *The Oxford Illustrated Encyclopedia* carries a brief definition of "transnational relations" described as the "wide variety of relationships and activities between groups and individuals in different states that are not controlled by governments (non-state actors)" (Hoggart 1993:315)

course" practiced by "nonstate entities". Nye and Keohane note that the impact of "transnational actors" on world politics "has often been ignored both in policy-oriented writings and more theoretical works" (1972:ix,x,v,vi). The diminished nuclear threat to territorial integrity and national security after the demise of the Cold War has lessened the utility of disciplinarian rhetorical strategies in ritualized political jeremiads. Their purpose was to build up loyal support for a variety of state policies of the "redeemer nation" (Ernest Lee Tuveson), i.e. the US, relying on the nexus of apocalyptic paranoia, millennial utopia and collective achievement.

During the Cold War, the US sought to survive in an environment, which fostered a "genocidal mentality" and an ideology of "nuclearism" (Robert J. Lifton) centering around the atom bomb as fetish (Opitz 1993b:168-177,192-193). In general, the end of the Cold War has further weakened the military imperatives in the service of "national defense", which sustained the nation-state, and stimulated a revival of democratic "associationalism" (Hirst 1994:6-7,12-14).

The authors contributing to *Transnational Relations and World Politics* are interested in a wide variety of transnational phenomena such as multinational business enterprises and revolutionary movements; trade unions and scientific networks; international air transport cartels and communications activities in outer space; as well as international non-governmental organizations such as the *Ford Foundation* or the *Roman Catholic Church*. Interestingly, transnational relations between ethnic communities in immigrant-receiving countries and their home countries are not examined (1972:ix,x,v,vi). After the end of the Cold War, however, Walzer and Clough, as was shown, explicitly mention the role of "ethnic groups" and the "impact of ethnicity" in transnational arrangements and in US foreign policy. What had happened in the meantime? The effects of increased immigration, well documented in many studies,[26] had been taken into consideration in scientific thought on transnational relations.

Nina Glick Schiller, Linda Basch, and Cristina Blanc-Szanton point out that, according to an increasing number of anthropologists, immigrants live their lives across borders and maintain their ties to home. To describe this new way of life, they state, some social scientists have begun to use the term "transnational"(1992:1). Constance R. Sutton, for example, discerns the "emergence of a transnational sociocultural system" encompassing the Caribbean and New York City, which has become a "truly global city" (1987:15), while Elsa M. Chaney describes Caribbean life in New York City as the "product of the continuous circular movement of people, cash, material goods, culture and lifestyles, and ideas" to and from New York City and the islands of the Caribbean (1987:3). Glick Schiller et al. define transnationalism as the "processes by which immigrants build social fields that link together their country of origin and their country of settlement" (1992:1). Accordingly, this new type of migrants was described as "transmigrants".

In search of an analytic framework for understanding migration, they propose a synthesis of two diverging currents in social sciences, which had developed over the past several decades: First, descriptions of migrant behavior, which focused on each population as a discrete and separate phenomenon, as a bounded unit living in one place and bearing a unique and readily identifiable culture. And, second, "world sys-

---

[26] For the new immigration to New York, encouraged and facilitated by changes in US immigration policy as well as by complex economic and political factors, see Foner (1987) and Kraly (1987).

tem theory" (Immanuel Wallerstein), which allowed to link penetration of capital into previously non-capitalized sectors of production to the movements of people into the labor market. Thus the study of migrating populations, they argue, should combine an emphasis on social relations, understood to be fluid and dynamic, yet culturally patterned, with an analysis of the global context. In this view, transnationalism is simultaneously seen as a "product of world capitalism", as a "cultural flow", and as "social relations"; as social fields, in which transmigrants construct and maintain a wide range of complex racial, national, religious, ethnic, political, gender, and class identities to express their resistance to the global and economic situations that engulf them, even as they accommodate themselves to living conditions marked by vulnerability and insecurity (Glick Schiller et al. 1992:1-24).

In 1994, Basch, Blanc-Szanton, and Glick Schiller refined their framework for the study of transnationalism, which they base on four theoretical premises: (1) the requirement of analyzing transnational migration within the context of global relations between capital and labor; (2) the perception of transnationalism as a process, by which *migrants* create social fields that cross national borders; (3) the insight into the likely limitations of researchers´ ability of analyzing transnationalism by means of bounded social science concepts; and (4) the realization that transmigrants find themselves confronted with nation building processes of two or more nation-states, which are configured by hegemonic categories such as race and ethnicity (1994:23-46).[27] In their anthropological view of "deterritorialized nation-states", transnationalism is reduced *per definitionem* to the phenomenon of periphery-to-center migration and to what could be called *ethnic diasporic transnationalism* displayed by recent US *immigrant* populations. They abstain, however, from dealing with the question of how the variety of non-state "intersocietal interactions" examined by Nye/Keohane et al. could be termed. Their concept of transnationalism is therefore itself bounded. A 1990 study by Haitian-American anthropologist Carolle Charles on Haitian migrants in New York limits the term transnationalism somewhat further to a specific mode of incorporation *within* US society after the fact of emigration, resulting from a culture clash of differing meanings of social categories between immigrant and society at large (1990:3-19).

There are, however, scholars, who take yet another look at the subject of transnationalism. For Masao Miyoshi, for example, transnationalism is foremost an economic phenomenon and the direct product of colonialism, "even more active now in the form of transnational corporatism", which leads to a seemingly "borderless world" and the "decline of the nation-state". He argues that economic enterprises of highly mobile and increasingly autonomous "transnational corporations (TNCs)" from the First World, distinguished from "multinational corporations" by the higher degree of alienation from the country of origin, represent, for the time being, the final stage of denationalizing economic operations. By applying "post-fordist production methods", TNCs are able to move whole business systems overseas and cause, as part of the "third industrial revolution", a "huge demographic movement across the world". This global process of "denationalization and transnationalization", Miyoshi points out, became more visible in the 1980s, when the gross domestic product of 64 out of 120 countries was smaller than the annual sales of 68 TNCs in mining and manufacturing. He summarizes: "TNCs continue colonialism" (1993:726-751).

---

[27] For a detailed discussion of a variety of studies, which these premises draw upon, see ibid.

According to the 1997 World Investment Report of the *United Nations Conference on Trade and Development* (UNCTAD), there were 44,000 TNCs worldwide, with the 100 biggest, led by *Royal Dutch Shell*, holding one fifth of the capital stock of all TNCs combined. 30 of the top-100-list were headquartered in the US, 18 in Japan, 11 in Great Britain, and 9 in Germany. The first two TNCs from developing countries, South Korea and Venezuela, emerged among the top-100 in 1995. The UNCTAD-report spoke of a boom of direct investments by TNCs abroad, increasing by 10.3% in 1996. While the lion's share, $208 billon, still went into industrialized countries, developing countries were able to catch up. They attracted $129 billion, which amounts to an increase of 34% (SZ 09/22/97:23). The relative financial prowess of TNCs and nation-states, to which Miyoshi refers, is reminiscent of Hobsbawm's observation. He notes that major transformations in the international division of labor, especially since the 1960s, and the development of networks of global economic transactions, which are, for practical purposes, outside the control of state governments, have increasingly undermined territorially bounded national economies, the constitution of which was once thought to be one important function of "the nation" (1990:173-175).

As early as the 1970s, transnational economic processes and private international financial activities were seen as being able to restrict the freedom of governments to establish social priorities and seriously infringe on governmental sovereignty in highly developed and less developed states alike (Morse 1972:23;Krause 1972: 189). It is observed that multinational corporations may arouse nationalistic feelings by their predominant positions in less developed countries (Gilpin 1972:68), which are forced by the relative weakness of their local entrepreneurial class toward more centralized forms of economic organization in search of greater autonomy (Evans 1972: 341). The US is seen as gaining most from the continuation of the trend in increased economic interdependence and losing least from its interruption (Vernon 1972:369).

In the wake of Wallerstein's *The Modern World System* (1974), an increasing number of scientists explored the economic determinants of periphery-to-center migration under many theoretical premises. Especially Robert A. Pastor's *Migration and Development in the Caribbean* (1985) aroused considerable attention in the scientific community. A host of literature exploring the connection between the movement of people and economic conditions followed suit, in particular with regard to countries in the Caribbean Basin.[28] But far from being a contemporary phenomenon, moving from place to place in search of a better life has been an institutionalized strategy of survival and adaptation for more than 150 years, especially in countries of the anglophone Caribbean, the cultures of which generated a migration tradition dating back to the times of slavery.[29] In a global perspective, causes and consequences of economic migration in many other regions of the world have received scholarly attention in the 1990s as well.[30]

In comparison to Glick Schiller et al., a broader concept of transnationalism was introduced by Arjun Appadurai. In his thought, the crisis perceived by Clough in US

---

[28] See, for example, Richardson (1983); Levine (1987); Palmer (1990); CSIMCED (1990); Diaz-Briquets,Weintraub (1991); Grasmuck,Pessar (1991); Richardson (1992); and Palmer (1995).
[29] See, for example, Richardson (1983:5,7,10-16); Marshall (1987:15-18); Carnegie (1987:32-43); Chaney (1987:10); Sutton (1987:23); Richardson (1992:134-136); and Simmons,Guengant (1992:94,107-108).
[30] See, for example, Appleyard (1991); Kritz,Lim,Zlotnik (1992); and P.J. Opitz (1997).

foreign policy in particular takes the shape of a "current crisis of the nation" in general. According to him, the idea that we enter a "postnational world" is now a "recurrent theme" in studies of postcolonialism, of global politics, and of international welfare policy. The "nationalist genie" has become itself "diasporic", causing strains in the union of nation and state. With "deterritorialization" seen as one of the "central forces of the modern world", the relationship between states and nations has turned into an "embattled one", leading to disjuncture and difference in the global cultural economy. Under these new constraints, the US has evolved into a "federation of diasporas" that entertain a double loyalty to their nation of origin and to America, which might increase the choice of dual citizenship; into one "node in the postnational network of diasporas" comprising a variety of "delocalized transnations", whose members love America while engaging in "extraterritorial nationalism"; into a republic of "diasporic communities" entangled in the tension between the centripetal pull of Americanness and the centrifugal pull of "diasporic diversity". Similar conclusions evoke jeremiads authored by those who anticipate an imminent "disuniting of America" (Schlesinger 1992).[31]

Appadurai proposes an elementary framework as the foundation of a "chaos theory" of global cultural interaction by introducing five fluid, irregular, and interconnected "landscapes" as analytical terms: mediascapes, technoscapes, financscapes, ideoscapes, and ethnoscapes. The latter is broadly defined as "the landscape of persons who constitute the shifting world in which we live: tourists, immigrants, refugees, exiles, guestworkers and other moving groups and persons constitute an essential feature of the world and appear to affect the politics of (and between) nations to a hitherto unprecedented degree". He explicitly adds the phenomenon of politically motivated, forced migration when expressing his view that "refugee camps, refugee bureaucracies, refugee relief movements, refugee-oriented departments of nation-states, and refugee-oriented transnational philanthropies all constitute one part of the permanent framework of the emergent, postnational order" (1990:6-7,11,13,20;1993:411,413,419,423, 424-425). How different types of "transnationalism" relate to concepts such as civil society, economic exchange, foreign policy, nation-states, and refugee flows, will be shown further below.

2.2 Refugee Studies and Haitian Community Studies

Resonating Walzer´s, Salamon´s, Miyoshi´s, and Appadurai´s thesis of increasingly limited state sovereignty in a postnational world from an explicit refugee-related perspective, Howard Adelman, writing on "ethnicity and refugees", expresses his belief that "we are entering a new world order" after the demise of communism. In this new world order, "borders will no longer be sacrosanct", and the "danger of greater instability" will loom. With the refugee claims system increasingly perceived as a "back door for immigration", he observes that "Western states believe that they are

---

[31] Arthur Schlesinger identifies a destructive "cult of ethnicity" that threatened to transform America into a "nation of groups" structured along ethnic and racial lines and endangering the "balance between unum and pluribus" (1992:16-17,102,113,133).

losing control over their borders and their own rights to self-determination" (1992:11,7). And for Gil Loescher, there can be no doubt that "mass migrations as a global security problem" can "endanger social and economic stability and security", especially that of the poorest states on earth, which carry the "world's refugee burden (...) overwhelmingly". He states that the "spectre of mass influxes" resulting from both "South-North population movements" and "South-South population movements" is often invoked "as a threat to the national security of host governments" (1991:7-14). Thus both scholars recognize the potential effects of migratory and refugee flows - which are inherently of a transnational nature, as will be shown further below - on certain properties associated with the concept of the nation-state. But research on what Harto Hakovirta called "refugeeism", i.e. the causes and consequences of the world refugee problem as a subject for the discipline of international politics (1986:11-14), has rarely assumed an explicitly transnational angle.

Aristide R. Zolberg, Astri Suhrke, and Sergio Aguayo, however, note in their comprehensive work of 1989 on "conflict and the refugee crisis in the developing world" that the "new orientation" of putting a "transnational emphasis" on refugee-related examinations had led to a substantial recasting of the original framework of their study. As a consequence, one of the main conclusions of their book was "that the causes of life-threatening conditions in the developing world stem from an interpenetration of national and transnational, or global, processes". In the chapter on "Haitian Un-Development", they state: "Second, and better documented, is that the arrival of so many Haitians in the United States meant that many groups became involved and interested in the Haitians' situation, both in the United States itself and on the island. Some groups helped the Haitians in the United States but also agitated for change in Haiti, by funding local development projects, pressuring Congress, and denouncing human rights violations". Yet, they add that the "involvement of American NGOs in support of the local groups is yet another aspect of Haiti's recent history needing research" (1989:viii,33,197-198). In a similar vein, Virginia A. Hodgkinson observes that "[m]ore research is needed on the advocacy functions of nonprofit organizations and their impact on public policy" (1989:17).

If and how US immigrants of the same nationality as refugees seeking asylum in the US organized themselves is a question they do not raise. Other knowledgeable scholars in the field of refugee studies maintain in general, however, that US immigrants, including former refugees, have become active politically. Robert F. Gorman, for example, states: "Resettled refugees constitute a growing constituency in U.S. politics, while overseas refugee populations, by and large, lack a strong domestic lobby in the United States". He maintains further that "[c]ongressional, executive, and judicial agents leave different marks on the [U.S. refugee] policy, as do the private voluntary agencies, expatriate communities, and state governments that vie to influence its formation" (1990:140,132).

In a similar vein, Norman L. Zucker and Naomi Flink Zucker state that private, non-profit voluntary agencies ("volags") and their local constituents are "integral to the formulation and execution of refugee policy, and resettlement specifically, in general acting as the public's conscience; the private voluntary agencies testify before Congress on which, and how many, refugees should be permitted to enter. They also testify on what the refugees' status and benefits should be, and for how long those benefits should continue" (1987:101,121-122). Others observe that, in fact, US refugee policy is affected by concerns of domestic interest groups, which also include ethnic and other constituent groups within the country. In an *CRS Issue Brief* of 1990, Lois McHugh quotes Julia Taft, Director of the Office of Foreign Disaster Assistance during the Reagan Administration and a "long-term expert on refugee issues" as stating that "[e]thnic groups and their allies have become very successful in influencing Congress and the executive branch on the merits of continued admissions for their compatriots overseas". McHugh adds that "[t]hese domestic pressures can lead to competition over admissions between groups" (1990:12-13).

Zucker and Zucker further conceptualize an "iron triangle of U.S. refugee policy", consisting of three major components: first, the executive branch [the Coordinator for Refugee Affairs, the *US State Department* (USSD), the *Immigration and Naturalization Service* (INS) within the *US Justice Department* (USJD) and the *Office of Refugee Resettlement* (ORR) within the *US Department of Health and Human Services*]; second, the legislative branch (the appropriate Congressional committees and sub-committees in the Senate and the House of Representatives); and, third, pressure groups (religious and secular voluntary agencies, and representatives of states receiving refugees). They explicitly include "concerned ethnics" into the third component. They see this "iron triangle of interested actors" as being driven by a "second somewhat more amorphous triangle of shifting concerns: foreign policy, budgetary restrictions, and domestic pressures". The latter is defined as a "complex relationship of various attitudes", e.g. "racial and ethnic bias", which seems to only comprise attitudes held by non-minority members of mainstream US society. With regard to what they deem a failure of the 1980 Refugee Act as it was originally intended by Congress, they conclude that the "asylum process has devolved into an unending contest between the government, on the one hand, whose goal is to discourage, deter, and eventually deport asylum-seekers, and, on the other hand, refugee advocates whose goal is to prevent the hasty or ill-considered deportation of asylum-seekers" (1991:225,248). The role of "concerned ethnics" is not dealt with in detail.[32]

As far as Caribbean community studies are concerned, Roy Simon Bryce-Laporte deplores the "special invisibility" of a specific group of ethnics in the US, namely that of Caribbean origin, which he sees as being "reflected and perhaps caused by the dearth of studies". He ascertains that "[There has been no] significant research on the contributions, lives, and roles of Caribbean immigrants in this country or this city [New York], from a socio-scientific or an historical perspective. ... We have not (...) said it all. There are many questions which remain unasked" (1987:69). In the same vein, Susan Buchanan Stafford complains about the lack of research in this area by noting: "Although Afro-Caribbean immigrants form an increasingly large proportion of the immigrants currently settling in New York City, the effects of this immigration on the city, as well as on the immigrants, have only recently become the subject of

---

[32] Zucker and Zucker's essay appeared in *Refugee Policy: Canada and the United States*, edited by Howard Adelman in 1991, which is the most comprehensive comparative study in refugee affairs between the US and Canada to date. None of the contributors, however, write about the role of immigrant populations in refugee politics. Other noteworthy studies published earlier concentrate on the country-specific causes of "The Haitian Exodus" (Stepick 1987:131-151) by also focusing on the nexus of "Migration and Development in Hispaniola" (Preeg 1985:140-156).

scholarly attention" (1987:131).³³ Nancy Foner also indicates the fact that "surprisingly little research has yet been carried out" on the "enormous flood of new immigrants" into New York City (1987:28).³⁴ As early as 1984, Haitian-American anthropologist Michel S. Laguerre called on the scientific community to conduct more research on a sub-group of the Caribbean immigrant population: "It is my hope that others will join in this effort to help the Haitian-American community to understand its strengths and its weaknesses, and to recommend the best course of action for its survival and its integration in the mainstream of American society" (1984:159). What were the "contributions and roles" of Haitian immigrants in New York City during the Haitian crisis between 1991 and 1994 with its concomitant influx of Haitian refugees into the US? What were the "effects of this immigration" on New York City's Haitian immigrants? What were the "strengths and weaknesses" of the Haitian-American community during that time?

Ever since, there have been a series of essays as well as monographs on the Caribbean community in New York City in general and on the city's Haitian immigrant population in particular. Philip Kasinitz' 1992 study *Caribbean New York* focuses on what he calls "ethnicity entrepreneurs" in the Caribbean community, which he notes is "at the historical moment when [its] identity is being redefined" and when its "role in the city's political life is now in flux", with a "pan-West Indian identity" as a strategy of adaptation fast becoming a cultural and political force both in New York and in the Caribbean (1992:176-202,2,11). Haitians, however, are mentioned only sporadically, and refugee issues are not dealt with at all. In the same year, Glick Schiller et al. published the anthology *Towards a Transnational Perspective on Migration* cited above, which also contains essays on the Haitian immigrant population. Karen Richman reflects upon "inflections of transnationalism in the discourse of Haitian President Aristide" (1992:198-200), and Charles ponders "transnationalism in the construct of Haitian migrant's racial categories of identity in New York City" (1992:101-123), a summary of her 1990 study cited above. This comprehensive monograph also deals with "changing patterns of Haitian migration" and with "Haitian life in New York City" (1990:147-198,199-256), but it does not shed light on how Haitians organized themselves when confronted with large waves of refugees from their own home country. The same holds true for Rose-Marie Cassagnol Chierici's study *Demele* on "migration and adaptation among Haitian boat people" in the agribusiness of Rochester (NY).

The fact of the matter is that Haitian community studies thus far have not specifically focused on the refugee situation, while refugee studies have not specifically focused on the Haitian community. Besides Richard Miller's old study of 1984 on *The Plight of Haitian Refugees* and Jean-Claude Icart's study *Négriers d'eux-memes* of 1987 on Haitian boat people in Florida, Alex Stepick's often quoted *Haitian Refugees*

---

³³ Bryce-Laporte's "contextual statement" on Caribbean immigration and Buchanan Stafford's essay on Haitians' "language and identity" appeared in the anthology *Caribbean Life in New York,* which also includes Constance Sutton's essay on the "emergence of a transnational sociocultural system" as well as Elsa Chaney's essay on the "context of Caribbean migration" mentioned above. Other essays contained therein deal with residential patterns of Caribbean immigrants in New York City (Conway, Bigby 1987:74-83) and with "unity and diversity in Haitian organizing in New York" (Glick Schiller et al. 1987:182-201).

³⁴ Nancy Foner's book includes an essay by Susan Buchanan Stafford on the "cultural meaning of race and ethnicity" in the Haitian-American community (1987:131-158).

in the U.S. of 1986 concentrates on their specific situation. But the one-page chapter on "Haitians in the U.S." does not reveal the Haitian community´s attitudes and activities vis-a-vis the refugee problem. We only learn that "the Courts have been the most powerful ally of the Haitian boat people", when the *Haitian Refugee Center* (HRC) in Miami filed the case "Haitian Refugee Center vs. Civiletti" in May 1979, resulting in Federal Judge James King´s ruling of July 1980, which found INS procedures to be unlawful (1986:14-15). In 1987, Norman Zucker noted that the "Haitians (...) became a rallying point for both sides [exclusionists and refugee supporters] in the continuing refugee controversy", which he details with a focus on the relatively successful "challenges in the courts to government misconduct" (1987:178,179,177-205).

The most specific studies to date (late 1990s) are the 4-page essay "Exile, Ethnic, Refugee" of 1987 by Glick Schiller et al. and the 10-page essay "The Implications of Haitian Transnationalism for U.S.-Haiti Relations" of 1995, dealing with the refugee issue in the context of the Haitian community. The former concludes that "some Haitians have organized themselves first as exiles, next as immigrants belonging to a Haitian ethnic group, and then as political refugees" (1987:11), while the latter makes the questionable, categorical statement that "in 1992 the 10th Department [Haitian diaspora] embraced these [Haitian] refugees as a symbol of the Haitian people" (1995:118). Likewise, Basch et al.´s study *Nations Unbound* of 1994 cited above contains relevant information in the two chapters on the "establishment of Haitian transnational social fields" and on "hegemonic agendas, Haitian transnational practices, and emergent identities" (1994:145-180,181-224). It is important to note that the multitude of research questions posed by Glick Schiller et al. in 1992 did not include an inquiry into the ways immigrant populations themselves respond to an ongoing refugee crisis originating from their own home country (1992:xi-xiv). Such a study is even more desirable when considering that refugees have increased as a proportion of all immigrants between 1983 and 1994: There were about 11 refugees for every 100 immigrants admitted to the US in 1983, increasing to about 18 refugees per 100 immigrants in 1990 before easing back to 16 in 1992, and further to 14 in both 1993 and 1994 (ORR 1992:4;1993:6;1994:6). This study´s purpose is to fulfill this task.

2.3 A Relational Theory of Transnationalism

Keohane and Nye define "transnational interactions" as the "movement of tangible and intangible items across state boundaries when at least one actor is not an agent of a government or an intergovernmental organization". In other words, they consider "transnational" interactions as those involving non-governmental actors (individuals or organizations), which may also relate to governments. They contrast the transnational interaction pattern with the classic paradigm of interstate politics, which depicts interactions involving only governments as the agencies, through which societies deal politically with each other, either directly or indirectly through intergovernmental organizations. These state-to-state relations can also be termed "horizontal" relations, as Mark Gibney does with reference to Lea Brilmayer´s argument (1991:94). According to Keohane´s and Nye´s definition, interactions are to be considered as transnational, when individuals or organizations "bypass" their own governments

(1972:xii-xiv).[35] Thus, they define transnational interactions as *direct* relations between individuals or organizations in one country with individuals, organizations or governments in a foreign country. As we will see, this definition is too narrowly conceptualized as to adequately represent the new reality of diasporic communities of "deterritorialized nation-states"[36] engendered by large-scale movements of people since the late 1960s.

It is worthwhile spelling out the transnational interaction paradigm presented by Keohane and Nye while taking into consideration diasporic communities. These are defined from the perspective of the classical political science definition of nation-states, according to which nation-states are communities composed of three structural elements: the *people*, who belong to the nation-state as its citizens endowed with certain rights, the state *territory*, on which these people live, and the state government exercising authoritative *power* over its territory and people.[37] Accordingly, diasporic communities are groups of people with citizenships or nationalities not necessarily consistent with the state, on the territory of which they live. We hypothesize a two-society-system, Haiti and the US, depicted in a formalized matrix. The matrix consists of two components for each society: firstly, the state territory, from which transnational relations originate, and, secondly, the mobile transnational subject (individuals or organizations) holding a citizenship that may be or may not be congruent with the state, on the territory of which he/she stays. Combined, these components generate all

---

[35] Likewise, Behrens and Noack present a schematized chart depicting a two-state-system in order to differentiate between three possible types of relations. The inner structure of each state consists of a government (R) and several social groups (G). Both the level of international organizations (IO) and the level of transnational organizations (TO) are integrated into the system. Their model describes, firstly, the sphere of international politics between nation-states as represented by their governments; secondly, the field of transnational politics as relations between natural or juristic persons of various nation-states or between these persons and foreign governments; and, thirdly, the domestic process of the forming of volition in foreign affairs within each nation-state (1984:12-14).

[36] The technical term "deterritorialized nation-*state*" is inappropriate in that it only makes sense from the perspective of its dispersed people abroad, whose long-distance nationalism has become independent from the home state´s territoriality. Taken literally, however, the term is nonsensical from the perspective of the "deterritorialized nation-*state*" itself, as there is no physical disappearance of its territory. From this perspective, it would be more appropriate to speak of *depopularized* nation-state due to high rates of emigration regardless of high population growth, or else of *deauthorized* nation-*state* due to a relative loss of authoritative power over the emigrated portion of its people, who in case of refugees left their home country following arbitrary and violent use of state power. In the final analysis, the shortcomings of the term stem from the growing, migration-induced disjuncture between nation and state.

[37] Ever since the birth of the modern state in the *Peace of Westphalia* of 1648, the principles of territoriality and sovereignty constitute the foundation for international relations between states and for their independence from each other (Behrens,Noack 1984:43). Nationalists tend to emphasize the state´s capacity of providing security in its relation to the outside world, with the state being, as Anthony Smith put it, the "protective shell for their nation" (Smith 1983:178). The three structural elements mentioned above are, of course, not sufficient to constitute a nation. Joseph Stalin, for example, in *Marxism and the National and Colonial Question* of 1912, depicted, besides territoriality, language, economic unity, and culture as four necessary conditions for being a nation: "A nation is a historically evolved, stable community of language, territory, economic life and psychological make-up manifested in a community of culture" (Hobsbawm 1990:5). Various types of nationalism can be differentiated. For a definition of the terms *Staatsnation* and *Kulturnation*, between which the German historian Friedrich Meinecke distinguished, see Peter Alter (1985:19). For a typology of nationalisms, the most basic of which are "ethnic nationalism" and "civic nationalism", see Anthony Smith (1983:224-226).

those *direct* types of transnational relations that constitute citizen-to-citizen relations. Furthermore, when supplemented with both state governments in the two-society-system, it is possible to generate all those *direct* types of relations that constitute citizen-to-state relations. "Relations" are defined not only as direct eye-to-eye contact, but also as mediated contacts established through all sorts of communication vehicles such as letter, telephone or fax etc., and as publicly or semi-publicly uttered attitudes towards a potential communication partner, mediated by the press (e.g. demonstrations or panel discussions covered by the media). Theoretically, there are eight types of *direct* transnational citizen-to-(foreign) citizen relations between Haiti and the US:

(1) those relations of Haitian citizens organized in Haiti's society with US-citizens organized in US society,
(2) those of Haitian citizens organized in Haiti's society with Haitian citizens organized in US society,
(3) reversely, transnational relations of US-citizens organized in US society (partially Haitian immigrants) with Haitian citizens organized in Haiti's society,
(4) and those of US-citizens organized in US society (partially Haitian immigrants), with US-citizens organized in Haiti's society,
(5) those of US-citizens organized in Haiti's society with US-citizens organized in US society,[38]
(6) those of US-citizens organized in Haiti's society with Haitian citizens organized in US society,
(7) those of Haitian citizens organized in US society (mainly Haitian immigrants) with Haitian citizens organized in Haiti's society, and
(8) those of Haitian citizens organized in US society (mainly Haitian immigrants) with US-citizens organized in Haiti's society.[39]

When including the foreign governments into this matrix of transnational relations, i.e. the governments abroad belonging to the state territory, on which the transnational subject does *not* currently reside, there are another four direct types of relations that can be dubbed *reverse* "diagonal" relations in reference to Mark Gibney's definition (1991:94)[40] or citizen-to-(foreign) state relations:

(9) those of Haitian citizens organized in Haiti's society with the US-government,
(10) those of US-citizens organized in Haiti's society with the US-government,

---

[38] As NYT-correspondent Larry Rohter reported in July 1994, there were about 3,000 Americans, 2,000 Canadians, and 2,500 Britons, who decided to remain in Haiti, according to estimates by diplomats. Before the imposition of economic sanctions, there were more than 6,000 Americans living in Haiti (1994b:10;A3). In July 1994, Congressman Rangel referred to 10,000 people in Haiti as having dual Haitian-American citizenship (Merida 1994:A7). In October 1993, Alexander Fletcher Watson, Assistant Secretary for Inter-American Affairs at the USSD, referred to 10,000 American citizens, "nearly 9,000 of whom are dual nationals" (Cong5:2).
[39] See Figure 1 on page 45 for a graphical description of Citizen Relationships.
[40] Brilmayer and Gibney describe "relationships between the government of one country and the citizens of another country" as "diagonal analysis". Of particular concern to Gibney in the context of the creation of refugee flows are "coercive diagonal relationships" defined as "situations where intervention by an outside state will have severe negative consequences for individuals in the country where the intervention has taken place" (Gibney 1991:94).

(11) reversely, transnational relations of US-citizens organized in US society (partially Haitian immigrants) with the Haitian government, and
(12) those of Haitian citizens organized in US society (mainly Haitian immigrants), with the Haitian government.

Types 10 and 12 virtually represent domestic or "vertical" (Gibney 1991:94) relations originating, however, from foreign territory. Chidozie Ogene called types 9 and 11 "group-external government linkages" (1983:197). To complicate matters even further, one needs to take into consideration that, between 1991 and 1994, there were two Haitian governments claiming legitimacy: the military junta of the putschists, not recognized by the international community, but exercising *de facto* state authority; and the exile government under President Aristide, recognized by the international community and exercising state authority *de jure*. Thus the coup d´etat of September 1991 manouvered Haiti´s legitimate government into a hybrid position at the intersection between civil society and state sphere on non-Haitian diasporic territory.[41]

In addition to direct transnational relations, there are also *indirect* transnational relations, not taken into consideration by Keohane and Nye. They can be generated by combining both foreign and domestic governments into the equation. Indirect transnational relations to the foreign government (or to the society abroad) are established *through* the domestic government, i.e. the government of the state territory, on which the transnational subject currently resides. There are four relations of this type:

(13) transnational relations of US-citizens organized in Haiti´s society with the US-government (or US society) through the Haitian government, and
(14) those of Haitian citizens organized in Haiti´s society with the US-government (or US society) through the Haitian government,
(15) those of US-citizens organized in US society (partially Haitian immigrants) with the Haitian government (or Haiti´s society) through the US-government, and
(16) those of Haitian citizens organized in US society (mainly Haitian immigrants) with the Haitian government (or Haiti´s society) through the US-government.

These types of relations instrumentalize domestic governments in terms of genuine state-to-state relations (or diagonal, state-to-foreign citizen relations) as a tool of transnational politics. They aim at stimulating desired governmental policies that are to affect the government (or society) abroad. Types 14 and 15 are part of the domestic process contributing to the forming of volition in foreign affairs. Ogene calls these types "group-government linkages" and "group-general public-government linkages" (1983:197). Type 15 refers to Zucker´s and Zucker´s "iron triangle of U.S. refugee policy". Types 13 and 16 represent the field of ethnic lobbyism in foreign policy. From a US perspective, type 15 and, most of all, type 16 represent the field of ethnic lobbyism in US foreign policy, which Michael Clough is so concerned about. The history of foreign policy lobbyism by ethnic groups in the US was detailed in *Race, Ethnicity, and American Foreign Policy* by Alexander DeConde (1992). Type 16 is similar to direct

---

[41] In a somewhat similar situation, albeit on its proper state territory, was the Clinton/Gore team within the Democratic Party during the presidential election campaign in 1992.

type 9 in that in both cases, Haitian citizens address the US-government, albeit from different territory.

Finally, there is another *indirect* type of transnational relations with the foreign government (or with the society abroad), which bypass the domestic government. They are established in the sphere of interstate world politics *through* international organizations (OAS, UN) and their subunits seen as semi-autonomous entities.[42] There are another four relations of this type:

(17) transnational relations of Haitian citizens organized in Haiti´s society with the US-government (or US society) through international organizations,
(18) those of US-citizens organized in Haiti´s society with the US-government (or US society) through international organizations,
(19) those of US-citizens organized in US society (partially Haitian immigrants) with the Haitian government (or Haiti´s society) through international organizations, and
(20) those of Haitian citizens organized in US society (mainly Haitian immigrants) with the Haitian government (or Haiti´s society) through international organizations.

(21) *Direct* relations of Haitian citizens organized in Haiti´s society with the Haitian government, and
(22) *direct* relations of US-citizens organized in US society with the US-government (partially Haitian immigrants)

do not represent transnational relations, but "vertical" relations (Gibney 1991:94) within Haiti or the US, which are part of processes contributing to the forming of volition in domestic affairs.

Glick Schiller et al.´s definition of transnationalism seems to cover at least six direct types (3, 4, 7, 8, 11, and 12) out of the total of 20 transnational direct and indirect types of transnational relations possible. Similarly, Keohane´s and Nye´s transnational interaction paradigm covers only direct relations, but is not confined to ethnic diasporic transnationalism only. Walzer must have had types 1 to 8, types 17 to 20, and, to a lesser extent, types 9 to 12 in mind when writing about transnational formations of different sorts "above and below the level of nation-states". All communication levels of transnational relations were used during the Haitian refugee crisis between 1991 and 1994. All transnational relations originating from the Haitian community in New York City are paramount to this study. These relations correspond with types 3, 4, 7, 8, 11, 12, 15, 16, 19, and 20. With these types of transnational relations, albeit in varying intensity, Haitian immigrants in New York City responded to the stream of Haitian refugees after the coup of September 1991. It is important to note and significant to this study that the movement of Haitian refugees towards the US is nothing less than a transnational movement of people in need of protection. This movement corresponds to the types 1, 2, 9, 13, and 17. This is not to say that the decision to leave is always based on a determination *where* to flee to. Flight is more often than not a spontaneous desire to escape *from* violence and terror. Transnational refugee movements perceived

---

[42] Interestingly, this type is not conceived of in the model of Behrens,Noack (1984:43-44).

as endangering territorial integrity and national security of states are the subject, which Adelman and Loescher deal with.[43]

Keohane and Nye distinguish four major types of global interaction: communication (movement of information); transportation (movement of physical objects); finance (movement of money); and travel (movement of persons). Both international and transnational activities may involve all four types of interaction simultaneously (1972:xii). All four types, which seem to denote an *immediate purpose* of the activity, also played a role during the Haitian refugee crisis: disseminating information on the state of repression in Haiti or about the progress of international negotiations for the return of Aristide, transmitted in private by telephone or publicly by the Haitian-American press; providing Haitian compatriots in Haiti with necessities of daily life, having been short in supply as a result of the embargo (i.e. an *internationally coordinated* measure agreed upon by a group of states to prevent the *transnational movement* of merchandise into a given country); supplying Haitian compatriots in Haiti with funds by remitting money; and keeping people from traveling to Haiti in order to isolate the military junta, later instituted by the international community by means of a ban on air traffic. The latter of Keohane´s and Nye´s type (travel) corresponds the most with Appadurai´s "ethnoscape". This specific "landscape" seems to involve a variety of other purposes not listed by Keohane and Nye: pleasure (tourists), residence (immigrants), protection (refugees and exiles), and labor (guestworkers). As will be shown, tourism as a kind of transnational movement (*touristic transnationalism* or *transnational tourism*) played a certain long-term role during the Haitian refugee crisis.

Another way of distinguishing transnational activities is to ask who the transnational subjects are. Since Glick Schiller et al. are interested in transnational relations originating from diasporic communities of ethnic groups, I call this type *ethnic diasporic transnationalism*. Transnational relations originating from the Haitian community may be called *Haitian diasporic transnationalism*. What distinguishes the types of ethnic diasporic transnationalism in the US from, for example, *African-American transnationalism*, *WASP-American transnationalism*, or other kinds of *hyphenated American transnationalisms*, is that the transnational subjects belonging to the former type are engaged in nation building processes of *more than one* nation-state, to which they all feel loyal, as Basch et al. (1994) point out. In other words, they are engaged in "extraterritorial nationalism" (Appadurai) in contrast to the subjects belonging to the variety of hyphenated American transnationalisms, who feel loyal to the nation-state *only*, on the territory of which they were both born and reside, i.e. the US.

Haitian diasporic transnationalists´ engagement in nation building processes of more than one nation-state (Haiti and the US), as opposed to Haitians in the home country, who feel loyal to Haiti only, presupposes a cultural difference between the former and the latter. This difference has been discerned by many Haitians themselves, whose "triple minority status" in the US as black, foreign, and French- and Creole-speaking is in sharp contrast to Haitians in the home country (Laguerre 1984:9).[44]

---

[43] For a more comprehensive discussion, see A. Dowtry and Gil Loescher (1996), p. 43-71.

[44] Jean-Pierre, for example, as host of the weekly English and Haitian Creole program "Radyo Neg Mawon" on the short-wave radio station *Radio for Peace International* himself a member of the Haitian diaspora, hints at a difference between "Haitians on the outside" and Haitians who never left Haiti, which seems to be primarily informed by class: The "wealth of Haitian emigrants is a double-edged sword", he notices, because returning Haitians, easily recognized by their "'air of superiority'", have

Maintaining the myth of homogeneous nations, which Benedict Anderson calls "imagined communities" (1983), seems to be compounded by the condition of deterritorialization.

Yet another way of distinguishing is to ask from what societal sphere transnational activities originate. It is useful to follow the beforementioned three-part model suggested by Cohen and Arato, which distinguishes civil society from both state and economic society (1992:ix-x, chapter 1). Accordingly, it is possible to differentiate between *economic societal transnationalism* and *civil societal transnationalism*. The source of the former type are business enterprises, the source of the latter are non-profit, non-governmental organizations (NGOs). On a global scale, economic societal transnationalism is "transnational corporatism" (Miyoshi), carried out by powerful "global players" such as TNCs. NGOs are the agents in Walzer´s "nascent international civil society" and in Salamon´s "global `associational revolution´". Since ethnic groups are part of both civil and economic society,[45] both correspondent types of transnationalism can be further broken down along *ethnic* lines. Thus *ethnic diasporic transnationalism* interpermeates both *economic societal* and *civil societal* transnationalism.[46] Groups engaged in civil societal transnationalism organize around a variety of individual issues and pursue specific private agendas in non-governmental foreign policy.

The issue of human rights and refugee affairs embedded in transnational settings and seen from the perspective of Haitian migrants in New York as well as its intersectional links to economic society, to other ethnic groups, and to the level of the state is the "cultural theme" (Spradley 1979:186) central to this study.[47] It seeks to decode the culturally constructed *meanings* that the various transnational and intra-societal relations have for Haitian migrants in their organizing efforts. These varying meanings structured their social behavior during the Haitian crisis between 1991 and 1994 and led to preferences of one kind of relations over the other. The meanings of the preferred transnational and intra-societal relations were, as will be shown, more often than not informed by historically grown and culturally absorbed relations of power and can thus be explained by the concept of "hegemony". Coined by Gramsci (1971), the term was introduced into anthropological discourse in the late 1980s, encompassing in Basch et al.´s definition concepts of race, ethnicity, and nation. They are constantly

---

come to be "disparagingly" called "`diaspo`" because of their "`developed´" attitude, their "American lingo", and their "flashy material acquisitions" (1995:202). Likewise, black Haitian-American anthropologist Carolle Charles told me once that she was idenitfied in Haiti by a young Haitian girl as *blan* (white/foreign).

[45] The National Directory *Minority Organizations* lists thousands of groups according to 23 types. Many of them are situated in both economic society such as "Business development and chamber of commerce organizations" or "Professional organizations" and in civil society such as "Civil rights agencies" or "Social service organizations". Mixed types are, for example, "Community development and service organizations" or "Equal Employment and human rights agencies" (GPP 1992).

[46] Basch et al. contemplate about economic transnationalism in terms of "business connections". But these border-crossing business links are, again, confined to the life of migrants belonging to deterritorialized nation-states (1994:243-246).

[47] Spradley defines "cultural theme" as "any cognitive principle, tacit or explicit, recurrent in a number of domains and serving as a relationship among subsystems of cultural meaning". Cultural "domains" are defined as the "larger units of cultural knowledge" (1979:186,94).

redefined and reappropriated in arenas of contention between social classes linked by relations of domination (1994:12-14).

Figure 1: Citizen Relationships

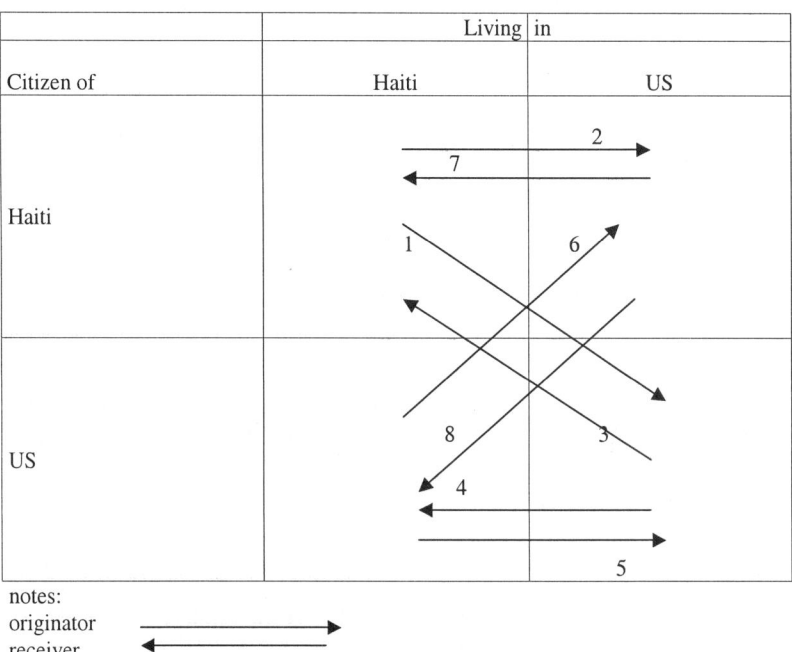

notes:
originator ———————▶
receiver ◀———————

2.3.1 "Nationalistic" and "Ethnic" Organizing in the Context of Refugee Flows

This study concerns itself with "nationalistic" and "ethnic" organizing by Haitian immigrants in New York City. These terms were coined by Glick Schiller et al. (1987:183) and are defined as courses of action "aimed at achieving recognition, status, and resources for an immigrant community as an interest group within the American political system" (ethnic) and courses of action "directed toward influencing the political system in the country of origin rather than attempting to establish a niche in American society" (nationalistic). These definitions distinguish between two opposite orientations used by transmigrants in their organizing activities: the former is directed at positioning one´s own ethnic group within US society, it refers to the "here". The latter is directed at the home country abroad, it refers to the "there". In the former case, the own ethnic group and the people perceived as its members are intended to benefit from organizing activities directed towards US society at large, including the US government. In the latter case, the country of origin is intended to be affected from organizing activities directed towards its society including the Haitian government. These definitions are ideal types, insofar as they do not occur in social practise without deviation. They often affect each other mutually, so that, for example, the Cuban exile community as an ethnic group within the US political system can also be strengthened by its opposing the Castro government.

This, however, does not say anything about the actual orientation taken in the first place. Theoretically, these orientations are mutually exclusive, dichotomous categories. But it is possible in social practise for the ethnic group to profit in one way or the other from nationalistic organizing, just as it is possible for the home country to be affected by unintended side effects of ethnic organizing. Ethnic organizing, for example, may result in achieving resources that improve the status of the ethnic group, which is therefore in turn better able to organize nationalistically at a later point in time. Yet, these reciprocal effects do not say anything about the orientations taken to begin with. An individual can orient himself or herself both nationalistically and ethnically, a skill Mohammed Ahrari called "paradoxical ability" (1987:xvi,156).[48] But if this same person is engaged in nationalistic activities, he/she is *not* engaged in ethnic activities at the *same* time, as far as the specific orientation is concerned. Since nationalistic organizing activities are aimed at influencing the political system in the country of origin, they correspond with direct and indirect transnational relations equivalent to types 11, 12, 15, 16, 19, and 20 as defined above. The term "influencing" should be understood as neutral in terms of comprising both supportive and adversarial transnational relations towards the Haitian government.

From the perspective of most Haitian immigrants in the US, the time period between 1991 and 1994 was, of course, characterized by political divergencies between diaspora and state. Thus their transnational relations are to be seen as adversarial. Insofar as the term "political system" includes Haitian groups organized in Haiti´s society as well, those transnational relations must also be considered, through which groups that aim to influence the Haitian government may be promoted. Those transnational relations correspond, most of all, with the direct types 3, 4, 7, and 8. When speaking of "nationalistic transnational organizing", "nationalistic" denotes the political *purpose* of organizing activities performed by members of diasporic communities that feel loyal towards their home country, whereas "transnational" simply denotes the *border-crossing form* of organizing activities performed by non-state entities. Nationalistic transnational organizing is "extraterritorial nationalism" put in action.

Ethnic organizing activities, on the other hand, manifest themselves in terms of domestic vertical relations of type 22, while US-citizens organized in US society (par-

---

[48] Ahrari observes that the "effectiveness of an ethnic group is also determined by its paradoxical ability to become assimilated into US culture yet still retain enough ethnic identification to pursue foreign policy objectives affecting its old country". In contrast to Irish-Americans, Jewish Americans "appear to have retained their paradoxical ability to assimilate enough yet still retain ample ethnic identification to pursue foreign policy goals affecting Israel" (1987:xvi,156). This paradox seems to be consistent with Herschelle Sullivan Challenor´s observation, made with reference to Michael Parenti´s similar thesis, that African Americans´ increased identification with Africa "exists at a time when blacks have greater access to equal opportunities while they are rejecting many American values" (1981:160). Furthermore, it seems to be in line with Basch et al.´s premise (4) for the study of transnationalism (1994:34-45).

tially Haitian immigrants considered to be integrated into US society to a higher degree) may be joined by Haitian citizens organized in US society (mainly Haitian immigrants) as well. Insofar as the Haitian diaspora is to benefit from direct transnational relations of type 9, which seems to be rather rare, this type is similar to relations of type 22, performed by Haitian citizens organized in US society. When speaking of "ethnic vertical organizing", "ethnic" denotes the political *purpose* of organizing activities performed by members of an interest group belonging to US society, whereas "vertical" simply denotes its non-border-crossing, *intrastate form*. Nationalistic organizing is carried out by a member of a diasporic community, who feels to be part of the nation abroad, at which his/her organizing efforts are directed. Ethnic organizing is carried out by a member of an ethnic group, who feels to belong to the nation, in which his/her organizing activities are presently carried out. Ethnic organizing in the US of today is largely performed under the paradigm of multiculturalism granting - in contradistinction to the old WASP-centric assimilationist ideology of the "melting pot" as well as the concept of cultural pluralism under white supremacy - some recognition to the barriers of race (Basch et al. 1994:286-287;Ostendorf 1992:3-4,7-8).

At this point, we see that both kinds of organizing activities may overlap in that the experiences made and the methods used to establish *indirect* transnational relations of types 15 and 16 (Haitian ethnic lobbyism in US foreign policy) can be implemented to more successfully establish domestic vertical relations of type 22, so that the ethnic group may benefit from nationalistic organizing activities, when it comes to their ethnic organizing efforts. But again, while the methods of both kinds of organizing activities may be similar (lobbying before the domestic government), the orientations taken respectively differ. Since *indirect* transnational relations of types 15 and 16 resemble ethnic vertical relations in that both types are directed against the domestic government, it is possible to conceive of, reversely, ethnic organizing activities carried out in certain policy arenas with the *ulterior motive* of additionally generating, at a later point in time, a certain foreign policy behavior by the same government, which is thereby *indirectly* lobbied to influence the *home* government. In both areas of organizing, nationalistic and ethnic, diasporic communities may choose to forge alliances and coalitions with a variety of other groups within the US, which Ogene calls "inter-group linkages" (1983:197).

As will be demonstrated, the refugee issue represents such a policy arena. For some civil societal and hyphenated American transnational activists in particular, the return issue was the *hidden agenda* underlying the publicly pursued refugee issue. The common bond they felt with the Haitian refugees was predicated upon diverse motivations, be they humanitarian, racial, historical, or empirical. As members of interest groups within the US political system and in cooperation with or without Haitian activists, they *indirectly* lobbied their *own* government in order to influence the Haitian government abroad. It may be hypothesized that this kind of organizing requires a thorough knowledge of the political process in the US, including the institutional principles and cultural idiosyncrasies governing this process as well as its strengths, weaknesses, and historically derived vulnerabilities. As a consequence, the more acculturated and integrated into US society the transnational subject is, the more he/she is capable of performing this kind of organizing. In other words, the "paradoxical ability" of both hyphenated American and Haitian diasporic activists must be balanced to the extent of having as much identification as necessary and as much identification as possible with the US *and* with Haiti, respectively. Both activist groups can be assumed to be socially situated at different stages in a reciprocal adjustment process of unconscious cultural exchange called "creolization" (Ostendorf 1992:6-7). In the final analysis, transnational organizing by both activist groups is a product of this tension between inclusion and exclusion.

Where, however, to draw the line between "ethnic" and "nationalistic" when dealing with refugee streams originating from the ethnic group's own home country? It is useful to choose the US state border as the preliminary dividing line between both orientations, because it is there that a "refugee" assumes the status of an "asylum-seeker" with all concomitant legal consequences. This border line is derived from the way nation-states developed in general, and from interstate practices with respect to international refugee law in particular. In order to determine when the transition between nationalistic and ethnic organizing occurs, it is further useful to envision various stages in a refugee's flight. From the perspective of the Haitian community in the US, this flight presents itself as a continuum that extends from "there" to "here": from an Aristide-supporting Haitian citizen in Haiti to an adversary of the *de facto* regime, from a victim of human rights violations to an internally displaced person in hiding, from a refugee belonging to the boat people to an intercepted Haitian national aboard a USCG cutter, from an internee on the US military base at Guantanamo to an INS-determined screened-in refugee, from an asylum-seeker on US-territory to a client of a private voluntary agency placed for resettlement, from an approved asylum-seeker to a member of the Haitian community, from a residential alien to a US-citizen.

Consequently, the farther the refugee moves from Haiti and the closer he/she moves towards the US, the more he/she changes from an object of nationalistic organizing to one of ethnic organizing. The closer the refugee moves towards the Haitian community in the US, the more he/she is perceived as a potential member of this community. In this process, the US state border is the most decisive barrier on the refugee's flight from "there" to "here", on his/her way out of the Haitian state authorities' sphere of influence towards the US state authorities' sphere of influence. In Haiti, the refugee is more directly associated with human rights abuses as a cause of his/her escape. In the US, the need of resettlement and care for the refugee is more salient. In Haiti, he/she is politically active in the field of Haitian domestic politics (type 21), though affected, to varying degrees, by foreign policies of state governments abroad. In the US, he/she is present in the area of US politics (types 16 and 22). In Haiti, he/she is victimized by state institutions, such as the Haitian army. Getting closer to the US, he/she is subjected to the treatment by US-authorities (USCG, US military, INS, US asylum courts etc.). To further distinguish between both orientations, it is useful to differentiate between "cause" and "consequence". Organizing activities directed at removing the *immediate causes* of the refugee's outbound flight (Haitian army etc.) are nationalistic in character, since they are oriented towards the home country.

Organizing activities, on the other hand, oriented towards the *circumstances* (treatment by US-authorities) and the *consequences* (need of resettlement in the US) of the refugee's flight are rather of an ethnic nature.[49] Obviously, the US state border as

---

[49] Hence the so-called "return issue", i.e. the demand for removal of the military junta and Aristide's reinstatement as Haiti's legitimate president, is rather "nationalistic". The so-called "refugee issue", i.e. the demand for protecting their rights and for granting them asylum, is rather "ethnic".

theoretical dividing line between nationalistic and ethnic orientations is problematic, since in practise US state power extends *beyond* its proper state territory. In other words, the range of US state authorities´ sphere of influence is wider than the range of Haitian state authorities´ sphere of influence, resulting from differential power relations. This is evident with the USHIA of 1981, which erected an additional barrier for Haitian refugees in international waters. Furthermore, it is evident with the installation of so-called In-country Processing Centers for refugee applications set up by the US within Haiti. Thus ethnic organizing in conjunction with refugee issues is not confined to US state territory within its proper borders. It comprises the US state power´s sphere of influence projected across its own state border. Hence, it is necessary to distinguish between *intra-territorial* and *extra-territorial* organizing of an ethnic orientation.[50]

To complicate matters further, distinguishing between nationalistic and ethnic organizing can be deemed useless for the analysis of mobilization efforts by US immigrants for the following reasons: One can argue that the emergence of a "transnational socio-cultural system" (Sutton) between the Caribbean and the US merged Haiti and the US to the extent of not being able any longer to properly distinguish between both states. US dominance of the Caribbean has transformed the region into one single, highly integrated unit. As a result of this synthesis, the "Haitian state" is not discernible any longer as an autonomous entity. This process can be seen as having culminated in the US occupation of September 1994, converting Haiti into a US-protectorate. Consequently, nationalistic organizing cannot be directed towards the Haitian state, since it is entirely usurped and absorbed by US state power. In the final analysis, nationalistic organizing therefore amounts to ethnic organizing; both orientations are equivalent. US hegemony over Haiti, this argument concludes, outdates these categories to the point of irrelevance.[51]

There can be no denying the fact that the US has had, past and present, an immense impact on both the Caribbean and Haiti (Peek,Standing 1982;Pastor 1985;Knight 1990;Trouillot 1990;Plummer 1992). One climax of this impact was the Marine Occupation between 1915 and 1934 (Schmidt 1995), which moved Haiti further into the orbit of US influence. Yet, I hold the thesis of a vanished Haitian state to be exaggerated. The Haitian state´s inherent weakness has been a function of its brutality and, in part, the result of external intrusion and interference. But influence of US state power over internal matters of Caribbean countries has not been as ubiquitous and omnipotent as it sometimes seems to have been. After all, external forces could not prevent the overthrow of the Duvalier regime in 1986 and Aristide´s election in 1990! Haiti as a country at the periphery is dependent on countries in the center in many ways. But dependence is not synonymous with the entire loss of national sovereignty and with the total absence of latitude in the exercise of state rights. The occupation of Haiti in 1995 is doubtless evidence of US power in the Caribbean. But it was met with considerable resistance from other countries in the international community, from the Haitian military junta, from the US public, and from a variety of transnational actors

---

[50] Projecting US state power is not, of course, limited to refugee-related measures and authorities, but includes, *inter alia*, USAID, and the CIA. Conversely, the concept of the *10th Department* put in action also amounts to projecting Haitian state power into US territory. Those diagonal relations are, however, embedded in differential power relations.

[51] I owe these considerations to an exchange of thoughts with Carolle Charles, with whom I had the pleasure to meet again in person on September 17, 1996.

alike. The use of "nationalistic" and "ethnic" orientations as analytical instruments is warranted by these observations.

From a contemporary point of view, human rights abuses in Haiti during the time period under investigation were not perpetrated by US state representatives *per se*, even though one can justifiably argue that they were tolerated through neglect.[52] Conversely, human rights violations on Guantanamo (due process etc.) and on the high seas (forced repatriation etc.) were neither perpetrated by representatives of the *de facto* regime (nor by representatives of Aristide's exile-government), even though *de facto* regime representatives might have approved of them. While "nationalistic" organizing is directed toward the former abuses as the *immediate causes* of the refugee's outbound flight, "ethnic" organizing is directed towards the latter as the *circumstances* of the refugee's flight. From a historical point of view, human rights abuses in Haiti as the *immediate causes* of the refugee's outbound flight are the consequence of the September 1991 coup. The coup, in turn, had causes as well, reaching back into Haiti's history, in which the US played, as mentioned above, a decisive role. In historical perspective, the *mediate* causes of the September 1991 coup are the cumulative factor for the *immediate* causes of the refugee's outbound flight. In other words, the mediate causes can be seen as the backward-directed prolongation of the immediate causes going back in time. To put it yet another way, US influence in Haiti's history can be seen as part and parcel of the complex of mediate causes of human rights abuses producing refugee flows.

This means, the more one tends to interpret the time period under investigation from a historical point of view, the more irrelevant the distinction between nationalistic and ethnic orientations becomes. On the other hand, the more one tends to interpret the time period under investigation from a contemporary point of view, the more relevant the distinction between both orientations becomes. But even if one follows the argument of a vanished Haitian state, distinguishing between nationalistic and ethnic organizing makes sense. While the latter is, now and before, directed at positioning one's own ethnic group within US society, the former is also aimed at promoting groups within Haiti's society in their quest to position themselves vis-a-vis the dominance of US state power in Haiti's internal affairs. In other words, it does not matter if one decides to conceive of either two autonomous states *de jure* or of one overarching state comprising both territories *de facto*. In both cases, differentiating between both orientations makes sense. Ultimately, the contradictions between both orientations seen as ideal types cannot only be used to analyze the way Haitian immigrants in New York City organized against the backdrop of the refugee crisis. It can also be used as a benchmark for measuring the degree, to which the transnational socio-cultural system in the Caribbean has become one highly integrated unit.

---

[52] It is important to note, however, that human rights abuses in Haiti may have been welcomed and even encouraged by US state representatives, as the CIA-FRAPH connection shows (see further below).

3 Methodological Considerations Regarding the First Level of Analysis

As stated above, this study reflects an interdisciplinary approach designed to explore the Haitian refugee crisis on three different levels of analysis: first, the level of bilateral relations between Haiti and the US embedded, as they are, in an international context; second, the level of nationalistic organizing by Haitian immigrants in New York City mainly oriented toward the country of origin, and, third, the level of ethnic organizing predominantly directed toward the host society. The first level of analysis treats the Haitian refugee crisis as a foreign policy problem of the US and provides the bulk of information serving as a foil, against which nationalistic and ethnic organizing must be interpreted. It depicts the major events and decisions of various actors by means of a process analysis, which remains descriptive in nature for the most part.

News articles published in the NYT between September 30, 1991 and October 16, 1994 on the subject of "Haiti" were chosen as the pool of data for the first level of analysis. There are three major methodological reasons for this choice: First, NYT-articles promise to meet the most important requirement for the first level of analysis in that they serve as a relatively unitary source of information covering news that were made available by a variety of state-run news outlets both within the US and abroad. Second, given the criticism regarding the NYT often uttered by Haitian immigrants in the US, the manner, in which the Haitian crisis was covered by the NYT, may be contrasted with the way Haitian immigrants organized. Third, the NYT as a daily press publication also used to a certain degree in the Haitian community of New York may well have affected Haitian immigrants´ outlook on the crisis. All three points will now be discussed in detail.

3.1 The *New York Times* as a Newspaper Relying on Governmental Sources

Opting for the NYT as a source of information makes sense methodologically when considering theories of mass communication in the US. Noam Chomsky and Edward S. Herman, for example, suggest in *Manufacturing Consent* a "propaganda model" for the analysis of the "political economy of the mass media". Their theory posits that there are five news "filters", built into the system of the US mainstream media, which determine newsworthiness: (1) the size, concentrated ownership, and profit orientation of the dominant mass-media firms; (2) advertising as the primary income source of the mass media; (3) the reliance of the media on information provided by government, business, and experts funded and approved by these primary sources and agents of power (sourcing);[53] (4) "flak" (i.e. harsh criticism) as a means of disciplining the media; and (5) "anticommunism" as a national religion and control mechanism.

---

[53] Chomsky and Herman note with regard to the third filter that the Pentagon was publishing 1,203 periodicals in 1982. In sharp contrast, the scope of public-information operations of the *American Friends Service Committee* (AFSC) and the *National Council of the Churches of Christ* (NCCC), two of the largest non-profit organizations critical of the views of the Pentagon, was a tiny fraction of the overall public-information program under the assistant secretary of defense (Chomsky 1988:20). The AFSC and CWS, a unit of NCCC, are also members of NCHR.

The limits of these filter constraints, the theory holds, exclude alternative bases of news choices to the detriment of professional news values such as "objectivity" and result in a "systematic and highly political dichotomization in news coverage based on serviceability to important domestic power interests" (1988:1-35).[54] If the propaganda model is correct, one may expect in NYT-articles a high incidence of news originating from governmental institutions such as the White House, the USSD, the Pentagon, the US Embassy in Port-au-Prince, the INS, the USCG, or other US state authorities significant in the Haitian crisis.

Chomsky applied his theoretical assumptions to the case of Haiti in two essays: "The Tragedy of Haiti" (1993b:197-219) and the "Introduction" to Paul Farmer's *The Uses of Haiti* (1994:13-44). He presents quotes from an arbitrary series of news articles on the Haitian crisis written by journalists of major US newspapers, including Barbara Crossette and Howard French of the NYT, ignoring NYT-editorials, however. He tries to prove that there was a tendentious and biased news coverage on the Haitian crisis in the US mass media favoring the official US position on issues such as the advisability of the trade embargo or Aristide's human rights record.[55] Chomsky's conviction of the US media's one-sidedness in reporting on Haiti is corroborated by a score of Haiti-experts.

Catherine Orenstein of the New York-based *North American Congress on Latin America* (NACLA), for example, ascertains that the US media essentially function as the "public relations arm" of the USSD: "By depending on State Department sources, the mainstream media runs the risk of becoming its mouthpiece".[56] Over 35% of sources used in NYT news articles from September through December 1991 were US officials, another 10% were unnamed diplomats. This "preferential sourcing" was almost double the count of all Haitian sources combined. During the two-week period after the coup, the NYT spent over three times as many column inches discussing Aristide's alleged transgressions of human rights than it spent reporting on the ongoing violence of the army. She stresses that, in contrast, the NYT did not report on the failure of the embargo and the deplorable conditions at the Guantanamo Bay refugee camp in Cuba. Moreover, the "unbalanced use of epithets and adjectives" was one of the subtle ways the mainstream media imposed "a U.S.-centric perspective" on the Haitian crisis (1995b:103-105). In addition, writer Amy Wilentz[57] describes vividly the familiarity of the international press corps in Haiti with spokespersons of Western embassies and relates her experiences with the desire for sensation in foreign reporters usually accommodated in the Grand Hotel Oloffson in Port-au-Prince. The blurb on the cover of her book *The Rainy Season* tells about the "international press corps who jet in

---

[54] For a short critique of the propaganda model, see Michael Schudson's *The Power of News* (1995:4-6). The NYT is in the peculiar position of being both a *state-oriented* and a *market-oriented* organization situated between *civil society* (third sector) and *economic society* (private sector): It is an organization of the *third sector*, because it represents freedom of expression institutionalized; it is an institution of the *private sector*, because it is organized as a for-profit corporation; it is *state-oriented* by virtue of its preferential sourcing; and it is *market-oriented* due to its reliance on advertising.

[55] For a presentation of some of the results from a press review by *Boston Media Action* regarding coverage of human rights abuses in Haiti, see Chomsky (1993a:154).

[56] According to Orenstein, Serge Beaulieu, spokesman for the Haitian military at Governors Island, greeted Howard French on June 30, 1993, with "Our foreign minister! Welcome!" (Farmer 1994:233).

[57] At one point, Amy Wilentz was a member of NCHR.

when they smell a coup, and leave the minute it´s over" (1989:21-23,47-49,300-303). With regard to the inclination of the US media for preferential sourcing, NYT-articles are an appropriate source of information for the first level of analysis.

3.2 The *New York Times* as a Repository of American Cultural Values

Chomsky´s view seems to be backed by renowned US anthropologists of the Caribbean. Paul Farmer, for example, discerns in the US media´s preoccupation with Aristide´s alleged human rights violations "a major trend in U.S. reporting on the violence in Haiti" (1994:188). More generally, Robert Lawless states in *Haiti´s Bad Press* that "most of the works on Haiti that the public reads are based on myths ... Since the late 1960s ... [t]he press has responded by muting its more blatant racism". Lawless quotes Sidney Mintz who remarks that "[f]ew countries in modern times have received as bad a press at the hands of foreign observers as Haiti". Gerald R. Murray complained in the 1970s that "Haiti still has a uniquely poor press as New World societies go". In describing the "ethnocentric assumptions" of US journalists and their "more unconscious prejudices", Lawless discusses attributes associated with the Haitian boat people, the stigmatization of Haitians with AIDS, and their stereotyping as cannibals and zombies (1992:xiii,1-27).

Similar views were expressed by some of my Haitian-American informants, by HP, which is usually very critical of the NYT´s coverage of Haitian affairs, and by other Haitians quoted in HP. Philippe Généus, for example, reported for HP on plans to establish a Committee for Cultural Affairs in the *Haitian Consulate* in Boston. There, the Haitian Consul-General, Jean Généus, said on August 22, 1991, a few weeks before the coup, that the Committee´s task was to "exploit the cultural and artistic potentials of the Haitian people to change the negative image certain journalists, out of ignorance or malice, project of our country" (HP 1:9). In late 1991, HP derided the NYT and qualified the *Washington Post* (WP) as a newspaper "not even having the liberal touch of the NYT" (HP 123:14-15).[58]

News can be understood as a "form of culture", as a "cultural product", and indirectly as a "social force", related to ideology and information. Michael Schudson calls this quality of the US news media, which tend to be deeply nationalist, "public knowledge". The political views of the Washington and New York-based news elite tend not to be as close to those of Americans in general as to the political views of US journalists at large. In general, the mood and values of white, middle-class society are reflected in the mainstream press, the consensus of which stems from the broad class and racial bias in US society as a whole.[59] Schudson agrees with Chomsky that "offi-

---

[58] Using WP-articles as the basis for the first level of analysis was ruled out for the following reasons: As I experienced during my field work first-hand, the WP is neither available at news stands in Manhattan nor in Brooklyn, it is not a New York-based newspaper, and subscribing to it from New York is both difficult and expensive. The WP does not seem to be an alternative for potential readers in the New York marketplace. As the views on the US media expressed by Haitian immigrants refer in part to concrete events covered by the NYT, they will not be discussed until after the first level of analysis.

[59] According to statistics published in a brochure informing on the databank *Ethnic NewsWatch* by the company *SoftLine Information, Inc.* in Stamford, CT, US mainstream media does not reflect US diver-

cials remain the subject of news as well as its source". Views at the margins get little coverage.[60] Among three ethnic minorities, blacks feel most alienated from the mainstream media and are most critical of media coverage, followed by Hispanics and Asian-Americans (McAneny 1994:31-32). The "trickle up" of significant news stories is rather rare as opposed to stories that trickle down from elite outlets to others. Journalists operate within a cultural system, a "reservoir of stored cultural meanings and patterns of discourse" and produce news that incorporate "assumptions about what matters". The "what", to which a news story answers, is equally a product of cultural presuppositions. Just as different firms have distinctive corporate cultures, different newspapers establish different historical traditions. The WP is known as a "writer's paper", the NYT as an "editor's paper". Schudson sums up: "News is culture" (1995:3,6-9,11,30,14-16,31).

NYT-articles on the subject of "Haiti" may uncover a certain culturally conditioned structure of selection treating preferred aspects of the Haitian crisis. It may be assumed that the NYT is more or less representative of other US newspapers in that regard. The selection structure of the NYT on the one hand and the perspectives of Haitians in the US diaspora on the other can be juxtaposed to examine convergences and divergences of two different so-called *folk models*, the former American, the latter Haitian. A *folk model* is a representation of reality, a simplification of the world, partially determined by cultural beliefs and varying from society to society, which allows us to reduce an undifferentiated mass of daily informational stimuli to a manageable degree that makes sense and that is held unquestionable. Data gained from NYT-articles as processed in the database *Proquest* may provide some clues regarding the nature of the Haiti-related *folk model* of the US mainstream media as well as, to a lesser extent, of US society at large, as it manifested itself during the Haitian crisis. The second and third levels of analysis of this study shed light on the Haitian *folk model*. The juxtaposition of both *folk models* constitute the *analytical model* providing some explanations for the reasons why Haitian immigrants organized the way they did.[61]

---

sity: 45% of mainstream newspapers in the US have no minority journalists on staff, who comprise barely 10% of the industry, and less than 2% of management in mainstream media is minority, even if the African American, the Hispanic, and the Asian American populations increased considerably between 1980 and 1990 (SoftLine 1994). See also Bogart (1989:103). In the case of the NYT, the only editorial staff member writing on Haiti, who could be identified as minority employee, is Haitian-born Garry Pierre-Pierre.

[60] The mere existence of a Haitian ethnic press composed of HM, HO, and HP is an expression of the fact that views at the margins don't get enough coverage. These newspapers supply a market with Haitian-specific news, the demand of which is a function of a perceived deficiency of the mainstream media, as is also reflected by the existence of other minority news media.

[61] For a discussion of the two terms *folk* and *analytical models* that go back to the anthropologist Paul Bohannan, see Lawless (1992:xiv-xviii).

3.3 The *New York Times* as a Newspaper Possibly Affecting Haitians´ Views

Norman and Naomi Zucker´s "iron triangle of U.S. refugee policy" (1991:225) lacks another integral component. Refugee and asylum policy is not only forged in a direct way as the result of an interplay between the executive, Congress, and pressure groups. For these three components also communicate indirectly in a contested public sphere mediated by the press. The media transform the "iron triangle" into a "rectangle". Constituting the fourth component in the system, it functions as a passive mirror by covering refugee-related events and the concomitant public debate among the three other components. In addition, it functions as an active agent through its very capacity to represent, interpret, and, to a certain degree, distort reality in one way or the other. It also exerts this function by publicizing opinions on refugee matters in its own right. This role of the media has some kind of an effect, albeit hard to measure, on the "complex relationship of various attitudes", including "racial or ethnic bias" or the "perception of the migrants" in US society at large, of which "concerned ethnics" are a part (Zucker 1991:225).

It is all too easy to exaggerate the effect of the news media on its audience, which is made up of ordinary people and government officials alike. Some observers, like the sociologist Herbert Gans, hold that they are primarily messengers of their major sources rather than autonomous setters of the political agenda. But through their capacity to organize not just information but audiences, the media amplify the public and stimulate social interaction. Perhaps their most important feature is their "capacity to *publicly include*" (Schudson 1995:19,20, 25). Newspapers have a socially integrative function by providing a common pool of information. They tend to reduce social distance and to eliminate social differences (Bogart 1989:101-102). Public media visibility is deemed to be of enormous importance, no matter how many people actually bother to read or watch the news. Political actors must reckon with a more or less amorphous attention-paying public (Schudson 1995:25), which accounts for an undetermined influence of the news media on the political agenda. The same holds true for Haitians in the US, however. They must also be concerned about the way they, or issues important to them, are portrayed in the media. The more they are exposed to the contents of the media on a regular basis, the more salient this concern may be hypothesized to be.

It is impossible to infer from NYT circulation statistics, which are not broken down by race or ethnicity, the actual newspaper readership of Haitian immigrants in New York: Between 1991 and 1995, penetration of the NYT weekday edition in the estimated households of Kings County (Brooklyn), where most of the Haitians live, was rather steady and fluctuated between 5.5% (1994) and 6.5% (1993). In contrast, penetration in New York County (Manhattan) was highest and fluctuated between 29.7% (1993) and 30.7% (1992). In Queens County, where most affluent Haitians live, penetration was higher than in Kings County and fluctuated between 8.3% (1995) and 9.6% (1991). The numbers suggest that Haitian immigrants in New York are not very likely to buy the NYT regularly (ABC 91,92,93,94,95).[62] This conclusion does not say anything about secondary readership, however.[63]

It is likewise difficult to directly infer from general statistics on newspaper reading patterns according to social categories such as income status, education, sex, race, and age to the actual reading behavior of Haitian immigrants in New York. But they allow, at least, for a mixed set of educated guesses on this matter: People of higher income and education are more likely to be heavy users and seekers of information, and newspapers are read far more often by people at the upper end of the social scale. For those lower on the educational scale, the newspaper as a major institutional power appears more remote and impersonal. Even if blacks have been ignored or underrepresented in news coverage historically, daily newspaper readership is somewhat lower among blacks than among whites, but nonetheless strong. As among whites, newspaper readership among blacks is greatest among people of higher income and education (Bogart 1989:94-96,103,105). Even though a majority of Haitians in Haiti do not have access to it, "education is highly valued" (Civan 1994:15).

Access to both Western culture and resources as well as opportunity in Haiti is accomplished through education. It is therefore an important parameter of social location. Education gets even more value in defining social location in the US, where economic mobility is strongly desired by Haitian immigrants[64] and, even more so, by the social strata making up the leadership of most Haitian organizations in New York, according to a survey in the mid 1980s. Among Caribbeans, Haitian migrants have a high rate of educational attainment and come closest to the educational level of native-born New Yorkers (Charles 1990:310-311,327,209). As among whites, newspaper readership among blacks is greatest among people living in larger metropolitan areas, while people who are active in civic affairs and who participate in voluntary organizations rank above average in newspaper readership (Bogart 1989:97,105). Of the approximately 250 Haitian organizations existing in the New York metropolitan area between 1985 and 1987, 91 organizations were interviewed in the survey referred to above. The majority of these (54.9 %) were located in Brooklyn, with Queens (24.2%) following second and Manhattan (15.4%) ranking third (Charles 1990:300,302-303).

Even though the distinction between what is local and what is not is increasingly hard to make and the line between national and international news is increasingly blurry, local community news ranked high (84%) in 1987 with both frequent and infrequent readers when asked which three things in the paper they most like to read, followed by international/world news, news briefs/summaries, news about President/Congress, and local governments/politics etc. Interest in local news was greatest among older people, whose roots in the community go deep. Among both men and

---

[62] For more detailed circulation statistics, see ibid.
[63] My landlords in Brooklyn, for example, asked me eagerly if I could let them have the NYT, which I used to buy every day, second-hand for their own use. It is possible that Haitians pool resources in a similar way to afford buying the NYT - or another comparable newspaper in the metropolitan area - on a regular basis.
[64] My Haitian roommate, a very busy "gipsy" cab driver, often took advantage of his leisure time to educate himself by studying Latin with the help of an old school book. After having lived in their house for a few months already, my male landlord seemed to be embarrassed one day to admit that his time-consuming job as a yellow cab driver did not allow him yet to study administration at one of the colleges of New York, something he seemed to desire very eagerly.

women, interest in national and international events increases with education and income. Local news is of greatest interest in rural areas and of least interest in large metropolitan areas (Bogart 1989:324,391-320,325).

According to the *1992 Media Guide*, the New York Times newspaper group suffered a 52% drop in profits in the first quarter of 1991. The NYT responded to this challenge by repositioning itself in the New York marketplace with a greater emphasis on features and local news. Increased emphasis was put on city news (Wanniski 1992:95). Total average paid circulation for the NYT throughout the world for 1995 was 1,124,328 for the weekday and 1,720,284 for the Sunday edition. 676,251 was the total for the weekday edition circulated within the New York DMA (New York City and suburbs). In Haiti, 43 weekday and 58 Sunday editions were sold in 1995 (ABC 1995).

In conclusion, the NYT might have been read by Haitians in New York by virtue of their general aspiration for education and economic mobility, their higher income status in Queens, their higher proclivity for civic participation in Brooklyn, and their assumed tendency for secondary readership. In addition, the increased attractiveness of the NYT as provider of local news in conjunction with the fact that newspaper readership is principally high in metropolitan areas, might have induced Haitian residents in New York to read it. Furthermore, what seems to be even more important is the tendency of the Haitian ethnic press to substantiate their news stories with information obtained from the US mainstream media.[65] HP, for example, often utilizes quotes from the NYT and other newspapers, sometimes commenting on them. The same can be assumed not only for HO and HM, but for the numerous Haitian-owned radio stations in New York as well.

Kim Ives, HP staff member, insisted in July 1993 that the Brooklyn-based Haitian weekly was the market leader at that time with a circulation of about 78,000,[66] thereby disputing the circulation of 50,000 to 60,000 claimed by HO. While HP has subscribers on every continent, it sells "most" of the issues in the New York metropolitan area, with about 12,000 copies sold in Haiti, Ives said (French 1993b:D8). Consequently, the Haitian ethnic press functions in part as a multiplier of news originating from the US mainstream media, albeit partially transforming it in the process. The NYT has thus a certain potential to affect the views Haitians in the US had on the crisis.[67] Frank of *Haitian Centers Council* (HCC), who does not hold US citizenship, tes-

---

[65] It is, of course, very likely that Haitians in New York were exposed to other mainstream media types as well (local tabloids, TV news shows or radio stations) that refer to information obtained from the NYT.

[66] In two letters dated January 29, 1997, and March 10, 1997, I asked Jeanie Loubet, *Rédactrice en chef* of HP, and Maude LeBlanc, *Co-Directeur* of HP, respectively, if they could provide me with HP circulation statistics for the whole time period under consideration. Regrettably, even one follow-up telephone call did not result in obtaining the requested information. According to Jean-Pierre, circulations of the three Haitian weeklies range from ten to fifty thousand each. He also states that these papers´ influence is "somewhat muted", as the majority of Haitians did not read French, for which reason radio "seems to be the optimal medium of communication among the diaspora" (1995:201). Besides the technical impossibility of analyzing reports that were aired on Haitian radio a long time ago, it is quite possible that some radio stations in New York based their reporting, to a certain extent, on articles published in HP.

[67] The Haitian ethnic press´ relying, in part, on information disseminated by the NYT and other mainstream media testifies to the methodological difficulty to differentiate clearly between the two folk mod-

tified that he watches TV news and reads US and Haitian newspapers such as the NYT, HO and HP "[f]rom time to time". He asserted that he had learnt about Haitian refugees taken to Guantanamo after the coup "from the media" in general, putting an emphasis, though, on what he had been "seeing on TV, those parents crying about this situation" (Frank 1995;Frank 1993:128-129,158).

---

els. They rather cross over to a certain extent, since the NYT also published a few news stories, more often than not written by Haitian-born staff member Garry Pierre-Pierre, which mostly dealt with opinions of ordinary Haitians in New York vis-a-vis current events unfolding on the level of international politics.

Radio announcer in Brooklyn (courtesy Maggie Steber)

4 The Haitian Crisis in the Context of International State Relations

The detailed process analysis of the Haitian crisis as covered by the NYT is published in the microedition of this study (Opitz 1999). Supplemented with OAS and UN resolutions pertaining to the crisis, it depicts bilateral relations between Haiti and the US, embedded in an international context, and is based on a pool of 570 NYT-abstracts. Only those abstracts were selected that contain information on statements, decisions, and actions by government officials and governmental institutions or that explicitly identify governmental actors as information source.[68]

The process analysis covers the initial responses by the international community, including the US, the OAS and the UN, to both Aristide's overthrow and the ensuing refugee crisis. It describes the OAS-sponsored negotiations leading to the "Washington Protocols" signed in February 1992, the so-called "Villa d'Accueil Tripartite Agreement", Bush's "Kennebunkport Order" on Haitian refugees, the "Florida Declaration" initiated by Aristide, the OAS-Special Mission to Haiti in September, and the US elections in November. Moreover, it covers events surrounding Clinton's inauguration in January 1993, the *UN/OAS International Civilian Mission* to Haiti (UN/OAS-ICM [or MICVIH]) launched in February to monitor human rights, the UN Oil Embargo and the beginning of the Governors Island process in the summer leading to the signing of the GIA on July 3, the breakdown of the Governors Island process, the CIA's role, and Aristide's failed return as scheduled for October 30, 1993.

It furthermore describes the growing tensions between Aristide and the Clinton Administration at the end of 1993, Aristide's so-called "Miami Conference" in January 1994, and further negotiation attempts, a new wave of violence in Haiti, growing pressure on Clinton leading to changes in his policy on Haitian refugees in May, and Washington's first invasion threats. It finally covers the UN authorization to invade Haiti in July, the new scheme for processing Haitian refugees, and US preparations for an invasion of Haiti; the Carter-Mission to Haiti leading to the US-led occupation of Haiti in September, preparations for Aristide's return including the planning for Haiti's future, and the resignation of the Haitian junta paving the way for Aristide's return on October 15, 1994.

4.1 The *New York Times'* Folk Model: Representing the Haitian Crisis

News articles published in the NYT between September 30, 1991, and October 16, 1994, were chosen as the pool of data for the first level of analysis. During this time period, the NYT published, according to the database *Proquest*, 1,011 articles on the subject of "Haiti", which are summarized in form of abstracts of varying length. The research-related advantage of this database is that each record is preceded by a data head composed of eleven headings that contain relevant information about the

---

[68] The pool of 570 NYT-abstracts amount to 56.4% of the total of 1,011 NYT-abstracts prepared by *Proquest*. The abstracts selected were boiled down to the core content, slightly rewritten, and combined to a fluent text, supplemented in footnotes with excerpts from declarations and resolutions on the Haitian crisis, issued by the OAS or the UN.

article in condensed form. The first four headings represent formal background information secondary to the content of the article. These are "Access No", "Title", "Authors", and "Source" composed of "Date", "Sec", "Type" (Commentary, Correction, Editorial, News) and "Length" (long, medium, short). The following four headings represent primary information about the content of the article itself. These headings are "Companies", "Names", "Geo Places", and, most importantly, "Subjects".[69] An analysis of these headings permits important insights into the way the NYT represented the Haitian crisis. They reveal the focus of the NYT´s coverage.

In summary, the NYT´s reporting on the Haitian crisis was dominated by editorial staff member Howard French, who wrote 208 news stories. Ranking second was Larry Rohter, whose name is listed 58 times, followed by Garry Pierre-Pierre, a NYT minority employee of Haitian descent, who is the author of 36 pieces.[70] Their news stories and all other article types totaling 1,011 were published in varying quantities in the course of time.[71] On average, 27.7 articles per month were published during the 36.5 month period. 82 articles were published in 1991 during the three months after the coup, which equals 0.08% of the total. In 1992, during Bush´s 12 remaining months in office, only 144 articles, or 14.2% of the total, appeared in the NYT. In 1993, during Clinton´s first 12 months in office, the number went up to 324 articles equaling 32.1% of the total. And in 1994, during the 9.5 month period ending with Aristide´s return, the NYT published the large number of 461 articles on Haiti. This equals 45.6% of the total, even if the remaining 2.5 months of the year are not accounted for. In short, there was a steady increase in quantitative reporting on Haiti between the coup and Aristide´s return. The quantative emphasis was on Clinton´s term rather than on Bush´s.[72]

According to *Proquest*, the NYT described the Haitian crisis as a process, in which a total of 51 "Companies" played a certain role. This process is dominated by the "United Nations", mentioned 68 times and followed by the "Organization of American States", for which there are 24 entries. The "United Nations Security Council" is listed 20 times. This ranking is in line with the quantitative reporting results, as both the UN and the UNSC did not come into play until 1993. Furthermore, the process is dominated by one person, "Jean-Bertrand Aristide", whose name is mentioned 324 times. Out of a total of 112 "Names", Aristide is followed by "Bill Clinton" (153 entries) and "Raoul Cedras" (71 entries). This ranking is compatible with the quantative reporting results as well on account of the saliency of Clinton. Not surprisingly,

---

[69] See the print-out of complete *Proquest* record samples in the appendix. In comparison to another database by the name of *Dow Jones News* that carries 1,348 NYT-abstracts on the subject of "Haiti" during the time period under consideration, *Proquest* is better to work with as a research tool. For abstracts in *Dow Jones News* are not preceded by a data head that allow to make inferences as to the way NYT-articles, in their totality, represented all aspects of the Haitian crisis. *Proquest* is publicly accessible in the Library of Congress´ Newspaper and Current Periodical Room.

[70] There was a total of 91 authors writing on Haiti. By and large, they wrote 753 news stories. This means that 258 articles, including 24 "Correction"-articles, were published without giving the authors´ names.

[71] Only 146 articles are "Length: Short", including all 24 "Correction"-articles. This number amounts to 16.9% of the total. Of these 146 short articles, only 19 are on the subject of "Refugees".

[72] For an overview of NYT´s coverage of the Haitian (refugee) crisis in relation to other indicators such as USCG statistics, see the chart in the appendix.

the process takes place geographically in "Haiti" (1,019),[73] followed by the "United States" (199) and by "Port-au-Prince" (24), but also in a total of 56 different "Geo Places". Finally, *Proquest* interprets the NYT´s coverage of the process as touching upon 266 different "Subjects", with "[US] Foreign Policy" (211) topping the list, followed by "Refugees" (nominally 203) and "International relations" (200).

What is remarkable is the closeness between "Foreign Policy" on the one hand and "Refugees" as well as "International relations" on the other. According to *Proquest*, the NYT thus treated the Haitian crisis as a foreign policy problem of the US, strongly marked by the wave of Haitian refugees and involving the international community. Immediate causes of this refugee stream, as expressed in subject headings such as "Coups d´etat" (105) or "Human rights" (35), rank 5th and 19th respectively.[74] By the same token, means employed by the international community to solve the Haitian crisis, centering around subject headings such as "Embargoes & blockades" (93) or "Military occupations" (79), fall behind the refugee issue as well.[75] The Haitian diaspora in the US is dealt with in 31 articles amounting to only 3.1% of the total.[76] Since the focus of reporting appears to have been on the immediate effects of the crisis, the perspective assumed by the NYT can be dubbed "ethnic" pursuant to the definition mentioned above. In addition, the reporting is ahistorical, since the subject heading "History" is mentioned 6 times only, thereby indicating that longer-term causes of the Haitian crisis were not a focus, either.[77]

The real number of 216 articles[78] dealing with the refugee issue amounts to nearly 22% of the total. In other words, every fifth of the 1,011 articles deals with the Haitian refugees, while all other 265 subjects cover different aspects of the Haitian crisis. To put it yet another way, the NYT spent about 8 months of the 36.5 month time period under consideration for reporting on the Haitian refugee crisis. In 1994, there were only 61 of a total of 461 articles published on the refugee issue that year, which is much less than the average of 22% for the whole time period. This proportion equals 13%. In the month of September 1994, 169 articles appeared in the NYT, the highest number per month ever during the whole time period, with only 3 articles deal-

---

[73] Due to double counts, the number includes 8 more than the overall total of 1,011.

[74] There are, of course, other subject headings that refer to the human rights situation in Haiti, but they don´t figure prominently, either. These are, for example, "Violence" (14), "Police brutality" (12), "Paramilitary groups" (11), "Political persecution" (9), "Assassinations & assassination attempts" (8), "Terrorism" (8), "Arrests" (5) "Atrocities" (3), "Shootings" (3), "Massacres" (2), and "Torture" (2).

[75] "Embargoes & blockades" rank 6th, with related subject headings being "Sanctions" (56), "Assets" (6), and "Frozen assets" (5). "Military occupations" rank 8th, with related subject headings being "Military policy" (66), "Military deployment" (37), and "Peacekeeping forces" (23). "Negotiations" were mentioned 24 times only, and "Peace negotiations" as well as "Amnesties" only 14 times.

[76] Indicators for this observation are headings such as "New York City", "Brooklyn", "Miami", "Expatriates", "Immigration", "Minority & ethnic groups", "Expatriates", "Aliens", "Emigration", "Public Opinion", "Hispanic Americans", and "Exile".

[77] Other indicators for this observation are headings such as "Dictators" (8), "Duvalier, Francois (Papa Doc) (1907-71)" (5), and "Duvalier, Jean-Claude" (3).

[78] The nominal number of articles on the subject of "Refugees" is only 203 including 4 "Correction"-articles. But 5 articles on the subject of "Immigration" (total of 89) and 12 articles on the subject of "Political asylum" (total of 62) dealing with the refugee issue are not listed in combination with the subject heading "Refugee", thus adding up to the real number of 220 articles dealing with the refugee issue. After taking out the 4 "Correction"-articles, one ends up with the number of 216 articles dealing with the refugee issue. Of these, only 19 articles, or 8.8% of the total, are "short" articles.

ing with the refugee issue. During that month, the US intervened militarily in Haiti. In 1993, only 55 of a total of 324 articles published that year (13%) deal with the refugee issue, thus equally falling below the average of 22% for the whole time period. In the month of October 1993, 88 articles, the second highest number per month ever, appeared at a time when the first attempt of returning Aristide to Haiti failed. Only 3 articles on the refugee issue were published that month. Both in 1994 and 1993, the "return issue" prevailed over the "refugee issue".

In 1992, however, 74 articles, the highest number of articles on the refugee issue per year ever, appeared in the NYT. This number amounts to an unparalleled 51% of the total of 144 articles published that year, thus surpassing the average of 22% for the whole time period by far. 20 of a total of 32 articles (62.5%), the highest number of articles on the refugee issue per month ever, appeared in the month of February 1992, when the House of Representatives voted on the Rangel/Mazzoli bill, which would have provided relief for Haitian refugees. Consequently, the "refugee issue" prevailed over the "return issue" in 1992. In summary, according to *Proquest*, the NYT´s coverage of the Haitian crisis mirrored, and contributed to, a political climate in 1992 which was characterized by a major focus on the refugee crisis. This political climate, so it seems, ushered in a time period in 1993 marked by the Governors Island process. This process was finally superseded in May and June of 1994, when the refugee issue was gradually pushed to the forefront again for the time being. In those months, 16 and 15 articles respectively appeared in the NYT on the Haitian refugees, amounting to 34% of the total of 47 articles published in May and to 31.9% of the total of 47 articles published in June. Subsequently, the public debate was increasingly dominated by the US military intervention of Haiti that materialized in September and led to Aristide´s return in October.

It is not enough, however, to merely outline the NYT´s selection structure of preferred aspects of the Haitian crisis, because this structure does not reflect the way the newspaper assessed the major issues of the Haitian crisis. To better evaluate the NYT´s folk model, it is necessary to examine the newspaper´s stand on those issues along an axis of pros and cons. What is the NYT´s position on the plight of Haitian refugees? What is its standpoint regarding the embargo, the negotiations, and US military intervention etc.? Editorials, in which opinions are published in an explicit way, promise to be the best source to assomplish this task. The NYT published a total of 58 editorials on the Haitian crisis. Of the total of 3 published in 1991, 1 dealt with the Haitian refugees. In 1992, 10 of 17 dealt with this issue, and in 1993, 6 of 17. In 1994, only 3 of 21 dealt with the Haitian refugees.[79]

My own review of *Proquest*-abstracts of NYT-editorials revealed, in sum, that 20 of them dealt with the refugee side of the Haitian crisis, focusing on 1992. All of these reported on the Haitian refugees in a positive and compassionate way, opposing

---

[79] According to the subject headings assigned by *Proquest*, 21 of the NYT-editorials treated the Haitian crisis as having to do with "Foreign policy", followed by the subjects "Refugees" (16), "International relations-US" (9), "Sanctions" (8), "Political Asylum" (6), "Coups d´état (5), "Embargoes & blockades (5), and "Military policy" (5). Combined with other subject headings such as "Military deployment" (3), "Military engagements" (1), "Military occupations" (3), the US-military aspect of the crisis figures prominently with a total of 12 subject headings on that aspect.

the US policy of forced repatriation.[80] Despite the shortcomings in Barbara Crossette´s and Howard French´s reporting on the Haitian crisis as documented by Chomsky,[81] the NYT seems to have assumed a position in many ways critical of official US policy towards Haiti. Whether or not the NYT´s preoccupation with the refugee aspect of the Haitian crisis and the solutions to the refugee problem advocated by the newspaper reflected the concerns of the broader US public or rather those of the Haitian community, becomes clear in the following chapters.

---

[80] Moreover, 12 editorials are pro-embargo, 11 are pro-Aristide, 9 are pro-negotiation, 6 are contra-US invasion, 2 are pro-Clinton, 1 is contra-Clinton, 2 are pro-peaceful intervention, 1 is pro-US military, 1 is contra-US military, 1 is pro-democracy in Haiti, and 1 is contra-CIA.
[81] Chomsky´s propaganda model expects news stories about "worthy and unworthy victims" and about "enemy and friendly states" to differ in quality, with refugees and other dissident sources being heavily used in dealing with enemies (Chomsky 1988:34). If one follows this logic, the US must have considered Haiti led by the military junta as enemy state, since the NYT reported heavily on the Haitian refugees. This is, however, repudiated by Chomsky in the essays referred to above.

5 Nationalistic and Ethnic Organizing: Responding to the Haitian Crisis

The coup d´etat in Haiti of September 30, 1991 shocked the Haitian people all over the world. In the US, the Haitian diaspora reacted quickly by demonstrating in the streets for the return of Aristide. But not until a few weeks into the Haitian crisis did leaders of the Haitian community in the US publicly discuss what strategy to pursue to tackle the crisis. The Haitian Consul-General of New York City, Wilson Désir, confirmed the spontaneous response by his Haitian compatriots at a "public debate" at *Barea School* in Boston on November 3, which was attended by nearly 1,000 people.[82] He said that "mobilization" in the streets was "indispensable". Haitians would stand upright on the side of "Tidid" (Aristide), because they had clearly expressed their will by voting for him. Philippe Généus, coordinator of the group *Rezistans Demokratik Ayisyèn*, which had organized the event, reported that "all aspects of the crisis such as the OAS-mission, the effects of the embargo, and the role of the Haitian army after the coup etc. were touched upon" (HP 43:16;HP 244:7).

Généus predicted that "Cédras, Honorat, Jean-Claude, Michel Francois and Co." would be driven into exile with a "three-pronged strategy", which he dubbed "resistance-embargo-mobilization" (HP 43:16).[83] He thereby reiterated what Haitians in Philadelphia had articulated a few weeks earlier, when they expressed, with a long list of signatures, their wish that the "inner resistance, the mobilization of Haitians of the 10th department as well as the international mobilization would finally force the authors of the coup to accept the return to power of Father Aristide, the only legitimate president of Haiti" (HP 16:14).

Aristide himself made it clear, which part of the deterritorialized Haitian nation was to engage in "resistance". Speaking on November 22 on *Radio Tropicale*, a Haitian radio station with 50,000 subscribers, he called upon the people in Haiti to act in an examplary way vis-a-vis the international community by *not* leaving the country and by resisting peacefully: "Résistez sur place. Ne quittez pas le pays pour aller échouer dans la mer. Résistez comme toujours, sans violence, pacifiquement. Tenez-vous la main. Montrez au monde entier que vous préférez rester chez vous, en résistant sans violence, plutôt que d´aller échouer en mer dans la gueule des requins" (HP 53:15;Dreyfuss 1993:81).

HP-journalist Angèle Tecumseh agreed that this is the only way to go. She added that "mobilization" is the part for the Haitian diaspora to play in order to reverse a coup, in which the US, seemingly ready for a military solution of the crisis, was probably implicated in the first place: "Lá est bien en effet la seule voie véritable car *seule la résistance* et la lutte nous permettront de venir à bout du macoutisme ... Parallèlement *aux Etats-Unis*, nous avons *notre propre partition* à jouer et elle passe par des *pressions* intenses *sur l´administration Bush* pour qu´aucun *réfugié ne soit refoulé* dans les circonstances actuelles ... Nous ne demandons pas aux Etats-Unis d´aller jouer

---

[82] Besides Désir and others, Bostonian poet Jean-Claude Martineau, Aristide´s future spokesperson, was present at the event (HP 43:16). It was Martineau, who invoked the image of "Lavalas" (deluge) in his celebrated 1975 freedom song "Ayiti Demen" (Haiti Tomorrow) to describe an utter destruction of the Duvalier state (Richman 1992:189).

[83] Jean-Jacque Honorat, who became Haiti´s first Prime Minister in the *de facto* government, and Joseph Michel Francois, the Port-au-Prince Police Chief, participated in the coup against Aristide (see further below and the NYT of 10/15/91:A11 and of 09/09/93:A5).

aux Rambo en Haiti et de remettre de l'ordre à leur facons dans notre propre pays. L'*intervention militaire, nous n'en voulons* à aucun prix ... ce que nous voulons c'est une position claire des dirigeants nord-américains qui ne peuvent jouer indéfiniment leur jeu ambigu. Sont-ils, comme ils le prétendent officiellement, en favour du *retour du gouvernement constitutionnel*, ou n'essaient-ils pas plutôt de *maintenir l'homme* qui a peut-être été *leur carte* pour évincer Aristide du pouvoir? (HP 53:15;author's italics).[84]

HP assented to Tecumseh's strategical considerations in early December by opining that "the struggle is fought on two fronts": On the one hand, the "granting of political asylum in the US" for Haitian refugees; on the other hand, "the struggle for the return of Aristide", which HP appreciated as the "sole means to regulate the problem definitely". HP echoed Tecumseh's fear that Aristide's return might be accomplished through "foreign intervention". For Haitians, however, the "objective is not the replacement of internal colonization by external occupation". Since "the US knows all too well that the wave of refugees came to a trickle under the Aristide government inspite of economic difficulties that continued to exist" (HP 57:6,16-18), addressing the root causes of the problem by returning Aristide must also be in the interest of the US. Consequently, at a *10e of New York*-organized "soirée de réflexion" in *St. Francis Church*, Brooklyn, on February 8, 1992, representatives of different organizations spoke about the necessity to organize the struggle, to create political unity, to understand the fundamental role of liberation theology, the role of women as well as artists, and the importance of solidarity between oppressed peoples (HP 74:10).[85] The role of Haitian refugees in the struggle was not discussed.

In most of the first half of 1992, leading Haitian community organizations including the *Haitian Consulate*, Aristide's exile government, and HP-editor Benjamin Dupuy, the Aristide government's Ambassador-at-Large, were, by and large, uniform in terms of the strategy to be pursued. "Resistance" in Haiti, "mobilization" in the Haitian diaspora, pressure on the Haitian military junta by means of the international "embargo" and a favorable "world opinion" were to bring about Aristide's return; a collective endeavor to be guided by the central ideas of the Lavalas movement: transparency, justice, and participation, as HP's Jeanine Loubet put it (HP 100:16-17). But "world opinion" was not only to add pressure on the *de facto* government, but to rein in what was perceived as an intervention-prone US Administration accessory to the coup to begin with. It was nevertheless cautiously pressured on the refugee front. The strategical unity began to crumble in the second half of 1992, even more so after Bill Clinton's election in early November, and in particular after signing of the GIA. This occurred for a variety of reasons, which had been increasingly verbalized in the course of time.[86]

---

[84] The term "macoutisme" refers to the dreaded members of Duvalier's secret police, the *tonton makouts*. In everyday speech, it has taken on a broader meaning, signifying Haitians with a reactionary, undemocratic, and opportunistic mind set with a propensity to violence.

[85] The event was hosted by the 10e's founding member Jocelyne Mayas as well as by Raphael Pierre of AEH, and attended by more than 300 people (HP 74:10).

[86] For detailed information on the GIA and the events surrounding it, see the NYT-abstracts following the one of 07/04/93:1/1, including the corresponding footnotes, in the detailed process analysis included in: Opitz 1999.

Late November 1992, HP assessed the assumption nurtured by certain Haitian media that Clinton´s arrival at the White House could prefigure Aristide´s return to Haiti as illusory and "extremely dangerous", since one had to realize that both US parties represented "two faces of the same imperialist system". In contrast, politicians within Haiti like Victor Benoit, Secretary-General of KONAKOM, were "a bit more prudent". HP reported that his party conveyed a message of congratulation to the Democrats, but was not willing to make the return to democracy in Haiti entirely dependent on US foreign policy. Benoit said on *Télé Haiti* (11/06/92): "[W]e at KONAKOM think that ... it is the political forces in this country that need to unite". Likewise, Pierre Canel Joseph Rindal, representative of the *National Front for Change and Democracy* (FNCD), warned on *Télé Haiti* (11/04/92) "not to hope great things from Bill Clinton in the Haitian cause ... it is up to the Haitians to unite in order to solve the problems of Haiti" (HP 153:6).[87]

Aristide, on the other hand, came to prioritize "negotiation" and "compromise" under US leadership. HP more and more criticized this route by advocating in early April 1993 a "resolute struggle" that counts on the "force of the people" inside and outside of Haiti: "Lá encore, il y a bien sûr l´argument selon lequel le peuple a les mains nues, n´ayant rien pour se défendre et encore moins pour attaquer. ... les efforts ont été bien plus tournés vers les tractations en tous genres que vers l´*organisation systématique du peuple à l´intérieur*. Et dans la mesure où a été écarté le secteur militant, cela n´a fait qu´aggraver les choses, y compris *dans le `dixième´* où les potentialités sont loin d´être exploitées au maximum" (HP 202:14;author´s italics). HP did not mention the refugee card anymore, when it called on to work for a "rupture with imperialism" as well as with the Haitian bourgeoisie: "Bien sûr, un petit pays comme Haiti ne peut se targuer de tenir seul tête à l´impérialisme mais cela n´empêche pas pour autant que la voie à suivre soit celle de la *résistance*, de la *mobilisation* et de l´*organisation* car à suivre la *bourgeoisie*, nous ne ferons au´aller de *tragédies* en tragédies". Passing from Duvalier to Aristide was a "magnificent trajectory", and the Haitian people would never accept to be "enslaved" again (HP 202:14;author´s italics).

Not until late January 1994, HP-correspondent Guy Roumer found fault with the dearth of strategical thinking that also takes into account the refugee issue. At that time, HP´s voice did not reflect the political leadership of the Haitian community anymore. Roumer reported that the refugee issue was put on the back burner at the Miami conference in the last moment, even if the refugee problem "resurfaces on every occasion". He advocated to use the issue again as a means to pressure the US: "Une vraie discussion sur le sujet aurait pu pour le moins *démontrer* un minimum ou non de bonne foi du *gouvernement des Etats-Unis* dans la résolution de la crise haitienne.

---

[87] The social democratic KONAKOM is the standing body of the *National Congress of Haitian Democratic Movements*, organized by a group of Haitian "center-left intellectuals" in Port-au-Prince in January 1987. Representing the more militant sector of the popular movement, the *National Popular Assembly* (APN) was founded by HP´s Dupuy and others in March 1987 as a popular alternative to KONAKOM, which had laid the groundwork for the center-left political party FNCD. On February 4, 1991, Aristide antagonized FNCD and KONAKOM by building an independent political structure, the "Lavalas Organization" (Chamberlain 1995b:22-23;Chamberlain 1995a,52-53;Hooper 1995:172; Aristide,Richardson 1995:194,185-187).

D´autant plus que dans ce cas précis, Clinton ne peut évoquer l´interférence d´aucune tierce partie" (HP 227;author´s italics).[88]

In summary, the political elite of the Haitian community in New York City favored direct transnational citizen-to-citizen relations especially during the first third of the crisis when putting a strategical emphasis on "resistance" within Haiti and "mobilization" within the Haitian diaspora for the sake of Aristide´s return. Second ranked indirect transnational citizen-to-state relations to elicit international measures such as the economic "embargo" and the double-targeted pressure of "world opinion" emanating from outside the territorially dispersed Haitian people. The strategical potential of the refugee issue for the return of Aristide was assessed positively at first, but later came to be more and more discarded for a variety of reasons. How those reasons worked together to shape Haitian organizing in the course of time, will be shown in detail on the following pages.

5.1 Responses to the US Mainstream Media´s Coverage of the Haitian Crisis

As Wilentz reported, the USSD, suddenly concerned with "human rights and the rule of law" during Aristide´s seven months in office, circulated an unprecedented "thick notebook" immediately after the coup. It documented alleged human rights violations under his term. According to Canadian journalist Linda Diebel of the *Toronto Star*, Cédras presented to OAS negotiators the "thick bound dossier", to which the former Canadian fighter pilot Lynn Garrison, now living in Los Angeles, provided much of the "evidence". It derived from Aristide´s diary, some paintings, and a statement from a "psychiatrist". Garrison reportedly "masterminded the smear campaign" in close contact with "military attaché" Pat Collins of the US Embassy. Alvin Adams, US Ambassador to Haiti, reportedly used the dossier to brief major US journalists in private meetings on October 3, 1991. Tales about Aristide´s alleged "meager" democratic credentials and psychological defects soon began to emerge in headlines of leading US newspapers (Farmer 1994:33-34,223-224).

Far from being "monopolized" by US journalists (HP 8:16-23), Aristide worked to neutralize the adverse effects of the post-coup media campaign. As NCHR reported, he "telephoned our New York office from Venezuela to acknowledge receipt of a copy of the report" *Haiti: The Aristide Government´s Human Rights Record*. NCHR´s report, which "boldly countered charges ... that the Aristide government had deserved to topple", was released to provide an "independent assessment of charges" that Aristide himself had condoned political violence. It thereby challenged what NCHR called "the [Haitian] army´s cunning public relations strategy" composed of widely aired allegations, which were "meant to legitimize Aristide´s overthrow". While still in his first exile in Caracas, Venezuela, early in the crisis, "in an OpEd column in the *New York Times* Aristide had cited NCHR statistics ... in an effort to bolster his claim for immediate reinstatement" (NCHR5:15-17).

Writing from Port-au-Prince, Dupuy responded to Haiti´s resurfacing "bad press" (Lawless), as reflected in an October 6, 1991 WP-editorial and an October 7

---

[88] There is a total of 37 HP-articles, for which no page numbers can be provided for technical reasons.

article by WP's Lee Hockstadter. HP translated into French Dupuy's letter to the editor, published in WP on October 13, and reprinted it at length. It noted that "the criminals, who have killed hundreds of our compatriots, have found intellectual complices" in the US and Canadian media "to multiply their mendacious and shameful propaganda" in order to "justify the crime perpetrated against the new democracy of Haiti" by painting "Aristide as a despot". Dupuy wrote that "necklacing" ("Père Lebrun"),[89] one of the phony accusations, did not occur during Aristide's term until the day of the coup. He repudiated Hockstadter's assertion that Aristide "divided Haitian society" (HP 19:8).

Individual Haitian - and maybe even more so non-Haitian - activists followed Duyuy's lead in criticizing the US media's reporting on Haiti. At a mass protest in Washington in mid-October 1991, Worth Colley-Prost of the *Washington Office on Haiti* (WOH)[90] and a speaker of the *Quixote Center/Quest for Peace* (QC/QP) stressed the campaign of misinformation by the US press (HP 25:16-19). *Pax Christi USA* had HP publish telephone numbers not only of US governmental institutions, but also of WP, "which tends to misinform the public" (HP 18:8,11). Ramsey Clark, founder of the *Haiti Commission*, deplored at an event in New York on November 1 that the US mainstream press had ignored the bicentennial of the slave revolt in Saint-Domingue (HP 36:8). *Haiti Commission*- member Pat Chin observed at a soirée on November 21 that "as soon as the US decided not to support Aristide anymore ... all news pertaining to Haiti stopped" (HP 51:10).

The Haitian community at large soon joined the protest against the US mainstream media, foremost by taking to the streets in big numbers. As part of the *10e of New York*-organized February 7 celebrations of 1992 in favor of Haitian democracy, about 15,000 Haitians participated in a UN-bound march, which also stopped in front of the NYT-building (HP 80:12-13). As late as October 1994, Haitian protesters deemed it necessary to demonstrate against the NYT's coverage of Haiti, accusing the newspaper of being "the voice of the State Department" (Orenstein 1994:103). Haitian protesters seem to have always been aware of the media publicity potential of mass demonstrations. This is especially obvious in HP-correspondent Fanfan Latour's report on a rally in Manhattan on March 5, 1994 with about 7,000 Haitians (HP 236:1,17). But HP complained with regard to yet another protest march of 10,000 demonstrators in early May 1994 that the "number of participants was, as usual, largely underestimated" (HP 257:17), while Clinton's refugee-related decision of May 8, 1994 "provoked a media hype in his favor" (HP 258:1).

HP-correspondent Carl Gilbert especially criticized Howard French for describing in a March 15, 1992 article the situation in Haiti "in sibyllic language" as a "climate of general violence". He countered that it was "systematic repression - contrary to what the New York Times wants to make us believe - that awaits [Haitian] refugees" (HP 91:8). At the so-called "day of the press" in early June 1992, however, Marie Laurence Lassègue, the legitimate Minister of Information, linked the "pressure of the 10th department and the tour of president Aristide" in Boston, Washington, New York,

---

[89] Placing a motor tyre around a victim's neck, then setting it on fire, is called "necklacing". Père Lebrun" is the name of a motor tyre dealer in Port-au-Prince.

[90] According to Cynthia Peters, WOH was founded in 1984, "in part to examine the question of why so many Haitians were fleeing their country" (1995:208-209).

and Miami in late April 1992 to a new "tendency of being a bit more objective" on the side of US journalists covering Haitian refugees and decisions by the Bush Administration (HP 126:9-10).

Some of my Haitian informants uttered similar views. Relating what he had observed in Port-au-Prince harbor in October of 1993, NCHR´s Aphaly Coradin complained about the "sloppy work" by US journalists relying on accounts given by US Ambassador Stanley Schrager "without any investigations of the facts" (Coradin 1995). 32-year-old Ninaj Raoul, executive director of HWHR in Brooklyn, said that "Haitians in general" were "only portrayed negatively": "[There are] ... taboos that Haitians have been slapped with by the mainstream media" (Raoul 1995). Mayas speculated that the US mainstream media "were biased toward the refugees, and it was all dictated by the American government!" (Mayas 1995). According to Guy Victor, US media coverage of Guantanamo turned negative after the US government had implemented the HIV-testing procedure there (Victor 1996).

At the same time Lassègue discerned a "minimum of professionalism", HP surprisingly agreed with a well-known regular of the NYT. Anthony Lewis had described in a commentary (05/21/92) the lawsuit brought by numerous human rights organizations against the US Administration´s refugee policy as a "travesty of justice" (HP 124:20). Latour would later acknowledge Lewis´ news analysis of December 13, 1993, in which he alluded to a double game in Washington, played by key personalities working to prevent Aristide´s return behind a facade of verbal support (HP 218:12). Based on information in the NYT (05/28/92), HP foresaw a "new wave of repression" in June 1992, following the assassination of George Izméry, the brother of Aristide-supporter Antoine Izméry, and the arrest of Port-au-Prince mayor Paul, but cautioned that the US press tends to cover it inadequately as a principle (HP 124:20).

At the time of Clinton´s inauguration, HP saw this principal tendency confirmed: NYT´s Howard French (01/09/93) used Cédras´ argument that the coup was justified as "an attempt to block the recourse to violence Father Aristide threatened with". For HP, French and Jack Anderson, who wrote in WP (01/07/93) about Aristide´s "violent rhetoric", were examples of how "pieces of accusations" were manufactured to get rid of a political enemy. HP suspected that such "propaganda articles" would multiply in the days to come with new accusations, threats, and appeals to compromise: Reiterating the opinion voiced by "diplomats", French wrote that Aristide had "refused to engage himself in efforts of negotiations" (HP 168:6,14,16).

HP´s suspicion was further nourished by a WP-article (01/24/93), which the Haitian weekly qualified as overall anti-Aristide, since it detailed once again all known pieces of misinformation (HP 174:17). At a time, when the working relationship between HP and Haiti´s exile government was long in the doldrums, HP sometimes used NYT-articles to make a point in defiance of conservative voices, for example with regard to the Miami conference in January 1994 (HP 217:13). Moreover, HP used the US press to learn about the policies of both Aristide and the White House. But even if HP recognized the NYT´s indication in an editorial (01/08/94) that this was not the right time to abandon Aristide, it still insisted that "this does not change anything about the general tendency" of this particular newspaper (HP 222:1,16) and the "foreign press" in general (HP 228:15).

Kim Ives, both a member of the *Haiti Commission* and a journalist of HP, opined in early December 1993 upon his return from a trip to Haiti that the international press conveyed the false image of a people there waiting for deliverance through foreign troops to establish order (HP 215). By mid-July 1994, when the threat of an invasion of Haiti had become a reality, HP criticized that the subject of Aristide's return was always presented in the context of foreign intervention (HP 284:8). A few weeks later, Ives complained that the "private press" with its "constant bashing" presented an invasion of Haiti favorably (HP 301:11).

In sum, many Haitian political activists in the US evaluated the mainstream media's coverage of aspects of the Haitian crisis, centering around the "return issue", as inadequate and biased overall, especially with regard to Aristide's human rights record, the severity of repression in Haiti after the coup, and the desirability of foreign intervention. But interestingly enough, their verdict differed, when it comes to the "refugee issue": Tecumseh wrote in late November 1991 that "one has to acknowledge on that matter that the press is, all in all, in favor of refugees". She noted that the NYT "has also published several articles on Haitian refugees on the first page" (HP 53:12-15). This observation is in line with the NYT's folk model of the Haitian crisis, as analyzed above, but deviates from the view espoused by Chomsky and others.

Referring to William Raspberry of the WP, Tecumseh concluded with some reservations: "One can see that the US media are perfectly able, if they wish, to expose the hypocrisy of US leaders, even if they do not miss to wave in considerations of `compassion´, supposedly one of the principal moral values of the US, or other remarks nourishing the feeling of superiority of Americans vis-a-vis the `poor´ countries, to whose rescue they come" (HP 53:12-15). Gilbert confirmed the high incidence of news stories on Haitian refugees in late 1991 when observing that "[n]o single day passes without discussion of this subject in the press" (HP 56:10,24). HP used this kind of information to counter what it perceived as the US media's deficiency in reporting on Haiti's human rights situation: "In deed, US newspapers are currently full of reports on refugees, which explain to what sort of brutal repression they have been exposed" (HP 57:6,16-18).

HP's assessment of the US media's performance regarding the refugee issue was rather mixed throughout 1992. In a report in late February 1992, the Haitian weekly acknowledged that the NYT (02/11/92) had given certain examples to prove that Haitian refugees have a "well-founded fear" of persecution (HP 79:1,20). But soon later, HP lamented that the US mainstream press paid only minimal attention to a "friend of the Haitian people": 82-year-old Katherine Dunham, the famous African-American dancer and choreographer, who went on a hunger strike to protest US refugee policy vis-a-vis Haiti (HP 83:1,18). HP found it "interesting" that the WP (05/23/92) refuted a number of arguments used by Bush in defense of his Kennebunkport Order, e.g. the overcrowding of Guantanamo. WP referred to Bill Frelick, senior policy analyst of the *United States Committee for Refugees* (USCR), and Lionel A. Rosenblatt of *Refugees International* (HP 123:14-15). After Clinton's election, however, HP observed a panic "fabricated and orchestrated by the US mainstream press and the Coast Guard on the subject of a `massive´ and imminent exodus of Haitians towards the US" (HP 156:9).

In late January 1993, HP noted with relief that there were still more realistic reports in the US press on the issue of a "massive exodus" (HP 173:8). It reported that the Haitian refugees "continue to be the subject of debate in the US mainstream press and in the middle of the 10th department". As HP admitted, numerous editorials in the

US press guessed that the solution to the human tragedy of refugees was the return to power of Aristide (HP 169:8). In attacking Clinton for his "spectacular turn" in refugee policy, HP quoted editorials of the NYT (01/17/93) as well as the WP (01/16/93), which both called the policy cruel and illegal (HP 172:6,14-16). This is in line with my own before-mentioned findings regarding the way NYT-editorials covered the refugee side of the Haitian crisis.

Surprisingly, HP even extended its praise to Howard French: Tecumseh stressed that French, on February 2, 1993, related in detail the case of a 27-year-old guitarist named Ferleau Nordé, who, after having been tortured by the military of Dame-Marie, took refuge in the capital, but was not accorded a "reasonable fear of persecution" by US authorities (HP189:10-13). What Tecumseh probably did not know was that French, on January 22, interviewed asylum-seeker Nordé at NCHR's office in Port-au-Prince, which resulted in two articles (NCHR18:1). Thus NCHR itself sought to exert influence on a press-mediated public sphere, strongly contested by the US executive branch, Congress, and pressure groups alike, which all constitute Zucker and Zucker's "iron triangle of U.S. refugee policy" (1991:225).

NCHR realized the strategical value of publicity early on in the crisis, "[u]sing the media to rally support for Haitian refugees". In the three months following the coup, the group reported to have been "especially successful" in disseminating information on refugee issues through general and Haiti-specific as well as national and local media. This effort, which was extended in 1992, involved frequent public appearances and media interviews (NCHR5:6-7;NCHR6:1). According to McCalla, NCHR staff was featured in many TV news shows as well as in several newspaper articles and appeared on several radio talk shows (NCHR13:3).

In particular following the aborted attempt in June 1993 to strategically utilize the US judiciary system (USSC ruling), NCHR increasingly turned to "the court of public opinion". Hoping to keep the refugee issue in the "public eye", the group maintained longstanding ties with the media by periodically distributing press releases to some 150 outlets and several "powerful publications", including the NYT (NCHR19:5). NCHR's Human Rights Program activities in 1993 also aimed at providing "an informed perspective" on events in Haiti to the US public via the media, which reportedly had "few comparably informed sources" (NCHR14:1). In 1994, NCHR staff again worked regularly to influence "the media's `spin´ on Haiti issues" (NCHR24:2). The partial chronology of "public appearances, media outreach and other advocacy" by NCHR staff in 1994 comprises over 13 pages (NCHR26:1-14).

HP came to report with concern in June 1994 that the US Embassy in Port-au-Prince "intensified its propaganda against Haitians fleeing the brutal repression" by boat: "Indeed, the US ability to control the Haitian media has reached alarming proportions. Tele-Haiti, an independent station, now broadcasts video stories put together by the US government, including stories on refugees" (HP 278:13). In an effort to keep Haiti's free press and exiled Haitian journalists loyal to Haiti's legitimate government, activists of the 10th department organizations and Aristide government officials did not only warn about transnational terrorism by armed civilians from Haiti, as will be shown further below. For Lassègue did not miss any opportunity to publicly remind of the necessary work to counterbalance misinformation on a daily basis (HP 212:8).

But defensive rather than offensive in nature, these community-internal efforts were designed to inoculate Haitians against the harmful effects of external misinformation. This was done by either presenting in HP an alternative account of Haitian reality or by correcting in commentaries distortions of Haitian reality by non-Haitian journalists. By so doing, HP functioned as multiplier of news produced by the US mainstream media. The weekly´s and the NYT´s records suggest that Haitian activists rarely sought to directly influence US journalists as mediators of Haiti-related information, as NCHR did with a focus on the refugee issue. Members of HEAR insisted, however, that they "tried to shape public opinion" to exert pressure on the US government by faxing press releases to newspapers (HEAR 1995). Similarly, Mayas stressed that "we kept pushing! But some of the media never really picked up on the Haitian issues" (Mayas 1995).

5.2 Fighting the Cause I: Working for Aristide´s Return from Within Through Resistance and Mobilization (Direct Transnational Relations)

Haitians in New York City were among the first in the Haitian diaspora of the US to respond to the shocking news of the coup. HP reported that "permanency was prescribed" by the *10e of New York*, which, since September 30, "incessantly sensitized the community on radio and television waves to demonstrate its support of and its solidarity with Tidid and the Lavalas government". On October 3, more than 8,000 people participated in a rally and applauded New York Mayor David Dinkins, who promised to support Aristide (HP 15:14,25). On October 5, Ben Dupuy, the Aristide government´s Ambassador-at-Large and HP-editor, addressed a Haitian and Caribbean audience at an urgency meeting in Brooklyn entitled "Haiti in Crisis: Popular Democracy or Military Dictatorship" (HP 17:14).

5.2.1 Starting to Get Organized: Street Rallies as Emotional and Moral Support

In other US cities with a large Haitian presence, the initial response was similar. There were more than 500 spontaneous demonstrators in Boston, who gathered downtown on September 30, "confident that a handful of power-hungry macoutes and mercenaries will not take away the victory of December 16, 1990" (HP 11:14), the day Aristide was elected president. An estimated 25,000 to 30,000 people shouting the slogan "We want Aristide" were mobilized by Ray Flynn, Mayor of Boston. They were addressed, among others, by the Consul-General of Boston, Jean Généus, and his Vice-Consul Jean-Robert C. Victoria. At the end of the "ceremony", people sang "We shall overcome" (HP 13:11).

On October 11, about 10,000 people demonstrated again downtown Boston in front of the Government Center. In the presence of Kathy McAfee of *Oxfam America*, Généus explained the measures taken regarding the arrest of popular Haitian singer Manno Charlemagne. Among the many organizations alerted by the case were *amnesty international* (ai) and the *Mexican Commission of Human Rights Defense*, a coalition of various Mexican organizations (HP 21:10). In California, the *10th Department Organization* organized a mass of 800 people on October 13 to commemorate the coup victims. Haitian priest Jacuqes Fabres admonished that now, after the coup, "it is up to us, on foreign soil, to contribute to the efforts of the Haitian people" (HP 20:9). In late November, Philippe Généus noted the "bitter resistance" within the country getting "more organized, day after day", while "the outside" of the country "maintains a mobilization unremittingly" (HP 43:16).

In the third week of October, HP presented reports issued by two Catholic organizations of different national origin, in which the coup was "denounced categorically". *Pax Christi USA* published its report in Erie, Pennsylvania, and the *Haitian Commission Justice et Paix* (CJP), or *Justice and Peace Commission*, published its in Port-au-Prince.[91] Anne McCarthy, *Pax Christi*'s national coordinator, promised not to cease showing "solidarity with the people of Haiti" and encouraged the general public to participate in demonstrations organized by the 10th department (HP 18:8,11). The next opportunity to engage in this kind of direct transnational relations came, when the spontaneous public outcry in the Haitian community of New York City became more organized on October 11.

On that day, the "grand demonstration of honour and dignity", as Latour put it, took place. He reported on this "historic date in the annals of struggles waged by the Haitian people" in a lyric 6-page article, describing how a crowd of staggering 150,000 to 200,000 people from "all the corners of New York", from "all over the territory of the 10e" gathered at Grand Army Plaza to march over Brooklyn Bridge into Lower Manhattan. They were the " the people of the `10e´, the same people that are killed in Haiti". Latour marveled that "[N]ever before, the ground of Brooklyn trembled so much under the weight" of such a rally. The "masters of ceremony" were Sabine Albert and Vice-Consul Ferdinand, who asked the crowd "What do we want?" to receive the answer "We want Aristide". The numerous speakers came from "all political horizons, allied by a common denominator: denouncing the disgusting crime against the Haitian people, demanding the return to democracy, to legitimacy, the unconditional return of president Aristide" (HP 22:14-18).[92]

The Haitian campaign of mass protests was soon extended to include Washington, home of a sizable Haitian community in its own right. Latour, himself a member of the 10e in Philadelphia, covered the event of mid-October for HP in a 4-page article. He ascertained that "mobilization is the only word of order, the only leitmotiv". In his uniquely dramatic diction, the deterritorialized Haitian nation melted into one, united behind the return issue, the "only refrain from New York to Washington: Democracy for Haiti. One half of the Haitian heart beats in Haiti. ... The other half beats throughout the `10e´, ardent, pugnacious, determined" (HP 25:16-19).

Speaking at the rally, Rolande Dorancy, executive director of HRC in Miami, said proudly: Cédras "could, under no circumstances, gather as many people as there were at the demonstration".[93] Haitian singer Farah Juste of Florida said desparately: "We want the return of Aristide, but we want to know how". Wilson Désir sought to intimidate the military junta in Haiti by alluding to the territorially dispersed Haitian people: "We demand from young Haitians who serve in the US army, in the French

---

[91] CJP is the human rights arm of the *Haitian Catholic Conference of Bishops*, which is most active in the Artibonite, Central Plateau, and Grand Anse departments of Haiti (HRW/A,HCHR 1993:91).
[92] For a list of the many speakers, see footnote 18 in the microedition of the study (Opitz 1999).
[93] In an interview with HP´s Latour in March 1992, Dorancy described HRC as a "center with a political character occupied with the lot of Haitian refugees" (HP 88:10,21).

army, in the Canadian army, we also demand from the army of Haiti to organize ... it is up to us, other Haitians, to clarify this question ... it is high time for radio stations to announce that the Forces of Haitian Resistance have taken action within Haiti...". Latour attached to his report a message from Aristide (HP 25:16-19).

According to HP, demonstrations had become routine by the beginning of November, with one succeeding the other. On October 26, for example, about 2,500 to 3,000 people participated in a rally on Eastern Parkway, organized by the *Alliance des Émigrés Haitiens* (AEH), known in the Haitian community as *Wilson Désir's Office*. The Haitian nationalist Désir, who enjoyed broad backing in New York's Haitian community,[94] said he was not impressed by the Honorat-government's revoking of his post as Consul-General. The crowd was addressed by members of a delegation from AEH, which had just returned from a trip to Venezuela, where it met with Aristide before his departure to France. The delegation had had a message from Aristide read by various radio stations (HP 26:9).

In covering mass demonstrations as one important "mobilization" effort organized by Haitians in the US, HP strengthened the "resistance" in Haiti and gave Haitians in the home country an idea of how big the political, emotional, and moral support for them in the diaspora actually was. Patrick Norzéus, Deputy of Barradères, made this point at an event on November 22, 1992 in the *10e of New York*'s office, organized by the *Comité Contre la Répression en Haiti* (CCRH). He said that the "solidarity between the exterior and the interior of the country since September 30" manifested itself not only financially, as will be shown further below, but also in "moral and psychological" ways (HP 159:7). In identifying the need for emotional support for their compatriots, the Haitian diaspora was also joined by US citizens.[95]

In addition to making public political, emotional, and moral support, HP also allowed single groups in the Haitian community to publish messages giving advice, which were directed at specific segments of Haiti's population. The New York sport

---

[94] Two parishioners of the *Église de Dieu/Church of God, Inc.* in Flatbush described Désir to me as the "leader of the community" (09/18/94), and NYT's Donatella Lorch called him "the community's unofficial leader for more than 20 years" (1991:A12). He felt this backing, when he told me with self-confidence that "[a]fter President Aristide, I am one of the most popular Haitians living in this time inside and outside the country". Désir was a graduate from Haiti's military academy coming to work for the Haitian Coast Guard as Leutinant. He fled to the US in 1970 after participating in a failed attempt to overthrow the Duvalier regime. He had been the founding president of the multi-service office AEH, before being nominated by Aristide as New York's Consul-General (Désir 1995). Désir was part of the first cohort of Haitian migrants leaving Haiti for New York, after Francois Duvalier had taken power. They were opposition political leaders and their closest supporters, who perceived New York as a place of transit. The agenda of the majority of these political exiles clearly defined the priority of activities in the Haitian diaspora of New York, which was national politics. Brooklyn was the center of these activities (Charles 1992:112-113;1990:244-246).

[95] Two "human rights activists", for example, decided to protest against Washington's Haiti policy late in the crisis. As HP reported at the beginning of February, 1994, the "US citizens" John and David, both founders and co-directors of *Beyond Borders*, a Philadelphia-based organization offering financial aid and technical assistance in the field of education to local communities in Haiti, started an "open-ended fast". Calling their initiative "Hunger for Justice", they suggested that 4 thousand people - one for each Haitian killed by the military - fast at least one day per month to let the Haitian people know that they were not forgotten and that people in the US would work for their liberation. Inspired by their "belief in Christ", they called on every witness to the repression in Haiti to make available photos and other evidence for an exposition, to be mailed to an address in Washington (HP 231:8).

club Don Bosco, for example, appealed in Creole to all students to refuse to return to school (HP 23:9). And the *Amicale des Anciens du Collège Immaculée Conception des Gonaives, Inc.*, a "New York-based non-profit organization dedicated to the moral and spiritual revival of the youth in Gonaives", extended its support to the "bold position" adopted by the *Organization of Students of March 6 in Gonaives* and called on the students to boycott school under the Honorat-regime (HP 28:9).

Speakers at street demonstrations did not only stress the necessity to maintain the mobilization, "the only veritable key for the return of Aristide", as Dupuy put it. He spoke on April 6, 1992 at a rally in the streets of Manhattan co-organized by HEAR. Dupuy also mentioned the lot of 900 repatriated refugees (HP 102:8). Explaining that "in the back of people´s mind was that the solution to the refugee problem would come from what happened in Haiti", members of HEAR professed to me that picket-signs used in this rally referred to the plight of Haitian refugees as well: "As a matter of fact, we had six of the refugees from Florida ... we let them tell their stories". HEAR´s objective was to shed light on Haiti´s worsening human rights situation in an attempt to win the support of the "democratic country" US for its democratic neighbor in the Caribbean (HEAR 1995).

Henry Frank of HCC admitted that "[s]ometimes the refugees were used to demonstrate for Aristide and his return to Haiti" (Frank 1995). And Pére Paul Dorsinville, executive director of *Haitian Americans United for Progress* (HAUP), a member organization under the umbrella of HCC composed of eight "Haitian centers",[96] confirmed that "they would welcome them [i.e. the refugees] in terms of speaking out at rallies" only (Dorsinville 1995). Letting Haitian refugees speak at demonstrations seems to have been the exception rather than the rule. Raoul of HWHR, which also shipped supplies to a small clinic in Port-au-Prince, observed that leading Haitian community organizations "were more involved with the political situation in Haiti ... they clearly concentrated on getting Aristide back to Haiti" (Raoul 1995).

Haitian refugees were more often than not used as an instrument to keep the spot light on the "political situation in Haiti" rather than on US refugee policy. As Guy Victor told me: "We never demonstrated for refugees *per se* ... but we had large demonstrations for the return, restoration of democracy, because ... once Aristide is returned, automatically the question of refugees would be more or less addressed properly" (Victor 1996). For HP, there was even a positive side to repatriated Haitian refugees, because they returned to the benefit of the resistance within Haiti: Having been confronted with "the cynicism of the US", they would "make the engine of revolution turn faster" (HP 71:8,17). HP agreed with HEAR´s organizers of the April 6 rally: "Haitians need to make New York tremble" (HP 102:8).

Another more important purpose of a massive presence of Haitians taking to the streets was to directly encourage Haiti´s legitimate government. On the day of Aristide´s speech before the UN prior to the coup, around 3,000 people carrying posters reading "Titid we are with you" took possession of Ralph Bunche Park in front of UN Plaza Hotel, where Aristide stayed (HP 8:16-23). Similarly, HP reported shortly after

---

[96] The other members are the *Bedford Haitian Community Center* (Joseph I. Dormeus), *Evangelical Crusade* (Rev. Philius Nicolas), the *Haitian Community Center/BRAHGS* (Marcus Mordan), the *Flatbush Haitian Center* (Jean-Claude Belizaire), HNSC (Guy Vigne), HACSO (Dameus Denis), and the *Haitian Community Center of Stamford, CT* (Robert Jean-Baptiste) (HCC 1995).

the coup that the *Haitian Advancement Association* of New Jersey planned a bus trip to Washington to morally and politically support Aristide before the OAS-meeting of Foreign Ministers (HP 14:11). The "flame of mobilization" during the first anniversary of the coup produced yet another "human flood" (Latour) originating in Brooklyn and surging into Manhattan to join more demonstrators in front of the UN-building. There, Aristide addressed the 47th session of the General Assembly of the UN (UNGA), while protesters shouted "No Aristide, no Peace" (HP 147:8-9).

Likewise, when Aristide met with several human rights organizations in the offices of *Human Rights Watch/Americas* (HRW/A) in Manhattan in late May 1992 to discuss Haiti´s past and present human rights situation, including individual rights of Haitian refugees,[97] hundreds of Haitians demonstrated outside (HP 127:13). After having "noisily taken over 42nd Street on June 27", 1993, *10th Department organizations* announced that they would demonstrate in support of Aristide during the UN-mediated talks with the Haitian military in New York. As Aristide recalled, the military was so "frightened" by the announcement that it succeeded in moving the talks to Governors Island in the port of New York (1996:124). And during the Miami conference in January 1994, again hundreds of Haitians demonstrated outside. HP regretted that Aristide did not deem it useful to address them directly: "ce sont eux qui méritaient le plus d´être remerciés" (HP 224:17). In the same vein, Latour commended the "grand political and patriotic party" celebrated by *Veye Yo* in front of Hotel Intercontinental, where the conference took place (HP 226:9).

McCalla evaluated street demonstrations as part of a mission aimed at "trying to speed up as much as possible Aristide´s return to Haiti". In general, "the demonstrations in New York were organized by the so-called `10th Department´, ... [which] was transforming into (...) a support base for the Aristide government" (McCalla 1995). Frelick of USCR said he was impressed by "the [Haitian] bus loads ... there has been a significant increase in Haitian involvement (...) in terms of street demonstrations" (Frelick 1994). Emile Milne, Congressman Rangel´s Legislative Director, who had been in touch with Haitian activists during the crisis, commented: "... the Haitians? They can only take to the streets in great numbers". He conceded, however, that the electronic media impact of Haitian mass protests contributed to the efficacy of advancing Haiti-related legislative initiatives in Congress (Milne 1995).[98]

While Ronald Aubourg of NCHR, later HCC, underscored the importance of Haitian "street ambassadors" (Aubourg 1996), demonstrations came to Guy Victor´s mind first when asked about means of pressure used by Haitians to promote Aristide´s return (Victor 1996). For Désir, "mobilization" in the streets was generally "indispensable" (HP 43:16). He thereby emphasized the strategical value of Haitian diasporic

---

[97] Among the human rights organizations were NCHR, *Physicians for Human Rights* (PHR), the *Lawyers Committee for Human Rights* (LCHR), the *American Jewish Congress* (AJCs), *amnesty international´s* section of New York, and the Immigration and Refugee Service of the Lutheran church (LIRS). HRW is a non-governmental organization established in 1978 to monitor and promote the observance of internationally recognized human rights in Africa, the Americas, Asia, the Middle East, and among the signatories of the Helsinki accords (HRW/A,NCHR 1994a:52). Its Americas division, formerly called *Americas Watch*, was established in 1981 to monitor and promote observance of human rights in Latin America and the Caribbean (HRW/A,NCHR,CR 1991:36).

[98] During my research stay, I met Emile Milne a couple of times. After returning to Munich, I conducted two short telephone interviews with him on January 21, 1997 and on March 25, 1998.

transnationalism of a public, massive, and open kind. As Basch et al. observed, "the continuing agitation of Haitian transmigrants" in the US hindered the military regime in Haiti "in its attempt to establish legitimacy" (1994:274). Invoking the liberal tradition in America, Haitian activist Josaphat Large appreciated the US as a "country where they grant the right to demonstrate to whomever wants to perform demonstrations" (HP 49:11).

5.2.2 Broadening the Effort: Outside Help in Denouncing the Military Junta

Not only Haitians in Haiti and the legitimate government were in need of assurance in the post-coup chaos, which seems to have disrupted the "intense network and constant communication with parents and relatives in New York, Montreal, Miami and Haiti" (Charles 1990:215).[99] Among the early protesters, for example, was Micheline César from Queens Village, who worried about her husband Camille. Mme César's husband, an Aristide-supporter, was still in Port-au-Prince. She called friends and family in New York, Miami, Boston and Canada as well as Désir at the *Haitian Consulate*, who said he could offer little comfort to the hundreds of callers desperate to learn of their homeland and their relatives (Gonzalez 1991:B1,5). By October, Frank registered an increase of people, "at least ten times" higher than usual, who called HCC for assistance. Most of the "hundreds and hundreds of calls" in the four months after the coup were made by relatives of those endangered in Haiti (Frank 1993:98-99,175,120,101,112). According to Gilbert, a practicing physician residing in Philadelphia, the situation in Miami's Little Haiti was no different (HP 56:10,24).

One of the most important lifelines for Haitian transmigrants in the US to their Caribbean island was operative, though embattled by the political leadership of New York's Haitian community: On October 26, the *10e of New York* organized a picketline at JFK airport to protest against the resumption of *American Air Lines* flights. Guy Victor, "coordinator of the *10e of New York*", indicated that Haitian "compatriots" without any intention to fly had made reservations to reinforce the boycott (HP 26:9). By boycotting *American Air Lines*, the 10e took on the air transport industry, which "operates transnationally" and whose "operations often affect governments". A "force for intersocietal contact, both for pleasure and business" (Thornton 1972:2002,203), the airline was pressured to help isolate Haiti's military junta further.

At the end of October, the Haitian community's cause was endorsed by a prominent figure in US politics. Former US Attorney General, Ramsey Clark, initiated the formation of the Manhattan-based "Commission Indépendente d'Enquête sur le Coup d'Etat du 29 Septembre", in short *Haiti Commission*. Clark described its purpose as contributing to the "struggle of the Haitian people to accelerate the reinstallation of Aristide to the presidency". HP lauded Clark and ascribed to the group's founders, whose "integrity is beyond doubt", the "advantage of being able to mobilize, to a large extent, public opinion". HP appealed to "all Haitian compatriots both in Haiti and in

---

[99] This network of communication through visit, letter, telephone, and remittance has been examined since the early 1980s (Larose 1984:229-230;Laguerre 1984:80-82;Charles 1992:111).

the 10th department" to "collaborate actively with the Haiti Commission that needs a maximum of precise data to document the repression" (HP 24:10).

The *Haiti Commission*'s first public activity was a fund-raiser on November 1. In his address, Jean Casimir, Haiti's Ambassador in Washington, thanked "progressive Americans" for their support and assured them that "they have not worked in vain". Their efforts would contribute to the mobilization of Haitians both in Haiti and in the 10th department. A short film project by US film-maker Rudi Stern was launched. In HP, the *Haiti Commission* appealed once more to Haitians to come forward with information for an inventory of coup victims (HP 36:8). In the second week of November, HP published a "partial list of persons killed during and after the coup d'état", which had been compiled by the *Haiti Commission*. The list included the names of more than 100 fatal coup victims. HP stressed that the *Haiti Commission* "has a very important role to play in cornering the gang Honorat/Cedras and in shedding light on the atrocious crimes committed since September 29" (HP 37:9).

The Haitian community expressed its grief in a score of church masses: A ceremony in commemoration of the more than 1,000 coup victims was celebrated at *St. Patrick Church* in Manhattan on November 16. Attended by Désir, Fritz Longchamps, UN Ambassador of Haiti, it was opened by Aristide-supporter Cardinal O'Connor. Père Guy Sansaricq delivered the sermon, in which he stressed the repressive character of the Cédras/Honorat/Nerette regime (HP 45:9).[100] On November 24, another mass was celebrated in Sansaricq's *St. Jerome's Catholic Church* in Brooklyn. Guest of honor, the Rev. Jesse Jackson of the *Rainbow Coalition* assured that he would show his solidarity with the struggle of Haitians in the 10th department (HP 50:8).[101] Yet another ecumenical mass was celebrated at *Holy Cross Church* in Brooklyn on November 29, at which many notabilities of the 10th department rose to speak. Guy Victor, who had left Haiti for political reasons in 1965 to come to the US, expressed his conviction that Aristide would return to power (HP 55:9,25;Victor 1996). Furthermore, a "special mass" at *St. Patrick Church* for Haitian refugees was celebrated by Cardinal O'Connor on December 22. According to Milne, O'Connor had met three days before with a group of "Haitian leaders", to whom he emphasized that he was acting in response to Rangel's urging (Rangel91a;Owens 1995). The group did not only include Pères Sansaricq, Darbouze and Frank, but also Guy Victor and McCalla. The latter two rather rarely interacted in the course of the crisis.

The *Haiti Commission*'s denouncing of the military junta was joined by Louis Roy, ex-member of the Constituent Assembly in 1987, who HP called the "father of the Constitution". Writing from Montréal on November 7, Roy registered his "protest" and noted that "nothing in the Constitution provides for a coup of force waged against a democratically elected president". He did so in response to members of parliament such as Déjean Bélizaire, president of the Senate, or Guy Beauduy and Julio Larosilière, who had justified the coup on constitutional grounds (HP 40:10). Joseph Préval, Vice-Consul of New York, published an open letter in HP in February 1992 to testify to his "mistrust" of the "honorable Senators and Deputies" (HP 72:9). The

---

[100] Supreme Court Justice Joseph Nerette was the *de facto* regime's first provisional president until Bazin's inauguration on June 19, 1992 as the regime's second Prime Minister (see the NYT of 10/09/91:A1, 10/15/91:A11, and 06/20/92:A3).

[101] Jackson was accompanied by Manhattan Borough President Ruth Messinger, Rangel, Owens, Guy Victor, and Désir (HP 50:8).

Counseil d´Administration du Barreau de Philadelphie (CABP), on July 23, 1992, called on the Haitian *de facto* regime "to respect the law" (HP 148:8). Lassègue and André Chérilus, president of the Haitian Supreme Court,[102] reiterated at a "political-cultural soirée" on March 27, 1993 that the Constitution constituted the frame of reference to denounce the crimes committed by the putschists (HP 199:8,16).

Jesse Jackson redeemed his promise of November 24, 1991 by traveling to Haiti after Clinton´s inauguration in January 1993 to put pressure on the military junta. HP noted that his visit was met with "a sort of euphoria" in the Haitian community. Speaking at the Hospital Workers Union *Local 1199* in Manhattan on January 25, Jackson reported that the Haitian army had "fear" of "père Lebrun" committed by "Aristide´s partisans". HP criticized the well-known African-American civil rights activist, suspecting his motivation to be purely personal: "Un séjour qui porte la marque de la démagogie propre à Jesse Jackson, affectionnant ce genre d´action spectaculaire où il se projette à l´avant-scène et crée un courant autour de lui, qui lui donne un regain de popularité, en jouant notamment sur la `solidarité´ raciale qui a toujours une certaine presse dans un pays aussi racialement structuré que les Etats-Unis" (HP 174:1,16).

In sharp contrast to Clark, HP sometimes viewed Jackson as a competitor rather than an ally. This is surprising at first sight, given Clark´s and Jackson´s different racial backgrounds. The explanation for this is both historical and cultural: Haitian migrants see the US both as a place to work and as a country of whites. Both perceptions are informed by a nationalist preoccupation that fosters the creation of a separate identity from black Americans. Haitians cannot understand how black Americans have accepted conditions of oppression in a white society for so long, whereas Haitians´ defeat of Napoleon is taken as evidence of their power as a people and as a race. Haitians´ tendency to develop forms of identity with a "marked pattern toward disaffiliation" from black Americans is expressed in the common saying "I don´t want to be black twice". A mode of resistance, the saying affirms an own Haitian definition of blackness (Charles 1992:114;Charles 1990:257-280)[103]. This unique race-pride based on their historical experience often informs the observed tendency of Haitians to regard the US system of racial classification as illegitimate, as applied to them. Often holding negative stereotypes about black Americans, Haitians frequently let whites know that they come from a country that has been independent for more than two centuries (Buchanan Stafford 1987:147-149).

The Haitian Revolution as well as French education and culture make Haitians equal to whites. Perceiving the successful slave revolt as having regenerated the African race and its descendants, Haitians still project Haiti as the spokescountry for all blacks in the African diaspora. The Haitian Revolution and Haiti as a black nation came to symbolize the dignity and pride of the black race. This concept of race-pride has served as the basis for nationhood and for cultural nationalism (Charles 1990:97-99). Jackson´s direct and independent activism in Haiti´s national affairs, circumventing the exile government and the Haitian diaspora, challenged the leadership of Haitian activists in the US. It feared Jackson´s popularity with Haitian migrants. Even if HP

---

[102] Aristide-appointed chief justice Chérilus was replaced by Emile Jonassaint after the coup, who later became the second *de facto* president and the third *de facto* Prime Minister following Jean-Jacques Honorat and Marc Bazin (HP 263:13).

[103] In more general terms, Owens referred to this tendency as a "defensive mechanism employed by immigrants of color", which might be stronger in the case of Haitians (Owens 1995).

concluded that Jackson´s mission was a success, HP suspected him to be Clinton´s "official emissary", who also stressed the putschists´ demands (HP 174:1,16). Jackson´s location in the US power center called Washington, as opposed to Clark´s proximity to the Haitian community in New York,[104] further fueled Haitians´ suspicion towards the former. Whereas the work of Clark´s *Haiti Commission* was, by and large, in line with the nationalist agenda of Haitian community leaders, the latter´s suspicion towards Jackson extended to his pursuit of a political agenda, which somewhat deviated on issues such as refugees and military intervention, as will be shown further below.

In its quest for publicity, the *Haiti Commission* also embarked on a trip to the Haitian-Dominican border to obtain new information, which it presented in the auditorium of *Baruch College*, Manhattan, on November 21. A short video on the fact-finding mission was shown as well as footage taken by independent film-makers. Present was Senator Wesner Emmanuel. He talked about death threats he himself had received, the mobilization of the 10th department, and the suffering of the refugees (HP 51:10). Almost half of all NYT-articles dealing with the Haitian crisis that month covered the refugees (see chart in appendix).

According to Manno, the *Haiti Commission* was instrumental in his release. In a telephone interview conducted by HP with the exiled Haitian singer after his arrival in Miami on December 29, he stated that besides the *Haiti Commission*´s "important role" in exerting continued high-level pressure, "numerous artists" contributed to his release (HP 63:9,15). These artists had organized themselves as *Resistance Movement of Artists* two months earlier. On November 3, the group had arranged its first event, a "soirée" at *Erasmus High School* in honor of Manno (HP 35:8).

The organizational unity between Aristide´s exile government, the Haitian diaspora and HP during the first half of the crisis is exemplified by the way demonstrations and a myriad of other activities were organized for September 30, 1992 in commemoration of the coup. Through his private secretariat, Aristide asked the community activists at the grassroots level of the 10th department to send him propositions for a calendar of events (HP 143:9). HP published the calendar of events scheduled to take place in a variety of locations such as Ottawa, Montreal, Boston, New York, Long Island, New Jersey, Stamford (Connecticut), Miami, Chicago, Detroit, St. Louis, Philadelphia, and Paris. Events in New York included a meeting with Lassègue, John Brittain, president of the *National Lawyers Guild*, and Dupuy (September 27) as well as a mass at *St.-Patrick Cathedral* in memory of the victims of repression (HP 142:7).

On his visit to New York in late 1992, Aristide met with 45 "members of the Lavalas family" on November 21. As Latour reported, the principal topic of the meeting was "ORGANISATION". Aristide proposed a "working technique of the different groups ... for efficient, optimal and rapid results". On a piece of paper, Aristide drew "peripheral circles (CP) around a central core (NC)", with each CP representing an organization either in Haiti or in the 10th department. Each CP was to name a delegate reporting to the core of coordination (NC) on the decisions taken (HP 157:10-12). At

---

[104] Many Haitians and Americans in New York seem to have trusted Clark and the work of the *Haiti Commission*. Otherwise, five physicians affiliated with the *Harlem Hospital* at *Columbia University* would not have asked him for help. In a letter to Clark, published by Gilbert in HP at the end of March 1994, they asked him to petition the US Embassy in Haiti with a view to work for engineer Jacques Dorcéan release. Dorcéan had been illegally arrested and imprisoned by the military regime on March 5, 1993 along with other Haitians (HP 238:6,17).

St. Francis Church in Brooklyn on March 27, 1993, Lassègue said that it was necessary to reinforce those structures already in existence (HP 199:8,16). Six days earlier, democratic elections of the *10e of New York*'s 9-member executive committee had taken place in the organization's offices in Brooklyn. Guy Gérald Victor was elected president in what were periodic organizational elections (HP 197:8). To some critics like Mayas, these were dominated by "nepotism" (Jean-Pierre 1995:203).

One month later, on April 25, legitimate Prime Minister René Préval seemed to be content with the state of mobilization, insisting that the "coup d'etat a été mis en échec par la mobilisation populaire". He spoke at yet another "political-cultural soirée" at *Wingate High School* in Brooklyn on the occasion of the International Day of the Woman. Florence Bonhomme Comeau of *Komite Pou Zafè Ayisyen/Haitian Affairs Committee* (KOZA) looked already ahead. She encouraged all mothers in Haiti "to furnish a solid civic education to their children" to prevent the emergence of future putschists (HP 210b:8). Reflecting on the "task to hope" in the new year of 1994, Latour felt encouraged by thousands of Americans supporting democracy and veritable justice in Latin America (HP 218:12).

HP, on the other hand, did not share this optimism. Foreshadowing its outright disapproval of the exile government's changed strategy, HP lauded itself in April 1993 to be a "magazine, whose influence and authority is uncontested in certain areas of the popular sector, while the bourgeois sector of Lavalas rejects its analyses" (HP 202:10). Writing in the January/February 1994 issue of *Report on the Americas*, the journal of NACLA, HP-journalist Kim Ives,[105] also a member of the *Haiti Commission*, detailed the reasons for the decision of HP-editor Dupuy to give up his post as Ambassador-at-Large of the Aristide-government.[106] Dupuy resigned on June 23, six days before negotiations with Cédras began on Governors Island (Ives 1995c:80). The strategical and organizational unity between Aristide's exile government, the 10th department organizations, allied groups such as the *Haiti Commission*, and HP ceased to exist. Communication between Aristide and many activists in the Haitian diaspora came to a virtual standstill. Thus Michael Ratner, a white American and well-respected human rights activist and refugee advocate of the *Center for Constitutional Rights* (CCR), issued an appeal to Aristide in an open letter dated January 10, 1994. He recommended to get out of Washington more often in order to get in touch again with the Haitian diaspora (HP 229:8).

After the Miami conference in January 1994, HP perceived an increasing danger of disintegration and demoralization of the popular sector in Haiti, created by the repression and by a lack of "really combative leadership". According to Gilles Danroc of CJP, this situation accelerated the departure of Haitians (HP 228:14). In an interview with *Newsday* (ND), McCalla of NCHR would later say with regard to the absence of organized armed resistance in Haiti that "the only time there was a certain form of organized resistance" was in the 1960s against Duvalier. HP qualified this statement as a "cynical lack of inhibition" (HP 299:14). There were a few Haitians like the pharmacy-owner in Brooklyn, Luc G. Olivier, who advocated armed resistance. He told the

---

[105] Notwithstanding all political differences, there is an interesting familial connection between HP and NCHR: Dupuy is the father-in-law of both Ives and McCalla.
[106] Ives' piece was later republished in NACLA's *Haiti: Dangerous Crossroads*. The special Haiti issue was originally intended to contain a foreword by Jean Casimir (HP 274:13). The non-publication of Casimir foreword is symptomatic of the political split in the 10th Department.

NYT´s John Kifner that "[w]hat we need is permission for training somewhere in the United States to use arms ... they have all the weapons. It just isn´t fair" (1993:14). But opinions like those were rather scarce.

A group formed by US citizens and supporting the Haitian cause early on was *Americans for Aristide* (AfA). The New York-based organization invited to a "soirée informelle" in Manhattan with Haitian Ambassador Casimir on October 25 (HP 31:9). It was attended by only 75 Haitians and Americans, whose donations of $50 each were dedicated to *Voye Ayiti Monte* (VOAM), an organization officially commissioned to collect funds for the Lavalas government (HP161:16). Questions asked by the audience concerned the embargo, the reforms of the army, the role of the Dominican Republic, the future of the corrupted members of the Haitian parliament, and a possible intervention (HP 32:11). It does not seem that the event inquired about the plight of Haitian refugees, 49 of whom arrived in the US on October 22 (HP 30:10). Gilbert opined two weeks later that the "flight towards Miami of numerous Haitians", nearly 500 boat people since the coup, was a "phenomenon" produced by the illegal regime (HP 42:15). Instead, Casimir contemplated Haiti´s future after Aristide´s return. He proclaimed that a special bank account could be established for the 10th department to receive bonds destined for development projects in Haiti (HP 32:11).

St. Jerome´s Roman Catholic Church in Brooklyn (by Götz-Dietrich Opitz)

5.2.3 Showing Monied Muscle: Material Support for the Victims of Repression

The Haitian Embassy in Washington soon published an announcement in HP, informing other Haitian diplomatic headquarters about the opening of a special bank account in the near future. It was, however, also designed for the purpose of collecting voluntary contributions in the Haitian diaspora to finance the foreign service of the legitimate Haitian government and the resistance within Haiti (HP 33:11). The monied muscle of the Haitian diaspora had already helped Aristide in his political endeavors. In 1990, he extended the Haitian electoral process across national borders to the US, Canada, France, and beyond, where "Lavalas for Home" or the "Bank of the Diaspora", as he put it, was mobilized to finance his campaign (Richman 1992:190,196). Two-thirds of the $300,000 spent on Aristide´s presidential bid came from the 10th Department, which raised additional $600,000 to support a score of development projects after his election (Jean-Pierre 1995:202).[107]

The financial prowess of the Haitian community in New York City, which could have, according to sociologist Josh DeWind, produced an estimated $99.5 million worth of remittances sent to Haiti in 1987 (Charles 1990:217), has also been utilized for other purposes. After a 1991 Dominican government decree had resulted in the forced repatriation of 7,000 Haitians working for the *Dominican State Sugar Council*, followed by the "voluntary" return of 25,000 to 50,000 more (USCR 1995:177), the *10e of New York* mounted, in cooperation with the *Haitian Consulate*, a two-day fundraising campaign in favor of the "compatriots of the interior", a "marathon of solidarity" with "our brothers and sisters" deported to Haiti (HP 2:9;HP 3:10;HP 74:10).

In mid-February 1992, HP published an appeal from CCRH to Haitians in the 10th department to help finance the distribution of cassettes with Aristide´s February 7 message calling on all Haitians to engage in active resistance. Dupuy, founding member of CCRH, announced the project on the air (HP 75:10). During Aristide´s visit to New York City in late April 1992, the "Commission-Finance du Comité de Coordination de la Tournée du Président Jean-Bertrand Aristide dans la Région métropolitaine de New-York" also engaged in fund-raising activities. On April 25, for example, a $150-per-plate dinner-party at Marriot Hotel, planned by different popular organizations from New York, Connecticut, New Jersey, and by the *10e of New York*, took place (HP 109:11;HP 111:10). The Finance Commission soon announced gladly to be able to transfer a surplus of $33,096.00 to the legitimate government for the benefit of "the victims of the repression in Haiti" (HP 117:8). Nevertheless, Aristide believed it necessary to find better techniques to raise funds (HP 114:16).

At the end of July, Henry-Claude Ménard of Aristide´s private secretariat proclaimed the president´s authorization to form a "General Finance Committee" with the task of collecting funds in a bank account, which resulted from activities by Haitian groups in the 10th department or from other friendly organizations, in order to assist in the return of Aristide (HP 131:8). In late September, the Regional Finance Committee of New York published an appeal to the Haitian community to "contribute generously" in support of the victims within Haiti. Seeing the Haitian people´s struggle at a difficult

---

[107] Haitian governments before Aristide already tried to tap the financial resources of the Haitian diaspora, for example with the help of the Arlington-based think-tank and operations firm named *New TransCentury Foundation* (North 1994:1).

crossroads, Ludovic Dauphin, coordinator of the General Finance Committee, stressed that participating in street demonstrations was not enough, for the lack of financial means might push the oppressed in Haiti into resignation or even collaboration. Therefore, direct financial aid to the victims was so important (HP 137:9). It was designed to keep them from defecting to the enemy. A "community meeting" on February 6, 1994 in *Wingate High School* on the subject of "Urgency Funds" for Haiti disclosed the money flows from the 10th department to Haiti between 1991 and 1993. It was also to inform about other fund-raising activities planned for the near future. A report by Aristide´s secretariat detailed how the funds were utilized. According to Latour, none of the speakers at the event had any doubts in terms of the way the funds had been used as well as regarding the probity of the operations (HP 232:8,19). [108]

Dauphin´s stated correlation between repression and impoverishment was confirmed by Père Yvon Massac, both a first-hand witness and a victim of the deteriorating human rights situation in Haiti after the coup. On a brief sojourn in the US, he spoke in mid-May 1992 at *Wingate High School*, Brooklyn. Massac, who had been arrested in February, indicated that it was impossible, due to repression and gagging of the press, to pronounce in Haiti the slogans voiced in the diaspora. Repression in Haiti augmented the material misery of soldiers, who in turn extort money from peasants: "Thus the peasant is obliged to make a compromise with the military officer. He gives him 20 or 30 Dollars not to be arrested" (HP 119:9). Massac thus corroborated Alex Stepick´s observation that in Haiti "motivations for migration can only be labeled as both economic and political" (1986:9). As one HEAR-member put it, the Haitian junta´s bad "political actions reflect[ed] on the economy ... The idea that people like to leave their country is not true" (HEAR 1995).

As early as in the second week after the coup, "[l]oss of jobs and fear of economic hardship were probably a contributing factor" in the internal exodus of Haitians seeking refuge in the countryside from the ubiquitous Port-au-Prince military (HRW/A,NCHR,PHR 1991:5). Extorting bribe money from individuals sympathizing with Aristide and looting the savings of organizations active in Haiti´s civil society was part of the military repression early on (HRW/A,NCHR 1993:17,21,69,121,124).[109] Many other cases of human rights abuses directly resulting in financial burdens suf-

---

[108] In one of the panels, Guy Victor presented a balance sheet of a fund-raiser organized in May 1991, which yielded $437,558.55. VOAM in Port-au-Prince received $424,179.69 of that amount. According to Dauphin, coordinator of the General Finance Committee, donation drives between July 1992 and July 1993 resulted in a net total of $113,456.00: "L´utilisation de ces fonds a toujours relevé du secrétariat de la présidence, à des fins d´aide aux victimes de la répression en Haiti". Yvon Proux of AEH reported on funds resulting from a "Rafle de la déliverance", organized by about 15 organizations and individuals. They collected a total of $58,377.00 before expenses and $39,877.00 after expenses (HP 232:8). Speaking on *Radio Tropicale* in late February 1992, George Wilson ("Moumousse") indicated that the economic support furnished by the 10th department did not achieve a lot, because it did not really reach the refugees (HP 84:9).

[109] On October 1991, for example, soldiers ransacked several buildings of the *Movement Paysan de Papaye* (MPP), taking the group´s safe, which contained between $11,100 and $55,500 (HRW/A, NCHR 1993:17,21,69,121,124). According to a report on the activities of the paramilitary group *Front pour l´Avancement et le Progrès d´Haiti* (FRAPH) in two public markets, issued by *Solidarite Ant Jen/Veye Yo*, members of the army-backed organization extorted between 15 and 50 Gourdes (1 - $3.50) from each market woman every week (HP 247:9).

fered by the victim were documented in the various editions of NCHR's monthly bulletin *HaitiInsight* issued during the crisis.

In general, the breakdown in the constitutional order, the dislocation and internal displacement caused by extensive and pervasive persecution, the ensuing disruption of services and spiraling corruption, and the termination of most foreign assistance resulted, to a large extent, in Haiti's economic woes (HRW/A,NCHR 1994a:49). In hindsight, NCHR deplored in 1994 that repression had been largely overlooked as a cause of impoverishment and misery of Haitians. The escape of a family's principal income-earner often resulted in an abrupt cut-off of a family's means of subsistence. Departures in rural areas meant that fields were left untended and crops ungathered. On the other hand, families sheltering victims of abuse took on the burden of supporting an extra person. High levels of displacement also exacerbated government delivery of and public access to services and greatly reduced the scope and effectiveness of the work of non-governmental development and humanitarian organizations (HRW/A,JRS,NCHR 1994:24-25). NCHR developed a "modest effort" in 1992 to aid persecuted Haitians in Haiti, who needed emergency cash assistance for basic needs and medical care after having been ill-treated in prison (NCHR11:2). William O'Neill of NCHR exemplified the connection between state-sponsored violence and economic misery by pointing to an Aristide-supporter in the countryside forced to flee Haiti, because the military burnt down his house as an act of repression (O'Neill 1995).[110] In 1994, NCHR's staff in Port-au-Prince had meetings with US Ambassador William Swing, which eventually led to the establishment of a US-sponsored Fund to assist victims of human rights abuses (NCHR24:2).

Similarly, HP stressed the political end of the problematic continuum, long discussed by experts of refugee affairs, but often erroneously dichotomized in terms of "economic versus political" (Zolberg 1989:30-33;HP 60:10,16). In contrast, *Télé National* tried in April 1992 "to make us believe" that it is not repression that pushes people to leave, "witnesses" reported (HP 108:9). HP reported how Haitians, forced to flee, easily fell prey of profiteers of all sorts. According to *TROPIC FM* (07/25/92), an operation was mounted by a group of travel organizers, who made believe that they were able to procure a trip to Florida. 500 people were trapped by the offer of work in the tomato harvest season there, with the organizers gaining $80,000. The army, after having been informed by the organizers, stopped the peasants from leaving. Most could escape, but a few were arrested and imprisoned (HP 133:1,22).

According to the Port-au-Prince-based coalition *Plate-forme des Organismes Haitien de Défense des Droit Humains* (Platform), the problem for returned Haitian refugees began with their reception by the *Haitian Red Cross*. It can serve as yet another example of the inextricable mix of political and economic causes. The institution, whose new director, Dr. William Fougère, came to be installed by the *de facto* authorities, gave the returnees a direly needed donation, which was limited to $10 in November 1991 (HP 54:12-15). Paul Déjean, director of *Centre Karl Lévêque* in Port-au-Prince,[111] did "not hide his mistrust with regard to this institution", since Fougère

---

[110] O'Neill believes that Haitians escaped to the US, since the country still was the exemplar of freedom (O'Neill 1995). In contrast, some of my Haitian informants told me that one pull factor for Haitian refugees attracting them to the US was the Haitian diaspora.

[111] *Centre Karl Lévêque* is an organization that cooperated with local human rights groups such as CJP and *Programme pour une Alternative the Justice* (PAJ).

had been a functionary in Haiti's ex-regime under president Prosper Avril (HP 53:14). Fougère is a Duvalierist physician affiliated with Haiti's torture chamber Fort-Dimanche (HP 65:9).

In April 1992, Honorat was said to have asked the US to provide $100 - instead of the maximum of $15 per refugee paid at that time - to better reintegrate them (HP 81:8,17).[112] Apparently, the military junta took advantage of the economic plight of repatriated Haitian refugees. Not surprisingly, when a ship of the *International Red Cross* arrived in Haiti on February 6, 1992 with 565 tons of food granted by Canada, the US, and other countries to aid refugees, according to the bulletin "Résistance et Démocratie", HP suspected this to be "nothing else than assistance to the de facto government", in case the *Haitian Red Cross* would be in charge of distributing it (HP 81:8,17). HP quoted Kenneth Roth of HRW/A as saying in the NYT that "the Haitian Red Cross can hardly be considered an independent institution" (HP 60:10,16).

Haitians in New York did by no means rely solely on official channels to make a pledge. As Caribbean migrants, who were described as belonging to "remittance societies", they also relayed money privately within the bounds of kinship networks that represent a "Haitian survival strategy" (Basch et al. 1994:31,166). Support payments from relatives in New York and Miami wired by "large international money-transfer companies" such as *Boby Express* and *Hatrexco* were estimated to be worth at least $250 million a year, "by far Haiti's largest source of income", as Howard French reported.[113] He quoted an unnamed Haitian economist as saying that "[f]or years, the biggest foreign-exchange earner in Haiti has been cash sent home, not exports sent out", adding that "[t]his is the main explanation why, when they imposed a trade embargo on the hemisphere's poorest country, it didn't crush this place". French reached the inexplicable conclusion that "it is ordinary Haitians themselves who ... have provided the funds that pay for critical imports and keep the exiled leader's enemies afloat" (1992d:A13).

However, when a Haitian Embassy official was asked why Washington had not prohibited the money transfers under the terms of the OAS-embargo on Haiti, he replied that the "idea was to make an impact on the coup makers, but not to totally suffocate the country that is the poorest in the hemisphere" (1992d:A13). French himself reported as early as January 1992 that the trade sanctions had a devastating effect on the Haitian farming community. The US relief agency CARE intensified its operations at that time (1992a:A3). French, however, did not accuse CARE of indirectly supporting Haiti's military junta. According to the *Platform*, the argument that the embargo predated the departure of the boat people was denied by the facts. It refuted the thesis, in a report issued in November 1991, that Haitians deciding to leave Haiti did so for economic reasons (HP 54:12-15).

The international trade embargo contributed to a recession, with Haiti's GDP declining by nearly 20%. Per-capita-income dropped to $ 260 in 1994, the national Gourde depreciated an average 20% nominally, inflation increased to 52%, unemployment topped 60%, and the lack of petroleum products accelerated deforestation.

---

[112] For more information, see also the NYT of 10/28/93:A16. In the 1991 December 4-11 issue of HO, Honorat said sarcastically about repatriated refugees that "it is an act of solidarity to welcome them" (HP 60:10,16).

[113] The maximum amount of money allowed to receive from the US was reportedly limited by the *de facto* regime to $50 for some time (HEAR 1995).

These developments effectuated a reversal of traditional city-bound migratory movements and generated waves of economic migrants (ECLA 1995:235-241).[114] By October 1993, more than 850,000 people in Haiti already depended on foreign aid to survive, according to relief workers. CARE estimated to provide the main meal for 620,000 Haitians (NYT 10/18/93:A6). The NYT´s Larry Rohter reported in August 1994 that relief efforts became an essential lifeline due to the strict economic embargo. Together with the *Catholic Relief Services* and the *Adventist Development and Relief Agency*, food programs fed more than one million Haitians, one of every seven people in the country (1994c:16).[115]

In sum, in addition to political, emotional, and moral support extended to Haitians in Haiti, the Haitian diaspora in the US collateralized its assistance for the "resistance" within Haiti by supplying victims of military repression and repatriated refugees with needed funds. They helped mitigate the economic effects of both human rights violations and international trade sanctions. By doing so, they enabled would-be refugees to stay in Haiti, "rather than ending up in the shark´s mouth" after leaving the "country to fail at sea", as Aristide warned in his 1991 November 22 message on *Radio Tropicale* (HP 53:15). On the other hand, Gilbert quoted one Haitian refugee as saying: "I prefer to die on the sea rather than dying in Haiti" (HP 56:10,24). For Gilbert, Haiti had turned into "a vast prison" (HP 91:8).

Haitian migrants in the US relayed their material assistance in form of indirect citizen-to-citizen relations, either mediated by transnational business enterprises such as money-transfer companies or by community-based representatives of Haiti´s legitimate exile government. Consistent with many observers advocating a long-term policy of supporting the democratic movement in Haiti by encouraging grassroots development programs, Rangel came to recognize in 1993 the advantages of transnational citizen-to-citizen relations within the deterritorialized Haitian nation-state. This was reflected in his legislative agenda (Taft-Morales 1993:14,15).[116] One of Owens´ central concern in forming *Brooklyn for Aristide* (BfA) in March 1993 was to promote closer "people-to-people and group-to-group communication" between Haitians and others in the US in order to support a variety of projects in Haiti (Owens 1995).

Haitian immigrants may also have participated in the "largest citizen-to-citizen network linking Haiti and the United States, the Adopt-A-Parish Program" initiated by Haitian priest Rénald Clérismé (Haiti1:6),[117] or in projects such as the "H.E.A.D.D. for Haiti Open Forum", organized by the *Haitian-Americans for Economic Alliance and Democratic Development for Haiti* in Rockland County, New York (Rangel92a:1).

---

[114] On International Youth Day on March 27, 1994, a high school student group in Port-au-Prince called *Zafè Elèv Lekòl* complained that prices were 200 to 350% higher now than when Aristide was in power (HP 247:9).

[115] For the "status of humanitarian conditions in Haiti" and the "actions and policies needed to address these conditions" (Cong2:1) in 1992, see the Congressional hearing of June 11.

[116] Inspired by the euphoria set off by the imminent Governors Island process, he introduced a bill on April 29, 1993, providing for "a program established by a nongovernmental organization under which Haitian Americans would help the people of Haiti recover from the destruction caused by the coup" (Taft-Morales 1993:14,15).

[117] Aristide´s inauguration is said to have stimulated a "burst of interest" among Americans, also revitalizing the transnational network "Adopt-A-Parish Program" (Haiti1:6). Clérismé seems to be a leading member of the peasant group *Tèt Kole* (HP 46:9;HRW/A,NCHR 1993:10,11,14).

Haitians in the US also sent in-kind contributions by mail, as my host family in Flatbush did (Loueur 1995). Delivering goods in person became too dangerous after the coup. Members of HEAR, for example, which took care of 250 children at Kenscoff in Haiti by paying their fees for a boarding-school, would usually travel to Haiti once or twice a year to bring along money and contributions in-kind. But since September 1991, those trips had to be interrupted (HP 125:8).[118] According to Dupuy at the end of 1992, donations and demonstrations were the most important contributions of Haitians in the diaspora, unparalleled in its history. Thanks to Aristide´s concept of the "10th department", the successes of the "diplomatie du béton" had been considerable (HP 161:6).

Désir, who kept his Haitian citizenship until his death in 1996, stressed the importance of organizational and financial independence. In his opinion, groups such as NCHR or HCC lacked the political freedom necessary to fight the Haitian cause successfully as "militant" organizations: "They cannot have the same positions as the Alliance of the Haitian Émigres, which refuse, still today, to receive funds from the US government to operate. When you receive federal funds, you do not have your freedom and you can be infiltrated" (Désir 1995).[119] This explains why Dorancy reiterated several times in an interview with Latour that HRC did not receive federal funds from the US government, which allowed the organization "to take a militant stance, to define its own political orientation in order to be able to join the struggle inside Haiti" (HP 88:10,21). Désir´s principle did not apply, however, with regard to Haiti´s legitimate government. On the contrary, all leading political organizations of the Haitian community´s third sector were rather state-oriented, albeit in a reversed relationship: Instead of depending on state funds themselves, these groups helped keep the exile government afloat.

Désir´s principle of independence from the US government seems to have mattered as well in terms of funding by private US sources, often seen to be close to US economic society. For there was no Haitian political organization in New York City which applied for funds with US foundations, according to the *Foundation Grants Index*. Service-providing organizations and HRC seem to be an exception to this rule, since its principal source of funds, according to Dorancy, was the *Ford Foundation*, followed by private donations from other US sources (HP 88:10,21). In contrast, WOH, an inactive member of NCHR and initiator of a project called "Haiti National Network" (HNN),[120] successfully applied for a $18,500 grant in 1993 to "build network of grassroots organizations in support of democracy in Haiti" (Foundation2:1189).[121]

---

[118] HEAR´s new crew was introduced to the public in May 1992 at the group´s office in Brooklyn. Among the invitees were representatives of HP and Guy Victor, president of the *10e of New York* and founding member of HEAR (HP 125:8). HEAR also supported an orphanage in Haiti (HEAR 1995).

[119] One HEAR-member told me that "McCalla is a big hat, when it comes to refugees ... most of his money, ... he got it from the [US] government" (HEAR 1995). While it is true that HCC received a refugee services grant from ORR (HCC 1995:1), NCHR was not funded by US federal government sources (Harris 1995).

[120] HNN was launched after a January 1992 "international conference" entitled "Dignité et Démocratie" in Washington´s *Howard University*, organized by WOH (HP 68:10;Haiti5:11).

[121] Moreover, Massachussetts-based *Grassroots International* secured a $25,000 grant from the *John Merck Fund* in 1993 for "continued support of financial and technical assistance to Human Rights Platform, coalition of Haitian organizations", the Haitian group mentioned above. GI received another grant

Insofar as some foundations can be defined as transnationally active NGOs, Skjelsbaek´s observation might still be valid. He states that "less developed countries partake much less in NGOs than do developed countries, and they are especially poorly represented in the central organs of these organizations". Hence they are "open to the suspicion of neo-colonialism" (1973:91). According to Peter D. Bell, the *Ford Foundation*, for example, has been perceived as an instrument of the *Ford Motor Company*'s public relations or, "at worse, as a more or less sophisticated attempt to maintain the status quo, including the capitalist system" (1973:124).[122]

---

worth $25,000 in 1993 from the *ARCA Foundation* "[f]or emergency assistance to Haiti´s democratic movement" (Foundation2:1198,1188).

[122] *Ford Foundation* CEO Franklin A. Thomas, an African-American, called his organization a "global institution" with a "global view", working on "issues of poverty and discrimination and opportunity" seen as problems "not limited by the borders of the United States" (Daniels 1989:21).

Cargo Express Shop in Brooklyn (by Götz-Dietrich Opitz)

5.2.4 NCHR's First Post-Coup Reports: Human Rights Before, After the Coup

Aristide's overthrow came as a "painfully unwelcome surprise to NCHR". The human rights organization's "rapid response" consisted of a press release issued jointly with HRW/A, condemning the violence in Haiti. NCHR's New York office provided the English-speaking public with a translation of Aristide's urgent message to the Haitian people. These earliest efforts were followed by the dissemination of many human rights advisories, news releases, and formal declarations in response to hundreds of media requests (NCHR5:15,17;HP 11:14). Writing in *HaitiInsight*, NCHR board member Amy Wilentz, author of *The Rainy Season: Haiti Since Duvalier* (1989), supposed that Aristide may become the "third world's first deposed democratic leader ever to be reinstated" because of "intense pressure from the Haitian community living abroad" (Haiti3a:6). NCHR noted in the winter issue that its staff had "received hundreds of phone calls from concerned individuals asking what they can do to highlight human rights violations in Haiti". One of NCHR's many recommendations was to "[p]ress local media to cover events in Haiti and to editorialize in favor of President Aristide's restoration" (Haiti4:6).[123]

When the *Haiti Commission* carried out its first public event on November 1, NCHR published its report *Haiti: The Aristide Government's Human Rights Record*, co-authored with HRW/A and the Barbados-based group *Caribbean Rights*.[124] The report was based on several fact-finding missions to Haiti (HRW/A,NCHR,CR 1991:35-36) and on extensive "contact throughout the year" with what NCHR calls "our network of indigenous sources" in Haiti. The report was "distributed broadly" to "agencies promoting human rights and humanitarian service, as well as the international press" (NCHR5:16). It explicitly mentions as informant the "Haitian Human Rights Center (CHADEL)" headed by Honorat, until his joining the *de facto* regime "perhaps Haiti's pre-eminent human rights monitor" (HRW/A,NCHR,CR 1991:11,12,2). Honorat was chosen as recipient of the *American Bar Association*'s (ABA) first annual Human Rights Award on August 13, 1991 (Haiti2:5).[125]

The report discussed the "positive steps by the Aristide government" such as extending civilian control over the military, abolishing the system of *Section Chiefs*,[126] attempts to curb military impunity, measures toward prison reform, seeking justice for past crimes, creating a civilian police force, and the President's personal security guard. It also sought to document "ongoing abuses under President Aristide" vis-a-vis a continuously weak justice system such as military abuse, land conflicts, and popular violence. Concerning the last point, the report stated that "[w]e cannot hold Aristide responsible for inciting reprehensible actions by his followers since the violent crowds acted quite spontaneously". Yet, "[m]ost disturbing is that on two occasions Aristide

---

[123] In 1992, NCHR was able to increase circulation of *HaitiInsight* by more than 500 subscribers and the number of pages from 8 to 12 (NCHR11:2).

[124] HRW/A's name prior to the sixth report *Terror Prevails in Haiti* issued in 1994 was referred to as *Americas Watch* (HRW/A,NCHR 1994a:52).

[125] Honorat founded CHADEL in 1983 while in exile in New York. NCHR's *HaitiInsight* relied on its monthly bulletin "as the starting point for its list of monthly human rights violations" (Haiti2:5).

[126] The *section chief*, who represented the government for the approximately 75% of Haitians living in the countryside, had life and death power over the residents of his section, serving as *de facto* executive, legislature, and judiciary for the areas under his command (LCHR 1990a:34-35).

seemed to endorse the practice of Père Lebrun [necklacing] ... As the head of state (...), President Aristide had a duty to refrain from any statement that could be understood to support" the practice.[127] The report concluded that "[o]verall, violence in Haiti of all sorts ... dropped conspicuously" during his tenure" (HRW/A,NCHR,CR 1991:23,24,28,5).

Nevertheless, the NCHR-CHADEL connection came to tarnish NCHR's reputation in the Haitian community. Three weeks after the coup, HP pointed out that Honorat utilized "his `reports´ emanating from his organization CHADEL" to slander the goverment Aristide-Préval (HP 18:8,11). In December, HP complained that US Ambassador Adams preferred "without doubt to rely on reports by CHADEL" rather than on the *Inter-American Commission for Human Rights* (IACHR) (HP 57:6,16-18). Moreover, the widely publicized film documentary "Killing the Dream", released in April 1992, juxtaposed the inquiry realized by the *Haiti Commission* and the declaration made by Mme Honorat, who came to actually head CHADEL. She assured that there were only "rumors", with nobody reporting cases of abuse to her (HP 104:10). In late May 1992, Aristide himself called on the human rights community in the US to reverse the distinction accorded Honorat by the ABA in the field of human rights before his ouster (HP 127:13).

Consequently, HP described HRW/A as "an organization well known for denouncing `human rights violations´ under Aristide" (HP 60:10,16). In August 1994, when the situation was emotionally very charged in the face of an imminent US invasion, HP noted that it had been a long time since McCalla "gave himself authority to discredit Aristide". HP reminded that the "imperialist propaganda arguments about the usage of `père Lebrun´" was presented in the report of NCHR, which was "not very remote from CHADEL". HP alleged that CHADEL was financed by the *United States Agency for International Development* (USAID), "which reaped the fruits of its investment when [Honorat] became the putschists `premier minister´ No. 1" (HP 299:6).[128] After Aristide's return, I was instructed about the NCHR-CHADEL connection by Donna Plotkin Coupeau and Michelle Karshan, both members of AfA. They defined NCHR as a "mainstream" organization.

NCHR justified the timing of issuing the report with concerns raised by a UN representative, who said that an independent assessment of charges that Aristide himself condoned political violence was needed. "NCHR responded swiftly to the grave need for concrete data" by releasing the report in an effort "to set the record straight" (NCHR5:15-16). In the report, NCHR declared that "we have no intention to lend our voice to those responsible for [Aristide's] ouster or to those working to prevent his return to power", thereby testifying to the group's "conviction that President Aristide must be returned to power" (HRW/A,NCHR,CR 1991:2,3).[129] As McCalla told me,

---

[127] Placing a motor tyre around a victim's neck, then setting it on fire, is called "necklacing". "Père Lebrun" is the name of a motor tyre dealer in Port-au-Prince.

[128] In February 1992, WOH requested "permanent prohibition of any U.S. government funding to CHADEL", which had been slated for significant expansion of funding under USAID's planned Democracy Enhancement project (Cong1:101).

[129] NCHR stated that it had to "redefine(...) its role in promoting human rights in Haiti" at the beginning of 1991. NCHR had joined UN and OAS monitors "in judging free and fair" the "first democratic election in Haiti's history", on which NCHR reported in *Haiti: The Birth of a Democracy*, published jointly with HRW/A, CR, and the *Luterhan World Federation* in September 1991. Fuller and McCalla ac-

NCHR as a politically independent organization planned to issue a report on the Aristide government long before the coup. There was no way to foresee that both events would coincide (McCalla 1995).

NCHR´s second report *Return to the Darkest Days: Human Rights in Haiti since the Coup* was better received than its first. HP´s review concluded overall that "the account presented by these human rights organizations has the advantage of giving US public opinion an overview of the current regime of terror" (HP 65:9). The report, released at Washington´s *National Press Club* on December 30, 1991, was co-authored with HRW/A and the Boston-based group *Physicians for Human Rights* (PHR). It resulted not only from information acquired through telephone and fax contact with a "broad-based network of indigenous rights advocates in hiding", but also from a mission to Haiti from December 3-10, 1991. The delegation of human rights activists met with a wide range of Aristide supporters and other individuals as well as with US Embassy officials, Evans Paul and Honorat (NCHR5:18). The latter justified the coup by insisting that "police brutality is not specific to Haiti; I saw the videos of what happened in Los Angeles" (HRW/A,NCHR,PHR 1991:18).

The report shed light on the high casualties, with educated estimates indicating that "at least 1,000 people were killed in the first two weeks of the coup and perhaps another 500 after that". It assessed the medical consequences of the repression, which led to an "alarming deterioration in the already abysmal state of health care in Haiti",[130] and revealed that many leading Duvalierists had been freed from prison during the first hours of the coup. It furthermore detailed the targets of the repression, victimized by returning *Tontons Macoutes* and restored *Section Chiefs*.[131] Finally, the report described post-coup Haiti as a "nation of refugees and displaced persons", with an estimated 250,000 people fleeing Port-au-Prince for the countryside by December, a "smaller, but significant movement" by leaders of grassroots peasant and church-based organizations to the city, thousands of people taking to sea in leaky boats, and a "perhaps higher number" fleeing east to the Dominican Republic. NCHR thanked the *Platform* consisting of 9 members[132] for providing "essential and reliable information" for the report (HRW/A,NCHR,PHR 1991:2,4,14,6-14,5-6,i).

According to NCHR´s Planning Committee, the group´s having developed "enough links and credibility with human rights advocates in Haiti" was one of two crucial factors in the group´s ability to rise to the challenge posed by the coup. Beginning in 1986, NCHR encouraged support of several Haitian human rights groups in Haiti, formed in the wake of Duvalier´s departure, by giving them access to US fund-

---

cepted "official invitations" to Aristide´s inauguration on February 7, the "fruit of decades of struggle for democracy by grassroots political groups in Haiti" (NCHR5:10,2,10-14).

[130] In May 1994, Dr. Claude Jean-Francois, Minister of Health under the Aristide government, presented a somber picture of the health system in Haiti (HP 268:8).

[131] After the coup, the "communal police agents" under the Aristide government were removed from office and the old section chief system was reestablished (HRW/A, NCHR 1993:104).

[132] These are the *Alternative Justice Project* (PAJ), the CJP, the *Commission for Legal Assistance of the Haitian Religious Conference* (CORAL), the *Legal Assistance Group* (GAJ), the *Center for Economic and Social Research and Training for Development* (CRESFED), the *Karl Leveque Center*, the *Karl Leveque Cultural Institute*, the *Office of Research for Development* (BRD), and the *Legal Aid Agency of the Haitian Association of Voluntary Agencies* (HAVA) (HRW/A,NCHR,PHR:i).

ing sources.[133] The *Ford Foundation* and the *Gilmore Foundation* were among the US foundations, from which funding was secured (NCHR21:5-6). The former was recounted as a "transnational actor" in its own right, which has made US Embassies "sometimes unhappy about [its] assistance to 'anti-American´ or `subversive´ groups". Modern foundations like the *Ford Foundation* can influence "national actors which, in turn, affect domestic and world politics" (Bell 1973:128,115,125). The Planning Committee indicated that NCHR´s focus shifted after the coup from monitoring human rights to the problem of Haitian refugees facing strict US policy measures.

The second factor was paraphrased as the "broad experience in working on behalf of refugee rights with Congress and the Administration" by NCHR members (NCHR21:6). In all eight human rights reports published during the crisis, the organization portrays itself as follows: NCHR "is composed of forty-seven legal, human rights, civil rights, church, labor, and Haitian community organizations working together to seek justice for Haitian refugees in the United States and to monitor human rights in Haiti". The coalition boasts a diverse member composition in terms of ethnic origin and issue area: It has encompassed Jewish, African-American and Hispanic groups as well as research, immigration and refugee resettlement agencies (volags), and a score of individuals. They are all firmly embedded in different sectors of US civil society. The intensity of cooperation between NCHR´s staff and its membership varied from organization to organization, which pursued their own Haiti-related agendas during the crisis independently from NCHR.[134]

NCHR´s institutional link to New York´s Haitian community is manifested in the membership of four Haitian-American organizations: HCC (headed by Henry Frank), HAUP (headed by Paul Dorsinville), the *Haitian American Cultural and Social Organization*/ HACSO (headed by Dameus Denis), and Pére Guy Sansaricq of *St. Jerome´s Roman Catholic Church* in Brooklyn, representing the Haitian Apostolate, are all NCHR-members.[135] In addition, there are three other Haitian organizations, which are not headquartered in New York, among them the *Haitian Refugee Center* (HRC) in Miami (Rolande Dorancy, later Guy Victor).[136] NCHR letter heads during the Haitian crisis also list Père Antoine Adrien as a member. Adrien, who returned to Haiti after the fall of Duvalier, is one of the Catholic Haitian priests committed to liberation theology, who had been part of HCC in the early 1980s, when it described itself as "the voice of the Haitian community" (Basch et al. 1994:208,204). Yet, almost all NCHR staff members interviewed alleged that most of the Haitian organizations in New York have not been active members. Pére Sansaricq, however, presented himself

---

[133] The *Haitian Lawyers Committee* was partly created at NCHR´s suggestion (NCHR21:5).
[134] The number "forty-seven" does not reflect the exact number of NCHR-members. See the list of members in the appendix. Especially between 1991 and 1993, NCHR members and allied groups communicated by way of two types of telephone conference calls, one was NCHR-internal, the other also included non-members (McCalla 1995).
[135] At one point, the three New York-based groups *Evangelical Crusade of Fishers of Men*/ECFM (Rev. Philius Nicolas), the *Charlemagne Peralte Center*/CPC (Emmanuel St. Hubert), and COCHE (Alex Etienne) had been members of NCHR, according to a list included in the yearbooks. The two latter, however, do not exist anymore. See the list of members in the appendix.
[136] The other groups are the *Coalition for Haitian Concerns* (CHC) in Willow Grove, PA (Gerard Ferere), and the *Pierre Toussaint Catholic Center* (PTCC) in Miami (Rev. Thomas Wenski).

as NCHR's most important link to the Haitian community of that city (Sansaricq 1995).

The deficient rootedness of NCHR in the Haitian community was deplored by McCalla, who noted in 1992 with regard to the organization's constituencies: "Haitians in America have the potential to influence positively the policies of this country. ... the energy of that constituency remains to be tapped to its fullest" (NCHR13:3). And the Planning Committee reminded that "NCHR correctly aimed to promote Haitian community advocacy in coordination with Haitian organizations, not in their stead" (NCHR21:1,8). Mario Toussaint of BfA and BHRAGS, who once came to work for NCHR at the end of the 1980s through its former executive director, Michael S. Hooper, confirmed that the group is not well-known among Haitians in New York. He criticized that under McCalla, NCHR concentrated too much on (pre-coup) Haiti at the expense of the Haitian community (Toussaint 1995).

NCHR was established in 1982 in the wake of the Mariel boat lift by 23 Haitian and non-Haitian organizations. The organization's first draft of by-laws referred to the arrival of the "Pilgrims more than 360 years ago", the US Constitution, and "the laws of the land" as sources of legitimacy for its mission, which was of a predominantly ethnic character: "... an end to the United States policy of unreasonable detention of Haitians and their interdiction on the high seas", the defense of "basic due process rights of Haitians under United States law", and the deepening of "our understanding of the underlying social, economic, and political causes" of Haitian migration. The group's second objective of investigating into human rights conditions in Haiti "grew out of necessity", according to the Planning Committee. NCHR's first executive director was Dr. Susan H. Buchanan, a renowned US sociologist, who was later succeeded by (Mike) Hooper, a lawyer working on immigrant human rights issues. In October 1986, NCHR became a non-profit, tax-exempt organization under section 501(c)(3) of the Internal Revenue Code. When Hooper died of cancer in 1988,[137] McCalla became NCHR's third executive director. He qualified the group's "narrow focus" as one of its key advantages (NCHR1;NCHR21:3-4;McCalla 1995).[138]

When I got in touch with NCHR in the spring of 1995, it had a total of seven professional staff members, four of whom are of Haitian origin. McCalla, who does not have US citizenship, praised what he called "ethnic mix" of NCHR's staff as its second major advantage. The organization thus seems to be different from other NGOs, which generally display what Skjelsbaek called a "Northwest bias of their membership composition". In their central organs, less developed countries were "especially poorly represented" (1973:91). NCHR's staff constitutes the intermediary between the broad spectrum of members within US civil society and the "network of indigenous sources" within Haiti's young civil society. This link makes up the transnational nexus between the two countries, which are also tied together by other NCHR-members.[139] It is noteworthy that NCHR's contacts to groups within Haiti were much more intense than to Haitian organizations in the US.

---

[137] In the microedition of my dissertation (Opitz 1999), a wrong cause of Hooper's death is stated.

[138] The same year saw the enactment of the Immigration Reform and Control Act (IRCA) containing a Cuban-Haitian Adjustment provision, which NCHR had been promoting since 1982 (NCHR21:4).

[139] In 1993, for example, the *Lawyers Committee for Human Rights* (LCHR), provided a lifeline to human rights advocates working clandestinely within Haiti by creating an "international fax network" to

NCHR staff in offices downtown New York City (by Götz-Dietrich Opitz)

Pierre Toussaint Center in Brooklyn (by Götz-Dietrich Opitz)

---

circulate their information. LCHR was founded in 1978 and is "dedicated to advancing human rights and the rule of law throughout the world" (LCHR 1993:13).

5.2.5 The Role of Haiti's Free Press and the *Macoute* Onslaught in the US

In the first weeks of the crisis, Haiti's free press declared its solidarity with Aristide in his pursuit to return to Haiti. In the second week of November 1991, HP published an open letter to Aristide by Patrick Jean Baptiste, journalist of *Radio Cacique* in New York. He assured him of his support with regard to the coup (HP 39:10). The exile government knew how important this endorsement for the mobilization of the Haitian community was, with which the *10e of New York*, through its press committee, tried to stay in touch by cultivating its press relations (HP 105:8).

The backing of the Haitian press was even more vital in the face of growing opposition within the Haitian diaspora: On November 15, 1991, two Haitians were shot at by three armed individuals during the daily demonstration organized by the 10th department of Orlando. Activist Large concluded in HP that the "macoutes" had now crossed the borders in order to spread terror in the middle of Florida (HP 49:11). One cab driver killed in March 1993 was the fourth cab driver slain in Boston since 1991. Three of the four were Haitian (Thorpe 1993:1). Three radio personalities in Miami known for their strong views were gunned down soon after Aristide had been overthrown. Two of the radio talk show hosts were outspoken Aristide supporters. Another pro-Aristide radio talk show host, Dona St. Plite's, was killed in October 1993 (Fiagome 1994:17). His murder occurred at a time when Miami was reported to have supplanted New York as the most dangerous US city (Newport 1993:2). Suspicion of some Haitian voluntary organizations in the 10th department was big early on. In March, 1992, HP reported on a group called *International Congress of Resistance and Return* (CIRR) of Father Aristide, headed by Philippe Jules. HP mistrusted Jules' political record, as he had been a member of the official *Conseil Electoral Provisoire* in 1987. HP thus qualified Jules as a "perfect opportunist about to recycle himself according to changing political conjunctures" (HP 90:10).

When Dona St. Plite's murder occurred in October 1993, the paramilitary group *Front pour l'Avancement et le Progrès d'Haiti* (FRAPH) began to emerge as what Howard French later called the fastest growing political movement in Haiti (1994:A4). Many of the worst abuses of the post-Governors Island period had been carried out by the neo-Duvalierist group, which functioned as a surrogate for the military. Led by Emmanuel Constant, son of an army commander under Duvalier, FRAPH claimed to have 300,000 members by January 1994, among them so-called *attachés*, thugs, and former *Tontons Macoutes*.[140] Whereas FRAPH's national network owed a great deal to the old *Tontons Macoutes* organization, which had been created to serve as a counterweight to the army, FRAPH and the army worked hand in hand (HRW/A,NCHR 1994:11). In 1994, FRAPH opened up chapters in New York. In September, FRAPH reportedly even sought to weaken Aristide-supporter Rangel, who accused his chief political rival, Councilman Adam Clayton Powell IV, of having received campaign support from the Haitian right-wing group (Browne 1994:4).

On March 9, 1994, the fourth pro-Aristide activist, Daniel Buron of the Miami-based political group *Veye Yo*, which had organized many demonstrations seeking the

---

[140] "Attachés" are omnipresent civilians employed, armed, and directed by the Haitian military and police. Attachés abuse their enormous discretionary powers through murder, torture, arrests, beatings, extortion, imprisonment, and rape (HRW/A,NCHR 1994b:11).

return of Aristide, was assassinated in Miami's Little Haiti. Spokespersons of the Haitian community were said to see his and the previous three deaths as acts of terrorism exported by coup leaders in Haiti to Miami (Fiagome 1994:17). Buron's death was followed by "fears of assassination", particularly in Little Haiti, as the NYT's Rohter reported. Coinciding with a "campaign of terror in Haiti", Buron's killing was interpreted as a warning to the "more than 100,000" Haitian exiles in Miami to halt their anti-macoute marches, speeches, and broadcasts, which could sometimes be heard in Haiti. Beverly Bell, spokeswoman for Aristide's exile government, confirmed the widely held belief that "transnational terrorists", supported by Haiti's military junta, were also responsible for other acts of violence against Haitians in Miami, New York, Boston, and Montreal (1994a:22).

Buron was gunned down a few days after his name had appeared on an anonymous hit list circulating in Little Haiti (NYT 03/11/94:A18). The name of HRC-director Dorancy was on the hand-written document, which also named Aristide, his Cabinet, and exiled pro-Aristide journalists (NYT 10/26/93:A13). Radio talk show hosts were at risk in particular. As the NYT's Pierre-Pierre reported, many Haitian-Americans rely on radio as the "primary source of information". The military junta's henchmen must have noticed the importance of radio among Haitians in the US, which has its roots in Haiti, where the illiteracy rate is about 80% (1993e:B3).

March 19 was dedicated to Buron's funeral at *Notre Dame d'Haiti Church*. Aristide had paid a visit to members of Buron's family (HP 239:7). Funerals consumed an increasing amount of organizing energy in the Haitian community, the longer the crisis dragged on. On March 1, 1993, students in Brooklyn organized a funeral service for a Haitian student from *Brooklyn College*, who had been murdered in the night of February 20 to 21 in his parents' home in Fontamara, Port-au-Prince (HP 188:9). On September 3, 1994, the Haitian community of New York mourned at *St. Innocent Church* in Brooklyn for Père Jean-Marie Vincent assassinated in Haiti on August 28 (HP 317:8). Another mass in commemoration of Vincent was celebrated with Mgr. Romélus, on his stop-over in New York, at *St. Grégoire Church* in Manhattan on September 18 at the initiative of Père Joseph Darbouze (HP 327:14,15).[141]

The exile government itself sought to cultivate its relations to Haiti's free press, a task confided to Lassègue, Minister of Information. In late April 1992, Aristide proclaimed that a new basis for information policy had been launched with the daily broadcast of *Radio 16 Décembre* (HP 114:16). According to Lassuège, the radio station was to counter misinformation on Haiti and to better inform the people in Haiti (HP 126:10). In 1992, Lassègue planned a "day of the press" scheduled for June 7, the day freedom of the press had become a reality in Haiti six years before. The idea was to assemble all Haitian journalists, scattered around the US in Boston, New York, Miami, and in Canada, as well as "foreign journalists" in the 10th department of New York (HP 126:9,10). In Haiti, the press had been a main target of censorship right after the coup. Especially the broadcast media were targeted. Army attacks on radio stations drastically restricted press freedom early on (HRW/NCHR 1993:107-118). In December 1991, HP reported that the brutal closure of *Radio Galaxie* assured *Radio Nationale* the entire monopoly of information (HP 60:10,16).

---

[141] Other participating priests were Rollin Darbouze, Pierre Etienne, Wilkens Lampy, and Carl Sansaricq. Vincent's sister, Marie-José Kersaint, was also present (HP 327:14,15).

According to Lassègue, numerous journalists had to leave the country, after certain media had been demolished by the military junta (HP 126:9,10). In October 1993, the NYT′s Pierre-Pierre reported that Haitians had to rely on foreign broadcasts like the *Voice of America* (VoA) and CNN, since news organizations practiced fear-driven self-censorship, while many Haitian journalists stopped working altogether (1993f:A18). Lassègue said that three in four journalists were currently outside of Haiti, where they had not established themselves, yet. The "day of the press" was to counter their isolation by providing the opportunity to exchange information on their experiences both in Haiti and in the 10th department in order to make their common work more efficient (HP 126:9,10).[142] When still in Haiti, Haitian journalists were also instrumental in giving would-be refugees and *de facto* refugees the opportunity to voice their motivations to flee (HP 173:8). Haitian radio journalists also occasionally reported on Guantanamo (HP 192:16;Dreyfuss 1993:81;Pierre-Pierre 1994a:A3).

On November 1, Lassègue met again with journalists together with members of the Haitian community in Brooklyn. Lassègue talked about the priority of "mobilization" and "resistance". Aristide and democracy were the overarching themes (HP 151:8). The event took place only a few days before the US presidential elections, which was followed by an upsurge in USCG interdictions: Whereas 141 Haitian refugees had been intercepted in September, the number was 1,016 in November (see chart in appendix). It seems that the refugee issue as one "means" of transforming the "resistance" into "democracy" was not discussed at the event.

At the *10e of New York*′s first annual dinner party in Queens on December 26, the political leadership of the Haitian community demonstrated its working relationship with media representatives by handing over "diplomas". Guy Victor awarded them to HP, the New York-based radio program *Moment Créole, Radio Soleil d′Haiti*, "progressive US journal" *Workers World* as well as *Local 1199*, the *Haitian Consulate*, and to unionists Leroy and Francine Louis (HP 164:8). HP and Aristide themselves sought to mitigate tensions with other important media in Haiti. At the dinner-party for Aristide on April 25, 1992, both Aristide and Dupuy embraced Jean Dominique, director of *Radio Haiti Inter*, who had criticized the former "for political or ideological reasons" (HP 111:10). When HP celebrated its tenth anniversary on May 1, 1993, Lassègue took advantage of the opportunity to remind her audience of the daily work by Haitian journalists counterbalancing misinformation. In its report, HP extended its gratitude to Aristide, who had congratulated HP in a public message. Furthermore, HP thanked other notabilities in the exile government and the political leadership of the 10th department as well as "all the friends of the US community" (HP 212:8). [143]

---

[142] The "day of the press" was also to pay hommage to *Radio Enriquillo* for its work during the previous eight months and in particular to journalist Jean Mario Paul, correspondent of *Radio Antilles*. Paul, whose case attracted international attention, had been arrested, tortured and jailed for months on charges of burning down the Grand Goâve police station. In April 1992, Paul was awarded the prize "PEN Freedom to Write" sponsored by *PEN International* in New York. He was honored with a ceremony at *St.-Francis School* in Brooklyn on August 28. According to HP and Lassègue, the international press and "foreign friends" exerted strong pressure on the *de facto* authorities for his liberation (HP 126:10;HP 138:9;HRW/A,NCHR 1992:15).

[143] Among them Lassègue, the band *FOULA*, Farah Juste, Guy Victor, Wilson Désir, Guy Ferdinand, Antoine Brutus, director of the tourism office in New York, Ben Dupuy, Sò Ann, Cauvin Paul, former director of HP, and Me Grognard as well as Rudi Stern of *Crowing Rooster Productions* (CRP), Pat

The publicly demonstrated harmony between the exile government, Haiti´s free press, the 10e and various US friends was even more needed in the face of what HP called "advanced macoutization" of the 10th department. HP warned in late January 1994, when it had already broken with Aristide, that the putschists attempted to infiltrate the Haitian community, just as Duvalier had heavily invested in espionage in the Haitian diaspora. HP reasoned that the "putschist sector" in the city, "taking the offensive" in the 10th department since October 30, 1993, felt emboldened by the replacement of Dinkins by the conservative Republican, Rudolph Giuliani, as mayor of New York. Giuliani "particularly benefited" from HO´s support, HP noted. In late December 1993, HO had published a note by FRAPH conveying "its kind regards to the community" with the signatures of its "coordinators" in New York" (HP 225:7). After a pro-putschist demonstration on January 13, announced by FRAPH in HO as "a protest against the embargo", HP took pride in remarking that the group *Comité Béton* had saved the "honour of the community" by dispatching "counter-demonstrators" (HP 225:7). Likewise, the demonstration on March 5, 1994 was presented by Latour as a "counter-demonstration" against the putschists "in the heart of the Haitian community of New York" (HP 236:1,17).[144]

According to HP, *Radio Tropicale* was the first of the Haitian-American media to fall victim to the FRAPH-attack. As the NYT´s Pierre-Pierre reported, Arioste Denis, director of the Manhattan-based *United Haitian Association of the USA* (UHA/USA), a grass-roots political organization, aired anti-Aristide shows on the radio station. HP referred to *Radio Tropicale´s* coverage of a meeting on August 29, 1993, over which Léon Veillard presided - a "criminal macoute", who had been denounced by Père Gérard Jean-Juste for years, when he was still executive director of HRC.[145] HP suggested that the "democratic media´s" resistance could be coordinated by a new group, the so-called *Comité d´Action Unitaire* of New York (HP 225:7;Pierre-Pierre 1993e:B3).

In late April 1994, HP reported that right-wing US organizations "in service of the putschists" attempted to occupy more and more political terrain outside Haiti. This could be seen with the *National Freedom Institute* (NFI). The oganization of the "extreme right", which HP believed coordinated its strategy with Clinton, Dominican president Balaguer, Cédras, and Michel Francois, invited eminent members of the putschist sector to Washington in February. Salvatore Imburgio of NFI sent a letter of invitation to HP´s Maude Leblanc to participate as journalist in another public meeting planned for April 9, to which individuals like Emile Jonaissaint were invited. HP evaluated the event as part of "anti-embargo operations" of the same kind as demonstrations organized by Denis of UHA/USA (HP 245:8). In June, the 10th department was aided by CCR in resisting the terror of FRAPH. Alerte Bélance, who was ab-

---

Chin of *Workers World*, Bryan Williams of the *Socialist Workers Party*, and representatives of *Pathfinders*.

[144] Père Gérard Jean-Juste, General Coordinator of the 10th department on the five continents, certified the official establishment of the *10e of New Jersey* in early February 1993 (HP 179:11). But Haitians in the US at that time were not exclusively mobilized in defense of growing "macoutization" in the Haitian community. This is in evidence with the demonstration "in solidarity with the internal resistance" in front of the White House on December 16, 1993, three years after Aristide´s landslide victory (HP 216:8,17).

[145] Jean-Juste was later appointed "General Coordinator of the 10th department on the five continents".

ducted on October 16, 1993 and attacked by men armed with machetes, filed a lawsuit against FRAPH. The plaintiff, represented by CCR´s Ratner, had always accused members of FRAPH to have been her torturers. FRAPH by then had also established itself in Miami, Boston, Chicago, and in Canada. The lawsuit was filed at a time, when another lawsuit against Haiti´s ex-president Prosper Avril entered its final stage in Miami (HP 270:7).[146]

FRAPH´s transnational terrorism and the macoute onslaught in the Haitian diaspora of the US opened up yet another battle front. On this front, the political leadership of the Haitian community increasingly concentrated its energies. This struggle required keeping exiled Haitian journalists loyal to Haiti´s legitimate government, since they were needed to mobilize the 10th department for the sake of the resistance within Haiti. Accordingly, less time was available to focus on the refugee side of the crisis, on which Haitian journalists had reported when still in Haiti. Raoul of HWHR hinted at the casual development of a division of labor avoiding duplication by saying: "[M]aybe Johnny McCalla thinks it would have been great, if we all supported his advocacy issues. ... we just don´t have enough power to do it all at once " (Raoul 1995). Members of HEAR confirmed this view by exclaiming "we have so much to deal with ... We do not limit ourselves" (HEAR 1995).

---

[146] Ever since Ratner brought before US courts the case of Avril charged with torturing Evans Paul and others, he represented Haitian refugees (HP 229:8) The lawsuit against Avril was initiated on February 28, 1991, when Avril still resided in Miami Lakes, Florida. On June 6, 1994, federal judge Wilkie Ferguson decided in favor of the plaintiffs. Avril escaped to Haiti in January 1993 (HP 272).

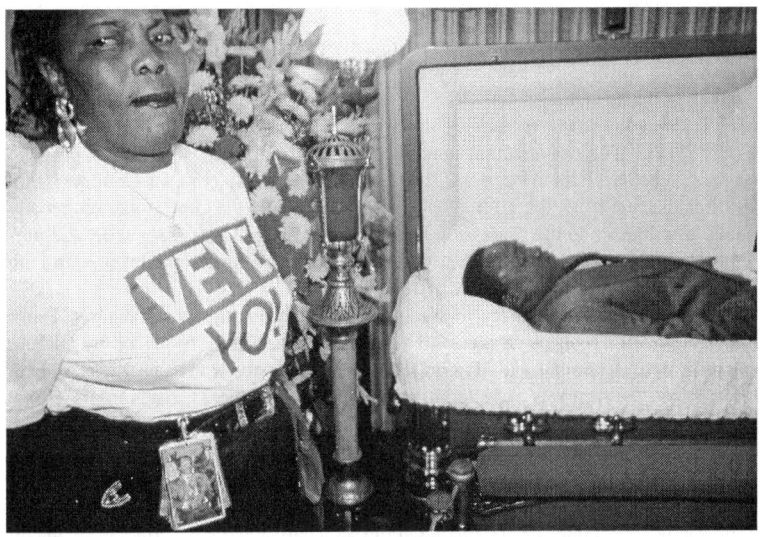

Funeral of journalist Fritz Dor in Little Haiti, Miami (courtesy Maggie Steber)

5.2.6 The Aid of Moving Pictures: Documenting the Repression in Haiti on Film

At the *Haiti Commission*'s first public activity on November 1, 1991, a Haitian-American short film project headed by US film-maker Stern of *Crowing Rooster Productions* (CRP) was launched (HP 36:8). The production team seems to have been able to take advantage of "four months of investigation" conducted by the *Haiti Commission* (HP 78:11). The organization announced ahead of time a "soirée" at *Columbia University*, scheduled for March 11, 1992, to report on its complete findings (HP 85:10). For the first time, the 30-minute video "Haiti Under the Gun" containing many accounts of witnesses to the repression and an interview with Honorat's wife was presented to the public (HP 95:9). The film was shown another time at the event with Père Massac at *Wingate High School* on May 15, 1992 (HP 119:9).

The pre-test performance of the bigger production, the documentary "Haiti: Killing the Dream", took place on April 5, 1992 in Manhattan. Produced by CRP in cooperation with American and Haitian film directors Stern, Katherine Kean, Babeth and Hart Perry, the film was expected to be submitted to the next Cannes Film Festival and to be shown soon in many large US cities, as Ives reported. The film is narrated by Ossie Davis with background music by Charlemagne as well as by the Haitian bands *Boukman Eksperyans* and *Ram*. It depicts the trajectory of the Lavalas movement until the carnage of the September 30 coup. It illustrates the savagery of the Haitian army and shows the resistance of the people both in Haiti and in the 10th department. Among the many people interviewed in the film are bishop Romélus, Père Joachim Samedi, and Père Adrien (HP 104:10).

"Haiti: Killing the Dream", shown across the country and reviewed by many newspapers as part of the Haitian campaign to win over public opinion within the US (Basch et al. 1994:215), was one among three Haitian movies presented at the New York Film Festival on Human Rights between May 8 and 17, 1992 (HP 113:9). "Haiti: Killing the Dream" also helped keep the 10th department mobilized, and so did "Haiti under the Gun", which was shown on May 17, 1992 in the 10e's offices in New York. The evening started out with personal accounts by three refugees, witnesses to the terror in Haiti after the coup, who also remarked the racism and the disdain by US authorities, to which they were exposed on Guantanamo (HP 121:10). NCHR reported that "Haiti: Killing the Dream", a "great educational tool for grassroots organizations or concerned individuals", was aired on most PBS stations on the coup anniversary (Haiti6:12). At a "socio-cultural activity" on March 7, 1993, organized by the *10e of New York*, yet another video testifying to the "aggression perpetrated by attachés and military macoutes against Mgr. Willy Romélus" was presented (HP 191).

The actual formal première of "Haiti: Killing the Dream" did not take place until September 27 in the auditorium of *Medgar Evers College* in Brooklyn under the patronage of the *Haiti Commission*. In front of an audience of more than 1,000 people, Jean Oriole, activist of *Assemblée Populaire Nationale* (APN) and member of Aristide's security service, related episodes of the day of September 27, 1991. Dupuy was co-founder of APN in 1987 (Aristide,Richardson 1995:188,194). In its report on the event, HP published the telephone numbers of the *Haiti Commission* and CRP to order copies of the film (HP 146:10), which was also used to mobilize union members and African-Americans during "Black History Month" in 1993 (HP 185:7;HP 186:7).

At a film show at *Brooklyn Museum* on April 24, 1993, another movie on Haiti was shown to an "enthusiastic crowd", as Alix Charlemagne reported. "This Other Haiti", directed by David Knob, illustrates the "relentless determination" of the Haitian rural masses to overcome their misery. The film show was organized by BfA and Congressman Major Owens, head of CBC's Haiti Task Force (HP 210a:8). BfA, a loose and informal association of Haitian groups run from Owens' district office, was founded in early March 1993 at the Congressman's sole initiative (Owens 1995).

In addition to the rather unknown film-makers mentioned above, HP sometimes reported on US celebrities, firmly established in the mainstream entertainment industry. HP lauded those Hollywood figures, foremost Jonathan Demme ("The Silence of the Lambs") and Susan Sarandon, as "agents of pressure" (HP 203:9,16;HP 246:9). They mainly concentrated on the refugee side of the Haitian crisis, however, and did not entertain a working relationship with political leaders in the 10th department. Hollywood celebrities were loosely organized as *Artists for Democracy in Haiti* (ADH) at the initiative of Demme out of his New York-based production firm *Clinica Estetico*. Demme is a NCHR-board member. In 1994, there were 229 "members of the arts, entertainment, and literary communities", underwriting ADH's "statement of intent", among them Harry Belafonte, Spike Lee, Paul Newman, Julia Roberts, and Steven Spielberg (ADH 1994).

Local 144 Poster on West Indian American Day Parade 09/05/94, Brooklyn (by Götz-Dietrich Opitz)

Haitian Truck on West Indian American Day Parade, 09/05/94, Brooklyn (by Götz-Dietrich Opitz)

5.2.7 The Haitian Diaspora and US-Haitian Economic Societal Transnationalism

ADH-member Sarandon put a rather neglected aspect of the crisis into the spot light on April 14, 1994, when she portrayed ADH on the "Phil Donahue TV Show". Referring to a study conducted by the *National Labor Committee* (NLC), she was outraged by the fact that in Haiti a worker was then paid 2 cents for manufacturing one baseball, which sold for $7.49 in the US. According to Demme, there were more than 24 trade unions in the US protesting against the import of baseballs and the increase in trade with Haiti during the crisis (HP 249:15). The unions called on the Clinton Administration to end the forced return of Haitian refugees and to tighten the embargo (HP 248:9).[147] This appeal was as old as the crisis itself, with the *10e of New York* noting with concern at the end of October 1991 that "[a]ir and naval lines of private companies continue to transport merchandise to Haiti" (HP 27:9). Hence the 10e´s campaign to boycott *American Air Lines* (HP 26:9).

Since the inception of the hemispheric embargo, transnational economic interests from European countries not party to the sanctions had helped keep Haiti´s economy afloat. But surprisingly, the unilateral easing of the embargo by Bush in early February 1992 went almost unnoticed in the Haitian community. HP touched upon the US measure to spare the US assembly industries as affecting 240,000 people in Haiti. The weekly connected the move to the refugee problem, lamenting that it would "support the putschists, thus perpetuating the vicious circle of repression and exodus" (HP 70:1,16). Aristide himself deplored the "fine-tuning" (Margaret Tutwiler) of the sanctions, since "[i]t was a feast for the criminals". He warned that it would increase repression in Haiti and spur an even greater exodus of Haitians (Farah 1992:A43). However, no Haitian community action followed this insight during the first half of the crisis, so it seems.

Unlike both HP and the NYT, the WP gave some background information on how the Bush Administration´s decision had come about: Approximately 50 private US-owned assembly businesses operating in Haiti´s textile, garment, electronics, and sporting goods industries waged an "intense campaign" to persuade the US government about the harmful effects of the embargo on "American jobs". The companies were organized in the Washington-based non-profit group *Caribbean Latin American Action* (CLAA) that promotes private-sector-led development in the Caribbean Basin. Elliot Abrams, former assistant secretary of state under President Reagan and a member of CLAA´s board of directors, was central in the lobbying effort coordinated by CLAA. In Miami, businessmen were reported to have told Bernard Aronson, Assistant Secretary of State for Inter-American Affairs, on December 4, 1991 that "the U.S. government had been urging American firms to invest down there for years and then turned around and, in eight weeks, destroyed what it had taken eight years to build up". US officials justified the decision to lift the embargo out of concern that it was harming about 40,000 poor workers fueling the exodus of Haitian boat people (Kamen,Goshko 1992a:A1,A11;1992b:A26).

---

[147] In early May 1993, HP published an announcement by *Workers World Party* on a May Day Rally in Manhattan on the occasion of the Inernational Workers Day on May 1. Among the demands printed in the ad figured "Asylum for Haitian Refugees" (HP 211:8).

CLAA, whose executive committee and board of trustees include Bob Graham, US Senator from Florida, Dante B. Fascell, chairman of the House Foreign Affairs Committee at the time, and Frank Guarini, another member of Congress, stated to have pursued the "twin objectives of keeping the [Haitian] economy alive while supporting restoration of the democratic process" in 1991 and 1992. Its ongoing efforts included "fostering dialogue between the various factions within Haiti" (CLAA 1992:6-7,9). In 1993, CLAA shifted its emphasis to the "longterm challenge of rebuilding the country once constitutional government is restored" (CLAA 1993:9,18).

According to CLAA, the US government began to encourage the development of non-traditional industries in Haiti and elsewhere since the early 1970s and especially since the early 1980s under the so-called Caribbean Basin Initiative (CBI). The concept entailed foreign firms starting up an assembly line for the price of the inputs and a manager, while a local firm would assume most of the risk of providing the physical plant and training the workforce (CA 1992:13).[148] In Haiti, a "triple alliance" had been formed by the early 1970s among the second Duvalier regime, foreign capital, and the Haitian mulatto bourgeoisie. As subordinate partner, it accepted "the conditions imposed by the U.S. manufacturing assembly contractors and by acquiescing to and collaborating with the regime" (Dupuy 1989:168-169).

The annual Miami Conference on the Caribbean on December 2-6, 1991 provided leading US manufacturers and their Haitian counterparts the opportunity to portray themselves as "the sacrificial lambs under the new U.S. policy" towards Haiti, as CLAA´s president Frederic H. Brooks put it (CA 1992:13). Jean-Edouard Baker, president of the *Association of Haitian Business*, told CLAA that the Haitian business community would be laying off all 65,000 workers it employed. Fewer than 600 workers at only four plants operated at the low point in early 1992. In CLAA´s view, "the embargo´s burden of suffering ha[d] fallen on Haiti´s poor", instead of Haiti´s elite. As part of a "concerted action" by companies most involved, 26 US firms joined CLAA in running a quarter-page ad in the WP of December 22, 1991.

The open letter warned that continuing the embargo would not only cost thousands of additional jobs, but also risk starvation, epidemic disease, economic collapse, and "perilous attempts to flee by boat for the people of Haiti". CLAA thus utilized the refugee issue successfully in having the US Administration grant export-import licenses on a case-by-case basis, for which over 170 US companies applied by May 1992 (CA 1992:14-16). The *US Treasury Department* (USTD) did, in fact, hand out licenses to companies controlled by well-known coup organizers (NLC 1994:135). CLAA´s success corroborates the observation that non-governmental groups such as US business companies with so-called "tangible interests" in visible and substantive goals like economic or financial benefit have been more influential than a wide range of groups with interest in "symbolic resources" (Ogene 1983:10,193-194).

The *American Federation of Labor/Congress of Industrial Organizations* (AFL-CIO), the umbrella organization of labor unions in the US and a member of NCHR, stressed that "Haitian democrats, including trade union leaders, believe the embargo

---

[148] Haiti´s combined production of goods, assembled offshore from US materials and exported to US markets under "Item 806/807", reached a high point in 1987, when some 300 factories employed 60,000 people and exported over $200 million worth to the US per annum. By 1991, the assembly sector had shrunk to 40,000 workers at about 200 plants (CA 1992:13).

needs to be strengthened not weakened" (AFL-CIO 1992b:1). As a result of a fact-finding mission to Haiti in mid-January 1992, the AFL-CIO informed the US public that worker rights such as freedom of association and freedom of assembly had not been spared the ruthless control of the Haitian military, with "round-the-clock surveillance of trade union offices" being the norm. The AFL-CIO delegates returned in March to offer assistance to the trade unionists and monitor the persistent violations of human rights (AIFLD 1992:1;AFL-CIO 1992a:1).

After Aristide´s return, CLAA anticipated to "bring the business constituency into the rebuilding dialogue" as part of "shaping the new Haiti" (CLAA 1994:9). An alternative development plan for Haiti´s future, relying to a large measure on economic society within the Haitian diaspora, was already contemplated by Aristide long before. During his visit to New York City shortly before the coup, he repeatedly called on the "sector which has money" to invest in order to create jobs in Haiti (HP 8:16-23). The opening of a "Haitian development bank" was announced by the Haitian Embassy one month after the coup to serve this long-term end (HP 33:11). Resorting to the "bank of the diaspora" was occasioned by the coopting of a large part of Haiti´s business community under the umbrella of the *Center for the Promotion of Investment and Export* (Prominex), founded by USAID in 1986. USAID had organized opposition to the Aristide government´s labor reform efforts aiming at a modest minimum wage increase and chose Andre Apaid, a wealthy Haitian businessman, as president of *Prominex*. Apaid attended CLAA´s annual Miami Conference on the Caribbean in December 1991, where he responded to the prospect of Aristide´s return by saying: "I´d strangle him" (NLC 1994:143-149).

Seven months into the crisis, Aristide kept calling on the Haitian business community in the US to plan for Haiti´s future. At a meeting on April 26, 1992, Deslande Rincher, spokesperson for Haitian business people, said that "[w]e can contribute greatly to the development of the country... The role of government is to guarantee security for investments". Aristide said that this meeting could be but a beginning to becoming what the Jews, in "their proper 10th department", represent for Israel. He encouraged the Haitian business community to "organize the way the Jews do", who control politics by virtue of their economic prowess (HP 116:12). In 1993, however, Aristide, when he met with CLAA trustees at the June Board meeting in Washington, seems to have partially abandoned his nationalistic development strategy within the confines of Haitian deterritorialized economic society as a long-term alternative to the offshore assembly industry in post-coup Haiti (CLAA 1993:9). In order to show that he would be "open to neoliberal economic policies" upon his return to Haiti, he hosted a "Haiti Government/Business Partnership Conference" in Miami with the support of organizations such as CLAA. According to Ives, many of the 200 attending people from both the merchant and technocratic sections of Haiti´s bourgeoisie had helped finance the coup and break the ensuing embargo (1995d:83).

HP, the *Haiti Commission*, and several New York-based US unions such as *Local 1199* (Estela Vasquez) and *Local DC 1707* (Ray Laforest) or the US magazine *Workers World* cooperated closely in denouncing Haiti´s military regime. But HP, in its section "Dizième Département", rarely reported on Haiti´s labor unions, which were "never strong", according to HRW and NCHR (HRW/A,NCHR 1993:53).[149] Taking stock of the Miami conference in late January 1994, however, HP noted the presence of Haitian unionists, who, the weekly complained, had themselves integrated into the current of "national reconciliation". HP mentioned Jean-Claude Lebrun of the *Confédération des Travailleurs Haitiens* (CTH), a national trade union federation with a significant peasant component (HRW/A,NCHR 1993:54), as embracing this idea (HP 228:14). After the funeral of *Veye Yo* activist Buron in March 1994, Aristide met with a delegation of union activists from Haiti. It included two representatives of the *Central Autonome des Travailleurs Haitiens* (CATH). The delegates conveyed a proposition, "which had the air of having left the baracks of the Haitian army", as HP put it. They demanded that the embargo be lifted and to meet directly with Cédras, with the unionists acting as mediators. Aristide rejected the proposal, and so did HP labelling the unionists as "substitutes for Caputo" (HP 239:7). Dante Caputo was the Special UN/OAS envoy to Haiti.

The only unionist denouncing the proposition was Cajuste Lexiuste of CGT (HP 239:7), the *Centrale Générale des Travailleurs* (*Central of Haitian Workers*) founded in 1986 and "the most militant of Haiti´s three federations of unions". A representative of CATH, also founded in 1986 to become "the most powerful federation of unions in the country" (Aristide,Richardson 1994:70), told HRW and NCHR in early 1993 that most of the local unions organized by CATH were not functioning, partly because many factories had closed under pressure of the embargo (HRW/A,NCHR 1993:53). According to the AFL-CIO´s *American Institute for Free Labor Development* (AIFLD) office in Port-au-Prince, most of the unions had been decimated, losing 40 to 50% of their membership. In 1993, only a "few trade union leaders still believe[d] that the embargo might work" (AIFLD 1993a:1,2).[150]

In late April, 1994, HP discussed the report issued by NLC, a New York-based labor research group formed by several US unions. The report resulted from a visit to Haiti of a delegation in March 1993. It gained access to the *Vetex* factory, a joint venture between the wealthy Haitian Mevs family and *RSK Industries, Inc.*, an apparel firm headquartered in New York. The *Haitian Sugar Company*, owned by Fritz Mevs Sr., was one of the Haitian corporations, which joined CLAA in running the anti-embargo ad in the December 1991 WP-issue (NLC 1994:134-136). The delegation also visited the baseball-producing firm *Home of Champions* (HoC). The report stated that, overall, the US imported $154 million worth of goods from Haiti in 1993 in spite of the embargo, up almost 50% from the 1992 figure of $107 million. More than 2.54 million softballs and 675,000 baseballs were imported in the first ten months of 1993 alone (HP 248:9). Since the early 1980s, virtually all baseballs destined for consumption in the US had been stitched together by Haitian women (Stepick 1986:7).

HoC, which runs two factories with 600 workers, is partly owned by the Mevs family as well, and, to a larger share, by US businessman Julius Tomar. NLC noted that in 1993, Fritz Mevs paid $100,000 to the US law firm *Williams and Connolly* in Washington to lobby the Clinton Administration to maintain the loopholes in the OAS-

---

[149] According to Charles, many Haitians are active in US trade unions. She mentions unions such as the *National Union of Hospital and Health Care Employees*, the *Fur and Leather Machine Workers Union*, and ILGWU (1990:212).

[150] According to Greg Chamberlain, AIFLD is "CIA-linked" (1995b:24), and Plummer states that the institute has a "history of ... [CIA] ... support" (1992:224).

embargo (HP 249:8). As AIFLD reported, on May 11 and 12, 1992, fifteen trade unionists were fired from HoC located in Cité Soleil. The manager told them that now was not the proper time for unions (AIFLD 1992:3-4).

According to HP, unions were officially banned in HoC. A worker testified to NLC that workers, most of them women, were suspected to be Lavalas when talking about unions. Under Mevs, HoC seems to have specialized in circumventing the embargo effectively. Thus businessman Antoine Izméry in Haiti denounced the company before the USTD for violating the embargo in multiple ways. Mevs, who lives in Miami, where he also owns *Star Sports*, shipped 1.45 million pounds of merchandise to the factories of HoC. According to Izméry, the Mevs did not only contribute to financing the coup. He also maintained that the Mevs funnelled "money directly to colonel Michel Francois" (HP 249:15). Izméry had to pay with his life for his assertiveness. During a mass on September 11, 1993, he was dragged from the church and shot point blank in the head (HRW/A,NCHR 1994a:12).[151]

Even if rather late in the crisis, HP recognized the potential of the myriad transnational links between Haitian and US economic societies as political weapon when suggesting "une vaste campagne de boycott contre les compagnies nord-américaines". NCL named five US companies as targets in such a "campaign of boycott". Among these, the most important was reported to be *Star Sports* as one of the largest softball and baseball importers controlling 19% of the market and being the main supplier of the US army. HP estimated that a boycott could have a large impact in the US, where baseball is the number one national sports (HP 249:15).

Whereas the Bush Administration's unilateral easing of the embargo was not immediately followed by Haitian community action aiming at US-Haitian economic societal transnationalism, the NLC-report seems to have triggered some activism. At a press conference held by the *Comité Contre l'Intervention en Haiti (Haiti Anti-Intervention Committee*/HAIC) in New York on December 10, 1993, Lexiuste described how he had been arrested and tortured in April. He said that "employers form a unity with the military regime". Another form of repression against the workers in Haiti were the "ridiculous wages". Laforest spoke about the role of USAID in spending $26.7 million to prevent a minimum wage increase (HP 215). On May 6, 1994, Kernighan of NLC spoke at a conference in New York. The event was organized by various US unions such as the *Amalgamated Clothing & Textile Workers Union* (ACTWU), the *United Paperworkers International Union* (UPIU), and the *International Ladies Garment Workers Union* (ILGWU). The latter is also a member of NCHR. Kernighan exhibited two samples of dresses manufactured in Haiti by *H.H. Cutler Company* and sold in the US by *Walmart* and *K-Mart* with an enormous margin of profit. He announced an action of civil disobedience in front of the White House on May 11 (HP 259).

The first real public activity taken on the issue in the Haitian community was a protest by a group of about 100 people, who demonstrated against *Sears* and *Walmart* on May 28 in front of a store in Brooklyn. They denounced the exploitation of Haitian workers "under the cover of the political crisis and the embargo". *Sears Roebuck's* gross revenue totaled $56 billion in 1990, which was 34 times the size of Haiti's entire

---

[151] Izméry was a founding member of the *Helping Hands Committee to Spread the Truth* (KOMEVEB), formed in May 1993 to spur resistance to the coup (HRW/A,NCHR 1994a:12).

GDP in 1991 (HP 267:8;NLC 1994:138). Needless to say that the rally, which was organized by HAIC, did not stop the usage of Haiti as a pool of cheap labor, nor did it prevent an invasion of Haiti at this late point in time. The relative neglect of US-Haitian economic transnationalism during the crisis is symptomatic of the "postmodern death of justice" in class relations between capital and labor in the US (Harvey 1994:211,205-227;own translation).

The link between the embargo and increased migration had already been successfully presented by CLAA for its own purposes by equating strict sanctions with economically motivated migratory flows. Repudiating this theory required linking relaxed sanctions and increased refugee streams with repression. The role of keeping the spot light on the specific repression against workers in the assembly industry should have first accrued to Haiti´s unions. However, unions were increasingly unable to fulfill this function, because they were not only continually reduced in strength as a result of the embargo´s broad effects, which led many unionists to doubt the advisability of economic sanctions to begin with. Unions were also targeted by the military junta and the assembly industry management, both emboldened by the relaxation of the sanctions. This dilemma was exacerbated by the exile government´s initial preference to promote long-term transnational Haitian-to-Haitian development strategies, later partially abandoned in favor of approaching organized interests of the US offshore assembly industry. NLC´s attempt to mobilize Haitians on the devastating effects of US-Haitian economic societal transnationalism came too late to have an impact on the course of events.

5.2.8 NCHR´s Further Post-Coup Reports: Repression and Dislocation in Haiti

The impact of US-Haitian economic societal transnationalism on Haiti´s human rights situation was not a specific focus of NCHR. In a footnote to *The Aristide Government´s Human Rights Record*, NCHR remarked that "[i]t is beyond the scope of this report to discuss the achievements of the Aristide administration outside the realm of human rights", while acknowledging the Administration´s devotion to addressing the needs of Haiti´s poor (HRW/A,NCHR,CR 1991:4). In its fourth report, however, the group dealt with repression against CATH, CTH, and other trade unions, which were found to have been "weakened considerably since the coup" (HRW/A,NCHR 1993:53-56); and in its sixth report, it documented the arrest in April 1993 of Haitian unionists Fabonor St. Vil, Sauveur Aurélus, and Lexiuste on the basis of interviews (HRW/A,NCHR 1994a:16-17).[152]

In accordance with its basic shift after the coup from monitoring human rights in Haiti to the problem of Haitian refugees facing strict US policy measures, NCHR co-published with HRW/A *Half the Story: The Skewed U.S. Monitoring of Repatriated Haitian Refugees* on June 30, 1992 (HRW/A,NCHR 1992:4-5). In writing this 16-page

---

[152] In a Task Force conference call on February 4, 1992, McCalla asked to consider that the lifting of trade sanctions on the assembly industry would send the message to the Haitian military that "we support the coup government and don´t much care for reinstating democracy" (NCHR12:1). About one month after the easing of the embargo, McCalla told *USA Today* that baseball manufacturing had been a mixed blessing for Haiti (Richards 1992:3).

report, NCHR possibly benefited already from the opening of an own permanent office in Port-au-Prince, which "greatly expanded" NCHR´s capacity to monitor human rights conditions in Haiti (NCHR6:1). NCHR´s goal of establishing an office in Haiti managed by Haitians, which was made possible with grants from the *Ford Foundation* and the *McDonnel Clark Foundation*, dates back to May 1991 (NCHR11:2). The Washington-based *ARCA Foundation* awarded NCHR a grant of $25,000 in 1992 "[f]or human rights monitoring efforts of newly established Port-au-Prince office" (Foundation1:80).

NCHR reported that it had taken charge in 1992 of a drive to unite scores of NGOs in the US, providing them with solid documentation of "the Haitian army´s dismantling of what had been until the coup an increasingly vibrant civil society". To this end, NCHR continued to consult with many of the "key players" in Haiti´s struggling popular movement (NCHR6:2,4). NCHR and HRW/A documented "the destruction of civil society in Haiti" in the report *Silencing a People*, the "most comprehensive picture to date of the repression in Haiti". The two human rights organizations introduced the 136-page book, which was later distributed in French in Haiti, at a joint press conference in Washington on February 11, 1993 with McCalla, Roth, and Wade Henderson of the *National Association for the Advancement of Colored People´s* (NAACP) Washington-chapter (NCHR14:2;NCHR18:1). The result of a two-month long investigation in Haiti in June and July 1992, the report was based on both interviews with 250 witnesses and on reports released by the CJP of the Diocese of Gonaives and the *Platform* (HRW/A,NCHR 1993:x).

The report explained that Jean-Claude Duvalier´s flight to France in 1986 created a "profound opening" for independent associations, taking, in part, the form of an assortment of political parties, which had been banned during most of the 29-year Duvalier dictatorship. These political parties left a vacuum in the countryside, which was "filled by a variety of groups that responded more directly to local needs". Known broadly as "popular organizations", the members of these groups came mostly from the country´s vast poor majority, which often organized with support from abroad.[153] Haiti´s civil society, the strength of which NCHR considered to be its breadth and diversity outside the narrow realm of electoral politics, had provided the base of support for Aristide´s electoral victory in 1990. Following the coup, the Haitian army cracked swiftly down on all signs of public dissatisfaction with military rule, including the mere possession of opposition newspapers or leaflets, while voluntary groups were as much the target of the army´s repression as was the Aristide government (HRW/A,NCHR 1993:3-4,9-124).[154]

NCHR´s work during 1993 was, to a large extent, dedicated to educating the US public on events in Haiti. This effort involved cooperation between NCHR´s New York staff and its staff in the Haiti-office. The latter began to draw on the new contacts it had established with international observer teams spread all across Haiti´s nine prov-

---

[153] The report informed that "a large group of foreign nongovernmental organizations sponsor popular efforts to improve agricultural methods, rebuild livestock populations, promote reforestation, dig wells, and develop farming collectives in Haiti" (HRW/A,NCHR 1993:27,25,52)

[154] In the report, NCHR focused on peasant organizations, rural development projects and groups, community and popular organizations, women´s organizations, youth groups, trade unions, literacy groups, students and educators, the press, individual dissenters, Aristide government officials, and the popular church movement (*Ti Legliz*) (HRW/A,NCHR 1993:79).

inces as part of the UN/OAS-ICM. Mainly as a result of this improved access to human rights data, NCHR-staff in Haiti drafted at least once each month letters of protest outlining action with reference to specific cases of abuse. They were sent to the *de facto* regime from NCHR´s New York-office "by electronic means" in order to afford an "increased measure of protection" for its staff in Haiti and to illustrate the "strength of international opinion" behind the demands in the letters. On October 11, the day of the USS-Harlan County incident, McCalla and NCHR´s recently hired human rights advocate Coradin travelled to Haiti to investigate the steps taken by the Haitian military to prevent the restoration of Aristide scheduled for October 30 pursuant to the GIA. After having met with Prime Minister Malval, Minister of Education Victor Benoit, and Justice Minister Guy Malary prior to his assassination, NCHR´s New York staff left Haiti along with the UN/OAS-ICM (NCHR14:1,2,4; NCHR18:4).[155]

As yet another token of NCHR´s shift in focus, the group co-published along with HRW/A and the *Jesuit Refugee Service/USA* (JRS) the report *No Port in a Storm: The Misguided Use of In-Country Refugee Processing in Haiti* one month earlier. NCHR became directly involved in the US in-country refugee processing program (ICP), which "informed the analysis" provided in the group´s 38-page report, its "most comprehensive critique to date" of the ICP-program (NCHR19:8;NCHR16:4). The report relied on a transnational set of governmental and non-governmental informants based in both Haiti and the US, including named and unnamed Haitian asylum-seekers (HRW/A,NCHR,JRS 1993:37).

NCHR prided itself in 1994 on being "the only non-Haitian rights group to maintain offices in Port-au-Prince" and on having become "an increasingly important reference point for international and non-governmental organizations and agencies concerned with human rights in Haiti". Staff at the NCHR headquarters in New York worked in "close collaboration" with the office in Haiti, where the group observed "a steady growth of increasingly brutal human rights abuses, including an average of 50-60 killings per month, as well as rapes, torture and forced disappearances". Representing the context for the refugee exodus, these abuses were documented in NCHR´s crucial sixth report *Terror Prevails in Haiti: Human Rights Violations and Failed Diplomacy*. Published jointly with HRW/A, the 52-page report was formally presented at an event on April 14, sponsored by the *United Nations Association* (NCHR24:5,2). The report also contained data compiled during a mission by NCHR, HRW/A, and HRW´s Women´s Rights Project in February 1994.

Informants in Haiti included "hundreds of individual Haitians", the UN/OAS-ICM, and an array of indigenous sources (HRW/A,NCHR 1994a:51-52). The report profiled FRAPH, described the assassinations of Izméry, Malary and others, and documented abuses against trade unionists, Aristide-supporters, congregations and religious leaders, as well as attacks on popular organizations, reprisals against displaced persons returning home, and violations of press freedom. The report detailed in eighteen specific paragraphs the violence leading up to Aristide´s scheduled return on October 30, 1993 pursuant to the GIA as well as the continuing terror thereafter, and assessed the policies implemented by international actors, including the work of the

---

[155] Victor and Malary were part of Malval´s cabinet, which was approved by the Haitian Parliament on August 25 as a precondition for lifting the UN oil embargo. Malval had been nominated by Aristide as Prime Minister on July 24. Malary was shot dead on October 14.

UN/OAS-ICM (HRW/A,NCHR 1994a:8-48). Information gathered during the February mission was also included in the last two reports published before Aristide's actual return on October 15, 1994. *Rape in Haiti: A Weapon of Terror*, co-authored by HRW/A and NCHR, was released in July, and *Fugitives from Injustice: The Crisis of Internal Displacement in Haiti*, co-authored in addition with JRS, in August. Research for the latter 31-page report, which also testified to NCHR's shift in focus, was conducted by a team composed of NCHR's associate director, Anne Fuller, Pierre Espérance, and Connie Walsh, both of NCHR's office in Haiti. Informants in Haiti included, *inter alia*, the *Plateforme des Organisations Populaire* (PLANOP).

NCHR referred to the sources in Haiti, which contributed information to the 28-page report *Rape in Haiti*, as "women's rights groups" and "human rights organizations". The report detailed cases of sexual assault by the military, by army *attachés*, and by "zenglendos", armed criminal groups, which usually operate at night and particularly in the slums and working-class districts of Port-au-Prince. It further assessed official complicity and corruption, the fear of reprisal, the failure to investigate, procedural hurdles, and the role of discrimination and stigma as factors contributing to impunity and the non-report of rape (HRW/A,NCHR 1994b:28,7-25). According to NCHR, the exposé proved to be "especially influential", as its findings were reported on widely in US print and electronic media (NCHR24:7).

Rape in Haiti, which also assessed the US asylum process, was NCHR's only human rights report containing explicit recommendations for both Haiti's military regime and the Aristide government.[156] It demanded that the military leaders publicly denounce the use of rape, investigate allegations of abuse, and prosecute those responsible. It called on the Aristide government to pledge to prosecute cases of rape aggressively, to include acts of rape into any amnesty provision, and to undertake to disarm *attachés* upon its return to power (HRW/A,NCHR 1994b:27). NCHR began in June 1994 to advocate, as part of the restoration of democracy in Haiti, the inauguration of a "Truth Commission" designed to promote accountability of human rights violations and to prevent anti-Aristide forces from portraying Aristide's return as "synonymous with an occasion of vigilantism". A full-time consultant on human rights issues, O'Neill, who is of Irish descent, was recruited by NCHR largely as part of this effort. He prepared an option paper on the Truth Commission, which he later used to advance the concept during direct consultations with Aristide's staff in Washington (NCHR24:8).

---

[156] In the introduction to *Silencing a People*, NCHR had already criticized Aristide's "exclusive focus on General Cédras and a small coterie of senior officers", disagreeing with his "apparent willingness to ignore abuses committed by junior members of the army" (HRW/A,NCHR 1993:2).

5.3 Fighting the Cause II: Working for Aristide's Return from Without by Means of Sanctions and World Opinion (Indirect Transnational Relations)

As shown above, one important "mobilization" effort organized by Haitians in the US was the campaign of mass protests. It was designed to strengthen the "resistance" against the repression within Haiti by demonstrating the diaspora's political, emotional, moral, tactical, and financial support. The same support was extended to the Aristide government, thereby encouraged in its attempt to return to power, while the campaign further sought to intimidate the *de facto* regime. However, the "three-pronged strategy" of "resistance-embargo-mobilization" (Philippe Généus), pursued by the Haitian community in the US (HP 43:16), did not only translate into direct transnational citizen-to-citizen and citizen-to-government relations, but aimed as well at the level of the "international community" at large, in which the US government plays an important role. Consequently, the strategy aiming at creating a favorable "world opinion" required indirect transnational relations.

5.3.1 From Initial Euphoria over Successes to First Signs of Skepticism

The second thrust of Haitian organizing manifested itself spontaneously right after the coup and became apparent in the deliberately chosen locality of protest. As early as September 30, 1991, approximately 4,000 Haitians gathered at a place in New York, where "the new world order" is determined: In front of the UN building, the protesters trustingly called on the UNSC "to study the problem [of the coup] and to make recommendations". HP quoted a Haitian taxi driver as assuring that "this demonstration will be copied at places all over the world, where one can find Haitian patriots" (HP 9:12,28). The "permanency", prescribed by the *10e of New York*, was realized in front of the UN building, where the biggest crowds of demonstrators could usually be seen after work at 5 pm (HP 15:14,25). In Miami's Little Haiti, Haitians shouting "We want Aristide" took to the streets "to let the whole world know that the response would not cease", as the Haitian weekly reported (HP 10:12).

The Haitian diaspora's anger was immediately transformed into concrete demands vis-a-vis the international community. In the morning of September 31, 1991, almost 4,000 people gathered in front of the Federal Building downtown Boston, where they were addressed, among others, by Dessima Williams, ex-Ambassador to the OAS from Grenada. In the afternoon, the "We want Aristide"-shouting crowd marched to the office building of US Senator John Kerry, member of the Senate Foreign Relations Committee. A delegation gained access and spoke to one assistant to the Senator, demanding that the Cédras "puppet government" not be recognized by the US and that all bank assets of the Aristide government be frozen to prevent the military junta from seizing them (HP 11:14). Haitian activists in Boston thereby anticipated two measures in resolution MRE/RES.2/91, agreed upon one week later in a meeting of the OAS-Ministers of Foreign Affairs in Washington (HP 14:11).[157]

---

[157] HP would later encourage all "compatriots" to assemble again in front of the OAS building on November 27, when the Permanent Council convened to discuss the crisis in Haiti, in order to make their

According to HP-correspondent Généus, the 25,000 to 30,000 protesters later mobilized by Mayor Flynn, "ally of the Haitian people", came together "to fulfill the historic task that the compatriots of the interior have transferred to the 10th department: keep up the pressure by all means to convince the international community, the OAS, the UN, and the US government in particular, to demand expeditiously the unconditional departure of the new Pinochet of Port-au-Prince, Raoul Cédras". Speakers like Flynn, Kerry, and a representative of *The Nation of Islam* made the "international solidarity for our struggle" visible, as Généus put it (HP 13:11). The Haitian CJP´s report mentioned above, which detailed the events leading to the coup and from which HP quoted extensively, was distributed by *Pax Christi USA*. *Pax Christi* called on HP´s readers to mobilize the US public and to write to one´s Congressman, while HP published the telephone numbers of the US Embassy in Haiti, the White House, Capitol Hill, the USSD, and the UN (HP 18:8,11).

On a rally in New York on October 11, Dupuy was able to triumphantly read from resolution A/RES.46/7 voted on unanimously by the 166 member states of the UNGA the same day, which condemned the coup and called for the restoration of legitimate power in Haiti (HP 22:14-18). Haitians early confidence towards the world body might have been informed by the aftermath of a general climate characterized by a "vastly increased respect" for the UN, according to a Gallup poll taken in October 1990 (McAneny 1992:12). Dupuy wrote in his letter-to-the-editor two days later: "We hope that ... leading US politicians will ... listen to the Haitian people´s choice" (HP 19:8). In his report on the Haitian mass protest in Washington one week later, Latour could now proudly declare that the mobilization centered around the final objective: the return of "the only President known and *recognized by international opinion* and conscience, Father Jean-Bertrand Aristide" (HP 25:16-19;author´s italics).

But Haitian singer and activist Sò Ann insisted on the necessity of a permanent vigilance in front of the UN building (HP 25:16-19). A group of Haitians in New York picked up the idea: On February 8, 1992, Geneviève Dalzon, spokesperson for the so-called "diplomates du béton", said that the group would maintain its daily vigil in front of the UN building (HP 74:10). Guy Victor maintained that the UN later took the *New York Police Department* (NYPD) to court because of the disturbing Haitian mass demonstrations there, which caused UN officials "headaches" (Victor 1996). The crowd of 15,000 people on October 11 moved from the Capitol building toward the White House and stopped in front of the OAS building. Latour commented: "Aujourd´hui, nous sommes rassemblés ici à Washington ... pour réclamer l´aide de la communauté internationale et l´aide de tous les gouvernements" (HP 25:16-19).

After Clark of the *Haiti Commission* had sent to members of Congress, in particular to those of the CBC, a letter dated October 18, asking them to join his organization (HP 24:10),[158] the *10e of New York* launched a "telegram campaign". HP encour-

---

demands (HP 52:10). For further information on a variety of resolutions issued by the OAS and the UN during the Haitian crisis, see the excerpts in the footnotes of the detailed process analysis (Opitz 1999) as well as the list of resolutions in the appendix of this study.

[158] In a hectographed letter to Rangel dated November 11, 1991, Clark called the addressees "Dear Haiti Commission Supporter[s]" (Rangel91b:1). But Clark´s organization does not seem to have received broad support from members of Congress. The only Congressional figure, for example, participating in the group´s fact-finding mission to Haiti between December 15 and 21 (HP 78:11) was an aide to Congressman Dellum. On the other hand, in a staff briefing on H.R.3844 on February 13, 1992 with Clau-

aged its readers to participate by writing to Bush in the White House and to James Baker in the USSD, "dans le cadre des pressions exercées sur le gouvernement Bush". The text of the appeal stated that "despite the executive order No. 12775 of President Bush, dated October 4, 1991, which `prohibits certain transactions with Haiti´, the US-Administration has not applied the embargo up to the present. Air and naval lines of private companies continue to transport merchandise to Haiti" (HP 27:9). The campaign was buttressed by a demonstration of about 3,000 protesters at Wall Street, organized by the *10e of New York* (HP 34:7). 10th department organizations such as the 10e in Michigan established contact with CBC-members (HP 41:10). As Philippe Généus reported from Boston, slogans such as "We want Aristide" and "No Aristide, no Peace" aimed at "the international community" had become a "leitmotive" (HP 43:16), which manifested itself in a score of public events throughout November (HP 45:9; HP 48:10).

According to Tecumseh, the international embargo was totally accepted by the Haitian people, who preferred this kind of hardship to a dictatorship Duvalier-style. She quoted one Haitian in Haiti as saying that "...we will be victorious. If the embargo is lifted, Father Aristide will never return". Tecumseh also referred to Père Massac, who had said that people in Haiti were not discouraged by the embargo (HP 53:14,15). Howard French reported that many poor people in Haiti continued to support "any measure", which would bring about Aristide´s return. He quoted 23-year-old Frankie Gentil as saying that "I´d rather never eat if it meant we could get our liberty back ... The embargo is our *only* weapon" (1992c:A3;author´s italics). Honorat was reported as having said on October 30 that the US had to be prepared to receive a lot of refugees as a result of the embargo - "as if it was the embargo that forced the people to escape from Haiti", Gilbert commented. He noted that, "according to sources in Haiti, the `kantè´ [boats] leave every day" (HP 42:15). In Tecumseh´s mind, the "means of preventing the people from leaving is to give them hope that Titid will return rapidly" (HP 53:15).

Even if Janvier echoed Latour when proudly stating that "[w]e enjoy the respect of the international community" (HP 48:10), the Haitian community engaged in the so-called "Vote for Democracy" of December 15 (HP 59:8). It was ushered in by a rally of nearly 10,000 demonstrators in front of the OAS building in Washington on December 13, 1991, three days before the first anniversary of Aristide´s election. The protesters came marching from the White House, the "White Grave", as Latour put it. He noted with self-irony that Bush did not need a translator, because there were picket-signs that "say all too well in the language of Shakespeare everything that one thinks in terms of superstitious people, who fear Friday 13" (HP 58:1,17). NCHR was informed about the event. McCalla reminded Conference Call participants in early December of the "march in Washington on behalf of the refugees and the return of constitutional rule in Haiti" and urged them "to make an effort to attend" (NCHR2:1-2). Conference Call participant Père Sansaricq qualified the rally on December 12 as a "significant demonstration" of Haitians "coming from all over". According to the minutes, *TransAfrica*´s and Congressman Rangel´s offices organized African-Americans "to lead" (NCHR4:2).

---

dette Werleigh, former high-ranking official in the Aristide government, which was organized by Rangel´s office, it was planned to show the video initiated by the *Haiti Commission* (Opitz 1992:2).

In his report on the WOH-organized January 1992 conference "Dignité et Démocratie" in Washington´s *Howard University*, Latour stressed that the "most important moment" was a speech given by Casimir. He stated that the political crisis had created "a space of international solidarity" for Haiti (HP 68:10). But Casimir´s, Latour´s, and Janvier´s euphoria about "international solidarity" had already been crosscut by skeptical views on the role of international organizations, with the US mainstream media´s "campaign of misinformation" in high gear. The *Platform* observed in its November 1991 report, written to also inform "all international organizations", that the repression in Haiti had especially aggravated since the arrival of the OAS-mission (HP 54:12-15). According to Charlemagne, OAS-negotiator Augusto Ramirez Ocampo, reportedly "never favorable to Aristide", was "anti-Haitian" indeed. He mentioned a recent reunion in the Argentinian Embassy of diplomats with a representative of US Ambassador Adam, Prime Minister-designate René Théodore, and the Dominican Ambassador, who said that his choice of Prime Minister would be Marc Bazin (HP 63:9,15).[159]

Measured against these early skeptical views, HP´s review of NCHR´s *Return to the Darkest Days* sounded more positive. The weekly gave the authors the credit that the account "has the advantage of giving US public opinion an overview of the current regime of terror" (HP 65:9). Influencing the US government through the public at large was, however, against the odds in the light of a rising isolationist mood: At the turn of the year, a "huge majority" of Americans had shifted from an international to a domestic agenda, with 82% wanting the US to concentrate on internal issues and to scale down involvements abroad (McAneny 1992:12).[160] In a more general sense, influencing the US government was exacerbated by the fact that Anglo-Americans, who constitute the nation´s ethnic core, retained dominance in the shaping of foreign policy due to their longtime majority status for over 200 years of successful ethnic politics (DeConde 1992:194-199).

HP´s review of NCHR´s report concentrated more on how US policy was evaluated: Since the authors pointed to the diminished monitoring capacity as a result of personnel reductions in the US Embassy to explain why Washington had not denounced human rights violations in Haiti so far, HP questioned their objectivity. The weekly deplored that the human rights groups did not want "to go any further in their taking a position" vis-a-vis the role of Cédras, who was "a pawn in the global US plan for the Caribbean in general and against Aristide in particular" (HP 65:9).

5.3.2 NCHR´s Role in US Foreign Policy, Toward International Organizations

In *Return to the Darkest Days*, NCHR did not view the coup plotters as tools in a "global US plan" opposing the return of Aristide, but linked the Bush Administra-

---

[159] After the first day of OAS-mediated talks with opposition leaders in Cartagena, Colombia, on November 22, 1991, Aristide accepted the Haitian Senate´s choice of René Théodore as prime minister in late December; see the detailed process analysis (Opitz 1999).

[160] Nevertheless, another Gallup poll taken one year later in March 1993 found a "strong humanitarian impulse toward Bosnia" and 67% of Americans interviewed in favor of the US decision to air drop relief supplies to the beleaguered former Yugoslavian republic (Saad 1993:22).

tion´s transformation from "an outspoken proponent of human rights and democracy in Haiti to a shameful apologist" with the refugee issue: The "radical shift in its human rights policy" was seen as the result of "a desperate attempt to stem the tide of refugees heading for the Florida coast". Obviously "fearful that continuing honest and outspoken criticism of military abuses in Haiti would jeopardize the legal defense of its interdiction efforts ... the Administration stopped public criticism altogether". The report concluded: "The timing of the sudden silence left the impression that the Administration was more concerned with avoiding lending support to the growing number of Haitians claiming to flee persecution than with pressing the military regime to stop the violence and killing" (HRW/A,NCHR,PHR 1991:2,19).

NCHR´s press release, jointly issued with HRW/A and immediately following Aristide´s overthrow, condemned the violence in Haiti. It also advised the Bush Administration to remind Haiti´s army of US laws forbidding foreign aid to nations, whose duly elected head of state has been replaced through a coup. The human rights organization shared information with both elected and appointed US policy makers. In particular members of Congress were kept informed on the "twin emergencies" of human rights in Haiti and of Haitians fleeing repression by providing written documentation and holding staff briefings.[161] UN and OAS officials, acknowledging NCHR´s "expertise in analyzing human rights and political conditions in Haiti", are reported to have sought the group´s "guidance" in the wake of the coup. NCHR staff responded accordingly. For example, NCHR´s *The Aristide Government´s Human Rights Record* was distributed to UN and OAS officials as well as to US Congressional leaders (NCHR5:7-8,15,16).

In 1992, NCHR "advised the international community" on the ongoing destruction of Haiti´s civil society by publishing three reports and by many other means of communication. Its staff and representatives from the OAS, the UN and UNHCR discussed how to promote "international cooperation in support of Haitian democracy" (NCHR6:3-4). NCHR´s main target during that time was the legislative branch of the US government, trying "to obtain meaningful legislation on behalf of the Haitian refugees" (NCHR13:1,2). The organization´s report *Half the Story* was part of that effort. Like other advocacy groups, NCHR used Congress as a channel to transmit opinions, as the seat of decisionmakers authorized to formulate foreign policy, and as a potential ally to establish support from other policymakers (Watanabe 1984:48,61).

Pursuant to its mandate, the international embargo was not a major focus for NCHR. One of its members, the *Lawyers Committee for Human Rights* (LCHR), on the other hand, started already during Bush´s term to call for "global sanctions" (LCHR 1993:13).[162] And the AFL-CIO, also a NCHR-member, publicly condemned the Bush Administration´s decision "to lift a highly effective economic embargo" (AFL-CIO 1992b:1). In *Terror Prevails in Haiti*, NCHR demanded that sanctions be targeted "more carefully". All other countries should be called upon to join in "similar targeted sanctions" against those individuals, who "deserve international stigmatization". The UN and the OAS were called upon to monitor the effects of the embargo

---

[161] In its winter issue of *HaitiInsight*, NCHR recommended its readers to become a member in one of the many groups working on Haiti and to contact members of Congress and Bush (Haiti4:6).
[162] The *ARCA Foundation* awarded LCHR a grant of $25,000 in 1992 "to encourage high-level U.N. involvement" in Haiti (Foundation1:80). In 1993, LCHR received a grant of $25,000 from the *ARCA Foundation* "[t]o evaluate U.N. and OAS involvement in Haiti" (Foundation2:1188).

(HRW/A,NCHR 1994a:50,51). In *Fugitives from Injustice*, NCHR explicitly remarked: "Human Rights Watch, the NCHR, Jesuit Refugee Service/USA have strongly advocated the imposition of internationally-enforced targeted sanctions". The Clinton Administration´s gradual expansion of those sanctions in May and June 1994 was thus a "long overdue measure". It added that "... we continue to monitor [the global economic embargo´s] effects on Haiti´s poorest sectors, as well as international humanitarian assistance to alleviate those effects" (HRW/A,NCHR,JRS 1994:5,4).

At the end of 1992, NCHR´s focus shifted towards the US executive branch. "Clinton´s shocking reversal on his Haitian policy established the framework for NCHR´s advocacy throughout" 1993, the group summarized. While rallying scores of NGOs in the US to criticize the Administration on its refugee policy, NCHR staff also joined in discussions with policy-makers from the Pentagon, the *National Security Council* (NSC), the USSD, and other key agencies as well as with UN officials (NCHR14:2). The group was able to deliver "by way of unofficial channels" a foreign policy position paper to UN representatives and the Clinton transition team.[163] It called on the new Administration "to take strong steps to signal its support for democracy in Haiti". In NCHR´s judgement, the paper´s "contents may well have influenced discussions between Clinton aides and those U.N. representatives who subsequently endorsed a UN presence for monitoring human rights in Haiti" (NCHR6:2).

NCHR´s further discussions with UN officials later led to the group´s "direct involvement in the planning" of the joint UN/OAS-ICM and to its "critical role" in relation to some 240 human rights observers. McCalla joined with LCHR´s former deputy director O´Neill and Roth of HRW in a committee advising the UN and the OAS on the establishment of the international group. It was designed to lay the groundwork for "democratic institution-building" (NCHR14:2,1). O´Neill, who "spearheaded" LCHR´s work on Haiti, would later be appointed legal director of the mission (LCHR 1993:13). O´Neill embodies the successful establishment of a border-spanning arrangement between a US civil societal transnational formation and an entity in the realm of international organizations by circumventing the level of the nation-state (Walzer 1993), on which influence had been exerted.

Before entering the field to help prevent human rights violations against the Haitian people, the UN/OAS rights monitors underwent an "intensive training" and a "vital orientation. It was arranged by a small team led by NCHR´s associate director Fuller (NCHR14:1,2).[164] The *ARCA Foundation* awarded NCHR a grant of $25,000 in 1993 for the "new training program for Haitian human rights monitors" (Foundation2:1188). Guy Malary cooperated with NCHR in this effort, before he became Haiti´s Justice Minister. He also agreed to serve as *pro bono* counsel in the lawsuit against Avril. According to Ian Martin, previously Secretary-General of ai, who became the director for human rights of the UN/OAS-ICM from April to December 1993, international human rights observers succeeded somewhat in encouraging Haitians to assert their freedom of expression. But the repression continued (Martin

---

[163] The paper was drafted by McCalla after consultation with HRW, LCHR, WOH, and the *Washington Office on Latin America*.

[164] In general, LCHR, for example, lends its legal expertise to assist local advocates in devising strategies to document violations and challenge local authorities. The group helps these local NGOs, which are reported to increasingly demand a meaningful role in the consideration of human rights at the UN, gain access to international forums and present their views there (LCHR 1993:i).

1994:72,79,80). At the end of 1993, NCHR planned to also "[a]ctively engage policymakers in international fora" such as those provided by the UN and OAS human rights commission (NCHR20:3,4).

In *Silencing a People*, NCHR applauded the Clinton Administration for its cooperation in enlisting the support of the UN "to bolster the largely ineffectual diplomatic efforts" of the OAS (HRW/A,NCHR 1993:125). In *No Port in a Storm*, however, the group denounced Clinton for strengthening the "policy of forced return" of Haitian refugees by surrounding Haiti with a naval blockade following the withdrawal of the military vessel USS-Harlan County (HRW/A,NCHR,JRS 1993:2,5). NCHR demanded in early 1993 that the UN/OAS-ICM allow its members to spread out throughout Haiti's countryside to build a "climate of confidence" for further negotiations, deter further military attacks on Haiti's civil society, and to reassure the Haitian army "that it will not face popular reprisals" (HRW/A,NCHR 1993:6, 126). NCHR also demanded from Washington that "serious abuses" of human rights be denounced "immediately and publicly" and "without regard to the public-relations effect on U.S. efforts to limit the flow of boat people". US support "should be lent to efforts to purge the Haitian army of its most abusive elements" while resisting the "temptation to view the Haitian army as the sole vehicle to stability and development". Democracy "cannot be built on a foundation of impunity for murder and torture", the authors recommended. The Clinton Administration was thus advised to "make its top priority in Haiti the protection of ... civil society" (HRW/A,NCHR 1993:6-7,128).

Consequently, with negotiations on Governors Island underway, NCHR opposed a number of policy positions backed by the US: The group discouraged the UN and the OAS from negotiating a settlement violating the "duty to hold gross abusers of human rights accountable for their crimes". NCHR shared its perspectives with UN/OAS envoy Caputo and others involved in the ongoing talks (NCHR14:3-4). In a three-page letter to Caputo, NCHR and HRW/A condemned as illegal the proposed amnesty for military leaders in Haiti (French 1993a:A11). NCHR reiterated this concern again in June and July, when the US also offered Cédras "restored military aid" in return for Aristide's reinstatement. McCalla challenged Clinton's proposal "to offer U.S. dollars for what has been referred to as the `professionalization of the Haitian military'". He advocated instead the "complete dismantling of the Haitian armed forces" (NCHR14:3-4). NCHR had already insisted before that a "training" program to "professionalize" the Haitian army would only "produce more skillful murderers" (HRW/A,NCHR 1993:127). Hence Demme's motion to send letters to the OAS, the UN, the USSD, and to the White House to express NCHR's concerns regarding the GIA's negation of the rights of victims was adopted on the NCHR Board of Directors meeting of July 13, 1993 (NCHR16:1).[165]

After the collapse of the Governors Island process, members of ADH, the group organized by Demme, criticized in its "statement of intent" that US and UN officials continued "to turn a blind eye to the on-going infusion of oil and other supplies enjoyed by the junta" and that the CIA and the Pentagon had been candid about their "preference, over President Aristide, of Haiti's military rulers" (ADH 1994:2). For HRW, the Clinton Administration's "capitulation to a murderous military regime in

---

[165] After the USS-Harlan County incident, NCHR's human rights staff briefed officials on Capitol Hill about the situation in Haiti, which led to further "high-level advocacy" in late 1993 (NCHR14:4-5).

Haiti", while summarily turning back boatloads of Haitians fleeing political persecution, proved "the need for a constant HRW vigil on U.S. policy, no matter which party is in office" (HRW 1993:7).

NCHR´s "integrated approach to advocacy on refugee concerns and human rights in Haiti" was reported to be a "uniquely successful one in influencing U.S. policies". After the issuance of *Terror Prevails in Haiti* in April 1994, NCHR advocated before the NSC. Its staff in New York had "periodic consultations" with Clinton Administration officials as well as with members of Congress, particularly of the CBC. On a July 14 press conference in Washington, NCHR and other "prominent human rights and social justice organizations" urged "an aggressive international push to settle Haiti´s political crisis" (NCHR24:1,2,4). NCHR qualified *Terror Prevails in Haiti* as a "crucial report" that identified the "roles played by international actors in the worsening Haitian crisis". The group stated proudly that "... the report played a key role in spurring on changes in U.S.-Haiti policy" (HRW/A,NCHR 1994a: 38-49).[166]

The report was especially critical of Ambassador Swing. A cable, for example, signed by Swing, sent to Secretary of State Warren Christopher, and reported upon by NCHR, had declared the Embassy´s suspicion of false reporting of abuses by human rights groups. This criticism led Swing to initiate a dialogue with NCHR and Haitian human rights groups. He suggested the establishment of a US-sponsored Fund for human rights victims and asked NCHR´s Fuller to serve as official member of its advisory board. But Fuller denied the offer and urged US Embassy officials instead to do more to ensure the "prevention" of human rights abuses (NCHR24:6,7). As HP reported, the nine Haitian groups making up the *Platform* that represented "almost all the indigenous groups working on human rights in Haiti", had already been urged by the US Embassy to attend "roundtable" discussions on the one-million-dollar "Human Rights Fund". The groups boycotted the discussions, however, and signed a letter dated July 29 instead. It identified the need to preserve its "independence of action, thought and movement". The *Platform* implied that the Fund could be used "to dedicate choices or orientations ... of Haitian organizations" (HP 309:9).

NCHR´s continued "close collaboration" with the UN/OAS-ICM served this kind of preventive purpose. The group engaged the latter´s leadership and field observers in regular exchange of information and case referral. Following the ICM´s return to Haiti on January 31, 1994, O´Neill left his post as the director of the ICM´s legal division in order to assume a role in New York as NCHR consultant in June 1994. But he maintained a close link to the UN, the OAS, and ICM´s directors Colin Granderson and Tiébelé Dramé (NCHR24:6).[167] *Terror Prevails in Haiti* recommended to the UN, the OAS, and to Caputo to redeploy a "significantly enlarged" ICM to Haiti, to review the "entire UN/OAS strategy for restoring democracy to Haiti", and to create a Truth Commission (HRW/A,NCHR 1994a:51). In *Rape in Haiti*, NCHR recommended to

---

[166] HP reported on NCHR´s report in late April 1994, stressing in particular that the group called on Clinton to fire Pezzullo and to provide information on CIA funding of the Haitian *National Intelligence Service* (SIN), "a drug trafficking and death squad organization" (HP 247:9).

[167] The UN has reportedly been getting better at working with NGOs in humanitarian endeavours linked closely to UN peace operations in the field (Malone 1996:27). LCHR, for example, enjoys consultative status with the UN, which allows it to receive UN documents and reports and to participate in key human rights meetings (LCHR 1993:2).

include "gender-specific abuse" in the ICM´s training of human rights monitors (HRW/A,NCHR 1994b:27).

The release of *Terror Prevails in Haiti* was followed by a letter to Clinton dated April 20 and signed by McCalla and representatives of eight other human rights organizations in the US.[168] "To avoid letting the facts come in conflict with both the power-sharing proposition and the refugee policy", they jointly explained, "U.S. officials have downplayed the human rights crisis" in Haiti. This was evident in the Haiti entry of the *State Department Country Reports on Human Rights Practices for 1993*, which did not even mention FRAPH. As a "clear signal" to the Haitian *de facto* regime, the signatories demanded five measures, among them the US Administration´s support of a "full deployment" of the UN/OAS-ICM (NCHR28:1-3). HP characterized the letter´s conclusion as a "rather eloquent accusation" of the Clinton Administration and its content as "explicit enough" (HP 250:8).

In NCHR´s judgment, seven of the nine recommended changes in *Terror Prevails in Haiti* were implemented by the US: 1) ending the summary repatriation of Haitian boat people, 2) abandoning the policy of downplaying human rights abuses, 3) replacing US Special Envoy Pezzullo, 4) advancing the return of Aristide, 5) calling for the return of an expanded ICM, 6) more targeted economic sanctions, and 7) promoting a regionally-based response to the refugee crisis. Calls for opposing any broad amnesty for Haitian military officers and for denying military aid for the Haitian armed forces remained very much in question at the writing of NCHR´s 1994 annual report. Only NCHR´s demand for the release of information regarding CIA activities in Haiti had been "met with complete silence" (NCHR24:6,5). In addition, NCHR demanded in *Rape in Haiti* that US officials publicly retract statements expressing the US "embassy´s skepticism about the veracity of allegations of politically-motivated rape", made by human rights organizations (HRW/A,NCHR 1994b:27).

As has been demonstrated above, NCHR´s human rights reports were a valuable method to criticize the conduct of international actors and they constituted an important part of the non-governmental human rights organization´s civil societal transnationalism. These reports resulted from the long-term cultivation of direct inter-societal transnational relations and facilitated the operation of indirect transnational relations via the UN and the US government against the backdrop of the current Haitian crisis.

5.3.3 Exposing a Hypocritical US at the Bar of Public World Opinion

In February 1992, the President of Venezuela, Carlos Andrés Pérez, narrowly thwarted an attempted army coup against his civilian government (Constable 1992:188). For HP, the coup attempt was evidence that the putsch in Haiti constituted an example for Latin American militaries. The paper thus demanded: "The rallies throughout the 10th department should be demonstrations of our fighting strength. ... On February 7, the community must mobilize on a massive scale" (HP 70:1,16). About

---

[168] Among the other eight representatives were Charles Norchi, executive director of the *International League for Human Rights*, and Kerry Kennedy Cuomo, executive director of the *Robert F. Kennedy Memorial Center for Human Rights* (NCHR28:3).

15,000 Haitians followed HP's appeal, marched to the UN building as part of the February 7 celebrations of 1992, and denounced the Bush Administration's Haiti policy, as Latour reported (HP 80:12-13).

The location of the demonstration in front of the world assembly was not coincidental. Dorancy of HRC explained in HP that the US strategy vis-a-vis Haiti consisted of a "double game: an official position ... on the side of law and democracy, but uniquely destined to deceive international public opinion ... In one word, this is a policy of cynicism". In her mind, the US had an interest in using the refugee problem as a pretext to dilute international sanctions (HP 76:11). While the Bush Administration's unilateral easing of the embargo was not immediately followed by Haitian community action directed against US-Haitian economic societal transnationalism, it did trigger mass protests targeting the UN. The bar of "world opinion" was to add pressure not only on the *de facto* regime, but also on the US Administration which was seen as playing a hypocritical role. Besides the UN, the Haitian community was called upon to aim at the US public also, which was to be educated on the real conditions in Haiti. In his report on the pre-test performance of "Haiti: Killing the Dream" on April 5, 1992, Ives noted that "it is important that, as quickly as possible, hundred thousands of people in the US watching TV can understand a bit better the Haitian reality through this film" (HP 104:10).

Both the US public and OAS member states had already been addressed in a full-page advertisement published in the NYT of March 16, 1992. The advertisement was signed by 3,500 individuals and organizations representing all 50 states, the District of Columbia, Puerto Rico, and four foreign countries, including Haiti. Many organizational signatories reportedly represented large national constituencies, including several religions, denominations, Central American solidarity activists, the anti-apartheid movement, students, and human rights and refugee groups. The advertisement was initiated and sponsored by QC/QP, "an organization with a decade of experience in rallying thousands of citizens to challenge U.S. policies toward Nicaragua", according to the *Big Red News*. The Rev. William R. Callahan, coordinator of the US group, was quoted as saying that "[l]ike his predecessor, Mr. Bush is long on rhetoric and short on action when it comes to real democracy in the hemisphere" (1992:4). The ad's headline stated in bold letters: "Restore Democracy in Haiti", and "Welcome Haitian Refugees". The text declared: "We call upon the governments of the U.S. and all members of the OAS to: 1) Condemn publicly and repeatedly the military repression... 2) ... abolish the Haitian military... 3) Reinstate a strict embargo... 4) Offer Temporary Protected Status [and] 5) Commit to a program of ... economic development" (NYT 03/16/92:A11).[169]

The advertisement can be seen as a response to the OAS-mediated Washington Protocols of late February and further to the USSC decision on Haitian refugees of late January 1992. Many Haitians in Port-au-Prince criticized that the agreement offered no punishment for the killing of hundreds during the coup and no firm commitment to bringing Aristide back to Haiti. According to Howard French, a man in a downtown

---

[169] Among the many individual and organizational signatories from New York were AfA, CRP, Jonathan Demme, the *Haiti Commission*, HP, NCHR, the *National Center of the Haitian Apostolate* (Père Sansaricq), Père Darbouze, Ira Gollobin (NECLC and NCHR) as well as Michelle Karshan and Donna Plotkin, both of AfA (NYT 03/16/92:A11).

street said that "[p]eople are not happy about this agreement". A woman working for the government-owned telephone company was quoted as saying that "[t]hat agreement is nothing but a piece of paper" (1992b:12). By voicing pessimism about the possible success of political negotiations mediated by international organizations, this private citizen preferred direct transnational relations in an effort to return Aristide to Haiti, as did a growing number of Haitians.[170]

Aristide also helped mobilize individuals and organizations of US civil society, committed to the strategy of influencing world opinion, during his visit to New York in late April 1992. At the Conference of Baptist Pastors at *Baptist Church*, Aristide was welcomed by Pastor V. Simpson Turner. According to Latour, Turner was convinced that "the UN does not do what it could do" (HP 122:12). A meeting at the church *House of the Lord*, administered by the Rev. Herbert Daughtry, the well-known black activist priest of New York, also served as a get-together with US popular organizations. CBC-members Ed Towns and Major Owens as well as Jean Vernet of the *Haitian Solidarity Network* (HSN) and HEAR were present. Latour concluded full of hope: "Il [Aristide] a semblé avoir fait un vigoureux effort en vue de faire pression sur l'administration américaine, par le biais de maintes personnes et organisations civiles et religieuses. La mobilisation, organisée et bien structurée doit continuer, assortie de pression constantes, diplomatiques et `bétonnantes´ (HP 122:17).

Dupuy elaborated some more on Latour's notion of the relationship between "pressure of diplomacy" and "pressure of the street" at the event with Père Massac at *Wingate High School* on May 15, 1992. Dupuy talked about the significance of the OAS Foreign Ministers meeting on May 17. He stated that Aristide and the diplomats were "convinced that negotiations alone will not allow the return of the president". Confirming the still existing unity between the exile government and the whole political leadership of the Haitian diaspora, Dupuy stressed that "the stronger the popular resistance is, the better fares the diplomatic corps" (HP 119:9). Turning the argument upside down, HP quoted in some detail Massac to demonstrate that the positive effects of a strong popular resistance on the performance of Haitian diplomacy might not necessarily be true in reverse. In this view, the US Administration's Haiti policy of both negotiations and embargo appears as deliberately designed to weaken Haiti's popular resistance: "Ce n'est pas seulement la peur qui empêche les gens de se mobiliser. Ce qui les en empêche aussi, ce sont les négociations ... C'est ca l'objectif des négociations, l'objectif de l'embargo panier percé: réduire le peuple à l'extrême et, lorsqu'il est à bout, jouer au sauver ... j'aimerais ... que tous les Américains vivant aux Etats-Unis comprennent à quel point est négative la politique de leur gouvernement" (HP 119:9).

These Haitian concerns were forcefully expressed in two petitions circulated by a "coalition of organizations" and published by HP in the first week of September. The petitions were in protest against the first round of negotiations between representatives of Bazin and Aristide at the OAS headquarters in Washington scheduled for September 1. As HP reported, the proposal caused a "hue and cry" in the 10th department, "in

---

[170] According to a delegation of the Caribbean and Latin America Office of the *National Council of Churches*, however, which visited Haiti from August 27-31, Haitians expressed "strong support for an international `democracy mission´ to guarantee security through a period of negotiations" (NCC/CLAO 1992:6).

New York in particular". The first petition was addressed to OAS Secretary-General Soares and stated that inviting Bazin for negotiations was "an insult to the Haitian people, who rejected Mr. Bazin clearly" on December 16, 1990. The second was addressed to Aristide (HP 139:9). Haitian concerns of this sort were also voiced during the rally in front of the UN building, organized on the occasion of the first anniversary of the coup on September 29, 1992. While listening to Aristide´s speech before the UNGA, protesters shouted slogans such as "George Bush: KKK", "No negotiations with murderers", and "Liberty or Death". Likewise, a "grand rally" of hundreds of protesters took place on September 30 in front of the USSD offices in New York. Slogans denounced the "bad faith and the cynicism" of the US government. Following a mass of almost 2,000 people at St. Patrick Cathedral in the late afternoon, celebrated by Pères Sansaricq, Bien-Aimé, and Arick Joseph, the crowd headed once again to the UN building. Latour detailed other events taking place in Montreal, Boston, Miami, New Jersey, Philadelphia, and in Chicago, with thousands of participants denouncing the "perverted hypocrisy of the Bush administration" (HP 147:8-9).[171]

Many Haitians remained skeptical after Clinton´s election. At the event on November 22 in the office of the *10e of New York*, for example, Deputy Norzéus blamed the international community for not realizing that it is impossible to negotiate with criminals like the putschists (HP 159:7). But all skepticism notwithstanding, Haitians in New York were still quite content with regard to diplomatic successes won on the level of international organizations. In its report on the role of the UN in the Haitian crisis early December 1992, HP labelled the UNGA resolution of November 24 (A/RES.47/20A) as a "victory of the legitimate government over the camp of the enemy", because it opted for the reinforcement of the "weapon chosen by the legitimate government: the embargo". HP attributed this success not only to the incontestable legitimacy of Aristide, but also to the "exemplary resistance of the Haitian people"; Haitians fought against overwhelming odds, which were confirmed in a report (A/47/621 of 11/06/92) by Marco Tulio Bruni Celli, Special Rapporteur of the *UN Economic and Social Council* (HP 158:6).

Referring to the UN resolution, HP warned that the concept of humanitarian aid "cuts both ways", because it "might well turn out to be an indirect instrument to sustain the de facto government". The legitimate government reportedly appeared to be vigilant on that subject during a November 25 meeting of the OAS Coordination Committee for humanitarian aid to be distributed through NGOs. It asked to consider that there were two types of NGOs: "il y a ONG et ONG ... certaines ONG ne sont autres que des ministères déguisés du gouvernement de facto". The legitimate government therefore proposed that the OAS Civilian Mission play a "preponderant role in the distribution of that aid", HP explained (HP 158:17).

HP´s suspicion vis-a-vis international organizations resurfaced in its report on Jackson´s visit to Haiti in January 1993, which had resulted in the putschists´ acceptance of international observers. In contrast to NCHR, HP was afraid that the observers could be designed to demand more respect from the Haitian people rather than from the putschists: "... cela signifie en clair que la mission d´observateurs se verra accorder

---

[171] At a mass in Port-au-Prince for the coup anniversary, Père Jean Bruni urged the 500 people attending to rely on their own efforts rather than counting on international organizations to rescue Haiti (Haiti8a:3).

le mandat de *réprimer le peuple*" (HP 174:17-18;author's italics). Typically, at an event hosted by MC Ricot Dupuy of *Radio Soleil d'Haiti* on January 31 in the auditorium of *Medgar Evers College* in Brooklyn, Désir stressed the role of mobilization. Jean-Robert Sabalat, on the other hand, Aristide's new Minister of Foreign Affairs, focused more on the role of the OAS/UN during current negotiations with Caputo. This divergence foreshadowed the disunity between the exile government and Haitian activists in the 10th department. Sabalat pleaded for an "international observation" in Haiti by arguing in an enlisting manner: "Je suis sûr d'une chose: s'il n'y avait pas eu une présence étrangère avec des observateurs civils, les élections (du 16 décembre 1990) n'auraient pas eu lieu" (HP 178:11). But in HP's view, the December 1990 elections were organized for Bazin "in complicity with imperialism" (HP 172:6,14-16).

Jackson, whose activism was closely followed by HP, kept a high profile on the Haiti issue in the months to come. At a press conference on February 2, he presented a report on the situation in Haiti, which was issued by six groups, and called on the US government to adopt a "new policy" vis-a-vis Haiti. He proposed an ultimatum of 90 days for the putschists to relinquish power, a measure which only the UNSC could make compelling. Reporting on the press conference, which was organized in Washington by WOH, HP added with concern that Caputo was exposed to a hostile climate, with anti-UN demonstrations organized by the putschist sector before his arrival in Haiti (HP 175:1,22). WOH successfully applied for a $18,500 grant in 1993 to "bring Haitian opposition leaders and human rights victims to brief U.S. policymakers" (Foundation2:1189).

One of these policymakers was Congressman Rangel. He told the *New York Amsterdam News* (NYAN) that he was encouraged by the strong initiatives the Clinton team had undertaken with the UN and the OAS to put in place several hundred human rights observers. Rangel's support for Clinton, NYAN remarked, "both surprised and shocked political observers in the Black community" (Browne 1993:1). Other leading CBC members gave Clinton the benefit of the doubt, too. This is reflected in Owens' founding of BfA in early March 1993 as well as in two bills in support of Haitian democracy, introduced by Moseley-Braun and McKinney on April 1 (S.Res.89) and September 22 (H.Con.Res.149). HP criticized this development, exclaiming that the motto of the day was thus "All behind Clinton" (HP 174:16). Jackson, on the other hand, called on Haitians in the US to redouble their pressure on the Clinton Administration to restore democracy in Haiti (HP 180:8).

Political mass protests for the return of Aristide were the avenue most Haitians in the US chose to buttress diplomatic efforts in the international arena, when they gained momentum after Clinton's arrival in the White House. For example, Jackson was among the main speakers at a demonstration in Miami's Little Haiti. About 7,000 people formed a 25 block-long human chain along 54th Avenue between the HRC and the INS buildings and shouted "Aristide, Aristide". The rally was part of many events organized by Haitians in Paris, Montreal, Philadelphia, Washington, New York, Chicago, Boston, and in the Dominican Republic to commemorate February 7, 1991, as Latour reported. In New York, 1,500 Haitian compatriots demonstrated in front of both the INS and UN buildings on February 6. One day later, Père Adrien and Elie of Aristide's private secretariat spoke at *Clara Barton High School* (HP 180:8-9). And again, "the different organizations of the 10th department" announced in HP that they would organize a "colossal demonstration" in Washington in front of Capitol Hill and the

White House on April 2. The announcement stated the telephone numbers of coordination committees in 17 locations in North America including the Caribbean (HP 184:7). As Désir told me in hindsight: "When President Clinton and the State Department saw the determination of the Haitian people, who had been demonstrating all over the world, then they had to accept the fact that President Aristide should return" (Désir 1995). Guy Victor supported this philosophy saying that "the will and the determination of the Haitian people both in Haiti and abroad" made Aristide's return possible by putting pressure on the international community (Victor 1996).

On the other hand, the achievement of what Gilbert called "small victories" emerging on the refugee front only appeared as a "drop in the ocean" without the prospect of restoring democracy in Haiti. Gilbert mentioned Clinton's announced intention to lift the ban on immigration for HIV-carriers soon or the improvements brought about in the wake of the 22-day-old hunger strike by Haitian refugees detained at Krome, the INS-run Detention Immigration Facility in Miami. Strangely enough, Gilbert substantiated his case by referring to McCalla, the proponent of the refugee issue strategy, whom he quoted as saying on the air on February 4 that creating a "social, pacific environment permitting the development of democracy in Haiti" was impossible, if Clinton adopted the "same logic as his predecessor" (HP 181:11,18).

5.3.4 Growing Mistrust of International Organizations Seen as US-Dominated

Despite general satisfaction with the "victory" of UNGA resolution A/RES.47/20A of November 24, 1992, Haitians in New York voiced reservations concerning the role, which international organizations might play in the Haitian crisis in the months to come. What was "more important" for HP about the UN resolution was what Longchamp had referred to at a press conference on November 25: "paragraph 5, which gives the UN Secretary-General a mandate to take all necessary measures in cooperation with the OAS Secretary-General". In HP's opinion, there was reason to fear the "power given to the UN Secretary-General", since he had developed the thesis of "preventive diplomacy". HP called into question the confidence put into Boutros-Ghali, whose proposition could "serve as theoretical justification for the will of the US" to interfere in the internal affairs of Third World countries (HP 158:6,16,17).

In fact, David Malone, Ambassador and Deputy Permanent Representative of Canada at the UN from 1992 to 1994, sees the US at that time at "the zenith of its power in the Security Council", particularly after Dayton (1996:29,27).[172] HP referred to Somalia as one example for concepts such as "limited sovereignty" and pointed out that Boutros-Ghali "racks his brains over justifying and favoring US interventions throughout the world". Quoting *The Globe and Mail* in Canada (11/29/92), HP warned that these concepts "would convert the UN into an instrument of US imperialism". It took an article by William Safire, "famous liberal US `columnist'", in the NYT (11/30/92) as proof of how far "interventionist theories" had already disseminated (HP 158:6,16,17).

---

[172] Malone was told by a UNSC Ambassador that the US is no longer "the last remaining superpower", but rather "the supreme power".

The mistrust of international organizations seen as being dominated by the US grew continually in the course of 1993. The more the UN got involved in the Haitian crisis, the more strained the relationship between the Haitian think tank HP and associated Haitian groups, on the one hand, and Aristide's exile government on the other became. Following the arrival in March 1993 of the UN/OAS-ICM, the "largest human rights monitoring mission ever deployed" (Martin 1995:73), and Clinton's announcement on April 23 to dispatch a "multinational police force" of 500-600 officers to "professionalize" the Haitian army, a "coalition of all the major popular organizations" in Haiti sent an open letter to Aristide on May 17. The letter expressed the hope that Aristide "will immediately take an official public position that is crystal clear in denouncing and condemning" Clinton's plan "to send a military police force to *occupy* the country" (Ives 1995c:79;author's italics). According to Martin, the UN forces, which were allowed to carry sidearms for self-defense, came to be portrayed by the Haitian military and ultranationalists in the official media as unacceptable foreign interventionists likened to the UN/US operation in Somalia (1994:79,87).

Hence Haitians on both sides of the political divide increasingly opposed UN involvement in the Haitian crisis, albeit for differing reasons. For those aligned with the military junta, it implied the threat of Aristide's return. For those in the popular pro-democracy movement, it heralded an era of stifling US occupation. Consequently, Haiti's popular sector saw the "gift" of the June 16 UNSC Resolution 841, calling for a mandatory global oil and arms embargo, as a "trap" for Aristide, Ives explained.

HP-editor Dupuy resigned his post as Ambassador-at-Large of the legitimate government on June 23. In a letter to Aristide, he stated: "... I think that it is extremely dangerous to put the national sovereignty of the country in the hands of an international organization whose real defense of the peoples' rights, and even its impartiality, can legitimately be put in doubt at this time". The *Haiti Commission* said in a June 26 statement: "Having usurped control of the crisis in Haiti, the UN and the United States have begun forcing Aristide into a corner.... The UN is trying to validate Cédras as a negotiating partner" (Ives 1995c:79-81). The strategical-organizational unity between Aristide's exile government, the 10th department organizations, HP, and groups such as the *Haiti Commission* came to an end. The split came as a result of differing strategical views concerning the role of international organizations in the Haitian crisis, not as a direct outcome of differing views concerning the strategical value of Haitian refugees. Conspicuously, in the month of Dupuy's resignation, the NYT's coverage of the Haitian refugee crisis was relatively high, with 14 out of 35 news stories on Haiti dealing with the issue (see table).

According to HP's competitors, the weekly's criticisms of Aristide "cost it dearly in readership and respect", as Howard French reported (1993b:D8). Even if it is possible that HP's analyses began to reflect a minority position, albeit sizeable, within the Haitian diaspora in the US, many Haitians, quoted by the NYT, uttered reservations and opinions similar to those held by HP. This can be seen as fallout of Dupuy's criticism of Aristide. Asked for the initial UN plan to use a naval blockade to enforce the oil embargo of June 1993, Marco Lamothe said that "[w]e are against all forms of intervention". He stressed that the solution to Haiti's problems would rest in the hands of Haitians abroad and at home. One week before the opening of talks at Governors

Island, the NYT's Pierre-Pierre noted that many Haitians felt "weary of international negotiations" (1993b:B3).[173]

One day before the signing of the agreement, Pierre-Pierre observed that after "nearly two years of disappointment", Haitians along Nostrand and Flatbush Avenues received the "sudden twist of events" in the talks with "guarded optimism" (1993c:A2). After July 3, the NYT's Rohter saw the previous "cautious optimism" in Port-au-Prince turn "to suspicion and skepticism". Quoting Père Jean-Juste, General Coordinator of the 10th departments, as calling the agreement "good news", he observed that Haitians in poor neighborhoods such as Cité Soleil, a "pro-Aristide stronghold", were "clearly not as pleased". They were "unhappy" about the four months' wait until Aristide's scheduled return and angry about the likelihood that the UN oil embargo would be lifted before that date (1993b:12).[174] According to the *Center for International Policy* (CIP), Caputo knew that the four months' wait would not be welcome to a "shocked" Aristide delegation (Morrell 1993:7). The NYT's Raymond Hernandez quoted Darbouze of *Holy Cross Church* on Church Avenue in Brooklyn as summarizing that "[p]eople are skeptical". Haitian immigrants in New York wondered about the "wisdom" to allow the military to remain in place until Aristide returned (1993:A4).

Haitians' skepticism turned out to be justified. The NYT's Kifner reported that the days after the retreat of the USS Harlan County were "days of frustration". He quoted Brooklyn pharmacy-owner Luc G. Olivier as saying in despair: "The United Nations says `Do this, do that´, but even the United Nations seems to be playing games" (1993:14). In Martin's view, the withdrawal of the USS Harlan County was indeed the "most stunning, but not the first, breach in" the determination of the US (1994:85). The role of the UN dominated the public debate on Haiti not only within the Haitian communities. During the month of October, the NYT published 88 articles on Haiti, of which only 3 dealt with the refugee problem, even though 371 Haitians, the second highest number in 1993, had been intercepted by the USCG the month before (see table). As the NYT's Ian Fisher observed, Haitians in New York felt the "gloom of smashed expectations, of hopes for their homeland deflated" in the face of the failed attempt to return Aristide to Haiti on October 30. "Thousands of Haitians" were reported to have flocked to the UN-headquarters, where Aristide requested a total blockade of Haiti (1993:B1,B2). Consequently, Haitians seem to have been much more occupied with questions of national sovereignty and destiny at the mercy of powerful international actors than with the plight of Haitian refugees.

Haitians in Haiti shared the disillusionment in the Haitian diaspora. Howard French reported from Léogane that people's faith in Clinton had "turned to scorn and despair" by early December. French quoted even a wealthy, anti-Aristide businessman as saying: "You get the feeling the United States is mocking us ... You have to ask yourself, `Do they really want Aristide to come back?´" (1993c:22). Two weeks later, French reported that "26 months of dashed hopes, wasted lives and abandonment by the outside world", many "half measures and false starts to diplomatic initiatives", and the "widespread perception" that the intended target of the sanctions, Haiti's wealthy

---

[173] Pierre-Pierre identified Lamothe as a spokesman for the New York-based *National Regeneration Movement*, a "grass-roots political organization" promoting "efforts to restore democracy in Haiti".

[174] On August 28, however, the NYT reported that "Haitians rich and poor alike were glad" about the UNSC's decision to lift the embargo (NYT 08/28/93:A2).

classes and the military, seemed scarcely to have been affected, left many Haitians "deeply skeptical" of the international community (1993d:A15).

Taking stock of the Miami conference late January 1994 in the wake of the breakdown of the Governors Island process, HP pointed out that the UN did not appear to deem the conference important, since high-ranking UN officials did not attend the conference. Pezzullo spoke of the probable reinforcement of the embargo and a $400 million international aid program. In HP´s judgement, Aristide was to be "punished" for his "bad will" and put once more into a "position of inferiority" relative to Malval. It was afraid that the possible succession of Malval by putschists like Julio Larosilière or Serge Gilles might lead to a "temporary stabilization of the crisis" and induce the UN to lift the embargo by presenting the situation as a step towards normalization. But this would not advance "one inch" the return of Aristide (HP 228:13,6).

At the end of January, HP discerned a growing danger of disintegration and demoralization of the popular sector in Haiti. According to Gilles Danroc of CJP, the unwillingness of the international community to work for the return of Aristide contributed to accelerating the departures of Haitians (HP 228:14). In a report issued on March 31, CJP criticized the US and the rest of the international community for displaying "great contempt": "It even appears that this systematic repression is part of a strategy to install `democracy´ without people. ... [the army] ... must have their master! And it is not difficult to identify him". The report was one of many released over the previous two weeks, as HP reported on the basis of information obtained from the *Haitian Information Bureau* (HP 247:9).

In refusing further endless negotiations mediated by the US and the UN, the 7,000 Haitians, who protested on March 5 at the rally in Manhattan, came together in front of the UN headquarters to reject the idea of naming a new Prime Minister to resolve the crisis (HP 236:1,17). Similar to many Haitians´ view, Martin opined that the UN´s "most serious mistake was to link itself too closely with" Washington in the case of Haiti. It became unable to achieve anything without support of the US, on whose dealings with Haiti´s army leaders the UN "became dependent" (1994:88). In Malone´s judgement, the US with its "growing weight" within the five permanent members of the UNSC was indeed the "predominant external actor" throughout the Haitian crisis (1997:126,134). Brian Urquhart called the "new enthusiasm", following the Persian Gulf War, of some permanent UNSC members for UN interventions in humanitarian and human rights situations "regardless of national sovereignty" a "source of unease", a trend that would be resisted in some parts of the world as a "new cloak for great power interventionism" (1991/92:25). In the case of Haiti, the fear of "great power interventionism" especially with regard to the UN/OAS-ICM often assumed, from an outsider´s uninformed point of view, slightly paranoid features. This can be explained, in part, by Haitians´ historical experience (see further below).

At the end of March, HP reported on the "offensive against the policy of Clinton in Haiti". It announced the CBC´s plans to hold a summit in Washington with numerous political and community leaders as well as religious and other personalities. The "most spectacular action" would be an open letter to Clinton to be published soon in the NYT (HP 237:18).[175] The CBC conference entitled "Community Empowerment:

---

[175] The letter was reported to be signed by members of Congress and a variety of other personalities in the US. Among these were Carol Moseley-Braun, Ronald Dellums, Patricia Schroeder, Henry Siegman,

A Formula for Change" took place on March 18 and 19 and dealt with the current situation of African-Americans. One work shop was dedicated to the Haitian situation. Rangel suggested that Aristide should wait for the international community to do something. HP commented angrily: "Cela fait trente mois qu'attend Aristide et il ne semble pas que le démagogie de Rangel puisse le mener plus loin". Owens announced that the CBC's "new offensive" would be introduced with Congressman Ron Dellums' piece of legislation calling for, *inter alia*, the termination of air traffic, a ban on visas for all putschists without exception, and a total embargo (HP 239:7).

Aristide, however, spoke what was in many Haitians' hearts when saying at *Northeastern University* on April 9 that "... [this] sham embargo ... was imposed to break the struggle of the Haitian people". At about the same time, 24 US trade unions called on the Clinton Administration to tighten the embargo (HP 248:9). In HP's judgement, the New York-based *Village Voice* (04/19/94) summarized the situation well by stating that "the principal violator of the embargo imposed on Haiti by the Clinton administration is the Clinton administration" (HP 249:8).[176]

HP documented for its readers the "widening gap between the Clinton Administration and Congress on US policy toward Haiti" in late April. A group of Democratic Senators led by Christopher Dodd (D-CT) had introduced a bill backed by more than 70 representatives that would tighten sanctions and provide at least some sanctuary for Haitian refugees. HP noted that the bill was similar to the piece of legislation sponsored by Dellums earlier that month (HP 252). These expressions of Congressional discontent were accompanied by the protest march of 10,000 demonstrators from New York, Miami, Philadelphia, New Jersey, Montreal, and other places in the Northeast in early May 1994. The demonstration was organized by the *Comité d'Action Unitaire*, the principal leaders of which were Guy Victor, Paul Tulcé, and Maxime Lorismé. The numerous speakers called for a breaking off of negotiations in order "to engage in other forms of struggle".

HP evaluated the demonstration a full success, because Clinton could not ignore the Haitian community's message. But HP was not satisfied at all with organizational matters: The demonstrators did not present demands in written form. There were no leaflets prepared to educate the US public. The organizers did not provide for a delegation demanding to be welcome in the White House or mandated to forward a message on behalf of the Haitian community. And it would also have been a matter of courtesy, as HP insisted, to send a delegation to the headquarters of *TransAfrica*, where Robinson had been on hunger strike for 22 days. HP issued its gravest criticism of Haitian organizers to date: "Si l'on accepte d'être dirigeant, cela implique certaines responsabilités ... il serait important de critiquer ceux qui continuent à privilégier l'improvisation, le spontanéisme, le flou, le manque de principes, l'amateurisme... Une improvisation qui se reflète dans tous les détails..." (HP 257:1,17).

In comparison, the demonstration was indeed, in some measure, a far cry from the gathering in Boston on September 31, 1991 (HP 11:14). Partially generated by their growing suspicion of the US's role and that of international organizations in the

---

executive director of AJCs, the musician Quincy Jones, actors and actresses Paul Newman, Joanne Woodward, Julia Roberts, Robin Williams, Danny Glover etc. (HP 237:18).

[176] HP referred to a letter to Clinton from the NLC, dated April 11, which denounced the US's trade policies following the coup. The letter stated that even after the "second OAS embargo was imposed on October 18, 1993 ... more than 60 US companies continue to trade with Haiti" (HP 249:8).

Haitian crisis, Haitian activists increasingly preferred to indirectly express their grievances towards these actors via the general public as covered by the media. This is what the record of HP's reporting seems to suggest. Lobbying through indirect transnational relations became even rarer as the crisis progressed.

Haitians' doubts about the UN's impartiality and neutrality in the conflict turned into open accusations in the weeks to come. The UN was increasingly seen as acting like an instrument of US interests in Haiti and was alleged to be implicated in a plot aimed at draining the ranks of the popular camp. In a common declaration issued in mid-July, 13 popular organizations in Haiti joined to expose the "double game of the international community".[177] Their analysis was summarized by HP. The "double game" was particularly manifested in the embargo. In sharp contrast to NCHR's view, the UN/OAS-ICM, rather than denouncing human rights abuses in Haiti, was accused of transforming into a "henchman of a policy designed to facilitate the departure of activists in order to dismantle popular organizations, while refugees are returned to the hands of the military without scruples". HP lauded the groups (HP 291:1,17).

Not surprisingly, Haitian organizing vis-a-vis international organizations became more desperate in these heightened times of crisis. On July 23, *Pawòl Fanm Son Radyo Solèy Dayiti*, a group of patriotic Haitian women in New York, organized a poorly frequented demonstration in front of the Catholic Mission at the UN. On a podium at Dag Hammarskjöld Plaza, Roger Etienne of KOZA coordinated the speakers. Maude Leblanc opined that Aristide could have been in Haiti a long time ago, if Haitians had directly attacked the Vatican, the CIA, and the USSD ever since the coup (HP 297:8). From an outsider's point of view, the title of HP's report on the rally, "New York: des femmes en tête de la lutte contre le Vatican", had a strange quixotic quality. It overestimated the small crowd's power and testified to a lack of contact with reality or an unbroken will for agitation. Yet the theme was picked up in the Haitian community. At Père Vincent's "symbolic funeral" on September 3, Pères Etienne and Clérismé denounced the complicity of the *Catholic Church*'s high hierarchy in Haiti. In its report on the event, HP unveiled plans of the groups *Ti Kominote Legliz* of New York and *Partisans de Jesus Christ* to organize a picket-line in front of *St. Patrick Cathedral* in Manhattan on September 4 (HP 317:8).

To many Haitians, the Carter-Mission to Haiti leading to the US-led occupation of the island in 1994 was frustrating. At the second mass in commemoration of Vincent on September 18, Mgr. Romélus said he was very disappointed to see the Carter delegation collaborating directly with the *de facto* president Emile Jonassaint. Reporting on the event, HP added that collaboration between the "military putschists" and the US was now going to be legitimized (HP 327:15). In sharp contrast, the NAACP "praised the Clinton Administration's weekend diplomacy" to restore Aristide. Dr. William F. Gibson, chairman of NAACP's Board, emphasized proudly: "We note, in particular, that the strong respect the Haitian people have for General Colin Powell apparently was a critical factor in producing this agreement" (NAACP 1994:1). At the NAACP's 1993 board meeting in Nassau, Bahamas, both Gibson and Dr. Benjamin F. Chavis, executive director of the 600,000 member organization, had demanded "full respect for the sovereign rights of the Caribbean nations" (NAACP 1993:3). Needless

---

[177] These groups were *Têt Kole*, APN, *Solidarité Entre Jeunes* (SAJ), *Veye Yo*, *Solidarité Paysans Haitiens*, *Konbit Komilfo*, *Komite Defans Enterè Nasyonal* (KODENA), and many others (HP 291:1).

to say that for many Haitians, "respect for the sovereign rights" of their country had not been acknowledged, when it was occupied by the US-led multinational force, even if that meant the return of Aristide.

5.4 Fighting the Effect: Solidarity with Haitian Refugees Detained at Guantanamo, Repatriated to Haiti, or Processed in Haiti
(Extra-territorial Ethnic Organizing)

As has been shown above, the observation made by McCalla of NCHR that the refugee crisis was "not an issue" for activists in the Haitian community is not correct if understood as a categorical statement, since there were indeed "demands for refugees". But the strategical value of those demands was assessed in a different way and, as a consequence, toned down for a variety of reasons. A set of reservations responsible for the different handling of the refugee issue can be discerned. According to McCalla, the strategical advisability of the refugee issue was obvious to NCHR. He contrasted this with the way the political leadership of the Haitian diaspora allegedly approached the issue: "[T]hey saw their mission as ... Aristide´s return to Haiti. And the thinking was that, of course, Aristide would not return without the support of the United States. So if they raise the refugee issue, in other words, they took on the United States over its bad refugee policy, then the likelihood that Aristide would have the support of the United States was null. So that´s one reason that they avoided the refugee issue, you know, very logical on their part, except that it was a wrong logic" (McCalla 1995).

NCHR, on the other hand, inferred the opposite conclusion from the facts of a "bad" refugee policy pursued by the US, as McCalla recalled: "It´s the politics of fear that is driving US policy, *fear of migration*, fear of refugees, fear of people of Haiti. ... So our emphasis was very clear: You focus on the refugees, you focus on migration. That´s the only way you are going to catch the attention from the Administration, that´s the only way you are going to catch the attention of Congress, that´s the only way you make them concerned" (McCalla 1995;author´s italics). Aubourg agreed that in the Haitian community, the "refugee camp was in the minority, indeed". Aristide´s Haitian advisors did not understand the refugee issue (Aubourg 1996). Likewise, Frank of HCC observed that activities in the Haitian community in support of Haitian refugees were "not strong at all ... They were less concerned with the problem of the refugees than the political aspects" (Frank 1995).

Lisa Daugaard, white American activist of ECHR and one of the students at *Yale Law School*, who were involved in the refugee-related lawsuit during the crisis, added one motivation for the stated "fear of migration" when explaining the strategy underlying the lawsuit: "[I]f we can undo the interdiction program and refugees begin arriving and get to the United States, ... that would force this kind of bizarre reactionary political pressure on Clinton and on Florida and New York and other Governors. And that would provide the constituency for resolving this problem in Haiti, and I think that worked! ... what we were trying to do is this sort of cynical gambit of playing on *domestic racism*" (Daugaard 1995;author´s italics).[178] As Ratner of CCR plainly stated: "One of the most efficient strategies [is] to pressure the US on the question of refugees" (HP 229:8). Likewise, Milne asserted that the tide of Haitian refugees had "the strongest impact on our government to act to restore Aristide" (Milne 1996).

In contrast, Désir said to me that "[t]here was a time, when some people [in the Haitian community] were of the opinion that we should not raise the refugee issue, because it was against the will of the State Department" (Désir 1995). Aristide´s return was "the topic to deal with" to have US-based Haitians come out in public, as Guy Victor told me. First you win the support of the international community, "then you bring the question of the refugees" (Victor 1996). What the international community was concerned about, however, was the flow of Haitian refugees, as is reflected in some OAS and UN resolutions issued during the crisis.[179]

Hence the strategical thrust of NCHR and other collaborating groups primarily concentrated on the one effect of the coup, in which the main stake of the US was believed to lie. US policy towards Haiti as primarily designed to halt the Haitian refugee stream was presumed to constitute the most vulnerable point of the US government, and the criticism of it the most effective political weapon. This approach required extra-territorial organizing activities of an ethnic orientation for the benefit of Haitian refugees. Utilizing indirect transnational relations, it relied on the possible consequent impact of these activities on the US government´s policies towards the Haitian military junta. A score of participant and non-participant observers corroborated the view that the main interest of the US in the Haitian crisis was the containment of refugees.[180]

---

[178] As Harold Hongju Koh, professor at *Yale Law School*, put it, the plaintiffs´ governing strategy in the case was "to provoke the articulation of norms by sympathetic judicial fora ... and then to transport those norms to other fora for use in political bargaining" (1994:2400).

[179] The OAS-Permanent Council resolution CP/RES.594 of November 10, 1992, the UNGA resolution ARES.47/20A of November 24, 1992, the OAS-Ministers of Foreign Affairs resolution MRE/RES.4/92 of December 13, 1992, and the UNSC resolution S/RES.841 of June 16, 1993, are all concerned about an "increase in the number of Haitians seeking refuge in neighboring member countries".

[180] From a multilateral viewpoint, Ian Guest of the *Refugee Policy Group* found that Haitian boat people "are one of the *unspoken reasons* why the international community has made a commitment to Haiti´s recovery" (1993:11;author´s italics). Latin American correspondent and foreign affairs reporter for the *Boston Globe*, Pamela Constable, asserted that the US "Justice and Defense Departments [we]re primarily worried about an invasion of `boat people´ across the Caribbean" (1992/93:184;author´s italics). According to Juan P. Osuna and Christine M. Hanson, editors of *Interpreter Releases*, the "Haiti crisis" represented the "most compelling refugee dilemma during the Bush years", which posed an "embarrassing problem for the U.S. government" (1993:42). James Morrell, director of research at CIP, noticed that the "specter of tens of thousands of poor, black refugees landing in Florida kept Clinton riveted on the realities of Haiti" (1993:3). And Elizabeth G. Ferris, Director of the Immigration and Refugee Program (IRP) of CWS, stated that the US "government´s policy toward the internal situation in Haiti has in fact been shaped by the desire to prevent a mass influx of Haitians arriving on Florida´s shores" (CWSW 1994b:1). Similarly adding an intra-societal dimension, Martin observed that the US "administration wanted U.N. involvement because of its compelling *domestic need* for a solution that would stem the refugee flow" (1994:88;author´s italics). For Frelick of USCR, "[i]t appeared at the time that U.S. policy was being driven by the fear of an influx of refugees into Florida, a critical State in President Bush´s reelection bid" (1993:680). In a similar vein, Koh explained both US Administrations´ being "soft on the illegitimate regime" with a "pattern of executive reactivity" nourished in part by Bush´s "*election-year-desire* to avoid a replay of the Cuban Marielito boat crisis" and by Clinton´s "prospective desire to avoid a refugee inflow that might distract attention from his ambitious *domestic*

McCalla´s "fear of migration"-thesis and Daugaard´s "domestic racism"-thesis were validated by a Gallup opinion poll taken in February 1992, which found a rising anti-immigrant sentiment since the mid-1980s. Public concern was greatest about immigration from the Third World, with 69% of Americans interviewed feeling that there was too much immigration from Latin American countries, followed by immigration from Asian (58%) and African countries (47%). Whites were more likely than non-whites to feel that there was too much immigration. The differences were largest in the case of Africa. 67% of Americans agreed with the US decision of that month to deport Haitian boat people rather than allowing them to "immigrate" to the US. Opinions were sharply divided along racial lines, with 70% of whites, compared with 42% of blacks, approving of the decision (Hugick 1992a:6).

NCHR´s strategy was reflected in the reasoning of an unknown number of Haitian refugees. Their transnational flight was in part motivated by a calculation centering around the US Administration. As HP reported in late January 1993, Haitian refugees either did not seem to have heard Aristide´s second appeal to stay in Haiti nor Clinton´s warning that they would be intercepted by the USCG. HP speculated that some of them could have as well made the conscious decision to test or defy the US blockade "Able Manner" in accordance with the following strategy: "Ceux qui ont décidé de défier les gardes-côtes étatsuniens semblent le faire dans un but précis: *exercer des pressions sur Clinton* ... pour que le prochain président travaille à la réintégration de `leur prêtre-président qu´ils (les réfugiés) avaient choisi et qui a leur confiance´ ... D´autres Haitiens qui sont restés à l´intérieur ont dit ... que si ... les négociations n´aboutissaient pas au retour physique d´Aristide au pays, ils prendraient la mer" (HP 173:8;author´s italics). One HEAR-member conceded that Haitian refugees "also created an atmosphere, where ... they triggered the return of Aristide" (HEAR 1995).[181]

The three clergy persons Raymond Mailhot, Dempsey Loarca, and Sister Santina Perin, who decided in July 1994 to take to the sea in solidarity with the Haitian boat people, redefined the term "resistance" to include the refugees´ flight: "Devant la répression militaire qui empêche une participation active et directe, une alternative est possible: la résistance. Face à toute tentative de dissuasion, les 16,436 réfugiés haitiens doivent être animés d´une conscience claire que leur résistance, patiente et courageuse, est un apport précieux au processus de changement" (HP 306:8). By means of their specific form of action, they contributed to publicly amplifying the transnational movement of Haitian refugees and broadened the officially coined concept of "resistance" confined to the territory of Haiti. In the same vein, NCHR´s strategy aimed at boosting the impact of the refugees´ transnational movement. As NAACP and *TransAfrica* put it: "[*D*]*ramatizing* the plight of Haitian refugees ... [is] part of the larger campaign to restore democracy to Haiti" (Rangel92f:1;author´s italics).

---

agenda". As he put it yet another way: "When boatloads of refugees started to come, the Bush administration began to view the *refugees*, not the regime, as the problem" (1994:2392,2410,2430;author´s italics). And one of the broad lessons that Malone drew from the Haitian crisis was that "Haitian refugees *heavily* influenced US policy" and "haunted his [Clinton´s] administration for the next 21 months, generating *pressure to resolve* the ongoing political crisis" (1997:134-135;author´s italics).

[181] Interestingly, Haiti´s elite was concerned about the boat people´s calculation after Clinton´s election, since a sudden refugee exodus could "re-energize Washington in its efforts to reinstate [Aristide]", as Howard French reported (1992f:A10).

HP´s strategical thinker Tecumseh agreed with Aristide early on in the crisis that "resistance" within Haiti, buttressed by "mobilization" in the 10th department, was basically the "only road" to success defined as the legitimate government´s return to Haiti. She thereby stressed the strategical value of direct transnational relations between the Haitian diaspora and Haiti, which included preventive measures against refugee-producing contingencies, as has been documented above. Subsidiary to that was the Haitian community´s role of putting "pressure on the Bush Administration, so that no refugee be returned under the present circumstances" (HP 53:15). She thereby suggested, as NCHR did, extra-territorial organizing activities of an ethnic orientation with their hoped for effects on the US government. Indirect transnational relations inherent in the second component of the "three-pronged strategy" of "resistance-embargo-mobilization" (Philippe Généus) focused on the international community.

However, Tecumseh attached a caveat to the secondary stratagem of focusing on the refugee issue, which she elucidated with regard to Congressman Rangel: "[I]l dénonce la politique raciste de l´administration Bush et fait du tapage sur les réfugiés. C´est *en notre faveur* car Bush est mis sur le défensive *mais* il ne faut pas non plus se mettre à la traîne de politiciens dont les contradictions avec Bush restent secondaire et qui ont *leur propre vision*" (HP 53:12;author´s italics). These reservations, as will be shown, derived in part from differing conceptions of race and differing perceptions of US power interests.

5.4.1 Initial Responses to the Refugee Crisis: Demarcating the Policy Arena

HP informed its readers continually on the refugee crisis. There were about 97 articles on the refugee issue, including a few announcements, published during 32 months of reporting. This amounts to about 3 articles per month on average, with the absolute numbers ranging from zero article in March 1994 to 10 articles in August 1994. Measured against the total of 331 articles included in the pool of HP-publications used for this study, articles on Haitian refugees accounted for approximately 29% of the total. The highest percentage occurred in 1992 with 39 articles or about 37% of all articles included in the sample for that year. There were 11 authors explicitly mentioned as being responsible for the news stories, most of which were written by Carl Gilbert.[182] It is striking that there are many more US human rights activists and US refugee advocates quoted on the issue than there are Haitian activists. The only exceptions to this rule were, by and large, Haitian-born McCalla of NCHR, Haitian-born Dorancy of HRC, and NCHR board member Père Sansaricq.

HP´s first article on the refugee side of the Haitian crisis appeared one month after the coup in the week of October 30, 1991.[183] Pointing to the double standard in US refugee policy, as manifested in the preferential treatment of Cubans vis-a-vis Haitians, HP informed that the INS had suspended all deportation procedures for Haitian

---

[182] With 67 articles, the name of the author was not given; 13 articles were written by Carl Gilbert; Of course, the 311 articles in the sample represent only a small fraction of all articles published in HP on the Haitian crisis. Consequently, the average percentage of 29% must actually be much lower.

[183] The NYT´s first article on Haitian refugees, entitled "U.S. Is Holding 200 Haitians on 2 Ships", was written by Howard French and appeared on November 8 (1991:A4).

boat people. The weekly assumed that this occurred "perhaps at the instigation of certain personalities like Senator Connie Mack, who had introduced a piece of legislation in Congress [S.Con.Res.71] providing for the temporary termination of these deportations by virtue of the bloody coup". HP quoted Cheryl Little, HRC-attorney at that time, and Peter A. Schey, executive director of the *Center for Human Rights and Constitutional Law* (CHRCL) to criticize the INS policy (HP 30:10).

One week later, Gilbert reported for HP that the nearly 500 Haitian boat people, who had fled since the coup, had been intercepted by the USCG. Rangel was now mentioned as being among "many personalities", who had raised their voice vis-a-vis the refugees´ plight. Pointing out that Rangel had introduced a piece of legislation in Congress providing for the temporary suspension of deportations (House Concurrent Resolution or H.Con.Res. 220), Gilbert stressed that "it is necessary to consider, as US Congressman Rangel does, that thousands of our compatriots are `desperate people, who feel in danger´" (HP 42:15). According to Gilbert, Dorancy of HRC felt "encouraged by the signs of apparent support by diverse organizations, which ... exert pressure on US officials". He listed NAACP, NCHR and the *Southern Christian Leadership Conference* (SCLC) as examples. Ray Fauntroy, president of SCLC in Miami, was quoted as saying that "this [US refugee policy] is racism pure and simple". Dorancy was reported demanding "from the 10th department to show its support, physical, moral and financial, in the current struggle for the respect of the rights of our refugees" (HP 42:15).

Dorancy´s "firm position" echoed the content of H.Con.Res.220 sponsored by Rangel on October 11. It called upon the US Attorney General, among other things, to temporarily "suspend the forced return of Haitian nationals in the United States during the crisis in Haiti" (MIS/MIN 1991). This provision is commonly referred to as Temporary Protected Status and known under the acronym TPS. As part of the landmark Immigration and Nationality Act (INA) of 1990, this legal term codifies the concept of safe haven for those aliens in the US, "who may not meet the legal definition of refugee but are nonetheless fleeing potentially dangerous situations" (Wasem 1992:3-4). On November 21, Congressman Romano Mazzoli (D-KY), chairman of the Judiciary Committee´s International Law, Immigration & Refugees Subcommittee, introduced at Rangel´s initiative House Resolution (H.R.) 3844, the so-called "Haitian Refugee Protection Act of 1991". The most important measures provided in the bill were TPS for Haitians fleeing their country´s violent turmoil and the reallocation of 2,000 federally funded refugee slots to Haitians (MIS/MIN 1991). In contrast to H.Con.Res.220, H.R.3844 would have been legally binding for the US executive branch if adopted by both houses of Congress.

The refugee definition derives from the 1951 United Nations Convention Relating to the Status of Refugees. It was modified by the 1967 Protocol (Martin 1991:30;46).[184] In the 1951 Refugee Convention, the concept of non-refoulement (Article 33), the prohibition of forced return of genuine refugees, is mandated. It is simi-

---

[184] That definition now provides that a refugee is a person, who "owing to a well-founded fear of persecution for reasons of race, religion, nationality, membership of a particular social group or political opinion, is outside the country of his nationality and is unable or, owing to such fear, is unwilling to avail himself of the protection of that country; or who, not having a nationality and being outside the country of his former habitual residence, is unable or, owing to such fear, is unwilling to return to it" (Convention Article 1(A)(2), 189 U.N.T.S. 137;Protocol 606 U.N.T.S. 267).

larly prohibited in section 243(h) of the INA. But the concept of asylum is neither mandated by the Refugee Convention nor by the INA, whose section 208 clearly makes the granting of asylum discretionary, a sovereign right of the contracting state to decide, who should be granted asylum (Frelick 1993:675-676). Asylum was therefore called a "scarce resource" (Martin 1991:34-37).[185]

Haitians in the 10th department responded to Dorancy´s appeal by joining a demonstration in the city in which HRC is headquartered. According to Dorancy, almost 70,000 Haitians and Americans attended the rally in mid-November, which was organized in Miami, as Gilbert reported. Along with "diverse organizations" and former US presidential candidate, Dr. Laura Fullani, the demonstrators expressed their anger vis-a-vis the hesitance, then the refusal of the Bush Administration to accept all Haitian refugees. Gilbert mentioned in his report for the first time the US naval base at Guantanamo Bay as the place, where a group of 483 Haitians was held in US custody. He reported that the USSD had announced on November 18 that it would send back Haitian refugees to Haiti, unless they were accepted by other countries. He quoted Rangel, who had met with members of the 10th department on November 15, as calling the new policy "disgusting, racist, and vicious ... a policy of double standard. This would not have happened, if the refugees were European". Gilbert concluded that democracy must have many meanings for the Bush Administration, depending on whether it deals "with Kuweit, the Curds, the Cubans ... or the Haitians". In his mind, the temporary stay of deportations issued by a federal judge in Miami as a result of HRC´s intervention was "another proof of the pugnacity of the 10th department" (HP 44:8). These developments indicate that in the early stages of the crisis, the Haitian diaspora´s center of activism in refugee affairs emerged in Miami rather than in New York City. Guy Victor confirmed that in contradistinction to New York, there had been various demonstrations in Miami organized just for the Haitian refugees (Victor 1996).

The "pugnacity of the 10th department" was later documented in an interview with Dorancy conducted by Latour in March 1992. Latour described the NCHR-member HRC as a "beehive" in the "very heart of Little Haiti" and Dorancy as the queen bee exhibiting "extreme devotion to the cause". Dorancy informed that after the "rupture" of its predecessor organization, HRC was founded in 1980 as a "center with a political character occupied with the lot of Haitian refugees".[186] She asserted that HRC "has become what it is today" thanks to its former executive director, Père Jean-

---

[185] International law and domestic law have kept the two concepts distinct: Article 33 of the Refugee Convention provides that "[n]o Contracting State shall expel or return ("refouler") a refugee in any manner whatsoever to the frontiers of territories where his life or freedom would be threatened on account of his race, religion, nationality, or membership of a particular social group or political opinion". Likewise, section 243(h) of the INA provides that "[t]he Attorney General shall not deport or return any alien ... to a country ... [where] such alien´s life or freedom would be threatened...". Section 208 of the INA provides that "... the alien may be granted asylum in the discretion of the Attorney General if the Attorney General determines that such alien is a refugee..." (Frelick 1993:675-676).

[186] In a classified ad published in HP in February 1993, HRC described itself as follows: "HRC is co-recipient of the 1992 Carter-Menil Human Rights Prize, was founded in 1973, and is a community-based, grass roots organization in Miami´s Little Haiti" (HP 89:9). A 1995 brochure stated that HRC is involved in a "variety of educational activitites directly related to its core responsibilities". It airs "matters of importance to the community" on three local radio stations in Haitian-Creole and holds "bimonthly meetings with interested community members" (HRC 1995:1,2).

Juste (HP 88:10,21), who would later be appointed General Coordinator of the 10th departments (Jean-Pierre 1995:202).

HRC´s staff at that time was composed of 13 persons assigned to legal tasks covering both the US and Haiti. Besides Dorancy, who studied law in the US, the staff included Ira Kurzban, an American and HRC´s legal counselor, and Cheryl Little, also of American origin and HRC´s chief advocate. Even though legal matters and human rights are HRC´s main concerns, Dorancy said that "people come here for all sorts of reasons, social, economic, familial". She said HRC was able to function "thanks to a network of Haitian solidarity, the great sanctuary of which ... is the ... mass organization *Veye Yo*". She stressed that HRC entertains good relations with Jewish religious organizations, various pastors, SCLC, NAACP and its president in Florida, Johnnie McMillan.[187] After HRC´s legal victories in 1982 and 1986, the Center considered "litigating against Secretary Baker". As a result, 3,400 refugees to date were allowed to file for political asylum in the US (HP 88:10,21).

Even if the initial center of activism on the refugee front was located in Miami, the Haitian community of New York City was not indifferent to the Haitian refugees´ plight. During the mass in memory of 152 drowned boat people, celebrated in *St. Jerome Church* in Brooklyn on November 24, Père Sansaricq denounced the INS policy as double standard. Guest of honor Jackson observed in his speech, as Alain St. Victor reported, that the US Administration´s discriminatory and racist policy vis-a-vis Haitian refugees was carried out in spite of the condemnation of the criminal coup on the international level (HP 50:8). He thereby implied a contradiction in the US Administration´s policies vis-a-vis Haiti. The highly respected *Haiti Commission* was also concerned with the refugee question. It did so from a decided political point of view. At the group´s "soirée" on November 21, its founder Ramsey Clark "categorically denounced the Bush Administration´s racist policy vis-a-vis Haitian refugees, which permits the entire world to see its support for the Honorat regime", as HP reported. US-member Pat Chin stressed the hypocrisy of the US in talking about alleged human rights violations under Aristide while treating the rights of Haitian refugees fleeing repression with contempt. And Dominican-member Vasquez along with US-member Ives condemned the deportations and the bad treatment of Haitians by Dominican authorities under Balaguer (HP 51:10).

In contrast to Jackson, Clark did not see a contradiction between Bush´s diplomatic and refugee policies towards Haiti: Rejecting Haitian refugees was simply a way of supporting the military junta. The US´s main stake was not believed to lie in the containment of refugee flows, as McCalla´s NCHR did, but helping keep the *de facto* regime in place through neglect. Tolerating the military junta was not seen as an unintended side-effect of containing the refugees, but stemming the flow of boat people was seen as a deliberate measure to support the *de facto* regime.

Whereas Clark - as well as Fauntroy, Rangel, and Jackson - predicated their criticism of US refugee policy concerning Haitians upon what they claimed to be racism in US society, Haitian strategists were rather reluctant to establish this link. In her

---

[187] The group´s 1995 brochure characterizes "[n]etworking with national and international organizations" as a "regular part of HRC´s work" and testifies to its "long-standing working relationships" with "legal agencies" such as NCHR, USCC, the *National Lawyers Guild*, the *National Immigration and Refugee and Citizenship Forum* (NIF), CCR as well as with NAACP and *TransAfrica* (HRC 1995:2).

report on the "drama" of Haitian boat people in late November 1991, Tecumseh cited Rangel, who had accused the Bush Administration of adopting "a policy à la David Duke". She commented: "Is it necessary to view the refusal to accept Haitian refugees as discrimination based on racism? This is certainly a susceptible aspect to bring into play, but it is very likely subordinated to an issue of ideological and political nature ... in the context of the Cold War". For Polish and Russian refugees had been accepted into the US in high numbers (HP 53:12). Similarly, HP opined that the bad conditions on Guantanamo were "neither neglect nor uniquely a consequence of racism, but rather a deliberate policy" (HP 57:6,16-18). In sum, many Haitian organizers in this early stage of the crisis stopped short of calling US refugee policy "racist", but preferred to label it "discriminatory" and politically motivated instead, especially with regard to well-received Cuban refugees fleeing Socialist rule. According to Mayas of HWHR, most US-based Haitians believe that Haitian refugees are not welcome in the country primarily because of the language barrier, followed by the fear of AIDS and illiteracy, with the color of their skin ranking last (Mayas 1995).[188]

In accordance with Clark, Tecumseh believed the Bush Administration´s position to be clear, which she implicitly compared with the Haitian diaspora´s strategy: The US "quietly whitewashes the putschists said not to be responsible for the exodus in any way" instead of seizing the refugee problem "as a *supplementary* means of driving into a corner the regime in place" (HP 53:15;author´s italics). The plight of Haitian boat people was to be used to shed *additional* light on the repressive character of Haiti´s illegitimate government rather than *primarily* taking advantage of the refugee flow by denouncing the related policy of the US government. This policy was believed to be secretly backing the military junta. Consequently, Tecumseh explained, Bush called the Haitians "economic refugees". He did not have "any second thoughts to send back those, who escape intense repression", but asked Third World countries to accept the refugees, not willing to accept that the US is the "country of first asylum". Tecumseh admitted, however, that Bush also "sees the specter of an `invasion´ - like president Balaguer in the Dominican Republic". She recalled the "merciless battle" in the 1980s "waged by organizations in defense of refugees to refute the thesis of `economic refugees´": "It is hard to see how to deny repression in a country, where there have been more than one thousand people killed in a couple of days and which lives the old days of Papa Doc; on the other hand, if it is right that the embargo augments the difficulties of the populace, it is a consequence of the coup ... the important question of why the refugees had not left right after the coup is in their [i.e. the US Administration´s] eyes proof that it is not the cause of their flight". Tecmuseh identified "the urgency of reaching the only solution to stop this wave of refugees: the return to power of Aristide" (HP 53:12,13).

The NCHR-informant and human rights coalition *Platform* was somewhat more detailed in criticizing US refugee policy in its report of November 1991, which was distributed on Capitol Hill. The nine member-organizations stated to be "preoccupied" with the conditions, under which the crucial asylum interviews were conducted on USCG cutters. They stressed that during the first months of the Aristide government,

---

[188] Mayas personally puts the factors into the following hierarchical order: race, the language barrier, illiteracy, and AIDS (Mayas 1995). Guy Victor of HRC said Haitian refugees were not welcome in the US, because they are "people of African descent" (Victor 1996).

the number of refugees decreased dramatically. The authors complained that they were not informed ahead of time about returning Haitians and, as a consequence, had not been able to meet them upon arrival. The *Platform* demanded "instantly from all authorities involved not to return any Haitian citizen as long as no notable change takes place in the political situation of the country" (HP 54:12-15). It thereby paraphrased the demand for granting TPS.

In early December, Gilbert picked up the concerns about the adequacy of asylum interviews on the high seas. He reported that advocates of HRC had been able to prove that the interviews conducted by the INS "with our compatriots" did not reflect at all the "conditions of fear, of persecution, of abuse, of repression" in Haiti. Kurzban, for example, listed members of a few groups, who did not have the chance to present their claims for political asylum. Gilbert noted that despite the ruling by judge Donald Graham in Miami, the refugees were not admitted onto US territory. Gilbert announced that on December 2, federal judge C. Clyde Atkins in Miami would hear the cause of Haitian refugees, for whom Little of HRC would seek a permanent injunction. He noted that about 30 organizations and personalities, among them archbishop of Miami, Edward A. McCarthy, signed a petition dated November 26. It called on Bush to suspend deportations of Haitian refugees until the restoration of constitutional order (TPS). And a dozen US Congresspersons as well as ABA, NAACP, ai, and UNHCR all denounced Bush´s refugee policy. Gilbert was confident that "our compatriots [i.e. the refugees] will certainly find the comprehension and the support of all the 10th department and of Haiti´s friends abroad" (HP 56:10,24).

As a matter of fact, one week later HP reported in a 4-page article on the successful "maintenance of mobilization in their favor": In Miami, "a rally took place this Sunday December 8 with 8 to 10,000 people" (HP 57:6,16-18). And at the rally of nearly 10,000 people in Washington on December 13, the diaspora´s demands relative to Haiti´s political crisis were followed by the demand of "political asylum for Haitian refugees" (HP 58:1,17).[189] Both rallies came after judge Atkins´ decision of November 19 to prolong the Temporary Restraining Order halting the forced return of interdicted Haitians for seven days. HP proudly quoted Dorancy of HRC as having told the *Herald Tribune* (12/04/91) "We have won". According to Kurzban (UPI 12/05/91), "INS officials have admitted that they were in ignorance about political leaders and conditions in Haiti as well as about US immigration law and the criteria for political asylum". HP characterized the INS hearings as interviews "with ignorant people, stuffed with biases" (HP 57:6,16-18).

On the subject of Haitian boat people detained at Guantanamo, HP quoted "eye witness" McCalla at length. McCalla said on ABC´s "Like it is" (12/08/91): "... the Americans cannot communicate with the Haitians in the first place ... We have learnt that they will eventually use police dogs to maintain control over the Haitians ... Practically, this is a prisoners of war camp ... similar to a *concentration camp*". HP commented: "Why not using an observation tower?". It quoted Haitian-American Fritz Martial of the New York-based radio station WLIB as saying on *Moment Créole* on December 8: "A pig fattened to be sold lives in better conditions than they do". He

---

[189] Rangel attended the December 13 rally, where he would say that Julna Albert, the "first person to die while in detention at Guantanamo Bay", died from "complications of pregnancy" after having arrived at the camp on December 2 (Rangel91c:1).

indicated that there were 2,500 US soldiers on the naval base. HP mentioned the death of a 32-year-old pregnant Haitian woman, Julna Albert, in the hospital at Guantanamo on December 8. HP summarized that "the conditions, in which thousands of Haitians live, hemmed in tents on Guantanamo Bay, don´t compare with those at Krome... there the refugees could at least feel close to their parents, their friends and acquaintances, protected by the community". HP referred to the NYT (12/08/91), which explained the "new tactics" of discouraging the refugees and of pushing them to demand their voluntary repatriation. Part of this strategy was to exceed the capacity of the camp, which could hold more than 10,000 people (HP 57:6,16-18;author´s italics).

Another method was replacing fresh meals with MRE (Meals Ready to Eat). Paraphrasing a remark made by a US official quoted in the NYT, HP realized that the US "is about to defend itself against a horde of invaders". It reported that in Camp Bulkeley, where nearly 2,500 refugees were detained, US soldiers were mostly operation Desert Storm veterans, who had already established refugee camps for the Curds in Iraq. At the same time, the UN was reported to be in the process of negotiating an accord with Cuba to have Haitian boat people establish themselves permanently in the Cuban city of Guantanamo. HP lauded the country: "[T]he Cuban government has thus not reacted with the cynicism, which the US has exhibited" (HP 57:6,16-18).

The first riot on Guantanamo occurred in a Cuban context. It was reportedly triggered by the rumor that Fidel Castro had ordered to have Haitian refugees killed, if they did not leave within 5 days. In view of UNHCR´s "accord of cooperation" with Cuba for the benefit of Haitian refugees, HP suspected US-owned *Radio Marti* to be the author of this "counter-propaganda campaign". Castro had denounced the installation of a "concentration camp" (HP) for refugees on what Haiti´s island neighbor called "Cuban territory illegally occupied". At the same time, the Bush Administration tried on December 12 to nullify judge Atkins´ decision with the assistance of its top lawyer, Solicitor General Kenneth Starr. He declared in the 11th Circuit Court of Appeals in Atlanta that the federal court in Miami had no jurisdiction in that case due to the fact that the Haitians were intercepted in international waters. Kurzban commented that "the question is not about entering the US. [But] ... if or if not ... these people will be confronted with death upon returning to Haiti". Nonetheless, the US had conceded 911 claims for political asylum out of a total of 7,104 Haitians intercepted, as HP pointed out, contrary to the "economic refugee" thesis (HP 60:10,16).

HP further mentioned the "odd proposition" made by Stein of *Federation for American Immigration Reform* (FAIR) in a NYT-commentary (12/14/91). Stein suggested that "we must tackle the selection process [of "genuine" political refugees] in Haiti, not on the high seas".[190] HP commented on the proposal with irony: "Good idea, but it remains to be known, where the refugees would present themselves: at the US Embassy? One would have to talk to `Bourik Chaje´ [US Ambassador Adams] and one needs to ask, if it would be `feasable´ in the current climate of terror" (HP 60:16). The proposal was picked up by the Bush Administration. Having Haitian refugees file asylum claims directly at the US Embassy in Port-au-Prince came to be referred to as "In-

---

[190] FAIR presents itself as a "non-partisan organization", which was formed in 1979 "with the express purpose of advocating a `zero population growth´ position for U.S. immigration quotas". Guided by a national Board of Directors and a National Board of Advisors of "distinguished Americans from all political persuasions and points of view", FAIR is funded by over forty foundations and has 50,000 due paying members all across the US (Cong6:223).

Country Processing" (ICP), a procedure, which was "utilized in peace times for a non-communist country for the first time", as HP quoted the NYT (01/31/92). The Haitian weekly called the idea a "gross mockery" and a "cynicist strategy to divert attention" from the US policy of forced repatriation. Aronson was reported to have testified before the Appeals Court in Atlanta that "perhaps up to 20,000 Haitians or more are about to mass together at the coasts of Haiti, ready to leave for the US on sea" (*Miami Herald* 01/31/92). In HP´s eyes, this was misinformation designed to "incite panic and to put the Supreme Court on the spot". After the USSC´s decision of January 31, overturning with a vote of 6 to 3 judge Atkins´ third TPO after lengthy hearings in Atlanta on January 22, the Haitian weekly commented that the highest US court finally "cave[d] in with the desires of the [US] government" (HP 64:22;HP 71:8,17).

By the end of 1991, HP had gradually informed its readers about the complete set of locations and actors playing a role in the Haitian refugee crisis: the US Administration, the US Congress, the judicial branch of the US government, independent groups embedded in US civil society, and the Haitian diaspora in the US. This policy arena geographically encompassed Haiti, Guantanamo, and the US and centered around the legal and ethical legitimacy of US refugee policy vis-a-vis Haitian nationals concerning Guantanamo, the practice of forced return, and the ICP-program. The Haitian community´s center of activism in refugee affairs in the early stages of the crisis emerged in Miami rather than in New York City and involved direct relations to the US judicial branch by HRC and to the US Congress, especially to CBC-member Rangel, as well as indirect relations to the US Administration in terms of mass protests on the streets of Miami. It is striking that the *10e of New York* did not seem to have openly joined the chorus of criticism vis-a-vis US refugee policy at this point in time.

5.4.2 NCHR´s Initial Steps in its Refugee-oriented Strategy: Targeting Congress

Consistent with its basic shift after the coup from monitoring human rights in Haiti to the problem of Haitian refugees, NCHR claimed to have assumed "leadership of an intensive public education campaign to end interdiction and to secure protected status for Haitian refugees". NCHR´s strategy in 1991 involved "public education efforts" targeting in particular Capitol Hill, federal courts, immigrant communities, and various organizations promoting human rights. As part of the latter, NCHR counted IACHR. Meanwhile, CHRCL´s Schey continued to represent before the court (IACHR) a number of allied groups including NCHR in a suit challenging the US government´s interdiction policy. In response to an emergency application filed by CHRCL on behalf of these groups, the OAS sent a cablegram to Secretary of State Baker, requesting that the US "suspend its policy of interdiction of Haitian nationals". These measures were adopted, after McCalla had met with Aristide months before the coup to outline, in vain, options available to Haiti´s new democratic government, should it decide "to withdraw its consent" from the decade-old USHIA of 1981 (NCHR5:4-5,2). Also NCHR and LCHR had both documented the establishment and operations of the USHIA long before. It was made with Jean-Claude Duvalier in the wake of the Mariel boatlift to deter Haitians from fleeing to the US (LCHR 1990b:10-15;Fuller 1989:1-2).[191]

After the resumption of forced repatriations, part of NCHR´s "refugee advocacy projects" was the issuance of an "emergency declaration" reminding Bush of ongoing terror in Haiti and urging him "to halt this inhumane [interdiction] policy immediately". It was issued by its member organizations, including HRC. These depended upon evidence of human rights violations compiled by NCHR staff in affidavits submitted by McCalla. His post-coup collaboration with the HRC-team had been evident in undertaking a joint fact-finding mission to Guantanamo, during which depositions were taken to further buttress the case against repatriation. The federal court case permitted INS procedures to be scrutinized, which led to an "exponential increase" in the number of refugees selected to enter the US, with approximately 2,000 applicants "screened-in" by the end of 1991 (NCHR5:5,6,7). Faced with an obdurate US Administration unwilling to change its policy of forced return, NCHR increasingly turned to the US government´s legislative branch to produce political clout.

This strategy became even more urgent in the face of the negative USSC decision of January 31, 1992. Following its interest in sharing with members of Congress information on Haiti´s "twin emergencies", NCHR employed a technique, which Charles Lindblom called "partisan analysis". This technique is designed to influence policymakers through persuasion by connecting the non-governmental activist´s desired policy with the latter´s fundamental dispositions or values. It requires what V.O. Key called an "intelligence function": the surveillance of developments in a variety of arenas both in the US and abroad, in and outside of Washington, in and outside of ethnic communities. Activists thus often perform an "educative role" that can partially counter the preponderance of executive branch information by supplying a variety of documents. Their reputation for accuracy and expertise can be enhanced by consistently communicating insightful, original, and credible information. The sternest test faced in this task by non-governmental sectors is demonstrating the compatibility of their views with the policymaker´s perception of the national interest (Watanabe 1984:59,54-55,62,63).

NCHR worked "especially closely" with Rangel. After McCalla had joined the Congressman at a press conference on Haitian refugee issues on November 18, 1991, Rangel was invited to attend a NCHR Board Meeting on December 4. There he outlined his "legislative agenda" with regard to the Haitian refugee crisis, in particular H.R.3844 (NCHR5:6,8). Rangel insisted on the need to increase pressure on the executive branch, whose strong defense of its interdiction policy he interpreted in the context of Bush´s campaign for re-election. He cited his own efforts to reach out to religious, Jewish, and African-American leaders to mobilize support for TPS (NCHR3:1).[192] As NCHR emphasized, Rangel co-sponsored H.R.3844 on November

---

[191] Under the USHIA, the USCG was authorized to board and inspect on the high seas private Haitian vessels suspected of transporting undocumented Haitians, most of whom were determined by INS officials aboard USCG cutters to be "economic migrants" rather than political refugees and thus returned to Haiti (LCHR 1990b;Fuller 1989).

[192] The meeting, at which Haitian Senator Art Austin substituted for Wesner Emmanuel to give a report on Haiti, was attended by more than 30 participants. Among them were the Haitians Alex Etienne of COCHE, Gérard Férère of the *Coalition for Haitian Concerns* (CHC), Henry Frank of HCC, Pére Guy Sansaricq and a representative of HAUP (NCHR3:1).

21. One day before, McCalla had appeared at a House Immigration Subcommittee hearing set up by Mazzoli, where he testified regarding the situation of Haitian boat people. His invitation to the hearing resulted from NCHR's "campaign to educate" Congressional staff, which was reportedly instrumental in the subsequent drafting of two similar Senate bills: S.2026 by Mack (R-FL) and S.2091 by Dennis DeConcini (D-AZ) (NCHR5:8). In mid-November, NCHR conference call participants, among them Sansaricq, had found Mazzoli to be still "wavering" on the issue and thus agreed on drafting a "sign-on letter" supported by 37 organizations and on "doing op-ed pieces for Mack and Rangel" (NCHR4:1,2).

NCHR advocated for these pieces of legislation by mustering support within the broad refugee and civil rights community in the US.[193] The *Lutheran Immigration and Refugee Service* (LIRS), the *United States Catholic Conference* (USCC), and the *National Immigration Forum* (NIF) in Washington reportedly helped NCHR encourage other groups to sign a letter endorsing the measures in the Rangel/Mazzoli bill (NCHR5:8). LIRS and USCC are both volags. At the time of the crisis, they were members of NCHR, represented by Ralston H. Deffenbaugh Jr., LIRS executive director, and Rev. Richard Ryscavage, executive director of USCC's Migration and Refugee Services (MRS).[194] MRS is accountable to the *National Conference of Catholic Bishops'* (NCCB) Committee on Migration, whose Immigration Division Liaison is headed by His Eminence Anthony Cardinal Bevilacqua, Archbishop of Philadelphia (USCC/MRS 1991:1,27). Bevilacqua is also Chairman of NCHR's executive committee. Pastoral care, one of four different levels, on which MRS worked with Haitian boat people following the coup, was provided on Guantanamo by Scalabrini Father Jacques Fabre, a Haitian-American, and in Miami and throughout the US by Père Sansaricq, Rev. Thomas Wenski of *Pierre Toussaint Catholic Center* (PTCC), and the network of pastoral agents (USCC/MRS 1991:17).[195]

NIF was "particularly helpful" to NCHR by facilitating conference calls and communicating information to local and regional immigrant groups (NCHR13:3). Its executive director Frank Sharry was part of NCHR's 16-member Task Force on Haitian Refugees suggested by Gollobin during the December 4, 1991 Board Meeting. Led

---

[193] See also the list of 13 communication levels, on which NCHR exerted influence, in the appendix.

[194] LIRS is a "nonprofit organization ministering to refugees, asylum seekers, undocumented persons and immigrants" (LIRS:199?). USCC is the "public policy and social action agency of the Catholic Bishops" of the US, within which the Migration and Refugee Services (MRS) is the "lead office responsible for developing Conference policy on migration, immigration, and refugee issues" (USCC/MRS 1991:1). Founded in 1982, NIF is a non-profit membership organization dedicated to "preserv[ing] America's tradition of welcoming refugees and immigrants". Among its seven priorities figured "Immigration and Asylum Policy" and "Race and Ethnic Relations". NIF lists as type of members "individuals, ethnic organizations, major religious institutions, national voluntary agencies, civil rights groups, trade unions, local service providers, regional coalitions, and representatives of state and local governments" from throughout the US (NIF 1995:1).

[195] According to HP's Gilbert, Father Fabre is a Haitian-American (HP 145:8,11). Rev. Wenski is of the Archdiocese of Miami, representing PTCC as a member of NCHR. In the wake of the Haitian crisis in the early 1980s, the NCCB advocated the creation of a national office for the Haitian Apostolate, and this was opened in 1990. Pére Sansaricq was nominated coordinator of the Haitian Apostolate and the director of its office accountable to USCC. Mentioning the pastoral care within USCC's MRS Office, Pére Sansaricq said to me: "This is where I belong". Before becoming the priest of *St. Jerome* in 1994, Sansaricq's parish was a church in Cambria Heights, Queens (Sansaricq 1995).

by McCalla, the Task Force's purpose was the coordination of "political and legislative initiatives through conference calls and meetings" (NCHR3:3).[196] NCHR released a report explaining TPS and other relevant provisions, which it sent to about 30 "Haitian refugee associations" in the US. Comprising a "large united constituency", NCHR's member organizations, other community groups, and volags determined to advocate further Congressional hearings in early 1992, to be used "as a forum of promoting deeper understanding" of Haiti-related issues (NCHR5:8-9).

As Paul Watanabe observes, the willingness of Congress to perform the "role of judge" is a "crucial consideration" for non-governmental sectors including ethnic groups, which may find their desires at odds with the Administration. Representativeness, accessibility, and a pronounced activist inclination by key factions in the legislative branch make Congress an "alluring partner" for these sectors. Congressional personnel tends to be more responsive to the types of concerns commonly associated with ethnic groups than Administration personnel. Close working relationships quite often extend to both staff and committee personnel, who may evolve into experts in particular issue areas (Watanabe 1984:39,56,41,61,65). Hearings constitute an important part in that role of Congress. McCalla was reported to have continued to assist the House Human Rights Caucus and aides to Rangel in developing an appropriate agenda for such hearings (NCHR5:8-9). The key contact person for McCalla in Rangel's office on Capitol Hill was the Congressman's legislative director Milne. A "small core of dedicated individuals" involved in "legislative action" was composed of Carol Wolchok of ABA, Michael Hill of USCC's Office of Government Liaison, John Fredriksson of LIRS, and Rick Swartz of *Swartz & Associates* in Washington, the former president of NIF (NCHR11:iii;Haiti9:1). McCalla especially emphasized Gollobin's time-honored experience in advocacy work within the legislative branch and his personal influence with members of Congress, which he had been able to skillfully apply in terms of the refugee issue strategy (McCalla 1995).

NCHR's and its allied groups' "coordinated advocacy efforts" were most visible at a NCHR press conference moderated by McCalla and hosted by Mayor Dinkins at New York's City Hall on December 21, 1991. As NCHR reported, "numerous prominent citizens", among them Lenore Miller, President of the *Jewish Labor Committee* (JLC) and new board member of NCHR, called on the US to ensure safe haven for Haitian refugees (NCHR5:7). According to Milne, the Jewish community was in the forefront of supporting various legislative initiatives throughout the crisis (Milne 1997). One day before the NCHR Board Meeting, JLC, the "liaison organization between the organized Jewish community and the trade union movement",[197] issued a statement by Miller condemning the Bush Administration's policy of interdiction by using a strong moral argument: "In the spring of 1939, over 900 Jewish refugees fleeing from Nazi Germany on the ship `St. Louis' were refused entry to both Cuba and

---

[196] Gollobin's affiliation is with the New York-based *National Emergency Civil Liberties Committee* (NECLC) founded in 1951, "a non-partisan organization that initiates and supports court cases to safeguard existing civil and political freedoms and extend the boundaries of justice and equity in American life" (NECLC 199?:1,2). Gollobin is one of HCC's *pro bono* lawyers, who have helped Haitians in immigration matters for years, as Frank testified (1993:82).

[197] According to Arieh Lebowitz, JLC Program Associate, the organization, founded in 1934, works "to maintain and strengthen the support of the Jewish community for matters of concern to the free trade union movement" (JLC 1995:1).

the United States. As a result, virtually all passengers on the ill-fated voyage returned to Europe, many of them ultimately dying during the Holocaust" (JLC 1991:1). A broad spectrum of Jewish organizations spoke out against the US policy of forced repatriations, bombarding Congressional and media offices with a flurry of faxes.[198]

At the Haitian-organized rally of nearly 10,000 protesters in front of the OAS building on December 13, Rangel intended to pick up the powerful St. Louis comparison. He was advised to state that the "U.S. attitude toward the Haitians is reminiscent of its actions just prior to World War II when the U.S. ... refused ... the St. Louis" (Rangel91c:2). He would reiterate this point many times on the House floor and in Congressional hearings, in particular during the early and final stages of the Haitian crisis.[199] In HP's record, there is no mention of Haitian activists taking advantage of the St. Louis comparison. Only three times, the weekly pointed to US activists using the argument.[200] Perhaps the reason for this is the tendency of many Haitians in the US to refrain from publicly establishing a link between US refugee policy and racism in US society. Maybe a thankful relief for having found sanctuary in America is another reason. Cajuste Carelus, for example, the president of the *Haitian Community Association* (HCA) in Huntington, Long Island, an advocacy group for Haitian immigrants, told the NYT in late May 1992 that the battles he fought in Haiti against the Duvalier's regime had been more dangerous than casual racism in Long Island (Schemo 1992:7).

Rangel often effectively added to the Jewish experience of persecution the collective memory of African-Americans in the US. Commenting sharply on the Bush Administration's refugee policy, he lashed out in early February 1992: "We are acting like old-time slave-drivers, who dragged runaway slaves back onto the plantation to punish them" (Opitz 1992:3).[201] *TransAfrica* joined the African-American leadership to decry US refugee policy in racial terms. Executive Director Robinson asserted on February 4, 1992, that the USSC decision "smacks of political and racial discrimination" (TA 1992a:1). "Discrimination on the basis of race seems to be a crucial factor in President Bush's repatriation criteria", he concluded on the eve of a joint press conference on Capitol Hill one day prior to the House vote on H.R.3844 (TA 1992b:2). According to Herschelle Sullivan Challenor, *TransAfrica* is recognized as the "key institutional voice in the black community on foreign affairs" (1981:172).

---

[198] Among those were the *Council of Jewish Federations*, the *Greater New York Coalition for Soviet Jewry*, the *American Jewish Committee* (AJC), the *Jewish Community Relations Council* of New York (JCRC), the *Union of Orthodox Jewish Congregations of America*, three New York Hasidic groups, the *American Jewish Congress*, the *Anti-Defamation League*, the *National Jewish Community Relations Advisory Council*, the *Women's American Ort*, the *Union of Orthodox Jewish Congregations of America*, the *Council of Jewish Federations*, and the *Hebrew Immigration Aid Society* (HIAS), which is also a NCHR-member (various sources in Mr. Rangel's Capitol Hill office).

[199] It is likely that Rangel's colleague Ted Weiss (D-NY) was the source of the comparison. He told Rangel about the St. Louis during a rally at the Statue of Liberty on February 29, 1992, attended by "prestigious US personalities" (Cong6:51-52, HP 87:8).

[200] At the end of May 1992, the weekly referred to Cardinal Bernard Law of Massachusetts (HP 123:15), and in late January 1993, it mentioned Jackson. Latour called the camparison made by Jackson "particularly stirring" (HP 226:8). The only Jewish US activist HP referred to was Bialkin, president of JCRC (HP 127:12).

[201] Jackson labelled the forced repatriation policy in the wake of the USSC decision an "act of genocide" (HP 70:1,16).

There was also a host of US church organizations, which saw race as a factor influencing US refugee policy. The *Diocese of New York of the Episcopal Church*, for example, was concerned, in a resolution of February 4, by the "apparent racial dimension" in the "refusal of refuge to our Haitian brothers and sisters" (Rangel92c:1). In a telegram dated February 10 and signed by 50 national and regional executives, the 1.6-million-member *United Church of Christ* (UCC) with headquarters in Cleveland discerned a "pattern of racial discrimination" in US immigration policy (Rangel92d:1). On December 9, 1991, Benjamin Chavis, executive director of the Commission for Racial Justice of UCC had taken the "hypocritical and racially discriminatory policies" of the INS vis-a-vis Haitian refugees as "yet another example of the racist inhumanity of U.S. domestic and foreign policies toward the people of Haiti" (Rangel91d:1). Using less harsh language, the *Church World Service's* (CWS) Immigration and Refugee Program of the *National Council of the Churches of Christ* in the US called the forced repatriation of Haitian refugees in a letter to Bush dated November 20 "shameful" (Rangel91e:1). CWS, "one of two voluntary agencies in the United States [besides USCC/MRS] involved in resettling Cuban and Haitian refugees" (CWS 1991:2), is also a member of NCHR represented by Kay Bellor. Likewise, Winter, Director of USCR, in a letter to Bush dated November 19, called the US policy "discriminatory and shameful" (Rangel91f:1). USCR, the "public information arm of IRSA", is a "program of the Immigration and Refugee Services of America, a private, nonprofit organization" (USCR 1994:i,174). It is also a member of NCHR, which is represented by Winter.[202]

NCHR and its allied groups increasingly discussed the best Congressional advocacy strategy in conference calls beginning in January. They agreed to "target key congressional leaders on house and senate side" to "be contacted at the local level in their offices before".[203] The participants discussed the positions of a variety of legislators, whose views on the issue they knew from many sources (NCHR12).[204] A staff briefing on February 13, which I was in charge of organizing along with an organization called *Global Exchange* (GE), sought to muster more Congressional support for H.R.3844 with the help of Claudette Werleigh, former advisor to Prime Minister Préval (Opitz 1992:1-2).[205] It took until February 27, 1992 for the House to vote on H.R.3844, after amendments had been adopted. 217 representatives voted for and 165 against the bill, which had 46 current cosponsors in its final stage (MIS/MIN 1991). For NCHR, the House vote was an "unprecedented success in affecting public attitudes toward Haitian asylum-seekers" in spite of the Senate's subsequent failure to pass cor-

---

[202] Another volag, the *New York Association For New Americans* (NYANA), called on House Speaker Thomas Foley in a letter dated November 26, 1991 to schedule a vote on Rangel's bill. NYANA is the "largest local Jewish refugee resettlement agency ... responsible for assisting approximately half of the Soviet Jews" admitted to the US (Rangel91g:1).

[203] Anticipating the argument later used by Rep. John Bryant (D-TX) of eventually having to grant TPS to "all Haitians" other than the ones on Guantanamo, given that there are an estimated "70,000 undocumented Haitians" in the US, the activists were aware that they had to compromise. As one participant put it: "[S]omewhere in [the] process usually you must narrow [the] scope of [the] bill...".

[204] Discussions cited in conference calls of January 8, January 10, January 15, and February 4, 1992.

[205] I organized the staff briefing in cooperation with Joan Heckscher at GE's Washington-office (Opitz 1992:2). The group assisted Werleigh in Haiti-related public relation work in the US. According to NCHR, GE is a San Francisco-headquartered organization promoting "people-to-people exchange with third world countries and U.S. locations" (Haiti3b:7).

responding legislation. "[F]or the first time in our decade-long history, at least one branch of the U.S. Congress passed a bill calling for the suspension of the longstanding [USHIA]", the organization rejoiced (NCHR6:1). The Jewish-American evocation of the St-Louis incident, the African-American reference to racism, and the description of Guantanamo as a concentration camp successfully converged to verbally castigating the Bush Administration as an ideological heir of the spirit of Nazism in its policy vis-a-vis black nationals from Haiti. The combination of verbal strategies drew an evolutionary line from the past US executive branch as negligent towards the Holocaust in Europe to the present US Administration as a neglectful collaborator in a current small-scale genocide in Haiti.[206]

This ethically powerful attack was simultaneously embedded in a legal context of international and national refugee law and attracted unparalleled media attention.[207] Guy Victor told me that he was part of a joint delegation of the *10e of New York* and AEH, which joined activists from *TransAfrica* and other US groups with "experience in lobbying". They talked to more than 300 Congresspersons on Capitol Hill a few days prior to the vote. According to Aubourg of NCHR, who accompanied the delegation, there were "less than two dozens" Haitian activists (Victor 1996;Aubourg 1996). Rangel nevertheless drew the lesson that a "National Haitian Lobbying Network" was needed to advocate more effectively for Haiti-related issues in US politics (Rangel92b).

Participation of Haitian organizations in the US in advocating the Haitian refugees in the halls of Congress seems to have been rather low indeed. As part of a 31-member delegation of the New York-based *Campaign for Peace and Democracy*, Yanique Joseph, "long-time Haitian activist" of the *Green Policy Group*, was the only Haitian to go to the Haitian and the US Missions to the UN on November 26 to express support for both the return of Aristide *and* to demand an end to forced repatriations. The group stated that the US "seems to believe that if one is poor or black one cannot be a political refugee" (Rangel91h:1,2). In a sign-on letter of 29 organizations to Rangel dated January 29, 1992, the *Haitian American Institute*, the *Haitian Chamber of Commerce*, the *Haitian Neighborhood Service Center* (HNSC), HAUP and HCC were the only Haitian organizations expressing appreciation to the Congressman's "exemplary efforts to date". The groups, which urged Congress-persons to co-sponsor H.R.3844, presented themselves as members of the *New York Immigration Coalition*, an "umbrella organization for over sixty groups which represent or work with New York City's immigrant and refugee communities" (Rangel92e:1,2).[208]

HP reported on the House vote in the first week of March. The Haitian weekly observed that lawmakers pro and con "utilized habitually and passionately their politicians' jargon". Some legislators compared "our compatriots" with East European Jews, oppositionists from the former Soviet Union, from Cuba, Lebanon, Kuwait or with Vietnamese boat people (HP 86:1,19). McCalla testified to US-based Haitian activists'

---

[206] Not until late April 1994, Aristide would denounce the Clinton Administration as "contributing to a holocaust". See the NYT of 04/22/94:A1.
[207] The media attention culminated in 20 out of a total of 32 NYT-articles on the refugee issue in February 1992, the highest number per month ever in the course of the Haitian crisis (see chart).
[208] Other co-signatories were, *inter alia, Catholic Charities,* the *Center for Immigrants Rights* (CIR), the *Church Avenue Merchants Block Association* (CAMBA), ILGWU, LCHR, NCHR, NYANA, and the *NYC Mayor's Office of Immigrant Affairs* (Rangel92e:1,2).

unfamiliarity with the skillful implementation of advocacy techniques when stressing that they did not know how to play what he called "soft ball and hard ball" (McCalla 1995). Aubourg agreed that "in a larger context, it may be right", since the professional advocacy work was done by NCHR, *TransAfrica*, HRC, ABA, USCC, and CWS. But he nevertheless commended Haitians´ lobbying efforts in the halls of Congress by insisting that they did an "excellent job" (Aubourg 1996). One HEAR-member said that part of the group´s strategy was lobbying for Aristide´s return in cooperation with Rangel: "We took numerous trips to Congress", where lawmakers listened to them, because "they were tired of marches" in the streets packed with "dedicated" Haitians with "a vision to bring Aristide back" (HEAR 1995).

5.4.3 Isolated Initiatives from Haitians in the US: Guantanamo and Litigation

HP made observations similar to those made by Rangel. In late January 1992, HP identified what it called "a period of slackness in the activities taken on the level of the 10th department in defense of the Haitian refugees". The Haitian weekly suggested that what was needed was "taking the offensive again, ... And these are thousands of compatriots bored to death at the US base of Guantanamo, who count on the pressure of the 10th department to guide them out of that hell" (HP 67:9). In its report on Haitian refugees shortly before the USSC decision, HP reiterated its first doubts about the attitude of Haitians in the US towards the refugee issue. The newspaper referred to Kurzban of HRC, an unnamed attorney of UNHCR, and to ai in insisting that one "needs to continually take on the Bush Administration, to demask it, to denounce it". But, HP continued, "one needs to wonder once more, if the 10th department is at the height of its task at the present time, because there seems to be a waning of mobilization in favor of refugees. Mobilization that would permit to exert global pressure on the US" (HP 69:8,18). HP thereby indirectly criticized the political leadership of the *10th Department Organizations*.

In contrast, in its report on the "new battle" in Congress in early February, HP acknowledged the *American Jewish Committee* (AJC), NAACP, and USCC as being among the "numerous organizations in the US" in favor of the Haitian boat people (HP 70:1,16). The newspaper identified the House vote on H.R.3844, albeit threatened by Bush´s veto, as the only resort in the wake of the negative USSC decision. But it did not have anything to report regarding Haitian lobbying for the bill in the halls of Congress (HP 83:1,18;HP 84:9). In early March, the Haitian weekly foresaw difficulties in passage of the Senate version of the bill. It quoted Dorancy of HRC, who had called on all Haitians in the 10th department via VoA to write to their Senators to encourage them to vote for the bill (HP 86:1,19). In mid-February, on the other hand, Latour reported that "all speakers" of the February 7 celebrations in New York City had "unanimously denounced and condemned the unfair and racist wheelings and dealings of the US government vis-a-vis the 12,000 Haitian refugees (and even more), who are about to be `repatriated´ to certain death".[209] But he stressed in this context the

---

[209] Among them were Désir, Dany Toussaint of Aristide´s secret service, Dazòm (or Dalzon) of the *Diplomates du Béton*, and a Haitian activist named Moses St. Victor (HP 80:12-13).

speeches given by two Americans, Marc Wally of "WLID" and Dr. Fulani of the *New Alliance Party* (HP 80:12-13;author´s italics).[210] In the same issue, Dorancy proudly proclaimed that the virtual disappearance of the phenomenon of boat people during Aristide´s term had been the "basis of courageous and indefatigable action of numerous Haitian compatriots and national institutions, in particular the Haitian Refugee Center in Miami" (HP 76:11). It is possible that the diverging assessments by HP and Dorancy regarding Haitian activism on the refugee issue resulted from the differing degrees of this activism in New York City and Miami.

In late December 1991, HP probably would have shared Dorancy´s assessment, since the newspaper seemed to have been rather optimistic at that time when calling on Haitians in the US to support "Operation Hope" for the benefit of Haitian refugees detained at Guantanamo (HP 61:10). About 7,000 refugees at the US naval base were the target group of a drive launched by two New York-based black-owned radio stations, WLIB and WBLS. The Haitians were to profit from an airlift of 16 tons of Christmas presents donated by New Yorkers. The idea for the campaign originated from a visit at the refugee camp by a delegation composed of Jackson, Rangel, and Percy Sutton, chairman of the board of *Inner City Broadcasting* (ICB). The visit led to appeals for donations on the two radio stations owned by ICB (Gruyson 1991:I/34). HP portrayed "Operation Hope" as a campaign organized by Martial (HP 64:1,22), a Haitian-American and ICB´s vice-president (Dreyfuss 1993:81).[211]

In its announcement of "Operation Hope", HP asked all "patriots" to donate money for the purchase of all sorts of cloth and to give contributions in-kind. Members of HEAR stored donated cloth in their basement office in Crown Heights. HP informed that the Haitian musical band *Phantom* was scheduled to host a Christmas dinner at Guantanamo and to forward Christmas gifts to the refugees (HP 61:10;HEAR 1995). In early January 1992, HP reported that the Bush Administration had cancelled "Operation Hope" a couple of times, a move the weekly called a "policy of harassment". The *New York Post* embarrassed the Bush Administration by effectively labeling Defense Secretary Dick Cheney as the "Scrooge" in Charles Dickens´ "A Christmas Carol". The Christmas gifts could not be delivered to the refugees until their inspection by US military officers. "This is the base. They can do what they want", HP quoted Martial as saying (HP 64:1,22). It is not clear whether a low turn-out of Haitians in "Operation Hope" was the reason for HP to deplore the "waning mobilization" in the Haitian community regarding Haitian refugees. But the campaign could not have competed yet with the official fund-raising activities in the 10th department for the "benefit of the victims of the repression in Haiti", since it did not begin in earnest until April 1992 (HP 117:8).[212]

---

[210] Among the "US friends" at the rally were Rangel, Al Sharpton, and Ramsey Clark (HP 80:12-13).

[211] WLIB has been one of a few non-Haitian radio stations broadcasting Creole-language programs in the New York area (Pierre-Pierre 1993e:B3), in particular *Moment Créole*. A "highly influential commercial Haitian radio program", *Moment Créole* became transnational in its programming following the overthrow of Duvalier in 1986. At the same time, it continued its efforts to build a constituency of Haitian voters in the US (Basch et al. 1994:205). Martial was among the Haitian leaders, who organized the first major march of 50,000 Haitians in New York City on April 20, 1990 (Dreyfuss 1993:81), which served a marked ethnic purpose.

[212] A 11-member NAACP delegation led by Hooks went to Guantanamo on January 28 to distribute several tons of material to the refugees. The items had been collected through the volunteer efforts of

HP referred to Gladys Dupuy to describe the "unbearable situation" for Haitian refugees on Guantanamo. Mme Dupuy, member of the group *Association des Mères Haitiennes*, was part of a delegation of 24 people representing several religious US organizations. There was only reduced access to medical services. Legal representation during the INS asylum interviews was not available. A prepared card written in French and Creole reading "I am fine at Guantanamo, and I do not have any problems, I am hopeful to leave from here" was circulated among the refugees. They were said to be forced to sign the card, which was then sent to their families. Many refugees said that they had participated in Aristide´s presidential campaign, showing their FNCD membership cards. Mme Dupuy referred to accounts given by a Haitian working for the INS (HP 64:1,22). Gilbert reported in March that journalist Roger P. Chabot, writing in *The Church World*, had quoted a Guantanamo refugee, Louis Nixon, as saying that "they watch us like cattle" (HP 91:8).

The Haitian Mme Dupuy must have worked as an INS interpreter. As Gilbert reported, the two USCG cutters Confidence and Steadfast had only two interpreters aboard capable of speaking Haitian Creole (HP 42:15). McCalla corroborated the lack of translation aides working for US authorities on Guantanamo. Martial indicated that the US military leadership of the refugee camp had appealed to a small group of Haitian-born soldiers stationed in the US marine in North Carolina to serve as interpreters (HP 57:6,16-18). There was no shortage of interpreters for English-speaking staff working for HRC, though. When Kurzban was among a team of four attorneys accompanying court officials on a two-day fact-finding mission to Guantanamo and aboard seven USCG and Navy vessels docked there to get depositions from Haitian refugees and from INS officials alike, he was assisted by four translators (Warren 1991:3A). The lack of Creole-speaking INS interpreters would turn out to be the gateway for an unknown number of activists from the Haitian diaspora in the US. The INS turned into the focal point, in which a small portion of Haitian diasporic transnationalism penetrated the US state sphere extraterritorially.

Jocelyne Mayas from Queens was one of the first Haitian-Americans to apply as interpreter with the INS. She told me in 1995 that she had spent "for the past four years" a total of "seven months in Guantanamo". When she first got there, for a whole month she had to live "just as the refugees live: under a tent, with no plumbing, no electricity, we slept on a cot, we walked fifteen minutes to the john, we walked fifteen minutes to take a shower". As voluntary INS interpreter, she was not allowed to communicate with the outside world. But she decided to ignore this condition: "I took my chance, I made phone calls ... somebody had to do it!" (Mayas 1995). In early February 1992, HP referred, for the first time, to unnamed interpreters on Guantanamo working for the INS as sources of information. Three of them reportedly furnished information on the conditions, under which asylum interviews were conducted. Moreover, they reported that hundreds of dossiers got lost in the camp (HP 79:1,20).

After the USSC decision of January 31, 1992 marking the end of "Haitian Refugee Center vs. Baker", law students at the *Allard K. Lowenstein International Human Rights Clinic* at *Yale Law School* sought to learn more about conditions on Guan-

---

"Women In the NAACP" (WIN) headed by Frances D. Hooks, national WIN Coordinator. Mrs. Hooks, who was part of the delegation along with Henderson and McMillan, said that WIN would continue its efforts to assist the refugees (NAACP 1992a:1-2).

tanamo and to explore alternative legal claims on behalf of the Haitian refugees. As three of "over one hundred past and present Yale Law students who worked on behalf of the Haitians" related, Guantanamo refugees' relatives in the US and Creole interpreters under INS contract told them about plans to interview screened-in Haitians a second time by applying the higher standard of a "well-founded fear of persecution" (Clawson et al. 1994:2350-2351). According to HP, the US military was now "ready for brutal repression" on Guantanamo (HP 71:8,17). In an interview with VoA, Dorancy expressed her grave concerns about an incident involving a young Haitian refugee at Guantanamo accusing a US soldier of rape (HP 79:1,20).

The law students, among them two of my would-be informants, referred to a "sympathetic contact", through which a request for counsel by "screened-in" Haitians on Guantanamo was faxed to *Yale's Lowenstein Clinic* in March 1992. The Clinic was founded by several Yale Law School students and Professor Koh in 1991. From its inception, it collaborated with the *Center for Constitutional Rights* (CCR) in furthering the use of US courts as a forum for challenging international human rights abuses suffered by victims from foreign countries. It did so on the basis of the so-called Alien Tort Claims Act. While helping litigate the lawsuit "Paul vs. Avril", students in the Clinic had developed a special interest in Haiti and also established contact with the young Aristide government. In addition to relatives of the refugees and to INS interpreters on Guantanamo, three Haitian service organizations wishing to represent the refugees also contacted the law students. They reported to have been the ones, who "initiated and litigated" the case after approaching Koh and Ratner to discuss the possibility of filing a lawsuit (Clawson et al. 1994:2337,2342,2338,2350,2351). Among the three Haitian service organizations was HCC.

Frank of HCC, who was confronted with an increased case load in immigration assistance, testified to have received "a lot of phone calls" from parents and "relatives of people that were in Guantanamo" about "three months after the coup". One of the "main families" in Brooklyn approaching HCC was the family of Mireille Berger. Frank contacted the advisory board of HCC to convene a meeting in late February 1992. The board discussed the "problem of the refugees" and the "position we were going to take". In early March, Frank personally contacted the *Center for Immigrant Rights*, CCR, Daugaard of the "group at Yale University", and "our pro bono lawyers" in order to ask "what could be done because of the problem in Guantanamo". He asked Ratner, in "what capacity his center could help us in suing the Government in order to allow those clients ... to have counsels" (Frank 1993:158,101,168,101-103,159,121,134,122). From its outset in 1982, HCC "looked publicly like a black ethnic organization with the sole purpose of incorporating Haitian immigrants into life" in the US (Basch et al. 1994:204). But besides providing ethnically oriented community services, HCC is also nationalistically oriented, as it has plans to open an office in Haiti, which would be, as Frank told me, an "extension of what we have here" (Frank 1995).[213] Due to his political biography, Frank was hardly considered an Aristide-

---

[213] Moreover, former Haitian president Ertha Trouillot, the interim president preceding Aristide, came to power with the backing of a coalition of forces that included the Haitian priests, who founded HCC. Frank, former director of HCC-member HNSC in Manhattan, was later appointed by Trouillot as Haitian Consul of New York. Raymond Joseph, conservative editor of HO, was named representative of the Haitian government in Washington (Basch et al. 1994:209).

follower during the Haitian crisis.[214] As Guy Victor and Dr. Pierre-Louis of HCAIDS told me, he had only been accepted as a community leader within the framework of the Haitian centers (Victor 1996;Pierre-Louis 1997).

According to Koh, the Clinic "felt obliged" to test certain academic assertions in practice, when the INS finally determined in March to reinterview, without lawyers present, some 3,000 Haitians with "credible fears of persecution" held incommunicado at Guantanamo. These assertions made by Ratner and Koh, who both taught a clinical course at Yale, centered around what Koh called "transnational public law litigation". He argued that private litigants increasingly turn to US courts to enforce internationally recognized human rights standards against foreign and US government officials as part of an emerging "transnational analogue" to the domestic phenomenon of "public law litigation". Koh, Ratner, their co-counsels, and the law students (Yale team) filed suit against an array of US officials in Brooklyn Federal Court on behalf of the class of "screened-in" Haitian refugees and several service organizations, which sought to give the refugees legal advice (right-to-counsel) (Koh 1994:2394-2396).

The lawsuit was ultimately captioned "Haitian Centers Council v. McNary" due to the fact that HCC was the only one of the three organizational plaintiffs in the case with headquarters in Brooklyn. One of the two other plaintiffs was NCHR (NCHR13:3).[215] The lawsuit ended up on the desk of Judge Sterling Johnson, Jr. of the Federal District Court for the Eastern District of New York, which is located in Brooklyn. Given that Johnson was a former Marine, whom the Yale students said had served on Guantanamo, he seemed to be disadvantageous compared with the judge originally desired.[216] NCHR asked HCC, due to its location, to act as the main plaintiff in the case. But beside that, HCC´s role in the lawsuit was minimal (McCalla 1995;Clawson et al. 1994:2355). As the lawsuit unfolded, the narrow right-to-counsel case expanded into a broad legal challenge ranging from extra-territorial refoulement of Haitians to the sustained offshore internment of HIV-infected Haitians on Guantanamo. Over time, the original party set composed of US officials, Haitian aliens, and refugee service organizations came to embrace a broad array of

1. intergovernmental organizations
2. international human rights NGOs
3. domestic civil rights groups
4. "rule of law" proponents
5. refugee advocates, and
6. members of Congress.[217]

---

[214] In contrast to Glick Schiller, HP contended that Trouillot was "imposed on Père Adrien" by US Ambassador Adams. HP´s headline was "Ertha Trouillot: A President made in USA" (HP 202:13).

[215] Besides NCHR and HCC, the Immigration Clinic of the *Jerome N. Frank Legal Services Organization* of the *Yale Law School* belonged to the original group of plaintiffs. They asserted that the First Amendment protects advocacy organization´s right of access to the Guantanamo Haitians to disseminate legal advice. In the beginning, the lead defendant in the case was the Bush Administration´s INS Commissioner Gene McNary, who was substituted under Clinton by Chris Sale (Koh 1994:2396,2395).

[216] As McCalla told me, NCHR originally planned to have the court of jurisdiction in Manhattan, because the judge was believed to be more likely to handle the case favorably. But the inofficial procedure he dubbed "court shopping" ultimately failed (McCalla 1995).

[217] For the numerous groups of the *amici curiae* supporting the plaintiffs in each category of actors, see

They comprised what Koh calls a

1. "sprawling transnational party structure" as one of five distinctive features of transnational public lawsuits. The remaining four are
2. a "transnational claim structure",
3. a "prospective focus",
4. the "transportability of norms", and
5. a process of "institutional dialogue" (Koh 1994:2396,2400,2399,2398).[218]

Since access to the US naval base was strictly controlled, the students in the Yale team found other ways to collect "more detailed information to fill out the emerging legal claims". The team gathered affidavits from people, who had worked as INS interpreters on Guantanamo. In addition, students at Yale´s Immigration Clinic with plans to work in March with HRC in processing Haitian asylum claims were asked to bring along to Miami a list of questions to ask refugees, who had just arrived from Guantanamo (Clawson et al. 1994:2352). At the same time, Ninaj Raoul and Marie-Lilly Serrat, two Haitian-Americans, who would later found HWHR in Brooklyn, decided to travel to Guantanamo to work as interpreters for the INS. They were joined by a Haitian woman named Nicole (Raoul 1995;Mayas 1996). HP quoted Serrat as someone, who "has worked in the camp of Guantanamo". Speaking on *Radio Tropicale* on February 22, she gave a few examples of how the US military sought "to discourage the refugees to stay ... They are mentally and physically weakened. And when they are in this state, they send them back to their country". HP quoted George Wilson ("Moumousse") as saying in the same broadcast that the US tried hard to isolate the Guantanamo refugees "like prisoners of war" by severing all outside contacts (HP 84:9).

On Guantanamo, Raoul and Serrat met Evelyne Longchamps, co-founder and Board member of the Brooklyn-based *Haitian Women Program* (HWP). Mme Longchamps would come to work closely with Mike Wishnie, one of the law students in the Yale team, when she also served as an interpreter (Wishnie 1995). The practical contributions of some US-based Haitians to the lawsuit should not be underestimated. As Frank of HCC put it in a more fundamental way: "If they [i.e. the refugees´ relatives] did not come for help, we would not have that lawsuit at all" (1993:156).

In March 1992, approximately 40 Immigration Clinic students came to help HRC file asylum claims for more than 3,000 Haitian refugees. Among them were not only students from Yale, but also from Case Western, Harvard, Columbia, Boston, Notre Dame, and Florida universities. They were assisted by an equal number of Haitian-American students from Miami Central High School, who were on "loan" to HRC. Their role was that of interpreter. As St. Paul reported, three of the students, "Petit", "Manoucheta Dieudonne" and "Shirley Augustin", grew up in the US and speak and understand English much better than they do French or Creole. HRC administrator Sharon Brown did not mind the slow pace of the interviewing process, which was due to the language barrier, since "[t]his could be an all-or-nothing shot" (1992:3A). The Immigration Clinic students stayed at the *Budget Inn* in the center of Miami´s Little

---

Koh (1994:2399). Koh is also a member of HRW´s Board of Directors (HRW 1993:i).
[218] For the definitions of the five distinctive features, see Koh (1994:2398,2403).

Haiti (Clawson et al. 1994:2352). Gilbert commended all the students´ contributions to HRC´s work in favor of Haitian refugees (HP 91:8).

According to sworn affidavits from interpreters, the number "screened in" or approved to pursue asylum in the US soared to 80% between December 1991 and January 1992, but pressure was then applied to "screen in" fewer Haitians.[219] One interviewer wrote: "Immigration let us know they were very unhappy with this higher approval rate. They began to accuse us of testifying on behalf of the Haitians ... (They) began hiding their notes from ... (the interpreters). We could no longer see whether the final translation was correct as we had before" (St. Paul 1992:3A). The Bush Administration claimed that INS adjudicators at Guantanamo had been deceived by human rights groups and the Haitians themselves, which is why INS reports called for "re-screening of the Haitians screened-in" (HRW/A,NCHR 1992:3). Mayas said that it was important for the interpreters to know how to "play the politics". "But you have to use the right attitude, because ... this is America! Take it or leave it! If you gonna live in it, if you can fight them, you gonna have to join them ... I was friendly with everybody, and that´s how I was gathering information" (Mayas 1995).[220] As Aubourg told me, INS officials did not believe Haitian refugees even before 1986, unless they saw "somebody with his ears cut off" (Aubourg 1996).

In a parallel development, the INS building in New York City was the site of a small action of civil disobedience, on which HP reported at the end of March. The *New York Coalition for a Free Haiti* and *Pax Christi Metro New York* had organized the sit-in of about 30 protesters. They came to denounce the deportation procedures, to demand the tightening of the embargo, and to support dancer Dunham in her hunger strike (HP 99:9). It seems rather unlikely that any Haitians were among the participants, given the line of reporting by Gilbert. He announced in the same HP-issue Dunham´s decision to end her 47-day-old hunger strike. As if to contrast her well-publicized activism with that of the Haitian diaspora, he emphasized that Dunham had not hesitated to put her life on the line to protest against the bad treatment accorded "her compatriots from her country of adoption: the Haitian boat people". To prove her credentials, Gilbert pointed out that Dunham lived 50 years of her life in Haiti.[221] In contrast, he continued, many "of our compatriots on foreign soil often tried, out of shame or a inferiority complex, to hide their origin" (HP 97:8).

In late February 1992, HP had mentioned Dunham´s hunger strike for the first time (HP 83:1,18). The *Haiti Commission*´s "soirée" at *Columbia University* on March 11 was dedicated to Dunham (HP 95:9). But other than that, there were no further visible signs of solidarity with the African-American dancer. Two weeks later, however, HP was able to report briefly on what it exaggeratedly called the "Haitian presence" at a mass demonstration in Washington on May 16. The protest march of 200,000 people was organized by a multitude of US groups proclaiming their solidarity with Rodney King under the motto "Save our cities, save our children". According to

---

[219] Through May 24, 10,562 Haitians, or 30%, had been found by INS adjudicators to have a "credible fear" of persecution if returned to Haiti, according to NCHR. These "screened in" refugees would be brought to the US, where they could apply for political asylum (HRW/A,NCHR 1992:3).

[220] When Guantanamo was reopened in 1994, Mayas added, the INS "would not hire us, because they knew ... we were helping the Haitian people!" (Mayas 1995).

[221] Dunham first went to Haiti in 1935 as an anthropology student from the *University of Chicago* and bought property there in 1947. She lived half of each year in Haiti (Brozan 1992:B7).

HP, one of the "most imaginative demonstrators" was Pierre Ilincier of HAUP, who impersonated Jesus Christ by carrying a cross wrapped in the national colours of the US in order to illustrate the situation of the Haitian refugees (HP 118:8). There were some tensions between Dorsinville and Frank over the question of allowing political activities within the framework of HCC.[222] The absence of any public signs of solidarity with Dunham is explicable when considering HP´s renewed reporting on Haitian refugees in late May. The Haitian weekly now associated some OAS members´ sudden urgency in May to recognize a "new kind of pressure" on the side of the US to resolve the Haitian crisis with the increasing outpouring of Haitian refugees. HP was afraid that the pressure emanating from the refugee stream might lead to a higher degree of collaboration between the US and the *de facto* regime. It inferred this from two statements made by Secretary of State Lawrence Eagleberger, the "architect of a plan providing for the `cohabitation´ of Aristide and Cédras".[223] In HP´s view, the putschists reacted to those signals by commencing to arrest Haitians wanting to leave the country (HP 120:10).

HP had expressed a similar concern one month earlier: The growing number of Haitian refugees in the Dominican Republic, which claimed to have arrived at levels of "saturation", might lead President Balaguer to threaten another massive deportation program. HP warned that Balaguer could make of "these compatriots" a "blackmailing object" permitting him "to influence at a maximum Haiti´s political orientation" (HP 101:20). Similarly, HP interpreted in mid-June the nomination of Marc Bazin as Prime Minister under the Bush Administration´s "final stage of its plan for Haiti", for it could now hope to resolve the Haitian (refugee) crisis soon: More than 500 Haitians were being returned to Haiti almost every day, the Haitian weekly reported (HP 128:8-9). This reasoning is quite different from the refugee issue strategy preferred by NCHR and its allied groups. As has been shown above, they also associated a "blackmailing" function with the refugee stream. But while they tried to utilize the refugees as a bargaining chip vis-a-vis the US government, HP was afraid that the US might use it as well to further tighten its grip on Haiti.

On the legal battle front, Judge Johnson of the Federal District Court in Brooklyn ruled, on March 27, that the INA provided the Haitians with a right to obtain legal counsel to assist them in their second interviews. He did so on the "solid basis" of three pieces of evidence provided by the Yale team for distinguishing the new case from HRC v. Baker.[224] In preparation for a preliminary injunction hearing to take place on April 1, Judge Johnson granted the legal team temporary access to Guantanamo. It was only allowed to go to the US military airport located on one side of the bay, to which the plaintiffs had to be brought from the detention camps. When the team ar-

---

[222] Dorsinville was more permissive by not objecting to groups having pro-Aristide meetings in the office of HAUP. Frank, on the other hand, had misgivings about these, referring to restrictions on political involvement mandated by law for certain non-profit organizations (Dorsinville 1995;Frank 1995).

[223] Eagleberger had declared, first, that "these people have to learn to live together" and, second, that "one cannot continue to do nothing" with regard to the refugee flow (HP 120:10).

[224] The Bush Administration´s position in the case was two-fold: First, it argued that the 1967 Refugee Protocol was not "self-executing" and therefore not applicable as a source of rights. Second, it maintained that neither section 243(h) of the INA nor Article 33 of the 1951 Refugee Convention applied extraterritorially such as in international waters, but only "within the territory of a contracting State" (Frelick 1993:679-680;Clawson et al. 1994:2346).

rived, the refugees feared repatriation and refused to board the boat that was to take them there. The US government agreed to let McCalla go to the refugee camps to convince the clients that the legal team was waiting for them to conduct depositions and affidavits that were to demonstrate to Judge Johnson the need for counsel in the second interviews. The team was composed of professors, students, court reporters, and interpreters (Clawson et al. 1994:2343,2354-2355,2337).[225]

In early April, HP mentioned the Yale team´s trip to Guantanamo of March 28 following Judge Johnson´s ruling. It called his verdict the "first victory in the legal battle" coming as the "result of mobilization initiated in many areas". HP quoted from a NCHR press release of March 24, according to which "Ratner ... showed as evidence of [US] governmental intimidations a letter transmitted to him clandestinely and signed by representatives of the Association pour les exilés politiques haitiens ... an organization formed by refugees detained at Guantanamo [who] accuse [US] government officials of `employing strong pressure'" to have them abandon the asylum process (HP 101:8,20).[226] The six refugees, whom HEAR gave the opportunity to "tell their stories" at its rally on April 6, originally came from Guantanamo. A few of them were recruited by Mayas (HEAR 1995). According to HP, the longest part of the afternoon was dedicated to them (HP 102:8).[227] Stories from more recently arrived refugees interviewed by returning students in Miami confirmed and supplemented the information the Yale team had gained from what it called "our Guantanamo contacts". In addition, Guttentag, Ratner, and Tringali deposed INS officials in Miami and in Washington to come up with more "various bits of information". Pieced together by Koh in New Haven, it undercut the US´s argument that the refugee camps were humanitarian and orderly. Especially the story of "Marie Zette" established "irreparable harm resulting from the U.S. government´s policy and illustrated the human costs of the government´s administrative errors". She was screened-in, mistakenly repatriated, and upon return killed by the Haitian military (Clawson et al. 1994:2356-2357).

Nonetheless, the USSC, on April 22, stayed the injunction granted by Judge Johnson on April 6 pending appeal.[228] One day later, the team received a covert call from a "high-level source" stationed on Guantanamo warning: "If there is anything you

---

[225] In hindsight, the students extended their "special thanks" to Aubourg, part of NCHR´s staff at the time of the Guantanamo trip, whom they called "our trusted interpreter and friend" (ibid.).

[226] In the same report, HP further noted that the majority of the 17,000 Haitians, who had left Haiti since the coup, had already been repatriated by the USCG, the new tactics of which was to deport the Haitians right after intercepting them (HP 101:8,20). While the Haitian *de facto* regime agreed to accept refugees from Guantanamo, it refused to comply with demands from the Cuban government to accept Haitians returning voluntarily. HP also reported on Judge Johnson´s ruling of April 6 in favor of Haitian refugees. Ratner was reported to have announced that an office would be opened on Guantanamo to secure legal counseling for the refugees. HP asserted that Bush and his Ambassador, "Bourik Chaje", knew exactly the reason for the new wave of refugees: repression by the Haitian military (HP 103:8,9).

[227] One of the exiled Haitians, Chéry Dupuy, sang a self-composed song relating the pitfalls of the Haitian people after the coup. Another, Victor Pierre, said that he was a refugee, "who has gone through misery because of George Bush and Raoul Cédras". And the Haitian director of the journal *Children Express* stated in addition that "[w]e have to tell them that they must not send back the Haitian people any longer". Among the speakers, who were coordinated by Guy Victor, was also Leblanc of HP in her capacity as representative of the *10e of New York* (HP 102:8).

[228] According to Koh, the USSC voted against the Haitians "no less than eight times" in 1992 alone (1994:2413).

can do for your clients, do it now; the government is beginning interviews and repatriations". Another "urgent call" told the team that 89 of the Haitians were being forcibly repatriated that night. The team learned later "from a Guantanamo contact" that the refugees refused to get off the USCG cutter upon arrival in Haiti, because they could see the Haitian military waiting. When Bush issued the "Kennebunkport Order" on Memorial Day 1992, refugee advocates agreed in a nationwide conference call that the Yale team was "the only team in position to challenge" the executive order (Clawson et al. 1994:2358-2359). According to Koh, the order was the "strongest U.S. assault ever against the nonrefoulement principle" (1994:2402), since it did away with the INS screening procedure altogether. By summarily returning all Haitian refugees to Haiti, the distinction between economic migrants and political refugees, which Bush had been willing to make on November 21, 1991, was gone (Frelick 1993:678,681). On May 27, Governor Clinton indicated, for the first time, his opposition to the Bush Administration's policy of summary repatriation of Haitian refugees (Clawson et al. 1994:2348), of whom the USCG intercepted 13,103 in May, an all-year-high.

In the first week of June, HP reported about Bush's Kennebunkport Order. Considered by his Administration as a "horde of barbarians or primates", the weekly opined, Bush had thereby declared "total war" on the refugees. HP saw the Bush Administration's real calculation as simply hoping that the refugees would drown. This point was made by Jean-Claude Bajeux of the *Centre Oecuménique pour les Droits Humains* (CODH), who was quoted by HP as dubbing the order's goal as follows: "Let them sail, let them sink". Cardinal O'Connor and Conyers were reported to have issued similar statements, with the latter calling the new policy in ND a "policy of drowning". In addition, HP identified the Guantanamo refugees as an "ideal pretext" for the Bush Administration to reinforce its military presence on Castro's Cuba. Referring to the NYT, HP mentioned that "US officials fear ... that human and civil rights groups might initiate a lawsuit" (HP 123:14). But having been stayed a second time on August 1 by the USSC, the Yale team now turned to "advocacy outside the courts" in the form of "refugee resettlement, Guantanamo client service, and media and political activism" (Clawson et al. 1994:2360).

5.4.4 NCHR's Lobbying with Haitian Refugees Until the Transition to Clinton

In a NCHR conference call of May 26, 1992, a synopsis was given of the nationwide conference call "yesterday with litigators". The minutes confirm that participants in that call considered it "more profitable" to ask Judge Johnson for "some relief". The seventeen NCHR conference call participants, among them a HRC representative, stated that their objective was to "stop [the] Executive Order". They said the order was "based on a lie" regarding the overcrowding of the refugee camp at Guantanamo, as the Bush Administration had alleged (NCHR13:3). According to Frelick, the "parameters of the discussion about refugee rights" were "radically changed" by the Kennebunkport Order (1993:681), which compelled refugee advocates to readjust their strategy accordingly. As McCalla put it: "In the process of trying to get meaningful remedies for Haitian refugees, we have been forced by the circumstances to depart from our long-standing position on interdiction per se" (NCHR13:2). NCHR had sharply denounced the executive order as a "heinous violation of both U.S. statutes and international law" in an immediately distributed press release (NCHR6:1). HP quoted from a corresponding letter to Bush dated May 27 and signed by "very numerous US organizations", among them NCHR, NAACP, and AFL-CIO, as the weekly stressed (HP 124:6,20). The letter provided some of the language for an Amicus Brief to be used in the trial to show "that the President stands alone", as McCalla informed the 26 potential signers of the Brief on June 10, among them Père Sansaricq (NCHR12:1)

NCHR used depositions taken of US officials in the course of litigating, especially of Gunther O. Wagner, as additional source of information for its report *Half the Story*.[229] Even though US officials including Aronson were caught in the "embarrassing position" of asserting that the US was able to monitor the safety of returned refugees despite a vast reduction of Embassy personnel, they maintained to have interviewed some 2,500 repatriates "without finding a single sustainable claim of reprisal or persecution related to repatriated status", the NCHR report stated. In conclusion, NCHR found that the "primary purpose" of the monitoring effort was "to discredit repatriates' stories" and to serve "a public-relations purpose" in defense of Bush's Kennebunkport Order (HRW/A,NCHR 1992:4-6,1-2).

NCHR's analysis found that the US Embassy cables revealed a "somewhat more serious effort" than the USJD-reports. The report by Wagner, a senior INS intelligence agent and the leader of at least three INS survey missions responsible for about 600 repatriate interviews, was found to be "more baldly prejudiced". NCHR criticized the "brevity of the interviews" lasting five minutes or less and the "very public nature of the inquiry". Another problem was the "skewed sample of repatriates".[230] In particular, investigators' "disturbingly frequent contact with Haitian military officials", who were notified in advance of the INS teams' intention to conduct interviews, made it unlikely for repatriates to emerge from hiding. Wagner was shown to have displayed a high "degree of credulity" toward Haitian authorities such as the *Immigration Identification Department* at the Port-au-Prince Police Headquarters or those at the *National Penitentiary*. The INS teams accepted biased views of local conditions, which resulted from what NCHR called "'fraud detection' priorities of the investigators" toward Haitians claiming to have credible fears of persecution (HRW/A,NCHR 1992:6-16). HP did not often report on the US government's efforts to monitor repatriated boat people in Haiti, which was possibly due in part to a lack of information resulting from many Haitian journalists' escape from Haiti.[231]

---

[229] Other sets of documents used for analyzing the US government's efforts to monitor repatriated boat people in Haiti were more than 200 pages of unclassified telegrams from the US Embassy in Port-au-Prince sent between mid-February and mid-May 1992, the 11-page "Special Intelligence Report, Haiti" of February 24, 1992 authored by Wagner, as well as the 11-page "Haitian Situation Report, Repatriation" issued by the USJD (ibid.).

[230] Those were excluded who remained in hiding, feared emerging in public, or lacked confidence in the *Haitian Red Cross*, the cooperation of which was sought by the INS.

[231] But in mid-February 1992, referring to a HRC press release, HP wrote about human rights violations perpetrated against returned Haitians, which it contrasted with Baker's testimony before the House Foreign Affairs Committee (HP 79:1,20). As to the US government's flawed monitoring efforts, HP opined one week later that it amounts to totally misjudging Haitian mentality to expect candid answers, if questions were asked by US officials, who were "currently perceived as the principal enemies of refugees" (HP 81:8,17).

In the conference call of May 26, other measures furthering NCHR's refugee-oriented strategy were discussed. Participants considered trying to have Congress "stop funding used to ship Haitians back". It was suggested that the Urban Aid bill could be an option for "stopping repatriation with funding" (NCHR12:1,2). Sen. Kennedy's bill, the "Democracy in Haiti Act of 1992" introduced on April 2, included a provision authorizing appropriations (MIS/MIN 1992). As early as January 29, participants in a Task Force conference call agreed that "we should find out how much Guantanamo costs per day" (NCHR12:2). A report by the *General Accounting Office* (GAO), later requested by Rangel, identified the costs of US involvement in Haiti. The GAO-report found that the largest US expenditures had been related to the interdiction, detention, processing, and/or repatriation of asylum-seekers by USCG and the Pentagon, accounting for $59.12 and $24.52 million through September 1993, respectively (1993:1-3).[232] The May 26 conference call participants further agreed that an "emergency aid vehicle" was needed in Congress: "We will try to attach something to this to override [Bush's] Executive Order", they devised (NCHR12:2).

NCHR's "efforts to obtain meaningful legislation" had resulted in three new bills by early July: H.R.3844 was now "at the Senate desk", H.R.5360 introduced by Stephen Solarz to overturn Bush's Kennebunkport Order was waiting for action at the House Foreign Affairs Committee, and H.R.5267 introduced by Conyers sought to grant TPS to Haitian refugees (NCHR13:2).[233] At the end of May, HP informed its readers that TPS was still the solution "generally preconceived by groups defending Haitian refugees" (HP 123:15). On June 11 and 17, the Subcommittees on Western Hemisphere Affairs and International Operations of the House Foreign Affairs Committee held a joint hearing and markup on H.R.5360. Among the witnesses invited to testify were five Congressmen and Koh from Yale, Helton of LCHR as well as Ryscavage of USSC/MRS.[234] Koh emphasized that the present total refugee quota of only 3,500 for Latin America and the Caribbean would be "quickly exhausted". And Helton described the US Administration's policy as "deviant", "hypocritical", "unlawful", and "parochial" (Cong3:v,71,95;USCC/MRS 1992/93:15). NCHR and its allied groups took advantage of the hearings by advocating, at the same time, in Congressional offices for the rights of Haitian refugees. They did so, for the first time it seems, along with an unknown number of the very people affected: "Lobbying with Haitian refugees", the ten participants of a Task Force conference call on June 17 noted with satisfaction, "went well. We could repeat the effort in a more planned and organized way" (NCHR12:1). After the hearing, refugee advocates sought to link the Solarz/Kennedy

---

[232] Between October 1, 1991, and March 31, 1993, ten US government agencies expended or obligated about $211 million for Haitian-related activities (ibid.). The US reportedly spent nearly $200 million by September 1994 for "rescuing Haitians" on the high seas and building camps (NYT 09/02/94:A9).

[233] Conyers' bill also called for US "support for the restoration of democratic constitutional government in Haiti", the termination of the USHIA, and the establishment by the US of "expanded processing facilities for Haitians seeking refuge" (MIS/MIN 1992). Solarz' H.R.5360 and its Senate version S.2826 introduced by Sen. Kennedy were no Haiti-specific bills, but were meant to codify the applicability of Article 33 of the Refugee Convention to areas outside US territorial boundaries in response to Bush's Kennebunkport Order (NCHR11:iii).

[234] Winter of USCR and Herbert W. Chilstrom, Bishop of the *Evangelical Lutheran Church in America*, submitted statements (Cong3:v).

bill to a piece of legislation such as the "Soviet Aid" bill considered to be "veto-proof" (NCHR11:iii).

But NCHR deemed it insufficient to bring Haitian refugees into play in the Congressional arena only, because the targeted bills were not really moving "despite important endorsements", and "very little" on Capitol Hill including the Soviet Aid bill really appeared to be veto-proof,[235] as Muzaffar Chishti of ILGWU observed at the Board of Directors Meeting of July 13. The participants realized that NCHR depended "on the goodwill of the American people in a time of economic hardship, when the prevailing mood seems to be against opening borders to refugees". They therefore considered it to be "crucial to keep the issue at the forefront of U.S. media attention".[236] NCHR´s "greatest weakness" was identified as being the failure "to attach human faces to the important issues of refugee protection". A considerable part of the meeting thus focused on a proposal for empowering a "Creative Outreach Committee" to work on building greater visibility for Haitian refugees in the US. The creation of such a committee was suggested by Demme (NCHR12;NCHR11:v,iii).

The May 26 conference call participants had already realized that they depended on outside help. They understood that "[g]rassroots/lobbying people need solid suggestions as what they can do besides just screaming out against [the] policy". They also recognized the need to "[g]et more leaders of [the] Haitian community in NY and elsewhere" (NCHR12:1,2,3). As NCHR´s Planning Committee recalled in mid-1993, the group urged leaders in the Haitian community to focus on US refugee policy. But fearing that demanding asylum for Haitian refugees would "somehow" deviate attention from efforts to reinstate Aristide, as the committee members recorded with some lack of understanding, the leaders initially refused: "The struggle for Haitian refugees was therefore developed largely with little input from the Haitian community, a striking difference with the refugee struggle in the 70s and early 80s" (NCHR21:7). In Guy Victor´s judgement, NCHR certainly "served its purpose" in putting "a lot of pressure on the US government". But not as much as the Haitian grassroots organizations that led the Haitian mass protests. The NYPD was "praying for Aristide to come back" in the face of streets congested with thousands and thousands of demonstrating Haitians, he told me in hindsight (Victor 1996).

The Planning Committee´s comparison is in line with Buchanan Stafford´s observation concerning African-American activism. She recapitulated that in the 1980s Haitians had "moved to establish closer ties, particularly political ones, with black Americans". She mentioned the "striking example" of "the support Haitians garnered from black American politicians", particularly those in the CBC, "for the Haitian refugee issue". In those instances, the "common racial identity" of black Americans and Haitians became "more salient than ethnic differences". Since the refugee issue was

---

[235] According to a single-page fax of July 29, 1992, included in Rangel´s "support" folder, but not stating any sender nor a text, the Pennsylvania-based *Coalition for Haitian Concerns* (CHC), also a member of NCHR, HCC, HRC, and HAUP were part of a "partial list of organizations urging Congress to amend the Soviet bill to allow for modest benefits for Haitian refugees". According to a brochure of 1984, the purpose of CHC, whose board displays an ethnic mix, is "[t]o work for the well-being of the Haitian communtiy, the Haitian refugees and other refugee groups…" (CHC 1984:8).

[236] The month of July, in which the Board of Directors Meeting took place, saw only 7 NYT-articles on Haiti published, including 5 on the refugee issue, which was a sharp decrease from 23 (17) articles in May, when Bush issued the Kennebunkport Order (see chart).

seen as "an example of racial discrimination and bias", issues affecting Haitians also became "a focal point for black American politicians". But she erroneously predicted that "perhaps these political ties ... will become closer", as more Haitians would become citizens and exercise their right to vote (1987:151-152). Transnational centrifugal forces since the early 1980s have increased the nationalist orientation of Haitians in the US, with the two significant milestones being Duvalier´s fall in 1986 and Aristide´s election in 1990. Conversely, African-Americans have been much more inclined to see the Haitian refugee issue as "an example of racial discrimination" than Haitians themselves, which is a function of the former group´s higher integration into the US social structure.

The construct of race/color in US society is conceptualized into mutually exclusive bipolar categories of black and white, which engenders the perception of a polarized society organized primarily along racial lines. In contrast, Haitians shun any fixed category of racial ascription as expressed in the distance from any total identification with African-Americans. There is rather a continuum constructed as a gradation along the lines of color, a fluidity in the meanings of blackness, which is closely connected to the changing dynamics of class relations. The overlapping of race and class and the possibility to change social identity is paraphrased in the common Haitian saying: "A rich black is a mulatto, and a poor mulatto is a black". With the successful Haitian slave revolution, racial meanings moved from the realm of social relations to the state. In the ensuing struggle to control state power, race was socially rather than genetically defined (Charles 1992:104-109;Charles 1990:74-99). To create a national consciousness capable of defusing tensions over the color issue, Article 14 of the Imperial Constitution of 1805 stated that all Haitians were to be referred to "only by the generic word black". Thus all popular racial categories deriving from the colonial classificatory system were incorporated in the Haitian concept of nationhood, which became equated with the broad category of blackness encompassing all social classes (Trouillot 1990:45;Charles 1990:71).

Bringing their understanding of class, race, and ethnic relations with them, Haitians in the US share the unique collective memory of race-pride based on their historical experience. Coupled with a limited incorporation into the US social structure, this uniqueness makes them cognizant of racism in US society, but at a distance: "As foreigners they have nothing to fear, they are external to the U.S. racial conflicts", as Charles explains (1992:114). Consequently, US organizations in New York, which worked with Haitian entrant programs in the early 1980s to further their agenda of incorporating Haitian immigrants into the social and political fabric of the US for the sake of national unity, largely failed. African-American professionals and politicians, who emerged as key players in these incorporative initiatives, served as mentors in the project of resettling Haitian boat people. In approaching the Haitian leadership as ethnic spokespersons for the broader Haitian immigrant population, they saw ethnicity and race as overlapping identities for Haitians, who were to give up their allegiance to Haiti and to become US citizens. But neither the leadership of Haitian organizations nor the Haitian immigrant population at large were "deterred from continuing and increasing their transnational practices" (Basch et al. 1994:201-203).

At the July 13 NCHR Board of Directors Meeting, Wolchock now suggested "pairing celebrities", e.g. from the entertainment industry, with "Haitian refugees who´ve passed through [Guantanamo] and sending them to Capitol Hill to meet with key legislators [and] aides". This would be a good way to solve the problems of getting access to legislative appointments, she said (NCHR11:v,iii;NCHR12). The first opportunity to test part of this proposal in practice came, when NAACP and *TransAfrica* organized a "demonstration of civil disobedience" on September 9 in front of the White House. Planning for the protest march began as early as July. African-Americans interested in participating were asked in a joint July 10 "Dear Colleague"-letter to be prepared to be arrested and to be willing to pay a $50 fine (Rangel92f:1).[237] *TransAfrica* was in contact with NCHR through telephone, fax, and occasional meetings for "policy planning", but not with any other "Haitian community organization", as I was told.[238] QC/QP, however, whose "Haiti Working Group" was in touch with both NAACP and *TransAfrica*, informed at least two Haitian organizations about the planned march (Rangel92h:2).

Deliberating on the prospects of H.R.5360, fourteen Task Force conference call participants not only agreed, on August 21, that NCHR staff was to be in charge of writing a "Dear Colleague"-letter on human rights abuses in Haiti to be distributed on Capitol Hill. They also consented that "[w]e must do some lobbying on [the] 9th and 10th of September. The 10th will be lobbying day". The participants were asked to "bring in Haitians", while NAACP and *TransAfrica* were expected to "bring in prominent members of organizations" (NCHR12:1).[239] At long last, 40 refugee advocates, including Haitian nationals, participated on September 10 in what USCC´s MRS called "Haiti Lobby Day", a "principal organizer" of which MRS claimed to be (1992/93:15). Aided by Creole interpreters, they visited about 96 Congressional offices to urge their support for H.R.5360. According to NCHR, "[e]ach of these consultations included an unusual opportunity, coordinated by our staff, for a Haitian asylum-seeker who had arrived from Guantánamo, to share her/his personal experiences with a congressional aide" (NCHR6:2). Besides NCHR and USCC/MRS, the *People for the American Way*, CWS, NIF, and AJC were among the groups participating. They seized on media attention generated by the NAACP/*TransAfrica*-led protest march the day before (Haiti8b:4,13). The protest was well-publicized in part, because 95 demonstrators were temporarily arrested for demonstrating in front of the White House, as the WP reported (Lee,Sinclair 1992:A9).

---

[237] NAACP and *TransAfrica* intended to employ a specific style of policy mobilization, which had been a standard of the civil rights movement of the 1960s. Recrafted by *TransAfrica* in the early 1980s, this style involved the symbolic arrest of well-known personalities from a broad cross section of races, religions, and occupation groups. It brought many, who were familiar with its use, back to march in the picket lines of what emerged as a political coalition, the "Free South Africa Movement" (FSAM), which was, indeed, similar to the old civil rights movement coalition. With the tactic of civil disobedience, *TransAfrica* and the managers of FSAM sought to transmit mass influence to the legislative and executive branches of the US government (Walters 1987:75-77,79). For some background information on the history, membership composition, and institutional structure of *TransAfrica*, see Watanabe 1984:70; Challenor 1981:143,170,171,172; and Walters 1987:74.
[238] Statement by Mr. Munthali of *TransAfrica* in a telephone interview on February 13, 1995.
[239] In preparation of a conference call scheduled for September 4, McCalla updated NCHR´s Haiti Task Force on the "latest progress" regarding the planned protest march: "[S]ome 22 Haitian asylum seekers will join us in Washington next week to participate in the activities scheduled for the 9th and the 10th". Moreover, "the celebrities who will be present ... will include Arthur Ashe, Katherine Dunham, and Academy Award winners Jonathan Demme and Edward Saxon" (NCHR12:1).

HP informed its readers about the demonstration not until the week of September 9 in an unrelated report (HP 140:9,18). One week later, Latour reported on the protest march of about 1,000 participants as a sign of "great Haitian-American solidarity". The long banner held by the protesters read: "Haitians locked out because they are black". Latour quoted Robinson at length regarding the low asylum approval rate for Haitians of 1.9% as testifying to "declared racism". Latour stressed that Haitians had been "present by and large" on the lawn of Lafayette Park, where they were "well visible" with their picket signs and slogans demanding a "humane policy for Haitian refugees". He interviewed some Haitian protesters like Père Sansaricq, Harry Fouché, Azela Lundi, and Marie-Thérèse Raymond. Bayyinah Bello said that the protest was "a real marriage between the American and Haitian community". Marie Bonne-Année of the *10e of New York* told Latour that "today, I feel proud to be Haitian ... We will return to Haiti" (HP 141:9,19). In contrast, Robinson told the NYT in marked ethnic terms: "For African Americans, this is not a foreign policy issue, this is a domestic issue" (Crossette 1992:19).

In a press release dated September 11, NAACP stressed the attendance at the rally of Haitian poet and singer Fritzner Pierre of the group *Lafanmi Reyini* and of five other Haitians standing in Lafayette Park (NAACP 1992b:3;HP 161:16). But those observations notwithstanding, the Haitian presence at the protest march was not large when compared to the total of participants. The "better liaison" with "leaders of [the] Haitian community in NY", which the May 26 conference call participants had called for, did not materialize for the sake of September 9. The most important exception was Bonne-Année of the *10e of New York*. With regard to the legislative branch of the US government, there was only minimal overlap between Haitian diasporic transnationalism on the one hand and NCHR's civil societal and African-American transnationalism on the other. The latter two were more engaged in ethnic extra-territorial organizing without loosing sight of the return issue, whereas the former was more inclined to nationalistic organizing while being aware of the refugees.

Even if encouraged by the opportunities to share directly the "harrowing and emblematic experiences of these refugees" with Congressional aides, NCHR and its allies saw no bill progressing beyond the "mark-up" stage in the 102nd Congress, since the US national election campaign made for an environment, in which neither major party was willing to embrace their legislative proposals (NCHR6:1-2). This explanation is reflected in the low number of only 4 NYT-articles on Haiti, including 3 on the refugee issue, published prior to the election in the month of October, the lowest number throughout 1992 (see chart). For Koh, who also participated in some nationwide conference calls, the passivity of Congress could be explained not only on political, but also on institutional grounds (1994:2412-2413). One participant in a Task Force conference call on September 16 suggested to "look ahead and start to make points with possible members of [the] new Congress". The advocates also saw the "need to encourage more letter-writing" by enlisting the "help of more grassroots organizations". They reiterated the "need to put a more human face on the plight of refugees" by having, for example, a Haitian refugee tour the US. They agreed that this "refugee tour idea" should probably "happen after the election" (NCHR12:1).

When H.R.5360 was in the mark-up stage, participants in a nationwide conference call on September 24 reiterated the appeal to "generate ... [p]hone calls and letters". Many Congressmen had told them "that they do not hear from their constituents". NCHR resolved to urge readers of *HaitiInsight* to "press the U.S. government to back President Aristide´s return and [to] support desperate Haitian refugees" by contacting members of Congress (NCHR12:1-2;Haiti4:6).[240] The call participants of September 24, who discussed "planning for after the elections", were kept posted that there was "a speaking tour for [Guantanamo] refugees in the works". There were also "more trips to Haiti planned, to generate coverage" (NCHR12:1-2). As of October 8, the speaking tour was "still in the discussion stage", with Seattle having been already "fairly planned out", however. The conference call participants of the same day, among them one HRC representative, were instructed in more detail on the concept of the speaking tour.[241] NCHR was tentatively chosen to be in charge of organizing the tour. Other groups mentioned to be called on for help were *Pax Christi*, ai, and QC/QP (NCHR12:2,3,4).[242]

After Clinton´s election, more than thirty refugee and human rights activists participated in a nationwide conference call on November 18. They discussed six policy proposals on US policy toward Haitian refugees and democracy in Haiti for later negotiations with the Clinton transition team (NCHR7;NCHR12:2). Conspicuously, the proposals submitted by McCalla and by Steve Forrester of HRC differed from the other proposals in that they stressed much more the political aspects of the crisis seen from a Haitian perspective.[243] On the other end of the spectrum was a 6-page proposal submitted by Frelick of USCR. It assumed a US point of view in demanding that the Guantanamo camp "no longer be a stepping stone" to the country in accordance with

---

[240] While it is difficult to determine if Dorancy reiterated her appeal of March to all Haitians in the 10th department to write to their members of Congress (HP 86:1,19) and if Haitians chose to act accordingly in the first place, Jean-Pierre expressed the conflicting view that "[m]any Haitians *routinely* contacted their U.S. political representatives", including the White House, the USSD, and the Pentagon (1995:203-204;author´s italics).

[241] The memorandum read: "Crew of people touring the U.S. with a refugee, a translator and a `cause spokesperson´. We would need to determine key areas to visit, where we already have coalitions who could help with footwork. We would want to visit schools, do radio talk shows, local shows and other forums ... especially where congressional support is needed" (ibid.).

[242] On October 30, shortly before election day, ai and QC/QP organized two related events. QC/QP launched an appeal to boycott the USSD´s annual Refugee Day ceremony in Washington, officially held "to give special recognition to the U.S. government for its commitment to refugees worldwide". At the same time, ai realized an "unprecedented symbolic action", sending from Miami a 64-foot fishing vessel to the Windward passage off the coast of Haiti. The crew of nine unfurled a 50-foot banner upon arrival that read "Refugee Rights: No Forcible Return" (Haiti8b:13).

[243] The 3-page proposal by Forrester recommended a public education campaign by the Clinton White House on the "political genesis of Haitian refugee flight" under a brutal military dictatorship in Haiti, "one of the most politicized countries in the world". It further recommended the "prompt restoration of Aristide coupled with the removal of Cedras" as the "only solution to the refugee issue" through public statements and private pressures, "as in the past", and possibly an oil-stopping naval blockade (NCHR10a:1-2). Likewise, McCalla´s 3-page proposal put emphasis on "an aggressive effort to re-establishing democratic rule in Haiti" as the "key to dealing with" a possibly "renewed exodus" of Haitians. Clinton was advised to change "the perception among Haitians of Bush and Reagan Administration policy", namely that the "US sided with the elite and preferred maintaining ... the status quo" in Haiti and that it "denied the existence ... of persecution ... both because it was not in its interest to see democratic progress take shape ... and because it was more interested in demonstrating to its constituency a strong commitment to reducing refugee flow[s]". The Clinton Administration should pursue talks with all parties to the conflict, including "members of the Haitian democratic community (in and out of Haiti)" (NCHR8a:1).

"Clinton´s presumed interest in avoiding another Mariel-like exodus" (NCHR7:1). The other three proposals occupied the middle ground. In the conference call, representatives of the Yale team reported on the lawsuit. The litigators said they would try to get in touch with the "Clinton camp" to receive a statement on the 275 refugees remaining at Guantanamo. The team was concerned that they might "try to kill themselves". Participants were advised to "take Sandy Berger seriously". Berger was the "director of [the] national security team for the transition", who had been involved in putting together Clinton´s "proposal on Haitians during his campaign". Participants generally agreed that it was necessary to "stress [the] return of Aristide as the best resolution to the refugee problem", because it was "conceivable to restore Aristide rather quickly with Clinton´s initiative". One voice cautioned, however, that it would be "hard to get consensus from large organization[s]" within the US refugee advocacy community on this demand; activists should rather "stick to [the] refugee problem because that´s where our expertise is". There was heated discussion on what position to take on the issue of "forced return" (NCHR12:2,3,4).

On December 1, NCHR presented to President-Elect Clinton´s transition staff a "concise position paper" hammered out during the previous conference calls and drafted by McCalla. It constituted a "cohesive, unified policy position" endorsed by eighteen "influential religious, labor, human rights and civil rights organizations" (NCHR6:3). The 3-page paper, which was mailed to Little Rock, Arkansas, stated: "We believe that if your administration signals early and clearly its determination to achieve the prompt re-establishment of the democratically-elected government of Haiti, it will be able to avert a renewed and uncontrolled refugee outflow from Haiti". The letter recommended seven "interim steps" with respect to Haitian refugee protection: an end of "automatic repatriation" by rescinding the Kennebunkport Order, the establishment of additional ICP-sites "in each Haitian province", an increase of refugee slots for Haitians, the opening-up of a safe haven enclave in the Caribbean Basin, an expansion of VoA´s Haitian Creole programming to repeatedly inform Haitians of Clinton´s commitment to the proposed policies, the settlement of pending litigation and the admission of the Haitians held in Guantanamo, as well as the granting of temporary status to the 11,000 Haitian refugees already paroled into the US. The signatory organizations requested an opportunity to discuss these matters (NCHR27:1-3).[244]

This opportunity came in Washington on December 14 at a roundtable discussion sponsored by the *Carnegie Endowment for International Peace* (CEIP). According to Doris Meissner, Senior Associate at CEIP, the roundtable would provide "an off-record opportunity for key private, NGO, government and incoming administration officials" to debate "immigration and refugee matters, foreign policy, and international legal and humanitarian precedents". Among the 29 invited participants were Nancy Soderberg, Deputy Assistant Director for National Security and Foreign Policy at the Presidential Transition Office, James Cheek and Eric Schwartz, both of the Department of State Transition Team, as well as McCalla and Milne (Rangel92g:1-3). Repre-

---

[244] These groups included AFL-CIO, ACTWU, the *American Immigration Lawyers Association* (AILA), the *Florida Rural Legal Services* (FRLS) coordinating all Haitian-Guantanamo cases in Florida, *TransAfrica*, and USCC, as well as NCHR-members *American Council for Nationalities Service*, AFSC, AJC, CWS, HRW, ILGWU, IRC, LCHR, LIRS, NAACP, and the *National Council of La Raza* (NCLR) (NCHR27:3-4).

sentatives of both the Bush and Clinton USSDs and a "small number" of refugee advocacy groups attended the meeting (NCHR6:3).

Robert Rubin of the Refugee Rights Project at the *San Francisco Lawyers' Committee for Civil Rights* and Guttentag of the *American Civil Liberties Union's* Immigrants' Rights project in New York, both co-counsels of the Yale team, were appointed as consultants to President-elect Clinton's immigration transition team (Clawson et al. 1994:2373). At about the same time, Robert E. White, the former Ambassador to El Salvador and president of CIP, who had been advising President Aristide since 1991, submitted a "Haiti action plan" to Clinton's transition team. It stressed that Aristide's restoration offered the only permanent solution to the refugee dilemma. The proposal came after Clinton had been handed "a CIA psychological profile of Aristide which put in technical garb the U.S. national security establishment's deep distrust of a Third World populist leader" (Morrell 1993:3). Gaining access to the Clinton transition team constituted an important partial victory for the civil societal transnationalism of the US human rights and refugee advocacy community in its quest to reformulate US state policy towards Haiti. All the more disappointing was Clinton's announcement two weeks into the new year to continue unabated Bush's refugee policy, a reversal, which NCHR called "shocking" (NCHR14:1-2).

5.4.5 The Role of "Our Guantanamo Contacts" in "Client Services"

One of the rare articles on Haitian refugees published by HP between June and October 1992 appeared in early July 1992. The Haitian weekly reported that Martin of ai castigated US refugee policy at the organization's annual conference in Los Angeles. It hailed the group by noting with pride that "our compatriots have won an important victory with the unequivocal condemnation of the Bush government's policy" (HP 129:8,15). At the end of the month, HP stayed focused on California and covered a rare event in support of Haitian refugees, which was very different both in terms of its spectacular form and its Haitian participation: On August 12, about 40 non-refugee Haitians aboard a boat called "Saturna" had themselves been intercepted by the USCG in the San Francisco Bay in protest of the policy of interdiction. At the same time, 150 people at the beach, among them Lorenzo Carlisle, pastor at *Oakland United Church of Christ*, demonstrated against the US authority. The protest was organized by a coalition of groups, which included the *Haitian-American Council* of the Bay area, the *Bay Area Peace Navy*, *ACT UP San Francisco*, the *Coalition for Immigrant and Refugee Rights*, and GE (HP 135:13).

HP did not miss covering the legal battle, either. In the third week of June, it reported the latest decision of June 5 issued by Judge Johnson, whom HP called "Pilate" (HP 128:8-9). Judge Johnson had denied another Temporary Restraining Order requested by the Yale team in the wake of the Kennebunkport Order. But he saw the new US policy "unconscionable", since it rendered Article 33 of the Refugee Convention "a cruel hoax and not worth the paper it is printed on". As the legal team watched Guantanamo being transformed into what it called "an HIV detention camp", it entered settlement negotiations with the USJD in September by taking advantage of the publicity surrounding the tragic death of one refugee infant, Ricardo Success. After receiving the promise of the release of HIV-positive pregnant women, the team also pressed for access to Guantanamo to explain the settlement offer to the refugees in person. The US government finally agreed, allowing the activists to meet all their Guantanamo clients for the first time after almost a year of litigating. Wanting to learn more about the "internal dynamics" at the refugee camp, the team established contact with three refugee "camp representatives" there (Clawson et al. 1994:2360,2361,2364).

The students had heard from what they referred to again as "our contacts on Guantanamo", presumably Haitians under INS contract, that there were "political divisions" among the refugees. They named the camp representatives, who in turn identified to the students Michel Vilsaint as the person recognized by the refugees as the "camp president". He had been elected in military-sponsored elections. Haitian input into the first phase of what the students called "Guantanamo client services" also consisted of the help of three interpreters recruited by the students to accompany Ratner, Koh, Daugaard, and three other interview-experienced students for the three-day trip starting on October 7. Having also heard from "our Guantanamo contacts" that some US officials on the base had told the refugees that the Yale team was responsible for their continued detention, Koh tried to break the ice at the first encounter in an airplane hangar between the delegation and the small group of refugees reported to be "distrustful of authority figures" in general. A first-generation American of Korean decent, Koh said: "You must be asking yourselves if this Korean guy is an American. ... Like you, my father sought refuge in the United States. It is because of my father that I fight for you" (Clawson et al. 1994:2364,2365).

The following days, the refugees began to tell the three teams "story after story" of their misery: "One man showed us a photograph of his dead wife lying in pool of blood, which he had taken in an effort to substantiate his asylum claim as he fled his home in Haiti", the students recalled. Within weeks following Clinton's victory, the refugees' mood "changed dramatically". They had hopefully watched the election returns and now wondered why they still had to be on Guantanamo. The Yale team explained over the phone that US activists were working with Clinton's transition team until his inauguration in January to secure their release. Two suicide attempts preceded the second trip to Guantanamo by a new legal team in mid-November, led by Tringali and Guttentag. The team, which was finally granted access to Camp Bulkeley, included four students, three interpreters, and a Haitian-American doctor. The team had realized after its first trip that it was critical for the Haitian refugees to discuss their medical conditions with a doctor they could trust (Clawson et al. 1994:2366,2368,2369).

Dorancy of HRC complained as early as the beginning of February that the US military had prohibited HRC's staff from being accompanied to Guantanamo by Haitian physicians to better evaluate the living conditions there (HP 79:1,20). As Frank of HCC testified in February 1993, Dr. Marie Carmel Pierre-Louis, a Haitian health counselor, went to Guantanamo sometime after March 1992. As HCC's only staff member to do so, she asked Frank for authorization to make the trip. Confronted with US military personnel "not cooperative at all", as Frank reported, she had been first denied access to both the HIV-infected refugees and to their medical records. Later she had "a chance to speak to a few of them just to try to calm them down", after "our lawyers" had gone to Guantanamo "trying to ... convince the people to let them speak to them" (Frank 1993:55,144-145,152-153). Dr. Pierre-Louis is the director of HCAIDS, which was created in the early 1980s by HCC and health professionals, who are organized in the *American Association of Haitian Physicians* (AAHP) (Dorsinville 1995:2;Pierre-Louis 1997).[245]

The first news story on the inadequate health care facilities on Guantanamo broke in the WP-issue of August 7. The article was based on information, which the Yale team had received from "a contact on Guantanamo". The informant had told the students in July that a demonstration by the refugees against arbitrary punishment had ended in a violent military crackdown. Students´ interest in expanding the legal team´s advocacy to include media activism dates back to March 1992, when irresponsible US reporters covered court sessions extensively. Fearing that media coverage would expose the refugees to repercussions in Haiti, the students started to provide the media with their own perspective. The terms "Kennebunkport Order" as well as "Floating Berlin Wall" describing the US policy of ringing Haiti with USCG cutters in the wake of Bush´s executive order are creations of the students´ "media relations team". They were later used by McCalla and by Aristide. The students started to use publicity as "the most effective way to get people off Guantánamo" during the appellate process of the court cases (Clawson et al. 1994:2370-2372).

The first major instance of press coverage serving this purpose was started on November 18 by the NYT´s Anna Quindlen, after the students had arranged for her to visit Sillieses Success at the Varick Street Detention Center in New York. In September, the HIV-positive refugee was paroled from Guantanamo into the US along with her baby Ricardo born at the camp in May, who suffered from pneumonia caught during the rainy season. Further press coverage coupled with "protests outside the jail by the Haitian community in New York", as the students recounted, spurred her release just two days before Christmas (Clawson et al. 1994:2372,2361). HP was informed of the planned Haitian protest ahead of time. At the end of October, the Haitian weekly briefly announced the "picket-line" scheduled for October 30 in front of the INS detention center. The unnamed organizers were reported to demand "political asylum for the 288 AIDS-infected Haitians" still at Guantanamo. For further information, Guy Victor´s and Réjin Sterlin´s Brooklyn telephone numbers were stated (HP 150:8).

The Yale students´ "media relations team" was also involved in "political activism" outside the court rooms (Clawson et al. 1994:2360,2371). As Daugaard told me, her white American fellow student Mike Wishnie was the one in the team, who "took primarily responsibility for initiating this grassroots mobilization" (Daugaard 1995). Wishnie told me that, after returning from Guantanamo and moving to New York, he initiated political meetings in his own apartment in Brooklyn. He did not only invite Haitians, who he had met through Mme Longchamps and other contacts, but also some of his friends, who were part of the AIDS activist community in New York. He identified the invited Haitians as "members of organizations, some of them were private citizens, just a mixture, not too many, maybe 20 or 30 people at most". From these meetings, he continued, "was born a sort of grassroots political effort in New York". The group was first dubbed *Emergency Coalition for Haitian Refugees* (ECHR) and was

---

[245] Frank, in his capacity as HCC´s executive director, did not receive any correspondence from HRC. Communication between the two NCHR-members was virtually nonexistent (1993:137-141).

later renamed *Shut Down Guantanamo Coalition* (Wishnie 1995).[246] After the first few meetings, Victor of the *10e of New York* joined the coalition, the initial goals of which were holding "community education forums in Brooklyn and Manhattan". Wishnie explained that after the US government had begun releasing "the very sick refugees" and pregnant women from Guantanamo at the end of the summer 1992, ECHR went "to Varick Street once a week to have a little protest" in lower Manhattan, where the INS detention facility is located (Wishnie 1995). Curiously, HP did not report on the course of the protest of October 30. This is all the more conspicuous as the event was one of the first activities in protest of both extra- and intra-territorial US refugee policy with significant Haitian participation and involving a high-profile representative of the *10e of New York*. It is possible that Victor first joined ECHR as a private citizen, not in his capacity as president of the *10e of New York*.

Dupuy, Bonne-Année of the *10e of New York* and others did publicly denounce US refugee policy at the rallies on April 6 and September 9. But it now seemed that too much publicity surrounding Guantanamo refugees infected with HIV was not desired in the Haitian community, even if the *10e of New York* encouraged the Haitian community in late December to send Happy-New-Year post cards to the refugees at Camp Bulkeley. HP published the announcement along with a brief description of ECHR, which it wrote was "formed by several Haitian and American organizations". HP informed that ECHR organized weekly meetings. On December 13, one of those meetings took place in the auditorium of *St. Francis Church* in Brooklyn, in which Guy Victor, Raoul, Ratner, a Haitian named Rigaud Mélinette, and Daniel Coughlin, journalist of the *Village Voice* and *QW Magazine*, participated (HP 162:8).

Coughlin was among a group of journalists, for whom media publicity was a major concern. They introduced in a New York federal court a legal action against the US government charged with violating the Constitution by denying the press access to Guantanamo since May 1992. On November 9, the plaintiffs convened a press conference in Manhattan, on which Gilbert and Ives reported. The group was further composed of Steven Rendall of *Fairness and Accuracy in Reporting*, Richard Lingeman, executive director of *The Nation*, Stern of CRP, and a Haitian journalist of radio *Heure Haitienne* named Lionel Legros, also affiliated with a Haitian group abbreviated SELA. Writing on refugees of all nationalities since 20 years, Legros said that "the possibility to realize interviews with the refugees is a crucial element for the human dimension of reporting" (HP 154:9;HP 22:14-18).

The Bush Administration lifted the prohibition of press access to the base in early December (HP 163:17). Nearly one hundred copies of a ten-page press packet entitled *The World's First HIV Detention Camp: Haitian Refugees Imprisoned at the U.S. Naval Base at Guantánamo Bay, Cuba*, produced by several students of the Yale team at the end of November, were sent to press contacts all over the US, including CNN. As a consequence, a team of reporters traveled to Guantanamo with their cameras on December 11, "the first team to do so since Guantánamo had become an HIV

---

[246] According to Daugaard in a letter dated September 27, 1995, the most important members of ECHR were Esther Kaplan of *ACT UP New York*, Patricia Benoit of HWP, Suzanne Shende of *Black AIDS Mobilization* (BAM), Guy Victor of the *10e of New York* (and WLIB radio), Raoul of CWS and HWHR, free-lance journalist Dan Coughlin, Rejin Sterlin of HWHR, and Ray Laforest of *Local DC 1707*. Wishnie added the *Gay Men's Health Crisis* (GMHC), representatives of HEAR, of the *Haitian Teachers Association*, and of the *Comité Charlot Jacquelin* (Wishnie 1995).

camp", the Yale students recalled. This turned the tide towards more personalized media coverage sympathetic to Haitian refugees, who were now "allowed to speak to the world with their own voices" (Clawson et al. 1994:2373). Only two days later, HP took advantage of the new press access. The camp visit resulted in a piece on the living conditions at Camp Bulkeley, published in the third week of January 1993 and written by Ives. The article displayed pictures of mural paintings with political slogans and photos of Aristide. Since the establishment of a Joint Task Force (JTF) under Commander Joe Trimble and later under Colonel Stephen Kinder, some reforms had been put in place that hint at a "change in attitude" and a "more liberal administration", Ives reported. But recalling the rally organized by the refugees on July 17, 1992 to protest the miserable conditions of detention, he emphasized that stories of repression reported by the refugees abound.[247] For Ives, the JTF´s psychological strategy was to encourage "American values such as the `work ethic´, individual responsibility, and the taste of private enterprise". For example, a "primitive form of slave wage" for work had been introduced (HP 171:10-11).

One week after election day, HP pondered Clinton´s prospective Haiti policy. It quoted a USSD official as saying to the NYT (11/06/92) that his principal concern was that an exodus in the order of Mariel "could be the first big foreign policy crisis Clinton faces". HP thus doubted that Clinton would keep his campaign promise in the face of "such pressures" (HP 153:6). HP commented in the third week of November that the refugees´ hopes had been revived by Clinton´s election victory "to a very high degree". But HP still saw no indication that Clinton would respect his campaign promises after his inauguration on January 20 (HP 155:9,10). The weekly observed one week later that a panic "on the subject of a `massive´ and imminent exodus of Haitians towards the US" was fabricated within Haiti by people like the OAS´ "`semi-governmental´ functionary" Dorfeuille or by Lesley Délatour, former Finance Minister under former Haitian president General Henri Namphy (HP 156:9).

In the third week of December, Gilbert noted that in the US, talk about a "massive wave of Haitian refugees after January 20" continued. He reported that FAIR had run radio and TV spots encouraging people living in Miami to urge Clinton in writing to let the deportations of Haitians continue. Dorancy of HRC said that adovocates of Haitians responded in the media with counter-attacks (HP 163:9,17). Shortly before Clinton´s inauguration, HP mentioned with regret that he and Bush "now work hand in hand". In the weekly´s view, the "price for the return of democracy" was the containment of a "new wave of refugees". Suspecting that Clinton might resort to Bush´s methods by maintaining his Kennebunkport Order, HP concluded: "Voilà donc tout le monde d´accord, en premier lieu sur le fait que les réfugiés ne doivent en aucun cas atteindre le sol nord-américain" (HP 168:6,14,16). Several days before his inauguration on January 20, 1993, Clinton indeed announced that he would maintain Bush´s policy of summary return. As the Yale students recollected, "refugee advocates across the country were devastated" (Clawson et al. 1994:2374). HP corroborated that the disappointment following Clinton´s "spectacular turn" was very strong, in particular with refugee advocates, who were "extremely shocked" (HP 172:6). HP discerned an attitude of "wait-and-see" in the 10th department, where the February 7 celebrations

---

[247] Ives quoted Frantz Limen, a young activist of KONAKOM, poet Elmo Verdieu, and Jean Benjamin of *Mouvman Jenès Site Solèy* (ibid.).

were organized with a lack of "ardor". HP made out a feeling of "resignation" prevailing over "real hope", since everybody knew that the "ordeal" was not over, yet. This could be seen with the news of 400 Haitians perished on the sea at the end of December (HP 168:6,14,16).

5.4.6 "Shut Down Guantanamo": ECHR's Limited Success in Mobilizing

Clinton explained his new policy directly to Haitians in Haiti in a message transmitted in Creole by VoA on January 14. In HP's judgement, this would have been unimaginable during the Mariel boat lift of 1980. The newspaper called the officially declared intention to save lives as "especially hypocritical" in the case of Haiti, where undoubtedly a dictatorship ruled. Promising to extend ICP as Clinton did, from which only a minority could benefit at the expense of illiterate peasants, meant resorting to a policy of "punishing the victims" (HP 172:14-16). The aerial photographs showing a "multitude of boats" under construction did not distinguish between boats constructed for fishing and those destined for maritime commerce. Nonetheless, the "wall" of the USCG was erected in the Atlantic ocean, while Bazin wanted to pass for "good Dady" by distributing candies to repatriated refugees (HP 173:8).

As has been noted above, HP uttered serious concerns at Jackson's mission to Haiti following Clinton's inauguration. The Haitian weekly, which suspected him to be Clinton's "official emissary", was especially critical of the possible effect Jackson's skillfulness might have within the Haitian community (HP 174:16). The "common racial identity" of black Americans and Haitians identified by Buchanan Stafford in the 1980s (1987:151) now receded relative to "ethnic differences" between the two groups. Among these differences figured differing perceptions of US power interests, with many Haitian leaders seeing Cédras as the "pawn in the global US plan" (HP 65:9). Black American civil societal as well as legislative leaders became increasingly associated with official US executive power. Their rival rallying around the refugee issue was interpreted by some Haitian leaders as mere lip service, at least temporarily.

Rangel's "willingness to give Clinton a little time for his policy to work", as Milne put it shortly before Clinton's inauguration, intensified Haitian suspicions. Rangel's legislative director advised his Congressman "to make it clear to the Clinton people that you are holding back a dam of criticism in the Black community". Guy Victor told Milne that he was "understanding of our position", assuring him to refrain from commenting publicly on Clinton's policy announcement by canceling scheduled radio interviews. But "shortly after Inauguration Day he [i.e. Victor] would be forced to lead his people in demonstrations to condemn" the Clinton policy. The NYAN's editor Don Rojas told Milne that "there was a lot of anger out there in the Haitian community" (Rangel93a:1). The African-American newspaper reported that "many local Haitian leaders, as well as human rights activists, were sharply critical of the Clinton reversal" (Browne 1993:1). Victor's rather dramatic warning conveyed to Rangel did not materialize until early February, at least in part. As the NYAN's Charles Baillou reported, Haitian activists participated in a Sunday night "militant forum" in a Manhattan bookstore. Moise St. Louis of HEAR, who had been in Haiti two weeks before to attend an international human rights conference, described the severe military repression there. Claude Fequiere of the *10e of New York* was quoted as saying that "[w]e are still fighting for the return of the unconditional democracy in Haiti". Mme Success also participated in the forum. She contended that the US authorities at Guantanamo had neglected to give adequate health care to her infant. As Baillou surprisingly stated, speakers at the forum had maintained that Haitians see the US as "the only country in this hemisphere capable of addressing their wretched circumstances" (Baillou 1993:4).

In March, Owens formed BfA. Its purpose was to make it possible for him to exert additional political pressure by referring to a seemingly unified Haitian base in his Brooklyn district when pushing for Haiti-related legislative initiatives (Owens 1995). One of the African-American politicians, who introduced race into the pluralist paradigm governing the incorporative initiatives of the early 1980s, Owens had already sponsored the formation of the *Haitian Americans Citizens for Action* (HACFA). Founded by Haitian priest Père Darbouze, HACFA was designed to encourage the participation of Haitian immigrants in US politics as Haitians. But neither Owens nor Darbouze were able to build a core of activists fully committed to entering US politics in the wake of Duvalier's fall in 1986 (Basch et al. 1994:205-206). Similarly, Owens came to realize a lack of support by certain BfA members, which even took the form of obstructionism within the umbrella organization. He attributed this in part to the deficient leadership qualities of BfA's chairman Toussaint (Owens 1995), who confirmed that the group was not well-known among Haitians in New York (Toussaint 1995). But unlike HACFA with its ethnic design, BfA failed to organize Haitian immigrants *in spite of* its rallying around a nationalistic goal. This was "to organize the people and the organizations of Brooklyn in everyway possible to support the return of President Aristide", according to its "Agenda for Organization and Action".[248]

Victor's warning to Rangel further materialized in early March. HP reported on a rally of only about 40 demonstrators, organized by ECHR in front of the Federal District Court in Brooklyn on March 8 to demand the immediate release of the 266 Haitian refugees detained at Guantanamo. The Haitian weekly remarked that the protesters intended to gather on a regular basis until the end of the court proceedings (HP 190). On the same day, refugee camp president Vilsaint gave an interview with *Radio Soleil d'Haiti*. He said that several refugees had "mental troubles" from the adverse living conditions on Guantanamo. Identifying him in his official capacity as "coordinator of the *10e of New York*", HP quoted Victor as saying on *Moment Creole* (03/14/93) that he had found out about the existence of mines as part of a delegation that visited the camp last December (HP 192:16,17). By that time, Rangel had already revised his post-election strategy by resorting once more to the refugee issue to exert pressure on Clinton. According to Tecumseh, he told the *New York Daily News* on March 7 that he was "at the end of patience. ... I implore the President to return to the policy he espoused before the elections. You cannot have a policy for one group and another one for the Haitians". For Tecumseh, it was clear that Clinton was not different from Bush,

---

[248] It is important to note that for Owens, transnationalism is a "very positive phenomenon ... for the [US] culturally and socially, and it could be politically and economically in the future". Up until Aristide's emergence in the comparatively secluded lives of Haitians, he observed, "their society has been isolated from the rest of the black community" (Owens 1995).

because one of the Bush's officials, Maureen E. Mahoney, now defended the Clinton Administration's refugee policy before the USSC (HP 189:10-11).

The Yale students recalled that on March 8 "Judge Johnson's courtroom was filled with Haitian and AIDS activists" (Clawson et al. 1994:2383). According to HP, "certain demonstrators" outside read from open letters written by Guantanamo refugees to their families in Haiti. Yolande Jean wrote to her children and her relatives: "I send you two pictures that will show me for the last time" (HP 190). Jean was one of the camp leaders, who had not eaten for nearly a week. She was among a certain number of refugees on strike, who did not follow the advice of the Haitian doctors brought to Guantanamo. Among them was Adrien Marcel, as Daugaard told me. Prior to their trip, camp president Vilsaint unexpectedly called the Yale students to inform them that all refugees had begun a hunger strike to protest Clinton's broken promises, "their own agenda" to respond to his turnaround, as the students put it (Clawson et al. 1994:2374,2375;Daugaard 1995). The Yale students now also "began working with organizations long committed to fighting for the rights of Haitians". They officially contacted, *inter alias*, the *10e of New York* to encourage their members to attend rallies in support of the Haitians (Clawson et al. 1994:2377).

The Yale team further agreed on the need for a continuous presence of the legal team on Guantanamo, which it was able to maintain throughout the spring. Some refugees would threaten to commit mass suicide by invoking the Branch Davidian tragedy in Waco, Texas. This forced the students to recruit more volunteer attorneys, interpreters, and doctors to go to Guantanamo. As Raoul told me, the new-founded, community-based HWHR cooperated with the Yale team since early 1993 by providing interpreters. Back in New Haven, the Yale students took a cue from the Haitians' hunger strike and intensified their efforts on the political front. At a pro-Aristide "march for liberty and democracy" on February 6 in Manhattan with hundreds of Haitians, they asked Jackson to travel to Guantanamo in order to persuade the refugees to stop their hunger strike. Jackson disembarked on Valentine's Day, bringing along "a congresswoman, and other prominent black leaders". After his visit, Jackson announced that he would join the refugees in their fast. He was joined in turn by other activists like the Rev. Al Sharpton, basketball player Olden Polynice, and a group of thirty Yale law students, most of whom were not members of the litigation team (Clawson et al. 1994:2375-2377,2379;Raoul 1995;HP 176:8,23;Powell 1993:67).[249]

Jackson was later arrested in a pro-refugee rally in downtown New York, along with Demme and Sarandon, who read Jean's goodbye letter to her children before TV cameras (Clawson et al. 1994:2377). HP reported on the event, which took place on March 15 in front of the USSD offices in Manhattan.[250] According to the Haitian weekly, "hundreds of policemen" arrested 41 people charged with "civil disobedience" (HP 194:17). Neither the Yale students nor HP disclosed who the organizers of the protest on March 15 had been. But it seems likely that ECHR organized the event, since HP complained yet another time about a certain lack of mobilization in the Haitian community in the week of March 10. As Tecumseh noted: "Et l'on en vient pres-

---

[249] In early March, HP informed that Jackson was also joined by Mgr. Frederick Stevenson of Wallingford (PA) and Cardinal O'Connor (HP 187:8).
[250] The Rev. Daughtry, Dennis Rivera, president of the hospital employees union (*Local 1199*), Manhattan borough president Ruth Messinger, the Rev. Ford of the *National Council of Churches* as well as Ratner and others participated (HP 192:16).

que à ce demander si le *monopole des protestations* a été laissé aux seuls *groupes américains*, aussi positifs soient-ils" (HP 189:10-13;HP 184:7;author´s italics). HP lauded the organizers, however, by observing: "Si les réfugiés de Guantanamo en réchappent et sont finalement autorisés à venir aux Etats-Unis, c´est *bien seule cette mobilisation intensive* qui aura eu raison de Clinton. ... il faudrait le maintien de pressions extrémement fortes pour sauver les Haitiens et Haitiennes qui subissent le calvaire de Guantanamo" (HP 192:16;author´s italics).

HP did not put their desired release and transfer to the US in the larger context of restoring democracy to Haiti. In Koh´s opinion, however, the "public outcry" in the face of Clinton´s "betrayal of the Haitian refugees", which became a "grassroots political issue" in early 1993, "hastened the signing of the Governors Island Accord" for the return of Aristide (1994:2403).[251] But while the widely publicized refugee issue definitely helped put pressure on Bush for the benefit of Clinton during his election campaign in 1992, the media publicity in June 1993 was perhaps too forceful during the negotiations at Governors Island. As Malone recalled, "[t]he UN and the US administration put tremendous pressure on both Aristide and Cédras to obtain signatures on the GIA in July 1993. Boutros-Ghali was reported to have told Aristide, who requested more time to study the draft text: `Don´t study it, sign it!´" 1997:136).[252] Some Guantanamo refugees entertained the idea of committing suicide not only out of genuine despair. They also figured that their deaths might shock Clinton and US Attorney General Janet Reno to the point of releasing the rest of the group. "[T]he more tragedy there was on Guantánamo, the more the press would keep the story alive", the Yale students summarized the refugees´ "perverse logic" (Clawson et al. 1994:2376). Having their letters read in public to move people to tears would serve the tactical purpose of "dramatizing" (NAACP/*TransAfrica*) their plight. For the Yale students, the HIV-positive status of the Guantanamo refugees was a "especially sensitive" issue causing among them "ambivalence toward media coverage" (Clawson et al. 1994:2370). The tricky tactical question was, whether or not their HIV-positivity added to their "tragedy" in the public eye.

The group of thirty Yale law students, who fasted with Jackson, were successful in turning their efforts into a nationwide movement spreading from school to school across the US (Clawson et al. 1994:2377-2378). HP reported that the students set up an imitation of Guantanamo on the campus of *Yale University*. Two days after the ECHR-organized rally of March 8, the students were relieved as hunger strikers by those at Harvard (HP 190). In early April, HP informed that there were not only "progressive lay and religious US organizations", but also students from prestigious US universities, who declared their solidarity with "our brothers and sisters imprisoned at Guantanamo" by organizing hunger strikes and "sit-ins" (HP 200:9;author´s italics). In

---

[251] An observation made by HP´s Ives at the end of March seems to corroborate Koh´s view. He referred to a "rumor" that the US army, parts of the USJD as well as the INS were "unhappy" about the attention on the international level accorded the plight of the Guantanamo refugees (HP 195:20).

[252] It is true that half (10) of the articles on Haiti published in the NYT in January 1993 (20) dealt with the refugee issue. But the proportion further diverged from 33% (21:7) in March to a ratio of 27:1 in July, when the GIA was signed. This means that public pressure transported via the refugee issue actually subsided giving way to coverage of the Governors Island process, i.e. the return issue. In June, however, when the USSC upheld the Clinton Administration´s refugee policy, the number of NYT-articles published on the refugee issue (14) was the highest per month in all of 1993 (see chart).

early April, Marie-France Latour reported for HP in more detail on the student protest advocating the closure of Guantanamo.[253]

The trial in the Guantanamo case, which Yale law student Anthony Van Jones said was also known as "Operation Harriet Tubman", started in Brooklyn on March 8. The Yale students, led by Daugaard, argued that due process mandates adequate medical care for all persons held in official custody. During the two months before trial, the students had gathered supporting evidence to demonstrate the inadequacy of medical care on Guantanamo.[254] "Guantanamo survivor" Fritznel Camy took the stand to testify as the first witness. He described Guantanamo as "a park for pigs". The doctors testified about the inadequate medical care. Depositions of Haitian refugees still confined on Guantanamo were read into the record (Clawson et al. 1994:2381-2383;HP 204:8). Needless to say that NCHR was part of the lawsuit, too. According to its account, "[p]ublic education in parallel with high profile litigation" on behalf of the Guantanamo refugees "was at the forefront" of the human rights organization's advocacy during the first six months of 1993. Playing a "major role" in securing their ultimate release, NCHR staff's "primary function" involved serving as a "liason between the detainees themselves and our legal counsel working on the case". The group supplemented this "direct advocacy" through a "public information campaign" providing information on the situation at Guantanamo to US and international media and to various grassroots groups across the US (NCHR19:2,3). Representing one of the main plaintiffs, McCalla testified on March 8 in Brooklyn, featuring excerpts from a deposition by a Guantanamo refugee (NCHR18:2).

On July 10, 1993, McCalla observed that "[s]upport for Haitians in the US has never been more favorable, yet Haitian communities remain relatively impotent, thus weakening broader efforts on the refugees' behalf" (NCHR16:ii). As Daugaard told me, the relationship between McCalla, who "is regarded in the Haitian community as ... not of the community", and Guy Victor was virtually non-existent. She also said that Victor "was never ... unsympathetic with the idea that focusing on the repatriations was an effective strategy" (Daugaard 1995). But when asked in person, Victor assessed the refugee issue strategy rather negatively, since the international community was "not too much interested" in Haitian boat people as "people of color". He nevertheless acknowledged the work of ECHR, *TransAfrica*, and NCHR (Victor 1996). McCalla might have been in contact with some students in the Yale team. But he told me that he had never heard about a group called ECHR (McCalla 1995).

---

[253] Latour stressed that about one hundred students at *Columbia University* had started a hunger strike the week before, making New York the fourth stop of the movement following Harvard, Brown, and Michigan. Howard, Georgetown, Pennsylvania and about 20 other universities were to follow suit (HP 204:8).

[254] On Guantanamo, some of the students worked with Rubin to interview and make depositions on behalf of several of the refugees. In New York, Boston, and North Carolina, some of them interviewed and prepared potential witnesses, who included former government employees and immigration lawyers, and also Guantanamo-experienced Haitian-American doctors. The students claim they "searched incessantly" for them. The list of potential witnesses further included Haitian refugees, who had been medically evacuated from Guantanamo and resettled in the US. Since the students were able to develop a trusting relationship with them, they were willing to testify on behalf of those still held at Guantanamo (Clawson et al. 1994:2381-2383).

A delegation of Haiti´s constitutional government, headed by Minister of Social Affairs Célestin and Minister of Health Dr. Claude Jean-Francois, went to Guantanamo before the opening of the trial. While the trial was proceeding, HP published an interview conducted by Gilbert with Dr. Edouard Hazel, specialist of infectious diseases, who was part of the delegation. Dr. Hazel reported that there were 200 US army officers in the camp, who provided for a tight police regime involving tanks and even aircraft. This was a "very traumatic experience, especially for the children", he emphasized, adding that after the successful legal fight for press access to the camp, the situation ameliorated somewhat. Dr. Hazel warned with "members of the CDC", the US authority *Centers for Disease Control*, that the situation on Guantanamo could become explosive.[255] The CDC had warned months before that Camp Bulkeley was medically unacceptable. He called on the Haitian community to lobby the US government. Gilbert agreed with him that the Guantanamo refugees deserve "our respect and our continued assistance" (HP 193:9,14;Clawson et al. 1994:2384) .

But the only Haitians making "a lot of noise about this affair" (Dr. Hazel) were the refugees themselves. In the night of March 11, approximately 11 refugees escaped from Camp Bulkeley, but were caught by the US military the next day and thrown into a military jail. They were later released again, as Ives reported. According to Margaret Henessy, a refugee advocate, the refugees protested against the fugitives´ imprisonment. As a response to the attempted escape, the US military conducted a raid in the early morning of March 13, involving 300 to 400 heavily armed soldiers with police dogs, who patrolled the camp. Moreover, several refugee women testified to have been subjected to "vaginal searches". Some of the refugees began throwing rocks at the soldiers and put some huts in the camp on fire. 31 alleged rock throwers were incarcerated in the military jail since March 20, among them Yolande Jean. They were officially charged with assault against JTF personnel and vandalism against US government property (HP 195:1,20-21). Barred from seeing both the fugitives and the rioters in the military jail, the Guantanamo Yale team immediately informed the litigation team at the court in Brooklyn about the raid and the ensuing riot (Clawson et al. 1994:2384-2385).[256]

In his report, Ives referred to the court proceedings, stressing that "the final decision will not only hinge on the Judge, but also on the degree of general mobilization of Haitians and community organizations". Ives´s report was the result of a trip to Guantanamo on March 20 by a delegation of approximately 20 journalists, photographers, and advocates, headed by Jackson and Dorancy. Ives stated that since Clinton´s election, the refugees were subjected to "the harshest repression since last July and August". For the new JTF commander, colonel Myher Paulson, put an end to reforms such as the removal of barbed wire and access to telephones and TV sets. Paulson justified the severely limited access to the camps for refugee advocates under his command with security problems. Ratner said this was "the first time that we faced a situation, where we did not have the possibility neither to negotiate, nor to reach a compromise with the chief commander". Returning with 40 refugees from a short stay at

---

[255] For a statement by a CDC-official to this effect, see (Clawson et al. 1994:2384), foot note 175.

[256] According to Lieutnant Dillman from Guantanamo, who testified in Brooklyn, there were only six Creole speakers among the hundreds of soldiers dressed in full riot gear to explain the "head count of the migrants" following the escape the previous night. This information further demonstrated the abuse of the refugees´ rights in the Guantanamo trial (Clawson et al. 1994:2384-2385).

the camp to "McCalla Field", where the journalists had to wait, Jackson described the atmosphere at the camp as "desperate". The journalists took pictures of the refugees, the soldiers took pictures of the journalists. The refugees, among them Berthony Dupont, Success´ husband, were then forced into a yellow school bus. They demonstrated spontaneously by shouting "Aristide, Aristide". In front of running cameras, they repeated: "We are no criminals". Upon his arrival in Miami, Jackson indicated: "President Clinton ... could put an end to the misery of these people and prevent our nation from having the blood of Haitians on its conscience" (HP 195:1,20-21). One week later, journalist Payen of *Radio Soleil d´Haiti* reported on the "life of suffering endured by our compatriots" in Guantanamo, as HP put it, and said "... they live like animals". He spoke at the "political-cultural soirée" in *St. Francis Church* in Brooklyn with Lassègue, where Petit-Homme of the *10e of New Jersey* and ECHR´s Coughlin also rose to speak (HP 199:8,16).

On March 25, Judge Johnson issued an "interim order" calling for the release of all Haitians on Guantanamo fitting the two clinical definitions of AIDS (Clawson et al. 1994:2385). In early April, Gilbert reported on the ruling: It had to be implemented by the Clinton Administration within six days. Ratner declared that those refugees, to whom no adequate medical treatment could be provided at Guantanamo, would be transferred to US hospitals (HP 201:9). One week later, Gilbert reported that actor Tim Robbinson and Sarandon had denounced the "inhumane policy" of the US refugee policy when receiving an Oscar in Los Angeles on March 29. 75 million people watched the show on TV. The Yale students recalled that Sarandon and Robbins "shocked [the] Academy Awards audience" (HP 203:16;Clawson et al. 1994:2377). Following the arrival of the first group of refugees in New York on April 5, ECHR continued its political activism. The group organized a demonstration in front of the Federal Building in Manhattan to protest the detention of 200 HIV-infected Haitian refugees, who remained on Guantanamo. About one hundred people had followed ECHR´s call to participate, among them a "bon nombre de Nord-Américains", as Alix Charlemagne reported for HP in late April. Haitian Jean-Bernard Hérard, ex-detainee at Krome, said: "This camp is not a prison, it is hell".[257] At the end of the two-hours rally, seven US citizens, mostly students, were arrested at the Statue of Liberty for having tried to unroll a picket-sign demanding the release of all Guantanamo refugees (HP 207:8).

On June 8, 1993, Judge Johnson issued a final decision ordering the immediate release of all Haitians on Guantanamo. Camp president Vilsaint responded with "enthusiasm, glee, and relief" to the news relayed to him by the Yale students. Three days later, the first planeload arrived at New York´s La Guardia Airport. Greeted "with applause, flash bulbs and hugs", the refugees were "hungry for the enormous Haitian meal waiting them in the airport lounge", as the students recalled. The NYT´s Tabor reported that 158 Haitians were affected by the court order. Within two and a half weeks, the detention camp was empty. The students summarized: "The case began as a class action to impose legal discipline on governmental policy. As we responded to our clients´ changing needs, the case evolved into an effort to influence legislators and executive officials through various forms of political action, and a client service opera-

---

[257] The list of speakers included Victor, "coordinator" of the *10e of New York*, Daniel Simidor of *Solidarité Mouvement Populaire*, and a member of *Black Aids Coalition* (HP 207:8).

tion including medical evacuation, refugee resettlement, and political asylum applications" (Clawson et al. 1994:2386,2388;Tabor 1993:B6)

5.4.7 Clinton's Reversal and NCHR's Activism: Guantanamo, Repatriation, ICP

NCHR's initial response to Clinton's "shocking" policy reversal was the issuance of a news release, which "bluntly criticized" his plans. Signed by some fifty organizations in the US, the written statement set forth six recommendations detailed in the previous "consensus-based position paper" (NCHR19:2). The group expressed its concern "that the new administration's policies on the repatriation of Haitian refugees, without a hearing on their claims for asylum, will remain essentially the same as those of the Bush era". Clinton's intention to expand ICP did not justify continuing this "illegal and discriminatory" policy, NCHR declared (Browne 1993:1). But NCHR also lauded the incoming Administration's "professed commitment to restoring democracy to Haiti as a means of curtailing the human rights abuses there", thereby addressing "the root cause of [the] Haitian refugee exodus" (NCHR19:2.1).

Clinton's turnaround forced refugee advocates to return to the courts. Because of Clinton's campaign pledges disapproving of automatic repatriation, it was "widely presumed" that the incoming Democratic Administration would choose not to defend Bush's Kennebunkport Order in an appeal before the USSC (NCHR19:4). But after Clinton's announcement, the Yale students "hurried" to write an *amicus brief* and to coordinate twelve others filed in the non-return case. One of these was written by the "Haitian Service Organizations". The only brief supporting the US government's arguments was filed by FAIR (Clawson et al. 1994:2379-2380).[258] As HP reported, the USSC attended to the US repatriation policy on March 1 (HP 187:8). When the students drove to Washington to hear Koh's argument before the USSC scheduled for March 2, they knew that their last chance "of prevailing at the Court were slim". Koh argued that the US government's reliance on the Executive's emergency power in foreign affairs under two sections of the INA was tantamount to arguing that the President could shoot the refugees on the high seas in order to discourage their flight. Invoking the INA as the statute to return Haitians, without the accompanying constraint not to return *bona fide* refugees as provided in the same statute, was illicit. After Koh's argument, the Yale team was greeted by Jackson, Rangel, CBC-member Kweisi Mfume, and a throng of reporters next to a huge ai-banner protesting Clinton's policy. The students were "dismayed three months later", when the USSC upheld the Kennebunkport Order with an eight-Justice majority, with Justice Blackmum "voicing the lone dissent" (Clawson et al. 1994:2380-2381).[259]

---

[258] Before a House Subcommittee hearing on July 30, 1992, Stein of FAIR had testified that "[o]ur refugee admissions program is in the process of becoming a back-door immigrant admissions program" (Cong4:179). FAIR was the only US non-governmental organization active during the crisis, which McCalla would categorize as an opponent of NCHR, of its allied groups, and of the Haitian community at large (McCalla 1995).

[259] Justice Blackmum challenged the majority by noting that "whether within the United States or not, a refugee may not be returned to his persecutors". In concluding that Congress had intended to extend statutory protection only to aliens physically present within the US, i.e. in denying extra-territorial ap-

With US-based litigation against automatic repatriation thus "no longer a viable strategy", NCHR returned to the Guantanamo-case. As presidential candidate, Clinton had pledged in private conversations with AIDS activists and refugee advocates that, if elected, he would close down the prison camp. The group also returned to the "court of public opinion", taking advantage of its "longstanding ties with grassroots groups, the media and policy-makers" (NCHR19:5,3). One way of helping the Guantanamo Haitians in the legislative arena was by attempting to get Congress to lift the HIV travel ban. It excluded by law the admission into the US of persons "determined ... to have a communicable disease of public health significance". Before returning to the courts, the Yale legal team worked with lawmakers to draft and circulate a "Dear Colleague"-letter in support of this initiative (Koh 1994:2397;Clawson et al. 1994:2378). According to Yale law student Powell, the HIV exclusion had "never been applied to refugees seeking political asylum" nor "to other asylum-seekers" such as Cubans (1993:59). Following a "special effort" begun in the fall of 1992 to educate AIDS service providers and activists such as members of the *National Commission on AIDS* (NCAIDS) about the HIV-camp at Guantanamo, NCHR prepared a "background document", which was "widely disseminated" in early 1993. The exposé was also distributed to the International AIDS Task Force of the US Congress as well as to individual US Senators and representatives (NCHR19:3-4). The joint effort to have the HIV exclusion lifted ultimately failed on February 18 (Clawson et al. 1994:2378). Tecumseh reported that only 34 Democratic Senators voted in favor of the legislative proposal (HP189:10).[260] There was no mention in HP of any Haitian lobbying efforts in support of the bill.

NCHR was chosen to be in charge of organizing the Haitian refugee tour, which had been planned since September 1992. Guantanamo camp leader Jean was chosen to tell her story. The first event of this campaign was an "asylum and safe haven conference" for one hundred participants, organized by NIF in Washington on April 1. On April 26, Jean appeared in the "Phil Donahue" talk-show dealing with the question "Should HIV Positive Haitian Refugees be Admitted into the United States?" (NCHR18:3). The speaking tour attracted US print media attention as well. The NYT, for example, published a commentary written by Quindlen on May 30, in which she illustrated Jean´s experiences (Quindlen 1993:4/11). The *New Yorker* described Jean on June 7 as a "Haitian political activist" from Cité Soleil, hunted down and tortured after Aristide´s ouster. She resettled in Flatbush and became a nominee of the 1993

---

plication of both the INA and the 1951 Refugee Convention (Article 33), Koh concluded, the USSC placed the lawsuit "atop a line of recent Supreme Court precedent misconstruing international treaties" (1994:2413-2419).

[260] According to Gilbert, among the 76 senators, who voted for keeping the restrictions, were many Democrats like Al D´Amato of New York and Joe Lieberman of Connecticut. Gilbert invalidated the senators´ concerns by referring to opinions expressed by experts of the CDC, the *National Academy of Science*, and Dr. June Osborn of NCAIDS, who had declared that a lift of the ban would not constitute a health threat to the US public. In addition, a 1991 NCAIDS report refuted the argument of high economic costs involved in eventually treating immigrants sick with AIDS (HP 182). In late March, HP reported that the House of Representatives had voted with an even bigger margin of votes than the Senate in favor of the HIV exclusion (356:58). Among the representatives voting in favor were 185 Democrats. According to HP, Congress determined that HIV-infected immigrants were only allowed to enter the US for the period of 30 days for family visits, vacation, conferences, business, and medical treatment (HP 192:6,16).

Reebok Human Rights Award and also received the Michael Hirsch Award in 1993 (Brothers 1993;Kamins 1994:3). Jean travelled the West coast beginning in June. She first spoke at a public address at a Beverly Hills reception for Aristide on June 17 (NCHR18:3). Aubourg, who was her interpreter, told me that she moved many people in the audience to tears, among them celebrities like Harry Belafonte and Demme (Aubourg 1996). A couple of radio appearances followed in California, where she spoke on AIDS-discrimination, abusive conditions at Guantanamo, and the USSC ruling. During a Texas speaking tour in late October at a time when the Governors Island process came crushing down, Jean made public addresses and had media interviews in many cities (NCHR18:4-5). Jean, who was featured in the music video of Bruce Springsteen´s Academy Award winning song "Philadelphia", also visited other US cities like Boston and Washington (Kamins 1994:3).

The design of NCHR´s speaking tour with Jean was quite different from the thoughts on Haitians living in the US made by successful Haitian-American Joel Dreyfuss of New York. The editor of *PC Magazine* published a lengthy essay in the NYT of May 23 in an effort to achieve recognition and status for the "invisible immigrants". He was eager to deconstruct stereotypes such as "Voodoo. Poverty. Papa Doc", which he believed many Americans have about the Haitian immigrant population. Dreyfuss stressed that "we Haitians have established ourselves in the United States as an industrious, upwardly mobile immigrant group with a strong work ethic". He quoted "one Haitian immigrant" as saying that "[t]he boat people are a tragic aspect of Haitian life ... we hate being lumped with them". Dreyfuss confessed that he is able to "understand his anger", since the majority of Haitians arrive in the US "by plane". This reflected the wide range of Haitians living in the US: those "returning from visiting relatives back home", the "prosperous upper-middle class Haitians", the "working-class immigrants", and the "new arrivals" (1993:20,80).

NCHR´s Haitian refugee advocacy was a costly enterprise. In 1993, the group was successful in securing a number of grants from certain foundations. In sharp contrast, HEAR is run as a community-based organization solely depending on the voluntary contributions by its members. To them, NCHR appeared as "compromising" (HEAR 1995). Wishnie told me that NCHR was "criticized from the left" within ECHR. When the members discussed whom to invite as sponsors of the group´s platform, the following happened: "... as soon as I said NCHR, a number of the ... Haitian groups jumped up ... and they said `NCHR is a CIA-organization. If they sponsor, I take my name off ... He works for the American government, he has no contact with the Haitian community´" (Wishnie 1995). NCHR´s Harris said, however, that the organization only accepts funds from *non-governmental* donors, individual or organizational,[261] who were not in a position to influence NCHR´s work and objectives (Harris

---

[261] The group was able to secure a $25,000 grant in 1993 from the *Joyce Mertz-Gilmore Foundation* in New York "[f]or [its] Refugee Advocacy Program". And the New York-based *Aaron Diamond Foundation* awarded NCHR a $20,000 grant in 1993 "[f]or refugee advocacy and human rights activities" (Foundation2). The lion´s share in NCHR´s 1993 budget came from the *Ford Foundation*, which is likewise headquartered in New York. It awarded a total of $475,000 in 1993, which NCHR as formal receipient had to share with USCC, CWS, HRC, the Immigration Project of NLG, and *TransAfrica*. Besides a host of other private foundations, NCHR also received some smaller individual donations from private citizens, among them Bruce Springstein. Membership contributions amounted to only $7,850 (NCHR17:i).

1995). Other groups in the national Haitian advocacy network were successful in applying for grants, too.[262]

Among them were the denominations. According to Ferris, they continued in 1993 to advocate together through CWS´s Immigration and Refugee Program (IRP) "on behalf of Haitian asylum seekers" (CWSW 1993:14). In general, the group "advocated for an end to the backlash against immigrants" in the US (CWS 1993:11). Bellor of CWS/IRP called on "friends" in February to act on behalf of the Guantanamo refugees by sending a prepared postcard to Clinton. She also asked Clinton in a letter to waive the HIV exclusion (Bellor 1993). In 1993, Rev. Ryscavage of USCC/MRS was elected chairman of the refugee-resettling volags in the US, which are organized under the umbrella of *InterAction*.[263] Collaborating with NIF and the other volags, the agency reported to have made the "resourcing of increased grass roots advocacy efforts and increased media relations" a "top priority" in 1993 to promote a pro-immigration and refugee viewpoint (USCC/MRS 1992/93:9,10,15). The Most Rev. Theodore E. McCarrick, Archbishop of Newark and chairman of NCCB´s Committee on Migration, warned of the "specter of racism in our own society" in a letter in support of the Guantanamo refugees to National Security Advisor Anthony Lake (Rangel93b:1).

A Gallup poll taken in July 1993 validated USCC´s prioritizing. It found that Americans interviewed were "decidedly more opposed to new immigrants" than they had been three decades before. The "fear of cultural erosion" was mentioned as the one attitude predicting Americans´ position on immigration best. Ranking second was the fear of the "economic impact on local communities" by immigrants in their utilization of tax money in terms of government benefits. Haitians were bottom of a table comparing the popularity of nine nationalities. Only 19% of Americans interviewed believed that the presence of Haitian immigrants in the US benefited the country, down from 31% in 1985 (Moore 1993:2,5,6).[264] In 1993, USCC/MRS thus "continued to advocate strongly for a change" in the US government´s policy of "interdiction at sea and forcible return" of "Haitian asylum-seekers". At the same time, it signed a "Cooperative Agreement" with the USSD´s Bureau for Refugee Programs that year to establish an

---

[262] *TransAfrica* secured a $25,000 grant in 1993 from the *Ruth Mott Fund* in Flint (MI) "[f]or [a] public education campaign of Haiti". The same foundation awarded the QC/QP a $15,000 grant in 1993 "[f]or [the] Haiti Reborn project, to increase citizen involvement in shaping U.S. policy toward Haiti". Max V. Aristide and Laurie Richardson were coordinators of QC/QP´s "Haiti Reborn" campaign (Aristide,Richardson 1994:64). The $18,500 grant, which WOH secured in 1993 from the *Arca Foundation*, was also to "build [a] network of grassroots organizations in support of democracy in Haiti" (Foundation2:225,1207,1201,1189).

[263] *InterAction* is a Washington-based coalition of secular and religious voluntary organizations involved in disaster relief, refugee protection, assistance and resettlement, long-term sustainable development, educating the American public about the developing world, and public policy and advocacy (USCC/MRS 1992/93:9).

[264] 65% of them felt that the number of immigrants admitted to the US should be decreased, whereas only 33% felt that way in 1965. 55% said that diversity "mostly threatens" US culture. Of those, even 82% said that immigration should be curbed. Among the majority of 56%, who feared the "economic impact", 78% said that immigration should be cut. Yet the percentage of Americans concerned that there were too many immigrants from Latin America slightly decreased from 69% to 62% between February 1992 and July 1993. 75% said that the presence of Irish immigrants benefited the US. The Irish thus ranked first. 65% of Americans interviewed believed that Haitians´ presence generally created problems for the US (1985:35%), while only the Iranians (68%) ended up worse (Moore 1993:2,5,6).

ICP-center in Cap Haitien, Haiti, to assist in the preparation for INS interviews (USCC/MRS 1992/93:9,10,15).

The ICP-program, which was to be administered through the US Embassy in Haiti´s capital, had been established by the Bush Administration in February 1992. It became "the only option for victims of Haiti´s repressive military regime" (HRW/A, NCHR,JRS 1993:2). A few months later, the USSD indicated its intention to establish a "Joint Voluntary Agency" (JVA) in Port-au-Prince to serve as a communication channel with resettlement agencies in the US. NCHR was hesitant about the USSD´s invitation, as it posed a conflict to the group: Regardless of its opposition to the entire ICP, a failure to participate in the JVA´s establishment would, firstly, deprive NCHR of a channel providing inside information on the ICP system´s shortcomings and it would, secondly, probably leave Haitian applicants served worse. After denying USSD´s offer, NCHR´s July 13, 1992 Board of Directors Meeting reached agreement on the joint statement that ICP "is no substitute for the U.S. meeting its obligations under international law" (NCHR12:7-8;NCHR11:v). As with the US government´s flawed efforts to monitor repatriated Haitians, HP did not often report on the ICP program.[265]

NCHR´s and its allied groups´ position paper for the Clinton transition team also concerned itself with an expansion of ICP in Haiti. This demand was one of the three major provisions in H.R.5360, which called for the establishment of a certain number of sites outside of Port-au-Prince. Shortly after Clinton´s inauguration, NCHR´s Fuller and Esperance briefed a combined USSD/INS technical team about ICP in Haiti. With the enlargement of ICP´s scope, NCHR staff came directly involved in the program by assisting an increasing number of Haitians with various aspects of their applications. This direct involvement "enhanced" the group´s capacity to monitor the effectiveness of ICP, which it had surveyed since its inception. In September 1993, the group criticized the program in its comprehensive report *No Port in a Storm* (NCHR19:7-8).

ICP was not intended by Congress in the 1980 Refugee Act as "a sole means of protection". NCHR thus assumed in the report that the "driving force" behind the

---

[265] Having called ICP a "gross mockery" and a "cynicist strategy" (HP 60:16;HP 71:8,17), HP consulted in late May 1992 the expertise of "refugee advocates", who had stated in the NYT (05/22/92) that having to go to the US Embassy to file a request would render Haitian applicants vulnerable to repressive acts by the military (HP 123:15). Commenting on a US official, who had suggested that Haitians fearing persecution could as well call the US Embassy on the phone, the weekly stressed that Haitians in Haiti remained "confined by illiteracy" without reach of telephones in the countryside (HP 124:6,20). Latour found it noteworthy that one of the speakers at the demonstration with Aristide at Central Park in late April 1992 was Raymond Toussaint, "one of the rare refugee-exilees to have benefitted from a visa into the US issued at the US Embassy in Port-au-Prince" (HP 116:15;sic). After Clinton´s inauguration, Tecumseh reported in mid-March 1993 that the US Embassy in Haiti had announced that it would open an additional ICP-center on the fifth level of the *Banque National de Paris* building in Port-au-Prince. In her opinion, this was "but a pretext to justify the policy of massive refoulement". Tourist visas, issued again by the US Embassy since March 1, were "extremely difficult" to obtain (HP 189:10-11). Annie Wilson, director of *First Asylum Concerns*, a group that went to Haiti in January, was reported to be among those criticizing the ICP system as inadequate (HP 187:8). The Clinton Administration´s protesting the arrest at the Port-au-Prince airport of former Haitian soldier Williams on his way to Miami after having been granted political asylum was reported as an exercise in "diversionary tactics" vis-a-vis the plight of Haitian refugees on Guantanamo (HP 192:16).

"novel application" of ICP in Haiti was "the historically unshakable U.S. decision not to become a country of first asylum for Haitian refugees". The "operational structure" of ICP was dominated by the USSD as the "principal policy-making bureau" responsible for initial "vetting", i.e. the grading of applications into "priority categories", and contracting with the *International Organization for Migration* in Port-au-Prince as well as with USCC/MRS and *World Relief* as JVAs to run the newly opened regional centers in Cap Haitien and Les Cayes, respectively. The USSD´s role made for a heavy dependence of ICP upon "executive discretion" and US "foreign policy considerations". The report briefly outlined the ICP process, which resulted in 937 cases entering the US between June 1, 1992 and July 30, 1993 (HRW/A,NCHR,JRS 1993:8-14).

Following the USSD/INS technical team visit in January 1993, several improvements in the ICP process were implemented, among them the use of JVAs. The report still assessed the program very critically: A measure designed to mitigate and justify the policy of forced return, ICP represented "a desire to keep the numbers [of Haitian refugees] admitted to the U.S. to a minimum". The ICP program´s "conceptual inconsistencies" derived from substituting it "for traditional self-help remedies such as the ability to flee". The "central role and biased view" of the USSD was reflected, *inter alia*, in some INS personnel´s view that reports from human rights NGOs and UN/OAS-ICM were "totally unreliable". The ICP system operated in isolation from UN/OAS-ICM, UNHCR, and local human rights groups, "the real experts on local conditions". This generated inconsistencies in adjudication. The "most obvious weakness" of the program was the absence of a "safe haven component", so that a certain number of ICP applicants had been persecuted while awaiting final resolution of their cases (HRW/A,NCHR,JRS 1993:15-20). Among the "operational deficiencies" figured the system´s overloading, the problematic use of local Haitian staff from a different social class and political persuasion, and the inadequate vetting process heavily placing the burden of proof onto the applicant and providing for no privacy. The out-processing of approved applicants was often delayed and risky. A review of representative cases led NCHR to the informed assumption that "a significant group of asylum seekers" distrusted ICP. Considering the connection between interdiction, forced return, and ICP, NCHR recommended that the US government end the "refoulement policy", help develop alternatives, conduct an independent review of ICP, and use it as part of a broader plan (HRW/A,NCHR,JRS 1993:20-34,36-37).

In the "absence of any positive movement by the White House", NCHR took advantage of its knowledge about the "many flaws" in the ICP program when redirecting its advocacy work toward informing members of Congress. In an effort to "rekindle passion" against the US policy of forced return, the group held several "strategy sessions with refugee advocates" under the auspices of NIF. NCHR co-sponsored "a well-attended session on Capitol Hill to brief congressional aides" on the situation in Haiti, which deteriorated in the heightened military-inspired climate of terror between September and November. In hopes of securing the support of CBC members in NCHR´s "attempts to build a stronger constituency among African-Americans", the group enlisted the aid of Jackson. Relying on information and analysis contained in NCHR´s report *No Port in a Storm*, Jackson wrote to CBC chair Mfume in October to urge his colleagues to address "the ongoing tragedy of Haitian refugees" (NCHR19:8,7;NCHR16:2;NCHR20:2). He wrote the letter at a time, when the Governors Island process began to collapse.

NCHR´s legislative activities bore fruit on November 17, when McKinney introduced H.Con.Res.182, a resolution "concerning United States interdiction of Haitian vessels and individuals" (MIS/MIN 1993). The group also "worked closely" with aides to Congresswoman and CBC member Carrie Meek. She introduced on November 22 along with 34 co-sponsors the "Haitian Refugee Fairness Act of 1993" (H.R.3663). The bill provided for TPS. NCHR members sent out "action letters" to various advocates across the US, urging them to write to House members and to visit them in their districts. Despite these developments on Capitol Hill, officials of the NSC, the USSD, and the Pentagon denied "any need to consider other options for solving the refugee crisis" in a meeting with McCalla and Coradin in November. H.R.3663 became "a focal point in early 1994 for NCHR efforts to galvanize a national constituency in support of justice for Haitian asylum-seekers" (NCHR19:7). NCHR hoped "to get 60 more congressional sponsors" for a total of 100 by the time Congress reconvenes (NCHR20:3;NCHR25:2). The NYT´s Steven Holmes observed in mid-December that human rights groups and refugee advocates had "grown even louder" in recent weeks in denouncing US policy towards Haitian refugees (1993b:A17).

Another vehicle for NCHR to advocate the termination of the USHIA of 1981 as exacerbated by the USSC-backed Kennebunkport Order was IACHR. Following up-to-date testimony by NCHR in its capacity as plaintiff in the years-long case against US interdiction, IACHR urged the US government to review its policy of automatic repatriaton. It pointed out that the US is party to the 1967 Refugee Protocol and reminded of the Universal Declaration of Human Rights, which states that everyone has a right to seek asylum from persecution (NCHR19:5). Similarly, the *UN Human Rights Commission* explored, for the first time, resolutions addressing the plight of Haitian refugees. NCHR´s Coradin proposed a "safe haven enclave" to UNHCR´s Regional Director for the Americas and the Caribbean, Dessalegne Chefeke, and ensured collaboration by a number of NGOs concerned with the issue (HRW, USCR, USCC, and the *Refugee Policy Group*). Even if NCHR failed by year´s end to obtain commitment from UNHCR for an enclave within the Caribbean basin, the "groundwork had been laid for ongoing advocacy" (NCHR19:6).

NCHR´s activism in protecting the rights of Haitian refugees also included advocacy before the exiled Haitian government. Weeks after the new president´s inauguration, McCalla met with Aristide to outline "options available to Haiti, should his government choose to withdraw its consent from" the USHIA (NCHR5:2). NCHR endorsed "a proposal calling for Haiti´s elected government to reconsider its complicity with" the USHIA (NCHR19:6). At the turn of the year 1992, McCalla was in a position to report that NCHR´s endeavour to convince the Aristide government "to speak more openly about the problem" of Haitian refugees had begun "to bear fruit": After having "remained quiet about the US refugee policy", Aristide now called "for a conference in Miami on the rights of Haitian refugees to asylum" (NCHR20:3).

5.4.8 Mounting Pressure: From the Miami Conference to Robinson's Fast

The Miami conference was preceded by the demonstration of December 16, 1993 in front of the White House. The speakers gathered to denounce the "faithless hypocrisy and the cynicism" of the "White Tomb" residents across Lafayette Park, as Latour put it, and to denounce the "racist, inhumane policy of the Clinton Administration". Latour merged the assumed US "policy of drowning" and the fear of collaboration between the US and the *de facto* regime on the refugee front in a global context. Among the Haitian speakers was Dorancy of HRC and Yolande Jean. Dorancy raised the refugee issue in accordance with the strategy promoted by the African-American leadership. Ratner of CCR speculated that assassinated Aristide-supporter Izméry would have been turned back by the US, had he been a refugee (HP 216:8,17). Latour's accusation concerning the Haitian *de facto* regime as being "bought" by the Clinton Administration echoed a line of thought, which had become more prevalent in the Haitian community in the wake of the failed Governors Island process. "Former Ambassador of the Lavalas government" Dupuy pointed out that the "illegal naval blockade around Haiti" had been particularly designed to prevent the flight of Haitian refugees. The UNSC thereby created a "dangerous precedent" for future interferences in Third World countries: "l'ONU ... est devenu un instrument de la politique étrangère des Etats-Unis" (HP 215). Not only the military junta, but also the UN were now believed to have been "bought" by the US to keep Haitians from fleeing Haiti. Dupuy presented his analysis at the press conference on December 10, 1993, held by HAIC.

Interestingly, HAIC is the successor organization of the ECHR-turned *Shut Down Guantanamo Coalition*, as Daugaard told me. It transformed into a Haitian-dominated group preoccupied with questions concerning Haiti's sovereignty. The refugee issue was thus strategically interpreted within this governing frame of reference (Daugaard 1995). The plight of refugees was, of course, still of humanitarian concern. This is shown in a letter to Aristide written by Mayas at the end of 1993.[266] But it was more than ever ambiguous when used for strategical ends. Roumer, on the other hand, did not share the ambivalence regarding the refugee issue. On the eve of the Miami conference in January 1994, he advocated to use it again as a means to pressure the US by invoking the example of the Yale law students (HP 220:1,17).

HP covered the Miami conference in five news stories. The Haitian weekly quoted a press release issued by the Haitian Embassy in Washington in late December 1993. It announced that two issues had to be debated in Miami: "protecting the lives of refugees" and "the restoration of democracy". The refugee issue would be discussed not only by Haitian politicians, who had signed the New York Pact,[267] and by democratic groups from Haiti, but also by representatives of UNHCR and IACHR as well as by non-governmental refugee advocates and refugees themselves. HP referred to the WP (12/24/93) that stressed that the refugee problem touched a sensitive cord within the Clinton Administration, "which has always been afraid of a large-scale exodus" (HP 217:1). HP was right in assuming that Washington could not favor "such an initiative". Two weeks later, it reported that Aristide was pressured to transform the conven-

---

[266] She told him that "it was time that the Lavalas government takes care of its refugees" (Mayas 1995).
[267] For more information on the New York Pact of July 17, 1993, in connection with the GIA, see the NYTs of 07/17/93:A4 and 07/18/93:1/7.

tion into a kind of "national conference" (HP 222:1,16). NCHR's Coradin declared that this "political conference" was, of course, not what NCHR "exactly wanted" (NCHR25:2). Consequently, NCHR's Board of Director Meeting of January 14, at which Sansaricq, Dorsinville, Frank, and Jean participated, discussed the "[p]rospects for a change of position" by Clinton, Aristide, and the international community regarding the "automatic repatriation policy" (NCHR22:1).

After the Miami conference, HP observed that some people had been excluded from "certain work shops", including the one dedicated to the refugee issue (HP 224:17). Latour gave a list of all work shops dealing with the following subjects: the GIA and the New York Pact, the Haitian economy, the situation of individual rights in Haiti, the social crisis and the refugee crisis, Haitian and US civil societies, and the 10th department. He enumerated nine propositions, three of which addressed US foreign policy. According to NCHR, the staff of which attended the conference, a resolution calling on Haiti's elected government to rescind the USHIA passed with "overwhelming support" (HP 226:9;NCHR24:1). Taking stock of the Miami conference in late January, HP reiterated that statements made during the conference had been limited to officials of the US, the OAS, the UN, the *Caribbean Community and Common Market* (CARICOM), and CBC-members. No advocate defending Haitian refugees had been allowed to take the floor. Raoul of HWHR, who also participated in the conference, found it ineffective with regard to the "clearly racist policy" of the US vis-a-vis Haitian boat people. In the work shops, disorganization resulting from the control of the conference's orientation by the "official part of Lavalas" rendered the passed propositions inoperative. They were largely ignored (HP 228:13;Raoul 1995).

HP affirmed that the Haitian people still wanted to believe in a change of strategy. But the Miami conference was a "chimera", since all participants, "in particular on the level of the 10th Department", wanted to appear as members of the democratic sector. Instead, a set of factors accelerated new departures from Haiti by a certain group of Haitians, according to CJP's Danroc: "le *pays se vide* de tous ceux qui auraient pu travailler ... au changement" (HP 228:14;author's italics). Allegations of this sort were also made by KRIMPO, an organization reuniting religious people in the popular sector. The group had circulated a document at the Miami conference, accusing the US Embassy of complicity in the elimination of the "most combative sector" of Haitian society. It stated: "Faced with this wave of violence, activists look for asylum elswhere. ... [T]he authorities capable of issuing a visa to `empty the country´ conduct investigations that assist the forces of internal repression in finding the networks of resistance against the forces of dictatorship". HP suspected that the embargo could be part of this strategy of dismantling the popular resistance (HP 228:14).

This was a new quality in the Haitian debate on refugee affairs. These observations were, however, necessarily in conflict with demands for protecting the rights of Haitian refugees. Taking this interpretation of US policy seriously meant that demanding TPS, more effective ICP, and full immigration visa proceedings, as Frelick of USCR did, would amount to assisting the US Administration in its alleged attempt to intervene in Haiti's civil society. This interpretation thus posed a serious dilemma: Internal resistance was pitted against refugee rights. Quite contrary to assertions made since early May 1992 that the US tried to prevent the Haitians' flight (HP 116:15;HP 189:10-11;HP 215;HP 216:8,17), Haitian emigration to the US was now alleged to have increased through deliberate encouragement by the US for political purposes. It is hard to prove this allegation, or the opposite for that matter, by way of sheer INS statistics.[268]

Nevertheless, HP published another article written by Roumer in late January. He reiterated his appeal to use the refugee issue to pressure the US government (HP 227). Roumer was joined by no less a well-regarded and knowledgeable person in refugee affairs than Ratner. In his open letter to Aristide, Ratner affirmed that his return was the "only way to cease the blood bath". But he urged Aristide to acknowledge the necessity "to try out a new strategy. No amnesty. Show what the military really are: criminals" (HP 229:8). Ratner's advice to Aristide also included another point, which focused on the consequence of his ouster. He pointed out that the US Administration demanded from him "not to speak on behalf of the refugees". After all concessions Aristide had to make, he was "even forced to modify the program of the Miami conference". Ratner testified to his belief that Aristide's "return is closely tied to" US refugee policy. He explained: "Now that only a few Haitian refugees succeed in reaching US shores, Washington does not have any motivation, any interest to fight for your return to Haiti. He recommended: "Une des stratégies les plus efficaces serait de pressurer les Etat-Unis sur la question des réfugiés". HP commented that Ratner's thoughts on the current situation were "without doubt similar to those of many compatriots" (HP 229:8).

HP's comment could as well be related to the passage of Ratner's letter, in which he recalled the destiny of the popular movement in Nicaragua under Daniel Ortega well-documented in a book entitled *Poor People's Movements*. Ratner stated that in the end, Washington had always succeeded in destroying the movement of grassroots organizations in such countries for the sake of "stability necessary for commercial exchange". The US government "is simply too strong". Ratner did not mention refugee policy as the means employed by the US to accomplish that goal (HP 229:8).

---

[268] They show that the number of Haitian immigrants admitted between fiscal years 1991 and 1993 (ending 09/30/93) actually decreased: from 47,527 immigrants in 1991 and 11,002 in 1992 to 10,094 in 1993. Of the 1993 total, 9,899 were admitted from Haiti as the country of last permanent residence, which also constitutes a decrease relative to 1992 (10,756) and 1991 (47,046). Of the 1993 total, 8,195 were new arrivals entering the US at a port of entry and were subject to a numerical cap, while 1,899 were adjusted to permanent residence status by the INS within the US (INS 1994:31,28,43). However, of the higher 1992 total, the number of new arrivals was much lower (1,200) relative to 1993, while 9,802 were adjustment cases. This would corroborate Danroc's thesis. But of the even higher 1991 total, the number of new arrivals was much higher relative to 1993 (11,121), while 36,406 were adjustment cases, thereby contradicting Danroc's thesis (INS 1993:43;INS 1992:41). In other words, the number of new arrivals between fiscal years 1991 and 1992 decreased sharply, then increased again between 1992 and 1993, but without reaching the level of 1991. Of the 1993 total of 9,899 admitted from Haiti, 5,574 were admitted under the class of "family sponsored preferences" as opposed to only 65 admitted under the class of "refugee and asylee adjustment". Of the 1,899 adjusted within the US, the majority (1,124) were visitors for pleasure, with only 119 being "refugees and parolees" (i.e. aliens, whose allowed entry into the US under emergency humanitarian conditions does not constitute a formal admission, but confers temporary admission status only). Of the total of 10,094, the proportion of female immigrants (5,609) was higher (53.9%) relative to the proportion of male immigrants (4,484=46.1%). The age group of 15-19 years was prevalent in both sexes: 1,016 and 2,008, respectively. The preferred port of entry for new arrivals was New York (4,234), followed by Miami (3,762). The preferred state of intended residence for all immigrants (10,094), however, was Florida (3,724), followed by New York (3,643). 3,325 preferred the metropolitan statistical area of New York as intended residence, while 1,925 preferred Miami (INS 1994:47,49,54,59,61,65).

But Ratner echoed Haitian concerns about detrimental effects of negotiations as expressed in the two petitions of September 1992 (HP 139:9). HP does not seem to have endorsed Ratner's strategical position. But it continued to report on the refugee crisis on exclusively humanitarian grounds.[269]

The Aristide government publicly announced it would reconsider the USHIA on February 9. Ratner's, NCHR's, and other groups' advocacy before the exiled Haitian government contributed to this official announcement in appreciation of the refugee issue's strategical value. Gilbert reported that the USCG's returning to Haiti of 60 refugees on February 10 triggered protests by HRC and NCHR, while IACHR convened to review US refugee policy. He updated HP's readers on both the introduction in Congress of H.Con.Res.182 by McKinney and on the announcement issued by Lawton Chiles, Governor of Florida, in December 1993 that he would sue the federal government for reimbursement of exorbitant expenses spent on refugees in his state. In Gilbert's view, all this constituted a "means of pressure on Washington" (HP 233:18). He did not say, however, if this "means" could also be appropriate regarding the problem of Aristide's return. In late February, HP recalled Aristide's appeal prior to the Miami conference that "the voices of the refugees must be finally heard". It covered the "blood bath without end" endured by Haitian refugees in the Dominican Republic. At the same time, HP complained, Clinton would continue blackmailing the Aristide government (HP 235:8). The weekly also covered a "new tragedy of the sea" by detailing the destiny of a group of fleeing Haitians, who had capsized on February 20 on their way from the Bahamas. HP made mention of *TransAfrica*'s Robinson, who had declared that these waves of refugees were the result of the "irresponsible US policy in Haiti" (HP 234:8).

Robinson's appeal was part of *TransAfrica*'s "Haitian Education Campaign", which McKinney used in late February as an opportunity to advance H.Con.Res.182 (McKinney 1994:1). In contrast, the 7,000 Haitians, who demonstrated with Guy Victor and others at Grand Army Plaza on March 5 did not explicitly utter demands for Haitian refugees, as reported by Latour (HP 236:1,17). Two weeks later, the CBC gave a conference in Miami with Aristide in order to "extremely" criticize Clinton and to present a "new battle plan", as HP reported. CBC-member Dellums announced that he would introduce a piece of legislation (HP 237:1). Dellums' bill was the "centerpiece" of a "new and decisive offensive" for Haitian democracy launched by the CBC's Task Force on Haiti on March 17 (Owens 1994:1,2). Guy Victor would acknowledge the CBC as one among many groups that "worked very hard" to defeat the military dictatorship in Haiti (Victor 1996). Once again, HP raised concerns about the advisability to embrace the issue of race. It qualified this approach as a "discourse made to please the CBC-members". For the rhetoric of race was one of their "preferred battle horses" that has a "certain demagogical flavour". Incomprehensibly, HP concluded that intending to abrogate the USHIA was in contradiction to this rhetoric (HP 237:18;HP 174:1,16). The newspaper reported the CBC's plan to hold a summit in Washington. But the "most spectacular action" would be an open letter to Clinton in protest of his Haiti policy, signed by members of Congress and other personalities and soon to be

---

[269] The weekly reported in early February on Haitian refugees trying to reach Miami clandestinely after having left the "Haitian hell" for the Bahamas in order to use the country as a transit point (HP 230:8).

published in the NYT. HP demanded that those initiatives be complementary to a "coherent strategy" by the legitimate government (HP 237:18).

NCHR urged "African-American members of Congress" and organizations primarily concerned with the return issue "to campaign vigorously on behalf of Haitian refugees". The group explained to them that "this was the key strategy to reaching their objectives". "Periodic consultations" by NCHR's staff with lawmakers and their aides resulted in "several noteworthy advocacy opportunities on Capitol Hill" (NCHR24:1-2,3). One of two important bills for activist groups to rally around was H.R.4114, the "Governors Island Reinforcement Act of 1994", which CBC-member Dellums finally introduced on March 23. It called for, *inter alia*, the exclusion from US admission of "certain Haitians connected with the military", the freezing of their US assets, and for the termination of the USHIA (MIS/MIN 1994). This is exactly what Aristide decided to do on April 1: He notified Clinton in a letter of his intention to rescind the USHIA, which he argued the US had already breached by forcibly returning Haitians fleeing persecution. In NCHR's view, his "new stance" seemed to help "set the stage for further activism" (NCHR24:1;HP 246:9).

Part of this activism was one meeting between Robinson and McCalla. He "encouraged" Robinson "to have his agency assume a higher Washington profile on Haitian issues". As NCHR continues: "Robinson subsequently undertook a courageous and enormously well-publicized fast, focusing attention on the racist underpinnings of the United States policy vis-à-vis Haitian asylum-seekers" (NCHR24:2). According to the NYT, Robinson began his hunger strike on April 12 along with a group of celebrities (NYT 04/13/94:A15). His fast, which Owens told me was coordinated with the CBC (Owens 1995), attracted much more media attention than Aristide's important policy decision (NCHR24:3). NCHR's influential *Terror Prevails in Haiti* of April 14 reiterated the group's position on ICP, assailed the US Administration for undermining its ability to condemn human rights violations in Haiti by forcibly returning Haitian refugees, and exploited the embarrassing slip of John Shattuck, Assistant Secretary of State for Human Rights and Humanitarian Affairs (HRW/A,NCHR 1994a:42-44).[270] As Coradin told me, the month of April was the most crucial time of organizing that ushered in the eventual US policy change (Coradin 1995).

Newsweek interpreted this broad civil societal movement of a variety of activists in political terms as follows: "Robinson's hunger strike in April marked the beginning of an all-out offensive by the left ... [He] broke the policy deadlock in favor of the moralists by putting his life on the line to make Clinton honor his campaign pledge on refugees" (Masland et al. 1994:26-33).[271] This "offensive" entailed extra-territorial organizing activities of an ethnic orientation for the benefit of Haitian refugees, which in reality aimed at having a middle-term impact on US policy towards the Haitian military junta through indirect transnational relations. They resulted in the UNSC resolu-

---

[270] Shattuck said to the NYT (12/15/93:A7) that with human rights abuses increasing and the number of people leaving Haiti on the rise, the US should review its policy of forcible return.
[271] In late April, HP gave its readers background information on Robinson's hunger strike. It admitted that Clinton would "feel a bit the pressure from such a protest movement" (HP 251:8). As to NCHR's and other human rights groups' joint letter to Clinton of April 20, which called for an "end of interdiction and forcible repatriation" in connection with "regional safe havens" (NCHR28:3), HP was more critical. The weekly noted that "safe havens" would bring back "very bad momories" concerning Guantanamo and would leave a door of exit for Clinton (HP 250:8).

tion 940 and culminated in the US-led military intervention of September 19 with Aristide's subsequent return on October 15. HP first learned about Aristide's letter to Clinton through the WP (HP 242:19). The Haitian press was informed after the fact and through the "foreign press", HP complained. But the weekly now sounded more inclined to endorse the decision. It agreed that rescinding the USHIA could help "mobilize" the human rights community, the CBC, and the Haitian community. Further confusing cause and effect, HP added NCHR's *Terror Prevails in Haiti* as a product of Aristide's move. It also put Robinson's hunger strike and *TransAfrica*'s one-page-ad in the NYT (03/23/94) atop this list of allegedly Aristide-induced "new initiatives". The weekly discerned "certain positive aspects" with the refugee issue such as the mobilization of the Haitian community. "But who cares?", HP asked, since terminating the "unjust accord" USHIA did not "seem to shake the US severely" due to the notice of six months (HP 243:6,16;HP 246:9).

Unexpectedly, NSC representatives did finally "care". According to NCHR, NSC's Schwartz called the human rights organization within days of the release of *Terror Prevails in Haiti*. Subsequently, Schwartz visited Haiti's capital, confirmed NCHR's findings, and returned to the White House, "persuaded" that US refugee policy "could no longer be justified". In addition, NCHR's Haiti-based staff had consultations with the INS General Counsel and with Swing, while NCHR's New York-based staff had talks with Clinton Administration representatives like Meissner, now in her capacity as INS Commissioner (NCHR24:2). Aristide's warm welcome in the Haitian community during his speaking tour through New England between April 6 and 9 seems to suggest that his decision to abrogate the USHIA sat well with many Haitians in the US (HP 244:7).[272] Nullifying the agreement was "the moral thing for Aristide to do", as Guy Victor told me (Victor 1996). While one HEAR-member believed that Aristide's abrogating the USHIA earlier would have "backfired for him" (HEAR 1995), Désir observed that rescinding it so late was the result of his advisors' influence (Désir 1995).

With Robinson still being on hunger strike, the concept of "safe haven" and Dellums' bill were discussed at an *InterAction*-sponsored meeting in Washington on April 20. It was initiated to form a special Task Force on Haiti.[273] The meeting was followed by advocacy efforts on Capitol Hill, in which HWHR's Raoul participated, and an unauthorized sit-in in front of the White House on April 21 by six members of Congress (HP 256:8;Raoul 1995). UNHCR came to belong to those working more behind the scene. Coradin's efforts in laying the "groundwork" for advocating a stronger role of the international organization at the end of 1993 was expanded in early 1994 to include "regular consultations" with UNCHR's staff in Washington. They in turn "persuaded" Ogata to establish an "Office of the Special Envoy for Haiti" headed by Kofi Asomani, who was mandated to negotiate with the Clinton Administration. NCHR subsequently "worked closely" with Asomani for the annulation of the unlawful repatriation policy. In NCHR's view, it was "not coincidental" that Clinton's announce-

---

[272] Five Haitians in Mount Vernon, New York, did "care", too. They decided to follow Robinson's example by going on hunger strike between April 27 and 30, as HP announced (HP 254:8).
[273] Haitian-born Yull Celestin from Brooklyn, a representative of the New York-based EMM, whom I met there, participated.

ment of the cessation of automatic repatriations of May 8 came just one day before Ogata's annual official visit to the US (NCHR24:4).[274]

The cumulative pressure on Clinton was successful. But this time around, the US Administration took precautions against having to admit too many Haitian boat people. It tried to accomplish this through its refugee offshore screening scheme implemented onboard the US hospital ship Comfort in Kingston harbor, Jamaica. Whereas the bulk of translators at Guantanamo in 1992 had been composed of US-based Haitians and Haitian-Americans, the US now recruited interpreters from Haiti's bourgeoisie (HP 273). After Guantanamo had been reopened to detain some 14,000 boat people at the end of July,[275] some interpreters were reported to have connections to the Haitian army and intimidate the refugees during the asylum interviews. This was corroborated by Mayas of HWHR, who returned to Guantanamo as interpreter, but this time working for the NGO *World Relief*. She said that the Haitian refugees "pooped in their pants, because they recognized the same familiar faces they used to see in Haiti that intimidated them" (HP 300:15;Mayas 1995). Hiring what HP called "Macoute interpreters" was part of the US strategy of winning so-called "voluntary" repatriations. As a consequence of growing conflict between 15,400 refugees and camp guards, nearly 1,000 Haitians were in revolt at the end of August. At least 5 Haitians were reported to have died on the base, while Haitians from other refugee camps tried to escape. HP complained that "the major legal support groups" in the US had endorsed the Guantanamo safe haven policy (HP 308:9).

In addition, the US Administration was once more reported to be dissuading Haitians to leave the country. Paid messages in Creole broadcast from radio stations in Port-au-Prince called on them to go to ICP-centers instead (HP 281:14). Tecumseh discerned in late July, when plans for a US invasion of Haiti were already public, a growing tendency of the US to help drain the ranks of the popular sector by offering political asylum to leading Haitian activists needed for the "resistance" within Haiti. Tecumseh based her allegations on information obtained from *Movement Paysan de Papaye* (MPP)-leader Jean-Baptiste and Mayas of HWHR (HP 289:12).[276] Mayas was

---

[274] For more information on Clinton's changed refugee policy following Robinson's hunger strike, see the NYTs of 04/29/94:A1, 05/08/94:1/1, 05/09/94:A7, and 06/17/94:A3.

[275] Having secured a verbal agreement through Coradin to permit ongoing access to the Comfort, NCHR and a score of "like-minded agencies" undertook a summer-long monitoring mission to both Jamaica and to another US land-based screening site on Grand Turk island. On July 5, the Clinton Administration revised its Haitian refugee policy, announcing plans for a "network of safe haven zones" (NCHR24:3-4).

[276] Mayas reportedly stated on the same radio station (07/10/94): "c'est un *déblayage de terrain* ... ce sont les gens qui représentent des obstacles que l'on enlève ... Si vous prenez une organisation comme la Plate-Forme de Carrefour-Feuilles, elle est totalement détruite. Il y a une organisation en Haiti qui s'appelle PIRED (Projet Intégré pour le Renforcement de la Démocratie en Haiti). C'est une création de l'USAID. Elle offre de l'argent aux organisations populaires pour les aider à s'organiser. Et lorsque elle a approché ceux de la Plate-Forme de Carrefour-Feuilles, ils n'ont pas compris. Ils croyaient que c'était dans leur intérêt. On peut dire qu'ils ont vendu leur ame à PIRED qui les a démobilisés, déstabilisés. On apris leurs chef de file, leurs têtes de pont, et on les a fait partir. Et les autres, on les tués ou bien on les a obligés à *prendre un bateau*" (HP 289:12;author's italics). As HP reported, PIRED along with *America's Development Foundation* (ADF) were the two US organizations, through which USAID funnelled the money needed for the Human Rights Fund, "reportedly" designed to aid victims of the repression and to pay for progaganda campaigns urging "non-violence". PIRED, alleged to boast a budget of up to $15 million over six years for "democracy enhancement" work like "civic education", was also involved in

joined by the 13 popular organizations in Haiti accusing the UN/OAS-ICM in their common declaration of mid-July of being implicated in draining the ranks of the popular camp (HP 291:1). In this view, the US, the UN, and the OAS worked hand in hand in supporting the military regime by providing for a deadly recycling of Haitian activists through refugee processing and the repatriation policy. For the sake of maintaining the inner resistance, dropping the demand for political asylum would have been a logical consequence. This interpretation of US interest confirmed earlier held reservations towards exploiting the refugee issue strategically. In the final analysis, it rendered altogether nonsensical the demand of granting asylum to activists fearing persecution in Haiti, since this would lead to a "clearance of the field" to the effect of weakening the inner resistance.

---

assisting hundreds of Haitians to apply for political asylum in the US. According to HP, the fund was widely criticized for its declared objective to push the "rejection of violence as a political tool" by working with "responsible elements within the popular movement ... and even moderate Duvalierist factions". HP noted that *Oxfam America*, for example, called on Congress to freeze all USAID "non-humanitarian funding" and that WOH, in a June 24 letter, outlined USAID and ADF complicity in the violence in Central America in the 1980s (HP 309:9).

US Coast Guard return with Haitian boat people, Port-au-Prince, Haiti, Aug-Sept/87
(courtesy Maggie Steber)

5.5 The Primacy of History: US Responsibility and Liability

Haitians are a people proud of their country and its history, no matter where they may live. 1991 marked the 200th anniversary of the Vodoun ceremony in Bois Caiman ushering in the Haitian revolution against French colonial rule. Needless to say that Haitians in the US celebrated on this occasion. It made them aware of their country's status as the first independent black republic in the Americas, for which their forebears, inspired by the French Revolution's promises of Liberty, Equality, and Fraternity, had fought so long until 1804 in the only successful slave revolt in world history. On August 22, 1991, a few weeks before the coup in Haiti, Consul-General Généus invited the Haitian community of Boston to John Hancoc Hall to commemorate "this important event in our history". He opened the ceremony with a speech, in which he stressed the historic significance of Bois Caiman and its impact on liberation struggles later brought to Latin America by Simon Bolivar (HP 1:9;Plummer 1992:11; Wilentz 1989:75).

During his visit to New York prior to the coup in September 1991, Aristide took pride in the historical legacy of his country. He visited the *Schomburg Center for Research in Black Culture* in Harlem, where he was invited to admire the library's Haitian collection. It contains letters written by Toussaint Louverture, the self-educated slave rebel of colonial Saint Domingue, who had succeeded Vodoun priest Boukman, the master of ceremony of Bois Caiman, to lead the anti-imperialist revolt. In his sermon at *St. John the Devine Cathedral*, Aristide evoked, besides Toussaint, two other heroes of Haiti's history: Jean-Jacques Dessalines, the revolutionary general, who succeeded Toussaint to later become self-declared emperor of Haiti, and Charlemagne Péralte, the leader of the peasant "Cacos Insurrection", engaged in guerilla warfare against the Marine occupiers more than a century later. Aristide contended that they had been animated by the "force of love" that he now used to unite the Haitian transnation: "This is our history, ... nobody can take [our power] from us, because it is the power of seven million Haitians" (HP 8:16-23;Plummer 1992:11,21;Trouillot 1990:101;Wilentz 1989:75;Schmidt 1995:102-103).

The shocking coup against Aristide seems to have intensified Haitians' deep historical consciousness. The knowledge about Haitian history not only helped make sense of the excruciating events taking place in their beloved home country. It also provided the blueprint for action for Haitians in Haiti and, maybe even more so, for Haitians in the diaspora. The crowd of 150,000 to 200,000 people from "all over the territory of the 10e", who gathered at Grand Army Plaza in Brooklyn on October 11, 1991, had, as Latour reported, a "rendez-vous" with "Lady Liberty, that constant companion since that liberating night of August 14, 1791, until that liberating morning of February 7, 1991". The first date marks the Bois Caiman ceremony, and the second Aristide's inauguration, which Latour called Haiti's "second independence" (HP 22:14-8). In his open letter to the exiled president, *Radio Cacique* journalist Baptiste congratulated Aristide "in his capacity as chief of state on the decision reached not to accept troops on the soil of Dessalines, of Capois, and of Charlemagne Péralte" (HP 39:10). General Francois Capois was the hero of the final battles against the French (Trouillot 1990:73).

5.5.1 The Haitian Diaspora as the Modern Version of *Maroon* Societies

Aristide's radio address of November 22, 1991 on *Radio Tropicale* and the designs put forth by other Haitian strategists like Généus and Tecumseh were informed by Haiti's historical example. "Resistance" in Haiti and "mobilization" in the Haitian diaspora are reminiscent of the relationship between the black slaves subjected to the repressive labor system that was the colonial plantation and the *marrons*, or maroons, who managed to escape to safety to live in remote mountain enclaves as a form of resistance against plantation oppression. The runaway slave communities were emblematic of freedom from colonial violence. As Bonham Richardson notes: "It is probably safe to say that the freedom and independence associated with *marronage* was an irresistible and unending source of inspiration for the plantation slaves". Indeed common during slavery and an ubiquity throughout the Caribbean, they constituted the beginning of the slaves' liberation struggle in Saint Domingue. Numbering at least 3,000 in 1751, maroons also joined the black troops in their fight against the French. On the other hand, as Brenda Gayle Plummer notes, even though they were outlaws legally, in many instances "the colonialists honored their de facto autonomy in exchange for territorial concessions, assistance in recapturing other fugitives, or commercial privileges" (Wilentz 1989:76;Richardson 1983:5,7,15;Richardson 1992:134-136;Plummer 1992:12;James 1989[1963]:20).

The Haitian diaspora represented a modern version of maroon communites, whose "mobilization" efforts provided the political, emotional, moral, tactical, and financial support for the internal "resistance" against "internal colonization". For Latour, the crowd of Haitians protesting in front of New York's Madison Square Garden in July 1992 was a "marée de marrons" (English: "tide of maroons") (HP 132:9). Haiti's historical example predestined the priority given to direct transnational relations between diaspora and homeland. As Aristide himself put it: "From the era of plantations to the putsch, there is a common thread uniting all forms of resistance" (1996:146).

Haiti's history furnished the eldorado of verbal strategies designed to constantly motivate Haitians in the US. Latour sketched the significance of the February 7 celebrations of 1992 in historical terms that linked their organizing efforts in an evolutionary line to the sacrifices demanded by the Haitian revolution: The "tree of resistance" had grown bigger from "Makandal ... [to] Aristide", between 1791 and February 7, 1991, the "anniversary of our second independence" (HP 80:12-13). African-born Francois Macandal, sometimes also referred to as "Mackandal", who himself became a maroon, was notorious throughout colonial Saint Domingue for one example of slave resistance involving the poisoning of whites, whose entire population was gripped by the fear of magic. He was arrested and burned at the stake (Farmer 1992:157-158;James 1989[1963]:20-21).

During his visit to New York late April 1992, Aristide reminded Haitian business people of their patriotic duty, calling on them to share their "experience and knowledge to show that the children of Dessalines, young and old, know what it means to bring to fruition their money in building the new Haiti" (HP 116:12). The Haitian diaspora's youth was to be educated in that sense, too. In the 10e's offices in New York on May 17, the "Commission Jeunesse" related the history of resistance by the Haitian youth against various regimes in Haiti's past (HP 122:10). Fundraising drives by the Regional Finance Committee of New York also resorted to the Haitian community's historical awareness. Dauphin enouraged in September to "contribute generously". He stated: "Les petits-fils de Dessalines ont juré de poursuivre le combat jusqu'à la victoire". He announced that Aristide had decided to issue a "Diplôme de résistance" to Haitians not ceasing to demand the return of democracy to the "soil of Charlemagne Péralte" (HP 137:9).

The willingness of rank and file Haitians to respond to calls for mobilization was also expressed in reference to heroes of Haiti's past. At the demonstration in front of the White House on September 9, Latour quoted Haitian protester Lundi as saying that "the blood of Jean-Jacques Dessalines, Boukman, Capois la Mort runs in our veins" (HP 141:9). Conversely, the authority of historical precedence also served as a tool of criticism. HP, for example, deemed it dishonorable that certain members of the Haitian diplomatic corps "favor the concept of `limited sovereignty´". It asked in early December 1992: "Etait-ce la vision de Dessalines et Péralte dont se réclame le gouvernement légitime?" (HP 158:17). In early January 1994, there were signs of a new rapprochement of HP and Aristide, manifested in agreement on how to term the prospects for the upcoming year. HP stated that 1994 stood "under the sign of Dessalines". Evoking the two heroes of Haitian independence, Aristide had indicated: "Durant l'année 1993, le peuple s'est davantage appuyé sur Toussaint. Au cours de l'année 1994, il marchera plutôt au rythme de Dessalines" (HP 219:1). In contrast to Dessalines, an uneducated soldier, the historian C.L.R. James describes Toussaint as a hesitant leader with so much allegiance to France as to underestimate the French ruling class in its attempt to restore slavery. Instead, he sought to avoid a bloody war of independence by exchanging notes with Bonaparte to appease him. Dessalines' tenuous ties to French culture allowed him to be more uncompromising and radical until his proclamation of independence in 1804 (1989 [1963]:278-282,285-290,369-370).

Consequently, after some restraint in the course of 1993, Haitians now assured themselves again of their national heritage. Latour described the crowd of 7,000 Haitians taking to the streets on March 5, 1994 as "... le sang dessalinien de milliers d'Haitians ... la foule ... a traversé Manhattan au rythme Bois-Caimanais" (HP 236:17). At a "cultural party" at *Northeastern University* on April 9, Aristide justified the prior strategy of his exile government with reference to the two key icons in Haiti's history. Toussaint's "heroic deeds of diplomacy" and his "intelligence" in fighting against slavery had inspired the legitimate government. But, in addition, "the power of Dessalines" was needed as well (HP 244:7). At the demonstration in front of the Catholic Mission at the UN on July 23, Dorismé linked current developments with the beginnings of colonization in the West Indies. She denounced the *Catholic Church* as the Haitians' "first colonist": When Christopher Columbus landed at Môle St. Nicolas, he planted the cross "to rob the Indians". The Catholic Church "gave a green light to the colonists to import blacks from Africa to continue the genocide", she said, before the participants started singing the "Dessalinienne" (HP 297:8).

The manifold uses of important dates and national heroes of Haiti's past in the discourse between 1991 and 1994 hint at a marked disposition of Haitians to interpret the events leading to the coup and the developments following the coup in historical terms. Haitians in the US seem to have perceived the unfolding crisis through a historical lens and as if physically present in Haiti. This historical angle largely informed the *folk model*, on which Haitians in the US organized during the crisis.[277] The collective memory of Haitian history represented a hegemonic force structuring the organizing efforts by Haitians in the US. Submerged in this universe of thought, heroes of US history were reclaimed very scarcely either as an example for Haitians to follow or as a tactical weapon to morally pressure the US government.[278] Jewish-Americans and African-Americans have been mentioned as the two most important ethnic groups in the US, which were emulated by other ethnic groups in their political activities (Watanabe 1984:12;Ahari 1987:xiv-xv;DeConde 1992:157,165). Asked what examples they followed when organizing, some of my Haitian informants did refer to black American leaders. More often than not, these informants belonged to groups involved in the refugee issue. Frank, for example, mentioned Martin Luther King. McCalla found it rather ludicrous that Haitians in the US claimed to emulate American civil rights leaders as models. He rather believes that voluntary action in rural Haiti was the experience, upon which organizing in the US was based (Frank 1995;McCalla 1995).

5.5.2 The External Enemy: From the French Empire to the "American Plan"

Rhetorical references to heroes of Haiti´s history also signify the nature of the battle, for which they were meant to motivate. Especially Toussaint, Dessalines, and Péralte stand for courageous resistance against powerful forces invading the island of Hispaniola from outside or seeking to further intrude themselves into Haiti´s internal affairs. The foundations of the new nation were predicated upon the abolition of slavery, which the black leaders were in complete agreement with the masses of ex-slaves. Control over the entire island was essential to the security of the former colony. The ideal of liberty was manifested in the willingness to sacrifice everything for freedom and territorial integrity. Since Haiti remained a weak state and a small country, roughly the same size as the state of Maryland, warfare against a foreign aggressor could only be an ultimate, defensive venture. This necessitated an emphasis on diplomacy with European empires that still coveted the former colony´s novel agricultural goods (Trouillot 1990:44;Plummer 1992:21-24;Lawless 1992:xix;Mintz 1995:74-75).

Concern for territorial integrity was rooted in reality, for an independent Haiti was perceived as a major threat by white racist rulers of slaveholding societies. They saw a Caribbean nation controlled by blacks as a continual menace and a source of revolutionary contagion. These perceptions were more prevalent in the US than in European powers, which tolerated slavery only in their remote empires. To isolate the new state, these powers imposed a diplomatic and political blockade on Haiti. The Vatican and the US were in the forefront of ostracizing the new republic, with the for-

---

[277] It is therefore diametrically opposed to the *folk model* of the NYT, whose reporting on the Haitian crisis was, as shown above, markedly ahistorical.

[278] HP sometimes invoked the example of Martin Luther King. It did so with regard to USSC Judge Clarence Thomas and in late January 1994, when it recapitulated that thousands of Haitian demonstrators had "paralyzed the city of New York in proportions never seen since the era of Martin Luther King" (HP 86:1,19;HP 225:7;see also HP 226:8). In addition, at the Conference of Baptist Pastors in *Baptist Church* during his visit in late April 1992, Aristide said he felt the presence of Martin Luther King each time one utilizes his strategy of active non-violence (HP 122:12-13).

mer formally recognizing Haiti not until 1860 and the latter not until 1862. At the same time, Haitian-US commerce yielded substantial profits for US merchants. As early as 1792, the USSD exempted Saint Domingue from the prohibition to trade with the French Empire as mandated by Congress. By 1851, US trade with Haiti was greater in volume than US commerce with most Latin American states. In the post-Civil War period, Washington sent a score of black diplomats to Port-au-Prince, including Frederick Douglass and Henry Watson Furniss, to extend political influence over US control of the Haitian import market (Trouillot 1990:50-58;Plummer 1992:15,34-49).

While Plummer maintains that "[no] metropolitan state after 1825 [Monroe Doctrine: 1823] really wanted the onerous task and dubious reward of defeating and annexing Haiti", Rolph-Michel Trouillot ascertains that "Haitian territorial waters were violated more than twenty times in the second half of the nineteenth century by warships of various foreign powers" including the US in 1868 and 1891 (Plummer 1992:33;Trouillot 1990:57).[279] The trade-related politics of reciprocity, territorial concessions, and annexation were prone to harboring suspicions on either side. The so-called "Syrian invasion", the immigration of Levantine traders with useful business contacts in New York and Chicago into the Haitian market, further promoted US influence at the end of the century (Trouillot 1990:55-56). By that time, the US, ideologically driven by the Puritan-derived notion of "Manifest Destiny", had expanded territorially and grown more powerful economically (Knight 1990:124;Opitz 1993:58-59). Since producing for a world market required relations with the European powers and the emerging societies of the Americas, Farmer contends that speaking of a "century of isolation" with respect to Haiti´s first century is not accurate. On the contrary, it was a history of increasing domination by European powers and by the US. Foreigners played an ever more important role in the vicissitudes of Haitian politics and Haitian economic affairs. Haiti was isolated politically, but not commercially. As Farmer put it: Haiti "became a useful - and used - pariah" (1992:166-176;Wilentz 1989:77).

At the turn of the century, US interest in long-term stability in the Western Hemisphere were given precedence over economic penetration by American short-term business interests in the formulation of US policy toward Haiti. As Hans Schmidt states: "The main considerations in the decision to intervene in Haiti [in 1915] were strategic and, more specifically, military", the outcome of the battle between the four imperialist powers: Britain, France, Germany, and the US. Yet long-term stability was also a prerequisite to massive American investments needed to transform Haiti into a profitable economic satellite (1995:42-63,56). To establish a stable government amenable to the US, the Marine occupiers installed a puppet president, Philippe-Sudre Dartiguenave. To replace the first Haitian army, which claimed to defend the nation against foreigners, the Marines formed the centralized Haitian *gendarmerie* (later: *Garde*), pursuant to the treaty of 1915 as promulgated by the US. Fusing the roles of army and police, it was specifically created to control other Haitians alongside the Marines in the war against Péralte´s troops and would henceforth be an instrument for internal terror (Trouillot 1990:104-107;LCHR 1990a:203-204).

---

[279] Nancy and Robert Heinl even assert that the "United States Navy had been compelled to send warships into Haitian waters to protect the lives and property of American citizens" 25 times between 1849 and 1914 (1978:404-405).

The enforced Constitution of 1918, reportedly written by Navy Secretary Franklin D. Roosevelt, reintroduced, to the benefit of many US companies, foreign ownership of land, which had been outlawed by Dessalines (Farmer 1992:179). The US occupation of Haiti lasted from 1915 to 1934. It brought about long-term links between the US military and the Haitian army, revolving around training, equipment, and tactical doctrines (Weinstein,Segal 1992:33). The US "now substituted for France as the resented metropole", as was reflected in the Haitian literary movement *négritude* in the 1940s. The decade also saw, ironically, a growing number of private US visitors for pleasure following the establishment of the *National Tourist Office* in Port-au-Prince and the promotion of American travel industries by the USSD (Plummer 1992:126-127,131-135). Backed by the US-trained army and cynically appropriating black nationalist rhetoric and Vodoun beliefs, Francois Duvalier (Papa Doc) seized power in 1957. He transformed the authoritarian political model of the past into a totalitarian apparatus through a patronage system that reached deep into civil society and survived unprecedented 29 years. The system came to include a decapitated Haitian army and the *Volontaires de la Securité Nationale* (VSN). The VSN was an officialization of the dreaded *tonton-makout*, members of Duvalier´s secret police serving as a counterweight to the neutralized Haitian army (Trouillot 1990:148-152156-158,189-191).

The US preoccupation with communism in the Cold War and, after 1959, with the Cuban Revolution forms a leitmotif in US-Haitian diplomacy during the Duvalier dynasty years. Under President Eisenhower, the US was first interested in a strong Haitian army to keep VSN excesses in check. When liberal forces ousted ten dictators between 1956 and 1960, the Kennedy Administration regarded in Duvalierism a useful tool for excluding Cuba from the inter-American system and maintaining surveillance over the spread of revolution. While the CIA in the 1960s made halfhearted plans to abet Duvalier´s overthrow, US Administrations indicated a fundamental ambivalence about ousting him. He shrewdly exploited US anti-communist paranoia to receive financial aid from Washington. Pursuant to the Mann Doctrine of 1964, which reappraised militarism as a stabilizing institution, a period of cooperation and comparative generosity toward Haiti began with the incoming Johnson Administration. The additional desire to create security for US investments in Haiti met with Duvalier´s economic conservatism. Foreign light-assembly re-export industries appeared as early as the 1950s, but their attractiveness for the US was enhanced with the election of Richard Nixon. The creation of a new public image with the ascent of Duvalier´s son Jean-Claude (Baby Doc) in 1971 gave Washington a rationale for renewed financial support of the regime. The US´s blessing of Baby Doc formalized the alliance between the two governments (Plummer 1992:181-195;Trouillot 1990:202-204;LCHR 1990:205).

Washington´s blessing of Baby Doc helped consolidate the regime´s light industry strategy in alliance with Haiti´s local bourgeoisie. While the traditional exploitation of Haitian agricultural workers in a corrupt state continued during the 1970s, the decade also witnessed a growth in the number of tourists. By 1970, it was close to 100,000 rising to 143,538 by 1979. After US President Carter had tied aid to improvements in democratic rights, however token, Haiti remained politically isolated in the Caribbean Basin at the end of the decade, when leftist insurgencies in the region convinced US policymakers to return to traditional postures. The Reagan Administration´s CBI of 1981 promised economic aid to restive republics in exchange for their governments´ maintaining an anticommunist stance. Reagan´s advent facilitated the oppression of domestic dissidence by Baby Doc. The latter also hoped to better control community development projects by private voluntary organizations from abroad, which had proliferated during the past decade. By 1985, roughly four hundred separate agencies, among them those of the *Catholic Church*, operated assistance programs, thereby potentially threatening state influence. In an increasingly private environment, USAID indirectly spent some 57% of its funds on such programs. Following the "nationalization" of the Haitian clergy begun in the 1960s under Papa Doc, lower militant priests became more numerous. Church organizations ultimately provided the platform for them to call for radical reform of Haitian institutions. The *Ti Legliz* movement was born. According to HP, Mgr. Romélus particularly encouraged the formation of *Ti Legliz* (Trouillot 1990:204-216,219;Plummer 1992:197-205;Farmer 1992:145-146;HP 202:11-12).

Aristide´s inner city parish of *St. Jean Bosco* evolved into a major center of opposition. By 1985, he became a powerful voice in demanding change. The escalation of growing antigovernmental sentiment, which found expression in unprecedented demonstrations, paired with internal conflict within the Duvalierist system and the suspension of aid by the USSD within a more pragmatic Reagan Administration ushered in the Duvalier regime´s collapse in early 1986 (Plummer 1992:206-209). It was followed by "Dechoukaj", literally the uprooting of a tree, a folk term Wilentz describes as "the violent movement against the Tontons Macoute" and "the necessity of ridding the country of Duvalierism". Wilentz arrived in Haiti days before Duvalier´s ouster. She reported that "[t]he American Embassy hated him [Aristide], because he held the United States and its economic system responsible for much of Haiti´s economic woe, and thus for the misery of her people, his congregation". One US Embassy official described him to her as "[a] Marxist maniac" (1989:53,112,137).

At the end of 1986, Wilentz began hearing about the "American Plan". Aristide also talked about it and HP mentioned it in numerous articles. Wilentz first gathered from street talk that the "American Plan" was thought to be "a Machiavellian conspiracy to force Haiti to comply with U.S. economic and geopolitical needs in the region". In the narrow sense, the "American Plan" turned out to be a collection of quotes from US government documents, trying to prove that the US intended to transform Haiti into an export-oriented economy catering to US markets. Wilentz soon realized that the "American Plan" was used by Haitians as a paranoid-sounding catch-all phrase going beyond mere economics to include AIDS, toxic waste, and even every-day calamities (1989:269-271;Plummer 1992:225). A street boy named Wildek once told Maggie Steber, the famous American Pulitzer-prize-winning photographer, that "the Americans put the stars in the sky ... because everything American is bigger ... [but if God made the stars] ... then God must be American" (Steber 1991:56). NCHR took advantage of the resentful respect Haitians in Haiti have for Americans.[280] But based on the historical record,[281] Wilentz consented: "The American strategy for developing Haiti ... [is] ...

---

[280] In spite of the terror reigning in Haiti between 1991 and 1994, Fuller´s and her family´s lives were never in jeopardy (Fuller 1995). NCHR once had a young US college student working as staff assistant in Port-au-Prince. He was related to a Congressman in Washington, which added to his authority (McCalla 1995).
[281] This record includes the US-imposed Constitution of 1918 and the irresponsible aid policies of the American-run cooperative venture *Société Haitiano-Américaine de Développement Agricole* (SHADA) of 1941, as well as the USAID-supported swine-fever-eradication program replacing well-adapted Hai-

a restructured and dependent agriculture that exports to U.S. markets and ... a displaced rural population that not only can be employed in offshore U.S. industries in the towns, but is more susceptible to Army control". Aristide told her that "I cannot accept that Haiti should be whatever the United States wants it to be" (1989:264-284,282).

During the crisis, HP linked "le `plan américain pour Haiti´" with the current negotiations and Haitian political society. Assessing its "10 years of struggle" in early April 1993, the Haitian weekly defined the "American Plan" as part of the new US strategy for Latin America in the 1980s: the promotion of civilian governments supported by anti-communist political forces that oppose all sorts of socialist projects. HP stressed that this was the "type of democracy that they prepare for us right now". As evidence of the "continuity of the American Plan", HP pointed out that Lesley Delatour was now often mentioned as a possible candidate for Prime Minister (HP 202:11). Advocating fiscal conservatism and austerity for Haiti, Delatour was Finance Minister under the *Conseil National Gouvernement* (CNG), the provisional government that immediately succeeded Baby Doc. The US Embassy is reported to have played a major role in persuading US Army-trained general Henri Namphy to head the CNG as chief of state. Namphy´s adviser on military affairs became Avril, also a US-trained military man (Plummer 1992:218,220;Wilentz 1989:324).

Nicknamed the Americans´ "toutou" (English: "bow-wow" or "lap-dog"), "ultra-liberal" (HP) Delatour was a close associate of Bazin, who was also briefly Finance Minister in 1982. He tried to curb the excessive spending of the Bennets, the powerful family of Baby Doc´s wife Michèle Bennet, and was dismissed. After working in Washington as a World Bank economist, he returned to Haiti in 1987 to wage his campaign as one of eight candidates running for the US-financed November 29 elections that ended in bloody turmoil. Known as "Mr. Clean", Wilentz describes the "anti-Communist" Bazin as "almost as American as Bill Cosby" (HP 202:11;Plummer 1992:196,223;Wilentz 1989:87,294,340). Bazin ran against Aristide in the 1990 elections. The "congressionally funded" *National Endowment for Democracy* (NED) in conjunction with the USSD´s Office of Democratic Initiatives reportedly spent over $12 million to finance both the elections and Bazin. "[B]oth Bazin and Washington were unpleasantly surprised by the Haitian electorate" (Griffin 1992:669;Ives 1995:43).

In sum, rhetorical references to heroes of Haiti´s past in association with wide-ranging suspicions condensed in the political slogan of the "American Plan" reveal the collectively shared experience of a national history characterized by increasing foreign involvement. After 1804, Haiti´s territorial borders, the safeguarding of which had been one expression of the highly esteemed ideal of liberty, became increasingly porous. Hard-pressed by ill-disposed state powers in a hostile international environment, the country became increasingly permeated by representatives of various types of transnationalisms from varying national backgrounds. They added to the perception of

---

tian pigs with costly white American pigs, various contemporary USAID Country Development Strategy Statements and World Bank reports analyzed by sociologists Josh DeWind and David Kinley, Wilentz´ personal experiences with Haitians working for the assembly industry, the price-reducing and migration-inducing repercussions of the USAID-funded Agroforestry Outreach Project administered by CARE, seen in Haiti´s Northwest as implementers of the "American Plan", the Food-for-Work program using US-government-supplied surplus food, and the low-cost contraband "Miami rice", likewise seen as part of the "American Plan".

foreign infiltration, often for exploitative purposes. Haiti's ideal of collective liberty is reflected in what I called above "Désir's principle of independence": organizational and financial freedom from US infiltration, be it governmental or private (Désir 1995). This history-conscious experience corresponds with a feeling of marginalization and alienation resulting from a heteromonous loss of control, a loss of self-determination. Not surprisingly, Haitian historian Laennec Hurbon divided Haitian history into three periods: slavery (16th century - 1804), independence (1804 - 1915), and the epoch of American colonization spanning the time period from "1915 to present" (Farmer 1992:183). As Aristide noted, Haiti "has been operating as a colony! It is the anachronistic but caricaturish prolongation of colonialism!" (1996:81). Hurbon was writing in 1987. In that year, "[m]any Haitians", as Plummer reported, "held the United States *directly* responsible for sustaining the thirty-year dictatorship and holding Haiti hostage to the cold war" (1992:224;author's italics). Following the bloody massacre at Ruelle Vaillant during the November 1987 elections under US-backed Namphy, "rumors of an American intervention washed over the city" of Port-au-Prince as "[a]lways in times of crisis", as Wilentz remembers. "This time, the Marines will definitely come", many Haitians and sensationalist journalists from abroad believed. But the US intervention did not occur (1989:327-328).

5.5.3 Focusing on the Cause: Unmasking the US as Coup-Instigator

Généus was glad to report in August 1991 that the Haitian artists, who participated in the event commemorating the 200th anniversary of Bois Caiman, proved that Haitian art was well alive. There was no danger of "loosing our identity despite the cultural imperialism, of which we are victims" (HP 1:9). Haitians in the US generally seek to retain in their children as much identification with Haitian culture as possible. Observations indicating a socialization that departs from this orientation are commented with great concern within the community.[282] Given this climate, Haitians in the US mostly concentrated on the possible causes of the coup, not primarily on its consequences such as the refugee crisis. Many of them suspected the US government to have masterminded Aristide's overthrow. This mind-set had them organize as if physically present in Haiti. They focused on indirect transnational relations of type 16 resembling those of type 9 (see above) in that they are both directed, albeit from different territory, at the US government believed to be implicated in the coup to begin with.

The Haitians, who demonstrated for Aristide in Miami's Little Haiti early on in the crisis, carried picket signs accusing Bush and the CIA in front of TV cameras (HP 10:12). Writing for HP from Haiti, Sekon Salye confirmed that the coup was de-

---

[282] Mayas of HWHR sent her then five-year-old daughter to a French school in New York, before she proceeded to an American school (Mayas 1995). Aubourg lamented that the majority of Haitian parents in New York do not raise their children bilingually. But they teach their American-born children about Haitian history (Aubourg 1996). For the three American-born children of my host family, their strict Creole-speaking grand-mother, who could hardly speak English, constituted the most important link to Haiti's past. One of their grand-sons would insist that he feels both "Haitian and American". For first-generation Americans like Raoul and Serrat, identification with Haitian culture was strong enough as to organize for the benefit of both Haitian refugees and Haiti.

nounced at once by "our compatriots" in Miami, New York, and New Jersey, who blamed Bush, the CIA, and US Ambassador Adams for having instigated it along with the putschists. Trying to appear as saviours, the word was spread that the "imperialist countries" represented by the Ambassadors of France, Venézuela, and the US "negotiated" with the "rebels" to save Aristide's life (HP 12:14). Among the crowd of approximately 200,000 Haitian protesters in New York on October 11, 1991 were posters proclaiming "Aristide yes, CIA no". For the demonstrators, "their leader [was] toppled by a storm of military-macoute following orders from obscure forces from inside and outside" as Latour put it (HP 22:15). Haitians were not alone in suspecting the US behind Aristide's overthrow. Latour quoted the Rev. Lucas, who reportedly said at the same rally that "it is not hard to imagine that the implicated hands of the USA have taken part in this coup" (HP 22:18). Likewise, at the *Haiti Commission*-sponsored soirée at *Baruch College* on November 21, Clark said that the US "is also responsible for the overthrow of the elected president of Haiti.... The Haitian military would have never dared to oust Aristide without the consent of the US" (HP 51:10).

Strategist Tecumseh joined this line of thought. She ascertained that Cédras was well-known in the US, referring to the November 1991 issue of *Jeune Afrique Economie*. The magazine had pointed out that "[n]obody in Haiti makes a secret out of Cédras' sojourn in the US, just before the coup. Three weeks, during which he met with senior officials of special US services". Cédras appeared as the man, who was the US's "card to drive Aristide from power" (HP 53:14). Manno Charlemagne suggested another indication for the US's implication. In the telephone interview in early January 1992, he maintained that Michel Francois had the "logistical, financial, military, and political backing of the US Ambassador, who tells him what to do" (HP 63:9,15). Consequently, HP observed that the US ironically lamented about the "consequences of a drama it itself has created and tries to prolong" (HP 57:6,16-18).

For HP, it was evident that the US's objective was "not simply to get rid of the refugees", but to "attempt to stabilize the current dictatorship or to orient itself towards solutions that keep Aristide away from power" (HP 79:1,20). As a result, not the refugee issue, but the US's assumed involvement in the coup must have appeared as its most vulnerable point. The 15,000 Haitians demonstrating in Manhattan as part of the February 7 celebrations of 1992 were reinforced by a "clear verdict of high culpability of the Bush Administration", as Latour put it. Marc Wally of "WLID" was quoted as calling the coup "an obscenity, with the complicity ... of the US government" (HP 80:12-13). Ives chose similar words. He stated that the documentary "Haiti: Killing the Dream" put an emphasis on "the complicity of the Bush Administration in the events surrounding the coup" and speculated about the role of US Ambassador Adams (HP 104:10). Similarly, Stern declared that the Americans' ignorance pushed the filmmakers to produce the documentary depicting Haitian reality and "the deeds of the US government in Haiti" (HP 146:10).

At the demonstration on April 6, Henry Ambroise of HEAR and the *Haitian Student Association* maintained that Aristide was "a challenge to Bush's new world order ... We need to tell George Bush to *leave Haiti* immediately" (HP 102:8;author's italics). At that time, Haitians in the US were trying to make sense of the "Washington Protocols" of February 1992. Since the accord also provided for the "professionalization" of the Haitian armed forces (ESC 1993:28-29), some Haitians started to get suspicious. In early April 1992, HP's Loubet interpreted "professionalization" in the "global context of a new US strategy for Latin America": The US sought to put in place "`democrats´ of capitalism" made obedient to the "IMF with the help of local armies" (HP 100:17). Moreover, the fact that the US was willing to pay $40 million between the coup and May 1992 in handling the refugee exodus added to the suspicions, "if the Bush government", as HP wrote, "actively or tacitly encouraged Cédras´ army to effectuate the coup" (HP 117:8). In HP´s view, the US appeared as being "caught in its own trap", fallen victim to a "situation that it has contributed to create" (HP 120:10). The CIA kept on assuming metaphorical meaning in accusations of US complicity. In his report on the NAACP/*TransAfrica*-organized demonstration of September 9, 1992, Latour thanked the two organizations on behalf of the 10th department for protesting against the "politique CIAiste de Bush" (HP 141:9). Advisers to Aristide also asserted in public that the US had masterminded the coup, which was denounced in early October by Bush Administration officials (French 1992d:A13).

In late November, HP observed that a "vast majority of Haitians in the 10th department, in particular in Miami" welcomed Clinton´s victory "with joy". This was understandable due to the fact that Bush was "perceived by the Haitian community as *directly* responsible for the coup d´etat of September 30, 1991" (HP 153:6;author´s italics). But prior to Clinton´s inauguration, HP cautioned that the "machine of the coup d´etat" had already been put in place following December 16, 1990. It asked the rhetorical question: "Is this different with Clinton?" (HP 168:16). HP based its assessment on an analysis by WOH´s Cooley-Prost entitled "Democratic Intervention", intervention by the US in Haiti through "pseudo-NGOs" such as NED. The analysis indicated that "NED functions like an arm of the US government ... an instrument utilized by Washington to support its foreign allies of the private sector ... [in terms of] ... interventionist operations formerly conducted by the CIA". HP reminded that after the departure of Baby Doc, the US had launched a "vast offensive to assure the control of Haiti". It started in September 1986 with a conference in Puerto Rico, to which "different Haitian politicians and Democrats had been invited to participate". It was organized by the *National Democratic Institute for International Affairs* (NDI), "one of the branches of NED". General Namphy received a NDI delegation on December 9, 1986, which "arrived to investigate the electoral process in Haiti". HP stressed that NED "belonged to the Democratic Party" (HP 153:6).[283] In general, according to Marx Aristide and Richardson of QC/QP´s Haiti Reborn Campaign, the US government "attempted to contain and counter" Haiti´s popular movement by using NED, USAID, and the CIA under the guise of "democratization", "development", and "the war on drugs" to build "conservative alternatives" (1995:190).

Further suspicions of the Democratic Party and, by extension, towards Clinton were fueled by Congressman Robert Torricelli. Following a trip to Haiti, the Democrat from New Jersey had declared that the embargo against Haiti was useless and that "the return of Aristide is not non-negotiable". HP suspected that Torricelli could as well

---

[283] In March 1987, NDI, transmitting "directly orders from the US", proposed to the CNG to provide "immediate technical assistance" for the November elections. HP called "Ertha Trouillot: A President made in USA", while NED´s funding reportedly increased sharply in preparation of the December 1990 elections (HP 202:12,13; Aristide,Richardson 1995:190). HP alleged that the Haitian national union CTH was funded by NED (HP 228:14). Likewise, the conservative *Federation of Workers Union* is alleged to have enjoyed "strong financial backing" by NED (Chamberlain 1995b:24), and Honorat noted that his group CHADEL received $40,000 a year from NED (Ives 1995c:67).

have been Clinton's emissary, in which case the Clinton Administration would pursue a policy "fundamentally identical with that of his predecessor" (HP 156:9). US General Sheehan' mission to Haiti in early January was no indication for HP that the US had "really abandoned its putschist friends". Rather, he let the military high command know that it could reckon with "non-lethal aid" for the Haitian army in exchange for cooperation to prevent a massive wave of Haitian refugees. HP was afraid that the aid offered by Sheehan for the army's "professionalization" could be supplied without replacing the "criminals" implicated in the coup (HP 168:6,14,16). The demand for "professionalization" of the Haitian army was going to be included in the GIA, whose point 5 called for "international assistance in modernizing the armed forces of Haiti and establishing a new police force" (Res.862).[284] Suspicions harbored towards Jackson must also be seen in this light.[285]

Given the historical links between the US military and the Haitian army dating from the Marine occupation 1915-1934, proposals such as Sheehan's alerted many Haitians. These serious concerns seem to have eclipsed in part concerns for Haitian refugees. Even if the Haitian Constitution mandated the separation of the roles of army and police, the "so-called professionalization of the army" was in HP's mind part and parcel of a new approach it called "social appeasement". The resumption of military aid would rather be designed to "quell effectively all popular uprisings". Clinton would kill two birds with one stone when succeeding in returning Aristide pro-forma with a pro-putschist Prime Minister: firstly, he could satisfy US public opinion by getting rid of the refugees; and, secondly, he could reassure Latin American democracies that the US would not tolerate coups in the region. But in reality, he would complete the "enterprise of destabilization undertaken by Bush" (HP 168:6,14,16).

Washington's intimidating posture of sending USCG cutters to Haiti to build what the Yale students would term the "floating Berlin Wall" was commented by HP as a naval blockade established "not against the putschists, but against the Haitian people" (HP 172:6,14-16). The operation "Able Manner" designed to contain the wave of Haitian refugees is reminiscent of the many times the US sent warships to Haiti "to protect the lives and property of American citizens" (Heinl and Heinl), and it must have equally reminded many Haitians of this horrifying aspect of their country's history. HP referred to NCHR-associate Rick Swartz, who had said in the WP (01/16/93) that "blockades are an act of war", while a USSD historian, William Slaney, had reportedly declared that such an operation was without precedent in the US. HP expressed its hope that a comparison between the case of Haiti and that of Somalia alluded to in the WP (01/16/93) "will not go any further" (HP 172:6,14-16). Instead of

---

[284] A letter dated July 24, 1993 from the UN Secretary-General to the UNSC President (S/26180) conveyed "a proposal from the Government of Haiti requesting the UN to provide assistance in creating a new police force and in modernizing the Haitian armed forces" (Res.867).

[285] As has been shown above, Jackson was not exempted from assumptions of furthering a hidden agenda. Not only had he met with Christopher on the eve of his departure, his whole visit took place "under the aegis of the US Embassy". What is more, Jackson's sheer proximity to high-ranking members of the Haitian army during his visit made him somewhat untrustworthy: He had a three-hour-meeting with Generals Cedras, Philippe Biamby, Jean-Claude Duperval, and Max Mayard in the private residence of Lesley Alexander, the "chargé d'affaires" of the US in Haiti (HP 174:16). Philippe Biamby was the third of Haiti's top military leaders, who participated in the coup (see the NYT of 06/20/94:A1 and of 10/13/94:A8).

pondering its future-oriented usefulness in strategical terms, many Haitians still thought of the refugee crisis as a phenomenon, the roots of which had to be traced to its very origin, i.e. as a direct product of the coup, which the US at least helped to create. In other words, their outlook was diagnostic, rather than prognostic, even though a direct culpable entanglement of the US was hard to prove. As a result of this line of thinking, the refugee crisis, the coup, and the US government were linked with each other in terms of a backward-looking chain of causation.[286]

In July 1993, British journalist Greg Chamberlain, Paris-based publisher of the weekly newsletter *Haiti Hebdo*, told the NYT´s French that in his judgement, HP, HM, and HO were "a real job to read ... [t]hey see everything in terms of plots, usually by the U.S. against Haiti" (1993b:D8). "[G]reatly concerned about persistent rumors that the CIA itself either supported, or was involved in, the coup" and for a lack of hard facts, refugee issue strategist Rangel called on the CIA on October 27 to meet with interested Members of Congress to refute the charges. The agency was to answer questions such as "What role, if any, did the CIA play in the September 1991 coup ... including, but not limited to, financial assistance, political counsel, or logistical support" (Rangel 1993b:1). Haitian organizing seems to have been based, to a large extent, on coup-related assumptions informed by a historical experience characterized by foreign (US) domination. The verifiability of these assumptions was, however, rather elusive for a lack of hard facts. In contrast, the US Administration´s violation of international and national refugee law was provable.

At the December 16, 1993 rally in Washington, Rangel recalled the "bad treatment of Haiti by the US and the infiltration of Haiti by the CIA", as Latour reported (HP 216:8,17). While Rangel might have had mainly the CIA´s role in the attempted character assassination of Aristide in October 1993 and the agency´s creation of the Haiti-based *National Intelligence Service* (SIN) in the mid-1980s in mind, the listening Haitians could have as well thought of the CIA´s presumed role in the coup. Providing another non-Haitian view, Chamberlain states that while the US Embassy "must have seen [the coup] coming and done nothing to stop" it, "a CIA-sponsored coup, predictably a favorite explanation of many Haitians and foreign friends, makes no sense and only the shakiest evidence has so far been presented to support this theory. Aristide was not remotely a threat to U.S. interests in Haiti or elsewhere" (1995a:56). Similarly, Malone notes that "White House-sanctioned US sponsorship of the coup against Aristide, as adduced by some observers of the Haitian scene, seems highly unlikely" (1997:135).

During 1991-1994, the US Administration did not speak with one voice. As CIP´s Morrell put it, the US "simultaneously conducted two policies toward Haiti", with especially the Clinton White House supporting "democratic norms" as the best

---

[286] Steve Louis, for example, one Haitian activist, who demonstrated in support of Haitian hunger strikers in Krome on January 9, 1993, was quoted by Ives as saying: "... la cause du problème des réfugiés réside dans le coup d'Etat *perpétré en Haiti par les Americains* et les macoutes que Cédras, Bazin, Honorat, Nérette". Lavarice Goldin, member of *Veye Yo*, was quoted as saying: "Quand Aristide était au pouvoir, il n´y avait pas de réfugiés. Mais depuis *Bush a fait le coup*, les gens ne cessent de fuir le pays" (HP 170:9;author´s italics). Interviewed in his Brooklyn office by NACLA staff member Orenstein in June 1993, Dupuy said that "[w]ithout doubt, ... Adams, was active in the coup. ... if they engineered the coup[,] [t]hey had to accept the necessity of Aristide´s return, but under [their own] conditions... I think the Bush Administration was involved in the coup" (1995a:98,99,100).

way to "contain the refugees". The other policy was the "traditional U.S. embrace of the elite and military as a bulwark against waywardly leftist or nationalist popular movements". In the case of Haiti, "the CIA and Pentagon in effect conducted their own parallel and conflicting policy" (Morrell 1995a:1). In early November 1994, Owens called the US government's Haiti policy a "schizophrenic policy", because "we've allowed the CIA to keep its hand in there".[287] It seems, however, that the CIA could be rather assured of a well-disposed US public at large, when it set out for its public character assassination campaign against Aristide in October 1993.[288]

In late December 1993, Latour pointed to the US's responsibility for Haiti's human rights situation in another way. He made mention of the "infamous" *School of the Americas* in Georgia, where military personnel from Latin American countries get training (HP 218:12). Farmer noted that Colonel Francois was a *School of the Americas*-graduate (1994:314). According to Père Adrien in the *Birmingham Catholic Press*, Haitian military officers were seen at the US army base in Fort Benning, home of the *School of the Americas*, as early as October 1993 (Chomsky 1994:36). Ives indicated that "many officers and specialists" of the Haitian army had been trained in Fort Benning. After Aristide's return, he was concerned that candidates for a "professionalized" Haitian army could be recruited from this source (1995a:116). The historical links between the US military and the Haitian army were a constant companion during the crisis. Not surprisingly, Latour condemned the "cowboy mentality" of the US and encouraged the "Davids of the Third World" in their struggle against the "Goliath of the North". He commended the Haitian people, who had "fallen prey to an international conspiracy", to a "coup d'Etat *made in USA, benedetto per il Vaticano* [sic]" (HP 218:12).

At the Miami conference, Sister Anne McCarthy of *Pax Christi*, who was part of the work shop dealing with the role of civil society, demanded "to shed light on the role of the US government in the way it undermines democracy". These remarks led USSD representative Mike Kozak to leave the room, slamming the door (HP 224:17). Whereas Sister McCarthy's inquiry seems to have covered the period following the coup only, Latour reached back much farther. Pezzulo insisted at the conference that the US did not have a "special interest" in Haiti's future on account of its "territory or resources", but an interest in finding a "democratic process" serving the Haitian people. Latour ironically commented that in reality, this search had already begun in 1917 during the US occupation, "and the search continues..." (HP 226:8). HP made out a score of Haitian unionist at the conference it did not trust. Among them was Jean Nazaire Tidé, who reportedly said to have felt a "spirit of compromise" at the conference. HP linked him to PLANOP, which the weekly attributed to a group of Haitian organizations funded by USAID in 1993 through the *Projet Intégré pour le Renforce-*

---

[287] Statement by Owens at the "Haitian Community Leaders Meeting" of BfA on November 3, 1994.
[288] One indication for this assumption is that Americans appeared "surprisingly unconcerned" in early 1994 about the so-called "Ames scandal" involving the revelations of a former CIA agent and his wife accused of spying for Russia. Asked for their "overall opinion" of the CIA, a majority of 40% said to be "mostly favorable" towards the agency. The public was "evenly split" on whether the CIA should (48%) or should not (47%) work clandestinely inside other countries to weaken or topple governments unfriendly to the US (Moore 1994:17,20). For more information on the CIA's campaign in cooperation with Senator Jesse Helms to publicly discredit Aristide as drug addict and depressive, see the NYT of 10/23/93:A1, 10/24/93:1/7, 10/31/93:1/12, 11/01/93:A1, and 12/25/93:A10.

ment de la Démocratie en Haiti (PIRED). According to a USAID-document dated June 1993, from which HP quoted, PIRED was designed in 1991 to "support democracy" in Haiti (HP 228:14). In his open letter to Aristide late January 1994, Ratner seemed to agree on many points in the Haitian analysis of US foreign policy in the Caribbean Basin (HP 229:8).[289] Yet the many similarities did not keep him from constantly pursuing a strategy focusing on the refugee issue. Whether or not he foresaw the long-term consequences of this strategy in terms of a US-led multinational intervention, is unclear.

Faced with never-ending negotiations on the international level while the human rights and economic situation in Haiti worsened, criticism of the US and the international community grew more desperate in the months to come. Following the Miami conference, Aristide took again the offensive against Clinton's Haiti policy in a fashion that must have appeared to many Haitians as being more in line with his claim of following the example of Dessalines. At the CBC conference in Miami of March 18 and 19, he raised again the question of the US Administration's responsibility in the coup, using it as a means of pressuring the same: "Comment peut-on prétendre que *l'ambassade américaine* à Port-au-Prince n'était pas *impliquée dans le coup* d'Etat? ... le président Clinton a encore une chance de prouver que les Etats-Unis n'étaient pas, ou ne sont plus impliqués, en restaurant la démocratie". His spokesperson Martineau subsequently toned down the charge to the quality of a rumor (HP 237:18;author's italics).[290] Accusations of US responsibility were even publicly raised in most private moments. At Haitian *Veye Yo* activist Buron's funeral in Little Haiti on March 19, the crowd, as HP reported, attested to its "disgust of the CIA and the complicity of the US with the putschists" (HP 239:7). In what appears as a reflection of the private-public character of Buron's funeral, HP deplored in early September that the global phenomenon of refugee streams would be "depoliticized at a maximum" (HP 316:18).

For many Haitians, the phenomenon of "refugeeism" (Hakovirta) is not an academic and abstract subject matter, but an experience made either by themselves, by family members and friends, or by their ancestors. As Gilbert reported in late March 1992, Aristide had said before the UN that the living conditions of the Haitian refugees were reminiscent of "the slave trade of Blacks" (HP 91:8). Similarly, Tecumseh was appalled in late July 1994 to be a witness of negotiations involving "humilated" Panama as well as Caribbean islands such as Antigua, Jamaica, Turks and Caicos, and Caiman. They were pressured by the US Administration with the promise of financial aid to open up Haitian refugee processing sites on their territories. Haitian refugees were treated as a "commodity" and thus degraded to an "object of bargaining", Tecumseh complained, to a "kind of money exchange" reminiscent of the days of slavery. She said that this "slave trade" must be a "slap in the face" for Aristide seeing his people "sold by auction" and even perhaps returned "to the soil of Africa" (HP 289:12). As early as March 1992, Tecumseh explained that the Haitian hunger strikers on Guantanamo aimed at "reconquering their dignity" (HP 189:10,13).

---

[289] Ratner pointed out that he had fought for 20 years against US intervention, in Puerto Rico, Nicaragua, El Salvador, Guatemala, Grenada, and Cuba. The communist threat was but a pretext, which the current situation of Haiti illustrated, now that the USSR did not exist anymore (HP 229:8).

[290] According to Latour, Aristide framed his charge as a joke: "[P]ourquoi n'y a t-il jamais de coup d'Etat aux Etats-Unis? ... parce qu'aux Etats-Unis, il n'y a pas d'ambassade américaine" (HP 239:7).

As early as 1505, several black Africans were introduced to Hispaniola to replace the declining native population as laborers. During the growth of the sugar economy in the 16th and 17th century, about 4.5 million Africans were imported as slaves into the region. During the era of Atlantic slave trade, an estimated 1.7 million Africans were transported to the British Caribbean alone. More than 864,000 enslaved Africans were shipped to French Saint Domingue by 1791, the plurality of them after 1697 (Richardson 1983:10,14;Simmons,Guengant 1992:94;Mintz 1995:75).

Tecumseh enumerated the refugees´ sorrows and humiliations that "*we* are inflicted upon": They were "rejected without pity in the putschists´ hell, put in quarantine on Guantanamo, [and] treated with disdain in the US". She stressed that Haitian refugees have a "right for political asylum in the US", be they HIV-infected or not. The refugees never asked Clinton for a "special `humanism´". They rather demanded that an "illegal immigration´policy" be abandoned (HP 189:10,13;author´s italics). It is quite possible that many Haitians viewed NCHR´s Haitian refugee tour with Yolande Jean, designed to attach a "human face" to the important issues of refugee protection, as a humiliating exercise in currying of favors with the US public. This view must have been informed by the historical ideal of *marronage*. Instrumentalizing Haitian boat people, once called by Latour "the maroons of the sea" (HP 58:1,17), as bargaining chips for the sake of the return issue seems to have been tantamount to a sacrilege in the eyes of many Haitians. To put it metaphorically, a national hero like Makandal would not have begged for asylum.

Bearing the history of US-Haitian relations in mind, the next logical step would be to make the US liable for the injustices it inflicted on Haiti. Consequently, Tecumseh ascertained that there was "a special obligation" accruing to the US: "Et si les Etats-Unis ont une responsabilité principale, c´est du fait des *réparations* qu´ils nous doivent pour tous les *torts* qu´il nous ont causés, avant, *pendant* and après le coup d´Etat". Writing in March 1993, she called on Haitians in the US to mobilize in order to have the US fulfill its obligation, to have the US make "reparations" for the "torts" it committed (HP 189:13;author´s italics). The first measure of redeeming its historical debt was for the US to help restore Aristide, certainly a morally justified demand, which was, however, not backed up with any teeth.[291]

Conversely, there was another obligation seen on the side of the US, which did not result from torts, but from support given by Haitians to their neighbor country. This point was stressed for the first time by Aristide at the demonstration in Central Park in late April 1992. He reminded his audience that Haitians and Americans fought side by side in the American War of Independence (HP 116:16). In his report on the rally, Latour dwelt somewhat longer on this point, on that "day of victory" and "of liberty, when 2,400 valorous Haitian soldiers under General Leconte d´Estaing headed to

---

[291] While HP hoped in mid-June 1994 that Ratner´s lawsuit against FRAPH would also shed light on the US - the "real terrorists", who tolerated the group´s "undesirables" on its territory (HP 270:7), one shocking aspect of US responsibility in committing "torts", and thus the validity of Tecumseh´s demand, became visible only after Aristide´s return. In late October 1994, journalist Allan Nairn revealed in *The Nation* that Patrick Collins, then attaché of the *US Defense Intelligence Agency* (USDIA) in Haiti, had encouraged Emmanuel Constant in 1993, then working for the CIA-run SIN, to form FRAPH (Farmer 1995:222). As HP´s Ives put it: "The ... death squads of FRAPH were conceived, recruited and funded by the CIA and the ... [USDIA]" (1995a:112). The news confirmed the US´s "politique CIAiste" (Latour) in post-coup Haiti.

Savannah on October 8-9, 1779 ... In 1782, Haitian and American soldiers fraternized once again and fought until the Americans would have their independence" (HP 116:16).[292] Aristide would reiterate this idea at a student party at *Brooklyn College* in Flatbush (HP 122:15). Not only Aristide used this argument to put moral pressure on the US. At the Miami conference, Jackson added that the victory of Haitians over the troops of Napoleon had made possible the inexpensive purchase of Louisiana. He therefore pleaded for fair treatment towards Haiti (HP 226:8;Plummer 1992:4;Wilentz 1989:76;Lawless 1992:42).

Probably to many Haitians' chagrin, Aristide evoked one of Haiti's national icons in a much more sober way during his visit to New York in mid-May 1994, when a US-led military intervention seemed already to be unavoidable. He said that it would be impossible to prevent US troops from coming to Haiti by acting like Péralte (HP 261:8). HP, on the contrary, doubted as early as April that democracy could be imposed by military intervention, "let alone by the US military that created, armed and financed the Haitian army" (HP 252). Similarly, the *Haiti Commission*'s Pat Chin emphasized at an event in the *Local 1199* headquarters in Manhattan on July 28 that the triumph of the 1804 revolution and the overthrow of the Duvalier regime in 1986 had not been the result of a US invasion. Georges Honorat of APN said that a military US intervention would "legalize and finalize the coup" (HP 301:10). Aristide noted in retrospect that the "most persuasive educational methods ... will never get the idea out of Haitian minds that Alvin Adams was involved in the conspiracy" leading to the coup. "In Port-au-Prince, the American ambassador was informed" (Aristide 1996:49).

Upon Aristide's US-assisted return on October 15, HP repeated that it must be considered an "alarming naivety" to think that the US would finish with the "military macoutes", since the latter were formed by the former, they were their "proper agents" (HP 331:16). As early as June 1993, that is even before the signing of the GIA, Dupuy testified to his belief that "the ultimate goal of the United States is to get militarily involved in Haiti - to do it through international institutions like the OAS and the UN" (Orenstein 1995a:99). As a matter of fact, fears of US military intervention between September 1991 and October 1994 had been almost as old as the crisis itself. And those fears helped structure organizing efforts in the US-based Haitian community.

5.6 The Imminent Danger for Haiti's Self-Determination: US Military Power

As the NYT's Gray Jerry reported right after the coup, among the Haitians, who spontaneously demonstrated for Aristide in Miami's Little Haiti, were also "[s]ome demand[ing] American intervention to restore Mr. Aristide to power" (1991:A6). On October 4, Robert A. Pastor, professor for political science at *Emory University* and staff member of the *Carter Center* in Atlanta, argued in a NYT-commentary for collective military action by the OAS against the coup in Haiti (1991:A31). But contrary to vague reports in the US mainstream media that Aristide would "possibly even" ask the OAS for "foreign intervention" (Friedman 1991:A1), at the AfA-sponsored event in

---

[292] The volunteer unit participating in the battle of Savannah, the *Fontages Legion*, was composed of 545 mulattoes and blacks from Saint-Domingue (Plummer 1992:3).

Manhattan on October 25, Casimir responded unequivocally to questions from concerned participants: "Aristide will never demand that *foreign soldiers* come to target Haitian soldiers ... Now, that we are close to the return of Aristide, it would be crazy to envisage a *foreign occupation*" (HP 32:11;author's italics). On his way to the summit of francophone countries in Paris on November 17, Aristide gave a press conference at Travelodge Hotel next to JFK airport. Questions asked also concerned an eventual military intervention. Aristide answered that it was useless to evoke military intervention, since the embargo should suffice (HP 47:10,21). At the soirée at *Baruch College* on November 21, *Haiti Commission*-member Pat Chin not only pronounced herself against any suspension of the embargo, but also "against all military intervention" (HP 51:10). Coinciding with the US media's "campaign of misinformation", concerns over US foreign intervention in post-coup Haiti did not only emerge in the Haitian community of New York. Speaking before an audience of about 600 to 700 people at a soirée with Senator Wesner Emmanuel in *St. Mathieu Church* in Boston on November 15, Père Clérismé, the initiator of the Adopt-A-Parish Program and leading member of the Haitian peasant group *Tèt Kole*, stressed the important role of the 10th department and, at the same time, warned "against all foreign *military* intervention", as Généus reported (HP 46:9;author's italics).

About one week into the crisis, the NYT reported that Bush had "not favored military intervention, saying he wants to let" the OAS "fashion an appropriate response" (Gonzalez 1991:B5). This is consistent with information Milne used to prepare his Congressman for a meeting with Bush's National Security Adviser Brent Scowcroft, who had requested from Rangel recommendations for further actions concerning Haiti. According to Milne, Bush would have supported a "multinational force" organized by the OAS or the UN, "but not including American combat troops". He did, however, dispatch 300-400 Marines to Cuba to be used to evacuate US citizens from Haiti, if his "Administration determines that their security is in danger" (Rangel91j:2,1). Bush failed with his idea of a OAS-sponsored "multinational force", since the OAS' "preferred tool", as Malone put it, was economic sanctions. Even once sanctions failed, many OAS members were not ready to endorse "more coercive measures", as the memories of the 1965 OAS-approved US intervention in the Dominican Republic were reportedly still vivid (Malone 1997:136).

The OAS' response to the Haitian political crisis emanated from the "Santiago Commitment to Democracy" of June 1991 and the subsequent Resolution 1080. It recognizes - "with due respect for the principle of non-intervention" - representative democracy as "the form of government of the region". The Santiago Declaration was the joint attempt to counter some Latin American and Caribbean states' growing pessimism towards the Inter-American system at the end of the 1980s. At that time, observers attributed the discontent of those states' leaders to what was perceived as the US's historical "interventionism" and "imperialism" as well as its excessive "bilateralism" at the expense of "multilateralism" and to the detriment of the OAS (Han 1987:40,376-378). The coup in Haiti put the Santiago Declaration to its first test.

In a letter to Rangel dated November 11, 1991, Clark expressed grave concern over the Marine evacuation mission mentioned by Milne. Relying on a "documentary camera crew", which had recently returned from Haiti, Clark informed him that "several sources spoke of U.S. transport planes carrying tanks, ammunition and weapons" to be transported to a military airstrip near Jeremie, "a town which is a stronghold of opposition to the coup". Referring to an ai-report and information included in a *Granma*-editoral on US Marines "deployed toward the north of Haiti" by way of "six amphibious vessels headed by LPH-12 helicopter carriers", he stated that "[w]ether the military operations are for Haiti or Cuba is unclear; however, there is no question that they are an ominous development for both. We cannot stand idly by" (Rangel91b:1,2). In the light of alleged US preparations for an invasion of Haiti, the assumed US-assisted coup must have appeared as the conspiratorial pretext for the US to gain total control of the island nation by military means.

The perceived danger of an imminent US military intervention in post-coup Haiti was in the air in these times of crisis, and also Jackson picked up the theme. But he did so in a way that must have horrified and outraged many Haitians in the US. Probably not being aware of the historically charged negative connotation the term implies especially for Haitians, he "forthright favored military intervention to restore Aristide to power" at the mass in memory of 152 drowned Haitian refugees in Sansaricq´s *St. Jerome Church* in Brooklyn on November 24, 1991, as Alain St. Victor reported. In response, Victor judged Jackson harshly: "This position, which takes the form of a paternalist attitude with Jackson, has to be denounced without reservation, because it can play into the hands of imperialist forces that have never been in the interest of the Haitian people. ... [O]ne cannot follow him, if he favors military intervention by those forces that have historically been the tutors of the military-macoute to begin with" (HP 50:8).

Plainclothes police chase demonstrators to break up riot, Port-au-Prince, Haiti, Feb/86 (courtesy Maggie Steber)

Haitian army protest Aristide's attempted return on 10/29/93 (courtesy Maggie Steber)

5.6.1 The Linkage between the Refugee Issue and the Issue of US Invasion

HP alleged that Rangel made statements similar to those made by Jackson. These statements caused great mistrust by the Haitian strategist Tecumseh, whom HP granted pages to elaborate on the positions taken by both. While agreeing with Rangel on the merits of "making noise" on the refugee issue, she cautioned the 10th department against being "taken in tow by politicians, whose disagreements with Bush remain *secondary* and who have their own vision, for example that of a *military intervention* in Haiti". She continued: "We don't demand from the US to play Rambo in Haiti and to reestablish order in our own country as it sees fit". Tecumseh referred, *inter alia*, to a press conference in New York on November 24 with Rangel, Ed Towns, and Guy Victor, at which Jackson called for military intervention to restore Aristide by alluding to Saddam Hussein. She observed that "the democratic, liberal sector in the US" had "apparently taken the refugees as its cause". But she concluded that "the defense of refugees by such political figures thus cuts both ways ... [and that] ... the support for a `black people´ ... might turn out to be extremely dangerous, because it leaves a door of exit for the Bush Administration in terms of a solution [intervention]... that would definitely appear as the better means to guarantee its proper interests". Consequently, "the compatriots of the 10th department have to be vigilant vis-a-vis the allies, whose excesses of zeal are incontrollable,... What is important ... [is for the 10th department to know] ... how to utilize the *temporary allies* for its own benefit" (HP 53:12-15;author´s italics).

It seems that from now on the refugee issue was inextricably tied to the fear of US military intervention in post-coup Haiti, a linkage that seemed to be based on a cultural misunderstanding. Pressuring the US Administration for its unlawful handling of the Haitian refugee crisis therefore always entailed, to a certain extent, the danger of pressuring it *too hard*. The refugee issue strategy implied for the return issue a risky brinkmanship between US inaction and US overreaction. It posed a dilemma between humanitarian-patriotic concern for the plight of Haitian refugees and supposed strategical imperatives for the sake of Haiti´s territorial integrity and sovereignty. To put it in McCalla´s words, the *10e of New York* and a score of allied Haitian community-based political organizations in the US were not so much concerned that the "likelihood" for US support could be "null", but that there could be *too much* "support of the United States" for the return of Aristide, i.e. under conditions of a US military intervention. There was a concern that the US might use the refugee crisis as a pretext for an invasion of Haiti.

Understandably, the political leadership in the Haitian community watched carefully, what the next steps of their "double-edged" allies would be. In early December, HP reported that Rangel and Jackson had been to Guantanamo, with the latter "pursuing his interventionist propaganda". The weekly quoted him as having told AP (12/07/91) that "the Haitians should return to Haiti like the Kuweities were able to return to Kuweit". HP added that their concern for the Haitian refugee was an issue that "continues to be the number one of the press" (HP 57:17-18). Similarly, in his report on the rally of nearly 10,000 demonstrators in Washington on December 13, Latour reiterated the Haitian community´s demands, among them "political asylum for Haitian refugees ... and, *most of all*, no military intervention" (HP 58:1,17;author´s italics). Concerns over unilateral US military action must have especially reverberated in the

Haitian community, when popular singer Manno Charlemagne said in the telephone interview with HP on December 29 that the "lumpen bourgeoisie", allied to the army, "dreams but of intervention" (HP 63:9,15).

As far as Rangel is concerned, he did *not* call for military action in Haiti until the fall of 1993. He did call, however, for *diplomatic* intervention by the UN early on. The misunderstanding seems to have been based on the difference between intervention and *military* intervention. It also seems very unlikely that Jackson intended, at this early point in time, to push the Bush Administration to actually intervene militarily in Haiti in order to have Aristide returned to power, even with multilateral OAS/UN-backing. What seems to be much more likely is that he sought to put additional pressure on the Bush Administration, which had already begun its "slow strangulation" of Aristide by discrediting him as an instigator of "mob rule" (Ives 1995c:66). Jackson must have realized the rising isolationist mood in the US. An overwhelming majority of Americans wanted their government to *reduce* involvements abroad (McAneny 1992:12). At the same time, confidence in both the Presidency and the US military was diverging in a downward trend, with the former loosing more confidence relative to the latter (Newport,Saad 1994:5,6).[293] In the light of these sentiments, the political risks involved in sending US troops to post-coup Haiti in a full-scale military adventure were too high for Bush, provided there was a vital interest for him to do so in the first place. What appeared as a reflection of these conditions, Rangel alluded to the Gulf War in early February 1992, complaining that the Bush Administration would never have given up so quickly, "if Haiti had oil or raw materials" (Opitz 1992:3).

The benefit from Saint Domingue for imperial France was obvious in 1789. The colony represented what Knight calls "the epitome of the successful exploitation slave society in the tropical American world" (1990:202). Caribbean *land* captured from American Indians, know-how, managerial skills, military power and initial *capital* from Europe, and cheap African slave *labor* were the factors of production that made this "success" possible (Mintz 1995:74). According to Plummer, early Marine occupation policies by USSD officials, which were accompanied by open racism, indicate that Washington began to regard Haiti primarily as a "repository of cheap labor". Attracted by higher wages in Cuba and the Dominican Republic, cheap Haitian labor joined coffee and other commodities as a significant export during the occupation years. Considering cheap labor "Haiti´s most valuable asset", Haitian and US officials alike were concerned over the exodus. The revival of forced labor, the so-called *corvée*, which had been briefly employed in Haiti by King Henry Christophe and was now reintroduced for road building serving strategic purposes, is indicative of US appreciation of

---

[293] The growing isolationist sentiment in the US was reflected in a Gallup poll taken in November 1991. It showed less than half (46%) of registered voters saying that they would not vote to re-elect Bush, whose 10-percentage-lead over an "unspecified Democratic candidate" was down from his 22-point advantage only two months earlier. A "key factor" in the improved Democratic prospects for the 1992 elections was assumed to be "the precedence voters now give to economic and domestic issues over national defense and foreign affairs" (Hugick 1991:5). The growing isolationist mood correlated with the rising anti-immigrant sentiment especially with regard to influxes from the Third World including Haiti (Hugick 1992a:6). Out of a pool of 15 institutions, the US military generated the most confidence (69%) among Americans in October 1991, down from 85% in March 1991, when the Gulf War still raged. The Presidency, on the other hand, ranked fifth with 50% in October 1991, down from 72% in March 1991 (Newport,Saad 1994:5,6).

Haitian labor. The withdrawal from Haiti was marked by the pragmatic realization in Washington that open intervention would accomplish little (Plummer 1992:108,111,95,102,140).

With the availability of cheap labor being the prime determining factor for investment in peripheral developing countries with low wages, high unemployment, limited natural resources, low levels of unionization, and "politically stable regimes", multinational enterprises began in the 1960s to export what Helen Safa calls "runaway shops" to Asia, to Central America, and to the Caribbean (1981:418,423). Consistent with one component of the Mann Doctrine, the US re-emphasized at that time the traditional concern with maintaining a political climate favorable to US business interests, which reflected Johnson´s belief that Haiti meant little to overall US interests. His Ambassador to Haiti, Benson E. L. Timmons III, termed US policy non-interventionist. By 1971, the US government under Nixon had made a substantial aid investment in Duvalier´s Haiti, providing improved infrastructural facilities in support of the new light-assembly industry in Port-au-Prince. An array of US agencies spearheaded by USAID constructed an interdependence between Haiti and the US. "Their ideas about how the two countries could best cooperate", Plummer notes, "rested on the time-honored conception of Haitians as a source of cheap, docile labor who expected little and got less" (1992:175-177).[294]

Interconnected with internal migration, urbanization, and the decline of agriculture, the US offshore assembly industry in Haiti came to support about one-quarter of the population of the island nation´s capital by 1980 (Farmer 1992:184-188). The industry was further promoted in pre-coup Haiti, as was shown in chapter 5.2.7. CLAA´s success in convincing the Bush Administration to relax the OAS-sponsored embargo and the ensuing resumption of trade in ever higher volumes for the benefit of Haitian and American business interests in the offshore assembly industry is indicative of one key element in the overall US interest in Haiti: Haitian cheap labor. The US did not have a "vital interest" to invade Haiti during the crisis, because its interest was already met. In its letter to Clinton of April 11, 1994, NLC denounced the detrimental effects on the Haitian situation caused by more than 60 US companies´ continued trade with Haiti following the OAS´ re-imposition of the embargo on October 18, 1993. As HP agreed, this policy was part of the "American plan" for Haiti (HP 249:8).[295]

While McCalla called the alleged widespread belief in the Haitian community of US geostrategical interests in Haiti an anachronistic "myth", Guy Victor identified a US need of "strategical control" of the "triangle" formed by Jamaica, Cuba, and Haiti. But the "most important thing", he acknowledged, were US commercial interests not only in the Haiti-based assembly industry, but also in the export-oriented Dominican

---

[294] Mayas said that the US government had been disturbed by the Haitian politics of return in the wake of Aristide´s election, "because they were not going to have anybody to work those sweat shops for them. Nobody was going to work for ... minimum wage, except Haitians" (Mayas 1995).
[295] While Lexiuste, at the union-organized conference in New York on May 6, defined the "American plan" in a broader sense as a US policy designed to maintain the status quo in Haiti through the World Bank and the IMF (HP 259), a young Haitian cab driver, whom I met in 1994, pointed to real estate interests coupled with a will of revenge as Bush´s personal stake in Haiti. The US President allegedly intended to purchase a villa in the hills of Pétionville, the wealthy suburb above Port-au-Prince. However, his bid was rejected, the cab driver gloated with a grin. I met the cab driver in "Magguy´s Restaurant" at the corner of Utica Avenue and Empire Boulevard in Brooklyn on August 27, 1994.

sugar industry dependent on Haitian cheap labor. Similarly, one HEAR-member defined US interest in Haiti as the reliance on "three million people that would work for $3 an hour". In Raoul's view, Haitian cheap labor has "definitely an influence" on US interest in Haiti. For McCalla, transforming Haiti into the "Taiwan of the Caribbean" failed, wherefore the low wage level was the country's most valuable asset (McCalla 1995; Victor 1996; HEAR 1995).

Apprehension about US military intervention was continually expressed, generating friction between the political leadership in the Haitian community and the African-American leadership. Following the USSC's decision in early February 1992, Rangel condemned the recalling of the US Ambassador at a time when Haitian civilians were forcibly returned "to the same dangerous place". HP commented that "the declarations by politicians like Rangel and Jackson have to be taken with a grain of salt, as they are often accompanied by interventionist propositions" (HP 70:1,16). Those concerns were compounded by the "threat of military intervention" that the Bush Administration reportedly used "to force Aristide to come to terms with Cédras and the macoute sector". HP criticized that this policy "can only perpetuate the exodus of refugees and the sufferings of ... a people of martyrs" (HP 84:9).

In the early stages of the crisis, the pros and cons of military intervention also caused divisions within the political leadership of the Haitian community. Speaking for the press committee of the *10e of New York*, Magloire and Alain St. Victor opposed in early February "any foreign intervention" in Haiti. With the embargo not respected universally, they observed that "certain compatriots" lose courage. Among them was reportedly Désir, who, as they regretted, "on a radio program on Sunday, February 2, 1992 has promoted the idea of military intervention in our country". They deemed a debate necessary about "the historic disastrous consequences of various interventions made under the aegis of the UN, the OAS or the US" (HP 73:11). When the detrimental effects of the porous and blunt economic sanctions on Haiti become ever more visible, concerns over military intervention became also linked to the embargo as one pillar of the Haitian "three-pronged strategy". Reporting on US refugee policy in early June 1992, HP elaborated on the question whether or not the "sabotage of the embargo" could ultimately lead to "intervention" (HP 124:20). Those fears were additionally nutured by Ocampo, OAS mediator in Haiti, who reportedly favored in the presence of Aristide an intervention in the island nation. He justified his demand with the systematic violation of the embargo and "the old concepts of absolute sovereignty" as being "totally outdated". He spoke at the annual award reception on September 15, sponsored by *Inter Press Service* (IPS), a Third World press agency founded in 1964. In his report on the event, Ives reiterated that Ocampo's suggestion was "an option that president Aristide .. continuously and clearly rejected" (HP 144:13).

The exile government's strategy seems to have been influenced by a perceived threat of US military intervention. At a meeting with the *Jewish Community Relations Council* of New York (JCRC) in Manhattan during Aristide's second visit to New York in late May 1992, Aristide was asked by Ed Foxman, president of the *Anti-Defamation League*, why the US seemed to lack the will to help him. Aristide simply responded that "Jean-Claude Duvalier left Haiti after a simple telephone call ... without military intervention, a simple appeal on the telephone". According to Wilentz, Duvalier's actual departure was preceded by a premature USSD announcement about his ouster one week earlier, which "[p]erhaps helped encourage the President to leave".

The same was true for Namphy and Avril, Aristide stressed, insisting that the same kind of pressure could be effective again (HP 127:12;Wilentz 1989:21-22). At a meeting in *City College* on November 20, Aristide again rejected categorically every possibility of foreign military intervention. Latour quoted Aristide as saying that "a telephone call (to General Cédras) would be much cheaper" (HP 157:10-12). The perceived threat of US military intervention seems to have conditioned the cautiousness in handling the refugee issue. One of Aristide´s advisors, HRC´s legal counselor Kurzban, would later remind the participants in the nationwide conference call of November 18, 1992 that "one phone call got Duvalier out of power". It would thus be wrong to minimize the power of the US. The emphasis should be on the restoration of Aristide as a solution to the refugee problem (NCHR12:3). The "telephone call" metaphor became emblematic of the assumed scope of US power and was, as a matter of fact, reiterated time and again by many Haitians in the US interviewed in the NYT. Rohter would later dub it "`the magic phone call´ theory", which was also espoused by Haitians in Port-au-Prince (1994d:A2). It did not, however, answer the question of how to prod the White House to pick up the phone to begin with. The telephone metaphor signified both overestimating US power and US will to reinstall the legitimate Haitian government. For in the final analysis, it took more than a telephone call to oust the *de facto* regime, and it took more to urge the US to do so in the first place.

After Clinton´s election, Roumer identified the OAS Santiago Commitment to Democracy as a possible blue print for foreign intervention. For it contained "all elements of the scenario" required to push Clinton towards a solution "hoped for by the interventionist sectors in the US". Roumer referred to Pastor as a protagonist of this sector, who had published in the 1992 fall issue of *Foreign Policy* an essay entitled "Latin American Option". Pastor argued that a freely elected President´s calling on the OAS "should not be interpreted as an intervention but rather as a legitimate request for help". Roumer asked to be cautious by paying attention to the dangers of "interventionism" (HP 152:22). As the crisis dragged on, increasing UN involvement following UNGA resolution A/RES.47/20A of November 24, 1992 and the initial Haitian fear of imminent unilateral US military action in Haiti began to merge. As was shown in chapter 5.3.4., a fraction of the Haitian political leadership in the US led by Dupuy interpreted Boutros-Ghali´s concepts of "preventive diplomacy", "limited sovereignty", and "preventive deployment" as theoretical justification allowing the US by way of intervention "to recolonize the world, now that the Cold War is principally over". In this context, HP interpreted UN Charta Art. 24 pertaining to the "maintenance of peace and international security" in conjunction with Art. 53 stipulating "coercive measures", mandated by the UNSC and executed by regional organizations, as giving sole authority to the UNSC to undertake "a military action". The weekly concluded that the UN Charta could "open the door" for the UNSC "to take into its hands the Haitian case" in order to authorize "the eventual dispatch of an armed force" that could "unleash all types of armed intervention". HP therefore demanded: "Non, ... [à] une intervention armée étrangère ... on ne lutte pas contre les macoutes locaux en faisant appel aux macoutes internationaux". Singling out Haitian economist Paul Latortue as one proponent of this approach, HP showed itself to be surprised about the "incredible naivety" of certain members in the Lavalas camp willing to trust Clinton more than Bush (HP 158:6,16,17). Refusing to form a unity with the "propagandists of the American Plan", HP saw HM "totally aligned with Clinton" on the question of military intervention (HP

161:18). Following a more moderate line relative to HP, HM was reported to have given Aristide "unyielding support" (Jean-Pierre 1995:201).

According to HP, the NYT (01/24/93) reported that Jackson had pressured Cedras during his visit to Haiti in late January 1993 to accept the return of Aristide. The only question remaining was whether or not the "transition to democracy" would require "force". At the same time, Secretary of State Christopher made it clear at a press conference in New York that the Clinton Administration would support the dispatch of 400 to 500 OAS and UN monitors to observe human rights in Haiti. HP resented Jackson's "clear allusion towards a recourse to military intervention". The weekly made the Aristide government responsible for "the soon arrival of an observer mission" representing the "prelude to the eventual occupation of the country". The Clinton Administration's interest was to "pocket" the Haitian people by using Jackson and Rangel to gain acceptance for its "turnaround" on Haitian refugees. Referring to Evans Paul, HP warned that Caputo's "acceleration of the process" might "create an uncontrollable situation" justifying an "armed military intervention" as a last resort (HP 174:16,18). Jackson's subsequent activism on behalf of the Guantanamo refugees must have appeared to anti-interventionist Haitians as duplicity, as an exercise in rallying support in the Haitian community for his supposed interventionism, as a lure to persuade Haitians to follow his course. Yet Jackson and ECHR were not successful in mobilizing many Haitians for the cause of the Guantanamo refugees, as shown above. This either testifies to the effectiveness of HP's anti-interventionist campaign or it hints at other restraining factors that might have been in play. But HP continued to denounce any suggestions regarding threats of military intervention (HP 175:22).

Following the arrival in March of the UN/OAS-ICM, the dispatch in April of a "multinational police force" mandated to "professionalize" the Haitian army was seen in May by many groups of Haiti's popular sector as the US-driven attempt "to occupy the country" (Ives 1995c:79). In mid-April, for example, the 62-year-old founder and executive director of HCA in Huntington, Camille Germain, told the NYT that he preferred negotiations "instead of sending the Marines to Haiti, because Haiti is an independent country" (Guyther 1993:2). Préval, on a two-day sojourn in New York beginning on April 24, tried to diffuse those concerns at a press conference in the *Haitian Consulate*. He commented on reports circulating in the press about an eventual foreign military intervention: "[L]a question de la force multinationale n'est pas à l'ordre du jour pour nous" (HP 209:9). Dupuy's resignation as Aristide's Ambassador-at-Large on June 23 was, however, inevitable.

With the Governors Island process falling apart, Rangel went the other way by at least intimidating the military regime. Prompted by the murder of the Justice Minister, he called on the UN on October 14 "to intervene militarily in the Haitian crisis" in order for the body to "maintain its credibility around the world". Aware of Clinton's unwillingness to risk the lives of any US military personnel in the wake of Somalia, he announced that he would recommend to his colleagues in the CBC to join him in petitioning Clinton to immediately call on the UNSC for an international deployment. After his opposition of earlier invasions, Rangel now contended that in Haiti, the US had the full support of the international community and "has not been involved in clandestine activities with the CIA as we have in the past" (Rangel 1993a:1-2). At its 1993 board meeting in Nassau, Bahamas, on October 15, the NAACP called on the UN and the OAS to guarantee Aristide's security upon his return. But the group stopped short of advocating a full-scale intervention arguing that "too many lives will be lost in such a confrontation" (NAACP 1993:1). Nevertheless, a CBC-resolution dated October 27 recommended "[t]hat all necessary means, including protective military force, should be utilized to complete the objectives" of the GIA on schedule (CBC 1993:1).

5.6.2 Military Intervention After Governors Island: From Tactics to Reality

At the end of 1993, the perceived danger of US intervention became increasingly alarming as well as associated with the supposed responsibility of the US in the coup. The weight accorded the Haitian refugee crisis relative to other key aspects of the Haitian crisis as perceived by some leading 10th department organizations at the end of the year becomes clear when studying an announcement by HAIC published in HP in the first week of December. Informing about a self-organized demonstration in front of the UN building scheduled for December 10 on the occasion of the 45th anniversary of the Universal Declaration of the Rights of Men, HAIC listed its demands. The list can also be read as constituting a hierarchy: "s´opposer à *toute intervention nord- américaine* sous le couvert des Nations Unies, rejeter le *coup d´Etat téléguidé par les Etats-Unis* contre le président Aristide élu démocratiquement par le peuple haitien en exigeant son retour inconditionel, soutenir la lutte du *mouvement populaire* pour les droits humains et le changement social, demander la *fin des déportations racistes* et la détention illégale des réfugiés haitiens qui ont droit à l´asile politique sans conditions" (HP 214;author´s italics). At HAIC´s press conference in New York on December 10, the group sought to shed light on both the role of the UN and of the US. Ives, who had recently returned from Haiti, described the terror ruling there. He said that even though the international press conveyed the image of a people waiting for deliverance by foreign troops to establish order, the interviews conducted by the *Haiti Commission* would tell a different story. Stefanie Fumo, coordinator of HAIC, said that the right for self-determination and the right for political asylum would go hand in hand in international law, but they were violated by the US in the case of Haiti (HP 215). Fumo´s statement reveals the perception of running the risk to endanger Haiti´s right for self-determination when blaming the US for violating the rights of Haitian refugees.

HP´s coverage of the Miami conference in January 1994 exhibits the same crisis-long ambiguity, which manifested itself again in the way African-American activism was assessed. The most "combative intonations" had come from Rangel and Meek presenting themselves to be "combative enough" to demand the cessation of negotiations. However, HP complained that Rangel had subtly called for military intervention, while Meek had done so even openly (HP 224:17). Latour confirmed that Meek had demanded military intervention to finish with the thugs of the junta. In addition, he reported that Meek, Rangel, and Owens had attacked the US by criticizing that Washington did not define the drug traffickers of the Haitian military as a "national security threat", even though they defied the biggest world power (HP 226:9). HP reiterated its frustration with Rangel when reporting on the CBC conference with Aristide on March 18 and 19. The Congressman had suggested to the exiled president that he should wait for the international community to do something (HP 239:7). At this point in time, a majority of CBC members probably had already made up their minds in favor of military intervention; the first time, as Owens emphasized, that the CBC advocated US military action abroad (Owens 1995).

HP expressed the same ambivalence towards Robinson. Beyond all the praise for his hunger strike in protest of US refugee policy, the weekly was basically skeptical, as Robinson´s fast could as well turn out to be a "Pandora´s box": "Ainsi, Clinton pourrait être tenté de reconsidérer (!) l´option de *l´intervention militaire* en Haiti, ... La *grève de la faim* commencé par Randall Robinson, aussi noble qu´elle puisse être, peut donc se transformer en une *boîte de Pandore* n´allant pas nécessairement dans des intérêts du peuple haitien" (HP 251:8;author´s italics). In the same issue, HP mentioned David Obey´s call for a US invasion of Haiti in a Congressional hearing on April 14 (HP 252). Faced with the Pandora´s box threatening Haiti´s territorial integrity, activism in the Haitian community mounted slightly. In late April, HP briefly announced a political soirée scheduled to take place on April 29 in Harlem and organized by the *Coalition Patrice Lumumba* (CPL) "in solidarity with the struggle of the Haitian people for its independence" (HP 255:8).

What Haitian and non-Haitian anti-interventionists could not know at this point in time, however, was that the White House had already opted for a kind of solution of the Haitian crisis they so much opposed. As Morrell recalled, "Clinton made up his mind" to intervene in Haiti as early as April 1994. According to the staff member of ICP, Robinson´s twenty-seven-day hunger strike was one key element in Clinton´s decision making. He would have "faced real trouble from the American black community and wide sectors of public opinion", Morrell explained, had he attempted to "callously leave Robinson to die",[296] and he would have had to "endlessly appease the cold warriors in the Pentagon, CIA, and Congress", the Washington power centers that came, along with "the press", to oppose his decision (Morrell 1995b:4). After Clinton´s refugee policy revision of May 8, HP reported that Robinson had presented on ABC´s "Nightline" (05/09/94) the ultimate solution: "I think that at last resort, we will need a military intervention". The weekly desperately denounced "the liberal sector´s aggressive support pushing towards occupation" (HP 258:17). According to the NYT´s Pierre-Pierre, "all" Haitians he interviewed in Brooklyn and Queens following Clinton´s decision "opposed military intervention" by the US. Myrtho Volcy, for example, an Aristide-supporter living in Brooklyn, said that there were easier ways to deal with the military thugs in Haiti: "Just pick up the phone" (1994a:A3).

After a meeting with Haitian professionals at UN Plaza Hotel on May 14, the exiled president also met with the Haitian press and about 150 Haitians the following day. HP observed that the audience was, above all, interested in the possibility of foreign intervention, and questions were asked accordingly. Aristide reiterated that the Haitian Constitution did not give him "the right to demand military intervention". But he asked the audience to imagine the Haitian people´s "joy" upon being "liberated from the criminals". To HP´s chagrin, the audience was more inclined to approve of Aristide´s arguments "than to discuss realistically the crisis and the instruments to face it with". The weekly took Aristide´s position on military intervention as a sign that the Haitian people and its organizations did not have any clout anymore in the balance of power (HP 261:8). It is, however, hard to estimate, on the sole basis of this encounter,

---

[296] Robinson had to be hospitalized on May 4 "for severe dehydration" (De Witt 1994a:A5).

the size of the anti-interventionist camp within the Haitian community at large. Haitians in the US were probably rather evenly split on the issue. It is nevertheless striking that since February 1992, HP did not report on any moves possibly undertaken by the *10e of New York* regarding the question of military intervention. This might suggest that the organization aligned itself with Aristide´s position.

The HAIC-organized demonstration against *Sears* and *Walmart* on May 28 in Brooklyn, where speakers also condemned US preparations for an invasion of Haiti, suggests indeed a rather high degree of isolation, as the organizers could muster up the support of only about 100 people (HP 267:8). HP had no other choice than simply asking to consider that "there is no antagonistic relationship between the US and Haiti´s military leadership". The weekly did so in a late-May report on US military exercises by more than 40,000 US troops in the Caribbean and the southeastern US that possibly were a "mock invasion of Haiti" (HP 264:13). In early June, HP angrily complained that the hunger strike by Robinson led to "military exercises .... [that] certify the rumors that the potential occupier prepares to replace his indigenous surrogates" (HP 269:17).

On June 5, representatives of the radical camp within Lavalas met in *St. Jerome Church* in Brooklyn, which was organized by CCRH and hosted by HP´s Leblanc. Georges Honorat of APN, on a stop-over in New York, said that his coalition was against all forms of intervention. The popular organizations, the "revolutionary forces", were at a crossroads today and needed to unite on a minimum platform, he stressed. Lexiuste of CGT maintained that the legitimate government´s relying on the US for the sake of Aristide´s return had had the effect of demobilizing the masses. He warned that an intervention would have the objective of reinforcing imperialist domination (HP 271). In mid-June, HP made out the first signs of the imminent oppression of the popular masses. According to Mark Dow in *New Politics* (summer 1994), US government cables showed that a "master list", a "name-retrievable" database with "regional profiles" of Haitian refugees were being set up. A USJD legal opinion concluded "that information contained in the asylum files may be disclosed to FBI and CIA officials". HP speculated that the information on Haitians might as well be used to target the popular movement in Haiti (HP 275).

In late June, HP reported that UN plans to deploy an occupation force laying the basis for a US-led invasion of Haiti were "already being hammered out in New York" by the UNSC. According to HP, Haiti´s popular movement sharply criticized the *UN Mission in Haiti* project as a "violation of Haiti´s national sovereignty", which was, HP criticized, in conflict with the GIA (HP 279:13). In the light of confusion within the Clinton camp, the weekly noted that virtually every Republican Senator had come out strongly against an invasion. And the *US Chamber of Commerce* had slammed Clinton´s new special adviser on Haiti, William Gray. In a press release of June 17, it called him "a destroyer ... of the Haitian nation" for his cutting off US-Haiti air traffic (HP 280:13). The crisis-old linkage between the refugee issue and the fear of US military intervention in post-coup Haiti became especially evident, when HP reported that the US would plan to open processing centers in Turks and Caicos Islands on July 15. The weekly contended: "Mais la principale *conséquence de cet exode* ... est d´accroître à nouveau la possibilité d´une *intervention militaire* étrangère". HP identified one key motive behind US policy when concluding in a resignative tone: "Rapatriements forcés, réouverture de Guantanamo et, comme solution `finale´, *l´intervention pour mettre fin au flot de réfugiés*, voilà où l'on est après trois ans de coup d'Etat" (HP 281:1,14;author's italics). While Evans Paul was cited as not having a problem with "les Blancs" going into Haiti, HP maintained that "the end is not independent from the means": Foreign intervention would imply long-term foreign domination (HP 284:8).

On July 13, Rangel came out unequivocally and publicly in favor of "multilateral military intervention in Haiti to protect U.S. citizens and unarmed Haitian civilians" in the wake of the expulsion of UN/OAS-ICM observers (Rangel 1994:1).[297] CBC-member Moseley-Braun added another motivation to push for deposing Cédras through a US invasion, which could not have been more opposed to the views of Haitian anti-interventionists. In her mind, "the only reason why we haven't done it yet is because they are people of color. Clearly we wouldn't tolerate this kind of senseless violence so close to America otherwise" (Waldschmitt-Nelson 1996:95). Consequently, Clinton's new Haiti adviser Gray, former African-American president of the *United Negro College Fund*, claimed to speak on behalf of the whole Haitian community in the US when testifying before Congress on June 8. He substantiated US interests in Haiti with reference to, firstly, its being "a close neighbor", and, secondly, with reference to "approximately one million persons of Haitian descent resident" in the US. American citizens living in Haiti, drug-trafficking, the "massive outflow of Haitian refugees", and democracy in the Western Hemisphere followed (1994:4-5). Whereas US non-intervention in Haiti was for Moseley-Braun a sign of racial discrimination in US foreign policy, US intervention was for Haitian anti-interventionists a function of the color-blind will of the US to dominate over Haiti.

Meanwhile, resistance against US military intervention also began to grow in Miami. The *Militant Forum* unveiled plans to organize a meeting for July 16 on the subject of "Open the borders for Haitian refugees! No US intervention in Haiti", which ignored the causal link between the two issues (HP 285:8). *Strikti Otonòm Progresis Aysiyen* (SOPA) announced that it would organize along with "a group of other progressive compatriots" three events for the weekend of July 29-31 to commemorate the "anniversary of the Yankee occupation in Haiti in 1915" (HP 292:17). Likewise, a group called *US Hands off the Haitian People Coalition* informed the Haitian public that it would plan to present on July 24 the movie "Canne Amère" on the occasion of the "79th anniversary of the US occupation in Haiti" (HP 293:17). In Haiti, resistance against an imminent US military intervention grew in some measure as well. The mid-July declaration of 13 popular organizations in Haiti, among them APN, which questioned UN impartiality and neutrality in the crisis, also included an "anti-interventionist position". It maintained that a US invasion would "protect the criminals" of the coup (HP 291:1,17).

At the same time, HP noticed the "shaky support" for a US intervention in Washington. Interestingly, the weekly saw much of the opposition in Congress as stemming from the belief that an invasion would hurt the military regime and aid Aristide in returning to Port-au-Prince (HP 288:9). As Tecumseh observed, the Haitian strategist, who had established the doctrine that linked the refugee issue with the issue

---

[297] According to HP, many saw the July 11 order forcing some 90 observers to leave Haiti as an open request for a US military intervention, since the Haitian military was alleged to see it as a guarantee of protection against popular anger. The order was reported to have been used by the Clinton Administration and the UNSC to help lay the groundwork for a possible invasion of Haiti (HP 287:9).

of intervention: "[I]nterventionism", fueled by the exodus of Haitian refugees, was gaining territory in Congress, in particular among "liberal Democrats" and CBC members (HP 289:13). This time, however, her analysis was not based on a cultural misunderstanding, but on facts. Tecumseh noted with some nostalgia that "things were simple" with Bush. Clinton´s "inconsistencies" had been "more disastrous" now that the Haitian people face "an intervention that seems almost inevitable". In her analysis, the refugee issue took a subordinate place within the set of motives driving US policy towards Haiti. For the Clinton Administration´s policy was guided by two objectives: First, "avoiding an abrupt surge of refugees" that could be exploited by the Republicans domestically, and, second, "postponing as much as possible the eventual return" of Aristide, so that "the Haitian army may be the beneficiary". A military intervention had to occur as "retarded" as possible to assure the "transition of power to another government" during the parliamentary elections in November 1994. The refugee issue was "manipulated to serve as a pretext for an ultimate foreign intervention". The threat of the Haitian refugees´ "invasion" served as justification for a US invasion. It appeared more likely now that the 13-member CARICOM declared to support it if backed by the UNSC and implemented by a multinational force (HP 289:10-13). Gilbert analyzed the logic behind US policy as "killing two birds with one stone" similarly (HP 294).

The language used by Haitian anti-interventionists to denounce their opponents became harsher in early August. Reporting on McCalla´s interview with ND, HP called him "a spokesperson of the State Department" making "propaganda in favor of a US intervention". HP blamed him for identifying too much with Clinton, Lake, and Gray rather than with the "interests of the Haitian people". In contrast, "all progressive groups in the US, both Haitian and American" had denounced on July 28 military intervention on the occasion of the anniversary of the Marine occupation in 1915, the weekly stressed. QC/QP reportedly indicated in "Haiti Reborn" that intervention "could eclipse Haitian democracy for decades to come". HP called NCHR "the Trojan Horse infiltrated" in the midst of US refugee organizations. It was "vital" for the US government "in these times of `humanitarian intervention´" to be assured of someone like McCalla, a "perfect indigenous of service" in the guise of a human rights activist capable of "playing a double game" (HP 299:6,14-15). NCHR is reputed to have been financed by the CIA (Wishnie 1995). In *Fugitives from Injustice* published in August, the coalition officially stated that "HRW and the NCHR have not taken a position for or against a military intervention in Haiti, as a subject which falls beyond our mandates as human rights monitoring organizations" (HRW/A,JRS,NCHR 1994:5). Whereas HP opined that Haiti "is of much bigger importance to the US than countries in Europe or Africa" due to its location in the US´s "backyard", McCalla insisted that this was not 1915: "[T]his is 1994. The US has already conquered the region. Haiti has very little to offer to the US ... we are not going to be there for 19 years" (HP 299:14).

With mock invasion exercises conducted on the Caribbean island of Vieques as part of the Pentagon´s planning for intervention in Haiti (HP 298:9), "all progressive groups in the US", which HP had referred to in its criticism of McCalla, did not include the 10th Department organizations.[298] Conspicuously, they were also not among

---

[298] They did include HAIC, MOKAM, SOPA, SELA, APN, the *Comité pour une Alternative Progressiste*, the *Comité Contre la Répression*, the *Haiti Commission*, *Local 1199*, CPL in Harlem, the

the groups that organized a variety of events in opposition to a US invasion, which took place in Brooklyn, Manhattan, Miami, Boston, Detroit, Washington, Orlando, and San Francisco, as Ives reported on the occasion of the 79th anniversary of the Marine invasion. In one of those events, Pat Chin observed in the presence of almost 200 participants that "certain members of the right in the US oppose military intervention and we do, too". But "for entirely different reasons ... They fear what could result from an intervention, such as an uncontrollable popular uprising" (HP 301:10-11). The NYT´s Rohter, however, reported conflicting news from Port-au-Prince: In private, many Haitians, in particular among the poor, would "welcome the prospect of military intervention as the only certain way" to undo the coup (1994d:A1). Pierre-Pierre now saw Haitians in New York split over the use of force in Haiti (1994b:A3), an ambivalence that appeared to him as still existing in Brooklyn after Clinton´s TV-speech on September 15, in which he advocated an invasion (1994c:A8). In Miami, the NYT´s Karen De Witt saw Clinton´s speech eliciting "emotions ranging from hope and enthusiasm to anxiety and fear" (1994a:A11). In its report on a meeting in mid-August 1994, in which Aristide sought to dilute resistance against imminent foreign intervention, HP tried to counter these observations (HP 305:14).

In October, HP illustrated the danger it perceived by pointing to the 4-year embargo against Iraq, which the weekly opined resulted in a "real genocide" with 400,000 people dead, even if the country abided with all conditions imposed by the UNSC (HP 331:17). In contrast, Farmer, a medical anthropologist working in rural Haiti, observes in post-invasion Haiti of 1995 "widespread satisfaction with recent developments among Haitians of all classes". He finds a "new disjuncture" between assessments of the US occupation made by HP and those of his patients and friends in Haiti, who joined the popular enthusiasm and euphoria that accompanied the landing of troops. Citing Bajeux of CODH, Haitian writer René Dépestre, Jean-Baptiste of MPP, and progressive priest William Smarth, Farmer wonders if the US "may have been every bit as much" in post-invasion Haiti as in the early 1980s, when the CIA and USAID conducted an occupation as "proxy army" (1995:223-226). Moreover, Malone observes that while regional powers were "sensitive" to Washington´s seeking, for the first time, UN authority for a military intervention in the Western Hemisphere, the Clinton Administration was also "reluctant" to use force to reverse the coup "after the Mogadishu fiasco in Somalia of October 1993". He substantiates his observation with the dispatch of the Carter mission, the intention "to multilateralise fully" the intervention, and the implementation of the Clinton Administration´s "cherished `early exit´ strategy" (1997:137,135). Malone´s observation seems to be corroborated by Gallup polls taken in October 1994. For sending US troops into harm´s way apparently involved political risks for Clinton, as the military was still the one US institution in 1994 enjoying highest public esteem (Newport,Saad 1994:6,7).[299]

Coalition US Hands off the Haitian People, the *International Action Center,* HP, *Workers World Party,* the *Panamanian Human Rights Commission* and other groups (HP 301:10-11).

[299] 64% of Americans said in a Gallup poll that they have a "great deal" or "quite a lot" of confidence in it (Newport,Saad 1994:6,7). Consequently, a majority of 58% of Americans, who saw Clinton´s televised speech on September 15, did not feel that US troops should be sent to Haiti "simply to maintain U.S. credibility". A majority of viewers (51%) disagreed that the US has interests there that are worth protecting by sending US troops. One HEAR-member, however, believed that "Clinton needed a foreign policy success" furthering his reelection by showing his resolve to use force. While there was a pre-

For Congressman Solarz, the differences between 1915 and 1994 are "far more significant than the similarities". He observes that the US troops landing in Haiti "to restore democracy rather than to demean it" were greeted as "liberators". These also included "a significant number of Haitian-Americans ... fluent in Creole" (1995:ix-xv).[300] Similarly, Owens called the intervention the "Clinton liberation of Haiti" (Owens 1995). While this assessment misrepresents US interest in intervening militarily in Haiti as too altruistic, it is significant to note that persistent extra-territorial organizing of an ethnic orientation on the refugee issue eventually succeeded in breaking the reluctance to use the utmost manifestation of state power, the military (Schiller et al. 1992:7-8), to contain the flow of Haitian refugees by "complimenting" the *de facto* regime out of Haiti. The civil societal amplification of the undesired transnational Haitian refugee stream achieved the instrumentalization of US state power through indirect transnational relations.

5.7 The Eternal Probation: Haitian Pride of Capable Self-Government

For the anti-interventionist camp in the Haitian community, the US invasion of Haiti would crush all hopes for democracy in their home country. It would thereby virtually complete the coup committed by anti-democratic, Duvalierist forces more than three years ago. The coup sought to undo what Ives called "one of the most joyous episodes in Haitian history", Aristide´s electoral victory with 67.5% of the vote, which the last-minute candidate, propelled to power by the Lavalas alliance and a triumphant popular will, himself called "Haiti´s Second Independence" (1995b:45). Most Haitians in the US, who had in one way or the other supported Aristide´s presidential bid, shared the pride felt towards this unique event in Haiti´s history.[301] The 200th anniversary of the Bois Caiman conference celebrated in the Haitian diaspora on August 22, 1991 assumed new meaning in the light of this pride. Consul-General Généus said in Boston that day that Haitians wanted to "build irreversible democratic institutions in Haiti, because without them, there can be no justice" (HP 1:9).

---

speech majority (48%) opposing sending troops to Haiti, more than four in ten viewers remained "unconvinced" that Clinton should take military action despite a post-speech 16-point-jump in support. Even among those, who supported sending troops, 21% said that the US did not have interests in Haiti. Interestingly, the most persuasive argument Clinton used in his speech was stopping the abuse of human rights (67%), followed by reducing the flow of Haitian refugees, which 56% of interviewees endorsed (Moore,Saad 1994:16,17;HEAR 1995). A Gallup poll conducted late in the month found that US intervention in Haiti had yielded only a small "rally effect" for Clinton, whose overall job approval was only 5% higher than at the beginning of September. A majority of 61% saw likely an increase in the US´s prestige as a result of the intervention, followed by a "small majority" of 54% believing that there would be a reduction in the flow of Haitian refugees (Newport,McAnney 1994:18).

[300] According to the NYT´s Pierre-Pierre, there were about 700 Haitian-American soldiers participating in the intervention (1994:dA8). For the shortcomings of the US-dominated multinational force in establishing and maintaining "a secure and stable environment" as mandated by UNSC resolution 940, see HRW/A,NCHR (1995:2-26).

[301] And so did my landlord in Brooklyn. In late 1994, he ridiculed the US mid-term election results with a turnout of the popular vote of slightly over 30% compared with Aristide´s landslide victory.

After having been welcomed by the Haitian community several months before as a presidential candidate, Aristide, the symbol of Haitian democracy, was expected to come to visit New York City at the end of September 1991. It would be his first time as the President of Haiti. Aristide also "embodied anti-imperialism", which was directed against an elitist notion of "democracy" promoted in Haiti by the US. This notion was conceived by a US Embassy official as the "real American Plan" to be imposed on Haiti. Consequently, the executive committee of the *10e of New York* and HP called on "all compatriots" of the diaspora to meet in front of the UN building that day to let the US and the world know that Haiti was not a "neo-colonized country" anymore, but that its people knew how to elect a leader "of its own choice" (HP 5:1,26;Ives 1995:44;Wilentz 1989:276). All Haitians were invited to show the US public "our support for the first democratically elected president in Haiti" (HP 6:10).

Aristide's visit turned out to be a big success, because the Haitians were able to make the US "surprised", as Tecumseh reported. Haiti's powerful neighbor in the North "discovered yet another time that there were not only puppets in the Caribbean and in Latin America". Almost as if bearding the lion in his den, Aristide and his entourage went to Manhattan's Upper East Side, where "personalities belonging to the upper bourgeoisie reside". There he met with members of the *Council on Foreign Relations*, among them former special adviser to President Kennedy, Arthur Schlesinger Jr. Aristide explained to them the origins of Duvalierism and underscored the positive fact that the US had respected the electoral process in Haiti (HP 8:17). In his address before the UNGA, Aristide listed "liberty", "pride", "dignity", the "right to eat and to work" as well as the "legitimate defense of the diaspora, that is the 10th department" as five of ten "democratic commandments". Aristide also met with Assistant Secretary of State Aronson. This demonstrated, as Tecumseh emphasized proudly, "the importance the US actually accords our country". She cited the NYT-article of September 29 by Jerry Gray, which "details Tidid's visit long enough", as additional evidence. In her mind, "the US has an obligation to bow to our president and to feel a new respect with regard to the Haitian people" (HP 8:19-23).

The Haitian people's "respect and dignity" were trampled upon by the frustrating coup committed only a few days later. They took to the streets in droves in an angry attempt to regain their respect and dignity. Latour said about the impressive crowd of 150,000 to 200,000 Haitians demonstrating in New York City on October 11 that they were the "Haitians of the `10th Department'" having a "rendez-vous with mother democracy..." (HP 22:14-18). The solidarity needed to organize those mass gatherings and the solidarity felt as a result of them were in and of itself a stunning exercise in popular democracy. Mass gatherings were a counter-community, which was to show the usurpers of power in Port-au-Prince that popular democracy had grown roots. Reporting in mid-November on the latest events in Boston, Philippe Généus observed that "the nostalgics" of the Cédras/Honorat-regime "have not realized that the seven months of Lavalas government have permitted the people to compare 7 months of democracy with 34 years of dictatorship" (HP 43:16).

With the murderous putschists killing hundreds of Haitians in Haiti, with the insidious "macoutization" of the 10th department growing stronger, with the mainstream media's discrediting "campaign of misinformation" gaining momentum, with disappointing rumors about US implication in the coup spreading, and with desperate fears of US military intervention intensifying, Haitians were gradually forced onto the defensive. These external pressures were rising so high that they generated the need to re-assure oneself of the significance and the objectives of the hard-won and, indeed, new democracy and to embolden discouraged Haitians to hold on. At the *Haiti Commission*-sponsored soirée at *Baruch College* on November 21, for example, Haitian member of parliament Casséus said about Aristide's victory of December 1991: "This was a revolutionary process adopted by the people for changing ... the country". He encouraged the 10th department to keep up its mobilization (HP 51:10).

But despite the triumphantly noticed UNGA resolution A/RES.46/7 (HP 22:14-18), despite "the only [Haitian] President known and recognized by international opinion" called Aristide (HP 25:16-19), despite "the respect of the international community" enjoyed by Haitians (HP 48:10), and, in fact, despite all the other Haiti-related OAS and UN resolutions, which time and again condemned the coup and called for the restoration of democracy in Haiti, the Haitian community felt compelled to organize the so-called "grand jour avec le vote symbolique". The "Vote for Democracy" was to take place on December 15 in Brooklyn, Queens, Manhattan, Bronx as well as Long Island, Spring Valley, New Jersey, and Philadelphia, "marking the will to *reaffirm* the choice made by the Haitian people on December 16, 1990". The electorate could vote pro and con. The results of the vote would be forwarded to Aristide, to Baker (USSD), and to Joao Baena Soares of the OAS (HP 59:8;author's italics). A wide range of activities organized by "Operation 16th December", named after the day of Aristide's electoral victory, started already on December 12 (HP 59:8).

It is perhaps fair to say that this host of activities revolving around the reaffirmation of the Haitian people's choice of December 16, 1990, and indeed all following Haitian-organized events in support of democracy and the return issue, illustrate how deep the defensive posture ran. Particularly the mainstream media's "campaign of misinformation" in association with the Bush Administration's attempt to discredit and delegitimize Aristide constituted an insulting assault on Haitians' proudly felt capacity for popular self-government and the democratic choice they had made. They felt compelled to fight back by focusing their energies on the return issue, which had been called into question. The political leadership of the Haitian community thus conceived of the return issue as both the means and the end. The return of democracy was to be achieved by publicly rehabilitating what was to be returned. This defensive posture diverted much of its attention from other means, such as the refugee issue, which could have been employed more effectively to pressure the US government. The distracting battle front of the return issue increasingly consumed the energies of the Haitian community at the expense of recognizing the strategical potential of the refugee issue. Had the assault been directed at Haitians' capacity to attend to the incoming stream of Haitian refugees, Haitian organizing during the crisis might have taken a different shape. A multitude of events described in chapters 5.2 and 5.3 were the outcome, in part, of this specific set of circumstances. A certain number of activities were especially illustrative of the restraints generated by this environment. The dates chosen for those activities had, of course, to do with Haiti's new democracy. The Haitian community of New York celebrated on February 7, 1992 the first anniversary of Aristide's inauguration in 1991. In his report on the various activities, Alain St-Victor called the celebration a "historic event" (HP 74:10).

Naturally, the main target of the assault on Haiti's capacity for self-government, namely Aristide, the embodiment of Haiti's new democracy, felt obliged to lead the effort of relegitimization. During his visit in late April aiming at mobilizing individuals and organizations of US civil society, for example, he also went to a student party at *Brooklyn College* in Flatbush, Brooklyn, where he held a speech. He said: "If, in 1724, a German physician by the name of Fahrenheit invented the thermometer, we Haitians in 1992, we have invented the thermometer of resistance, the thermometer of democracy ... In 1752, the experience made by Franklin, who invented the lightning rod, reminds me of the experience that the Haitian people made in 1992, inventing its proper lightning rod against dictatorship" (HP 122:15). In his comments on Aristide´s visit, Latour spoke of a "balance" eventually turning towards democracy (HP 122:17). These statements hint at a latent outer-directed self-perception resulting, in part, from the crisis-specific external pressures mentioned above. Interestingly, HP published an analysis in mid-December 1992 of how the 10th Department had organized so far. It contains a critique addressed to the political leadership that foreshadowed the eventual split in June 1993. The weekly observed that many Haitians would restrain their criticism in Aristide´s presence, be it out of timidity, be it out of complaisance. But the positive fundamental role of criticism, HP emphasized, was the advancement of participative democracy. It added that Aristide had himself affirmed this role in form of a message on cassette, which was distributed to different organizations within Haiti on May 8. HP thus asked: "Il est une thèse dans les pays impérialistes selon laquelle les pays du tiers monde ne sont *pas encore mûrs* pour la démocratie, d´où la justification des dictateurs. Faudrait-il croire que les militants haitiens ne sont pas encore prêts pour la critique?" (HP 161:6;author´s italics).

Even though HP used the alleged immaturity of democracy in Third World countries as an ironic weapon to criticize the bourgeois camp within the Lavalas movement, the reference points to the existence of biases outside the Haitian transnation. They have, indeed, a long history of their own. Hence the observed latent outer-directed Haitian self-perception in defending democracy could have not only resulted from the crisis-specific external pressures, but also from prejudices that reach far back into the history of Haitian-foreign relations. The crisis-specific external pressures emanating from parts of the US mainstream media and the Bush White House may as well have been a manifestation of these time-honored biases. Not surprisingly, these prejudices have their roots in the hostile international environment, in which the Haitian Revolution occurred.

As shown in chapter 5.5, the former French colony Saint Domingue turned into a permanent threat for white racist rulers of slaveholding societies. For the example of the new independent Haiti controlled by former black slaves bore the potential of spreading revolution across its borders. According to Lawless, the historic event of Dessalines´ proclamation of Haiti´s independence in 1804 has to be understood within the context of the "folk models of racial superiority and inferiority". He describes the anger directed toward Haiti after 1804 as "a fear of black independence and self-government". Historians, writers, and commentators of post-revolutionary Haiti were torn between, on the one hand, admiring the extraordinary achievements especially of Toussaint and, on the other, demeaning and insulting other Haitian heroes like Dessalines, who "is forever associated with the slaughter of whites". To justify a social structure based on the master-slave relationship, a reversal of which was dreaded so much, US opponents of emancipation cautioned against the consequences of the misgovernment by blacks they perceived in Haiti. Fears of black rule and slave insurrections modelled after the Haitian example were especially prevalent in Louisiana, to where many of the French planters had escaped from Saint Domingue with their slaves (1992:39-41,44-45,47).

Biases against blacks and Haitians manifested themselves in the great debate on the abolition of slavery and the ability of blacks to govern themselves. Since Great Britain entertained diplomatic relations with the young island nation, Haiti´s "bad press" originated from English racists and antiabolitionists. The two most influential books in this debate, which argued about the question of self-determination of blacks, were written by W.W. Harvey (*Sketches of Haiti*, 1827), who offered a rather optimistic view, and by Charles MacKenzie (*Notes on Haiti*, 1830), who presented a racist discription. MacKenzie´s book came to dominate the debate and had an impact on St. John´s *Hayti: Or the Black Republic* (1884). It was the first "blood-curdling account of Voodoo and cannibalism", which became the most popular book in English on Haiti until the writings of Americans in the 1920s. In the US, many abolitionists seeing in Haiti a future model society, many free blacks eager to seek freedom from racial oppression, and white supremacists searching for solutions to racial conflict supported "emigrationism". It took the form of both voluntary expatriation and the forcible deportation of "surplus" blacks, for whom Haiti provided one desirable sanctuary. Many whites substantiated their interest in shipping free American blacks to Haiti by reference to black racial inferiority (Plummer 1992:26-31;Lawless 1992:45,51-53,56).

The desire to resettle the black US population also constituted an integral part of the debate over diplomatic US recognition of Haiti in the House of Representatives. Opposition in the question was predicated upon racism, charges of Haitian barbarity, and political instability as well as the general conception of Haiti as a republic without virtue. Recognition of Haiti in 1862 was rather motivated by the interest of the North to undermine the power of the rebel states in the South. Inspired by social Darwinist beliefs about the degeneration of inferior peoples and the notion of racial decay, the universal opinion of Haiti exacerbated at the turn of the century. Popular travel literature drew upon the long tradition of denigrating Haiti, merging "voodoo", cannibalism, political brutality, picturesque landscapes, and quaint customs into the concluding lesson that blacks lack the capacity to govern themselves. As Plummer notes, "[t]heir endurance, longevity, and omnipotence attest to their ideological utility in a racist and imperialist world system". It was not big a step from the Roosevelt Corollary claiming US responsibility to uphold law and order in the Caribbean, which mirrored the President´s conviction of non-white races´ inability to achieve prosperous and stable societies, to Wilson´s firm belief that radicalism and revolutionary succession in the Western Hemisphere testify to the need of a period of instruction and guardianship for politically backward nations (Plummer 1992:42-44,79-80,82-87).

Haitian political developments between 1913 and 1915 seemed to confirm the worst stereotypes in the US, where people ignored or did not understand the multiplex determinants of a postcolonial state´s history. Yet ending political anarchy and establishing democracy and civil liberties was but the official pretext for the US occupation in 1915. The Marine landing was coated in the language of a civilizing mission that ranged in practice from paternalism to overt racism. But initial rationalization of the US occupation was not confined to white Americans, the majority of whom paid attention primarily to the war in Europe. Booker T. Washington (1856-1915), for decades the major African-American spokesman in the eyes of white America, believed Haitians to be a backward people in need of discipline and enlightenment. And most African-Americans saw the occupation as a logical result of Haiti's political failures. This began to change gradually, however, after World War I with NAACP-secretary Walter White, African-American writers like Rayford Logan, Langston Hughes, and Mercer Cook as well as dancer Dunham. Yet autocratic Haitian president Elie Lescot, who came to power in 1941, seconded the belief that Haitians were too backward for democratic institutions by abolishing the national legislature (Plummer 1992:90,107-108,121,130-131,136,144;Trouillot 1990:104).

Plummer believes that "containment" has always been a "cornerstone of the U.S. attitude toward Haiti". She describes the "desire for political stability", equated with the promotion of regimes apt to neutralize popular discontent, as "a thick thread running through the fabric of U.S. diplomatic history". US historian and diplomat George F. Kennan, the architect of Soviet containment, doubted that the cultural gap between the US and Latin American countries, where the "Negro slave elements" had weighed "heavily on the chances for human progress", could be bridged. This pessimism succumbed to Cold War preoccupations following the Cuban Revolution, which increased the "desire for political stability" in Duvalier's Haiti. The advent in Haiti of offshore industries and the re-emergence in the US's postindustrial service economy of low wage sweatshops, which became more acceptable to the general public by domestic conservatism during the Reagan years, reinforced racist and sexist stereotypes about docile Haitian labor. The theme of "containment", isolation, and repulsion resurfaced in the stigmatization of Haitians with AIDS in the early 1980s (Plummer 1992:210-216).[302]

The variety of events organized in 1993 to commemorate February 7, 1991 was breath-taking. Latour listed in HP public activities planned to take place in Brooklyn, Manhattan, Rockland (NY), Miami, Boston, Chicago, Philadelphia, Detroit, Cincinnati, St. Louis, Orlando, Montreal, and Paris. Under the main theme of the "democratic Haitian cause", there were, however, also events focusing on the refugee issue in the wake of the Guantanamo refugees' fast and ECHR's activism. On February 5, for example, a "patriotic evening" took place at the *10e of New York*'s office at 531 Empire Blvd. with a debate on current developments and the video "Haiti, killing the dream" that also illustrates the Guantanamo situation (HP 176:8,23). The February 7, 1993 celebrations were ushered in by a major event on January 31 at the auditorium of *Medgar Evers College*, in which 300 people participated. Minister Lassègue presented the book entitled "Haiti, un an après le coup d'Etat". It was produced by the legitimate government to better understand the seven months of the Lavalas term. The impression of the book's obvious public relation purpose in white America was reinforced by Latour's detailed report on some of the events in commemoration of February 7, 1991. He insisted that on that day, the Haitian people "entered like a whip on the national scene, victorious, sovereign" (HP 178:11;HP 180:8). The innuendo regarding the slave revolt in Saint Domingue was conspicuous.

---

[302] And so it did in the repatriation of Haitian refugees as undesirables. In early December 1991, HP quoted one US officer on the Courageous as saying about Haitian boat people: "These are very good people, very humble people". The weekly commented: "The image of the `good savage' coexists with that of the underdeveloped brute" (HP 57:6,16-18). The overtones in charges of "mob rule" levied against Aristide recapitulated the old fears of independent black rule, which this time around threatened with a modest minimum wage increase in Port-au-Prince's assembly industry.

Part of the book-based PR campaign by the legitimate government was Aristide's latest book *Théologie et Politique*. The book was presented to the public on April 18, 1993 at *Wingate High School* in Brooklyn, which was organized by the *Haitian Consulate* and Lassègue's Information Ministry. Joseph stated that the methodology inherent in the book represents a "recherche-action" aiming at better understanding Haitian popular culture and the values that it carries. According to Renaud Bernardin, Planification Minister of the legitimate government, the book was a "guide pratique d'intervention", a "practical guide to intervention", needed in reaching out to all sectors of US society linked to the Haitian people (HP 208:8). The PR campaign to relegitimize and rehabilitate the Aristide government in the US public made sense with regard to an "American education", which "either dilutes or ignores the influence of Haiti on North American history" (Lawless 1992:42). In addition, Aristide maintains that the Haitian oligarchy used powerful connections in Washington to sway local pressure groups and to discredit the seven months of the Lavalas government in order to absolve the putschists (Aristide 1996:54).

In retrospect, it is, however, more than questionable, if this campaign could have succeeded soon enough in creating a favorable public opinion in the US that would have generated sufficient popular pressure on the US Administration to buttress the return issue, given the historically grown American attitude towards Haiti. The refugee issue seems to have taken this attitude into account more realistically. Moreover, the CIA was in a position with its character assassination campaign of October 1993 to destroy with one stroke whatever public credit the pro-Aristide campaign had been able to build up in a much longer period of time. More basically, why should a supposedly coup-implicated and intervention-prone US government be willing to be convinced by a refurbished public image to begin with? The treatment of the Guantanamo refugees indicated both the US Administration's lacking respect for Haiti's popular democracy and its fear of a backlash caused by them domestically. As HP put it, Clinton wanted to pass for the savior of democracy, but did not have "any scruples to let die" those at Guantanamo, who escaped a coup "orchestrated by those that have always been supported by the US". According to the weekly, the refugees' hunger strike was a form of resistance, which implied: "...nos compatriotes font preuve d'une dignité qui devrait faire honte à l'Amérique, et plus encore à celle de Clinton que de Bush" (HP 192:17).

The third anniversary of Aristide's electoral victory was commemorated by way of the demonstration in Washington on December 16, 1993. Latour reminded the international community and the decision-makers in Washington that the Haitian people were still held hostage by a handful of "narco-assassins" (HP 216:8,17). At this point in time, the return of democracy and of Aristide was indeed not accomplished, yet. But why demanding the "return of legitimacy", which had been confirmed time and again in many Haiti-related OAS and UN resolutions? The sheer longevity of the Haitian crisis indicates that there were almost unsurmountable limits in following a moral strategy of asserting that US state conduct is "contrary to U.S. principles of democracy and freedom", as suggested by Basch et al. (1994:275) - unless specifying freedom more clearly to include individual rights of Haitian refugees, which were verifiably violated by the US.

In the summer of 1994, Secretary of State Christopher used the term "failed state" to describe Haiti under the rule of the *de facto* regime. Defining it as countries "without governments, without authority, exposed to anarchy", HP interpreted the expression as the "new excuse for military intervention in Third World countries". Holding the "imperialist countries" responsible for the condition of Haiti, the weekly qualified the term as the usual exercise of "blaming the victim". After three years, the Haitian people had been pushed "on its knees", so that there now seemed to be no alternative to foreign intervention (HP 291:1). While it is true that the term is reminiscent of the old denial of Haiti's capacity in self-government, it served to justify the return of the democratically elected government to Haiti for the refugee flow to stop. Who would doubt that anarchy ruled in Haiti since September 1991?

HP opined that neither the coup nor Aristide's exile really implied a defeat for the Lavalas movement, because the Haitian people had already the "victory of legitimacy" on their side. Yet the Pentagon-assisted return of a legitimate president was a "humiliating spectacle", which represented a "blow to the heart" to all progressive people, to all those, for whom Haiti had become a "little dancing flame, symbol of rebellion". Wanting to make believe that the "occupying forces are their friends", whose real "objective is to liberate them", Aristide was blamed by HP as reinforcing an "attitude of dependence" by tending to "infantilize the people" and thereby displaying the "same paternalist attitude as the occupants, teaching the Haitian people how to behave in democracy". HP's judgement was harsh: The "master" did not only "triumph over the slave, but the slave also thanks him for it" (HP 331:16).

Haitian democracy stand at Wilson Désir´s Office on 10/15/94 in Brookyln (by Götz-Dietrich Opitz)

Haitian activists on stage at Wilson Désir´s Office on 10/15/94 in Brookyln (by Götz-Dietrich Opitz)

5.8 Haiti´s Messiah: Aristide´s Popularity with the Haitian People

Far from being the "slave" servile to the "master" called US, for the overwhelming majority of Haitian people, Aristide was the symbol of the country´s "second independence" and its capacity for popular self-government. HP was proud to announce that the major point in Aristide´s schedule during his expected visit to New York City would be a speech in the UNGA´s 46th session on September 25, 1991, the first time "Tidid" would make the leaders of the entire world listen to "the voice of the Haitian people" (HP 5:1,26). The *10e of New York* and HP underscored the historical importance of his visit by publishing a one-page ad with his picture (HP 6:10). In preparation of the "great moment" of his visit, HP wrote on behalf of the Haitian community that it "feels a legitimate arrogance to be represented by a president, who it can be proud of". On September 24, Aristide was welcomed at John F. Kennedy airport by Casimir, Longchamp, Désir, Jean-Juste, and a cheering crowd of about 200 applauding Haitians (HP 7:1,24). In her long 8-page report on his visit, Tecumseh used the theme Aristide had used in his sermon at *St. John the Divine Cathedral* to characterize the historic encounter as yet another episode of a "beautiful love story" between him and the Haitian people. The stops in his visit were emblematic of this "love story". He first paid a "symbolic visit" to *Resurrection Church* in Harlem, "the equivalent of St. Jean Bosco". In City Hall, Dinkins interpreted Aristide´s electoral victory as a triumph of the "ideas of liberty and self-determination" and honored him with the "symbolic key of the city", a privilege, which had only been accorded Nelson Mandela before him (HP 8:16-23).

After a "tête-a-tête" with UN Secretary-General Javier Perez de Cuellar, Aristide prepared to address the UNGA. "[T]wo to three hundred compatriots" crowding the galleries "cheered him warm-heartedly". Quoting the NYT (09/26/91), Tecumseh emphasized with pride that Aristide embarrassed the UN interpreters by speaking in nine different languages at one point in his 67-minute speech, before he introduced the "new language" of Haitian Creole to the UN. She proudly proclaimed that it was "undeniable that Aristide passed with style the stage of his acknowledgement on the international level and that he forced the admiration of everybody while being at the rostrum of the UN" (HP 8:16-23). Before his sermon at *St. John the Divine*, Aristide "was to meet the 10th department" for a reception at *Synod House* on the Upper West Side. It was attended by members of the *10e of New York*, of *Lafanmi Selavi*, and by others. One employee of HP, Denise Desroches, was the only person to receive "an ecstatic souvenir": a kiss from Aristide. An estimated "1,500 compatriots" in the cathedral and more of them outside "had but one and only desire: listening to Tidid, receiving Communion with him". While addressing the parish, Aristide sat high on a chair, which accentuated the "messianic character of his speech". Aristide´s popularity, Tecumseh noted, was "at its zenith ... This was an event that one has never seen before" (HP 8:16-23).

"Zenith" was an understatement. For Aristide´s overwhelming popularity seems to have mushroomed after the shocking coup against him. Haitians living as far away as California, for example, seemed to identify even stronger with him in this time of crisis. The Secretariat of the *10th department organization* in that state solemnly declared to support Aristide as "the authentic incarnation of the democratic legitimacy in Haiti" (HP 20:9). Aristide was revered as a charismatic leader imbueing his broad-based popular constituency with dignity, pride, and joy. Representing their long-held aspirations, he catapulted the historically most marginalized social strata of Haiti, the poor and the peasant population, into the international limelight by speaking in Haitian Creole to the diplomats and dignitaries of the world. At his press conference at Travelodge Hotel on November 17, nearly 4,000 Haitians hoped to see their beloved president at least for some minutes (HP 47:10,21).

He was one of them, but, at the same time, so far away, standing in solitary splendor above them as a "messianic" leader. As Wilentz reported, Aristide had received many death threats since the beginning of his political trajectory. He had survived many assassination attempts, including the massacre at *St. Jean Bosco* in September 1988; thirteen people were killed and at least seventy-seven wounded.[303] Aristide was "protected by his growing fame", Wilentz observed, the people were his bodyguards, as a progressive priest put it. Aristide was aware of this protective shield: "They think I'm protected. That I can't be hurt. That Jesus or the spirits are protecting me. That I am indestructible. This is great protection for me". Aristide had assumed the aura of invulnerability, which made him a hero. Many Haitians called him "Msieu Mirak" (Miracle Man). "Haitians love a victim", Wilentz noted, "because the corruption in the country is so widespread that only victimization proves purity" (1989:344-345,226-230,362,347-357,223,401,234,131;1991:6). In early 1986, HP had proposed Aristide as the political alternative and published the equivalent of a whole volume of articles dedicated to him. In fact, the weekly saw him as the leader of the Haitian people since its inception in 1983, according to Loubet (HP 100:16-17).

At the WOH-organized January 1992 conference "Dignité et Démocratie" in Washington, Cooley-Prost read from Aristide's book *In the Parish of the Poor*. As Latour reported, a mass was celebrated on Sunday morning, which he described as "the apotheosis ... of Father Aristide". The president personally attended the mass to instill in the participants the "serum of hope" (HP 68:10). Aristide could electrify the people, even in his absence. At the demonstration on April 6, Désir was able to stir the crowd up by hinting at Aristide's next visit to New York (HP 102:8). In late April, HP announced "with pride, joy and emotion" in a one-page-ad that the "Haitian community prepares to receive its president" (HP 109:11). The visit lasted three days (April 24-27). According to Latour, Aristide's "moral force" dominated the scene (HP 110:10). His "love story" with the Haitian people seemed to have no limits: Dauphin opined after the visit that hundreds of thousand people welcomed Aristide, which testified to his "*growing* popularity" (HP 117:8;author's italics).

HP published a total of 6 reports on Aristide's visit, most of them written by Latour. April 24 was dedicated to meeting business people and politicians as well as giving interviews for ABC and NBC. Rincher, the spokesperson for Haitian business people, said during breakfast with Aristide: "We have not had a leader since 1804". Aristide was hosted by the City Council of New York. Una Clarke praised Aristide as a "symbol of hope in the Caribbean". The City Council conveyed a "Proclamation" to Aristide in memory of this "historic morning". It stated that "Aristide, ... is perceived by his compatriots as the Prophet and the voice of the poor" (HP 110:10;HP

---

[303] The Haitian community in New York remembered the *St. Jean Bosco* massacre as well as Izméry's assassination on September 11, 1994 with a religious ceremony organized at the initiative of *Lafanmi Selavi* of New York led by Guy Sansaricq (HP 319:7,18).

114:12;HP 116:12,14,15). In the afternoon, he had a "fruitful encounter" with various groups of the 10th department, the first time that a "direct dialogue" with Aristide had been arranged. The 10th department was represented by about 20 Haitian organizations, among them the *10e of New York* and HEAR. HP called him a "man of ideas incarnate, of hopes of all the people hungry for change, hungry for democracy". The Haitian was "fundamentally a collective being", Latour exclaimed (HP 110:10,10;HP 114:12,15,16). In the evening of April 25 at Marriott Hotel, "beautiful ladies" and "elegant men" attended a "historic dinner-party" to "show their support, their attachment to their leader". Dauphin, the master of ceremony, had a hard time to rein in the "delirium" in the hall. Aristide proved once more to be a "routinized orator".

On April 26, Aristide received "particular attention" from local authorities of New Jersey. But the "apotheosis" of this weekend was the big rally at Central Park, which "nearly 100,000 Haitians and friends of Haiti, of democracy to be restored to Haiti, attended to listen to their leader". They had communion with the "only legitimate priest ordained by the Holy See of the Haitian people's will: Jean-Bertrand Aristide", receiving the "bread of unity and the wine of solidarity". The majority of demonstrators in Central Park was composed of Haitians from New York and its outskirts. But one could also see busloads of Haitians coming from Philadelphia, Connecticut, New Jersey, and Washington (HP 110:10;HP 111:10;HP 116:12,14,15). On April 27, Aristide had breakfast at the *Interchurch Center*, where he addressed Rabbi Block in Hebrew. Passing *Wilson Désir's Office*, Aristide also went to the *House of the Lord*, the church administered by Rev. Daughtry, where several leaders of liberation movements had been welcomed before. HP's editorial staff took also pride in receiving Aristide in its editorial offices in Brooklyn. He also met with religious groups before going to *Brooklyn College* in Flatbush, where he celebrated a party with Haitian students. Faustin Beaurevers addressed Aristide on behalf of the *Conféderation des Étudiants Haitiens* (CEH). Young students from *Sarah Garnett Junior High IS324* sang both the Haitian and the American national anthems. They also presented "The Star Banner" and the African-American hymn "Lift every voice and sing", performed by three African-Americans. One of them, Latasha Rutledge, said to Aristide: "God bless you, you are the president of all African people". Latour commented that this scene would be kept in memory, when "one could see the eyes of a young adolescent American shine with dignity, pride, and joy to belong to a noble cause" (HP 110:11;HP 122:13-14.17). Taking stock of Aristide's visit, Latour wrote: "On se souviendra longtemps de cette tournée du président Aristide... De son côté, Aristide a encore injecté une forte dose de courage dans la résistance à ses milliers de partisans" (HP 122:17). According to Dauphin, Aristide's visit to New York was a big success, for which he thanked the Haitian communities of New Jersey, Connecticut, Long Island, Westchester, Rockland, and the city of New York (HP 117:8).

The Haitian media frenzy accompanying Aristide's visit was appropriate, since the event was truly historic. But it helped build up, or at least reinforce, a personality cult surrounding the Haitian president. His popularity seems to have exceeded, for historical reasons, the popularity accorded heads of state from other countries. He was the first leader of the Haitian people "since 1804". He was introduced into Haiti's national shrine alongside Toussaint and Dessalines. He was even put atop the "tree of resistance" (Latour), which had grown ever bigger since Makandal. His impressive level of education, his ability to speak several languages, and his modest social background put the intellectual Aristide more in line with Toussaint. Ives stressed that (even) the NYT considered his Hebrew "impeccable" (HP 127:12).

What is more, he was not only regarded as the leader of Haiti and the Haitian diaspora, he was also celebrated as the leader of the African diaspora. The pressure put on him must have been immense indeed. High expectations were projected onto him, and he was expected to deliver. The virtue of "victimization" (Wilentz) would even enlarge his popularity with the people in the months to come. One HEAR-member told me that the Haitian "people were willing to do any sacrifice for him" (HEAR 1995). Guy Victor added that "he was the only issue that could rally all the Haitians together" (Victor 1996). Various groups in the US added to Aristide's extraordinary fame with the Haitian people by granting him a score of awards for his unprecedented achievements.[304] In the 1980s, the Haitian boat people did not have such superior competition in winning the goodwill of the Haitian diaspora. In a sense, Aristide's eminent and glittering sophistication and refinement eclipsed the plight of the miserable Haitian refugees to a certain degree.

Aristide'second visit to New York between May 28 and 31, 1992 did not attract as much media attention as the one before. According to Ives, this visit served a "very precise purpose". Aristide rallied support with a number of Jewish organizations, had talks at the UN, and also went to *St. Jerome Church* in Flatbush to attend a service in honor of the "fête des Mères". Even though his second visit did not have "the dimension of his recent tour last April", Ives concluded nonetheless that it increased the "anticipation and the sentiment of his imminent return" (HP 127:14). While Ives' judgement sounded rather sober in comparison to HP's coverage of Aristide's first visit, Latour still seemed to be upbeat in late September 1992, when he reported on the first anniversary of the coup. He stressed Aristide's "triumphant discourse" before the UN and added that "[a]ll Haitians worthy of that name had to feel proud when hearing the president making himself the mouthpiece of the Haitian people" (HP 147:8).

In late January 1993, when HP made out a lack of "ardor" and a feeling of "resignation" in the Haitian community in conjunction with the "price for the return of democracy" in the wake of Clinton's inauguration, the weekly's language went sour vis-a-vis Aristide. The left-of-center think tank criticized that his "strong popularity" and his "moral authority" had permitted him to neglect the "bases of organized resistance". Aristide was accused of not being in touch with ordinary Haitians anymore. Without doubt he did "not escape the confession of vanity", HP complained, since he had made himself "blind from his own aura". He had himself "carried away with his power over the people" and "prioritized his role of messiah". The weekly assumed that Aristide had not been "insensitive to all the honorary distinctions he was showered with". But this type of ceremony – receiving awards - had lost all its glimmer due to its "repetitive character" (HP 168:6,14,16;HP 261:8). Given that his analysis was correct, a share of

---

[304] On his tour through the US in March, for example, he received the "Social Justice Oscar Romero Award" sponsored by CHRCL in Los Angeles (HP 94:9). On May 31, the *Minnesota Lawyers International Human Rights Committee* awarded him a human rights prize (HP 127:14). On September 15, Aristide received the IPS-sponsored annual award (HP 144:13). At *Micheal's College* in Colchester, Vermont, he was given a honorary doctorate (HP 244:7). And during his visit to New York on May 14, 1994, following his participation in Mandela's inauguration in South Africa, Aristide was granted the "Hope Award" sponsored by the *Citizen Education Fund* (HP 261:8). Aristide also received the "Prize for Peace in Germany" and many others more (1996:99).

the blame fell on HP itself, because it had taken part in the construction of an inflated personality cult.

Nevertheless, on the occasion of the February 7 celebrations of 1993, patriotism prevailed over criticism. HP noted that the 10th department honored "the people inside, imprisoned" as well as Aristide, "in whom it always puts its whole confidence". For "the voice of the people is always the voice of their president: vox populi, vox Titidi" (HP 180:8). But the more the UN got involved, the harsher HP's language became. After the breach between Dupuy and Aristide in June, HP judged Aristide heavily and in an insulting fashion when taking stock of the Miami conference late January 1994. The weekly discerned in Aristide's moves a high "degree of infantilization" and accused him of letting himself be treated by the US as a "puppet" and a "protegé" exposed to "constant threats and pressure". The "Lavalas experience" demonstrated the impossibility to build a "veritable popular movement" around the "simple allegiance of one leader" (HP 228:13,15). In its report on Aristide's visit to New York mid-May 1994, HP regretted that so much hope had been raised and so much energy mobilized to only end up, for a lack of profound political work, with maintaining a "cult around president Aristide". In HP's view, the cult constituted a "handicap to heightening the community's political awareness". Adoration replaced political analysis and entertained a kind of passivity in waiting for a miracle to happen. HP opined that Aristide himself seemed much more to try to maintain a myth, just as Myriam Dorismé viewed in him the "Moses of Haiti" (HP 261:20). Reporting on Aristide's stop-over from Nicaragua in New York on July 6, HP observed that his entourage had abandoned all willingness to rely on popular mobilization a long time ago (HP 284:8,16).

HP's anger is instructive in two ways: First, it may be assumed that Aristide had by then endorsed the option of US military intervention, and, second, it also showed that Aristide's popularity must have been unbroken. As Guy Victor told me, since most Haitians were interested in Aristide's reinstatement, the political leadership of the Haitian community organized them around the return issue (Victor 1996). Aristide's return to Haiti was celebrated on October 15 by "hundreds of Haitian-Americans" in front of AEH's office on Eastern Parkway in Crown Heights, as the NYT's Ashley Dunn estimated (1994:20). At the celebration, I witnessed a group of Haitian participants, who almost got into a fight over Aristide-photographs distributed by activists. Given Aristide's popularity, many Haitians in the US must have followed his lead throughout the crisis. It is, therefore, necessary to take a closer look at the exile government's political choices.

Aristide supporters celebrating his return at Wilson Désir´s Office on 10/15/94 in Brooklyn
(by Götz-Dietrich Opitz)

Aristide supporter interviewed at Wilson Désir´s Office on 10/15/94 in Brookyln
(by Götz-Dietrich Opitz)

5.9 Negotiation and Compromise?: The Exile Government´s Strategy

Taken Aristide´s unabated popularity with the Haitian people and their will to follow him for granted, it may be assumed that a great deal of organizing efforts undertaken by groups in the 10th Department can be explained by way of illustrating in more detail the exile government´s strategical choices in the course of the crisis. At the AfA-organized event in Manhattan on October 25, 1991, Casimir sounded optimistic when declaring that "the question one has to ask is not if President Aristide will return to Haiti. The question is when". To that end, Haitian diplomatic efforts would center around the freezing of assets (HP 32:11). At Aristide´s press conference at Travelodge Hotel on November 17, questions asked also concerned the embargo and the upcoming negotiations with the presidents of both the Haitian Senate and the House of Commons in Carthagene, Colombia. Aristide praise the embargo as "the solution for the refugees. They will stay in Haiti, where there will be democracy" (HP 47:10,21). To this effect, Aristide appealed to would-be refugees in Haiti in his 1991 November 22 message on *Radio Tropicale* (HP 53:15). From the very beginning, the refugee issue as a political weapon was thus subordinated to the embargo and negotiations, which Aristide considered "an essential part" of the exile government´s strategy. Conspicuously, there is no mention of the refugee issue used against the US government in Aristide´s postcrisis list of "arms in the service of dignity and independence".[305] After the coup, Aristide "had to learn diplomacy ... [a] strange discipline for a liberation theologian". Yet he acknowledged in hindsight that "[s]topping the flow of boat people constitutes an essential motive for the American government in its attempts to get out of crisis" (1996:104,92,100,80).

Pondering the "role of the 10th department" in a climate resonant of rumors about US implication in the coup and of fears of US military intervention, Tecumseh expressed first concerns regarding US-Ambassador Adams´ presence in Carthagene. The "time-consuming negotiations" more and more appeared to her "as maneuvers aimed at impeding the return of Aristide and at organizing new `elections´" (HP 53:15). Nevertheless, HP published Aristide´s New Year greetings to the weekly (HP 62:9). As if confirming Tecumseh´s concerns, Casimir published "some clarifications" in late January 1992 on Aristide´s choice of Théodore as prime minister designate. The choice of the "leader of PUCH", who opposed the "government of December 16, 1990", "generated controversial reactions with certain compatriots", Casimir noted. He stressed that "Théodore does not constitute at all the choice of president Aristide. But the choice was the result of a give and take game". Aristide had to neutralize "the sectors that painted, in his opinion, a picture of an intransigent person responsible for blocking discussions or for their failure" (HP 66:9). In retrospect, Aristide posed the

---

[305] The "inventory of our essential military arsenal" included the "refusal to collaborate" with macoutisme, "denunciation and organized pressure from the exterior" originating from both "international opinion" and from the "Tenth Department" to isolate the *de facto* regime, "diplomacy", and "resistance within Haiti" (Aristide 1996). For Aristide´s belief in diplomatic pressure, see also the NYT of 03/16/93:A13 and 03/16/93:A21. Aristide paused criticizing US refugee policy between mid-February 1992 and late December 1993 (see the NTY of 02/10/92:A8 and 12/22/93:A5).

rhetorical question: "What trump could we play but good faith and respect for the rules of the game?" (1996:57).[306]

In early February, HP explained the recent outpouring of Haitian refugees with the refusal of Haitian parlamentarians to accept an invitation by the OAS to Washington as well as with the Nérette-regime's orientation towards elections: "[T]he flight out of Haiti is directly tied to the political situation and the issue of negotiations", the weekly observed (HP 69:8,18). Aristide understood, of course, the human costs of his exile government's strategy on the refugee front.[307] After the "Washington Protocols", criticism of the exile government's strategy involving negotiations on the international level mounted. In late April 1992, Loubet would qualify negotiations as "tortureous" (HP 100:17). And the press committee of the *10e of New York* published an official position emphasizing: The "failure of the negotiations has shown once more that macoutisme is hostile towards all dialogue" (HP 105:8). HP agreed by adding in its report on a new wave of refugees that "almost everybody seems to recognize" the "reason for the new exodus" by now: "the fact that the negotiations ... reached an impasse" (HP 108:9). HP predicted in early May that the "Villa d'Accueil" resolution, which did not provide for Aristide's return, would result in a surge of Haitian refugees (HP 115:8). Aristide himself felt immense pressure from his interlocutors in Washington, who were ready at any time to accuse him of being "inflexible, sectarian, intransigent" (1996:106).

Reflecting in part tensions over the question of negotiations, at the dinner-party on April 25, 1992 at Marriot Hotel, Aristide underscored the need for all Haitians "to discuss not only what divides them, but also what brings them together" (HP 111:10). As HP explained, two central themes guided Aristide's numerous addresses during his visit to New York in April: unity in the heart of the "forces of progress" and the necessary alliance between the political and economic forces (HP 114:12). After his arrival on April 24, for example, Aristide went to the World Trade Center to have breakfast with "master of ceremony" Roy Hastick of the *Caribbean Chamber of Commerce* and with numerous leaders of the black and Caribbean community living in the New York metropolitan area. Aristide took stock of the seven months his government had been in office. "In particular", he emphasized, "there were no refugees to flee Haiti". During his visit, Aristide was constantly confronted with the refugee issue.[308]

---

[306] The NYT described Théodore as Aristide's "political rival" and a "longtime Communist". He met with Aristide in Washington for talks leading to the "Washington Protocols" in late February 1992. Théodore supported a general amnesty. The accord was never ratified and completely dismissed by the "Villa d'Accueil Tripartite Agreement" (see the NYT of 01/09/92:A3, 01/11/92:A2, 01/12/92:1/9, 02/22/92:A2, 02/24/92:A3, 02/25/92:A1, 02/26/92:A3, 02/27/92:A8, 03/20/92:A3, 05/10/92: 1/12).

[307] After publicly criticizing US policy of repatriating Haitians and of offering Cubans political asylum at the same time (Brooke 1992:A8), he visited dancer Dunham's private residence in East St. Luois, Illinois, on March 16. As Latour reported, Aristide, who was accompanied by Jackson, had come to thank the "grande Dame" of "incomparable courage", but asked his "sister of combat" to suspend her hunger strike (HP 93:9).

[308] Rhoda Jacobs, for example, member of the New York State Assembly for the district of Flatbush, presented to Aristide the copy of a State Assembly resolution calling on the US government to stop the forced repatriation of Haitian refugees. Dinkins stigmatized Washington's indifferent attitude towards the Haitian crisis, adding that "inspite of constant and pressing appeals ... Washington did not stop to turn a deaf ear". During an interview at WABC-TV studios with Gil Noble for his show "Tel quel",

Part of the exile government's strategy was establishing close contact with groups embedded in US civil society.[309] In retrospect, Aristide noted that the "[v]aried and enthusiastic support" of the NGO community representing "a reservoir of unexpected solidarity" was "needed tremendously" (1996:54). At the Central Park rally, for example, Aristide sought to rally support by alluding to the Haitian participation in the US War of Independence. Latour summarized Aristide's point by noting that "this very solidarity (...) must lead to democracy in Haiti by means of effective pressure on the usurpers of power". Addressing the American people directly, Aristide said: "You know the role of your government in our problems. After seven months, it is time to act" (HP 116:16). At a press conference, he echoed the "three-pronged strategy" (Généus) when calling for a "real blockade" of Haiti (HP 114:12,13). He complained at the Conference of Baptist Pastors in *Baptist Church* on April 27, 1992 that "the rich have benefited from [the embargo] by even getting richer". Aristide called on the pastors to exert pressure on the US government, which would, in turn, exert pressure on the thugs of the coup. He did not recommend the refugee issue as a means of pressure. In Harlem, Aristide and his entourage went to WLIB studios for an interview with popular host Mark Riley. He pointed at economic and geopolitical advantages for the US in supporting democracy in Haiti. In contrast to the military regime, his exile government could provide "security to capital" for American investments in Haiti. Beyond that, "the virus" of the coup had spread to other countries in the Western Hemisphere such as Venezuela and Peru. At one point during his visit, Aristide voiced his belief that "if Jesus could change water into wine 2000 years ago, we can today change dictatorship into democracy" (HP 122:12-13,17).

While US intentions to close the Guantanamo refugee camp showed that there would be "no pity at all for the refugees", HP attested to Aristide's being "full of compassion with regard to the refugees" (HP 124 :6,20). The relationship between the exile government and HP was still intact at that time. In order to cultivate this relationship, Aristide and his entourage went to the offices of HP. Aristide appreciated HP's work by saying that the "river of information gushing out of the journal Haiti-Progrès" would commence "to flow into the interior of the country in order to purify it, to make it clean, to put things straight" (HP 122:16). In defending the information policy record of the Lavalas government, Lassuège lamented that there was a lot of talk about the people leaving Haiti, but that the situation prevailing *in* Haiti was not sufficiently covered (HP 126:10).

During Aristide's second visit to New York in late May 1992, he was maybe even more confronted with the refugee issue. He again sought to rally support with groups embedded in US civil society. The first day of his stay started with the meeting at JCRC in Manhattan. He testified to his conviction that "34 countries (OAS) can prove with sufficient resolve to stand in the way of a General and his accomplices". Interestingly, Aristide evaded one question posed by AJC's Gary Rubin, member of

---

Aristide reiterated that his return to Haiti hinged on the resistance within Haiti and on international solidarity (HP 112:14;HP 114:13,14,15).

[309] On April 25, 1992, for example, Aristide was guest of honor at a meeting of the 3-million-member organization *Association of Black Journalists* in the US (HP 110:10). On April 26, an ecumenical service took place in *Elizabeth High School*, New Jersey. As Latour reported, local Haitian and American "civilian authorities" demonstrated their "attachment to democracy". Mayor Thomas Dunn presented to Aristide the key of town Elizabeth (HP 116:13).

NCHR's Task Force on Haitian Refugees. He raised the question of US responsibility when asking what reprisals repatriated refugees could be exposed to. Aristide responded that under his government, poverty notwithstanding, "Haitians did not flee their country, because everybody enjoyed democracy, peace, and security ... without democracy in Haiti, there will continue to be piles of refugees". Asked by a woman, whether his approach based on "friendly words and persuasion" was not too "soft" and "utopic", Aristide responded that "we demand a real embargo that should be total and complete ... once there will be a veritable embargo, this will be a matter of days, not of weeks" (HP 127:12). Aristide's approach of "friendly words and persuasion" could have been partially based on the fear of US military intervention (see chapter 5.6.).[310]

In an interview, Longchamps appeared to put UNHCR in charge of the plight of Haitian refugees, pointing out that the organization "issued a declaration ... and expressed its disagreement with US policy". At the same time, he declared that "the OAS is in charge of Haiti. ... Aristide, on his part, has promised to do all that he can do for the UN and the OAS to find an area of cooperation". His interview came after Aristide had met with Boutros-Ghali, UNSC-president Peter Hohenfellner, and the *Council of Non-Aligned Countries*, while about 200 "diplomates du béton" gathered outside in Ralph Bunch Park (HP 127:13). At the end of July, 1992, HP warned that "[t]he perspective of the so-called negotiations must not bring the mobilization to a halt" (HP 133:22). Longchamps declaration foreshadowed Haitian concerns about detrimental effects of negotiations as expressed in the two petitions published by HP in the first week of September. The second petition, which was addressed to Aristide, stated: "[W]e are outraged by the latest news ... [about negotiations] with terrorists ... We demand from you instantly to keep word in your support of the Constitution of 1987" (HP 139:9). But the first round of negotiations between representatives of Bazin and Aristide at the OAS headquarters in Washington was reason enough for Casimir to throw a Thank You Party at the Righa Royal Hotel in New York on September 1. Emphasizing that "the list of concessions made by president Aristide is too long to be presented", he reminded of Baker's words at the OAS meeting of October 2, 1991: "[T]he coup d'Etat must not succeed, and it will not succeed". He pointed to the more than 3,000 deaths and the 40,000 refugees (HP 140:9,18).

The first coup anniversary made for an environment that required unity despite the tensions over negotiations. Consequently, at a meeting of regional delegates on September 16, Aristide demanded "from every Haitian, unless he is sick, to be present Tuesday 29 and Wednesday 30, 1992". He called on Haitians to exceed the number of demonstrators reached at the notorious rally on April 20, 1990. Speaking on behalf of those resisting within Haiti and those on Guantanamo, he encouraged to "reap" the fruits of democracy (HP 143:9). One day before, at the IPS-sponsored ceremony, Aristide made a remark followed by long applause. He had pointed to the 40,000 refugees returned to Haiti by the USCG on the eve of the first coup anniversary: "Today, one must be ashamed of those, who return the boat people" (HP 144:13). During his visit to New York in late November, Aristide publicly thematized the refugee issue again,

---

[310] On May 30, Aristide assisted in a service at the Jewish 600-member *B'nai Jeshurun Congregation*. Rabbi J. Rolando Matalon thought the refugee issue to be in the foreground when explaining: "You have seen the people aboard the little boats, who have been rescued and returned to certain death. That's why the president is here among us" (HP 127).

perhaps because the perceived threat of US military intervention diminished somewhat following Clinton's election. On November 19, he opened at *Hostos Community College* in the Bronx the "Alex Haley Conferences". Aristide said: "Les Haïtiens sont des réfugiés politiques ... La politique des Etats-Unis à leur endroit est une tragédie. Alex Haley ne l'aurait pas accepté. Malcolm X ne l'aurait jamais accepté, et, aujourd'hui, jamais nous ne l'accepterons". He advised Clinton to work on the return of democracy to Haiti, adding that Clinton could be assured that the refugees would stay in Haiti (HP 157:10-12).

Following UNGA resolution A/RES.47/20A of November 24, 1992, Longchamps said on a press conference that, in order to preserve human rights in Haiti, the UNGA might "demand from the Security Council to deploy [a] `peace-keeping force´". HP showed itself amazed that for certain members of the legitimate government "posing the Haitian question on the level of the Security Council seems to represent an ideal" (HP 158:17). HP did not trust the movement between the US, the OAS, and the UN with a view to solving the Haitian crisis, which Rangel reportedly called "fantastic" (HP 166:1,16). HP wrote extensively on the legitimate government's diplomatic moves. Taking briefly stock of the year 1992 in mid-January 1993, HP lamented that the legitimate government had not left its stamp on recent developments. Reminding that the OAS immediately prohibited international recognition of the *de facto* regime following the coup, HP gave the advice that the legitimate government would need "to take the OAS at its word" instead of "loosing its respect" and "selling out" its principal force by entering into the "political game" of negotiation and compromise. The effect would be disorientation "in the 10th department as well as in Haiti". With an entourage moved, in its majority, by purely personal ambitions of power, HP saw Aristide in danger of "selling" out his mandate to the bourgeoisie that had always cohabited or cooperated with Duvalierism. The current strategy consisted of an attempted "accommodation with imperialism". The struggle of the Haitian people could not be reduced to "diplomatic manoeuvers" (HP 167:15).

Analyzing the "price for the return of democracy" in late January 1993, HP discerned the danger that Aristide could become "Clinton's propagandist". It pointed to Aristide's speech on VoA, which he made to convince Haitians in Haiti that a solution was near and to dissuade them to leave the country. In HP's view, Aristide was poorly advised by his "principal political advisers" like FNCD's Evans Paul. Paul reportedly founded *Fondation Développement et Démocratie* (FONDEM) in September 1992 with funding from NED's local branch IRHED headed by Léopold Berlanger, a political friend of Bazin's. According to *Radio Métropole*, FONDEM was in favor of "a climate of social appeasement" (HP 168:6,14,16). HP concluded that Aristide was "surrounded by unscrupulous political sharks that completely share the American plan of total submission to imperialism and of capitulation before the putschists". Aristide's two key mistakes had been to believe, first, that "the more he proves himself to be conciliatory, the more he will be accepted by the US", and, second, to count too much on his popularity. Bearing "too high an image of himself", he forget about the one million Haitians in the diaspora (HP 168:6,14,16).

HP further believed that it was wrong for Aristide to abandon the position that the forced repatriation policy of the US is principally illegal under the "pretext" that Clinton offered a solution to the fundamental problem. For Aristide could turn out to be the next victim of the same betrayal, since Clinton was less motivated by "his fear of the refugees" than by his will to find a political solution fitting US interests. Clinton did not seem to have sufficient confidence in his "friend" Aristide in convincing his compatriots to stay in Haiti.[311] He therefore decided to employ the "impressing fleet" encircling Haiti to "prevent the Haitians manu militari from escaping" in the operation "Able Manner". Longchamps reportedly explained on *Radio Soleil d'Haiti* (01/15/93) Clinton´s preoccupation as "stemming from the fact that nearly 200,000 persons would be ready to come ... which could create a big political problem for him". HP was "alienated" by the degree, to which the legitimate government identified with Clinton´s "swing in opinion". Instead, the legitimate government "should identify with the refugees, victims of this turnaround". Vigilance had been "sent to sleep" with the result of confusion in the 10th department (HP 172:6,14-16). For Aristide, in contrast, the "deal" between him and Clinton - "I would discourage the boat people and he would favor the return of democracy" - was a "collaboration from which each side had something to gain". He counted Clinton among the ones, with whom he found "certain true solidarities" (Aristide 1996:79-80,110,103). Following Jackson´s visit to Haiti late January 1993, HP was surprised that nobody seemed to be shocked that the putschists could demand security guarantees (HP 174:17). HP held that the "eternal attempt of reconciliation with macoutisme" had already begun with the choice of Théodore over Benoit. One other "decisive step" had been the meeting in Miami in June 1992 resulting in the "Florida Declaration", which evoked, for the first time, a "gouvernement de concorde nationale" (HP 202:13-14).

On March 3, 1993, a delegation of the constitutional government, headed by the Minister of Social Affairs, returned from Guantanamo. It confirmed the squalid conditions, to which the HIV-infected refugees detained there were subjected (HP 187:8). In an interview with Gilbert, Dr. Edouard Hazel, who had been part of the delegation, said that its purpose was "to convey a message from president Aristide to the refugees". He said that Aristide had made their situation "one of the priorities of his government" (HP 193:9,14). In the first week of April 1993, HP published a message from Aristide to the Yale students, in which he mentioned his government´s fact-finding mission to Guantanamo. Aristide lauded the students´ "solidarity with my sisters and brothers" as an "act of love". By their participation, the students had become "members of the Lavalas movement" (HP 200:9). Wishnie of the Yale team recalled, however, that Aristide "made it very complicated", because he "remained the hero to all these [Haitian] political groups, and yet here he was being quiet about the refugees ... It was part of his diplomatic stuff to ignore the refugees" (Wishnie 1995).

It is rather unlikely that the extra-territorial problem of Guantanamo was a top priority for the exile government in direct talks with the US at this point in time. As Wishnie recalled, Rangel and Jackson "were disappointed with Aristide" (Wishnie 1995). The government did, however, join at least one effort of producing "pressure in favor of Haitians imprisoned in the US", as Gilbert reported in mid-April, 1993. Not only US students and Hollywood, but also the "10th department during the big demonstration on April 2" including the constitutional government had been "agents of pres-

---

[311] It must be noted that HP also preferred Haitians to stay in Haiti in an effort to make their oppressors rather than Aristide-supporters leave the country. The Haitian weekly suggested verbatim: "Aussi le peuple doit-il continuer à s´organiser, à résister activement contre la dictature, afin que ce soient les colons internes qui prennent la fuite, comme ils l´avaient fait le 7 février 1986" (HP 155:10).

sure". Between March 26 and 28, a governmental delegation including Préval and Kurzban visited 6 detention centers in Florida. It issued a preliminary report demonstrating that "our compatriots live under the yoke of a very strict carceral system" (HP 203:9).[312] Those measures could not, however, keep the relationship between Aristide and the 10th department from deteriorating. At the same time that the PR campaign to rehabilitate the Aristide government in the US public was launched, Préval came to New York. His two-day sojourn had obviously the purpose of renewing the Aristide government´s contacts with the Haitian diaspora. In the evening of April 24, for example, he assisted in celebrating HEAR´s 3rd anniversary in Grand Prospect Hall in Brooklyn (HP 209:9,17). In the meantime, NCHR continued its refugee advocacy before the Aristide government (NCHR19:6). Coradin, who was hired by NCHR in early October 1993, told me that "Haitians, to my personal chagrin, in this country have needed enormous prodding and enormous work to stand up and come out for the Haitian refugees". Since "Haitians in the US reflected, by and large, Aristide´s constituency in Haiti", he continued, they were "like sheep. If Aristide doesn´t tell them to do something, they won´t do it". Everyone in the Haitian community "knew about it, but no one gave a damn" (Coradin 1995).

After the Governors Island process came to a virtual halt in the fall of 1993, the legitimate government warned Clinton at the end of the year that it would reconsider Aristide´s support for the Administration´s policy of returning Haitian refugees (Holmes 1993a:A5). According to Roumer, Aristide said on December 21: "C´est le président qui doit retourner in Haiti, ce ne sont pas les réfugiés qu´on doit y renvoyer; ce sont les chefs du coup d´Etat qui doivent quitter Haiti, ce ne sont pas les réfugiés". This time, Roumer rejoiced, Aristide had taken the initiative (HP 220:17;HP 221). On December 23, Aristide announced that he was organizing the Miami conference for January 15, 1994 (Greenhouse 1993:A3). It was the last day of an ultimatum given to the Haitian military by the "four `friends´ of Haiti" to comply with the GIA (HP 217:1).[313] While Congressman Torricelli blamed Aristide in the WP for "encouraging a mass exodus to leave Haiti", HP observed that he had by no means launched such an appeal (HP 217:1,13). Aristide´s spokesperson Martineau said on VoA (01/04/94) that "this year, we are going to concentrate on mobilization. The Haitian people need to know that they are the key actor" (HP 219:1,7).

With the original design of the Miami conference abandoned, Aristide played the game of the putschists "without getting anything in turn" (HP 222:1,16). Even though workshop C at the conference dealt with proposals for ending the US interdiction program, Aristide´s adviser Michael Barnes of CIP declared that abrogating the USHIA was no option (HP 224:17). HP nonetheless called the thought expressed by Longchamps with regard to the possibility of abrogating the USHIA as "cynic" (HP 228:13). It considered it unnecessary to have assembled some 500 persons in Miami for a conference that only served, under the thumb of Pezzullo, to put new pressure on Aristide by calling for "reconciliation" (HP 224:1,17). Aristide reportedly still appreciated the GIA as the diplomatic road to go (HP 226:9). In HP´s view, the conference

---

[312] According to Tecumseh, "certain problems ... such as the incarceration of Haitian refugees in Krome" had already been identified by Aristide during his meeting prior to the coup with members of the *Council on Foreign Relations* (HP 8:17). They remained unsolved in the course of the crisis.
[313] The four "'Friends of the Secretary General" comprised the governments of France, Canada, Venezuela, and the US. See the NYT of 12/14/93:A8 and 12/15/93:A7.

was a "total failure in terms of concrete results". Comparing Aristide with PLO´s Yasser Arafat and referring to Edward Said, member of the National Palestinian Council, in *Z Magazine* (12/93), HP accused Aristide of exhibiting a "`nigger mentality´". His "submission to the dictates of the US" resulted from a "certain form of identification" and a "halo of prestige" following his electoral victory of December 1990 and the "innumerable prizes" he had received (HP 228:6,13,15). HP´s devastating and insulting criticism of Aristide is reminiscent of W.E.B. Dubois´s concept of "double consciousness" (1953:3).[314]

In retrospect, Aristide described the absurdity of pressuring him with proposals for a "union government" by posing the rhetorical question: "[W]ould President Mitterand place some neofascists from the Front National in his government, or would Bill Clinton reserve a few cabinet posts for the Ku Klux Klan? Would the Italian government look for a few authentic godfathers from the Mafia in order to combat organized crime better? Would the German chancellor seek a neo-Nazi ... in order to better assure the protection of foreigners?". At the same time, he was aware of the human costs of diplomacy: "How could I not be shaken by such a drama [of Haitian refugees perishing by drowning] and exasperated by the slowness of political solutions that would reduce the horror?" (1996:156,144). The Aristide government´s next steps have already been described in principle in section 5.4.8. They were preceded by Ratner´s letter to Aristide, in which he also suggested the example of Martin Luther King, who had ignored the pressure exerted by Johnson during the Vietnam war (HP 229:8). The Aristide government publicly announced it would reconsider the USHIA on February 9, 1994 (HP 233:5). NCHR´s, Ratner´s, and other groups´ advocacy before the exiled Haitian government seems to have had a long-term impact on Aristide´s strategical choices. Consequently, Aristide sought close contact with Haitian and American activists again as in the CBC conference on March 18 and 19 (HP 239:7).[315] In April, Aristide did get in touch again with the Haitian diaspora in the US. According to HP, his speaking tour through New England between April 6 and 9 was remarkable for two reasons: its length and the interest it aroused in the communities that he visited. Aristide had stop-overs in Massachusetts and in Vermont. Even though HP was not satisfied with the tour, it nevertheless testified to Aristide´s unabated popularity (HP 244:7). Aristide went on to Berkley on April 17, where he called US policy on Haitian refugees racist and a "clear violation of human rights" (HP 252).[316]

As was shown in chapter 5.6, Haitians in the US might have been evenly split on the issue of military intervention. But without Aristide´s tacit support, HP observed, calls for an invasion from the CBC would not have been as "strident". By asking the UNSC in June 1993 to take up the question of Haiti, HP continued, "Aristide opened the door to a multinational intervention into Haiti´s internal affairs" (HP 264:13). Tecumseh lamented in late July, 1994 that Aristide did "absolutely nothing to modify the course of events: ... no call to the Haitian community to mobilize" (HP 289:13). But on October 4, 500 Haitians and Haitian-Americans marched to the UN in a show of

---

[314] The black historian and sociologist described this concept as follows: "It is a peculiar sensation, this double-consciousness, this sense of always looking at one´s self through the eyes of others, of measuring one´s soul by the tape of a world that looks on in amused contempt and pity" (1953:3).

[315] Yet criticism of the Aristide government did not stop. Reporting on the succession of Joseph Yvon Feuillé as vice-consul of New York, HP accused it of nepotism (HP 240;HP 241:7,18).

[316] For similar statements and moves by Aristide, see the NYT of 06/24/94:A4 and of 06/29/94:A11.

support for Aristide, who was expected to address the world body (NYT 10/05/94). At a reception at the White House on October 13, Aristide already "hammered out" his motto "No to violence, No to vengeance, Yes to reconciliation". Upon his return on October 15, HP recalled that Manno Charlemagne once asked him during a meeting on November 21, 1992, if he would like to return to Haiti with a US plane or a US Navy ship. Aristide responded that he would not accept to return under these conditions. Only a few months ago, HP continued, he said that he would "never, never, never" accept to owe his return to foreign intervention. Now, he was accompanied by many of his "friends" from Washington, 35 people in the presidential plane and many more, including members of the 10th department (HP 331:6,16). Aristide insisted in hindsight that the "Tenth Department has never wavered in its support for Lavalas" (1996:89).

In sum, it may be assumed that many Haitians in the US diaspora followed their popular president´s exile government in its strategical choices.[317] As Frank of HCC said: "Whenever Aristide took a position on the refugees at that time, the refugees really had a lot of support" (Frank 1995). Critics of the 10th department felt that it had been "too directly linked to the Aristide government". Mayas said it could have accomplished more (Jean-Pierre 1995:203). In retrospect, Aristide felt to have been "more and more isolated from my people" as a result of "a distance between the impoverished people and those who had advocated the embargo" (Aristide 1996:59).

5.10 Socio-economic Class Differences in the Haitian Transnation

The mass demonstrations organized in New York City by Haitians right after the coup occurred in a specific urban environment. Latour characterized this setting in his report on the Haitian mass protest on October 11, 1991. It took place in a city he described as "the big apple of discord between big business that crushes, humiliates and kills, and the damned of assembly work, the refused goods of a liberalism diabolically perverted". New York City was the "metropolis of money and of the mess of world affairs". The torrent of 150,000 to 200,000 Haitians streamed from Grand Army Plaza in Brooklyn into "the core of Wall Street, the core of the very capital that made us see all colors, we the people of the Third World, tired of being marginalized by international capital and multinational corporations as well as their local puppets" (HP 22:14-18). At the mass protest in Washington, Haitian singer Juste said: "[T]he dirty bourgeoisie ... has preferred to spend $40 million to destroy the nascent democracy in Haiti ... this army ... has always been in the service of the 5 to 10% of the population that represent the upper classes" (HP 25:16-19). The "upper classes" in Port-au-Prince and the "core of Wall Street" are connected by economic societal transnational links described in section 5.2.7. The joint venture *Vetex* between the Mevs family and the New York-based *RSK Industries, Inc.* is but one example. Haiti´s economic oligarchy

---

[317] These ranged from advocating the international embargo and OAS-mediated negotiations, encouraging voluntary abstinence from fleeing Haiti and rallying support in US civil society, over advocating UN-mediated negotiations and the deployment of the UN/OAS-ICM, to finally utilizing the refugee issue as a pressuring device and condoning US-led foreign intervention.

has been accused of having financed the 1991 coup (HP 249:15;NLC 1994:135;Ives 1995:83;Bragg 1994a:14;Bragg 1994b:16).

Latour´s description is reminiscent of the analysis of New York as a "dual city" characterized by a tendency toward cultural, economic, and political polarization. According to urban sociologists, this tendency takes the form of a contrast between a comparatively cohesive core of professionals in the advanced corporate services[318] and a disorganized periphery fragmented by race, ethnicity, gender, occupational and industrial location, and the spaces they occupy. New York, where the minorities have become the majority in 1990, has been described as the product of a post-Fordist, post-Keynesian, postindustrial, and postmodern "World City" formation, which has condensed in it what probably is the largest and most diverse conglomeration of global cultures (Castells et al. 1991:400,402,415;Soja 1991:362-368). Since the early 1980s, New York has exhibited trends of economic informalization. Primarily located in densely populated areas with very high shares of immigrants, this expanding informal sector based on low-wage jobs within small units of production, including traditional sweatshop activities that compete with Third World factories, contrasts with the expansion of high-income jobs (Sassen-Koob 1989:60-63,73-76).

When riding on the number 2-train from Brooklyn into the Wall Street district crossing the East River, it is striking that the "periphery" is predominantly black and the "core" is predominantly white. Haitians, who represent 3% of New York´s foreign-born population (Kraly 1987:62), mainly live in the "periphery". Brooklyn-based Haitian anthropologist Charles notes that between 1965 and 1980, Haiti ranked 5th and then 6th among countries sending immigrants to New York. The Haitian work force in New York forms a large component in nursing facilities. With one important feature of the Haitian community in New York being its lack of unique concentration, most of the Haitians live in Brooklyn, followed by Queens, Manhattan, and the Bronx. In Brooklyn, they are primarily concentrated in Crown Heights, Flatbush, and East New York. They live in the midst of lower-and middle-income black Americans, Jamaicans, Trinidadians, Colombians, Hasidic Jews, and Italians. While there is a "clear collective consciousness of being Haitian", the existence of numerous Haitian organizations usually differentiated by regional place of origin, color, and class make for "a tendency of division and heterogeneity" in the Haitian community (1990:199-207).[319]

At the *Haiti Commission*-sponsored soirée at *Baruch College* on November 21, 1991, Garry Guiteau, member of parliament, wondered "how can we talk about the coup d´etat without talking about class struggle?". Casséus said that Aristide´s victory had been a revolutionary act by the people "for changing the political and socio-economic structure" of Haiti (HP 51:10). Consequently, Haitian-organized mass gatherings in support of Aristide were not merely an exercise in popular democracy. They were also a protest against socio-economic conditions seen as laying at the roots of the coup. The choice of Wall Street as the locality of protest was no coincidence, but made deliberately to show to those obscure economic forces the sheer numerical fighting strength of Lavalas in the 10th department. Often holding more than one or two jobs at

---

[318] These corporate services can be summarized with the acronym "FIRE", which stands for "Finance, Insurance, and Real Estate".

[319] The median family income for a Caribbean-headed household was $15,645 in 1980 compared to $17,361 for an American-born family (Charles 1990). Wishnie witnessed a huge "class difference in the Haitian community" (Wishnie 1995).

the same time in a post-industrial service economy, Haitian volunteers' limited time budget might well have been their most valuable resource in organizing. In that sense, political solidarity was congruent with class solidarity. Hence, HP was concerned about a diminished cohesion in street demonstrations early on. The weekly regretted in late October 1991 that street rallies had lost their "unitary character" (HP 26:9).

Haitian history provided the textbook that helped make sense of the coup. At the meeting on November 3, 1991 in Congressman Conyers' Detroit office, Dr. Jean-Claude Dutes, a psychologist affiliated with the *State University of Michigan*, East Lansing, gave a historical analysis of the current crisis. He stated that it derived from the colonial period and was "the product of a confrontation between the right of the majority and the dishonestly acquired privileges of a minority" (HP 41:10).[320] Exploitation and oppression in post-revolutionary Haiti were rooted in the peculiar tension-ridden amalgamation of people and interests in colonial Saint Domingue. In 1790, it had a racially and geographically fragmented population that totalled slightly more than 500,000. About 452,000 of them, roughly 80%, were black slaves, while only 40,000 were whites. The latter were subdivided into the most powerful *grands blancs* (planters and high officials) and less powerful *petits blancs* (small planters and local bureaucrats). An even smaller but nonetheless powerful minority was composed of about 28,000 *gens de couleur* or *affranchis* (free-born creole mulattoes), the light-skinned descendants of the unions between planters and their female slaves. Owning one third of the land and one fourth of the slaves in 1791, they competed with the *grands blancs* in their orientation to French culture and enjoyed a higher socio-economic status than the poor whites. When the proclaimed ideals of the French Revolution resonated in the colony, each of the three factions had its own interpretation of Liberty, Equality, and Fraternity. Being freedmen already, most of the *gens de couleur* picked out equality to define their own rights in relation to whites (Mintz 1995:76-77;Trouillot 1992:40-42;Knight 1990:202-203).

Yet the early revolutionary leadership, who would drive out the French masters and nearly all Europeans with them, included slaves and freedmen alike. The elimination of the white presence was to guarantee freedom and independence, which was primarily defined as the abolition of slavery. Beyond this point of consent, there were, however, sharp differences based on a "deep misunderstanding" as to the economic meaning of the ideal of liberty, as Trouillot explains. While the *anciens libres*, mostly *gens de couleur*, who were free before the revolution, opted for the maintenance of the plantation system, the *nouveaux libres*, those who gained their freedom during the economically destructive war, measured their liberty in the right to work autonomously on their own garden plots and to sell their produce in Sunday markets. The liberated masses of ex-slaves and their descendants preferred the increasingly marginal existence on those homesteads, which were continually subdivided by their heirs. This

---

[320] Furthermore, at the soirée on November 21, Senator Emmanuel spoke of "internal colonialism" as having been at the origin of the coup (HP 51:10). And at the "soirée de réflexion" on February 8, 1992, in *St. Francis Church*, Brooklyn, André Loroy spoke about the "historic importance" of December 16, 1990, reminding the audience that the Haitian people had been oppressed and exploited by two social classes since 1804 (HP 74:10), the year of Haiti's independence. As Mayas told me, the "big problem in Haiti is the class difference!" (Mayas 1995). One HEAR-member underscored the "social class difference" in the Haitian community (HEAR 1995). Owens saw the "class structure" as one reason why BfA's progress was stymied (Owens 1995).

preference was in fundamental contradiction to the plantation-based work regimen preferred by the plantation-owning leadership in the new state apparatus. It was temporarily instituted after independence by means of "militarized agriculture" to revamp productivity in the export sector. Color became the favorite idiom of rivalry within the leadership (Mintz 1995:79-80;Trouillot 1992:43-50;Stepick 1987:133).

In 1807, the contours of a fateful fiscal strategy were established. It was more dependent upon export duties on coffee than on sugar to be collected at customshouses. This system of indirect taxation, mediated through the middlemen, shifted the burden of state financing from the sugar-producing plantation-owners to the coffee-producing peasants and so was clearly unjust. By 1810, export taxes provided more than 50% of the national budget, while the entire budget depended on customs duties by 1887. This fiscal policy persistently siphoned off the resources of the peasantry drained by continued surplus extraction. According to Trouillot, "the state had chosen to live at the expense of the nation" characterized by agricultural production on minifundia.[321] This socio-economic organization divided 19th century Haiti into two distinct groups tied together in an unequal but complimentary relationship: the agricultural producers and the urbanites clustered around the alliance of rulers and merchants. It gave rise to the perception of a cultural dualism between elites and masses, rural and urban, *mulâtre* and black, French and Creole, or Catholic and Vodoun religion (Trouillot 1992:59-64,69-72,80-83). The central social imbalance in Haitian life took the form of chronic political instability marked by military coups since the early 19th century. The Marine occupation exacerbated the contradictions embedded in the socio-economic structure, which paved the way to totalitarianism in the corrupt Duvalier system called "kleptocracy". Even though 80-90% of Haiti's population remained rural in the late 1970s, 83% of governmental expenditures were in Port-au-Prince, while agricultural expenditures never exceeded 7-10% of the budget. Stepick calls the Haitian revolution a "pyrrhic victory" (Trouillot 1992: 102-104;Stepick 1987:133-134,140,147).

During the early months of his exile, Aristide often referred to the extreme socio-economic cleavages in his country. In his interview with WABC-TV in late April 1992, for example, he presented "statistics of injustice" illustrating this point: 45% of the land is possessed by a mere 1% of the Haitian population, while 45 families control almost the whole economic sector. On the other hand, there are only 1.8 physicians and 1.9 nurses for every 10,000 Haitians. Haiti's predominantly light-skinned elite, the top 1% of the population exempt from paying taxes, but appropriating half the nation's income in 1991, reportedly includes more than 100 millionaires, whereas 90% of the remainder earns about $120 a year on average (Bragg 1994a:14;Bragg 1994b:16;HEAR 1995). At Hemsley Palace Hotel on April 25, 1992, where he met with a group of prestigious businessmen belonging to the most influential companies in the US to discuss issues of infrastructural development and construction in Haiti, Aristide explained that the traditional elite in Haiti holds economic power, while the Lavalas movement holds political power. He relentlessly established a link between economic conditions in Haiti and those on a global scale: At the student party at *Brooklyn College* in Flatbush, he stressed the disparities between the rich North and the poor countries in the South. Aristide confirmed during his New York

---

[321] Minifundia: small garden plots or homesteads.

visit in April that "Haiti is the poorest country of the hemisphere" indeed. This phrase was the one recurring epithet of Haiti in the US mainstream media's coverage of the Haitian crisis (HP 114:12,14,15;HP 157:10-12;HP 147:8).

As early as April 1992, HP's Loubet cautioned against leaving the struggle in the hands of the "traditional bourgeoisie". Its only strategy was trying to appease the US, which sought to promote the "model of democratic capitalism of the neo-liberal type" under the total control of the IMF as embodied by Bazin. She added that it was not an empty word to talk about the "American Plan" in the case of Haiti (HP 100:16-17). HP's and other Haitian activists' usage of the term "bourgeoisie" seems to designate a set of people forming the dominant class in Haiti, which has lived off the extraction of surplus generated by the masses of agricultural producers from the time of the revolution (Basch et al. 1994:23,153). But the "traditional bourgeoisie" did not only exist in Haiti. It also loomed in the Haitian diaspora in the US, an area not easy to survey. Aristide added during his New York visit in late April that "if one observes the numerous relations of the Haitian community in the US, one will have to admit that what our population needs is the appropriate environment to be able to free itself from underdevelopment" (HP 114:12). For some Haitian activists, it was questionable, whether New York represented the "appropriate environment" for maintaining a cohesive class-based solidarity needed in the struggle, given the possibility to establish "numerous relations". This environment rather prompted manifold class-related suspicions.[322] There were fears that the Lavalas-leaning organizations in the Haitian diaspora could be undermined by the Haitian bourgeoisie.

First suspicions of this sort were expressed by HP following an event in Brooklyn in 1992. It was organized to commemorate the victims of the Ruelle Vaillant massacre of November 29, 1987 and attended by a score of representatives of the regional 10th departments, among them Dupuy and Guy Victor. Reporting on the event, HP regretted, however, that there had not been "more coordination to plan an activity together" (HP 160:8). HP's report was followed by a long analysis of the "way the 10th department has organized so far". It included a critique of "certain utilized methods" in the struggle against "macoutisme" waged by "two distinct sectors", as the weekly stressed: the "bourgeoisie and the popular camp". HP reminded that these two sectors merely formed a "tactical unity" after the December 16, 1990 elections, while preferring "fundamentally different approaches and methods". These "different conceptions of the struggle" were inevitably a "function of interests" and of "social classes that one identifies with" (HP 161:6). As Marx Aristide and Richardson put it, Haiti's popular movement, which strove to establish "a truly participatory democracy", was "embroiled in a dialectical struggle with the reformist sectors of Haiti's broader `democratic' movement". It was composed of "certain politicians, intellectuals and members

---

[322] At the "day of the press" in early June 1992, for example, Lassègue discerned two types of Haitian media in the 10th department: Certain professional weeklies and radio stations that use "good sources" in Haiti. And, on the other hand, a multitude of radio stations with journalists only eager to gain publicity. Composed of certain businessmen in New York, Boston, and Miami, who use means of communication only to make money, these journalists were not interested in the return of democray (HP 126:9). The danger of progressing "macoutization" in the 10th department had a socio-economic dimension. HP's Loubet characterized HM as a recycling enterprise, where one can find people, who once flirted with HO's Joseph (HP 100:16-17).

of the business elite", who sought to establish "formal democracy through elections and superficial reforms" (1995:182).

HP first pointed out that the Aristide government´s program "La Chance á Prendre" initially conceived of the Haitian diaspora as "une prolongation d´Haiti, une réserve stratégique dans la lutte pour la démocratie et pour le développement national". Père Jean-Juste had been nominated to structure the 10th department by way of forming an umbrella organization bringing together all 10th departments formed in each district. A "mini-conference" with delegates from different regions, which took place in New York on July 13 and 14, 1991, passed a final resolution stipulating: "Le 10e département est une confédération indépendante regroupant toutes les organisations du 10e dans les cinq continents". Several groups had already been integrated into this "vast unitary organization" with a "national orientation", among them "the oldest and the best known of New York" (AEH, HEAR, CCRH etc.). HP´s main criticism was that the original design had been abandoned in favor of a "totally different conception". The weekly maintained that the new concept had been put in place in New York on April 25, 1992 at a meeting in Hotel Hemsley between Aristide and 42 representatives of organizations, among them Frantz Jérôme, *Radio Digital*, Smith Georges, and Guy Victor (HP 161:6).

According to HP, Aristide declared at the meeting that he was not afraid of the sheer number of organizations. On the following meeting on May 10, the participants divided into four teams with one speaker each: James Monroe Rosefort of Anmwe in Miami, Bob Tolsiman of MOKAM, Fritzner Pierre of *Lafanmi Reyini*, and Ti Do of *Fè Koupe Fé*, who was later replaced by Roger Etienne of KOZA. At another meeting in New York on July 23 and 24 at Righa Hotel, Aristide defined anti-macoutisme and pro-democracy as the two minimal goals, around which the organizations should unite. But the organizational conception that remained was based on a great number of groups rather than on an umbrella type as originally planned. The new concept came to be called "`80 organisations´" according to the prospective total number of groups included therein. The "Organisation du Dixième" figured rather as "one among others". HP complained that the Lavalas movement thus attracted a score of opportunists, who want to position themselves by claiming to be the leader of a group (HP 161:16-18;HP 114:15). The Haitian community´s politico-organizational infrastructure steered for progressing fragmentation.

According to HP, the *10e of New York* started out to develop on a popular basis. But under the Lavalas government, that began to change with the creation of VOAM the weekly maintained: It was exclusively formed with members of the bourgeois sector like Père Adrien, Emmanuel Ambroise, Ambassador in Ottawa, Gladys Lauture, and Denise Fouchard. The organization soon tried, HP continued, to "short-cut" and "break" the "Organisation du Dixième" following Adrien´s arrival in New York in March 1991. He allegedly propagated the conception, after which the "Organisation du Dixième" was to be replaced by a conglomerate of groups. As a consequence, it was much easier for the bourgeoisie to manipulate the direction of the 10th department. The results were reportedly apparent at the third meeting with Aristide in New York on September 16, 1992 at Righa Hotel, from which the *10e of New York* was excluded. During that meeting, a change in route of a planned rally was agreed upon, which members of the *10e of New York* took as an attempt by the bourgeoisie[323] "to sabotage the demonstration" (HP 161:16-18).

At the last meeting in New York at Righa Hotel on November 21, 1992 with 45 invited individuals not mandated by or not affiliated with any organization, yet another concept called the "noyau de coordination" was hammered out, comprising Etienne, Tolsiman, Rosefort, Fritzner Pierre, Guilloteau, and Victor, leader of the *10e of New York*, who was thus outnumbered. While the 10e was itself criticized by Mayas for its lack of "transparency", HP complained that the "core" had not been formed on democratic principles. Its objective was the dismantling of the "Organisation du Dixième" by means of a "vast realignment" allowing the bourgeoisie to better impose its pawns. Consequently, activists on the grassroots level, those "on the concrete", were increasingly demobilized, because they would not identify with this kind of leadership. HP concluded that these developments had adverse effects on the "motivation of grassroots activists - in particular in New York". They were not inclined to work for the "notables from Queens" (HP 161:17-18;Jean-Pierre 1995:203).[324]

As one HEAR-member put it, they would not do "the dirty work" of grassroots mobilization in the streets (HEAR 1995). According to Guy Victor, Haitians in New York only trusted the three Haitian priests Adrien, Smarth, and Sansaricq as well as Désir and himself in terms of appeals to mobilize. But while the former two priests had returned to Haiti in 1986, Père Sansaricq did not want to be an organizer, Victor added. At the same time, Haitians in New York did not consider the heads of organizations working on the refugee issue "as leaders" (Victor 1996). HP rejected a form of unity with the "propagandists of the American Plan" and refused a concept of unity "under the hegemony of the right". In the long run, the cohabitation between the two sectors of the Lavalas movement could not prevent divergences on major issues such as military intervention, negotiations with Cédras or reconciliation with Duvalierism (HP 161:17-18). It is conceivable that the refugee issue belonged to those points of political contention aggravated by class ascription or socio-economic status.

In late December, 1992, HP called for a redefinition of the term "refugee" in the 1951 Refugee Convention on the grounds that it was impossible "to separate the political situation from the economic conditions". For "often these people flee their country because of social conditions created by dictatorial governments". But the "rich so-called industrialized countries" such as the US share responsibility in refugee flows. They were "not ready to accept the people of the Third World, who are often the victims of their cruel policy of domination and exploitation" (HP 165:8). The drama of the Guantanamo HIV-camp was seen as a "microcosm of the imperialist countries' attitude" (HP 192:17). Hence HP discussed the Haitian refugee phenomenon as one side-effect of the "American Plan" as defined above. This would imply that the "propagandists of the American Plan" in the Haitian bourgeoisie of the diaspora shared responsibility in refusing refugees.

---

[323] E.g. Marie-Thérèse Guilloteau of *Fanm Dayiti*, Roger Etienne of KOZA, Faustin Beaurevers of CEH, and Frantz Jérôme of *Mouvman Rezistans Queens*.

[324] HP blamed Dorancy of HRC for having collaborated with "opportunist" Biamby, former director of the *Haitian American Commuity Association of Dade* and member of CIRR, in forming "the core of coordination of the Florida district". HP also suspected the General Finance Committee under Déjean of New York to be "too visibly inspired by the bourgeois sector" (HP 161:17).

In early January 1992, HP referred to a letter-to-the-editor published in the ND (12/30/91). It maintained it was impossible for the US to accept Haitians, as there were millions of people unemployed in the US. HP was proud to refer to one "compatriot", Joseph Laurenceau, who responded (01/13/92) that "these Haitian refugees are those, who permit us all to have sugar free of cost, when we order our coffee in the morning" (HP 67:9). For "upwardly mobile" and "prosperous upper-middle class Haitians" like economically successful *PC Magazine*-editor Dreyfuss of New York, however, Haitian boat people were a "tragic aspect of Haitian life". In his essay in the NYT of May 23, 1993, he related in some detail his "haughty" social background, which is very instructive.[325] But "all that history and all that pride counted for naught in America", Dreyfuss regrets: "America - at least on matters of race - was a great social leveler" (1993:80-81). His latent aversion against black Haitian boat people is reminiscent of colonial Saint Domingue´s *gens de couleur*, who stressed the French revolutionary ideal of equality to define their own rights relative to whites. As Jean-Pierre explains, the "lighter the skin, the heftier the privileges" Haitians enjoy in Haiti. Some "Haitian mulattos found themselves grouped in the same category with the poorer, dark-skinned new immigrants" after coming to the US. Some "upper middle-class, light-skinned Haitians had to compete for the same manufacturing and cleaning jobs with people who were once their gardeners, cooks and maids" (1995:197). Class prejudices of earlier Haitian immigrants from the elite and middle social strata were, according to Buchanan and Glick Schiller, exacerbated in the early 1980s by "extremely pejorative representations of destitute and desperate Haitian boat people" (Richman 1992:192).

The same class-based social distance resulting in mutual alienation seems to have been at work during the Haitian refugee crisis under study. NCHR´s Coradin pointed to what he called "Haitian social dynamics, dynamics of class and color within Haiti". They were "transferred with the members of the diaspora, so middle-class professionals, educated Haitians, people like me, people who look like me and talk like me, may not ... identify with the Haitians that they see on CNN on a boat getting rescued ... Those people ... would not be considered peers in the social sense" (Coradin 1995). According to Celestin of EMM, there were Haitians among the boat people, who had even never seen an electric light bulb in their lives (Celestin 1996). Successful upper-class Haitian professionals in the US therefore seem to have been socialized in a very different context. Consequently, there had been, as Aubourg told me, "many Haitian attorneys that did not want to participate" in advocating the rights of Haitian refugees (Aubourg 1996). As Wishnie observed, the "professional class of the Haitian community in Brooklyn" was more concerned with what he called "typical immigrant

---

[325] His family was "typical of the ethnic stew that prevailed in Haiti´s middle class". His father, a Jew from Amiens, France, came to Haiti in the 1880s and "married into a fair-skinned and class-conscious family of South American and French origin, which traced its roots in Haiti" back to the 1700s. His mother came from "an equally haughty black family in Haiti´s north". Dreyfuss takes pride in his great-great-grandfather, who "had helped build the Citadelle", emperor Henry Christophe´s mountaintop fortress. His family settled in New York in the 1950s, when he was a 7-or-8-year-old. At that time, the Haitian community "was small, consisting mostly of the so-called elite. Many could be mistaken easily for White or Hispanic". Back home in Haiti, status was "a matter of history and family and circumstances, much more complex than the simplistic racial definitions" in the US. In Haiti, "middle and upper middle classes had their unique melting pot ... most light-skinned Haitians were members of the elite, but so were some very dark-skinned Haitians" (1993:80-81).

goals for America - in class terms, for them the refugees dragged them down" (Wishnie 1995).

Similarly, Mayas detected a class bias in the exile government. She told me that Aristide's entourage "did not really support the refugee business ... they don't want to have anything to do with them!". As to Haitian boat people, who came to the US on humanitarian and medical parole, she said that "the exile government would not help them. So we, the little people, tried to help them. And everybody was just like looking at us like we are all crazy for trying to help those people". Upon Aristide's return, she said that "the big shots of Haiti" responded to suggestions that the government establish a humanitarian support system for the Haitians returning from Guantanamo as follows: "[A]ll I heard was `who told those people to leave Haiti? Why didn't they stay? Why did they have to go? Now that they are back in Haiti, what makes them think that they should be treated special?´ I was so angry" (Mayas 1995).

According to Stepick, there might be a "bifurcation" in the Haitian community in the US: "There are those living out the American dream and those who, succumbing to anti-Haitian and racist prejudices, are merging into the underclass". Stepick is the director of the Immigration and Ethnicity Institute at *Florida International University* in Maimi, whose Haitian community in Little Haiti tends to be younger and poorer than in Brooklyn as well as greater relative to the total population of Miami (Sontag 1994:B4). The resultant social proximity to the Haitian boat people might be part of the explanation that the Haitian diaspora's center of activism in refugee affairs in the early stages of the crisis emerged in Miami rather than in New York City. As Wishnie speculated, "the poor Haitians ... they felt perhaps closer to the refugees" (Wishnie 1995). Similarly, HEAR's membership composition of young, financially weak students seems to have had the same bearing: "We are all refugees in a sense", one of them told me (HEAR 1995).

All things considered, it is quite possible that lower-class, dark-skinned Haitians in the Haitian community of New York were suspicious of NCHR as an organization run, in part, by lighter-skinned, educated middle-class professionals of Haitian origin like McCalla and Coradin.[326] While McCalla's Jamaican father migrated to Haiti in the 1930s or 1940s, families in Haiti's elite establishment such as the Powells, the Brandts, or the Wooleys trace their roots to Jamaica as well. Toussaint of BfA and BHRAGS criticized that under McCalla, NCHR neglected cooperation with the Haitian community: "He has been more occupied writing books than doing this kind of work" (Toussaint 1995). Wishnie speculated that McCalla might appear to ordinary Haitians as "a huge success of a Haitian", who differentiates himself by his manners: "... very professional, carries himself very well, very dignified" (Wishnie 1995). Even though an American human rights organization, the few Haitians in New York, who might have been aware of its existence during the crisis, spoke about NCHR as "McCalla's" or "Johnny's" organization. Many of the political parties, which were formed in the wake of Duvalier's ouster in 1986, were "no more than the vehicles for the advancement of a single politician", as NCHR stated in *Silencing a People*

---

[326] According to the Gallup poll taken in July 1993, Americans with lower incomes were somewhat more opposed to current immigration levels, while people, who are immigrants themselves, were more likely to support current immigration levels (Moore 1993:2). Translated into the Haitian equation, lower-class Haitian immigrants in the US must have been torn between those two conflicting trends.

(HRW/A,NCHR 1993:3). NCHR may have been viewed by Haitians as a vehicle for the advancement of McCalla, whose somewhat Americanized manners and access to Congress augmented their suspicions. To put it in HP's jargon, McCalla was into "elitist and individualist politics" conflicting with ideals of participatory democracy. In early August 1994, a few weeks before the intervention, the Haitian newspaper lashed out against McCalla, who even "got what it takes to be a new Jean-Jacques Honorat" (HP 299:15).

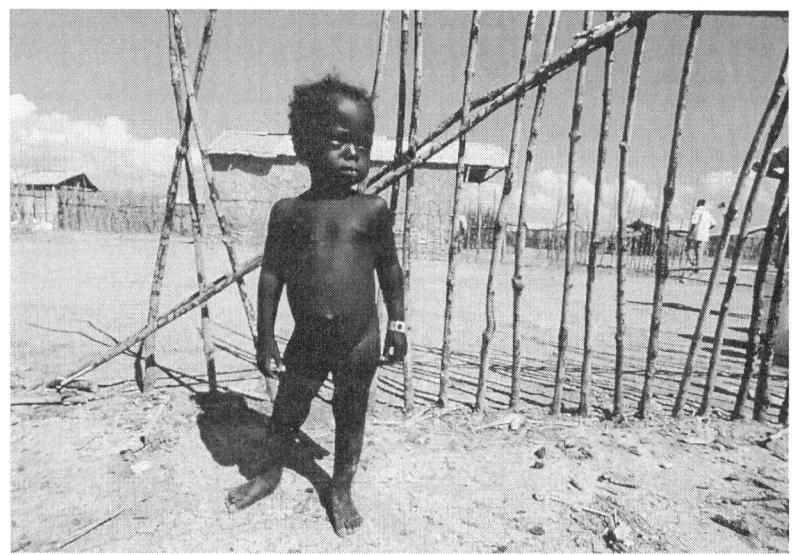
Starving child in dry Northwest, Gonaives, Haiti, Nov/93 (courtesy Maggie Steber)

Poverty in Haiti, 10/21/93 (courtesy Maggie Steber)

5.11 Getting Ahead in the US: The Stigmatization of Haitians with AIDS

A Gallup poll taken in May 1991 found a "substantial majority of Americans" interviewed continuing to favor AIDS testing for a score of "at-risk-populations" (Gallup,Newport 1991:25-26). Five months later, a majority of Americans agreed with the US decision to deport Haitian boat people, while Haitian immigrants were bottom of a table comparing the popularity of nine nationalities in the US in July 1993 (Hugick 1992a:6;Moore 1993:6).[327] Hence it must be assumed that much more than 10% of Americans agreed with the US decision to "isolate" on Guantanamo HIV-tested "foreigners" from Haiti, as declared in mid-December 1991 (French 1991:A3). HP was appalled by this decision affecting "compatriots" brought to the naval base. The weekly accused Washington of being guided by a "repressive policy obsessed by the sole objective of returning them to a regime of terror, utilizing all arms to create in US public opinion a sentiment of rejection towards them". One of these arms, HP opined, was the "question of AIDS", as some 200 Haitian refugees infected with the disease would be barred from entering the US (HP 60:10,16). Shortly before, Gilbert reported that Venezuela had tested 250, Jamaica 100, Honduras 100, and Belize 100 Haitian refugees for HIV as well, but accepted them nonetheless (HP 56:10,24).

For HP, it was "evident that the Bush government, yet another time, wants to create a climate of paranoia". Since US society was biased towards a disease associated with disgraceful fantasies and tied to racism and fears of joblessness (HP 60:16), Washington would "without doubt play on the phantasies surrounding AIDS in order to create a stream of unfavorable opinion". Little of HRC was cited as having indicated that the number of Haitians infected was overestimated (HP 84:9). Guy Victor agreed that "they [US government] had to create an issue ... [for Haitians to] lose their support from the American public opinion" (Victor 1996). The Yale team was concerned that a claim based on HIV status would elicit little sympathy (Clawson et al. 1994:2351). But whereas HP had reported in December 1991 that the group of Haitians on Guantanamo was "indeed infected with AIDS" (HP 60:16), the weekly contended in early February 1992 that the Haitians were detained "under the pretext that a score of Haitians attracted AIDS". The newspaper pointed to "the humiliations" the refugees had to endure "in being treated with gloves" (HP 71:8,17).

After three months, the Haitian weekly obviously did not trust anymore information issued by official US governmental sources. Within this time period, the mainstream media´s "campaign of misinformation", the rumors about US implication in the coup, and the fears of US military intervention had been pervasive. It was now be-

---

[327] The poll in May 1991 revealed at the same time that Americans´ overall "compassion and tolerance for AIDS victims" had increased since 1987. Among the groups presenting a "high risk of having AIDS or of transmitting it" figured immigrants applying for permanent status in the US and visitors from foreign countries. An "overwhelming" majority of Americans, 81% and 62%, respectively, felt that both groups should be tested upon admission. 10% of Americans agreed that people with AIDS should be isolated from society, down from 22% in 1987 (Gallup,Newport 1991:25-26). According to a Gallup poll taken in early September 1991, a majority of 35% of Americans interviewed was "not at all" concerned to get AIDS, followed by 25% of Americans, who were "very" concerned. 82% said that they do not know anyone with AIDS. Concern about contracting AIDS was less with white than with non-white Americans, 22% compared to 51% were "very" concerned. Concern about getting AIDS was highest in the lowest income bracket of $20,000 and under (GMP 1991:72).

lieved that the HIV-testing procedure on Guantanamo could be but a plot designed by the US government to incite the US public against the Haitian community. Traumatic memories in the Haitian community, "which has been despised by the US so much, in particular through its association with AIDS", had been eclipsed only five months earlier by feelings of a "legitimate arrogance" when Aristide was expected to visit New York in late September 1991 (HP 7:1,24). After the coup, those memories were revived. Latour stated with regard to the torrent of 150,000 to 200,000 Haitians protesting in New York against the coup on October 11, 1991 that it was "the second time that this mass of people renews the miracle of its force" (HP 22:14-18).

HP and Latour referred to the stigmatization of Haitian immigrants in the US with AIDS in the early 1980s and the broad-based protest by members of the Haitian community against AIDS-related discrimination at the end of the decade. As Farmer notes, Haitian immigrants denounced "the stigmatization of Haitians - *qua* Haitians - as 'AIDS-carriers'" as early as 1981. After the CDC reported in July 1982 that 43 Haitians residing in the US - among them Haitians living in the New York area - had been stricken with opportunistic infections, the CDC inferred on March 4, 1983 that Haitians *per se* were in some way at risk for AIDS. It declared Haitians as one of four "high-risk groups" along with homosexuals, hemophiliacs, and heroin-users. Speculations appeared soon in medical journals and other scholarly publications that the disease had actually been imported *from* Haiti.[328] The *US Public Health Service* recommended in March 1983 that Haitians should be excluded from donating blood. Following the CDC listing, Haitians were unable to find job placements, and their children were discriminated against in school. Gradually, resistance against US racism inherent in the devastating CDC classification briefly united the "fractious" Haitian diaspora in its struggle against AIDS-related discrimination. In the summer of 1983, the *New York City Department of Health* took Haitians from its official list of risk groups (Farmer 1992:209-216;Stepick 1986:17; Richman 1992:192).

The CDC followed in April 1985 by removing its Haitian-related designation, but the stigma remained and even more was to come. The US authority *Food and Drug Administration* (FDA) issued a decree on February 5, 1990, barring all Haitians from donating blood. Haitians in the US now reacted with unanimity and in greater numbers, with 5,000 Haitian-Americans marching outside the FDA office in Miami on March 14, 1990. On many banners, the FDA was renamed "Federal Discrimination Agency". After similar protest marches were copied in other cities, the movement culminated in what Farmer calls "mammoth rally" of far more than 50,000 Haitians in New York City on April 20, 1990, which had the support of a broad coalition of African-Americans, including Dinkins and Jackson. After setting up an advisory panel to reconsider its ruling and more concomitant Haitian rallies in Miami, Boston, Chicago, at the US Embassy in Port-au-Prince, and in front of the authority´s headquarters in Washington, the FDA rescinded its destructive ban in late 1990. Farmer demonstrates that there is no data suggesting that the American AIDS pandemic originated in Haiti. The available data on the epidemiology of HIV in the Caribbean rather suggest that the

---

[328] According to Farmer, "[f]ew countries have been more marked by association with endemic infectious diseases than Haiti", with Syphilis having been referred to by the Spanish as the sickness of Hispaniola. Thus he concluded that branding Haitians as AIDS-carriers "fed into preexisting stereotypes, long deployed by foreign commentators speaking of Haiti" (Farmer 1992:235-239).

virus came to Haiti *from* the US, "and perhaps especially through tourism" (Farmer 1992:217-220,259-260;Richman 1992:192;Farmer 1994:350).

As members of HEAR told me, FDA´s decree triggered the formation of the group, of which Guy Victor was a founding member. Haitian-American organizations such as HCC, HAUP, and AAHP were reportedly part of the formation process. Their members set out to wake up the "sleeping giant", as one HEAR-member put it, for the April 20, 1990 march in New York under the motto "No blood, no sweat". Besides Guy Victor, Martial, vice-president of ICB, was among the Haitian leaders, who organized the march that did not only stun New York´s political establishment, but the organizers themselves. According to NCHR´s Planning Committee, the demonstration was "the largest by people of color since the civil rights movement". It brought together a broad cross section of the Haitian community to rally around "an issue that affected their lives as Haitian-Americans, as Haitians in America". The Planning Committee underscored the demonstrators´ ethnic orientation by stressing that the issue was "not linked to the future of democracy in Haiti or to protest US policy toward the victims of persecution", but the "desire to build productive lives for themselves and their children in America dominated their concerns". AIDS-related discrimination, which affected all Haitians regardless of class and color, impeded their interest to work and to study as immigrants in the US (HEAR 1995;Pierre-Louis 1997;Victor 1996;HP 125:8;Dreyfuss 1993:81;NCHR21:7;Farmer 1992:220).[329]

As stated in chapter 5.4.6, the Yale students sensed in the spring of 1992 an "ambivalence toward media coverage", given the "especially sensitive" HIV-positive status of the Guantanamo refugees. These concerns centered not only around violating their privacy by exposing their status, but also around possibly provoking "a negative public reaction"even by a "sympathetic" coverage: "If the public saw the refugees only as black, poor, and HIV-infected, it would be more difficult for politicians to press for their release without risking public disapproval", the students explain. Thus they tried to draw media attention to the chaos on the camp (Clawson et al. 1994:2370-71). Concerns like these were vindicated in the light of statistics cited above. But these fears seem to contradict, at first glance, Daugaard´s "domestic racism"-thesis underlying the lawsuit. In the final analysis, the Yale students performed a tightrope walk: They had to drum up enough public sympathy for the refugees in support of politicians working for their release while retaining a public environment inducive to this racism-related "bizarre reactionary political pressure" (Daugaard) required to resolve the political crisis in Haiti.

While the Yale students seem to have had only the US public at large in mind, the question of concern here is what effect both mainstream and Haitian media coverage of the Haitian refugees including their HIV-positivity might have had on the Haitian community at large in terms of their motivation to come out for the boat people in public. HP continued to create some measure of publicity around the excluded HIV-infected Guantanamo refugees. In late April, 1992, it called the policy "cruel and capricious" using Judge Johnson´s words (HP 108:9). In late May, the HIV-infected refugees touched "the bottom of contempt and ostracism", because no medical treat-

---

[329] It is maybe no coincidence that Martial was among the organizers of "Operation Hope" in favor of the Haitian refugees at Guantanamo, which occurred, however, at a time, when the HIV-infection of some of them was not yet salient (HP 64:1,22).

ment such as AZT had been accorded (HP 123:15). In early September, HP reported on their protest at the camp, as they faced a "situation more and more intolerable" (HP 136:7).

But the "period of slackness" and the "waning of mobilization" in the Haitian community on the issue of the Guantanamo refugees, which HP had observed as early as January 1992 (HP 67:9;HP 69:8,18), was there to stay in the fall of 1992. Yet Gilbert exaggeratedly stated with regard to the Haitian-organized rally on September 29 in front of the UN on the occasion of the first anniversary of the coup that the refugees were "not forgotten", evidenced by a picture showing only two white young men and one black man with a poster demanding the closure of the "HIV-prison at Guantanamo" (HP 145:8,11). By that time, Wishnie's "grassroots political effort in New York" in the form of the Yale students' ECHR-turned *Shut Down Guantanamo Coalition* was firmly established with considerable input from Guy Victor. According to Wishnie, the group was formed in "an effort to bring together the Haitian community organizations, but most of them had no experience with AIDS or HIV, and to bring together the traditional AIDS and HIV organizations in New York, most of them had nothing to do with the Caribbean communities in Brooklyn. The AIDS groups were mostly white and the Haitian groups mostly had nothing to do with AIDS". The coalition conducted "education presentations" in churches in Manhattan and Brooklyn (Wishnie 1995;Daugaard 1995). Among the AIDS groups was the *AIDS Coalition to Unleash Power* (ACT UP), a radical and confrontational protest organization founded in 1987 by playwright Larry Kramer in the wake of the AIDS epidemic (Clawson et al. 1994:2377;Auerbach 1996:21,752).

Tensions within ECHR between Haitian activists and AIDS community activists were present throughout the organizing process and had become apparent from the very outset when discussing the wording of its platform: "Haitians would say: `who allegedly have HIV.' They did not believe the government ... they felt that if we acknowledged the refugees have HIV, that people in the Haitian community would not support them" (Wishnie 1995). Gilbert, a practicing physician residing in Philadelphia, must have thought otherwise. He reported again in early October 1992 on the "290 of our compatriots infected with the HIV-virus". They had published an open letter in HP (No. 21) to let the outside world know about the conditions on the base. Gilbert stressed that "the Haitians' dignity has constantly been treated with contempt" in that war prison. He referred to Haitian-American Father Fabre of MRS as one witness to the situation, which "no doubt reminds the refugees of the hell of their country" (HP 145:8). Yet Gilbert's sympathetic coverage did not seem to make a difference as to mobilizing the Haitian community. At the first encounter between the Yale team and the refugees on Guantanamo in early October, the Haitians asked questions such as: "Why is the government accusing us of having AIDS?". As the students recalled: "Over their months of detention, many of the Haitians had clung to the belief that they did not really have HIV, but that the government was conspiring to keep them out" of the US. Even if they were given AZT for AIDS and INH for tuberculosis by then, the US government doctors had broken the terrible news "You have HIV" whilst rendering little or no HIV counseling. For the first time, the Haitian refugees heard from the students as a source independent from the US government "that they might actually be ill" (Clawson et al. 1994:2366-2367). Haitian interpreter Longchamps of HWP, who is a nurse, confirmed to Wishnie that the records containing the test results were "valid medical files that showed these people had HIV" (Wishnie 1995).

But no matter if one was inclined to believe the US government or not, the link between AIDS and the Guantanamo refugees, held in what had already been transformed into "an HIV detention camp", had been established in the public eye. Even if HP does not seem to have reported extensively on Guantanamo in 1992, some news story did inform the Haitian public in the US on the HIV-infected refugees. Gilbert stated in late December that four of the Guantanamo Haitians had been denied transfer to the US for advanced medical treatment (HP 163:17). And in January 1993, Ives supplied official statistics, according to which there were 274 refugees, among them 221 HIV-positive Haitians. He explained that the refugees were in limbo: Neither could they be deported due to their valid claims of persecution, nor were they allowed entry into the US "under the pretext of their sero-positivity". Ives testified to the refugees' mistrust of the military physicians, who they likened to "charlatans" and "veterinarians". No other refugee group was subjected to HIV-tests, he lamented (HP 171:10,11). Haitian activists in the US still seemed to suspect the HIV-testing procedure on Guantanamo to be a diversionary tactic designed by the US government to distract attention from the crisis in Haiti.

Yet, in the Sunday night "militant forum" in a Manhattan bookstore in early February 1993, HIV-infected refugee from Guantanamo, Sillieses Success, was allowed to relate her story. She had been separated from her husband, who also had been labeled HIV-positive, brought to the US, and bandied about through Virginia, Washington, and New York City detention centers (Baillou 1993:4). By that time, the Lavalas movement's "bourgeois sector" with members of the Haitian middle-class had already come to dominate the organizational structure of the community. Nevertheless, the "march for liberty and democracy" on February 6, which had been organized by the *Noyau de Coordination de New York*, also included, as Latour stressed, a demonstration at Federal Plaza "against the bad treatment inflicted on the Haitian refugees" (HP 176:8,23). HP sought to prove regarding a demonstration organized on short notice by the *80 organisations* for January 16 in front of Grand Army Plaza that the "populist project" of the traditional Haitian bourgeoisie could merely integrate the people verbally, as only about 200 people showed up for the rally (HP 172:6,14-16).

But other "prosperous upper-middle class Haitians" seem not only to be unable to mobilize rank-and-file Haitians in New York, they also seem to be unwilling to do so. Dreyfuss, for example, added to the set of stereotypes in the US public, which he sought to deconstruct in July, 1993, the most recent ones: "AIDS. Boat People", with whom he disliked "being lumped". He noted: "For 12 years, the news media have dutifully reported the thousands of black people packed to the gunwales of leaky boats trying to make their way to Florida or, once there, quarantined because they are H.I.V. positive" (1993:20). The "sentiment of rejection" (HP) created around the refugee issue does not seem to have been confined to the non-Haitian public in the US. It is significant to reiterate that AAHP, an association composed of well-respected middle class Haitian-American health professionals, was one of the initiators of the April 20, 1990 march against the CDC listing - some of its members like Dr. Jean-Baptiste even testified in Congressional hearings on Capitol Hill - while it did *not* go public during the Haitian refugee crisis between 1991 and 1994 (HEAR 1995;Aubourg 1996).

What was the difference between AIDS-related discrimination in the early 1980s and AIDS-related discrimination after the coup of 1991? It may be assumed that the target group is the answer to this question. In the 1980s, *all* Haitians in the US *regardless* of class and color were victimized. As Mayas put it, "Haitians that are wealthy, not wealthy, upper class, middle class, down class, or no class, everybody was affected" (Mayas 1995). AIDS-related discrimination on Guantanamo, however, was limited to "black, poor" (Yale) Aristide-supporters, many of them from rural Haiti. According to the NYT's Deborah Sontag, the "monolithic image" of the Haitian boat people as "poor, illiterate, disease-carrying" people lent an "animus" to the debate over them (1994:1). To a certain extent, the Haitian version of this debate united Haitian immigrants from varying social backgrounds, who "busy themselves in the pursuit of the American dream", as Dreyfuss notes. He calls the US "the great equalizer" (1993:21;Jean-Pierre 1995:197). As Raoul of HWHR told me, Haitians in the US probably had not come out as strong for the HIV-infected refugees on Guantanamo as they would have for other issues "because of the taboos that Haitians have been slapped with by the mainstream media". She added: "Maybe people didn't want to be associated with that ... and the class structure ... all the people with money ... they don't associate with boat people" (Raoul 1995).[330] Coradin of NCHR opined that many Haitians in the US tend to adopt a negative media image of Haiti and Haitian boat people, reflecting "a deeper sentiment that Haitians - as poor, black, non-English-speaking aliens - are undesirable immigrants" to the US: "[I]t does have to do with general public perceptions and buying into those perceptions", he told me (Coradin 1995). In addition, the Guantanamo refugees may have been seen in conflict with the PR campaign to relegitimize and rehabilitate the Aristide government in the US public.

Betty Williams, a white American, who came to volunteer for the Yale students' "refugee resettlement team", established a connection between the April 20, 1990 rally and the Guantanamo "HIV detention camp". She told me: "[T]hat [i.e. the march] was not about helping people with AIDS, that was about 'get that AIDS-stigma off us', and they don't want it back in form of those people from the camp". Guy Victor disagreed by asking, "how could you separate both issues?". The HEAR-members I interviewed protested as well: "This is not true ... Just because a person is a refugee does not mean that the person is illiterate or has AIDS". Williams used to work on AFSC's Cambodian Refugee Program and worked in 1995 as what she called "volunteer client advocate of HWP". In her view, the AIDS-stigma was the main reason why the Haitian community at large did not focus on the refugee issue. She explained that "as Americans we were dealing with that piece that Haitians mostly don't want to deal with ... with this particular group of HIV-positive refugees, we have been really isolated. It has been Haitian Women for Haitian Refugees, Marie Carmel [i.e. Dr. Pierre-Louis of the] ... Haitian Coalition on AIDS, Haitian Women's Program, and that has really been it!" (Williams 1995;Victor 1996;HEAR 1995). Many of my informants corroborated Williams' statements.[331]

---

[330] HWHR's activities in the field of AIDS education included an "information and action forum" on December 9, 1992 to discuss the situation of the HIV-infected Guantanamo refugees, which the group sponsored along with NCHR, the *Brooklyn AIDS Task Force*, and the *Hunter College Center for AIDS, Drugs and Community Health* (Haiti6:12).

[331] Wishnie, for example, said that "the Haitian groups had a lot of AIDS phobia I think, because of the prior stigmatization of Haitians as carrying AIDS under the CDC definition in the mid 80s" (Wishnie

Even though it is all too easy to overemphasize this point, it seems to be plausible that Haitians' traumatic experience of having been stigmatized as HIV-carriers *per se*, led many of them to shun the refugee issue in public for fear of being yet another time exposed to AIDS-related accusations and discrimination. The US government seems to have indeed created a mood of quiet alertedness within the Haitian community, leading to passivity toward the refugee issue. Even if it did so unintentionally, this passivity worked for its advantage.

Based on her time-honored experience, Dr. Pierre-Louis indicated another, more basic reason for the Haitian community's state of denial in the field of AIDS. In contrast to cancer, which she said is considered "a clean disease", AIDS was "not something we talk about", because AIDS is mostly a sexually transmitted disease in the Haitian community (Pierre-Louis 1997).[332] The sense of shame attached to AIDS might have been touched upon by the way the Haitian media reported on HIV-infected Haitian refugees detained at Guantanamo. Even if the French term "promiscuité", which was used in a number of HP articles,[333] is not directly sexually connotated, its usage in combination with HIV-infection might have stimulated "fantasies surrounding AIDS" (HP) and thus a "sentiment of rejection" (HP) within the Haitian community. The "special attention" accorded the Guantanamo refugees was most likely marked by scruples.

Even if AAHP as an organization did not raise the Haitian refugee issue in public, it should be reiterated that a few Haitian-American doctors testified in Brooklyn court in early March 1993. It is further noteworthy that two unnamed Haitian physicians co-authored with NCHR staff a poster presentation at the IX. International Conference on AIDS in Berlin in 1993, after the group had issued an appeal to the Conference's Chief (NCHR19:4).[334] In comparison, however, these US-based Haitian physicians constitute only a small fraction of the professional group when considering what Mayas told me:. "We produced in these States more doctors, medical doctors than any

---

1995). NCHR's Harris, who used to work for HWP before getting on board of the human rights organization, agreed and added that many Haitians in the US exhibited what he called an "internalized homophobia" resulting from the AIDS-related stigmatization (Harris 1995). Dr. Pierre-Louis of HCAIDS and Aubourg of NCHR/HCC seconded these views. Dr. Pierre-Louis, who claims to be well-known in the Haitian community as the "AIDS-doctor" through radio and TV since 1989, added that she had received many phone calls in her office from concerned Haitians complaining: "You talk so much about it [AIDS], you are the one responsible for them [US government] saying that we have AIDS". She thinks that "the whole community is in denial" (Aubourg 1996;Pierre-Louis 1997).

[332] Dr. Pierre-Louis verbatim: "We don't talk about sex, we don't have sex ... even inside your family with your spouse", she described a prevalent attitude owing to strict Catholic moral values: "If you admit that you have AIDS, most of the time you are admitting that you had sex ... forbidden sex". Personal responsibility for attracting AIDS as a result of one's own behavior is sometimes denied by declaring it a "Vodoun spell, something they set on you, it's not your fault" (Pierre-Louis 1997).

[333] Tecumseh, for example, quoted Minister Célestin as saying about the conditions in the camp: "Nous avons visité les baraques, je dis bien: baraques ... *Promiscuité*, totale...tous sexes confondus" (HP 189:11-12;author's italics). HP summarized: "C'est dans cet universe cumulant à la fois répression carcérale, éloignement, *promiscuité et maladie* que vivent des compatriotes qui - dans la mesure où certains sont porteurs du *virus VIH* - devraient être traités avec une attention particulière" (HP 192:16;author's italics).

[334] As Gilbert reported, the World Conference on AIDS in June 1992 had protested against the INS policy of prohibiting all persons carrying the AIDS-virus to enter the US. It did so by relocating the site of the conference from Boston to Amsterdam (HP 177:11;HP 181:11).

other nationality" (Mayas 1995). All in all, NCHR´s *HaitiInsight*-editor Toni L. Kamins ascertained a "sorry lack of [Haitian] community support" in the US for HIV-infected Haitian refugees. Due to the "myriad myths of Haitians and AIDS", which Haitians had been unable to quash, Haitian community organizations did not make use, for example, of Jean´s multiple talents, Kamins observed (1994:3).

5.12 Who Gets Used?: Varying Assumptions in US Presidential Elections

Aristide´s ouster in the fall of 1991 coincided with the start of a US election year. US political society and US society at large engaged in the peak of activity in domestic politics as the sovereign expression of a democratic nation. At that time, Governor Clinton announced that he would seek the Democratic nomination, with his national name recognition among Democratic voters rising to 58% in November 1991 (Hugick 1991:6). Some Haitian activists in New York began to interpret the political and refugee crises of their country in terms of US electoral politics as influenced by factors such as race. The conclusions they drew had an impact on the way organizing efforts were shaped in the months to come. Tecumseh, for example, took a cautious position when analyzing the "drama" of Haitian boat people in late November 1991. She observed with interest that the US´s "discriminatory policy" towards Haitian refugees had been denounced by "numerous US politicians", even if they had done so "more for political (electoral) reasons rather than on the basis of principle". Referring to Rangel´s assertion of the Bush Administration´s refugee "policy à la David Duke", Tecumseh added: "[O]ne must not forget that in the US, the question of race is generally a welcome political weapon brandished by the members of the Black Caucus or by those courting the Black vote and immigrant minorities" (HP 53:12).

Electoral motives driven by pure self-interest were also attributed to assertions made by contenders, who had decided for a presidential bid in the Democratic race. With the Bush Administration being confronted with an "economic crisis" during a pre-election period requiring the search for "scapegoats", HP suspected that Senator Bob Kerrey´s labelling Bush´s refugee policy as "inacceptable" was guided by "political considerations", given his intention to run for the Democratic nomination (HP 67:9). Other Democratic contenders seized upon US refugee policy toward Haiti as well. Following the USSC´s decision of January 31, 1992, HP quoted Senator Paul Tsongas as saying: "I am happy that George Bush had not been president, when my parents arrived. They were economic refugees" (HP 70:1,16). The first activist publicly intervening in US electoral politics seems to have been Dr. Fulani of the *New Alliance Party*, who had been a first-hour supporter of the post-coup Haitian cause. As Latour reported, during the February 7 celebrations of 1992, Fulani denounced "the criminal silence" of US presidential candidates concerning the situation in Haiti (HP 80:12-13).

Referring to the NYT (02/11/92), HP reported that month that the Bush Administration´s policy toward Haiti might be driven by concerns to lose the electoral votes. In case immigrant-burdened Florida faced a massive wave of refugees, this would entail the risk of alienating conservative voters. According to polls, however, the weekly countered, 57% of Floridians (51% whites and 80% blacks) were in favor of granting refugee status to Haitians, and even the Cuban-American mayor of Miami, Xavier Suarez, launched a line-of-cars-campaign in support of Haitian refugees (HP 79:1,20;Constable 1992/93:184;HP 84:9). But regardless of the actual impact of Haitian refugees on Floridian electoral politics, the Bush Administration´s forced repatriation policy had become a wedge issue affecting the presidential race in the realm of US foreign policy. CBC-member Conyers, for example, asked the Democratic candidates, if the Bush Administration ought to return "economic refugees", which all of them - Tom Harkin, Jerry Brown, Clinton, Kerrey, and Tsongas - denied. While realizing the basic merits of intervening in this debate, HP also stressed a caveat informed by the crisis-old linkage between the refugee issue and the perceived threat of "foreign military intervention" (HP 81:8,17).

Beyond all theoretical assumptions, some Haitian activists began to practically incorporate the US election campaign into the transnational field of the pro-democracy struggle, thereby displaying an ethnic orientation. As Philippe Généus reported, three days before the US primaries in New Hampshire, a comparatively small crowd of 1,500 to 2,000 Haitians demonstrated on February 15 in Manchester to "denounce the two-facedness of the Bush Administration". At the head of the march, the Haitian flag was followed by two large picket-signs demanding TPS for Haitian refugees. At the end of the rally, candidates Brown and Harkin, Dorancy and Marie-Jo Luc of PNDPH, Dr. Fulani and a *TransAfrica*-representative as well as Robert White, former US Ambassador to El Salvador and CIP-president, denounced the Bush Administration, demanding Aristide ´s return (HP 82:10). QC/QP´s full-page ad in the NYT of March 16, 1992 was also motivated in part by considerations concerning US presidential politics. QC/QP´s Callahan told the *Big Red News* that it was "time for U.S. citizens to make Haiti an issue in this year´s elections" (1992:4). But HP remained skeptical about the effectiveness of concentrating on the US election campaign, as it was dominated by US politicians, whose hypocrisy it saw informed by *realpolitik*. In its report on H.R.3844, the weekly concluded that "... in this time of elections, all means are good for those, who want to `uproot´ Bush from the presidency" (HP 86:1,19). US groups such as AfA, on the other hand, called on Haitians in the US to send messages to the five presidential candidates, who had remained in the race by March: Brown, Clinton, Tsongas, Bush, and his Republican challenger Patrick Buchanan, a staunch and outspoken immigration restrictionist. The prepared message reprinted by HP in French as well as in English demanded both "increased diplomatic pressure for the immediate and unconditional return of president Aristide" and an "end to forced repatriation of Haitian refugees" (HP 92:8;Frelick 1993:680).

After the rally in New Hampshire, Haitians in New York also started to intervene in US electoral politics. The demonstration in the streets of Manhattan, sponsored by HEAR in collaboration with the *10e of New York*, was organized on April 6 to demand TPS and democracy, because on that day, Bush was expected to be in the city for the New York presidential primary (HP 96:9;HP 98:8). The date was chosen to put the candidates of the Democratic party, in particular Clinton and Brown, in the lime light. The crowd moved from Time Square close to Madison Square Garden, were the headquarters of the Bush campaign were accommodated. Demanding a total change in US policy toward Haiti, CBC-member Maxine Waters called on the crowd to vote for Clinton. HP cautioned against putting too much hope in this "electoral bickering", except in the general sense of demanding that "Bush must go" (HP 102:8). As the NYT reported the next day, thousands of demonstrators had reminded presidential candidates that the Haitian question "has not yet been resolved" (NYT 04/07/92:B6). In this specific climate, Clinton indicated on May 27, for the first time, his opposition to the Bush Administration's Haitian refugee policy (Clawson et al. 1994:2348). Morrell of CIP was certainly correct in observing that the presidential campaign "pitted a centrist Democrat against a centrist Republican, leaving them with practically nothing to argue about on foreign policy". Forced repatriation gave Clinton "one of the few issues on which he could differentiate himself from Bush" (1993:2).[335]

The Yale team's lawsuit was affected by US electoral politics as well, as HP noted. For Bush would try with his lawyer Starr to win the case "in order to make the American public believe, before the elections, that he has solved the problem of the Haitian refugees" (HP 129:8,15). In the light of these conditions, the Convention of the Democratic Party constituted an occasion for "general mobilization" in the Haitian community, which was summoned in front of Madison Square Garden. For July 13, 14, and 15, a picket line was scheduled, and for July 16, a big demonstration through the streets of Manhattan was planned.[336] The organizers came together to demand Aristide's return, the departure of the *de facto* regime, an oil embargo, no military intervention in "all forms", and TPS for Haitian refugees (HP 130:15). In his report on the demonstration, Latour noted that the presence of Haitians of the 10th department "sur le béton" was necessary to remind the Democrats that the case of Haiti was still on the agenda. With the "unconditional and irreversible return" of Aristide being the first demand by the Haitian people, Latour stressed that the 10th Department was the only political pressure group to demonstrate on a continuous basis for those four days (HP 132:9). The Democratic platform of the Clinton/Gore-campaign "Putting People First" came to include the promise to "[l]ift the current ban on travel and immigration to the United States by foreign nationals with HIV" (Clawson et al. 1994:2345), which would have benefited the Guantanamo refugees. A Gallup poll taken in January 1992 had found that 67% of all voters deemed a discussion about AIDS in that year's campaign very important. In April, voters preferred Clinton over Bush by a margin of 40% to 34% on the issue of AIDS (Hugick 1992b:2,3).[337]

After the Democratic Convention, which produced for Clinton the highest "post-convention bounce" in Gallup records (GMP 1992:25), many Haitian activists looked rather optimistically at the upcoming presidential elections: HEAR-members

---

[335] At the same time, HP pondered one election-related aspect of the Haitian refugee crisis, which was never mentioned again by Haitian activists. In its report of the "costly problem" of US refugee policy, the weekly noted that further expenses might incur as a result of aerial transport of admitted Haitians to be distributed throughout the US, who were granted $745 each for the first three months in the US. Deeming this money petty in the bigger scheme of the US budget, HP speculated that it could nevertheless have some weight in the balance of votes on election day, given US tax payers' mood of blaming Bush for being preoccupied with solving problems of other countries (HP 115:8).

[336] A partial list of organizers published in HP included the *10e of New York*, the *Lavalas organization of Long Island*, MOKAM, *Association de Travailleurs Haitiens* (ATH), MRAA, BRA, AEH, HEAR, and the *Haiti Commission* (HP 130:15).

[337] At NCHR's Board of Directors Meeting on July 13, Chishti proposed to draft a letter to the three main US presidential campaigns in order to influence the platform planks of the Democratic and Republican parties. But Rubin of AJC with experience in the platform area considered it too late (NCHR11:iii). The human rights organization was nevertheless encouraged because of the "fortright endorsement of elements of [its] agenda" by Clinton (NCHR6:3).

reported on a meeting convened by leaders of both the Haitian and black communities in New York, in which Hillary Rodham Clinton pledged that her husband was willing to work for Aristide's return if elected President (HEAR 1995). At the NAACP/*TransAfrica*-organized rally in Washington on September 9, Latour quoted Harry Fouché of Chicago as saying that "this demonstration is a way for the Haitians and their American friends to prepare the resignation of Bush". And Père Sansaricq described the purpose of the rally as follows: "... et enfin, une facon de faire campagne auprès de l'électorat américain en faveur du peuple haitien" (HP 141:9). In the fall of 1992, the Clinton/Gore-team began to actively seek the support of the Haitian immigrant vote. The team sent Jon-Christopher Bua to the rally in front of the UN building on September 29 on the occasion of the first anniversary of the coup. As a spokesman for Governor Clinton, he addressed roughly 10,000 Haitian demonstrators, promising that if elected, the Democratic candidate would reverse Bush's policy on Haitian refugees (Lewis 1992:A8).[338] As Bua told me, the Haitian organizers of the rally had invited the Clinton/Gore-team, which he said was committed to Aristide's reinstatement.[339] Aristide himself intervened in the election campaign in early October, urging his supporters not to vote for Bush in statements, which were immediately protested by Bush Administration officials (French 1992e:A9).

As Mayas told me, many Haitians in the US "force themselves" to become US citizens to sponsor relatives back home for US immigration, but they generally do not want to get involved in US politics: "[T]hey do not participate, they do not vote, they do not want to know when elections are taking place, they do not care!". But during the 1992 campaign, "[t]hat's the time they came out and voted, because we, this generation, we went out and motivated those people". Mayas co-organized seminars instructing Haitians how to register to vote. She said that Jean Vernet of HSN and HEAR produced a video in Creole and in English "to explain to those people how to vote". One of her friends lent them a voting booth, with which they taught Haitians at *St. Jerome Church* in Brooklyn on the eve of the election how to cast their vote: "[T]here were people, who have been here, citizens of the USA, for twelve, ten, fifteen years, they never voted, they never participated, because they did not understand that it is a power". The aim was simple: "We wanted Bush out! ... we campaigned against him, we voted him out of the White House" (Mayas 1995). Guy Victor insisted that there had been Haitians in the US willing to "help to organize elections of some Congressmen" in exchange for their assistance in Aristide's return (Victor 1996).

At about the same time, the Yale team visited Guantanamo, where camp president Vilsaint expressed concerns that Clinton might still lose the election. Several of the students would later inform the refugees over the telephone of developments in the US, including the latest presidential poll results. Having been watching the returns on Guantanamo, the refugees celebrated Clinton's victory a few days later. On the phone, Vilsaint shouted euphorically "Clinton! Clinton! Miami! Miami!" (Clawson et al. 1994:2367-2368).

---

[338] According to Louis L. Gerson, the US party system has been "the most important contributing factor in the hyphenization of Americans" by its persistent attention to the electoral support of ethnic groups (1981:24).

[339] Statement made by Jon Christopher Bua of the *Democratic National Committee* (DNC) in a telephone interview on February 2, 1995. Bua added that the DNC did not carry out a Haiti-campaign of its own.

Between 260,000 and 300,000 Haitian-Americans are reported to have voted overwhelmingly for Clinton in the 1992 election. Many activists, including those of the *10th Department organizations*, deserve credit for this turnout, according to Jean-Pierre (1995:203;Peters 1995:210). Regarding the observed role of ethnic electoral support as lure or electoral punishment as threat in the political calculations of members of Congress in the field of foreign affairs (Watanabe 1984:52,66-68), Owens candidly confirmed the importance of hoped for Haitian assistance at the polls. He stated that "politically, yes it´ll pay positive dividends for me". He added that his political activism "was rooted in the fact that many Haitians are my constituents" - there are approximately 100,000 Haitians in his district. In exchange, he emphasized, he "invested a lot of time and energy" in the cause of Haitian democracy while also making "a lot of enemies". But beyond that, the Haitian cause had become "a very important part of my soul". Interestingly, for the initiator of the Haiti-oriented coalition BfA, the issue of dual loyalty with regard to US-based Haitians does not pose a serious conflict of interest. Owens doubted that their maintaining close ties to Haiti "makes them disloyal" to the US (Owens 1995).

At the meeting with journalists and members of the Haitian community of New York on November 1 a few days prior to the election, Lassègue, however, cautioned the audience against expecting too much change in US foreign policy in case Bush was going to lose the elections (HP 151:8). Even if Roumer found two weeks later that Clinton´s three major campaign declarations in favor of Haitian refugees could not have been "more clear in one´s condemnation of the situation in Haiti", he feared that the new US president might "resort to traditional US interventionism" instead of choosing "the track of an easy success" (HP 152:22). At the end of the month, HP also opined that Clinton´s campaign promise to annul Bush´s Kennebunkport Order could have been designed to "panic-buy the Haitian-American vote" (HP 156:9). Lassègue´s, Roumer´s, and HP´s skepticism turned out to be justified. Within weeks, as the Yale students recall, the Guantanamo "refugees´ mood changed dramatically ... Why wasn´t Clinton keeping his promise ... Why are we still on Guantánamo?" Two suicide attempts preceded the students´ next trip to the camp. The refugees´ hunger strike in early 1993 was their answer to Clinton´s broken promises (Clawson et al. 1994:2368,2374).

In late January 1993, HP asserted that Clinton´s indication not to abandon Bush´s refugee policy had caused a "sentiment of anger" in "certain sectors of the 10th department", which the weekly found had "naively believed" in Clinton´s campaign promise (HP 169:8). Between Clinton and Bush, both seen as being subjected to the "imperatives of a system", existed only a difference in approach and methods used to reach the same objective (HP 172:6,14-16). The disappointment set in deeply not only with Haitian activists. Yale student Jones, according to HP organized in the *Coalition of Yale University to Liberate the Haitians*, explained why his group went on hunger strike in solidarity with the Haitian hunger strikers on Guantanamo: "We are ashamed that he (Clinton) be our president" after having worked for his election (HP 190). Similarly, Gilbert was void of any trust in the new US Administration. He believed that Clinton had secretly approved of the Senate vote on February 18 retaining the restrictions on issuing visas to HIV-carriers (HP 182). Tecumseh also took the Senate vote in conjunction with the unchanged US refugee policy as an example of Clinton´s tendency to reassure the conservative camp instead of responding to traditional Democratic voters' aspirations. She emphasized that denouncing Bush had not only allowed Clinton to win over the electorate of Haitian origin, but also the sympathies of the African-American community. She was certain that Clinton, who reckoned with the "confidence naively accorded by certain compatriots" during the election campaign, would not offer the return of democracy on a "silver tray" (HP 189:10,13).

In the long run, the disappointment of unkept campaign promises reinforced the strategical emphasis originally put on direct transnational relations: HP believed in early January 1994 with regard to the "new drama" of Haitian refugees that "only mobilizing on this issue" could stop Clinton's "cynicism" (HP 221). Faced with a possible US invasion in late July, Tecumseh recalled that Clinton had counted, above all, on "false hopes created by his campaign promises" and on a "certain capital of confidence" he used "to neutralize the opposition of the Haitian community in the US". Clinton did not only copy Bush, but went even further than his predecessor, displaying a "paternalism more dangerous than Bush's aristocratic disdain". Tecumseh's verdict was devastating in its emphasis on US culpability (HP 289:10). Nevertheless, Haitian-born political scientist Michel-Rolph Trouillot of *Johns Hopkins University* urged Haitians with US citizenship to exercise their power at the ballot box to bring about a positive influence on US foreign policy towards Haiti. He spoke at the NCHR-organized conference "Towards a Haitian-American Community Action Network" at *New York University* in October 1996: "We can't help Haiti until our community helps itself", he admonished. Refugee issue strategist McCalla agreed that it was necessary to build political clout: "Haitians living abroad must stop believing we can solve Haiti's problems without gaining political leverage in a country such as" the US that has "such a large influence on Haiti's present and future development" (Haiti9:1). Members of Congress are indeed sensitive to the opinions of constituents also in matters of foreign relations, in particular to pressure from lobbyists controlling "batches of votes" (DeConde 1992:195).

5.13 Representation and Resettlement: The Lack of Resources

By July 1992, more than 10,000 Haitian refugees had been paroled from Guantanamo into the US mainland. There they were allowed to file a formal application for political asylum within 90 days of arriving in the US. According to NCHR, there was "no precedence in the country for such a large number of asylum cases to be handled by *pro bono* attorneys", which caused an "enormous problem of resources". The group's "potential role in alleviating this emergency" consisted of providing information in support of asylum applications through a database of human rights violations in Haiti and of facilitating communications among agencies representing the refugees. 75% of them remained in Florida at that point in time (Haiti4:6;NCHR11:iv-v). A certain number were transferred to the Krome detention center. According to Dorancy, HRC assisted "3,000 of our refugees" by February 1992 in obtaining the right to come to the US to pursue asylum claims (HP 76:11).[340] In that month, 135 refugees allowed

---

[340] As a matter of course, HRC represented Haitian refugees detained at Krome already prior to the coup, for which purpose certain HRC-members had been permitted to enter the detention center, which

into the US were directly sent to Krome, where they were, as HP reported, "relatively less isolated" than on Guantanamo (HP 84:9).

Naturally, this unprecedented influx of Haitian refugees imposed constraints on HRC´s budget, which amounted to about $600,000 per annum. According to Dorancy, the *Ford Foundation* and other US sources far outstripped Haitian sources, from which only "very little" contributions derived. The latter nonetheless permitted "to reach more people and to help them", as she stressed in the interview with Latour (HP 88:10,21). It is likely that appeals for private Haitian donations to better service Haitian refugees admitted to the US was met with competition from the official fundraising activities in the 10th department for the "benefit of the victims of the repression in Haiti", begun in April 1992 (HP 117:8). The burden on HRC´s budget prompted Dorancy in mid-May to tell HP that "[w]e need help". The group announced plans to organize a musical concert featuring Dunham as special guest, which was designed to increase revenues (HP 115:8). Nevertheless, Gilbert emphasized in late March 1992 that HRC and the Haitian "diplomats of concrete" had "greatly contributed to ameliorating the lot" of Haitian asylum-seekers (HP 91:8). Those contributions could have consisted, in part, of translating for them. Following Judge Johnson´s ruling, HP noted in early April that "urgent appeals" had been issued to furnish interpreters for about 100 refugees, who had recently arrived in New York (HP 101:20). Some of those appeals were published in NCHR´s *HaitiInsight* that informed its readers that HRC was seeking volunteer attorneys and translators. USCC, CWS, and HRC were expected as early as winter 1991/92 to be the agencies supplying "the bulk of legal assistance" to Haitian refugees with the help of Creole interpreters, lawyers, paralegals, and general volunteers.[341]

In close cooperation with NIF throughout 1992, NCHR provided information including affidavits in support of asylum claims to a network of more than 100 agen-

---

is generally closed to the public. In August 1991, however, HRC-advocate Little was denied access to the prison to speak to her clients. A document prepared by HRC had listed human rights violations perpetrated by the INS in the facility. In that month, more than 330 Krome prisoners, about 2/3 of its total population, went on hunger strike to protest their ill-treatment by INS officers. In a protest letter signed by 120 detainees from 24 different countries including Haiti, Cuba, China, India, and various Latin American countries, they demanded, *inter alia*, that a bill introduced by Senator Graham calling for an end to their detention be applied (HP 4:10). After the coup, a group of 49 Haitian refugees detained on bail, in particular women, children, and those with parents in Miami, as Gilbert reported based on information obtained from Dorancy, was "liberated" from Krome "in this period of crisis" (HP 42:15). At the mass in *St. Jerome Church* on November 24, Jackson called Krome a "concentration camp", according to Alain St. Victor (HP 50:8).

[341] USCC´s "Catholic Emergency Legal Aid to Haitians" (CELAH), offering free legal services for Haitian asylum applicants in Miami, Patterson, Newark, Brooklyn, Boston, and Los Angeles, asked concerned individuals to make financial contributions or to volunteer as attorneys and interpreters. And CWS, providing free legal representation for Haitian asylum-seekers as part of its "Haitian legal services program", sought volunteers with knowledge of Haiti as well as multi-cultural communication and writing skills to help process asylum applications (Haiti4:6;Haiti5:11;HRC 1995:1,2;CWSW 1993:14;Bellor 1993). In FY 1992, CWS and USCC came to assume representation of nearly 5,000 and approximately 6,000 Haitians, respectively, who the two agencies continued to assist throughout 1993. EMM in New York resettled 14 Haitians out of a total of 2,619 refugees in FY 1992. CWS resettled in addition about 600 Haitian refugees in 1994, some coming directly from Haiti and some from Guantanamo (NCHR11:iv;CWSW 1993:14;CWS 1993:11;USCC/MRS 1992/93: 15;ORR 1993:C3,C5-7,C22;CWSW 1994a:13).

cies concerned with immigration and refugee affairs, "shared leadership of efforts" to facilitate the delivery of legal services "to some 12,000 Haitian asylum-seekers", and assisted in several training seminars for *pro bono* legal service providers (NCHR6:2;NCHR13:2-3). A variety of "adjustment issues" relevant to Haitian refugees from Guantanamo and their host families was another field of concern for NCHR. The group was part of a coalition of "Haitian community organizations", which sponsored a workshop on December 11 at *St. Francis Church* in Brooklyn. The panel was expected to discuss issues such as dealing with culture shock, coping with stress in the host family, learning English and other forms of further education, obtaining social and medical services as well as spiritual resources and the process of applying for political asylum. In an announcement published in *HaitiInsight*, Père Dorsinville at the *National Center of the Haitian Apostolate* (NCHA) was referred to as contact person (Haiti6:12).[342] In Père Dorsinville´s judgement, "many organizations that were active in the Haitian community ... in support of Aristide" were less interested in "the nitty-gritty of everyday services" for Haitian asylum-seekers. This special field of expertise "was not their cup of tea" (Dorsinville 1995). As Wishnie put it, "the Haitian groups were really there [ECHR meetings] more for the politics, not the refugees or the services to HIV" (Wishnie 1995). Their observations referred to the Haitian community of New York, which seems to have contrasted with communities in other US cities.[343]

But despite all free Haitian and non-Haitian legal assistance in the "long and expensive process" of applying for political asylum, Bellor of CWS/IRP informed the NCHR Board of Directors meeting of July 13, 1993 that there were not enough institutional and legal resources to serve some 11,000 Haitians paroled into the US. While the New York-based *Humanitas Foundation* awarded USCC/MRS a grant of $20,000 in 1993 for its "Haitians project", and while CWS was working with about 200 *pro bono* attorneys to file political asylum claims for the refugees in the New York area, only 20% of those resettled had formally applied for asylum. As of March 1993, less than 1% of all paroled refugees had been granted permanent asylum (NCHR16:2; Foundation2:1212;CWSW 1994b:3;Pierre-Pierre 1993a:26). USCC/MRS worked closely with the *Catholic Legal Immigration Network, Inc.*, the "bishops´ agency for providing legal services", as well as the *Catholic Charities* (CC) and MRS diocesan affiliates to resettle those, whose asylum applications were approved (USCC/MRS 1992/93:15).

CC in New York was in charge of Haitian refugees, who had arrived in the city to be transferred to homeless shelters as transitional housing sites. The best known of these was St. George Hotel, located on Henry Street in Brooklyn Heights. At the end

---

[342] On February 26, 1993, a similar NCHA-workshop was scheduled to take place (HP 183:7).
[343] The July 23, 1992 resolution of CABP in Philadelphia, for example, reveals that Haitians in that city seem to have been involved in at least the legal side of the "nitty-gritty of everyday services". According to Latour, the resolution dealt with the "attitude of the INS vis-a-vis Haitian refugees seeking political asylum in the US and the restoration of democracy in Haiti". Published in HP in late October 1992, it considered that members of the Council had represented Haitian refugees *pro bono* during the past years. Being aware of the "refusal of legal aid necessary for an effective representation of Haitians" and of the "apparent attempts designed to discourage the attorneys, who have volunteered to represent the Haitians", the organization of reportedly 12,000 members called on the US government, the USJD, and the INS "to encourage the pro bono attorneys to cater to the legal needs of Haitians in their quest for refugee status" (HP 148:8).

of April 1992, HP reported on the living conditions of a group of 19 Haitian asylum-seekers accommodated there. According to the weekly, they did not have the right to receive visitors in the hotel, the rooms of which were in bad shape. CC reportedly paid about $50 for each room per day, $1,500 per month, with funds allocated by the US federal government. One room was reportedly broken into, while the occupant was out to attend an English cours at *Holy Cross Church*. Among the refugees were unaccompanied children, whose parents disappeared in the course of the journey on the high seas. They were transferred to the *Bureau of Child Welfare* in charge of sending them to Foster Homes. Since those institutions did not have an excellent reputation in the US, as HP stressed, it would be desirable, if Haitian families would take care of the kids. Without being more specific, the weekly affirmed that the newly arrived compatriots nevertheless benefitted in the meantime "from the help and solidarity of certain members of the community" (HP 107:8).

The members HP referred to could have been Raoul and Serrat, the two Haitian-American founders of HWHR, who worked as INS interpreters. According to a pamphlet issued by the group, they first initiated a volunteer program servicing Haitian refugees after a visit to St. George Hotel. "When the Refugees articulated their many unmet needs", the pamphlet explains, "what started as an English class with volunteer teachers and donated books at St. Francis of Assisi [church] became HWHR" in early 1992. The group developed structurally after receiving "start-up funding" from the *New York's Women's Foundation* and, shortly thereafter, a grant from the *New York Community Trust* (HWHR 1995:1). A "Grantee Profile" in the foundation's newsletter noted that HWHR "started its first year of operation as a totally volunteer organization helping refugees". Mayas became the chair of HWHR (NYWF 1993:1). After "the word spread in the Haitian community", HWHR doubled its clientele within two years, expanding to also include residential Haitians and Haitian-Americans in its program of direct services ranging from literacy classes, English as a Second Language (ESL), job search and preparation, and referrals to a variety of other programs (HWHR 1995:1-2).

Other "members of the community" showing solidarity with paroled Haitian refugees were activists of HEAR. They told me that they had looked after twelve refugees accomodated by CC in a house in Crown Heights: "We provided counseling to them, we told them how to survive in this country". In addition, they provided shelter for a few refugees in the basement in Crown Heights, in which HEAR convenes on a regular basis. Insisting that Haitian refugees had been generally welcome in the Haitian community, one member stated that "[t]he Catholic Charities, they had the monopoly" in terms of logistics and government funding for refugee resettlement. He admitted, however, that community assistance "was not as organized as it should have been" (HEAR 1995).[344] According to Père Dorsinville, CC "did ask the Haitian community at large what could be done to help those Haitian people" to be resettled in the US, since public funding was only available for the time period of 90 days. But, he continued, "there was no coming together on this in the Haitian community itself". According to social workers at CC in Brooklyn, the agency's budget for resettling 365 Haitian refu-

---

[344] In contrast, Asfaha Hadera of the *African Service Committee*, which resettled a small number of Haitian refugees without relatives in the US as well as a few unaccompanied Haitian minors in New Jersey, lamented that his organization had received "no assistance from the Haitian community whatsoever". He had expected more help "for our Haitian brothers and sisters" after contacting unnamed Haitian groups (statement by Mr. Hadera in a telephone interview on June 6, 1995).

gees was $238,000 that year, including staff salaries and supplies. Dorsinville added that some political activists doubted the refugee status of screened-in Haitians, while others feared that helping them would render Aristide's return more unlikely. Echoing the NCHR Planing Committee's experience, the reasoning from the US government's perspective reportedly was: "If the people are being resettled, everything is fine, so why bother?" (Dorsinville 1995;Pierre-Pierre 1993a:26).

Père Dorsinville of HAUP, priest at *Sacred Heart Church* in Queens as well as chairman of HCC, stated that "there was not the same consensus as before" on the issue of resettling Haitian refugees as was the case in the early 1980s. HAUP was founded in 1975 by Pére Sansaricq and other leaders of the Haitian community, who realized that "they were a minority within the minority". Before opening a community center in Queens, "HAUP responded to emergencies" faced by the Haitain community: "In 1979, when thousands of our compatriots began to flee ... HAUP developed programs to advocate for the freedom of Haitian refugees, provided shelter, food and clothing and assist in their settlement. With federal, state, and city funding, ... HAUP developed an array of services for Haitian refugees". A 1986 information brochure issued by HAUP emphasizes the group's ethnic orientation by stating that it is a "non-profit community-based organization dedicated to building and serving the Haitian American community and integrating this community into the American life" (HAUP 1986). Père Dorsinville added that HAUP had been helped in these efforts by CWS and USCC, which extended "technical assistance in terms of setting up programs". He stressed that after the coup, non-profit Haitian service organizations such as the community centers associated under the umbrella of HCC, with "no funding available", were willing to give the refugees what they could, "with the available resources" (Dorsinville 1995).

Nevertheless, Raoul, who used to work at CWS "for a couple of years", commented that she and Serrat "were hoping that we were going to find places that already existed, that we just can refer people to ... But the problems grew and grew". Obviously identifying a deficiency within the Haitian community, she explained that "[t]here is a void". She made it clear that "[t]here is just no money allocated to this type of agencies ... Apparently, in the 1980s ... the community-based organizations I understand were better funded ... it was not the case this time" (Raoul 1995). In a similar vein, Frank of HCC pointed to a lack of resources within the Haitian community and to latent institutional discrimination when stating: "There is a tendency - even to take care of the Haitians, they will rather give the money to the Catholic Charities, not to the Haitian organizations ... and in terms of the Haitian community at large, a great deal of them are low-income" (Frank 1995). But Sansaricq, co-founder of HAUP and HCC, seemed to add lacking managerial skills when saying the following about the community centers: "I would say they have a history of passivity". He lamented that contrary to their beginning, they "have not produced ... as much as was anticipated ... they are up to their heads in debts ... the rent for their office was too expensive" (Sansaricq 1995). For whatever reason, it took until 1995 for HCC to be awarded a grant from the *Office of Refugee Resettlement* (ORR) to fund the so-called "New York City Haitian Refugee Community Strengthening Project" to service some 5,000 post-coup Haitian clients on Entrant Status in the city. In its application, HCC referred to its experience since 1981 in the implementation of programs promoting the self-sufficiency of newly arrived Entrants (HCC 1995:1,9).

The concentration of newcomers, most forcefully in the cities, raises tough questions regarding the financing of public services available, for example, in schools and hospitals. This even more so after public responsibility for incorporating newcomers had fallen, mostly by default, to state and local governments in the course of the 1980s (Fix 1993:1,8). This development is part of a broader pattern of reduced government-nonprofit collaboration initiated under the Reagan Administration despite the rootedness of this kind of cooperation in US history. The reduction forced nonprofit organizations to seek alternative funding or to curb their operations (Salamon 1990:226-238). As Dorsinville stated, this "less favorable environment" was compounded by the fact that "corporate and foundation funding depends on contacts and rarely exceeds three years" (1995:3). Obviously, these constraints exacerbated ethnic vertical organizing by Haitian community organizations in the US.

But there are a few service-providing Haitian organizations that were able to adapt to this new environment by applying successfully for funds from private US sources. In contrast to Haitian political organizations in New York, which followed Désir's principle of organizational and financial independence, these grants served purposes of a marked ethnic rather than a nationalistic character.[345] Staffed by Haitians, the ethnic orientation of HWHR, on whose board of directors also Ratner serves, is furthermore evidenced by its emphasis on "the educational aspect of assimilation" in an effort to adapt refugees "as much as possible" to life in the US (HWHR 1995:2;Raoul 1995). The examples of HAUP and HCC seem to suggest that the incorporative initiatives of African-American professionals and politicians on the refugee issue in the early 1980s were not as unsuccessful at least in certain sections of the Haitian community as Basch et al. seem to imply (1994:201-203).

Despite his criticism, Sansaricq also defended HCC when explaining that "a non-profit organization cannot be involved in political activities, especially concerning a foreign state - it was Haiti ... when HCC was not directly involved, HCC appeared to be indifferent to the main concern of the people, but according to the law, they could not be directly involved" (Sansaricq 1995). New provisions in the revenue act of 1987 extended excise taxes to publicly supported charities that engage in certain prohibited political or lobbying activities (Fremont-Smith 1989:82). Charitable nonprofits operating under Internal Revenue Code Section 501(c)(3) are "severely limited in their freedom to engage in lobbying or other political activities involving attempts to support or oppose a particular candidate or to influence legislation" (Weisbrod 1989:113). Consequently, Sansaricq added, the Haitian "population was focusing on the situation in Haiti" after the coup, "and they [the centers] were trying to focus on the situation here" (Sansaricq 1995).

After the three-month-period beginning with the refugee's admission, the "placement" phase was almost completed in early May 1992, when Gilbert detailed US refugee resettlement policies. Having the right to see a doctor or a dentist and to receive English lessons in special schools paid by governmental or local institutions, an admitted refugee received $745 from the federal government for this time period

---

[345] HCC's *Flatbush Haitian Center*, for example, acquired $25,000 from the *New York Community Trust* in 1994 to "expand delinquency prevention for Brooklyn youth". The *Haitian Community Health Information and Referral Center* (HCHIRC) got $20,000 from the *Aaron Diamond Foundation, Inc.* in 1993 for "final renewed general support", and HWHR obtained $10,000 from the same source in 1994 to "assist legal residents in becoming U.S. citizens" (Foundation2:324,841,1313).

through his or her intermediating sponsor to cover expenses for food and housing.[346] After the three-month-period, the refugee might benefit from an extension of his or her work permit until his or her asylum claim would be determined. Gilbert stressed vaguely that "it is doubtless the role of certain commissions of the 10th department to make sure that each refugee be treated with dignity and honesty" (HP 112:8).

In the spring of 1992, ORR started to place orphans from Guantanamo to towns in various regions within the US, where virtually no Haitians live, as part of a self-instituted shelter program. According to Mark Franken, operations director of USCC in New York, ORR justified the placements with costs involved. In criticizing ORR's policy, Dinkins demanded in the summer to allow 463 Haitian orphans to resettle in New York. He substantiated his demand in a letter to ORR with the existence in his city of an important Haitian community, which would be closer to the orphans culturally. HP assured that "in any case, the Haitian leaders of the community in New York want just as Dinkins that these children come to New York into the midst of their kind" (HP 134:11). The Yale students came to work with the City of New York following their successful settlement negotiations with the USJD in September for the sake of the release of HIV-positive pregnant women. They had to leave their families behind to deliver their babies in New Jersey (Clawson et al. 1994:2361-23).

Gradually, the students had to familiarize themselves with "appropriate care" for this specific clientele as a new area of research. Their resettlement team took advantage of contacts Wishnie had in New York in recruiting "Haitian organizations, housing providers, and AIDS advocates" to assist in resettling an increasing number of paroled refugees, among them Haitians, who had been granted medical evacuations. Resettlement placements were the condition, under which the Bush Administration was willing to release the refugees. The Haitian organizations had been HWP, HWHR, and HCAIDS represented by Patricia Benoit, Raoul, and Dr. Pierre-Louis, respectively. The housing providers had been *Housing Works* (HW) and the *Coalition for the Homeless* (CH). Williams, who worked for the former organization, was one of the AIDS advocates, while her friend William Broberg worked for the latter group as its "crisis intervention director". As the students stressed: "To our great relief, these two organizations soon took over all social services for the refugees once they entered" the US (Clawson et al. 1994:2349,2363;HP 193:14;Wishnie 1995;Daugaard 1995; Williams 1995;Pierre-Pierre 1993d:B1).[347]

---

[346] ORR's so-called Voluntary Agency Matching Grant Program provides an "alternative approach" to providing resettlement assistance and awards matching grants of up to $1,000 per refugee to volags, which agree to match the ORR-grant with equivalent cash or in-kind contributions (ORR 1993:28).

[347] According to its information brochure, HWP is an independent, non-profit organization founded in 1981 as a project of AFSC, supported by six public and private funders. With its target population being "recently arrived Haitian refugees and Haitian immigrants residing in Brooklyn", for whom there was a "scarcity of services", HWP from its inception "focused on the special needs of Haitian women and their families" to assist them "to adjust to their new environment". As HWP's receptionist told me, the organization's staff was composed in 1995 of eight Haitians and Haitian-Americans, who occasionally cooperate with the community centers under HCC and with HWHR. The *International Rescue Committee* (IRC), also a member of NCHR, as well as CWS and NYANA were among the volags, which referred Haitian refugees to HWP. Gabrielle Kersaint succeeded Sabine Albert to HWP's executive director in September 1994 (HWP 1995;statement by HWP's receptionist "Kathleen" in a telephone interview conducted on June 21, 1995). As shown above, Albert had cooperated with Haitian political organizations during the crisis in a certain number of events.

According to Wishnie, by the time Judge Johnson ordered the release of all HIV-positive refugees, ECHR had succeeded in building up a "track record" of resettling "30 to 40 people", since "providing the resettlement placements" was a precondition for their release. The group did so for free and in competition with CC and CWS, which had refused to resettle refugees without reimbursement of "$1,200 per head" - they would not "lift a finger": "[B]ecause they said No, we had to patronize those grassroots organizations sort of outside the main structures of refugee resettlement like Ninaj" Raoul's HWHR. Additional political support from Dinkins, mustered by New York's AIDS community, in conjunction with ECHR's local political activism "convinced the government to let people out immediately in April [1993] ... And then, when June came, when the final order came for anyone else, we already had a system in place". Without all these factors, Wishnie summarized, ECHR "would not have developed a relationship with the government, where they trusted us to resettle people" (Wishnie 1995). One of the plaintiffs in the lawsuit, NCHR cooperated with the Yale legal team in linking the Guantanamo refugees brought to the US with the "agencies qualified to assist in their resettlement" (NCHR19:4).

The relationship between ECHR and the US Administration was partially based on a mutual understanding concerning the potential impact of Haitian refugees' resettlement on public opinion: The US trusted ECHR "to ... keep it out of the news, keep it quiet" (Wishnie 1995). Daugaard's "domestic racism"-strategy was thus somewhat muted in 1993 by the trade-off between the intended refugees' release on the condition of non-publicity and the exertion of pressure on the US to solve the Haitian crisis. As the other students recalled, "We worked to keep news of arriving HIV-positive refugees away from the media, for fear that news reports would instill panic in the public and pressure the government to seek a stay of Judge Johnson's interim order". The first group of refugees, among them the most ill, arrived on April 5 at New York's La Guardia Airport, where they were welcomed by Yale's resettlement team in a "bittersweet reunion". However, the refugees' arrival did not escape the NYT. When the newspaper published a report the next day, the students' "worst fears seemed to be coming true. Luckily, the public outcry did not last, and the government complied with" Judge Johnson's order (Clawson et al. 1994:2386).[348]

Tecumseh had reported in mid-March 1993 on some 10,000 Haitian refugees already in the US, for whom life was "very difficult". A majority of them depended on agencies, "which cannot offer them a great deal". She quoted Harold Pirem, caseworker of CWS in Flatbush, Brooklyn, as saying in the NYT (03/06/93) that his work of finding housing for refugees was "gigantic". But those, Tecumseh stressed, who were taken in by parents or relatives, had "a good chance" (HP 189:12). The 27 Haitian refugees, who were flown from Guantanamo to the US on June 14, were "dressed in clothes sent them by relatives", as the NYT's Rohter reported. The 13 refugees, who arrived in New York, were "met with smiling faces and hugs from family members" and with the Yale students' resettlement team (1993a:A20). But as early as March

---

[348] In the students' account, there is no mention of a political delegation composed of Haitians welcoming the arrivals, while HP did not report on this first group of 20 refugees specifically. But it did mention them in a brief article on the second planeload of 33 "other compatriots", who arrived in Miami on April 8. The Haitian weekly informed that 8 of them stayed with relatives in Florida, while the remainder was brought to New York, where they were welcomed by Dinkins' "community council" (HP 205:8). Again, there was no mention of a Haitian delegation welcoming the refugees.

1993, CWS's Pirem, responsible for 250 refugees in Brooklyn, Queens and Long Island, told the NYT that "[n]ow we are dealing with something harder: sponsorship breakdown". Another CWS office in Manhattan dealt with refugees living there as well as those living in the Bronx and in Westchester. A certain number of cases in New York relied on relatives and friends, who had been in the US only a short time themselves, barely making a living. As a result, some refugees, who had been taken in by relatives or other immigrants, were turned out, their hosts unwilling or unable to keep supporting them.

According to the NYT's Pierre-Pierre, the volags' services also included employment and housing. Because many of the refugees spoke only Creole and had no relatives in the US, they often additionally relied on the volags' staff members to translate and explain documents, even though volags generally helped resettle Haitian refugees with relatives in the New York area (1993a:26). Cardinal O'Connor offered in March to open hospitals in his arch diocese to those refugees already sick and to help them find housing and jobs (HP 192:16).

In contrast to the traditional volags, CH generally helped to find housing for refugees without relatives in the area. As Broberg of CH told Pierre-Pierre, "administrative bungling" by the city of New York led to some 35 Haitian refugees' protracted accommodation in a motel near JFK airport one month after Judge Johnson's ruling, thereby "breeding resentment" in terms of "replicating" the situation on Guantanamo. This criticism was rejected by Burton Blaustein, deputy commissioner of the city's Human Resources Administration. His agency had two Creole-speaking caseworkers, who reportedly worked seven days a week (1993d:B1,B3). In addition, an unknown number of Haitian refugees without relatives in the area might have been assisted by HCA in Huntington, Long Island, where about 60,000 Haitians live (Schemo 1992:7;Guyther 1993:2).[349] Aubourg told me that he accomodated three HIV-infected Haitian refugees in his own apartment, since there had not been enough resources available to absorb them all (Aubourg 1996). All said, these Haitian refugees' personal odyssey from the carnage in Haiti to the hardships in New York is a tale of hegemonic forces shaping a transnational field.

---

[349] According to Carelus, who is also chairman of its multicultural center, HCA also helps refugees, who land in New York without money, housing or friends, providing them with food, shelter, and a lawyer. HCA was founded in 1982 by 62-year-old Germain (Schemo 1992:7;Guyther 1993:2).

Dennis Pottinger T-Shirt on West Indian American Day Parade, 09/05/94, Brooklyn
(by Götz-Dietrich Opitz)

6 Summary and Conclusions

Haitian organizing in New York City in response to the crisis in Haiti following the coup of September 1991 was guided by the "three-pronged strategy" of "resistance-embargo-mobilization" for the sake of Aristide´s reinstatement ("return issue"). In pursuing this strategy, the political leadership of the Haitian community in the US preferred *direct* transnational citizen-to-citizen relations and *direct* transnational citizen-to-state relations of a *nationalistic* orientation. These manifested themselves in the peaceful campaign of mass protests, which were the most important initial "mobilization" effort on the grassroots level. The protests were designed to denounce the illegal *de facto* regime and to strengthen the "resistance" against the repression within Haiti by demonstrating the Haitian diaspora´s political, emotional, moral, tactical, and financial support, which was also extended to Aristide´s exile government. They helped mitigate the psychological and economic effects of both human rights violations and international trade sanctions. This campaign, in which Haitian refugees were primarily used as instruments to keep the spotlight on the political situation in Haiti rather than on the illegal US refugee policy ("refugee issue"), enabled an unknown number of would-be refugees to stay in Haiti.

Part of the campaign consisted of reactive, internal community efforts to inoculate rank-and-file Haitians against misrepresentations of the "return issue" by the US mainstream media. It was further composed of energy-consuming efforts to fight transnational terrorism in the Haitian diaspora originating from paramilitary groups in Haiti. Their terror added to the paralyzing effects of mourning over a growing number of crisis-related victims in the Haitian transnation. In contrast, the detrimental effects of US-Haitian off shore assembly industry on the embargo and, consequently, on Haiti´s labor movement did not translate into immediate and large-scale action. Basically, "mobilization" in the Haitian community of New York was informed by what I called "Désir´s principle" of organizational and financial independence from US governmental and non-governmental actors alike. Haiti´s historical example seems to have predestined the priority given to *direct* transnational relations between diaspora and homeland. It furnished the plethora of verbal strategies used to constantly motivate Haitians in the US to organize. In this light, the Haitian diaspora represented a present-day version of maroon communities fighting against "internal colonization" in the home country.

Haitian activists in New York were nevertheless supported in their organizing efforts by a score of US groups. The relationship of trust underlying these direct cooperative alliances was based more on social proximity to the Haitian community and agreement with the nationalistic agenda of its political leadership than on racial or cultural affinities. Independent transnational activism by established civil societal and hyphenated American transnationalists such as NCHR and Jesse Jackson, both more closely situated to the power center of Washington, challenged the political elite of the Haitian community; Haitian diasporic transnationalists therefore watched those actors with some suspicion. This friction contributed to the eventual collapse of the strategical and organizational unity between Aristide´s exile government, the 10th department organizations, and allied Haitian and non-Haitian groups. The collapse resulted from diverging assessments of issues such as the refugee crisis as well as international negotiation and intervention, which had not been an integral part of the original "three-pronged strategy".

This strategy also required *indirect* transnational citizen-to-state relations, the utilization of which ranked second, however. They were to elicit international measures from outside the geographically dispersed Haitian people such as the economic "embargo" and a favorable "world opinion". The UN was to add pressure not only on the *de facto* regime, but also on a hypocritical US government, which was more and more openly suspected of playing a "double game" with a view to obstruct Aristide´s return. Initial euphoria over successes soon gave way to skepticism over the role of international organizations. The more the UN became more actively involved in the Haitian crisis, the more it was increasingly seen as US-dominated. After the failed Governors Island process, many Haitians came to question the UN´s impartiality and neutrality. Accused of acting as an instrument of US interests in Haiti advocating the *status quo*, the UN was finally alleged by some Haitian activists to be implicated in a plot to drain the ranks of the resisting popular camp in Haiti by means of blunt economic sanctions and the UN/OAS-ICM. The transnational stream of Haitian refugees was overshadowed by these concerns of national sovereignty perceived to be at the mercy of powerful international actors.

The strategical value of the "refugee issue" for the return of Aristide was assessed initially as positive, but as secondary to the "three-pronged strategy". The situation of Haitian refugees was to be used to shed additional light on the repressive character of Haiti´s illegitimate government rather than to primarily pressure the US government on its related unlawful policy. Since Washington´s main interest in the Haitian crisis was believed to be secretly backing the *de facto* regime through neglect, stemming the flow of boat people was seen as a deliberate measure to support the military junta. Tolerating the military junta was *not* seen as an unintended side-effect of halting an undesired wave of refugees. But regardless of all strategical caveats, the plight of Haitian refugees remained a distant humanitarian-patriotic concern. In contrast, the strategical thrust of NCHR and other collaborating groups, among them a few Haitian immigrants, mostly concentrated on the refugee side of the crisis. This major effect of the coup was believed to be the principal concern of the US. Containing Haitian refugees was presumed to constitute the US government´s most vulnerable point and the criticism of it the most effective political weapon. This approach relied on the potential impact of these efforts on the US government´s policies towards the Haitian military junta.

This strategy was also reflected in some Haitian boat people´s motivation to escape the tyranny in their home country. They were part of the set of actors playing a role in the Haitian refugee crisis understood as a policy arena that centered around the legal and ethical legitimacy of US refugee policy regarding the detention of Haitian nationals on Guantanamo, the practice of their forced return to Haiti ("refoulement"), and the ICP-program in Haiti. In "dramatizing" the refugees´ plight and by using information obtained from a transnational "network of indigenous sources", NCHR, a score of actors in the refugee and civil rights community in the US, as well as African-American and Jewish-American organizations first targeted the US government´s legislative branch to produce political clout vis-à-vis an obdurate US Administration unwilling to change its refugee policy. Many of these actors worked closely with Congressman Charles Rangel and the CBC, publicly denouncing the US Administration as being driven by racism and a fear of Haitian migration. They all did so against the backdrop of a rising anti-immigrant sentiment noticeable since the mid-1980s. After Clinton's election, the focus of refugee advocacy work, which was assisted by a score of screened-in refugees from Guantanamo, shifted temporarily to the US Administration in an effort to reformulate US state policy towards Haiti.

Participation by US-based Haitian organizations in this kind of Congressional lobbying was rather limited. This has to do with the unfamiliarity of advocacy techniques, the complexity of refugee law, the fear of a higher degree of collaboration between Washington and the *de facto* regime resulting from too much refugee-related pressure on the US, and many Haitians' hesitation to establish a link between US refugee policy and racism in US society. This reluctance is the product of differing constructs of race/color, which in the case of Haiti are *not* conceptualized into bipolar categories of black and white. The unique collective memory of race-pride based on their historical experience has them regard the US system of racial classification as illegitimate in its application to them. They are inclined to feel like external bystanders outside of US racial conflicts and tend to differentiate themselves from black Americans. In addition, the latter's leadership became associated increasingly with US executive power during the crisis.

There were, however, isolated initiatives by Haitians in the US concerning Guantanamo. As Creole-speaking INS interpreters, they contributed to a relatively high number of Haitian refugees paroled into the US. They accomplished part of the groundwork for HRC and later the Yale team and ECHR, which were assisted by a handful of Haitian-American doctors in litigating against the US government. The Haitian-led HRC in Miami is indicative of a casual division of labor in refugee affairs within the Haitian community in the US. After the Miami-conference in early 1994, US immigration and refugee policy was increasingly interpreted as a means exploited by Washington to intervene in Haiti's civil society. The US, the UN, and the OAS were seen as working hand in hand in supporting the military junta by providing for a deadly recycling of activists in Haiti's popular camp through refugee processing and the repatriation policy. This reading of events posed a serious dilemma: Internal resistance was pitted against refugee rights. Demanding TPS, more effective ICP, and full immigration visa proceedings amounted to indirectly weakening Haiti's inner resistance against the repression. In hindsight, some suspicions of Haitian activists proved correct with the CIA-assisted formation of the paramilitary group FRAPH.

This interpretation of US refugee policy was the result of Haitians' historical consciousness, which was intensified by the shocking coup. They perceived the unfolding crisis through a historical lens that largely shaped their folk model. Haitian history provided the blueprint for action for Haitians in the US diaspora; they organized as if physically present *in* Haiti. Rhetorical references to heroes of Haiti's history during the crisis point to courageous time-honored resistance against powerful external forces infringing on Haitians' highly-esteemed ideal of collective liberty. After the Haitian Revolution, the new black republic was isolated politically, but not commercially. Increasing foreign encroachment by various types of transnationalisms from varying national backgrounds culminated in 1915 in the Marine occupation by the US substituting the old French Empire as self-appointed arbiter over Haitian internal affairs. US governmental assistance to the Duvalier regime and manipulative interference into pre-coup Haiti's political, economic, and civil societies were condensed from a

Haitian perspective into the broad slogan of the "American Plan". The term connotes a feeling of marginalization and a loss of control. This historical interpretation of events was crucial: It led Haitians in the US to primarily focus on the possible *causes* of the coup, not on its *consequences* such as the refugee crisis.

Judged from this historical angle, many Haitians suspected the US government of having masterminded Aristide's overthrow. The assumed implication of the US in the coup appeared as its most vulnerable point. Consequently, the political leadership in the Haitian community sought to unmask and discredit the US as coup-instigator. It thereby predicated its strategy upon assumptions, the verifiability of which was rather elusive due to a lack of hard facts. In contrast, the US Administration's violation of refugee law was provable. Moreover, some Haitian activists were reminded of the days of slavery with regard to the refugee issue strategy, which seemed to degrade Haitian boat people to a "bargaining chip". Advocating the rights of Haitian refugees appeared as a humiliating exercise in currying of favors. In other words, Haiti's national hero Makandal would not have begged for asylum. The demand for help in Aristide's restoration as the solution to the refugee problem was therefore only backed up in moral terms: The historical debt obligated the US to reciprocate for Haiti's past support of its neighbor's War of Independence and to compensate for the torts it committed against Haiti. The history-conscious disposition made it difficult for Haitian activists to detect the US government's present-day vulnerabilities.

What is more, the assumed US-assisted coup and the concomitant refugee crisis appeared as the conspiratorial pretext for Washington to gain total control of the island nation by military means. This fear was triggered by early allegations of US preparations for an imminent invasion of Haiti. Consequently, the pros and cons of the Haitian refugee strategy meant for the return issue a risky brinkmanship: On the one hand, US action for Aristide's reinstatement was indispensable; but on the other hand one was afraid that the US could overreact in terms of intervening militarily. The widely used "telephone call" metaphor was emblematic of both overestimating US power and misperceiving US will in solving the political crisis. Ignoring the growing isolationist mood in the US and the successful harnessing of traditionally appreciated cheap Haitian labor in the wake of the "fine-tuned" embargo, the linkage between the refugee issue and the issue of US invasion increasingly generated friction between the Haitian community's political leadership and that of the African-American community. When the detrimental effects of international trade sanctions became ever more visible, the perceived threat of US military intervention was nourished by the belief that Haiti's economic condition could serve as an additional pretext for US invasion.

After Governors Island, the perceived danger for Haiti's self-determination by US military intervention mutated from a tactical demand, claimed by some African-American activists, into reality. The new offensive on the refugee front resulted in UNSC resolution 940 and culminated in Aristide's return in October 1994 with the help of US military power. Persistent extra-territorial organizing of an ethnic orientation on the refugee issue eventually succeeded in breaking the reluctance to use US troops to reinstate Aristide. The civil societal amplification of the undesired transnational Haitian refugee stream by means of indirect transnational relations via the US government achieved the instrumentalization of US state power to force the military junta out of Haiti. To the chagrin of Haitian anti-interventionists, US non-intervention in Haiti was for African-American transnationalists an example of racial discrimination in US foreign policy.

For Haitian anti-interventionists, US occupation would eclipse Haitian democracy for years to come. It marked the climax of a set of external factors operative since the beginning of the crisis, which gradually forced Haitians in the US to the defensive. One of those factors was the calling into question of Haiti's capacity for popular self-government as expressed by parts of the US mainstream media and the Bush White House. These doubts reflected prejudices that reach far back into the history of Haitian-foreign relations and are rooted in the hostile international environment in which the Haitian Revolution occurred. Haitians in the US felt compelled to fight back with their campaign of mass protests, which were in and of themselves a stunning exercise in popular democracy and Haitian solidarity. The recurring reaffirmation of the Haitian people's choice of December 16, 1990, in spite of a favorable world opinion confirming Aristide's legitimacy, illustrate how deep the defensive posture ran. The return of democracy was to be achieved by publicly rehabilitating what was to be returned. The Haitian community thus conceived of the return issue as both the means and the end. This tautology diverted much of the political leadership's attention from other means such as the refugee issue. The distracting battle front of the return issue suffered from a fundamental contradiction: Haitian activists thought they were able to persuade what they believed was a coup-implicated and intervention-prone US government into assistance by a refurbished public image of Haitian democracy.

Aristide was the incarnation of Haitians' pride in popular self-government. His overwhelming popularity with the Haitian people even ballooned after the shocking coup against him. Accordingly, Haitians in the US defended the first democratically elected president in Haitian history. He was revered as a charismatic leader, imbueing his broad-based constituency with dignity, pride, and joy. He catapulted the most marginalized social strata of Haiti, the poor and the peasant population, into the international limelight. Introduced into Haiti's national shrine alongside Toussaint and Dessalines and virtually celebrated as the leader of the African diaspora, Aristide was accompanied by a Haitian media frenzy reinforcing a personality cult that surrounded him as Haiti's invulnerable messiah. Aristide's sophistication and refinement eclipsed the plight of miserable Haitian refugees to a certain degree. In the early 1980s, the Haitian boat people did not have to compete with someone like him when winning the goodwill of the Haitian diaspora.

Many Haitians in the US were ready to follow Aristide unconditionally, whatever his political choices. From the very beginning, the refugee issue as a political weapon was subordinated to the embargo and negotiations, which Aristide considered "an essential part" of the exile government's strategy, in spite of mounting criticism in the Haitian community's political leadership. At the same time, he encouraged his compatriots back home in his radio address of November 22, 1991 to resist peacefully and to voluntarily refrain from fleeing Haiti. While rallying civilian support in the US for Haitian democracy, he repeated this appeal after the election of Clinton, with whom he reached a "deal". Aristide's approach of "friendly words and persuasion" was partially based on the fear of US military intervention and on advice given by his Haitian entourage and US consultants from groups such as ICP. They ruled out the abrogation of the USHIA for a long time. But NCHR's advocacy before the exiled Haitian government and that of other US groups such as Ratner's CCR had a long-term impact on Aristide's strategical decisions. On April 1, 1994, he employed the refugee issue again as a pressuring device while also condoning US-led foreign intervention.

Haitian-organized mass gatherings in New York were designed also to protest against socio-economic conditions in Haiti that were perceived as a root cause of the coup: The legacy of the peculiar mix of people in colonial Saint Domingue, who exhibited varying phenotypes, status, and interests, was oppression and exploitation in post-revolutionary Haiti. The political leaders of the new republic established a fiscal strategy that persistently impoverished the masses in the countryside. This socio-economic organization divided Haiti into two distinct groups: the agricultural producers, on the one hand, and the urbanites clustered around the alliance of rulers and merchants, on the other. Haiti's small and lighter-skinned economic elite are believed to have financed the coup of 1991. Part of the Haitian bourgeoisie living in the US managed to bring about a "vast realignment", which undermined the authority of the *10e of New York* and its popular base. The Haitian community's politico-organizational infrastructure moved towards progressing fragmentation. A class-based social distance increasingly alienated the changing political leadership from the "black, poor" Haitian boat people (Yale team). In Maimi's poorer and younger Haitian community, this distance was less pronounced. Conversely, NCHR's established Haitian staff seems to have been viewed by lower-class and darker-skinned Haitian activists with some suspicion.

The presumably popular US decision to isolate on Guantanamo HIV-positive Haitian refugees was speculated to be a plot designed by the US government to incite the US public against the Haitian community in its struggle for democracy. But the quarantine policy also affected the Haitian public in the US and contributed to the "waning of mobilization" in the community. Haitians' traumatic experience in the US during the 1980s of being collectively stigmatized as HIV-carriers led many of them to shun the refugee issue in public for fear of reoccuring AIDS-related accusations. Whereas in the 1980s *all* Haitians in the diaspora were victimized regardless of class and color, AIDS-related discrimination on Guantanamo was limited to "black, poor" Aristide-supporters from Haiti. In addition, Haitian HIV-infected refugees on Guantanamo were in conflict with the PR campaign to rehabilitate Aristide's exile government. In the Haitian community, the US Guantanamo policy resulted in a vigilant passivity towards the refugee issue.

The 1992 election campaign was waged in a national mood marked by growing isolationism and rising nativism. Influenced by the public debate on the Haitian refugees, Governor Clinton used the issue to score points in the foreign policy battle against the incumbent Bush by promising to help the Haitian boat people. Mobilized by a few compatriots conscious of US politics, a considerable number of Haitian-Americans and Haitians with newly acquired US-citizenship came to realize the merits of intervening in this debate. They took advantage of the power of the vote, to which legislative policymakers are basically receptive, in order to further the return issue. Aristide himself intervened in the campaign, urging his supporters not to vote for Bush. Haitian skeptics attributed pure self-interest to the electoral motives of contenders in the Democratic race. The disappointment over Clinton's unkept campaign promises devalued the strategical potential of the refugee issue and reinforced, in the long run, the emphasis originally put on *direct* transnational relations. During the Governors Island process, Clinton was much less exposed to refugee-related pressure than his predecessor. But his unkept promise could be re-instrumentalized in the new offensive on the refugee front in 1994 to push for Aristide's reinstallation.

Between 1991-94, some 11,000 Haitian refugees were allowed into the US to file asylum claims. They represented an "unprecedented" number of cases to be handled by *pro bono* attorneys and voluntary Creole interpreters. The need for legal assistance and refugee resettlement posed enormous problems of resources. These were compounded by reduced government-nonprofit collaboration dating back to the Reagan years. Service-providing Haitian community organizations formed in the early 1980s were especially hard hit by the restructuring in the nonprofit sector, which impeded ethnic vertical organizing for the benefit of asylum-seekers. Appeals for private Haitian donations to admitted refugees were met with competition from official fundraising activities for the victims of repression in Haiti. Consequently, established and nationwide operating US volags were primarily responsible for servicing the bulk of Haitian asylum-seekers. Some political Haitian organizations blamed them for having a "monopoly" status impeding Haitian-organized refugee services. But the Haitian political leadership was generally not interested in domestic and intra-community refugee issues. Accommodation of Haitian refugees with relatives in the US was provided on a family by family basis. The group of HIV-infected Haitian refugees were exclusively taken care of by older (semi-)Haitian community organizations specialized in services for refugees and AIDS-clients (HWP, HCAIDS) as well as by the newly formed HWHR cooperating with ECHR and New York housing providers.

Following are the conclusions from the findings summarized above: Whereas Haitians in the US organized "first as exiles, next as immigrants belonging to a Haitian ethnic group, and then as political refugees" (Glick Schiller 1987:11), they predominantly organized as Haitian nationalists between 1991 and 1994. Transnational centrifugal forces since the mid-1980s have increased their nationalist orientation at the expense of the refugee issue, with the four significant events being (1) Duvalier's fall in 1986, (2) Aristide's election in 1990, (3) Aristide's ouster in 1991, and (4) Aristide's reinstatement in 1994. Consequently, the categorical statement made by Glick Schiller that "in 1992 the 10th Department embraced these [Haitian] refugees as a symbol of the Haitian people" is very questionable (1995:118). The balance between nationalist and ethnic identities inherent in Haitian diasporic transnationalism was tipped in favor of the former with an emphasis on Haiti's political society.

Leading Haitian transnationalists' "paradoxical ability" (Ahrari) is underdeveloped on the ethnic end of the continuum. In contrast, their "extraterritorial nationalism" (Appadurai) is well-developed. Claiming the redemption of universal collective rights in the case of Haitian democracy was given priority between 1991 and 1994 over the demand of redeeming universal individual rights in the case of Haitian refugees. Notably, there was only minimal overlap between Haitian diasporic transnationalism on the one hand and US civil societal, African-American, and Jewish-American transnationalism on the other, with regard to lobbying and advocacy work before the legislative and judicial branches of the US government. As was shown above, a set of hegemonic forces structured Haitian organizing efforts.

US-based Haitians, who constitute a relatively young immigrant group, still have a long way to go to attain a high level of transnational sophistication that takes better advantage of indirect relations via the US government, but also via institutions at the intersection between US civil and economic societies (e.g. private foundations).

These relations are of an ethnic-nationalistic orientation that can be maintained in a dialectical relationship. If this orientation is to be harnessed for nationalist purposes, the corresponding kind of organizing requires a thorough knowledge of the US political process including its cultural idiosyncrasies. It presupposes a higher degree of acculturation and integration into US society.

In the case of Haitian transnationalism, the most significant roadblocks on this way seem to be the imposed constraints of race and the seduction of class in a binational context. The former will most likely keep Haitian transnationalism from reaching a high level of sophistication, while the latter might individually work to reach beyond this level to the point of indifference towards the *whole* Haitian populace, as the experience with economically successful Haitian-American professionals seems to suggest. In the example of Haitian transmigrants running for public office in the US, the question should not be dichotomized by asking "to which state do they give their allegiance?", as Glick Schiller does with regard to Bazin in Haiti (1995:120). For pledging *critical* allegiance is not necessarily a zero-sum-game when it comes to advancing Haitians´ paradoxical ability into an effective tool to benefit both diaspora and homeland in the deterritorialized Haitian transnation. In the long run, the most important task seems to be the construction of an ever broader-based middle-class in Haiti as the foundation for a viable democracy, Haitian style.

7 Bibliography (Primary and Secondary Sources)

ABC: Audit Bureau of Circulations.
199X *ABC Audit Report: Circulation 1991, 1992, 1993, 1994, 1995.* Statistics on the New York Times Average Estimated Paid Circulation, provided by Sandra McMillian of the New York Times Marketing Research Department in 1996.

Adelman, Howard ed.
1991 *Refugee Policy: Canada and the United States.* Toronto: York Lanes Press.

Adelman, Howard.
1992 "Ethnicity and Refugees". *1992 World Refugee Survey.* Washington, D.C.: The U.S. Committee For Refugees. p. 6 - 11.

ADH: Artists for Democracy in Haiti.
1994 "Statement of Intent". New York: ADH, June 3. 8 p.

AFL-CIO: American Federation of Labor - Congress of Indusrial Organizations.
1992a "Press Release: AFL-CIO Calls for Immediate Halt to Forced Repatriation of Haitian Refugees", by Lane Kirkland. Washington, February 4. 1p.

AFL-CIO: American Federation of Labor - Congress of Industrial Organizations.
1992b "Statement by the AFL-CIO Executive Council on Haiti". Bel Harbour, February 17. 1 p.

AFSC: American Friends Service Committee.
1994 *Introduction to the American Friends Service Committee.* Philadelphia: AFSC. 4 p.

Ahrari, Mohammed E.
1987 "Introduction", "Conclusions". *Ethnic Groups and U.S. Foreign Policy.* Mohammed E. Ahrari ed. New York: Greenwood Press. p. xi - xxi, 155 - 158.

Ahrari, Mohammed E. ed.
1987 *Ethnic Groups and U.S. Foreign Policy.* New York: Greenwood Press

AIFLD: American Institute for Free Labor Development.
1992 "Worker Rights in Haiti". Washington, May 21. 4 p.

AIFLD: American Institute for Free Labor Development.
1993 "Update on Worker Rights in Haiti". Washington, May 21. 2 p.

AJC: American Jewish Committee.
1991 "Statement on Haitian Boat People by Gary Rubin, AJC National Affairs Director", December 3. New York: AJC. 2 p.

Alter, Peter.
1985 *Nationalismus.* 1. Aufl. Frankfurt am Main: Suhrkamp. 179 p.

Anderson, Benedict.
1983 *Imagined Communities: Reflections on the Origin and Spread of Nationalism.* London: Verso. 160 p.

Anheier, Helmut K. and Wolfgang Seibel eds.
1990   *The Third Sector: Comparative Studies of Nonprofit Organizations.* Berlin, New York: Walter de Gruyter. 413 p.

Anheier, Helmut K. and Wolfgang Seibel.
1990a   "Sociological and Political Approaches to the Third Sector". *The Third Sector: Comparative Studies of Nonprofit Organizations.* Helmut K. Anheier and Wolfgang Seibel eds. Berlin, New York: Walter de Gruyter. p. 7 - 20.

Anheier, Helmut K. and Wolfgang Seibel.
1990b   "The Third Sector in Comparative Perspective: Four Propositions". *The Third Sector: Comparative Studies of Nonprofit Organizations.* Helmut K. Anheier and Wolfgang Seibel eds. Berlin, New York: Walter de Gruyter. p. 379 - 387.

Appadurai, Arjun.
1990   "Disjuncture and Difference in the Global Cultural Economy". *Public Culture.* Vol. 2, No. 2, Spring. p. 1 - 24.

Appadurai, Arjun.
1993   "Patriotism and Its Futures". *Public Culture.* II. p. 411 - 429.

Appleyard, Reginald T.
1991   *International Migration: Challenge for the Nineties.* Published for the 40th Anniversary of IOM. Genève: Imprimerie Genevoise. 84 p.

Aristide, Jean-Bertrand.
1996   *Dignity.* Translated by Carrol F. Coates. Charlottesville, London: University Press of Virginia. 210 p.

Aristide, Marx V. and Laurie Richardson.
1994   "The Popular Movement: Haiti's Popular Resistance". *The Haiti Files: Decoding the Crisis.* James Ridgeway ed. Washington: Essential Books. p. 64 - 71.

Aristide, Marx V. and Laurie Richardson.
1995   " Haiti's Popular Resistance". *Haiti: Dangerous Crossroads.* North American Congress on Latin America ed. Boston: South End Press. p. 181 - 194.

Aron, Raymond.
1966   *Peace and War: A Theory of International Relations.* Trans. Richard Howard and Annette Baker Fox. New York: Doubleday. 820 p.

Auerbach, Susan ed.
1996   *Encyclopedia of Multiculturalism.* 6 Vols. New York, London, Toronto: Marshall Cavendish.

Baillou, Charles.
1993   "Haitians Detained at U.S. Naval Base are Activists, Says Forum". *New York Amsterdam News*, Vol. 84, No. 6, February 06. p. 4.

Banks, Arthur S., Alan J. Day, Thomas C. Muller ed. "Haiti".
1995   *Political Handbook of the World: 1995-1996.* New York: CSA Publications. p. 391 - 397.

Basch, Linda, Nina Glick Schiller, and Cristina Szanton Blanc ed.
1994   *Nations Unbound: Transnational Projects, Postcolonial Predicaments, and Deterritorialized Nation-States.* Amsterdam: Gordon & Breach. 344 p.

Becker, Howard S. and Blanche Geer.
1970 "Participant Observation and Interviewing: A Comparison". *Qualitative Methodology*. Chicago: Markham. p. 133 - 142.

Behrens, Henning und Paul Noack.
1984 *Theorien der internationalen Politik*. München: dtv. 284 p.

Bell, Peter D.
1973 "The Ford Foundation as a Transnational Actor". *Transnational Relations and World Politics*. Robert O. Keohanne and Joseph S. Nye ed. Cambridge: Harvard University Press. p. 115 – 128.

Bellor, Kay, CWS/IRP.
1993 "Your Voice is Needed..." New York: CWS/IRP. 5 p.

Bogart, Leo.
1989 *Press and Public: Who Reads What, When, Where, and Why in American Newspapers*. 2nd ed. Hillsdale: Lawrence Erlbaum Associates. 376 p.

Bogdanor, Vernon ed.
1987 *The Blackwell Encyclopedia of Political Institutions*. Oxford, NY: Blackwell Reference.

Bragg, Rick.
1994a "Haiti´s Light-skinned Elite: The Tiny Minority Behind Aristide´s Ouster". *New York Times*, August 28. p. 14.

Bragg, Rick.
1994b "Haiti´s Elite: Resentful But Resigned". *New York Times*, September 25. p. 16.

Brenner, Michael.
1985 "Intensive Interviewing". *The Research Interview: Uses and Approaches*. London et.al.: Academic Press. p. 147 - 162.

Brooke, James.
1992 "Aristide Condemns U.S. Policy". *New York Times*, February 10. p. A8.

Brothers, Blood.
1993 "The Talk of the Town". *The New Yorker*, June 7.

Browne, J. Zamgba.
1993 "In Surprise Move, Rangel Backs Clinton´s Haiti Policy". *New York Amsterdam News*, V. 84, No. 4, January 23. p. 1.

Browne, J. Zamgba.
1994 "Rangel, Powell Spar". *New York Amsterdam News*, Vol. 85, No. 37, September 10. p. 4

Brozan, Nadine.
1992 "Chronicle: A Hunger Strike for Haitians". *New York Times*, February 12. p. B7.

Bryce-Laporte, Roy Simon.
1987 "New York City and the New Caribbean Immigration: A Contextual Statement". *Caribbean Life in New York: Sociocultural Dimensions*. New York: Center for Migration Studies. p. 45 – 73.

BRN: Big Red News, Anonymous.
1992 "Grassroots Groundswell Demands Democracy in Haiti". *Big Red News*, April 3. p 4.

Buchanan Stafford, Susan.
1987a "Language and Identity: Haitians in New York City". *Caribbean Life in New York: Sociocultural Dimensions*. New York: Center for Migration Studies. p. 202 - 217.

Buchanan Stafford, Susan.
1987b "The Haitians: The Cultural Meaning of Race and Ethnicity". *New Immigrants in New York*. Nancy Foner ed. New York: Columbia University Press. p. 131 - 158.

Bullock, Alan and Oliver Stallybrass ed.
1977 *The Harper Dictionary of Modern Thought*. New York et.al.: Harper & Row.

CA: Caribbean Action.
1992 "Firms in Haiti Struggle to Keep Economic Hopes Alive". *Caribbean Action: The Quarterly of Private-Sector- Led Development in the Caribbean Basin*. Washington: Pearson & Pearson. Published for CLAA. p. 13-16.

Carens, Joseph H.
1991 "States and Refugees: A Normative Analysis". *Refugee Policy: Canada and the United States*. Howard Adelman ed. Toronto: York Lanes Press. p. 18 - 29.

Carnegie, Charles V.
1987 "A Social Psychology of Caribbean Migrations: Strategic Flexibility in the West Indies". *The Caribbean Exodus*. Barry B. Levine ed. New York, Westport, London: Praeger. p. 32 - 43.

Castells, Manuel and John Mollenkopf.
1991 "Conclusion: Is New York a Dual City?". *Dual City: Restructuring New York*. New York: Russel Sage Foundation. p. 399 - 418.

CBC: Congressional Black Caucus.
1993 "Reaffirmation and Update of CBC Policy on Haiti". Washington, October 27. 2 p.

Challenor, Herschelle Sullivan.
1981 "The Influence of Black Americans on U.S. Foreign Policy Toward Africa". *Ethnicity and U.S. Foreign Policy*. Abdul Aziz Said ed. New York: Praeger Publishers. p. 143 - 181.

Chamberlain, Greg.
1995a "Haiti´s `Second Independence´: Aristide´s Seven Months in Office". *Haiti: Dangerous Crossroads*. North American Congress on Latin America ed. Boston: South End Press. p. 51 – 56.

Chamberlain, Greg.
1995b "Up by the Roots". *Haiti: Dangerous Crossroads*. North American Congress on Latin America ed. Boston: South End Press. p. 13 - 28.

Chaney, Elsa M.
1987 "The Context of Caribbean Migration". *Caribbean Life in New York: Sociocultural Dimensions*. New York: Center for Migration Studies. p. 3 - 14.

Charles, Carolle.
1990   *A Transnational Dialectic of Race, Class, and Ethnicity: Patterns of Identity and Forms of Consciousness Among Haitian Migrants in New York.* New York: UMI Dissertation Services. 359 p.

Charles, Carolle.
1992   "Transnationalism in the Construct of Haitian Migrant's Racial Categories of Identity in New York City". *Towards a Transnational Perspective on Migration: Race, Class, Ethnicity, and Nationalism Reconsidered.* Annals of the New York Academy. Vol. 645. New York: New York Academy. p. 101 - 123.

CHC: Coalition for Haitian Concerns.
1984   *The Haitian Drumbeat.* Willow Grove: CHC, May 15. 8 p.

Chierici, Rose-Marie Cassagnol.
1991   *Demele: "Making It": Migration and Adaptation Among Haitian Boat People in the United States.* New York: AMS Press. 333 p.

Chomsky, Noam and Edward S. Herman.
1988   *Manufacturing Consent: The Political Economy of the Mass Media.* New York: Pantheon Books.

Chomsky, Noam.
1993a   "Class Struggle as Usual". *Letters from Lexington.* Monroe: Common Courage Press. p. 149 – 159.

Chomsky, Noam.
1993b   "The Tragedy of Haiti". *Year 501: The Conquest Continues.* Boston: South End Press. p. 197 - 219.

Chomsky, Noam.
1994   "Introduction". *The Uses of Haiti.* Monroe: Common Courage Press. p 13 - 44.

Civan, Michele Burtoff.
1994   *The Haitians: Their History and Culture.* Refugee Fact Sheet Series No. 10. Washington: The Refugee Service Center. 34 p.

CLAA: Caribbean Latin American Action.
1992   *Annual Report 1991-1992.* Washington: CLAA. 19 p.

CLAA: Caribbean Latin American Action.
1993   *Annual Report 1992-1993.* Washington: CLAA. 19 p.

CLAA: Caribbean Latin American Action.
1994   *Annual Report 1993-1994.* Washington: CLAA. 19 p.

Clawson, Victoria, Elizabeth Detweiler, and Lauro Ho.
1994   "Litigating as Law Students: An Inside Look at Haitian Centers Council". *The Yale Law Journal*, Vol. 103, No. 8, June 1994. p. 2337 - 2389.

Clough, Michael.
1994   "Grass-Roots Policymaking". *Foreign Affairs.* Vol. 73, No. 1, Jan/Feb. p. 2 - 7.

Cohen, Jean L. and Andrew Arato.
1994   *Civil Society and Political Theory*. Cambridge: MIT-Press. 771 p.

Cong1: US-Congress, House. Com. on For. Af. Subcom. on Human Rights and Int. Org. and Western Hemisphere Af.
1992   *The Situation in Haiti and U.S. Policy*. Hearing, 102nd Cong., 2nd Sess., February 19. Washington: GPO. 101 p.

Cong2: US-Congress, House. Select Committee on Hunger.
1992   *Humanitarian Conditions in Haiti*. Hearing, 102nd Cong., 2nd Sess., June 11. Washington: GPO. 213 p.

Cong3: US-Congress, House. Com on Foreign Affairs. Subcoms on West. Hemisphere Affairs and Int. Operations.
1992   *U.S. Policy Toward Haitian Refugees*. Hearing, 102nd Cong., 2nd Sess., June 11 and 17. Washington: GPO. 172 p.

Cong4: US-Congress, House. Committee on the Judiciary. Subcommittee on Int. Law, Immigration, and Refugees.
1992   *Administration's Proposed Refugee Admissions Program for Fiscal Year 1993*. Hearing, 102nd Cong., 1st Sess., July 30. Washington: GPO. 194 p.

Cong5: US-Congress, House. Committee on Foreign Affairs.
1993   *Roundtable on Haiti-October 1993*. Briefing, 103rd Cong., 1st Sess., October 20. Washington: GPO. 39 p.

Cong6: US-Congress, House. Committee on the Judiciary. Subcommittee on Int. Law, Immigration and Refugees.
1994   *Haitian Asylum-Seekers*. 103d Cong., 2nd Sess. June 15. Washington: GPO. 504 p.

Constable, Pamela.
1992/93   "Dateline Haiti: Caribbean Stalemate". *Foreign Policy*, No. 89, Winter. p. 175 - 190.

Conway, Dennis and Ualthan Bigby.
1987   "Where Caribbean Peoples live in New York City". *Caribbean Life in New York: Sociocultural Dimensions*. New York: Center for Migration Studies. p. 74 - 83.

Crossette, Barbara.
1992   "2 Groups Plan Protest Against Haitian Policy". *New York Times*, August 23. p. 19.

CSIMCED: Commission for the Study of Int. Migration and Cooperative Economic Development.
1990   *Unauthorized Migration: An Economic Development Response*. Commission Report. Washington: July.

CWS: Church World Service.
1991   *Annual Report*. New York: CWS. 2 p.

CWS: Church World Service.
1993   *Annual Report*. New York: CWS. 14 p.

CWSW: Church World Service and Witness.
1993   *Annual Report*. New York: CWS. 29 p.

CWSW: Church World Service and Witness.
1994a *Annual Report*. New York: CWS. 28 p.

CWSW: Church World Service and Witness.
1994b "News Release: Interview with Elizabeth G. Ferris on Refugees, Immigration, July 13". New York: NCC. 7 p.

Daniels, George M.
1989 "The Crisis Interview: Franklin A. Thomas". *Crisis*, December, Vol. 96, No. 10. p. 20 - 23, 40.

Davidson, Roger H. and Walter J. Oleszek.
1990 *Congress and Its Members*. 3rd edition. Washington: CQ Press. 458 p.

De Witt, Karen.
1994a "Man Fasting in Haiti Protest is Hospitalized". *New York Times*, May 5. p. A5.

De Witt, Karen.
1994b "Exiles Favor Invasion but Fear for the Future". *New York Times*, September 16. p. A11.

DeConde, Alexander.
1992 *Race, Ethnichty, and American Foreign Policy: A History*. Boston: North Eastern University Press. 270 p.

Diaz-Briquets, Sergio and Sidney Weintraub ed.
1991 *Determinants of Emigration from Mexico, Central America, and the Caribbean*. Boulder, San Francisco, Oxford: Westview Press. 356 p.

Dorsinville, Paul.
1995 "A Perspective on Haitian Community Centers". New York: HAUP. 5 p.

Dowtry, A. and Gil Loescher.
1996 "Refugee Flows as Grounds for International Action". *International Security*, Vol. 21 (Summer), p. 43-71.

Dreyfuss, Joel.
1993 "The Invisible Immigrants". *New York Times*, May 23. Sec. VI, p. 20.

DuBois, W.E.B.
1989 [1903] *The Souls of Black Folk*. New York: Bantam Books.

Dunn, Ashley.
1994 "In Brooklyn, a Day of Celebration That Never Stops". *New York Times*, October 16. p. 20.

Dupuy, Alex.
1989 *Haiti in the World Economy: Class, Race, and Underdevelopment Since 1700*. Boulder. 245 p.

ECLA: Economic Commission for Latin America and the Caribbean.
1995 "Economic Trends in the Caribbean". *Economic Survey of Latin America and the Caribbean 1994-1995*. Santiago, Chile: UN. p. 115 - 241.

Evans, Peter B.
1972 "National Autonomy and Economic Development: Critical Perspectives on Multinational Corporations in Poor Countries". *Transnational Relations and World Politics*. Robert O. Keohanne and Joseph S. Nye eds. Cambridge: Harvard University Press. p. 325 - 342.

Farah, Douglas.
1992 "Aristide Denounces U.S. Moves on Haiti". *Washington Post*, February 13, p. A33,A43.

Farmer, Paul.
1992 *AIDS and Accusation: Haiti and the Geography of Blame*. Berkley, Los Angeles, London: University of California Press. 338 p.

Farmer, Paul.
1994 *The Uses of Haiti*. Monroe: Common Courage Press. 432 p.

Farmer, Paul.
1995 "The Significance of Haiti". *Haiti: Dangerous Crossroads*. North American Congress on Latin America ed. Boston: South End Press. p. 217 - 230.

Fiagome, Clemence.
1994 "Haitians Demand Federal Probe After Fourth Assassination". *Miami Times*, Vol. 71, No. 27, March 17. p. 1A.

Filstead, William J.
1970 "Introduction". *Qualitative Methodology*. William J. Filstead ed. Chicago: Markham Publishing Company. p. 1 - 11.

Fisher, Ian.
1993 "Haitians Living in New York are Digesting New Letdown", *New York Times*, November 1. p. B1,B2.

Fix, Michael and Wendy Zimmermann.
1993 *After Arrival: An Overview of Federal Immigrant Policy in the United States*. Immigrant Policy Program. Washington, D.C.: The Urban Institute. 39 p.

Foner, Nancy.
1987 "Introduction: New Immigrants and Changing Patterns in New York City". *New Immigrants in New York*. Nancy Foner ed. New York: Columbia University Press. p. 1 - 33.

Foundation1: The Foundation Center.
1994 *The Foundation 1000: In-Depth Profiles of the 1000 Largest U.S. Foundations 1994/1995*. New York: The Foundation Center. 2826 p.

Foundation2: The Foundation Center.
1994 *The Foundation Grants Index 1996: A Cumulative Listing of Foundation Grants Reported in 1994*. New York: The Foundation Center. 2266 p.

Frank, Henry.
1993 "Deposition of Henri Frank" in the Lawsuit Haitian Centers Council v. McNary at the United States District Court, Eastern District of New York, on February 8. Computer-aided Transcript provided by Tankoos Reporting Company, Inc. 182 p.

Frelick, Bill.
1993   "Haitian Boat Interdiction and Return: First Asylum and First Principles of Refugee Protection". *Cornell International Law Journal*. Vol. 26, No. 3, Symposium. p. 675 - 694.

Fremont-Smith, Marion R.
1989   "Trends in Accountability and Regulation of Nonprofits". *The Future of the Nonprofit Sector: Challenges, Changes, and Policy Considerations*. Virginia A. Hodgkinson, Richard W. Lyman ed. San Francisco, London: Jossey-Bass. p. 75 - 88.

French, Howard W.
1991   "H.I.V. Could Cut Haitian Entry to U.S". *New York Times*, December 14. p. A3.

French, Howard W.
1992a   "Land and Health Also Erode in Haiti", *New York Times*, January 28. p. A3.

French, Howard. W.
1992b   "Despite Agreement, Haitians Express Pessimism", *New York Times*, March 1. p. 12.

French, Howard. W.
1992c   "Plight of Haiti's Poor Brings Calls to Loosen the Embargo", *New York Times*, August 5. p. A3.

French, Howard W.
1992d   "Dollars from Kin in U.S. Now Sustain Haiti". *New York Times*, October 1. p. A13.

French, Howard W.
1992e   "U.S. Keeps Eye on Haiti, but Action Is Scant". *New York Times*, October 8. p. A9.

French, Howard W.
1992f   "Backers of Haitian Military Growing Nervous Over Refugees". *New York Times*, November 26. p. A10.

French, Howard. W.
1993a   "Two Rights Groups Protest Offer of an Amnesty in Haiti", *New York Times*, April 16. p. A11.

French, Howard W.
1993b   "In Haiti, a War of the Printed Word". *New York Times*, July 12, p. D/8.

French, Howard. W.
1993c   "In Haiti, a Growing Disillusionment with Clinton", *New York Times*, December 5. p. 22.

French, Howard. W.
1993d   "Haitians Bitterly Accusing Outside World of Desertion", *New York Times*, December 20. p. A15.

Friedman, Thomas L.
1991   "U.S. Suspends Assistance to Haiti and Refuses to Recognize Junta". *New York Times*, October 2. p. A1.

Fuller, Anne.
1989   *Injustice on the High Seas: U.S. Interdiction of Haitian Boat People*. New York: NCHR, March. 9 p.

Galens, Judy, Anna Sheets and Robyn V. Young.
1995   *Gale Encyclopedia of Multicultural America: Acadians - Iranian Americans*. Vol. 1. Detroit: Gale Research Inc.

Gallup, George Jr. and Frank Newport.
1991   "Large Majorities Continue to Back AIDS Testing". *The Gallup Poll Monthly*, May. p. 25 - 28.

GAO: US General Accounting Office.
1993   *Haiti: Costs of U.S. Programs and Activities Since the 1991 Military Coup*. GAO/NSIAD-93-252FS, August. 11 p.

Gerson, Louis L.
1981   "The Influence of Hyphenated Americans on U.S. Diplomacy". *Ethnicity and U.S. Foreign Policy*. Abdul Aziz Said ed. New York: Praeger Publishers. p. 19 - 31.

Gibney, Mark.
1991   "U.S. Foreign Policy and the Creation of Refugee Flows". *Refugee Policy: Canada and the United States*. H. Adelman ed. Toronto: York Lanes Press. p. 81 - 111.

Gilpin, Robert.
1972   "The Politics of Transnational Economic Relations". *Transnational Relations and World Politics*. Robert O. Keohanne and Joseph S. Nye eds. Cambridge: Harvard University Press. p. 48 - 69.

Glick Schiller, Nina and Lucie Brutus.
1986   *Directory of Organizations*. New York: Columbia University. 18 p.

Glick Schiller, Nina et.al.
1987   "All in the Same Boat?: Unity and Diversity in Haitian Organizing in New York". *Caribbean Life in New York City: Sociocultural Dimensions*. New York: Center for Migration Studies. p. 182 - 201.

Glick Schiller, Nina et.al.
1987   "Exile, Ethnic, Refugee: The Changing Organizational Identities of Haitian Immigrants". *Migration World*, Center for Migration Studies ed., Vol. XV, No. 1. p. 7 - 11.

Glick Schiller, Nina et.al.
1992   "Transnationalism: A New Analytic Framework for Understanding Migration". *Towards a Transnational Perspective on Migration: Race, Class, Ethnicity, and Nationalism Reconsidered*. Annals of the New York Academy. Vol. 645. New York: New York Academy. p. 1 - 24.

Glick Schiller, Nina.
1995   "The Implications of Haitian Transnationalism for U.S.-Haiti Relations: Contradictions of the Deterritorialized Nation-State". *Journal of Haitian Studies*. Vol. 1, No. 1, Spring. p. 111 – 123.

GMP: Gallup Monthly Poll, Anonymous.
1991   "AIDS: Fear of Contracting, Acquaintance With Victims". *The Gallup Poll Monthly*, September. p. 72.

GMP: Gallup Monthly Poll, Anonymous.
1992   "Post-Convention `Bounce´: Clinton´s Highest in Gallup Records". *The Gallup Poll Monthly*, August. p. 25.

Gonzalez, David.
1991   "Upside-Down Lives for New York Haitians". *New York Times*, October 7, p. B1,5.

Gorman, Robert F.
1991   "U.S. Overseas Refugee Assistance". *Refugee Policy: Canada and the United States*. H. Adelman ed. Toronto. p. 118 - 142.

GPP: Garret Park Press.
1992   *Minority Organizations. A National Directory*. 4th edition. Garret Park: Garret Park Press.

Gramsci, Antonio.
1971   *Selections from the Prison Notebooks*. Ed. and trans. by Q. Hoare and G.N. Smith. New York: International Publishers.

Grasmuck, Sherri and Patricia R. Pessar.
1991   *Between Two Islands: Dominican International Migration*. Berkley, Los Angeles, Oxford: University of California Press. 247 p.

Gray, Jerry.
1991   "Haitian´s Visit to New York Is a Celebration". *New York Times*, September 29. p. A6.

Gray, William.
1994   *U.S. Policy Toward Haiti*. Hearing of the House Foreign Affairs Committee. Testimony by the Special Adviser to the President and the Secretary of State. Washington: Federal Information Systems Corporation. June 8. 9 p.

Greenhouse, Steven.
1993   "Aristide Organizes Haiti Conference". *New York Times*, December 24. p. A3.

Griffin, Clifford E.
1992   "Haiti's Democratic Challenge". *Third World Quarterly*, Vol. 13, No. 4. p. 663 - 673.

Gruyson, Lindsey.
1991   "Haitian Refugees in Cuba Will Get Gifts a Day Late". *New York Times*, December 25, p. I/34.

Guest, Ian.
1993   *Repression in Haiti: A Challenge for Multilateralism*. Washington: Refugee Policy Group. 35 p.

Guyther, Mary Beth.
1993   "Assistance for Haitian Immigrants". *New York Times*, April 18. p. 2.

Haiti1: Anonymous.
1991   "Parish to Parish Exchange links Americans, Haitians". *HaitiInsight*, Vol. 3, No. 3, July/August. p. 6.

Haiti2: Anonymous.
1991   "Human Rights Activist Honored". *HaitiInsight*, Vol. 3, No. 4, September. p. 5.

Haiti3a: Amy Wilentz.
1991 "Coup d'Etat in Haiti". *HaitiInsight*, Vol. 3, No. 5, October. p. 1,6.

Haiti3b: Anonymous.
1991 "Calendar and Resources for Action". *HaitiInsight*, Vol. 3, No. 5, October. p. 7.

Haiti4: Anonymous.
1991 "You Can Help!". *HaitiInsight*, Vol. 3, No. 6, Winter. p. 6.

Haiti5: Anonymous.
1992 "Calendar and Resources for Action". *HaitiInsight*, Vol. 3, No. 7, March/April. p. 11.

Haiti6: Anonymous.
1992 "Calendar and Resources for Action". *HaitiInsight*, Vol. 4, No. 3, Fall. p. 12.

Haiti7: Anonymous.
1994 "Haiti Film to Premiere at Festival". *HaitiInsight*, Vol. 5, No. 2, April. p. 5.

Haiti8a: Anonymous.
1992 "Haiti´s Agony Continues". *HaitiInsight*, Vol. 4, No. 3, Fall. p. 3,14.

Haiti8b: Anonymous.
1992 "Last Hope Legislative Efforts Under Bush Administration Fail". *HaitiInsight*, Vol. 4, No. 3, Fall. p. 4,13.

Haiti9: Netlyn Bernard Samedy.
1997 "Haitians Launch Organizing Drive". *HaitiInsight*, Vol. 7, No. 2, Dec/Jan. p. 1,6.

Hakovirta, Harto.
1986 *Third World Conflicts and Refugeeism: Dimensions, Dynamics and Trends of the World Refugee Problem*. Helsinki: Commentationes Scientiarum Socialium 32. 160 p.

Hammersley, Martyn.
1990 *Reading Ethnographic Research: A Critical Guide*. London, New York: Longman. 172 p.

Han, Henry H.
1987 *Problems and Prospects of the Organization of American States: Perceptions of the Members States´s Leaders*. New York: Peter Lang. 528 p.

Harvey, David.
1994 "Klassenbeziehungen, soziale Gerechtigkeit und die Politik der Differenz". *Multikulturelle Gesellschaft: Modell Amerika*. Berndt Ostendorf ed. München: Fink. p. 205 - 227.

HAUP: Haitian Americans United For Progress.
1986 "A Description of the Purposes, Programs and Projected Needs of the Haitian Americans United For Progress, Inc. (HAUP)". New York: HAUP. 2 p.

HCC: Haitian Centers Council.
1994 Application Narrative of a "Community and Family Strengthening Grant under the Office of Refugee Resettlement´s Fiscal Year 1994 Omnibus Discretionary Social Services Grants Program for Services to Refugees". New York: HCC. 14 p.

HCC: Haitian Centers Council.
1995 "Service List". New York: HCC. 1 p.

Heinl, Robert and Nancy Heinl.
1978   *Written in Blood*. Boston: Houghton Mifflin Co. p.

Hernandez, Raymond.
1993   "Haitians in U.S. Hopeful", *New York Times*, July 5. p. A4.

Hirst, Paul.
1994   *Associative Democracy: New Forms of Economic and Social Governance*. Amherst: The University of Massachusetts Press. 222 p.

Hobsbawm, Eric J.
1990   *Nations and Nationalism Since 1780: Programme, Myth, Reality*. Cambridge: Cambridge University Press. 191 p.

Hodgkinson, Virginia A.
1989   "Key Challenges Facing the Nonprofit Sector". *The Future of the Nonprofit Sector: Challenges, Changes, and Policy Considerations*. Virginia A. Hodgkinson, Richard W. Lyman ed. San Francisco, London: Jossey-Bass. p. 3 -19.

Hoggart, Richard ed.
1993   *Oxford Illustrated Encyclopedia: Peoples and Cultures*. Vol. 7. Oxford, NY: Oxford University Press.

Holmes, Steven A.
1993a   "Exile Haitian rebuffs diplomat". *New York Times*, December 22. p. A5.

Holmes, Steven.
1993b   "Presure Builds Over Return of Boat People to Haiti". *New York Times*, December 17. p. A17.

Hooper, Michael S.
1995   "The Monkey's Tail Still Strong". *Haiti: Dangerous Crossroads*. North American Congress on Latin America ed. Boston: South End Press. p. 161 - 173.

HRC: Haitian Refugee Center.
1995   "Update: Haitian Refugee Center". Miami: HRC, February. 2 p.

HRW/A,NCHR: Human Rights Watch/Americas, National Coalition for Haitian Refugees.
1992   *Half the Story: The Skewed US Monitoring of Repatriated Haitian Refugees*. Vol. 4, Issue 4. June 30. 16 p.

HRW/A,NCHR: Human Rights Watch/Americas, National Coalition for Haitian Refugees.
1993   *Silencing a People: The Destruction of Civil Society in Haiti*. February. 136 p.

HRW/A,NCHR: Human Rights Watch/Americas, National Coalition for Haitian Refugees.
1994a   *Haiti: Terror Prevails in Haiti: Human Rights Violations and Failed Diplomacy*. Vol. VI, No. 5. April. 52 p.

HRW/A,NCHR: Human Rights Watch/Americas, National Coalition for Haitian Refugees.
1994b   *Rape in Haiti: A Weapon of Terror*. Vol. VI, No. 8. July. 28 p.

HRW/A,NCHR: Human Rights Watch/Americas, National Coalition for Haitian Refugees.
1995   *Haiti: Security Compromised, Recycled Haitian Soldiers on the Police Front Line*. Vol. 7, No. 4. March. 27 p.

HRW/A,NCHR,CR: Human Rights Watch/Americas, National Coalition for Haitian Refugees, Caribbean Rights.
1991   *Haiti: The Aristide Government's Human Rights Record.* Vol. III, No. 12. November 1. 36 p.

HRW/A,NCHR,JRS: Human Rights Watch/A., National Coalition for Haitian Refugees, Jesuit Refugee Service/USA.
1993   *No Port in a Storm: The Misguided Use of In-Country Refugee Processing in Haiti.* Vol. 5, Issue 8. September. 38 p.

HRW/A,NCHR,JRS: Human Rights Watch/A., National Coalition for Haitian Refugees, Jesuit Refugee Service/USA.
1994   *Fugitives from Injustice: The Crisis of Internal Displacement in Haiti.* Vol. VI, No. 10. August. 31 p.

HRW/A,NCHR,PHR: Human Rights Watch/Am., National Coalition for Haitian Refugees, Physicians for Human Rights.
1991   *Return to the Darkest Days: Human Rights in Haiti Since the Coup.* New York: December. 20 p.

HRW: Human Rights Watch.
1993   *Annual Report.* New York: HRW. 21 p.

Hugick, Larry.
1991   "Democrats Gain on Bush in 1992 Test Election". *The Gallup Poll Monthly,* November. p. 5 - 6.

Hugick, Larry.
1992a   "Immigrants Less Welcome in 1990s America". *The Gallup Poll Monthly,* March. p. 5 - 6.

Hugick, Larry.
1992b   "1992 Presidential Campaign". *The Gallup Poll Monthly,* April. p. 2 - 18.

HWHR: Haitian Women for Haitian Refugees.
1995   "Background Information". New York: HWHR. 2 p.

HWP: Haitian Women's Program.
1995   "Haitian Women's Program, Inc".. Brooklyn: HWP. 2 p.

INS: US Immigration and Naturalization Service.
1992   *1991 Statistical Yearbook of the Immigration and Naturalization Service.* Washington: US Government Printing Office. 169 p.

INS: US Immigration and Naturalization Service.
1993   *1992 Statistical Yearbook of the Immigration and Naturalization Service.* Washington: US Government Printing Office. 180 p.

INS: US Immigration and Naturalization Service.
1994   *1993 Statistical Yearbook of the Immigration and Naturalization Service.* Washington: US Government Printing Office. 183 p.

Ives, Kim.
1995a   "Haiti's Second U.S. Occupation". *Haiti: Dangerous Crossroads.* North American Congress on Latin America ed. Boston: South End Press. p. 107 - 118.

Ives, Kim.
1995b "The Lavalas Alliance Propels Aristide to Power". *Haiti: Dangerous Crossroads*. North American Congress on Latin America ed. Boston: South End Press. p. 41 - 45.

Ives, Kim.
1995c "The Unmaking of a President". *Haiti: Dangerous Crossroads*. North American Congress on Latin America ed. Boston: South End Press. p. 65 - 87.

James, C.L.R.
1989 [1963] *The Black Jacobins: Toussaint L'Ouverture and the San Domingo Revolution*. New York: Vintage Books. 426 p.

Jean-Pierre, Jean.
1995 "The 10th Department". *Haiti: Dangerous Crossroads*. North American Congress on Latin America ed. Boston: South End Press. p. 195 - 204.

JLC: Jewish Labor Committee.
1991 "Letter to President George Bush from JLC's President, Lenore Miller", December 20. New York: JLC. 1 p.

JLC: Jewish Labor Committee.
1995 "Letter to Author from Arieh Lebowitz, JLC Program Associate", March 8. 2 p.

Kamen, Al and John M. Goshko.
1992a "U.S. Plans to Ease Embargo on Haiti". *Washington Post*, February 5, p. A1,A26.

Kamen, Al and John M. Goshko.
1992b "U.S. Eased Haiti Embargo Under Business Pressure". *Washington Post*, February 7, p. A1,A11.

Kamins, Toni L.
1994 "Two Guantanamo Graduates: One Year Later". *HaitiInsight*, Vol. 5, No. 5, Summer. p. 3,6.

Kasinitz, Philip.
1992 *Caribbean New York: Black Immigrants and the Politics of Race*. Ithaca: Cornell University Press. 280 p.

Keohanne, Robert O. and Joseph S. Nye.
1972 *Transnational Relations and World Politics*. Cambridge: Harvard University Press. 399 p.

Kifner, John.
1993 "For New York Haitians, Hopes are Deflated", *New York Times*, October 17. p. 14.

Kimminich , Otto.
1994 "Minderheiten, Volksgruppen, Ethnizität und Recht". *Das Manifest der 60: Deutschland und die Einwanderung*. Klaus J. Bade ed. München: Beck. p. 180 - 197.

Knight, Franklin W.
1990 *The Caribbean: The Genesis of a Fragmented Nationalism*. 2nd edition. New York: Oxford University Press. 389 p.

Koh, Harold Hongju.
1994 "The `Haiti Paradigm' in United States Human Rights Policy". *The Yale Law Journal*, Vol. 103, No. 8, June. p. 2391 - 2435.

Kraly, Ellen Percy.
1987 "U.S. Immigration Policy and the Immigrant Populations of New York". *New Immigrants in New York*. Nancy Foner ed. New York: Columbia University Press. p. 35 - 78.

Krause, Lawrence.
1972 "Private International Finance". *Transnational Relations and World Politics*. Robert O. Keohanne and Joseph S. Nye eds. Cambridge: Harvard University Press. p. 173 - 190.

Kritz, Mary M., Lin Lean Lim and Hania Zlotnik ed.
1992 *International Migration Systems: A Global Approach*. Oxford: Clarendon Press.

Laguerre, Michel S.
1984 *American Odyssey: Haitians in New York*. Ithaca: Cornell University Press. 198 p.

Larose, Serge.
1984 "Transnationalité et résaux migratoires: entre le Québec, les Etats-Unis et Haiti". *Cahiers de Recherches Sociologiques*. Montréal: 2,2. p. 115 - 138.

Lawless, Robert
1992 *Haiti's Bad Press: Origins, Development and Consequences*. Rochester, Vermont: Schenkman Books. 261 p.

LCHR: Lawyers Committee for Human Rights.
1990a *Paper Laws, Steel Bayonets: The Breakdown of the Rule of Law in Haiti*. New York: LCHR. 215 p.

LCHR: Lawyers Committee for Human Rights.
1990b *Refugee Nonrefoulement: The Forced Return of Haitians under the U.S.-Haitian Interdiction Agreement*. New York: LCHR. 63 p.

LCHR: Lawyers Committee for Human Rights.
1993 *Annual Report*. New York: LCHR. 29 p.

Lee, Gary and Molly Sinclair.
1992 "Refugee Policy Protested: 95 Supporters of Haitians Arrested Outside White House". *Washington Post*, September 10. p. A9.

Levine, Barry B. ed.
1987 *The Caribbean Exodus*. New York, Westport, London: Praeger. 293 p.

Lewis, Paul.
1992 "Ousted Haitian Chief, at U.N., Denounces Vatican". *New York Times*, September 30. p. A8.

LIRS: Lutheran Immigration and Refugee Service
199? Undated LIRS Brochure Informing on the Voluntary Agency, written by Lily R. Wu.

Loescher, Gil.
1991 "Mass Migration as a Global Security Problem". *1991 World Refugee Survey*. Washington, D.C.: The U.S. Committee For Refugees. p. 7 - 14.

Lorch, Donatella.
1991 "Adulation Turns to Anger as U.S. Haitians Grieve". *New York Times*, October 2. p. A12.

Malone, David.
1996 "The Security Council and the Future of UN Peace-Keeping". *Oxford International Review*, Spring, Vol. VII, No. 2. p. 23 - 29.

Malone, David.
1997 "Haiti and the International Community: A Case Study". *The HHS Quarterly*, Summer. p. 126 - 146.

Marshall, Dawn.
1987 "A History of West Indian Migrations: Overseas Opportunities and `Safety Valve´ Policies". *The Caribbean Exodus*. Barry B. Levine ed. New York, Westport, London: Praeger. p. 15 – 31.

Martin, David A.
1991 "The Refugee Concept: On Definitions, Politics, and the Careful Use of a Scarce Resource". *Refugee Policy: Canada and the United States*. Howard Adelman ed. Toronto: York Lanes Press. p. 30 - 51.

Martin, Ian.
1995 "Haiti: Mangled Multilateralism", *Foreign Policy*, No. 95, Summer. p. 72 - 89.

Masland, Tom et.al.
1994 "How Did We Get Here?: The Inside Story of How President Clinton Stumbled into a Messy Showdown that Nobody Really Wanted". *Newsweek*, September 26. p. 26 - 33.

McAneny, Leslie.
1992 "Huge Majority Backs Shift from International to Domestic Agenda". *The Gallup Poll Monthly*, January. p.12.

McAneny, Leslie.
1994 "Ethnic Minorities View the Media´s View of Them": *The Gallup Poll Monthly Report*, No. 347, August. p. 31 - 41.

McClure, Marian.
1986 *The Catholic Church and Rural Change: Priests, Peasant Organizations, and Politics in Haiti*. Cambridge: Harvard University Press.

McHugh, Lois.
1990 "Refugees in U.S. Foreign Policy". *CRS Issue Brief*. Washington, D.C.: The Library of Congress. 19 p.

McKinney, Cynthia.
1994 "For Immediate Release: Congresswoman Cynthia McKinney Praises Haitian Education Campaign and Calls for Interdiction Legislation". Washington: February 24. 1 p.

Merida, Kevin.
1994 "Obey Calls for Invasion To Ouster Haiti´s Rulers". *Washington Post*, April 15, p. A7.

Miller, David ed.
1987 *The Blackwell Encyclopedia of Political Thought*. Oxford, NY: Blackwell Reference.

Mintz, Sidney W.
1995 "Can Haiti Change?". *Foreign Affairs*. Vol. 74, No. 1, January/February. p. 74- 86.

MIS/MIN: Member Information Service / Member Information Network.
1992   Entry for "House Concurrent Resolution 220", introduced by Hon. Charles B. Rangel on October 11, and entries for other Haiti-related legislation.

Miyoshi, Masao.
1993   "A Borderless World? From Colonialism to Transnationalism and the Decline of the Nation-State". *Critical Inquiry*, Summer. p. 726 - 751.

Moore, David W.
1993   "Americans Feel Threatened By New Immigrants". *The Gallup Poll Monthly*, July. p. 2 - 16.

Moore, David W.
1994   "Public Unfazed By CIA Spy Scandal". *The Gallup Poll Monthly*, March. p. 17, 20.

Morrell, James.
1993   "The Governors Island Accord on Haiti", *International Policy Report*, September. 11 p.

Morrell, James.
1995a   "A commentary by James Morrell, Research Director of the Center for International Policy". *CBS News, "60 Minutes"*. Transcript of the Interview on CIP´s Web Page. December 3.

Morrell, James.
1995b   "Haiti Success Under Fire". *International Policy Report*. Washington: CIP. January. 7 p.

Morse, Edward L.
1972   "Transnational Economic Processes". *Transnational Relations and World Politics*. Robert O. Keohanne and Joseph S. Nye eds. Cambridge: Harvard University Press. p. 23 - 47.

NAACP: National Association for the Advancement of Colored People.
1992a   "NAACP News: NAACP Visits Haitian Refugee Camp, Renews Call for Protective Status". Baltimore: NAACP, January 30. 2 p.

NAACP: National Association for the Advancement of Colored People.
1992b   "More than 1,000 Participants in Haitian Demonstration, 70 Arrested". Baltimore: NAACP, Sept. 11. 4 p.

NAACP: National Association for the Advancement of Colored People.
1993   "NAACP News: NAACP Supports Sanctions on Haitian Dictotarship; Calls for New US Policy in the Caribbean". Baltimore: NAACP, October 15. 3 p.

NAACP: National Association for the Advancement of Colored People.
1994   "NAACP News: NAACP Endorses U.S. Accord with Haitian Military: Praises Diplomacy of Carter, Powell and Nunn". Baltimore: NAACP, September 22. 3 p.

NCC/CLAO: National Council of Churches Caribbean and Latin America Office.
1992   "Report of an NCC Delegaiton to Haiti, August 27-31". New York: NCC. 7 p.

NCHR1: National Coalition for Haitian Refugees.
1982   "NCHR Yearbook, File 1982". New York: NCHR. 19 p.

NCHR2: National Coalition for Haitian Refugees.
1991   "Composition of Task Force". New York: NCHR. 2 p.

NCHR3: National Coalition for Haitian Refugees.
1991 "Minutes of Board Meeting, December 4, 1991". New York: NCHR. 6 p.

NCHR4: National Coalition for Haitian Refugees.
1991 "NCHR Yearbook, File 1991". New York: NCHR. 72 p.

NCHR5: National Coalition for Haitian Refugees.
1991 "Report On Program Activities During 1991". New York: NCHR. 19 p.

NCHR6: National Coalition for Haitian Refugees.
1992 "1992 Annual Report". New York: NCHR. 4 p.

NCHR7: National Coalition for Haitian Refugees.
1992 "Draft Policy Proposals for Wednesday's Conference Call Part I". New York: NCHR. 7 p.

NCHR8a: National Coalition for Haitian Refugees.
1992 "Jocelyn McCalla Proposal, NCHR: Draft Policy Proposals for Wednesday's Conference Call Part II". New York: NCHR. 3 p.

NCHR8b: National Coalition for Haitian Refugees.
1992 "LIRS Discussion Paper: Draft Policy Proposals for Wednesday's Conference Call Part II". New York: NCHR. 4 p.

NCHR9: National Coalition for Haitian Refugees.
1992 "Draft Policy Proposals for Wednesday's Conference Call Part III". New York: NCHR. 8 p.

NCHR10: National Coalition for Haitian Refugees.
1992 "Draft Policy Proposals for Wednesday's Conference Call Part IV". New York: NCHR. 6 p.

NCHR11: National Coalition for Haitian Refugees.
1992 "Minutes of Board Meeting, July 13, 1992". New York: NCHR. 7 p.

NCHR12: National Coalition for Haitian Refugees.
1992 "NCHR Yearbook, File 1992". New York: NCHR. 117 p.

NCHR13: National Coalition for Haitian Refugees.
1992 "Report on NCHR Activities over the Past Five Months, July 9, 1992". New York: NCHR. 4 p.

NCHR14: National Coalition for Haitian Refugees.
1993 "Haiti Human Rights Program Activities in 1993". New York: NCHR. 5 p.

NCHR15: National Coalition for Haitian Refugees.
1993 "Haiti / United States Relations in 1993: A Chronology of Political Events regarding Haiti During the First Year of the Clinton Presidency". New York: NCHR. 4 p.

NCHR16: National Coalition for Haitian Refugees.
1993 "Minutes of Board Meeting July 13, 1993". New York: NCHR. 7 p.

NCHR17: National Coalition for Haitian Refugees.
1993 "NCHR Yearbook, File 1993". New York: NCHR. 47 p.

NCHR18: National Coalition for Haitian Refugees.
1993 "Public Appearances and Advocacy by Staff in 1993". New York: NCHR. 5 p.

NCHR19: National Coalition for Haitian Refugees.
1993   "Refugee Advocacy Program Activities in 1993". New York: NCHR. 9 p.

NCHR20: National Coalition for Haitian Refugees.
1993   "Report of the Executive Director". New York: NCHR. 4 p.

NCHR21: National Coalition for Haitian Refugees.
1993   "Report of the Planning Committee". New York: NCHR. 8 p.

NCHR22: National Coalition for Haitian Refugees.
1994   "Agenda of Board Meeting January 14, 1994". New York: NCHR. 3 p.

NCHR23: National Coalition for Haitian Refugees.
1994   "NCHR Yearbook, File 1994". New York: NCHR. 57 p.

NCHR24: National Coalition for Haitian Refugees.
1994   "Report to the Board of Directors on NCHR Activities in 1994". New York: NCHR. 8 p.

NCHR25: National Coalition for Haitian Refugees.
1994   "Report to Board of Refugee Advocacy Campaign in Past 3 Months". New York: NCHR. 3 p.

NCHR26: National Coalition for Haitian Refugees.
1994   "Public Appearances, Media Outreach and Other Advocacy by Staff in 1994". New York: NCHR. 13 p.

NCHR27: National Coalition for Haitian Refugees.
1992   "Policy Position Paper on Issues Surrounding Protection of Haitian Refugeees: Letter to Clinton", December 1. New York: NCHR. 4 p.

NCHR28: National Coalition for Haitian Refugees et.al.
1994   "Letter of Nine Human Rights Organizations in the US to Clinton", April 20. 3 p.

NECLC: National Emergency Civil Liberties Committee.
199?   Undated Brochure entitled "In Defense of Freedom: The Work of the National Emergency Civil Liberties Committee". New York: NECLC. 2 p.

Newport, Frank.
1993   "Miami Supplants New York As Most Dangerous City". *The Gallup Poll Monthly*, September. p. 2.

Newport, Frank and Leslie McAnney.
1994   "Haiti Yields Clinton Small `Rally Effect'". *The Gallup Poll Monthly*, September. p. 18 - 19.

Newport, Frank and Lydia Saad.
1994   "Confidence in Institutions". *The Gallup Poll Monthly*, April. p. 5 - 6.

Newport, Frank and Lydia Saad.
1994   "After Clinton Speech: Public Shifts in Favor of Haiti Invasion". *The Gallup Poll Monthly*, September. p. 16 - 17.

NIF: National Immigration Forum.
1995   "The National Immigration Forum: Mission, Priorities". Washington: NIF. 1 p.

NLC: National Labor Committee.
1994 "Sweatshop Development". *The Haiti Files: Decoding the Crisis.* James Ridgeway ed. Washington: Essential Books. p. 134 - 154.

North, David S.
1994 *Using the Resources of the Diaspora to Build the New Haiti.* Arlington: New TransCentury Foundation. 45 p.

Norton, Anne-Lucie ed.
1994 *The Hutchinson Dictionary of Ideas.* Santa Barbara et.al.: ABC-CLIO.

NYT: Anonymous.
1992 "Restore Democracy to Haiti", *New York Times*, March 3. p. A11.

NYT: Anonymous.
1992 "Haitian Americans Demonstrate in Times Square". *New York Times*, April 7. p. B6.

NYT: Anonymous.
1993 "Haitians Express Relief", *New York Times*, August 28. p. A2.

NYT: Anonymous.
1993 "Embargo Adds to Old Woes", *New York Times*, October 18. p. A6.

NYT: Anonymous.
1993 "Haitian Radio Host, Backer of Aristide, is Killed in Miami". *New York Times*, October 26, p. A13.

NYT: Anonymous.
1994 "Haitian Exile Figure Shot to Death in the 3rd Such Attack Since 1991", *New York Times*, March 11. p. A18.

NYT: Anonymous.
1994 "Opponents of Policy on Haiti Begin Fast". *New York Times*, April 13. p. A15.

NYT: Anonymous.
1994 "Haitians march in New York", *New York Times*, October 5. p. A17.

NYWF: New York Women´s Foundation.
1993 "Grantee Profiles: Haitian Women for Haitian Refugees". New York: NYWF. 1 p.

Ogata, Sadako.
1997 "Geleitwort". *Der Globale Marsch: Flucht und Migration als Weltproblem.* Peter J. Opitz ed. München: Beck. p. 7 - 9.

Ogene, Chidozie F.
1983 *Interest Groups and the Shaping of Foreign Policy.* New York: St. Martin´s Press. 224 p.

Opitz, Götz-Dietrich.
1992 "'Papiergesetze und Stahlbayonette': Zur Situation der Flüchtlinge aus Haiti". Washington: March. Unpublished Manuscript.

Opitz, Götz-Dietrich.
1992 "Staff Briefing with Claudette Werleigh on Thursday, February 13, 1992, 10:00 to 12:00, room 1310 Longworth HOB". Memo to CBR, February 11. 2. p.

Opitz, Götz-Dietrich.
1993a "Die Unfreiwillige Nationalität". *Die Woche*, 8. Juli. p. 19.

Opitz, Götz-Dietrich.
1993b *Manifest Destiny im Kalten Krieg: Die Inaugurationsreden US-amerikanischer Präsidenten im Spiegel des rhetorischen Millennialismus.* Frankfurt/Main: Peter Lang. 274 p.

Opitz, Götz-Dietrich.
1994 "Dissertation Research Proposal". Unpublished Manuscript. München, April. 12 p.

Opitz, Götz-Dietrich.
1995 "Research Interim Report". Unpublished Manuscript. Brooklyn, January. 8 p.

Opitz, Götz-Dietrich.
1995 "Research Final Report". Unpublished Manuscript. München, August. 34 p.

Opitz, Götz-Dietrich.
1999 *The Haitian Refugee Crisis, 1991 - 1994: Transnationalism and State Politics.* Mikroedition. Marburg: Tectum. 427 p.

Opitz, Peter J. ed.
1997 *Der Globale Marsch: Flucht und Migration als Weltproblem.* München: Beck. 345 p.

Orenstein, Catherine.
1995a "An Interview with Ben Dupuy". *Haiti: Dangerous Crossroads*. North American Congress on Latin America ed. Boston: South End Press. p. 95 - 101.

Orenstein, Catherine.
1995b "Haiti in the Mainstream Press". *Haiti: Dangerous Crossroads*. NACLA ed. Boston: South End Press. p. 103 - 105.

ORR: Office of Refugee Resettlement.
1992/93 *Report to Congress.* U.S. Department of Health and Human Services. Washington, D.C.: Government 1994/95 Printing Office. 64 p.

Ostendorf, Berndt.
1992 *The Costs of Multiculturalism.* J. F. Kennedy Institut, Working Paper No. 50. Berlin: 1992. 30 p.

Osuna, Juan P. and Christine M. Hanson.
1993 "U.S. Refugee Policy: Where We've Been, Where We're Going". *World Refugee Survey.* Washington: USCR. p. 40 - 48.

Owens, Major R.
1994 "Memorandum: Recommendations for New Strategies and Actions on Haiti". Washington, March 17. 2 p.

Palmer, Ransford W. ed.
1990 *In Search for a Better Life: Perspectives on Migration from the Caribbean.* New York et al.: Praeger.

Palmer, Ransford W.
1995 *Pilgrims From the Sun: West Indian Migration to America.* London et.al.: Twayne Publishers. 101 p.

Pastor, Robert A. ed.
1985   *Migration and Development in the Caribbean: The Unexplored Connection.* Boulder, London: Westview Press. 443 p.

Pastor, Robert A.
1991   "Haiti Is Not Alone". *New York Times*, October 4. p. A31.

Peek, Peter and Guy Standing ed.
1982   *State Policies and Migration: Studies in Latin America and the Caribbean.* London, Canberra: Croom Helm. 403 p.

Pierre-Pierre, Garry.
1993a   "Haitian Refugees Find Welcome Wears Thin". *New York Times*, March 6. p. 26.

Pierre-Pierre, Garry.
1993b   "Émigrés are Holding off on Their Hopes for Haiti", *New York Times*, June 14. p. B3.

Pierre-Pierre, Garry.
1993c   "In Brooklyn, Guarded Optimism", *New York Times*, July 3. p. A2.

Pierre-Pierre, Garry.
1993d   "A Long Wait for a New Life Is Not Quite Over". *New York Times*, Juli 16. p. B1,B3.

Pierre-Pierre, Garry.
1993e   "For Haitian Immigrants, Radio Remains a Passion". *New York Times*, August 20, p. B3.

Pierre-Pierre, Garry.
1993f   "One More Shortage in Haiti: News". *New York Times*, October 19, p. A18.

Pierre-Pierre, Garry.
1994a   "In New York, Haitians Are Skeptical". *New York Times*, May 10. p. A3.

Pierre-Pierre, Garry.
1994b   "New York Haitians Split Over Use of Force". *New York Times*, August 2. p. A3.

Pierre-Pierre, Garry.
1994c   "New York Haitians Ambivalent Over Force". *New York Times*, September 17. p. A8.

Pierre-Pierre, Garry
1994d   "Double Role for Haitian-Americans", *New York Times*, October 13. p. A8.

Plummer, Brenda Gayle.
1992   *Haiti and the United States: The Psychological Moment.* Athens, London: University of Georgia Press. 303 p.

Powell, Cathy.
1993   "'Life' at Guantánamo: The Wrongful Detention of Haitian Refugees". *Reconstruction*, Vol. 2, No. 2. p. 58 - 68.

Preeg, Ernest H.
1985   "Migration and Development in Hispaniola". *Migration and Development in the Caribbean: The Unexplored Connection.* Robert A. Pastor ed. Boulder, London: Westview Press. p. 140 – 156.

Quindlen, Anna.
1993   "A Death Watch". *New York Times*, May 30. p. 4/11

Quixote Center / Quest for Peace.
1992   "Restore Democracy in Haiti, Welcome Haitian Refugees". *New York Times*, March 16. Paid Advertisement. p. B6.

Rangel, Charles B.
1993a "Press Release: Rangel Calls For U.N. Intervention in Haiti Crisis". Washington: CBR. October 14. 1 p.

Rangel, Charles B.
1993b "Press Release: Rangel Says CIA Undermines Clinton Policy in Haiti". Washington: CBR. October 27. 1 p.

Rangel, Charles B.
1994   "Press Release: Charles Rangel Calls For Multilateral Military Intervention in Haiti". Washington: CBR, July 13. 1 p.

Rangel91a: Folder "Support" with copies of Hon. Rangel's correspondence between 1991 and 1994.
1991   "Haiti/Cardinal O'Connor Meeting", Memo to CBR, 12/20/91. 1 p.

Rangel91b: Folder "Support" with copies of Hon. Rangel's correspondence between 1991 and 1994.
1991   "Letter from Ramsey Clark to Rangel", November 11. 2 p.

Rangel91c: Folder "Support" with copies of Hon. Rangel's correspondence between 1991 and 1994.
1991   "HAITI TALKING POINTS, White House / OAS Rally, 12/13/91". Washington. 7 p.

Rangel91d: Folder "Support" with copies of Hon. Rangel's correspondence between 1991 and 1994.
1991   "Press Release by Benjamin F. Chavis, Jr. of the Commission for Racial Justice at the United Church of Christ: U.S. Hypocracy and Racism Toward Haitian Refugees". Cleveland: UCC, December 9. 1 p.

Rangel91e: Folder "Support" with copies of Hon. Rangel's correspondence between 1991 and 1994.
1991   "Forced Return of Haitian Refugees Condemned". New York: CWS, November 20. 1 p.

Rangel91f: Folder "Support" with copies of Hon. Rangel's correspondence between 1991 and 1994.
1991   "Letter of Roger P. Winter, Director of the United States Committee For Refugees, to Bush". Washington: USCR, November 19. 1 p.

Rangel91g: Folder "Support" with copies of Hon. Rangel's correspondence between 1991 and 1994.
1991   "Letter by Mark Handelman, Executive Vice President of the New York Association For New Americans, to Speaker Thomas Foley: Urgent Action Needed to Protect Haitian Refugees". New York: CWS, November 26. 1 p.

Rangel91h: Folder "Support" with copies of Hon. Rangel's correspondence between 1991 and 1994.
1991   "Campaign for Peace and Democracy: Human Rights Delegation to Visit Haitian and U.S. Missions to U.N". New York: CPD, November 26. 3 p.

Rangel91j: Folder "Support" with copies of Hon. Rangel's correspondence between 1991 and 1994.
1991   "Memo to CBR from Emile: Haiti / Suggestion for Talk with Scowcroft", October 03. 2 p.

Rangel92a: Folder "Support" with copies of Hon. Rangel's correspondence between 1991 and 1994.
1992   "Letter by H.E.A.D.D. for Haiti to Rangel", December 7. 2 p.

Rangel92b: Folder "Support" with copies of Hon. Rangel's correspondence between 1991 and 1994.
1992   "National Haitian Lobbying Network: Memo from Gotz D. Opitz to CBR". Washington: April 22. 3 p.

Rangel92c: Folder "Support" with copies of Hon. Rangel's correspondence between 1991 and 1994.
1992   "Resolution of the Executive Committee of the Council of the Diocese of New York of the Episcopal Church Regarding Haitian Refugees". New York: February 4. 1 p.

Rangel92d: Folder "Support" with copies of Hon. Rangel's correspondence between 1991 and 1994.
1992   "Church Leaders Urge Bush to End Forced Repatriation of Haitians". Cleveland: UCC, February 10. 3 p.

Rangel92e: Folder "Support" with copies of Hon. Rangel's correspondence between 1991 and 1994.
1992   "Letter of the New York Immigration Coalition to Rangel". New York: NYIC, January 29. 2 p.

Rangel92f: Folder "Support" with copies of Hon. Rangel's correspondence between 1991 and 1994.
1992   "Joint Dear Colleague-Letter of NAACP and TranasAfrica on September 9 protest". Baltimore, Washington: July 10. 1 p.

Rangel92g: Folder "Support" with copies of Hon. Rangel's correspondence between 1991 and 1994.
1992   "Invitation of December 2, 1992 by Doris Meissner for Emile Milne to Roundtable on Haitian Migration Policy on Monday, December 14, 1992, 2:00 to 5:00 p.m. with List of Invited Participants". Carnegie Endowment for International Peace: Washington. 3 p.

Rangel92h: Folder "Support" with copies of Hon. Rangel's correspondence between 1991 and 1994.
1992   "QC/QP: Haiti Working Group". New York: QC/QP, August 21. 2 p.

Rangel93a: Folder "Support" with copies of Hon. Rangel's correspondence between 1991 and 1994.
1993   "Memo to CBR From Emile Re: Haiti/Blockade". Washington, 01/16/93. 2 p.

Rangel93b: Folder "Support" with copies of Hon. Rangel's correspondence between 1991 and 1994.
1993   "Letter by the Most Rev. Theodore E. McCarrick to National Security Advisor Anthony Lake". Washington, March 24. 2 p.

Richards, Rhonda.
1992   "Activist Calls Haitian Wages a Joke". *USA TODAY*, March 17. p. 3.

Richardson, Bonham C.
1983   *Caribbean Migrants: Environment and Human Survival on St. Kitts and Nevis.* Knoxville: University of Tennessee Press.

Richardson, Bonham C.
1992   *The Caribbean in the Wider World, 1492 - 1992: A Regional Geography*. Cambridge: Cambridge University Press. 235 p.

Richman, Karen.
1992   "A Lavalas at Home / A Lavalas for Home: Inflections of Transnationalism in the Discourse of Haitian President Aristide". *Towards a Transnational Perspective on Migration: Race, Class, Ethnicity, and Nationalism Reconsidered.* Annals of the New York Academy. Vol. 645. New York: New York Academy. p. 189 - 200.

Rohter, Larry.
1993a   "Haitians With H.I.V. Leave Cuba Base for Lives in U.S".. *New York Times*, June 15. p. A20

Rohter, Larry.
1993b "Haitians Remain Skeptical of Accord", *New York Times*, July 4. p. 12.

Rohter, Larry.
1994a "In Miami´s Little Haiti, Fears of Assassination", *New York Times*, March 20. p. 22.

Rohter, Larry.
1994b "Last flight out of Haiti strands some". *New York Times*, July 31. p. 10; "Americans in Haiti Fear an Invasion". *New York Times*, July 30. p. A3.

Rohter, Larry.
1994c "Haiti´s Hunger is Abundant while Food is Scant at Best". *New York Times*, August 7. p. 1.

Rohter, Larry.
1994d "Invasion That Never Comes Has Many Haitians Skeptical". *New York Times*, August 10. p. A1,A2.

Saad, Lydia.
1993 "Strong Humanitarian Impulse Toward Bosnia". *The Gallup Poll Monthly*, March. p.22.

Safa, Helen I.
1981 "Runaway Shops and Female Employment: The Search For Cheap Labor". *Signs*, Winter. p. 418 - 433.

Salamon, Lester M.
1990 "The Nonprofit Sector and Government: The American Experience in Theory and Practice". *The Third Sector: Comparative Studies of Nonprofit Organizations*. Helmut K. Anheier and Wolfgang Seibel eds. Berlin, New York: Walter de Gruyter. p. 217 - 240.

Salamon, Lester M.
1994 "The Rise of the Nonprofit Sector". *Foreign Affairs*. Vol. 73, No. 4, Jul/Aug. p. 109 - 122.

Sassen-Koob, Saskia.
1989 "New York City´s Informal Economy". *The Informal Economy: Studies in Advanced and Less Developed Countries*. Alejandro Portes, Manuel Castells, Lauren A. Benton ed. Baltimore, London: The Johns Hopkins University Press. p. 60 - 77.

Schemo, Diana Jean.
1992 "A Haitian Refugee Wonders When He'll Return". *New York Times*, May 31. p. 7.

Schlesinger Jr., Arthur.
1992 *The Disuniting of America: Reflections on a Multicultural Society*. New York: Norton. 160 p.

Schmidt, Hans.
1995 *The United States Occupation of Haiti, 1915 - 1934*. New Brunswick: Rutgers University Press. 303 p.

Schudson, Michael.
1995 *The Power of News*. Cambridge: Harvard University Press. 269 p.

Simmons, Alan B. and Jean Pierre Guengant.
1992 "Caribbean Exodus and the World System". *International Migration Systems: A Global Approach*. Mary M. Kritz, Lin Lean Lim and Hania Zlotnik ed. Oxford: Clarendon Press. p. 94 - 114.

Skjelsbaek, Kjell.
1973   "The Growth of International Nongovernmental Organizations in the Twentieh Century". *Transnational Relations and World Politics.* Robert O. Keohanne and Joseph S. Nye ed. Cambridge: Harvard University Press. p. 70 - 92.

Smith, Anthony D.
1983   *Theories of Nationalism.* 2nd ed. New York: Holmes & Meiers. 350 p.

SoftLine: SoftLine Information, Inc.
1994   *Ethnic NewsWatch: The other Side of the Stories.* A Brochure on the CD-ROM Database. Stamford, CT.

Soja, Edward W.
1991   "Poles Apart: Urban Restructuring in New York and Los Angeles". *Dual City: Restructuring New York.* New York: Russel Sage Foundation. p. 361 - 376.

Solarz, Stephen.
1995   "Foreword". *The United States Occupation of Haiti, 1915 - 1934.* New Brunswick: Rutgers University Press. p. ix - xv.

Sontag, Deborah.
1994   "Haitian Migrants Settle In With Memories Still Alive". *New York Times,* June 3. p. A1,B4.

Spradley, James P.
1979   *The Ethnographic Interview.* New York: Holt, Rinehart and Winston. 247 p.

Spradley, James P.
1980   *Participant Observation.* Orlando: Harcourt Brace. 195 p.

St. Paul, Omar.
1992   "Students Do Volunteer Work To Aid Haitians In Filing Claims For Asylum". *Miami Times,* March 26. Vol. 60, No. 30. p. 3A.

Steber, Maggie.
1991   *Dancing on Fire: Photographs from Haiti.* Introduction by Amy Wilentz. New York: Aperture Foundation. 96 p.

Stepick, Alex.
1986   *Haitian Refugees in the U.S.* London: The Minority Rights Group Report. No. 52. 20 p.

Stepick, Alex.
1987   "The Haitian Exodus: Flight from Terror and Poverty". *The Caribbean Exodus.* Barry B. Levine ed. New York, Westport, London: Praeger. p. 131 - 151.

Sutton, Constance R.
1987   "The Caribbeanization of New York City and the Emergence of a Transnational Sociocultural System". *Caribbean Life in New York: Sociocultural Dimensions.* New York: Center for Migration Studies. p. 15 - 30.

SZ: Süddeutsche Zeitung.
1997   "Boom der Auslandsinvestitionen: 100 größte Multis beschäftigen sechs Millionen Mitarbeiter". SZ, Montag, 22. Septmber. p. 23.

TA: TransAfrica.
1992a "News Release: TransAfrica Condemns Callous and Irresponsible U.S. Immigraiton Policy on Haitian Refugees", February 4. 2 p.

TA: TransAfrica.
1992b "News Release: TransAfrica Joins African-American Leadership to Decry the Bush Administration´s Inhumane Treatment of Haitian Refugees", February 25. 2 p.

Tabor, Mary B. W.
1993 "Judge Orders the Release of Haitians". *New York Times*, June 9. p. B4.

Taft-Morales, Maureen.
1993 "Haiti: The Struggle for Democracy and Congressional Concerns in 1993". *CRS Issue Brief.* Washington: Library of Congress, December 22. 16 p.

Thornton, Robert L.
1973 "Governments and Airlines". *Transnational Relations and World Politics*. Robert O. Keohanne and Joseph S. Nye ed. Cambridge: Harvard University Press. p. 191 - 203.

Thorpe, Richard.
1993 "Taxi killing brings grief to Haitians". *Bay State Banner*, Vol. 28, No. 26, March 18. p. 1.

Tocqueville, Alexis de.
1945 *Democracy in America*. Phillips Bradley ed. 2 Vols. New York: Vintage Books.

Trice, H.M.
1970 "The `Outsider's Role' in Field Study". *Qualitative Methodology*. William J. Filstead ed. Chicago: Markham Publishing Company. p. 77 - 90.

Trouillot, Michel-Rolph.
1990 *Haiti: State Against Nation: The Origins and Legacy of Duvalierism*. New York: Monthly Review Press.

Urquhart, Brian.
1991/92 "The United Nations: From Peace-Keeping to a Collective System?". *Adelphi Paper*, No. 265. p. 18 - 29.

USCC/MRS: National Conference of Catholic Bishops, Migration and Refugee Services.
1991 *Annual Report*. Washington: USCC/MRS. 29 p.

USCC/MRS: National Conference of Catholic Bishops, Migration and Refugee Services.
1992/93 *Report of Programs*. Washington: USCC/MRS. 32 p.

USCR: United States Committee for Refugees.
1994 *World Refugee Survey*. Washington: USCR. 176 p.

Vernon, Raymond.
1972 "Multinational Business and National Economic Goals". *Transnational Relations and World Politics*. Robert O. Keohanne and Joseph S. Nye eds. Cambridge: Harvard University Press. p. 343 - 355.

Waldschmitt-Nelson, Britta.
1996 "'From Protest to Politics': Schwarze Frauen in der Bürgerrechtsbewegung und im Kongreß der Vereinigten Staaten". Unpublished Dissertation, University of Munich.

Wallerstein, Immanuel.
1974 *The Modern World System*. 3 Vols. New York: Academic Press.

Walters, Ronald W.
1987 "African-American Influence on U.S. Foreign Policy Toward South Africa". *Ethnic Groups and U.S. Foreign Policy*. Mohammed E. Ahrari ed. New York: Greenwood Press. p. 65 - 82.

Walzer, Michael.
1993 "Between Nation and World". *The Economist: 150 Economist Years*. September 11 - 19. p. 51 - 54.

Wanniski, Jude.
1992 *The 1992 Media Guide: A Critical Review of the Media's Recent Coverage of the World Political Economy*. Morristown: Polyconomics. 663 p.

Warren, Michael.
1991 "Florida Judge Extends Haitian Deportation Ban". *Los Angeles Sentinel*. Vol. LVII, No. 33. December 04. p. 3A.

Wasem, Ruth Ellen.
1992 "Temporary Protections Under U.S. Immigration Law". *CRS Issue Brief*. Washington: The Library of Congress. 6 p.

Watanabe, Paul Y.
1984 *Ethnic Groups, Congress, and American Foreign Policy: The Politics of the Turkish Arms Embargo*. Westport: Greenwood Press. 228 p.

Weinstein, Brian and Aaron Segal.
1992 *Haiti: The Failure of Politics*. New York: Praeger. 203 p.

Weisbrod, Burton A.
1989 "The Complexities of Income Generation for Nonprofits". *The Future of the Nonprofit Sector: Challenges, Changes, and Policy Considerations*. Virginia A. Hodgkinson, Richard W. Lyman ed. San Francisco, London: Jossey-Bass. p. 75 - 88.

Werner, Oswald and G. Mark Schoepfle.
1987a *Systematic Fieldwork: Foundations of Ethnography and Interviewing*. Vol. 1. Newbury Park et al.: Sage. 416 p.

Werner, Oswald and G. Mark Schoepfle.
1987b *Systematic Fieldwork: Ethnographic Analysis and Data Management*. Vol. 2. Newbury Park et al.: Sage. 416 p.

Whyte, William Foote.
1984 *Learning From the Field: A Guide From Experience*. Beverly Hills, London, New Delhi: Sage Publications. 295 p.

Wilentz, Amy.
1989 *The Rainy Season: Haiti Since Duvalier*. New York: Simon and Schuster. 427 p.

Zolberg, Aristide R., Astri Suhrke and Sergio Aguayo.
1989   *Escape From Violence: Conflict and the Refugee Crisis in the Developing World.* New York, Oxford: Oxford University Press. ? p.

Zucker, Norman L. and Naomi Flink Zucker.
1987   *The Guarded Gate: The Reality of American Refugee Policy.* San Diego, New York, London: Harcourt Brace Jovanovich. 400 p.

Zucker, Norman L. and Naomi Flink Zucker.
1991   "The 1980 Refugee Act: A 1990 Perspective". *Refugee Policy: Canada and the United States.* Howard Adelman ed. Toronto: York Lanes Press. p. 224 - 252.

Haiti Progrès - Articles, 1991 - 1994

HP 1: Philippe Généus.
1991   "Commémoration du Bois Caiman: un succès pour le consulat de Boston", HP, 4 - 10 Septembre, Vol. 9, No. 23, p. 9.

HP 2: Anonymous.
1991   „New York: un marathon aux résultats quelque peu décevants", *Haiti Progrès,* 29 Août - 3 Septembre, Vol. 9, No. 22, p. 9.

HP 3: Wilner, Henriquez et Janvier, Jean-Joseph.
1991   „New York: invitation du 10e", *Haiti Progrès,* 11 - 17 Septembre, Vol. 9, No. 24, p. 10.

HP 4: Anonymous.
1991   „Miami: grève de la faim à Krome", *Haiti Progrès,* 4 - 10 Septembre, Vol. 9, No. 23, p. 10.

HP 5: Anonymous.
1991   „Aristide prochainement à l'ONU: le dixième département s'apprête à l'accueillir", *Haiti Progrès,* 18 - 24 Septembre, Vol. 9, No. 25, p. 1,26.

HP 6: Anonymous.
1991   „Bienvenue a Titid", *Haiti Progrès,* 18 - 24 Septembre, Vol. 9, No. 25, p. 10.

HP 7: Anonymous.
1991   „Aristide à l'ONU: Haiti Digne Face Au Monde", *Haiti Progrès,* 25 Septembre - 1 Octobre, Vol. 9, No. 26, p. 1,24.

HP 8: Tecumseh, Angèle.
1991   „Aristide à New York: nouvel épisode 'd'une histoire d'amour", *Haiti Progrès,* 2 - 8 Octobre, Vol. 9, No. 27, p. 16 - 23.

HP 9: Anonymous.
1991   „Le dixième proteste devant les Nation Unies", *Haiti Progrès,* 2 - 8 Octobre, Vol. 9, No. 27, p. 12,28.

HP 10: Anonymous.
1991   „Miami: les Haitiens protestent dans les rues contre le coup", *Haiti Progrès,* 2 - 8 Octobre, Vol. 9, No. 27, p. 12.

HP 11: Généus, Philippe.
1991 „Boston: manifestation contre le coup d'Etat fasciste", *Haiti Progrès,* 2 - 8 Octobre, Vol. 9, No. 27, p. 14.

HP 12: Salye, Sekon.
1991 „La fin d'un gouvernement ou le commencement d'une vraie révolution?", *Haiti Progrès,* 2 - 8 Octobre, Vol. 9, No. 27, p. 14.

HP 13: Généus, Philippe.
1991 „Boston: 30.000 personnes renouvellent leur appui au gouvernement Aristide", *Haiti Progrès,* 9 - 15 Octobre, Vol. 9, No. 28, p. 11.

HP 14: Petit-Homme, Edouard.
1991 „New Jersey: des manifestations en chaîne", *Haiti Progrès,* 9 - 15 Octobre, Vol. 9, No. 28, p. 11.

HP 15: Anonymous.
1991 „Permanence décrétée depuis plus d'une semaine face à l'ONU", *Haiti Progrès,* 9 - 15 Octobre, Vol. 9, No. 28, p. 14,25.

HP 16: Anonymous.
1991 „Les Haitians de Philadelphie solidaires du président Aristide", *Haiti Progrès,* 9 - 15 Octobre, Vol. 9, No. 28, p. 14.

HP 17: Anonymous.
1991 „New York: la communauté caraibéenne informée de la situation haitienne", *Haiti Progrès,* 9 - 15 Octobre, Vol. 9, No. 28, p. 14.

HP 18: Anonymous.
1991 „L'organisation Pax Christi USA et la Commission haitienne `Justice et Paix´ dénoncent le coup d'état", *Haiti Progrès,* 16 - 22 Octobre, Vol. 9, No. 29, p. 8,11.

HP 19: Dupuy, Benjamin.
1991 „Ben Dupuy, ambassadeur itinérant, écrit au Washington Post", *Haiti Progrès,* 16 - 22 Octobre, Vol. 9, No. 29, p. 8.

HP 20: Delva, Frantz, Marc André Roger, Regina Enriquez.
1991 „L'arrondissement de Californie continue sa mobilisation", *Haiti Progrès,* 16 -22 Octobre, Vol. 9, No. 29, p. 9.

HP 21: Généus, Philippe.
1991 „Boston: la mobilisation continue", *Haiti Progrès,* 16 - 22 Octobre, Vol. 9, No. 29, p. 10.

HP 22: Latour, Fanfan.
1991 „La grande manifestation de l'honneur et de la dignité", *Haiti Progrès,* 16 - 22 Octobre, Vol. 9, No. 29, p. 14 - 18.

HP 23: Don Bosco.
1991 „New York: protestation du club sportif `Don Bosco'", *Haiti Progrès,* 23 - 29 Octobre, Vol. 9, No. 30, p. 9.

HP 24: Anonymous.
1991 „Formation d'une commission indépendante d'enquête sur le coup d'Etat du 29 Septembre", *Haiti Progrès,* 23 - 29 Octobre, Vol. 9, No. 30, p. 10.

HP 25: Latour, Fanfan.
1991 „Un seul refrain de New York à Washington: Democratie pour Haiti", *Haiti Progrès,* 23 - 29 Octobre, Vol. 9, No. 30, p. 16 - 19.

HP 26: Anonymous.
1991 „Brooklyn: toujours le même cri de guerre `We want Aristide'", *Haiti Progrès,* 30 Octobre - 5 Novembre, Vol. 9, No. 31, p. 9.

HP 27: Anonymous.
1991 „Campagne de télégrammes pour faire pression sur le gouvernement Bush", *Haiti Progrès,* 30 Octobre - 5 Novembre, Vol. 9, No. 31, p. 9.

HP 28: Anonymous.
1991 „Solidarité avec les élèves des Gonaives", *Haiti Progrès,* 30 Octobre - 5 Novembre, Vol. 9, No. 31, p. 9.

HP 30: Anonymous.
1991 „Miami: Déportation des réfugiés haitiens suspendues en vertu du coup d'Etat", *Haiti Progrès,* 30 Octobre - 5 Novembre, Vol. 9, No. 31, p. 10.

HP 31: Anonymous.
1991 „`Americans for Aristide´: une soirée avec l'ambassadeur haitien Jean Casimir", *Haiti Progrès,* 23 - 29 Octobre, Vol. 9, No. 30, p. 9.

HP 32: Anonymous.
1991 „L'ambassadeur Casimir à New York", *Haiti Progrès,* 30 Octobre - 5 Novembre, Vol. 9, No. 31, p. 11.

HP 33: Anonymous.
1991 „Etats-Unis: ouverture d'un compte spécial pour le financement du service extérieur du gouvernement et la résistance interne", *Haiti Progrès,* 30 Octobre - 5 Novembre, Vol. 9, No. 31, p. 11.

HP 34: Anonymous.
1991 „New York: la communauté haitienne investit le quartier de Wall Street", *Haiti Progrès,* 6 - 12 Novembre, Vol. 9, No. 32, p. 7.

HP 35: Anonymous.
1991 „HOMMAGE A MANNO", *Haiti Progrès,* 6 - 12 Novembre, Vol. 9, No. 32, p. 8.

HP 36: Anonymous.
1991 „La commission indépendante d'enquête sur le coup d'Etat officiellement lancée", *Haiti Progrès,* 6 - 12 Novembre, Vol. 9, No. 32, p. 8.

HP 37: Anonymous.
1991 „Contribuez à faire la lumière sur les massacres des putschistes", *Haiti Progrès,* 13 - 19 Novembre, Vol. 9, No. 33, p. 9.

HP 38: Anonymous.
1991 „Premier résultats publics de la Commission d'enquête sur le coup d'Etat", *Haiti Progrès,* 13 - 19 Novembre, Vol. 9, No. 33, p. 9.

HP 39: Baptiste, Patrick Jean.
1991 „Lettre au président Jean-Bertrand Aristide", *Haiti Progrès,* 13 - 19 Novembre, Vol. 9, No. 33, p. 10.

HP 40: Roy, Louis E.
1991 „Le `père de la Constitution´ dénonce l´inconstitutionnalité du gouvernement de facto", *Haiti Progrès,* 13 - 19 Novembre, Vol. 9, No. 33, p. 10.

HP 41: Alcé, Jean.
1991 „„Mid-West: rencontre avec le congressman John Conyers", *Haiti Progrès,* 13 - 19 Novembre, Vol. 9, No. 33, p. 10.

HP 42: Gilbert, Carl.
1991 „Le régime de Cédras,Honorat provoque une vague de réfugiés vers les Etats-Unis", *Haiti Progrès,* 13 - 19 Novembre, Vol. 9, No. 33, p. 15.

HP 43: Généus, Philippe.
1991 „L´ambassadeur Jean Casimir et le consul Wilson Désir de passage à Boston", *Haiti Progrès,* 13 - 19 Novembre, Vol. 9, No. 33, p. 16.

HP 44: Gilbert, Carl.
1991 „Réfugiés: encore une fois la politique de deux poids deux mesures", *Haiti Progrès,* 20 - 26 Novembre, Vol. 9, No. 34, p. 8.

HP 45: Anonymous.
1991 „New York: messe à la mémoire des victimes du coup d´Etat", *Haiti Progrès,* 20 - 26 Novembre, Vol. 9, No. 34, p. 9.

HP 46: Généus, Philippe.
1991 „Le sénateur Wesner Emmanuel et Reynald Clérismé rencontrent la communauté haitienne de Boston", *Haiti Progrès,* 20 - 26 Novembre, Vol. 9, No. 34, p. 9.

HP 47: Anonymous.
1991 „Aristide de passage à New York: `il n´y a pas d´avenir pour eux", *Haiti Progrès,* 20 - 26 Novembre, Vol. 9, No. 34, p. 10,21.

HP 48: Janvier, Jean-Joseph.
1991 „Long Island réclame le retour de Jean-Bertrand Aristide", *Haiti Progrès,* 20 - 26 Novembre, Vol. 9, No. 34, p. 10.

HP 49: Large, Josaphat.
1991 „Orlande: les macoutes arrivent", *Haiti Progrès,* 20 - 26 Novembre, Vol. 9, No. 34, p. 11.

HP 50: Victor, Alain St.
1991 „Jesse Jackson: un soutien à double tranchant", *Haiti Progrès,* 27 Novembre - 3 Décembre, Vol. 9, No. 35, p. 8.

HP 51: Anonymous.
1991 „La Commission indépendante d´enquête dénonce le rôle des Etats-Unis dans le coup d´Etat", *Haiti Progrès,* 27 Novembre - 3 Décembre, Vol. 9, No. 35, p. 10.

HP 52: Anonymous.
1991 „Washington: réunion extraordinaire de l´OEA", *Haiti Progrès,* 27 Novembre - 3 Décembre, Vol. 9, No. 35, p. 10.

HP 53: Tecumseh, Angèle.
1991   „Réfugiés politiques ou réfugiés économique?: Une vieille polémique et un cynisme accru des Etats-Unis", *Haiti Progrès,* 27 Novembre - 3 Décembre, Vol. 9, No. 35, p. 12 - 15.

HP 54: Anonymous.
1991   „Des organisation de droits humans font une mise au point", *Haiti Progrès,* 27 Novembre - 3 Décembre, Vol. 9, No. 35, p. 12 - 15.

HP 55: Latour, Fanfan.
1991   „29 novembre 1991: manifestation du souvenir à New York", *Haiti Progrès,* 4 - 10 Décembre, Vol. 9, No. 36, p. 9,25.

HP 56: Gilbert, Carl.
1991   „Le drame des réfugiés haitiens se poursuit en mer et sur terre", *Haiti Progrès,* 4 - 10 Décembre, Vol. 9, No. 36, p. 10,24.

HP 57: Anonymous.
1991   „Guerre psychologique des Etats-Unis contre les réfugiés haitiens", *Haiti Progrès,* 11 - 17 Décembre, Vol. 9, No. 37, p. 6,16 - 18.

HP 58: Latour, Fanfan.
1991   „Résistance `manch long´ et pluie sur Washington", *Haiti Progrès,* 18 - 24 Décembre, Vol. 9, No. 38, p. 1,17.

HP 59: Anonymous.
1991   „New York: `vote pour la démocratie´", *Haiti Progrès,* 18 - 24 Décembre, Vol. 9, No. 38, p. 8.

HP 60: Anonymous.
1991   „Une lutte acharnée des Etats-Unis pour refouler les réfugiés haitiens", *Haiti Progrès,* 18 - 24 Décembre, Vol. 9, No. 38, p. 10,16.

HP 61: Anonymous.
1991   „`Opération Espoir", *Haiti Progrès,* 18 - 24 Décembre, Vol. 9, No. 38, p. 10.

HP 62: Aristide, Jean-Bertrand.
1992   „Le père Aristide offre ses voeux du Nouvel An à Haiti-Progrés", *Haiti Progrès,* 1 - 7 Janvier, Vol. 9, No. 40, p. 9.

HP 63: Anonymous.
1992   „Liberté et exil pour Manno Charlemange", *Haiti Progrès,* 1 - 7 Janvier, Vol. 9, No. 40, p. 9,15.

HP 64: Anonymous.
1992   „Une situation insupportable faite aux réfugiés haitiens", *Haiti Progrès,* 8 - 14 Janvier, Vol. 9, No. 41, p. 1,22.

HP 65: Anonymous.
1992   „`Retour aux jours les plus sombres´: un rapport sur les actuelles de droits humains", *Haiti Progrès,* 8 - 14 Janvier, Vol. 9, No. 41, p. 9.

HP 66: Casimir, Jean.
1992   „Qeulques précision de l´ambassade d´Haiti à Washington sur le choix de René Thédore", *Haiti Progrès,* 15 - 21 Janvier, Vol. 9, No. 42, p. 9.

HP 67: Anonymous.
1992 „A Guantanamo, l'attente angoissée des réfugiés se poursuit", *Haiti Progrès,* 22 - 28 Janvier, Vol. 9, No. 43, p. 9.

HP 68: Latour, Fanfan.
1992 „Les nouvelles racines d'Haiti: Dignité et Démocratie", *Haiti Progrès,* 22 - 28 Janvier, Vol. 9, No. 43, p. 10.

HP 69: Anonymous.
1992 „Plus d'un millier de réfugiés interceptés en un jour: une conséquence de la répression militaire", *Haiti Progrès,* 29 Janvier - 5 Février, Vol. 9, No. 44, p. 8,?,18.

HP 70: Anonymous.
1992 „Réfugiés: Vague de Protestations", *Haiti Progrès,* 5 - 11 Février, Vol. 9, No. 45, p. 1,16.

HP 71: Anonymous.
1992 „Réfugiés: de l'enfer de Guantanamo à celui de Cedras", *Haiti Progrès,* 5 - 11 Février, Vol. 9, No. 45, p. 8,17.

HP 72: Préval, Joseph.
1992 „New York: lettre ouverte du consul Joseph Préval aux parlementaires", *Haiti Progrès,* 5 - 11 Février, Vol. 9, No. 45, p. 9.

HP 73: Magloire, Jacques, Alain St-Victor.
1992 „New York: le `dixiéme s'oppose à toute intervention étrangére", *Haiti Progrès,* 5 - 11 Février, Vol. 9, No. 45, p. 11.

HP 74: Victor, Alain St.
1992 „7 février à New York: de la veillée patriotique à l'apothéose du festival", *Haiti Progrès,* 12 - 18 Février, Vol. 9, No. 46, p. 10.

HP 75: Anonymous.
1992 „Appel du Comité contre la Répression pour l'envoi de cassettes en Haiti", *Haiti Progrès,* 12 - 18 Février, Vol. 9, No. 46, p. 10.

HP 76: Dorancy, Rolande.
1992 „Réfugiés: la stratégie du gouvernement Bush mise à nu", *Haiti Progrès,* 12 - 18 Février, Vol. 9, No. 46, p. 11.

HP 77: Dorancy, Rolande.
1992 „Miami: le 7 février avec `Jeye Yo' et le Centre des Réfugiés", *Haiti Progrès,* 12 - 18 Février, Vol. 9, No. 46, p. 11.

HP 78: Anonymous.
1992 „New York: rencontre avec la Commission d'enquête sur le coup d'Etat 30 Septembre", *Haiti Progrès,* 12 - 18 Février, Vol. 9, No. 46, p. 11.

HP 79: Anonymous.
1992 „Persécutions contre les réfugiés rapatriés de force: Bush violemment dénoncé", *Haiti Progrès,* 12 - 18 Février, Vol. 9, No. 46, p. 1,20.

HP 80: Latour, Fanfan.
1992 „Vive le 7 février 1992! Vive le drapeau de la résistance", *Haiti Progrès,* 12 - 18 Février, Vol. 9, No. 46, p. 12 - 13.

HP 81: Anonymous.
1992 „Etats-Unis: les droits humains sont violés en Haiti, à l'exception de ceux des réfugiés!", *Haiti Progrès,* 19 - 25 Février, Vol. 9, No. 47, p. 8,17.

HP 82: Généus, Philippe.
1992 „1.500 à 2.000 compatriotes dénoncent à New Hampshire la duplicité de Bush dans la crise haitienne", *Haiti Progrès,* 19 - 25 Février, Vol. 9, No. 47, p. 10.

HP 83: Anonymous.
1992 „Réfugiés: la Cour suprême des Etats-Unis se fait complice de Bush", *Haiti Progrès,* 26 Février - 3 Mars, Vol. 9, No. 48, p. 1,18.

HP 84: Anonymous.
1992 „Une politique de plus en plus répressive à l'égard des réfugiés", *Haiti Progrès,* 26 Février - 3 Mars, Vol. 9, No. 48, p. 9.

HP 85: Anonymous.
1992 „La Résistance en Haiti", *Haiti Progrès,* 26 Février - 3 Mars, Vol. 9, No. 48, p. 10.

HP 86: Anonymous.
1992 „Le sort des réfugiés toujours débattu aux Etats-Unis", *Haiti Progrès,* 4 - 10 Mars, Vol. 9, No. 48, p. 1,19.

HP 87: Anonymous.
1992 „Réfugiés: la statue de la Liberté prise à témoin", *Haiti Progrès,* 4 - 10 Mars, Vol. 9, No. 48, p. 8.

HP 88: Latour, Fanfan.
1992 „Au coeur même de Little Haiti: le Centre des Réfugiés Haitiens", *Haiti Progrès,* 11 - 17 Mars, Vol. 9, No. 49, p. 10,21.

HP 89: Dean Daley.
1993 „Immediate Attorney Opening: Haitian Refugee Center", *Haiti Progrès,* 10 - 16 Février, Vol. 10, No. 46, p. 9.

HP 90: Anonymous.
1992 „Philippe Jules est-il un partisan du père Aristide?", *Haiti Progrès,* 11 - 17 Mars, Vol. 9, No. 49, p. 10.

HP 91: Gilbert, Carl.
1992 „Le rideau tombe sur le drame des réfugiés haitiens", *Haiti Progrès,* 18 - 24 Mars, Vol. 9, No. 50, p. 8.

HP 92: Anonymous.
1992 „Americans for Aristide: une nouvelle action de solidarité avec Haiti", *Haiti Progrès,* 18 - 24 Mars, Vol. 9, No. 50, p. 8.

HP 93: Latour, Fanfan.
1992 „Katherine, Titid: même combat", *Haiti Progrès,* 18 - 24 Mars, Vol. 9, No. 50, p. 9.

HP 94: Anonymous.
1992 „Aristide: de Los Angeles à Washington", *Haiti Progrès,* 18 - 24 Mars, Vol. 9, No. 50, p. 9.

HP 95: Anonymous.
1992 „Nouveau rapport de la Commission Haiti sur le coup d´Etat de Cedras", *Haiti Progrès,* 18 - 24 Mars, Vol. 9, No. 50, p. 9.

HP 96: Anonymous.
1992 „6 avril: manifestation à New York", *Haiti Progrès,* 18 - 24 Mars, Vol. 9, No. 50, p. 9.

HP 97: Gilbert, Carl.
1992 „Encouragée par Titid, Katherine Duham termine sa grève de la faim", *Haiti Progrès,* 25 - 31 Mars, Vol. 9, No. 51, p. 8.

HP 98: Anonymous.
1992 „6 avril: manifestation à New York", *Haiti Progrès,* 25 - 31 Mars, Vol. 9, No. 51, p. 8.

HP 99: Anonymous.
1992 „New York: une action de solidarité avec les réfugiés haitiens", *Haiti Progrès,* 25 - 31 Mars, Vol. 9, No. 51, p. 9.

HP 100: Loubet, Jeanie.
1992 „Réflexions autour d´un anniversaire", *Haiti Progrès,* 1 - 7 Avril, Vol. 10, No. 1, p. 6-7, 6-17.

HP 101: Anonymous.
1992 „Réfugiés: une victoire dans la lutte légale", *Haiti Progrès,* 1 - 7 Avril, Vol. 10, No. 1, p. 8,20.

HP 102: Anonymous.
1992 „`Lavalas´descend une nouvelle fois dans les rues de Manhattan", *Haiti Progrès,* 8 - 14 Avril, Vol. 10, No. 2, p. 8.

HP 103: Anonymous.
1992 „Autre victoire légale pour les réfugiés haitiens", *Haiti Progrès,* 8 - 14 Avril, Vol. 10, No. 2, p. 8,9.

HP 104: Ives, Kim.
1992 „`Killing the dream´: a-t-on vraiment tué le rêve?", *Haiti Progrès,* 8 - 14 Avril, Vol. 10, No. 2, p. 10.

HP 105: Magloire, Jacques, Alain St-Victor.
1992 „Prise de position du `dixiéme´ à New York", *Haiti Progrès,* 15 - 21 Avril, Vol. 10, No. 3, p. 8.

HP 106: Anonymous.
1992 „Réfugiés: l´exode n´est toujours pas tari", *Haiti Progrès,* 15 - 21 Avril, Vol. 10, No. 3, p. 8.

HP 107: Anonymous.
1992 „De Guantanamo à Brooklyn: le cas de 19 réfugiés", *Haiti Progrès,* 22 - 28 Avril, Vol. 10, No. 4, p. 8.

HP 108: Anonymous.
1992 „Réfugiés: une nouvelle vague de départs", *Haiti Progrès,* 22 - 28 Avril, Vol. 10, No. 4, p. 9.

HP 109: Anonymous.
1992 „New York: le dixième département recoit le président Jean-Bertrand Aristide", *Haiti Progrès,* 22 - 28 Avril, Vol. 10, No. 4, p. 11.

HP 110: Latour, Fanfan.
1992   „100.000 personnes accueillent le président Aristide à New York", *Haiti Progrès,* 28 Avril - 5 Mai, Vol. 10, No. 5, p. 1, 10 - 11.

HP 111: Gilbert, Carl.
1992   „New York: le dixème partage un dîner historique avec Titid", *Haiti Progrès,* 28 Avril - 5 Mai, Vol. 10, No. 5, p. 10.

HP 112: Gilbert, Carl.
1992   „Réfugiés: une hémorragie qui n'en finit pas", *Haiti Progrès,* 6 - 12 Mai, Vol. 10, No. 6, p. 8.

HP 113: Anonymous.
1992   „New York: trois film haitiens au festival sur les droits humains", *Haiti Progrès,* 6 - 12 Mai, Vol. 10, No. 6, p. 9.

HP 114: Latour, Fanfan.
1992   „Chaleureux accueil du dixième au président Aristide: '1ère partie", *Haiti Progrès,* 6 - 12 Mai, Vol. 10, No. 6, p. 12 - 17.

HP 115: Anonymous.
1992   „Réfugiés: un problème coûteux pour le gouvernement Bush", *Haiti Progrès,* 13 - 19 Mai, Vol. 10, No. 7, p. 8.

HP 116: Latour, Fanfan.
1992   „Chaleureux accueil du dixième au président Aristide: 2ème partie", *Haiti Progrès,* 13 - 19 Mai, Vol. 10, No. 7, p. 12 - 16.

HP 117: Dauphin, Ludovic et al.
1992   „Visite d'Aristide à New York: compte-rendu de la Commission Finances", *Haiti Progrès,* 20 - 26 Mai, Vol. 10, No. 8, p. 8.

HP 118: Anonymous.
1992   „Présence haitienne à la manifestation de Washington", *Haiti Progrès,* 20 - 26 Mai, Vol. 10, No. 8, p. 8.

HP 119: Anonymous.
1992   „Rencontre entre le père Yvon Massac et le `dixième´ de New York", *Haiti Progrès,* 20 - 26 Mai, Vol. 10, No. 8, p. 9.

HP 120: Anonymous.
1992   „Réfugiés: les Etats- Unis pris à leur propre piège", *Haiti Progrès,* 20 - 26 Mai, Vol. 10, No. 8, p. 10.

HP 121: St. Victor, Alain.
1992   „Organisation dans le `dixième´ à New-York: une activité de la Commission Jeunesse". *Haiti Progrès,* 20 - 26 Mai, Vol. 10, No. 8, p. 10. ?

HP 122: Latour, Fanfan.
1992   „Chaleureux accueil du dixième au président Aristide: 3ème partie", *Haiti Progrès,* 20 - 26 Mai, Vol. 10, No. 8, p. 12 - 17.

HP 123: Anonymous.
1992   „Bush face aux réfugiés: D'une politique de noyade à une politique de déportation massive", *Haiti Progrès,* 27 Mai - 2 Juin, Vol. 10, No. 9, p. 1, 14 - 15.

HP 124: Anonymous.
1992 „Etats-Unis: une politique sous le signe de l'hypocrisie", *Haiti Progrès,* 3 - 9 Juin, Vol. 10, No. 10, p. 6,20.

HP 125: Anonymous.
1992 „New York: `HEAR´ renouvelle sa direction", *Haiti Progrès,* 3 - 9 Juin, Vol. 10, No. 10, p. 8.

HP 126: Anonymous.
1992 „7 juin: la journée de la presse commémorée à New York", *Haiti Progrès,* 3 - 9 Juin, Vol. 10, No. 10, p. 9 - 10.

HP 127: Ives, Kim.
1992 „Aristide pour une deuxième fois croque la `Big Apple´", *Haiti Progrès,* 3 - 9 Juin, Vol. 10, No. 10, p. 12 - 14.

HP 128: Anonymous.
1992 „Une décision qui renvoie les réfugiés `dans les mâchoires´ de la répression", *Haiti Progrès,* 10 - 16 Juin, Vol. 10, No. 11, p. 9 - 8.

HP 129: Anonymous.
1992 „Le cas des interceptions et refoulements des réfugiés en appel", *Haiti Progrès,* 8 - 14 Juillet, Vol. 10, No. 15, p. 8,15.

HP 130: Anonymous.
1992 „New York: mobilisation générale les 13, 14, 15 et 16 juillet", *Haiti Progrès,* 8 - 14 Juillet, Vol. 10, No. 15, p. 15.

HP 131: Ménard, Henry-Claude.
1992 „Formation d'un Comité Général de Finances", *Haiti Progrès,* 15 - 21 Juillet, Vol. 10, No. 16, p. 8.

HP 132: Latour, Fanfan.
1992 „Convention démocrate et mobilisation du 10e", *Haiti Progrès,* 22 - 28 Juillet, Vol. 10, No. 17, p. 9.

HP 133: Anonymous.
1992 „Le naufrage des réfugiés a été provoqué par les militaris", *Haiti Progrès,* 29 Juillet - 4 Aout, Vol. 10, No. 18, p. 1,22.

HP 134: Anonymous.
1992 „Le maire Dinkins demande la venue des orphelins haitiens á New York", *Haiti Progrès,* 12 - 18 Aout, Vol. 10, No. 20, p. 11.

HP 135: Anonymous.
1992 „San Francisco: les gardes-côtes nord-américains interceptent de ´faux réfugiés´", *Haiti Progrès,* 19 - 25 Aout, Vol. 10, No. 21, p. 13.

HP 136: Anonymous.
1992 „Guantanamo: protestation des réfugiés haitiens atteints du Sida", *Haiti Progrès,* 2 - 8 Septembre, Vol. 10, No. 23, p. 7.

HP 137: Dauphin, Ludovic.
1992 „New York: Appel du Comité régional de finances", *Haiti Progrès,* 2 - 8 Septembre, Vol. 10, No. 23, p. 9.

HP 138: Anonymous.
1992 „New York: Hommage des journalistes haitiens à Paul Jean-Mario", *Haiti Progrès,* 2 - 8 Septembre, Vol. 10, No. 23, p. 9.

HP 139: Anonymous.
1992 „New York: pétitions pour protester contre toutes négociations avec Bazin", *Haiti Progrès,* 2 - 8 Septembre, Vol. 10, No. 23, p. 9.

HP 140: Anonymous.
1992 „New York: Le gouvernement légitime recoit ses amis américains", *Haiti Progrès,* 9 - 15 Septembre, Vol. 10, No. 24, p. 9,18.

HP 141: Latour, Fanfan.
1992 „Grande solidarité haitiano-américaine à Washington", *Haiti Progrès,* 16 - 22 Septembre, Vol. 10, No. 25, p. 9,19.

HP 142: Anonymous.
1992 „Calendrier des différentes commémorations du 30 septembre", *Haiti Progrès,* 23 - 29 Septembre, Vol. 10, No. 26, p. 7.

HP 143: Latour, Fanfan.
1992 „En marge du 30 septembre: rencontre avec le président Aristide", *Haiti Progrès,* 23 - 29 Septembre, Vol. 10, No. 26, p. 9.

HP 144: Ives, Kim.
1992 „Le président Aristide honoré par l'IPS", *Haiti Progrès,* 23 - 29 Septembre, Vol. 10, No. 26, p. 13.

HP 145: Gilbert, Carl.
1992 „Guantanamo: mise en quarantaine des réfugiés atteints du Sida", *Haiti Progrès,* 30 Septembre - 6 Octobre, Vol. 10, No. 27, p. 8,11.

HP 146: Anonymous.
1992 „`Haiti: du rêve au cauchemar´: succès monstre à New York", *Haiti Progrès,* 30 Septembre - 6 Octobre, Vol. 10, No. 27, p. 10.

HP 147: Latour, Fanfan.
1992 „29 et 30 septembre 1992: Kadans rezistans à travers le `10è´", *Haiti Progrès,* 7 - 13 Octobre, Vol. 10, No. 28, p. 8 - 9.

HP 148: Latour, Fanfan.
1992 „Le Barreau de Philadelphie prend position", *Haiti Progrès,* 14 - 20 Octobre, Vol. 10, No. 29, p. 8.

HP 149: Agnant, Marie-Célie.
1992 „Haiti-Progrès a su mériter le solidarité", *Haiti Progrès,* 21 - 27 Octobre, Vol. 10, No. 30, p. 8.

HP 150: Anonymous.
1992 „New York: picket-line en faveur des réfugiés haitiens", *Haiti Progrès,* 27 Octobre - 3 Novembre, Vol. 10, No. 31, p. 8.

HP 151: Anonymous.
1992 „Marie-Laurence Lassègue et la communauté haitienne de New York", *Haiti Progrès,* 4 - 10 Novembre, Vol. 10, No. 32, p. 8,23.

HP 152: Roumer, Guy.
1992 „Victoire de Clinton: quelles conséquences pour Haiti", *Haiti Progrès,* 4 - 10 Novembre, Vol. 10, No. 32, p. 1,19,22?.

HP 153: Anonymous.
1992 „Clinton: quelles solution pour Haiti", *Haiti Progrès,* 11 - 17 Novembre, Vol. 10, No. 33, p. 6,16.

HP 154: Gilbert, Carl et Ives, Kim.
1992 „Réfugiés de Guantanamo: un procès contre le gouvernement des Etats-Unis", *Haiti Progrès,* 11 - 17 Novembre, Vol. 10, No. 33, p. 9.

HP 155: Anonymous.
1992 „Nouvelles vagues de réfugiés vers les Etats-Unis", *Haiti Progrès,* 11 - 17 Novembre, Vol. 10, No. 33, p. 9,10.

HP 156: Anonymous.
1992 „Clinton fait marche arrière sur les réfugiés haitiens", *Haiti Progrès,* 18 - 24 Novembre, Vol. 10, No. 34, p. 9.

HP 157: Latour, Fanfan, avec Kim Ives.
1992 „Le président Aristide à l'honneur à New York", *Haiti Progrès,* 25 Novembre - 1 Decembre, Vol. 10, No. 35, p. 10 - 12.

HP 158: Anonymous.
1992 „ONU: Oui au renforcement de l'embargo! Non à l'intervention militaire", *Haiti Progrès,* 2 - 8 Decembre, Vol. 10, No. 36, p. 6,16 - 17.

HP 159: Anonymous.
1992 „Le 'député Patrick Norzéus à New York", *Haiti Progrès,* 2 - 8 Decembre, Vol. 10, No. 36, p. 7.

HP 160: Anonymous.
1992 „Le 29 novembre commémoré à New York", *Haiti Progrès,* 2 - 8 Decembre, Vol. 10, No. 36, p. 8.

HP 161: Anonymous.
1992 „Dixième Département: qu'est-ce qui ne va pas?", *Haiti Progrès,* 9 - 15 Decembre, Vol. 10, No. 37, p. 6,16 - 19.

HP 162: Anonymous.
1992 „New York: rencontre sur les réfugiés de Guantanamo", *Haiti Progrès,* 16 - 22 Decembre, Vol. 10, No. 38, p. 8.

HP 163: Gilbert, Carl.
1992 „Réfugiés: le probléme demeure entier", *Haiti Progrès,* 16 - 22 Decembre, Vol. 10, No. 38, p. 9,17.

HP 164: Anonymous.
1993 „New York: soirée de fête avec l'Organisation du Dixième", *Haiti Progrès,* 30 Decembre - 5 Janvier, Vol. 10, No. 40, p. 8.

HP 165: Anonymous.
1993 „Pour une redéfinition du terme 'réfugié'", *Haiti Progrès,* 30 Decembre - 5 Janvier, Vol. 10, No. 40, p. 8.

HP 166: Anonymous.
1993 „Accord entre Washington, l'OEA et l'ONU sur la résolution de la crise", *Haiti Progrès,* 6 - 12 Janvier, Vol. 10, No. 41, p. 1,16.

HP 167: Anonymous.
1993 „Bref Bilan de L'annee 1992", *Haiti Progrès,* 6 - 12 Janvier, Vol. 10, No. 41, p. 15.

HP 168: Anonymous.
1993 „Retour à la démocratie: à quel prix?", *Haiti Progrès,* 13 - 19 Janvier, Vol. 10, No. 42, p. 6,14,16.

HP 169: Anonymous.
1993 „Réfugiés: toujours un point chaud de l'actualité aux Etats-Unis", *Haiti Progrès,* 13 - 19 Janvier, Vol. 10, No. 42, p. 8?.

HP 170: Ives, Kim, Carl Gilbert trans.
1993 „Miami: manif de solidarité avec les grévistes de la faim", *Haiti Progrès,* 13 - 19 Janvier, Vol. 10, No. 42, p. 9.

HP 171: Ives, Kim, Fanfan Latour trans.
1993 „Le Haitiens à Guantanamo: Réfugiés politiques ou prisonniers de guerre?", *Haiti Progrès,* 13 - 19 Janvier, Vol. 10, No. 42, p. 10 - 11.

HP 172: Anonymous.
1993 „Clinton: 'un mur de Berlin flottant' contre le peuple haitien", *Haiti Progrès,* 20 - 26 Janvier, Vol. 10, No. 43, p. 6,14 - 16.

HP 173: Anonymous.
1993 „Des réfugiés sur les mers malgré la volte-face de Clinton", *Haiti Progrès,* 20 - 26 Janvier, Vol. 10, No. 43, p. 8.

HP 174: Anonymous.
1993 „Jesse Jackson: les retombées de sa visite en Haiti", *Haiti Progrès,* 27 Janvier - 2 Février, Vol. 10, No. 44, p. 1,16- 18.

HP 175: Anonymous.
1993 „Jesse Jackson réclame un ultimatim de 90 jours contre les putschistes", *Haiti Progrès,* 3 - 9 Février, Vol. 10, No. 45, p. 1,22.

HP 176: Latour, Fanfan.
1993 „Commémoration du 7 février 1991: Calendrier des manifestations", *Haiti Progrès,* 3 - 9 Février, Vol. 10, No. 45, p. 8,23.

HP 177: Gilbert, Carl.
1993 „Guantanamo: les réfugiés haitiens entament une grève de la faim", *Haiti Progrès,* 3 - 9 Février, Vol. 10, No. 45, p. 11,20.

HP 178: Anonymous.
1993 „New York: rencontre avec deux ministres du gouvernement légitime", *Haiti Progrès,* 3 - 9 Février, Vol. 10, No. 45, p. 11.

HP 179: Jean-Juste, Gérard.
1993 „L'Organisation du dixième officiellement établie à New Jersey", *Haiti Progrès,* 3 - 9 Février, Vol. 10, No. 45, p. 11.

HP 180: Anonymous.
1993 „7 février 1993: Vox Populi, Vox Titidi", *Haiti Progrès,* 10 - 16 Février, Vol. 10, No. 46, p. 8 - 9.

HP 181: Gilbert, Carl.
1993 „Une lueur d'espoir pour les réfugiés haitiens à Guantanamo et à Krome", *Haiti Progrès,* 17 - 23 Février 1993 ?, Vol. 11, No. 47 ?, p. 11,18,?.

HP 182: Gilbert, Carl.
1993 „SIDA: vote discriminatoire du Sénat américain", *Haiti Progrès,* 24 Février - 2 Mars, Vol. 10, No. 48.

HP 183: Anonymous.
1993 „New York: appel aux réfugiés venus de Guantanamo", *Haiti Progrès,* 24 Février - 2 Mars, Vol. 10, No. 48, p. 7.

HP 184: Anonymous.
1993 „2 avril: manifestation à Washington", *Haiti Progrès,* 24 Février - 2 Mars, Vol. 10, No. 48, p. 7.

HP 185: Anonymous.
1993 „New York: projection de `Haiti, killing the dream'", *Haiti Progrès,* 24 Février - 2 Mars, Vol. 10, No. 48, p. 7.

HP 186: Anonymous.
1993 „New York: soirée de solidarité avec la lutte du peuple haitien", *Haiti Progrès,* 24 Février - 2 Mars, Vol. 10, No. 48, p. 7.

HP 187: Anonymous.
1993 „Réfugiés: Clinton entend maintenir les rapatriements forcés", *Haiti Progrès,* 3 - 9 Mars, Vol. 10, No. 49, p. 8.

HP 188: Anonymous.
1993 „New York: un étudiant de Brooklyn College tué en Haiti", *Haiti Progrès,* 3 - 9 Mars, Vol. 10, No. 49, p. 9.

HP 189: Tecumseh, Angèle.
1993 „Réfugiés haitiens: la politique `humanitaire' de Clinton", *Haiti Progrès,* 10 - 16 Mars, Vol. 10, No. 50, p. 10-13.

HP 190: Anonymous.
1993 „Brooklyn: protestation en faveur des Haitiens à Guantanamo", *Haiti Progrès,* 10 - 16 Mars, Vol. 10, No. 50.

HP 191: Anonymous.
1993 „Femmes à New York", *Haiti Progrès,* 10 - 16 Mars, Vol. 10, No. 50.

HP 192: Anonymous.
1993 „Clinton: peu lui importe que 264 réfugiés périssent à Guantanamo", *Haiti Progrès,* 17 - 23 Mars, Vol. 10, No. 51, p. 6,16,17.

HP 193: Gilbert, Carl, avec Edouard Hazel.
1993 „De retour de Guantanamo, le docteur Hazel parle des réfugiés haitiens", *Haiti Progrès,* 17 - 23 Mars, Vol. 10, No. 51, p. 9,14.

HP 194: Anonymous.
1993 „New York: nouvelle action en faveur des réfugiés", *Haiti Progrès,* 17 - 23 Mars, Vol. 10, No. 51, p. 17.

HP 195: Ives, Kim, Marie-Célie Agnant trans.
1993 „Intense répression militaire contre les réfugiés de Guantanamo", *Haiti Progrès,* 24 - 30 Mars, Vol. 10, No. 52, p. 1,20-21.

HP 196: Anonymous.
1993 „Brooklyn: brutalités policières contre un Haitien confirmées", *Haiti Progrès,* 24 - 30 Mars, Vol. 10, No. 52, p. 8.

HP 197: Anonymous.
1993 „New York: élections dans le `dixième'", *Haiti Progrès,* 24 - 30 Mars, Vol. 10, No. 52, p. 8.

HP 198: Anonymous.
1993 „New York: épologue d'un meurtre", *Haiti Progrès,* 24 - 30 Mars, Vol. 10, No. 52, p. 8.

HP 199: Anonymous.
1993 „Brooklyn: soirée politico-culturelle autour de la Constitution", *Haiti Progrès,* 31 Mars - 6 Avril, Vol. 11, No. 1, p. 8,16.

HP 200: Aristide, Jean-Bertrand.
1993 „Message du président Aristide aux étudiants solidaires des réfugiés haitiens à Guantanamo", *Haiti Progrès,* 31 Mars - 6 Avril, Vol. 11, No. 1, p. 9.

HP 201: Gilbert, Carl.
1993 „Le gouvernement Clinton doit prodiguer des soins adéquats aux compatriotes de Guantanamo", *Haiti Progrès,* 31 Mars - 6 Avril, Vol. 11, No. 1, p. 9.

HP 202: Anonymous.
1993 „Haiti-Progrès: dix ans de lutte", *Haiti Progrès,* 31 Mars - 6 Avril, Vol. 11, No. 1, p. 10 - 14.

HP 203: Gilbert, Carl.
1993 „Pressions en faveur des Haitiens prisonniers aux Etats-Unis", *Haiti Progrès,* 7 - 13 Avril, Vol. 11, No. 2, p. 9,16.

HP 204: Latour, Marie-France, F.L. trans.
1993 „Protestation d'étudiants en faveur des Haitiens", *Haiti Progrès,* 7 - 13 Avril, Vol. 11, No. 2, p. 8.

HP 205: Anonymous.
1993 „Des réfugiés transférés de Guantanamo aux Etats-Unis", *Haiti Progrès,* 14 - 20 Avril, Vol. 11, No. 3, p. 8.

HP 206: Dow, Mark, Carl Gilbert trans.
1993 „Liberté sans conditions: résistance à Krome", *Haiti Progrès,* 14 - 20 Avril, Vol. 11, No. 3, p. 13.

HP 207: Charlemagne, Alix.
1993 „New York: manifestation en solidarité avec les réfugiés de Guantanamo", *Haiti Progrès,* 21 - 27 Avril, Vol. 11, No. 4, p. 8.

HP 208: Joseph, Fedner.
1993 „New York: lancement du livre `Théologie et politique`", *Haiti Progrès,* 21 - 27 Avril, Vol. 11, No. 4, p. 8.

HP 209: Anonymous.
1993 „Tournée du premier ministre René Préval à New York", *Haiti Progrès,* 28 Avril - 4 Mai, Vol. 11, No. 5, p. 9,17.

HP 210a: Charlemagne, Alix.
1993 „Projection du film `This Other Haiti´ à Brooklyn", *Haiti Progrès,* 28 Avril - 4 Mai, Vol. 11, No. 5, p. 8.

HP 210b: Joseph, Fedner.
1993 „Grande soiré politico-culturelle à Brooklyn", *Haiti Progrès,* 28 Avril - 4 Mai, Vol. 11, No. 5, p. 8.

HP 211: Anonymous.
1993 „May Day Rally", *Haiti Progrès,* 5 - 11 Mai, Vol. 11, No. 6, p. 8.

HP 212: Anonymous.
1993 „Haiti-Progrés: dix ans de présence, dix ans de lutte", *Haiti Progrès,* 5 - 11 Mai, Vol. 11, No. 6, p. 8,?.

HP 213: Gilbert, Carl.
1993 „Drames des réfugiés haitiens", *Haiti Progrès,* 1 - 7 Décembre, Vol. 11, No. 36, p. 8.

HP 214: Anonymous.
1993 „New York: manifestation contre toute intervention en Haiti", *Haiti Progrès,* 1 - 7 Décembre, Vol. 11, No. 36.

HP 215: Anonymous.
1993 „New York: les Etats-Unis et l´ONU sur la sellette", *Haiti Progrès,* 8 - 14 Décembre, Vol. 11, No. 37.

HP 216: Latour, Fanfan.
1993 „Le 16 décembre devant la Maison Blanche: Pour que vive la démocratie", *Haiti Progrès,* 22 - 28 Décembre, Vol. 11, No. 39, p. 8,17.

HP 217: Anonymous.
1994 „Washington s´oppose à la conférence de Miami", *Haiti Progrès,* 29 Décembre 1993 - 4 Janvier, Vol. 11, No. 40, p. 1,13.

HP 218: Latour, Fanfan.
1994 „Bilan au seuil de 1994: Le `devoir d´espérer", *Haiti Progrès,* 29 Décembre 1993 - 4 Janvier, Vol. 11, No. 40, p. 10-12.

HP 219: Anonymous.
1994 „1994 sous le signe de Dessalines", *Haiti Progrès,* 5 - 11 Janvier, Vol. 11, No. 41, p. 1,7.

HP 220: Roumer, Guy.
1994 „A la veille de la conférence de Miami: La question des réfugiés à l'ordre du jour", *Haiti Progrès,* 5 - 11 Janvier, Vol. 11, No. 41, p. 1,17.

HP 221: Anonymous.
1994 „Réfugiés: un nouveau drame frappe ces oubliés", *Haiti Progrès,* 5 - 11 Janvier, Vol. 11, No. 41.

HP 222: Anonymous.
1994 „Conférence de Miami: L'armée va-t-elle participer?", *Haiti Progrès,* 12 - 18 Janvier, Vol. 11, No. 42, p. 1,16.

HP 223: Roumer, Guy.
1994 „En guise de retour", *Haiti Progrès,* 12 - 18 Janvier, Vol. 11, No. 41.

HP 224: Anonymous.
1994 „Conférence de Miami: Quel impact sur le retour d'Aristide?", *Haiti Progrès,* 19 - 25 Janvier, Vol. 11, No. 43, p. 1,17.

HP 225: Anonymous.
1994 „No au macoutisme dans le dixième!", *Haiti Progrès,* 19 - 25 Janvier, Vol. 11, No. 43, p. 7.

HP 226: Latour, Fanfan.
1994 „Une autre conférence tenue à Miami", *Haiti Progrès,* 19 - 25 Janvier, Vol. 11, No. 43, p. 8,9.

HP 227: Roumer, Guy.
1994 „Réfugiés: un dossier impossible à classer", *Haiti Progrès,* 19 - 25 Janvier, Vol. 11, No. 43.

HP 228: Anonymous.
1994 „Bilan d'une conférence", *Haiti Progrès,* 26 Janvier - 1 Février, Vol. 11, No. 44, p. 6,13-15.

HP 229: Ratner, Michael.
1994 „Michael Ratner écrit au président Aristide", *Haiti Progrès,* 26 Janvier - 1 Février, Vol. 11, No. 44, p. 8.

HP 230: Anonymous.
1994 „Réfugiés: nouvelles tentatives de fuir Haiti", *Haiti Progrès,* 2 - 8 Février, Vol. 11, No. 45, p. 8.

HP 231: Anonymous.
1994 „Solidarité au-delà des frontières", *Haiti Progrès,* 2 - 8 Février, Vol. 11, No. 45, p. 8.

HP 232: Latour, Fanfan.
1994 „Branle-bas communautaire à New York", *Haiti Progrès,* 9 - 15 Février, Vol. 11, No. 46, p. 8,19.

HP 233: Gilbert, Carl.
1994 „Réfugiés: Aristide pourrait dénoncer l'accord avec les Etats-Unis", *Haiti Progrès,* 16 - 22 Février, Vol. 11, No. 47, p. 5,18.

HP 234: Anonymous.
1994 „Nouvelle tragédie de la mer", *Haiti Progrès,* 23 Février - 1 Mars, Vol. 11, No. 48, p. 8.

HP 235: Anonymous.
1994 „Réfugiés: hécatombe sans fin", *Haiti Progrès,* 23 Février - 1 Mars, Vol. 11, No. 48, p. 8.

HP 236: Latour, Fanfan.
1994 „Mobilisation tèt kale devant l'ONU", *Haiti Progrès,* 9 - 15 Mars, Vol. 11, No. 50, p. 1,17.

HP 237: Anonymous.
1994 „Offensive contre la politique de Clinton en Haiti", *Haiti Progrès,* 23 - 29 Mars, Vol. 11, No. 52, p. 1,18.

HP 238: Gilbert, Carl.
1994 „New York: des médicins dénoncent la détention de Jacques Dorcéan", *Haiti Progrès,* 23 - 29 Mars, Vol. 11, No. 52, p. 6,17.

HP 239: Anonymous.
1994 „Miami: de nombreux événements au cours du week-end", *Haiti Progrès,* 23 - 29 Mars, Vol. 11, No. 52, p. 7.

HP 240: Anonymous.
1994 „Un nouveau vice-consul à New York", *Haiti Progrès,* 23 - 29 Mars, Vol. 11, No. 52.

HP 241: Anonymous.
1994 „Un consul, un vice-consul et... Haiti-Observateur", *Haiti Progrès,* 30 Mars - 5 Avril, Vol. 12, No. 1, p. 7,18.

HP 242: Anonymous.
1994 „Aristide pourrait abroger l'accord sur les réfugiés: Une nouvelle de dernière heure", *Haiti Progrès,* 6 - 12 Avril, Vol. 12, No. 2, p. 1,19.

HP 243: Anonymous.
1994 „Quoi de changé pour les réfugiés?", *Haiti Progrès,* 13 - 19 Avril, Vol. 12, No. 3, p. 6,16.

HP 244: Anonymous.
1994 „Nouvelle tournée dans le dixième: Le président Aristide joindra-t-il le geste à la parole?", *Haiti Progrès,* 13 - 19 Avril, Vol. 12, No. 3, p. 7.

HP 245: Anonymous.
1994 „New York: une tentative pro-putschiste", *Haiti Progrès,* 13 - 19 Avril, Vol. 12, No. 3, p. 8.

HP 246: Anonymous.
1994 „Aristide Scraps Refugee Treaty", *Haiti Progrès,* 13 - 19 Avril, Vol. 12, No. 3, p. 9.

HP 247: Anonymous.
1994 „US `Complicity' Blasted", *Haiti Progrès,* 13 - 19 Avril, Vol. 12, No. 3, p. 9.

HP 248: Anonymous.
1994 „Playing Ball with the Putschists", *Haiti Progrès,* 13 - 19 Avril, Vol. 12, No. 3, p. 9.

HP 249: Anonymous.
1994 „Pas d'embargo pour les balles de baseball", *Haiti Progrès,* 20 - 26 Avril, Vol. 12, No. 4, p. 8,15.

HP 250: Anonymous.
1994 „Bill Clinton au banc des accusés", *Haiti Progrès,* 20 - 26 Avril, Vol. 12, No. 4, p. 8.

HP 251: Anonymous.
1994 „Grève de la faim en faveur des réfugiés", *Haiti Progrès,* 20 - 26 Avril, Vol. 12, No. 4, p. 8.

HP 252: Anonymous.
1994 „Congress Moves To Force Change In US-Haiti Policy", *Haiti Progrès,* 20 - 26 Avril, Vol. 12, No. 4.

HP 253: Gilbert, Carl, traducteur.
1994 „Alerte sur les réfugiés aux Bahamas", *Haiti Progrès,* 27 Avril - 3 Mai, Vol. 12, No. 5, p. 8.

HP 254: Anonymous.
1994 „Mount Vernon: action de solidarité avec Randall Robinson", *Haiti Progrès,* 27 Avril - 3 Mai, Vol. 12, No. 5, p. 8.

HP 255: Anonymous.
1994 „New York: soirée de solidarité avec le peuple haitien", *Haiti Progrès,* 27 Avril - 3 Mai, Vol. 12, No. 5, p. 8.

HP 256: Anonymous.
1994 „Washington: protestation devant la Maison Blanche", *Haiti Progrès,* 27 Avril - 3 Mai, Vol. 12, No. 5, p. 8.

HP 257: Anonymous.
1994 „10.000 manifestants devant la Maison Blanche: Message transmis à Clinton", *Haiti Progrès,* 4 - 10 Mai, Vol. 12, No. 6, p. 1,17.

HP 258: Anonymous.
1994 „Réfugiés: le rapatriement forcé maintenu", *Haiti Progrès,* 11 - 17 Mai, Vol. 12, No. 7, p. 1,7.

HP 259: Anonymous.
1994 „New York: solidarité syndicale", *Haiti Progrès,* 11 - 17 Mai, Vol. 12, No. 8.

HP 260: Anonymous.
1994 „Clinton Policy Change to High Seas Interviews Called `Cosmetic'", *Haiti Progrès,* 11 - 17 Mai, Vol. 12, No. 8.

HP 261: Anonymous.
1994 „Aristide à New York: des propos ambigus", *Haiti Progrès,* 18 - 24 Mai, Vol. 12, No. 8, p. 8,20.

HP 262: Anonymous.
1994 „Refugee Exodus Hits Peak", *Haiti Progrès,* 18 - 24 Mai, Vol. 12, No. 8, p. 13.

HP 263: Anonymous.
1994 „De Facto President #2 Installed By Military", *Haiti Progrès,* 18 - 24 Mai, Vol. 12, No. 8, p. 13.

HP 264: Anonymous.
1994 „Political and Military Maneuvers", *Haiti Progrès,* 18 - 24 Mai, Vol. 12, No. 8, p. 13.

HP 265: Anonymous.
1994 „Réfugiés: Clinton continue à bluffer", *Haiti Progrès,* 18 - 24 Mai, Vol. 12, No. 8, p. 13.

HP 266: Anonymous.
1994 „Réfugiés: l'ONU au secours des Etats-Unis", *Haiti Progrès,* 25 - 31 Mai, Vol. 12, No. 9, p. 6,16.

HP 267: Anonymous.
1994 „New York: une nouvelle action contre SEARS", *Haiti Progrès,* 1 - 7 Juin, Vol. 12, No. 10, p. 8.

HP 268: Gilbert, Carl.
1994 „New York: la HOHS organise son premier congrès sur la santé", *Haiti Progrès,* 1 - 7 Juin, Vol. 12, No. 10, p. 8,17.

HP 269: Anonymous.
1994 „L'embargo, pour quoi faire?", *Haiti Progrès,* 1 - 7 Juin, Vol. 12, No. 10, p. 8,17.

HP 270: Anonymous.
1994 „New York: un procès contre le FRAPH", *Haiti Progrès,* 8 - 14 Juin, Vol. 12, No. 11, p. 7.

HP 271: Anonymous.
1994 „Un représentant de l'APN à New York", *Haiti Progrès,* 8 - 14 Juin, Vol. 12, No. 11.

HP 272: Anonymous.
1994 „Avril condamné à payer des dédommagements à ses victimes", *Haiti Progrès,* 8 - 14 Juin, Vol. 12, No. 11.

HP 273: Anonymous.
1994 „Refugee Off Shore Screening Set to Begin", *Haiti Progrès,* 8 - 14 Juin, Vol. 12, No. 11.

HP 274: Anonymous.
1994 „NACLA Report on the Americas", 8 - 14 Juin, Vol. 12, No. 11; *Haiti Progrès,* 22 - 28 Juin, Vol. 12, No. 13, p. 13.

HP 275: Anonymous.
1994 „Refugees, The CIA And Intervention", *Haiti Progrès,* 8 - 14 Juin, Vol. 12, No. 11.

HP 276: Anonymous.
1994 „Clinton paie le prix fort pour se débarrasser des réfugiés", *Haiti Progrès,* 8 - 14 Juin, Vol. 12, No. 11, p. 13.

HP 277: Anonymous.
1994 „La politique de Clinton à l'égard des réfugiés: `encore une cynique plaisanterie'", *Haiti Progrès,* 22 - 28 Juin, Vol. 12, No. 13, p. 8.

HP 278: Anonymous.
1994 „Refugees Begin Middle Passage", *Haiti Progrès,* 22 - 28 Juin, Vol. 12, No. 13, p. 13.

HP 279: Anonymous.
1994 „UN Moves to Deploy Occupation Force", *Haiti Progrès,* 22 - 28 Juin, Vol. 12, No. 13, p. 13.

HP 280: Anonymous.
1994 „Confusion Reigns Again In Clinton Camp", *Haiti Progrès*, 22 - 28 Juin, Vol. 12, No. 13, p. 13.

HP 281: Anonymous.
1994 „Face à une forte vague de réfugiés: Clinton envisage de nouvelles mesures", *Haiti Progrès*, 29 Juin - 5 Juillet, Vol. 12, No. 14, p. 1,14.

HP 282: Anonymous.
1994 „New York: rencontre autour des problèmes des élèves haitiens aux Etats-Unis", *Haiti Progrès*, 29 Juin - 5 Juillet, Vol. 12, No. 14.

HP 283: Anonymous.
1994 „Après Guantanamo, une île au large du Panama pour y parquer les réfugiés", *Haiti Progrès*, 6 - 12 Juillet, Vol. 12, No. 15, p. 1,15.

HP 284: Anonymous.
1994 „Le président Aristide n'entend pas `mouri nan fim lan'", *Haiti Progrès*, 13 - 19 Juillet, Vol. 12, No. 16, p. 8,16.

HP 285: Anonymous.
1994 „Miami: forum sur la situation en Haiti", *Haiti Progrès*, 13 - 19 Juillet, Vol. 12, No. 16, p. 8.

HP 286: Anonymous.
1994 „Safe Havens - A Muderous Hoax", *Haiti Progrès*, 13 - 19 Juillet, Vol. 12, No. 16, p. 9.

HP 287: Anonymous.
1994 „Military Regime Ousts Observers", *Haiti Progrès*, 13 - 19 Juillet, Vol. 12, No. 16, p. 9.

HP 288: Anonymous.
1994 „Jockeying for Invasion", *Haiti Progrès*, 13 - 19 Juillet, Vol. 12, No. 16, p. 9,15.

HP 289: Tecumseh, Angèle.
1994 „Réfugiés haitiens: Les damnés de la mer", *Haiti Progrès*, 13 - 19 Juillet, Vol. 12, No. 16, p. 10-13.

HP 290: Kaye, Joe.
1994 „Les racines de la politique de Washington envers les réfugiés haitiens", *Haiti Progrès*, 13 - 19 Juillet, Vol. 12, No. 16, p. 16.

HP 291: Anonymous.
1994 „Le camp populaire dit: Non à l'intervention étrangére!", *Haiti Progrès*, 20 - 26 Juillet, Vol. 12, No. 17, p. 1,17.

HP 292: Anonymous.
1994 „Miami: week-end de solidarité avec la lutte du peuple haitien", *Haiti Progrès*, 20 - 26 Juillet, Vol. 12, No. 17, p. 17.

HP 293: Anonymous.
1994 „Miami: présentation du film `Canne amère'", *Haiti Progrès*, 20 - 26 Juillet, Vol. 12, No. 17, p. 17.

HP 294: Gilbert, Carl.
1994 „Réfugiés: un probléme en passe d´être régional", *Haiti Progrès,* 20 - 26 Juillet, Vol. 12, No. 17.

HP 295: Anonymous.
1994 „Mass Repatriation of Refugees", *Haiti Progrès,* 27 Juillet - 2 Août 1994 ?, Vol. 12, No. 18.

HP 296: Anonymous.
1994 „UN Ready to Sanction US Invasion", *Haiti Progrès,* 27 Juillet - 2 Août 1994 ?, Vol. 12, No. 18.

HP 297: Anonymous.
1994 „New York: des femmes en tête de la lutte contre le Vatican", *Haiti Progrès,* 27 Juillet - 2 Août, Vol. 12, No. 18, p. 8.

HP 298: Anonymous.
1994 „Puerto Rican Activists Denounce US Maneuvers", *Haiti Progrès,* 3 - 9 Août, Vol. 12, No. 19, p. 9.

HP 299: Anonymous.
1994 „Jocelyn McCalla: entre William Gray et Jean-Jacques Honorat", *Haiti Progrès,* 3 - 9 Août, Vol. 12, No. 19, p. 6,14- 15.

HP 300: Anonymous.
1994 „Réfugiés: le pire... et le meilleur", *Haiti Progrès,* 3 - 9 Août, Vol. 12, No. 19, p. 15.

HP 301: Ives, Kim, Guy Roumer trans.
1994 „28 Juillet: NON à une nouvelle occupation d´Haiti!", *Haiti Progrès,* 3 - 9 Août, Vol. 12, No. 19, p. 10-11.

HP 302: Anonymous.
1994 „Les trois religieux solidaires des réfugiés ne peuvent retourner en Haiti!", *Haiti Progrès,* 10 - 16 Août, Vol. 12, No. 20.

HP 303: Anonymous.
1994 „Réfugiés: le transfert vers d´autres pays mis en veilleuse", *Haiti Progrès,* 10 - 16 Août, Vol. 12, No. 20.

HP 304: Anonymous.
1994 „New York: réunion sur l´intervention nord-américaine en Haiti", *Haiti Progrès,* 10 - 16 Août, Vol. 12, No. 20.

HP 305: Anonymous.
1994 „Aristide `explique´ la résolution de l´ONU", *Haiti Progrès,* 10 - 16 Août, Vol. 12, No. 20, p. 14.

HP 306: Mailhiot, Perin, Loarca.
1994 „Témoignage des trois religieux sur leur voyage et leur séjour à Guantanamo", *Haiti Progrès,* 17 - 23 Août, Vol. 12, No. 21, p. 8,18.

HP 307: Anonymous.
1994 „Les Haitiens se révoltent à Guantanamo", *Haiti Progrès,* 17 - 23 Août, Vol. 12, No. 21.

HP 308: Anonymous.
1994   „Uprising Rocks Guantanamo", *Haiti Progrès,* 17 - 23 Août, Vol. 12, No. 21, p. 9.

HP 309: Anonymous.
1994   „Haitian Rights Groups Slam US Funding", *Haiti Progrès,* 17 - 23 Août, Vol. 12, No. 21, p. 9.

HP 310: Anonymous.
1994   „Letter to the Editor", *Haiti Progrès,* 17 - 23 Août, Vol. 12, No. 21, p. 9.

HP 311: Anonymous.
1994   „Nouveau mouvement de révolte à Guantanamo", *Haiti Progrès,* 24 - 30 Août, Vol. 12, No. 22, p. 1,18.

HP 312: Anonymous.
1994   „Le gouvernement légitime autorisé à aller à Guantanamo... pour un jour", *Haiti Progrès,* 24 - 30 Août, Vol. 12, No. 22.

HP 313: Anonymous.
1994   „Phantoms - Sweet Micky: Une perversion de l´art", *Haiti Progrès,* 31 Août - 6 Septembre, Vol. 12, No. 22.

HP 314: Anonymous.
1994   „Phantoms - Sweet Micky: Le spectacle de la honte", *Haiti Progrès,* 7 - 13 Septembre, Vol. 12, No. 24.

HP 315: Anonymous.
1994   „New York: manifestation en faveur des réfugiés haitiens", *Haiti Progrès,* 7 - 13 Septembre, Vol. 12, No. 24.

HP 316: Anonymous.
1994   „Guantanamo: frustrations et révoltes", *Haiti Progrès,* 7 - 13 Septembre, Vol. 12, No. 24, p. 1,18.

HP 317: Anonymous.
1994   „New York: les adieux de la communauté à Jean-Marie Vincent", *Haiti Progrès,* 7 - 13 Septembre, Vol. 12, No. 24, p. 8,?.

HP 318: Anonymous.
1994   „US Admits Collaborating with Haitian Military on Refugees", *Haiti Progrès,* 7 - 13 Septembre, Vol. 12, No. 24, p. 9.

HP 319: Anonymous.
1994   „Commémoration du 11 septembre, six ans après", *Haiti Progrès,* 14 - 20 Septembre, Vol. 12, No. 25, p. 7,18.

HP 320: Petit, Jean-Claude.
1994   „Principales demandes des réfugiés de Guantanamo", *Haiti Progrès,* 14 - 20 Septembre, Vol. 12, No. 25, p. 8.

HP 321: Anonymous.
1994   „US War Machine Gears Up", *Haiti Progrès,* 14 - 20 Septembre, Vol. 12, No. 25, p. 9.

HP 322: Anonymous.
1994 „Invasion Aims to Impose Neo-Liberal Program", *Haiti Progrès,* 14 - 20 Septembre, Vol. 12, No. 25, p. 9.

HP 323: Anonymous.
1994 „Chirac Launches Attack on Haitian Refugees", *Haiti Progrès,* 14 - 20 Septembre, Vol. 12, No. 25, p. 9.

HP 324: Anonymous.
1994 „Protestations aux Etats-Unis contre l'occupation", *Haiti Progrès,* 21 - 27 Septembre, Vol. 12, No. 26.

HP 325: Anonymous.
1994 „New York: forum sur l'occupation d'Haiti", *Haiti Progrès,* 21 - 27 Septembre, Vol. 12, No. 26.

HP 326: Anonymous.
1994 „New York: manifestation anti-intervention en Haiti", *Haiti Progrès,* 21 - 27 Septembre, Vol. 12, No. 26.

HP 327: Anonymous.
1994 „New York: hommage à Jean-Marie Vincent avec Mgr Romélus", *Haiti Progrès,* 21 - 27 Septembre, Vol. 12, No. 26, p. 14,15.

HP 328: Anonymous.
1994 „Les réfugiés peu enthousiastes pour retourner", *Haiti Progrès,* 28 Septembre - 4 Octobre, Vol. 12, No. 27.

HP 329: Anonymous.
1994 „Popular Organizations Denounce U.S. Occupation", *Haiti Progrès,* 28 Septembre - 4 Octobre, Vol. 12, No. 27, p. 9.

HP 330: Paraison, Edwin.
1994 „Réfugiés: un rapatriement inadéquat", *Haiti Progrès,* 28 Septembre - 4 Octobre, Vol. 12, No. 27.

HP 331: Anonymous.
1994 „Opération retour avec Tonton Sam", *Haiti Progrès,* 19 - 25 Octobre, Vol. 12, No. 30, p. 6,16-17.

8 Appendix

Contents:

Haitian-(American) Organizations in the New York Metropolitan Area (25)

Chronology and Interview Statitsics: November 1994 - January 1997

Chronology and Events Statitsics: September 1994 - July 1995

Example of Abstract of *New York Times*-Article Prepared by *Proquest*

Statitsics of NYT-articles: Period from October 1, 1991 until October 16, 1994
(share of articles on refugees, on 10e in US, on advocacy community; in analysis 1, editorials, USCG statitsics, major events)

Haitian Refugee Crisis 1991-1994: Chart on Coverage by the New York Times

Statitsics of *Haiti Progrès*-Articles Included in the Pool as Basis for the Study

Questionnaire for interview with Jocelyn McCalla/NCHR on February 15, 1995

Questionnaire for interview with Ronald Aubourg/HCC on September 19, 1996

Lits of Members of National Coalition for Haitian Refugees´ *Board of Directors*

13 Communication Levels, on which NCHR Exerted Influence

Haiti-Related OAS- and UN - Documents, 1991 - 1994 (chronological order)

Haitian-(American) Organizations in the New York Metropolitan Area (25)
(in alphabetical order, membership in brackets, research focus in bold letters, "-" = later focus)

Bedford Haitian Center (HCC)
BHRAGS/Haitian Community Center (BfA, HCC)

Brooklyn for Aritside/BfA

Coalition of Haitian Organizations

- **Emergency Coalition for Haitian Refugees**

Evangelical Crusade/Eglise Croisade Evang. De La Pentecote (BfA, HCC, NCHR)
Flatbush Haitian Center (HCC)
Haitian Affairs Committee
Haitian American Cultural and Social Organization/HACSO (HCC, NCHR)

Haitian Americans United for Progress/HAUP (HCC, NCHR)
Haitian Centers Council / - Haitian Coalition on AIDS (BfA, NCHR)

Haitian Community Association/Huntington
Haitian Community Center of Stanford/Connecticut (HCC)

- **Haitian Enforcement Against Racism**

Haitian Neighborhood Service Center (HCC)

- **Haitian Women for Haitian Refugees**
- **Haitian Women Program**

Haitain Women´s Organization/Kombit Famm Ayisyen (BfA)
Haitian World Autonomous Culture Movement/MOKAM
Haiti Information Center

National Coalition for Haitian Refugees/NCHR (New York Immigration Coalition)
St. Jerome´s Roman Catholic Church/Pére Guy Sansaricq (BfA, NCHR)

- **10th Department Organization of New York**
United Haitian Association

Haitian Consulate/Wilson Désir´s office/Alliance des Emigres Haitiens (BfA)

Chronology and Interview Statitsics: November 1994 - January 1997
Chronology

Date:	Informant:	Organization:
01: 11.16.94, 15:00,	Bill Frelick,	US Committee for Refugees (USCR)
02: 02.15.95, 10:00,	Jocelyn McCalla,	National Coalition for Haitian Refugees (NCHR)
03 02.22.95, 10:00,	Jocelyn McCalla,	National Coalition for Haitian Refugees (NCHR)
04: 03.12.95, 14:30,	Mario Toussaint,	Brooklyn for Aritside (BfA)
05: 03.29.95, 10:00,	Jocelyn McCalla,	National Coalition for Haitian Refugees (NCHR)
06: 04.11.95, 12:30,	Major R. Owens,	Member of Congress, CBC, BfA
07: 04.13.95, 10:00,	William O'Neill,	National Coalition for Haitian Refugees (NCHR)
08: 04.13.95, 12:00,	Anne Fuller,	National Coalition for Haitian Refugees (NCHR)
09: 04.26.95, 12:00,	Eileen Reilly,	Church Ave. Merchants Block Assoc. (CAMBA)
10: 04.27.95, 15:00,	Henry Frank,	Haitian Centers Council (HCC)
11: 04.28.95, 10:00,	Jocelyn McCalla,	National Coalition for Haitian Refugees (NCHR)
12: 04.29.95, 20:00,	Andetrie Smith,	Brooklyn Society for Ethical Culture
13: 05.04.95, 14:00,	Aphaly Coradin,	National Coalition for Haitian Refugees (NCHR)
14: 05.29.95, 15:00,	Henry Frank,	Haitian Centers Council (HCC)
15: 06.02.95, 10:00,	Jocelyn McCalla,	National Coalition for Haitian Refugees (NCHR)
16: 06.07.95, 11:00,	Paul Dorsinville,	Haitian Americans United for Progress (HAUP)
17: 06.11.95, 13:00,	Mario Toussaint,	Brooklyn for Aritside (BfA)
18: 06.12.95, 12:00,	Wilson Désir,	Haitian Consulate
19: 06.13.95, 15:30,	Henry Frank,	Haitian Centers Council (HCC)
20: 06.16.95, 15:00,	Guy Sansaricq,	Haitian Apostolate, St. Jerome Church
21: 06.22.95, 14:00,	Aphaly Coradin,	National Coalition for Haitian Refugees (NCHR)
22: 06.26.95, 11:00,	Paul Dorsinville,	Haitian Americans United for Progress (HAUP)
23: 06.27.95, 10:00,	Jocelyn McCalla,	National Coalition for Haitian Refugees (NCHR)
24: 06.28.95, 11:00,	David Harris,	National Coalition for Haitian Refugees (NCHR)
25: 06.30.95, 14:00,	Aphaly Coradin,	National Coalition for Haitian Refugees (NCHR)
26: 07.03.95, 16:00,	Jocelyne Mayas,	Haitian Women for Haitian Refugees (HWHR)
27: 07.11.95, 10:30,	Lisa Daugaard,	Yale-Team, Emerg. Coalition for H.R. (ECHR)
28: 07.11.95, 13:30,	Betty Williams,	Haitian Women Prog. (WHP), Housing Works
29: 07.12.95, 10:00,	Guy Sansaricq,	Haitian Apostolate, St. Jerome Church
30: 07.13.95, 18:00,	Ninaj Raoul,	Haitian Women for Haitian Refugees (HWHR)
31: 07.24.95, 10:00,	Carlo DeRege,	Catholic Charities (CC)
32: 07.25.95, 13:00,	Mike Wischnie,	Emergeny Coalition for H.R. (ECHR), Yale-Team
33: 07.27.95, 21:00,	Lisa Charles etc.	Haitian Enforcement Against Racism (HEAR)
34: 07.29.95, 18:00,	M. Loueur	Landlord, private (end of research stay)
35: 02.15.96, 18:00,	Guy Victor (phone)	10e of New York (currently: HRC)
36: 09.19.96, 16:00,	Ronald Aubourg	Haitian Centers Council (before: NCHR)
37: 09.20.96, 14:00,	Yull Célestin	Episcopal Migration Minitsries (EMM)
38: 01.09.97, 15:00,	Dr. Marie Carmel Pierre-Louis (phone)	Haitian Coalition on AIDS (HCAIDS) / HCC

Statitsics
(in alphabetical order according to last name of informant)

Nr.:	Informant:	Number:	Time (ca.):	Nationality:	"Race":
01.	Ronald Aubourg	1 interview	1 hour	Haitian	Black
02.	Yull Célestin	1 interview	2 hours	Haitian	Black
03.	Lisa Charles etc.	1 interview	1.5 hour	Haitian	Black
04.	Aphaly Coradin	3 interviews	3.5 hours	Haitian	Black
05.	Lisa Daugaard	1 interview	1 hour	American	White
06.	Carlo DeRege	1 interview	1 hour	American	White
07.	Wilson Désir	1 interview	1 hour	Haitian	Black
08.	Paul Dorsinville	2 interviews	2.5 hours	Haitian	Black
09.	Henry Frank	3 interviews	3 hours	Haitian	Black
10.	Bill Frelick	1 interview	1 hour	American	White
11.	Anne Fuller	1 interview	1.5 hours	American	White
12.	David Harris	1 interview	2 hours	American	White
13.	M. Loueur	1 interview	1 hour	Haitian	Black
14.	Jocelyne Mayas	1 interview	1 hour	Haitian	Black
15.	Jocelyn McCalla	6 interviews	11 hours	Haitian	Black
16.	William O'Neill	1 interview	1 hour	American	White
17.	Major R. Owens	1 interview	1 hour	American	Black
18.	Dr. Marie Carmel Pierre-Louis	1 interview	1 hours	Haitian	Black
19.	Ninaj Raoul	1 interview	2 hours	Haitian	Black
20.	Eileen Reilly	1 interview	1 hour	American	White
21.	Guy Sansaricq	2 interviews	2 hours	Haitian	Black
22.	Andetrie Smith	1 interview	1 hour	American	Black
23.	Mario Toussaint	2 interviews	2 hours	Haitian	Black
24.	Guy Victor	1 interview	1 hour	Haitian	Black
25.	Betty Williams	1 interview	2 hours	American	White
26.	Mike Wischnie	1 interview	1 hour	American	White

---

26   interviewees,   38 interviews, ca. 49 hours,   15 Haitian/Black
                                                    9 American/White
                                                    2 American/Black

1 hour = ca. 12 pages of text (verbatim transcript of interview with Bill Frelick)
->   49 hours = ca. 588 pages (+ 180 pages = ca. 768 pages)

- In addition, I conducted a couple of telephone interviews during my research stay as indicated in the text. Moreover, I met Emile Milne, Congressman Rangel´s Legislative Director, a couple of times during my research stay. I conducted a few telephone interviews with him after returning to Munich.
Statements made in the interviews are referred to in the text as "(informant year)":
(McCalla 1995) or (Victor 1996) or (Pierre-Louis 1997) etc.

Chronology and Events Statitsics: September 1994 - July 1995
Chronology

Date:	Time/Times:	Event:	Informant (Org.):	Proof:
01: 09.05.94	6 hours	West Indian American Day Parade, Carnival	participants	photos, material
02: 09.18.94	2 h../7 times until 03/95	*Eglise de Dieu / Church of God, Inc.*	parishioners	notes
03: 10.08.94	continuously 10/94-07/95	Living with a Haitian family	family Loueur; room mates	notes, photos
04: 10.14.94	1 hour	Celebration at *Désir's Office*/Aritside-return	participants	notes
05: 10.15.94	7 hours	Celebration at *Désir's Office*/Aritside-return	participants	photos, notes
06: 11.03.94	2 hours	*Brooklyn for Aritside*-meeting	members	tape, material
07: 11.12.94	4 hours	SuGTV `Washingtonia´ -Heimatabend"	Alpine Dancers	notes, material
08: 11.30.94	2 hours	Latin American and Caribbean Conference, *York-College* / Jamaica	participants	tape
09: 12.03.94	3 hours	Aritside-dinner, *Ethical Culture Society*	Major R. Owens, Michelle Karshan	tape, notes
10: 03.05.95	2 h./5 times	Haitian disco theque *4D*	landlord,	notes, guests
11: 04.09.95	2 hours	"How Can We Live Together?", *Hunter-College*	Aphaly Coradin	tape, material
12: 04.30.95	1 hour	"Pierre Toussaint," *St. Jerome Church*	Guy Sansaricq	tape, material
13: 05.08.95	1 hour	Presentation at *Hunter-College*	Aphaly Coradin	notes
14: 05.10.95	3 hours	Subcommittee on Immigration Hearing	wittnesses	tape, material

15: 06.18.95	2 hours	Procession on "Corpus Chritsi"	Guy Sansaricq	photos, material
16: 06.20.95	1 hour	Meeting, *Soc. Science Research Council*	Josh DeWind	notes
17: 06.29.95	2 hours	Immigration Seminar, *Russel Sage Found.*	Frank Scharry, Alex Stepick	tape
18: 07.04.95	1 hour	Haitian concert on Empire Boulevard	Jocelyne Mayas	photos
19: 07.07.95	1 hour	H.E.A.R.-meeting	members	notes
20: 07.09.95	3 hours	Haitian concert, "Summer Stage"	Boukman Eksperyans	photos, CD
21: 07.14.95	3 hours	NCHR-Board of Directors meeting	members, staff	notes, material

---

Statitsics

Sept. 1994 - July 1995	total of ca. 70 h.	21 different events, including 3 social situations	score of various informants	7 events on tape: ca. 15 h.

1 hour = ca. 12 pages (transcript of interview with Bill Frelick)
-> 15 hours = ca. 180 pages (+ 588 pages = ca. 768 pages)

Example of Abstract of *New York Times*-Article Prepared by *Proquest*

Access No: 01444772 ProQuest - Newspaper Abstracts
Title: Haiti's Military Assumes Power after Troops Arrest the President
Source: New York Times (NYT) ISSN: 0362-4331
    Date: Oct 1, 1991 Sec: A p: 1 col: 1
    Type: News Length: Long Illus: Photograph
Names: Aritside, Jean-Bertrand; Cedras, Raoul
Subjects: Coups d etat; Armed forces; Haiti

Abstract: Haitian Brigadier General Raul Cedras announced on Sep 30, 1991 that the military had ousted President Jean-Bertrand Aritside, the country's first freely elected leader. Diplomats said that Aritside flew safely out of the country.

Access No: 02356667 ProQuest - Newspaper Abstracts
Title: Haitian refugees find welcome wears thin
Authors: Pierre-Pierre, Garry
Source: The New York Times [NYT] ISSN: 0362-4331
    Date: Mar 6, 1993 Sec: A p: 26 col: 1
    Type: News Length: Long Illus: Photograph
Geo Places: New York City New York; Haiti
Subjects: Refugees; Aliens; Social conditions & trends

Abstract: The unsure fate of many Haitian refugees in New York City who are finding that their relatives and friends are unable or unwilling to further support them is discussed.

Access No: 03198113 ProQuest - Newspaper Abstracts
Title: Aritside, in a joyful return, urges reconciliation in Haiti
Authors: Kifner, John
Source: The New York Times [NYT] ISSN: 0362-4331
    Date: Oct 16, 1994 Sec: 1 p: 1 col: 6
    Type: News Length: Long Illus: Photograph; Map
Names: Aritside, Jean-Bertrand; Duvalier, Francois (Papa Doc) (1907-71)
Geo Places: Haiti
Subjects: Exile; Leadership

Abstract: Haitian President Jean-Bertrand Aritside returned to Haiti on Oct 15, 1994, touting his message of reconciliation without violence or vengeance. Following three harsh years of military rule, most Haitian citizens spent the day celebrating Aritside's return and the formal end to the system that has exitsed in Haiti since the Duvalier family dictatorship took power in the 1950s. A chronology of Haiti's recent hitsory is provided.

Statitsics of NYT-articles: Period from October 1, 1991 until October 16, 1994
in **bold**: highest score of articles source: *Proquest* NYT-abstracts
in *italics*: lowest score of articles article average = 27.7/month

Article #	Month	Score	on: refugees	10e in US	advocacy commuity	in analysis 1	Major events during the Haitian crisis
1994							
1,011.	Oct	77	3	5	2	34	Aristide´s return Haiti
934.	Sep	**169**	3	3	1	**83**	US-led intervention
765.	Aug	39	6	1	*0*	21	NCHR-rep 8, UNvote
726.	Jul	*12*	4	*0*	*0*	*6*	NCHR-rep 7
714.	Jun	47	15	1	*0*	37	Guantanamo reopened
667.	May	47	**16**	1	3	30	Clinton´s policy shift
620.	Apr	23	6	*0*	**5**	12	NCHR-rep 6,USHIA, Robinson´s fast
597.	Mar	*12*	*1*	2	*0*	*6*	
585.	Feb	18	4	*0*	*0*	13	
567.	Jan	17	3	1	*0*	11	Miami-conference
	sum:	461	61	14	11	253	
	=	100%	13%	3%	2.4%	55%	
	of 1011	45.6%					
1993							
550.	Dec	29	7	0	1	19	
521.	Nov	30	*0*	1	1	17	
491.	Oct	**88**	3	1	0	**55**	Aris.´s failed return
403.	Sep	18	1	0	0	13	NCHR-rep 5
385.	Aug	9	0	0	0	5	Malval-cabinet
376.	Jul	27	1	2	1	14	GIA signed
349.	Jun	35	**14**	3	3	21	Gov. Is., USSC-decis.
314.	May	*8*	1	1	0	5	
306.	Apr	20	3	1	2	13	
286.	Mar	21	7	1	1	10	Jdg Johnson´s decis.
265.	Feb	19	8	0	1	*3*	NCHR-rep 4
246.	Jan	20	10	0	3	11	Clinton continues Bush-policy
	sum:	324	55	10	13	186	
	=	100%	17%	3.1%	3.7%	57%	
	of 1011	32.1%					

Article #	Month	Score	on: refugees	10e in US	advocacy community	in analysis 1	Major events during the Haitian crisis
1992							
226.	Dec	4	3	0	0	3	transition team neg.
222.	Nov	9	8	0	1	2	Clinton´s elect. vict.
213.	Oct	*4*	3	1	0	2	
209.	Sep	10	*1*	0	0	6	NAACP/*TransAfrica*
199.	Aug	10	7	0	0	2	
189.	Jul	7	5	0	0	5	Democ. Convention
182.	Jun	12	4	0	**2**	6	NCHR-rep 3
170.	May	23	**17**	1	1	13	Bush´s exec. order
147.	Apr	8	*1*	1	1	5	
139.	Mar	11	3	0	**2**	4	
128.	Feb	**32**	20	1	0	**19**	House-vote, embargo, Washington accord
96.	Jan	14	2	0	0	9	
	sum:	144	74	4	7	76	
	=	100%	51%	2.1%?	4.9%	53%	
	of 1011	14.2%					
1991							
82.	Dec	*24*	**18**	*0*	**3**	15	NCHR-rep 2
58.	Nov	25	12	*0*	1	20	NCHR-rep 1, Guant.
33.	Oct	**33**	*0*	**3**	*0*	19	Haitian mass protests
-1.	Sep		1			*1*	Aritside´s ouster
	sum:	82	30	3	4	54	
	=	100%	37%	3.7%	4.9%	66%	
	of 1011	8.1%					
	totals:						
		1011	216	31	35	570	(= 56.4 % of 1,011
	=	100%	22 %	3.1%	3.5%	100%	

Statitsics of NYT-articles: Period from October 1, 1991 until October 16, 1994

in **bold**: highest score of articles source: *Proquest* NYT-abstracts
in *italics*: lowest score of articles article average = 27.7/month

Article #	Month	Score	on: refugees	editorials (on refug.)	USCG interceptions		Major events during the Haitian crisis
1994							
1,011.	Oct	77	3	4	22		Aristide's return Haiti
934.	Sep	**169**	3	**6**	131		US-led intervention
765.	Aug	39	6	*0*	1,345		NCHR-rep 8, UNvote
726.	Jul	*12*	4	1(R)	**16,086**		NCHR-rep 7
714.	Jun	47	15	2	5,603		Guantanamo reopened
667.	May	47	**16**	3(R)	1,451		Clinton's policy shift
620.	Apr	23	6	1(R)	613		NCHR-rep 6, USHIA, Robinson's fast
597.	Mar	*12*	*1*	1	274		
585.	Feb	18	4	1	345		
567.	Jan	17	3	1	63		Miami-conference
	sum:	461	61	21(3)	24,933	(yearly	total = 25,059)
	=	100%	13%	(14%)	37.1%		
	of 1011	45.6%					
1993							
550.	Dec	29	7	3(2R)	226		
521.	Nov	30	*0*	1	60		
491.	Oct	**88**	3	**4**	95		Aris.'s failed return
403.	Sep	18	1	1	371		NCHR-rep 5
385.	Aug	9	0	*0*	77		Malval-cabinet
376.	Jul	27	1	1	91		GIA signed
349.	Jun	35	**14**	3(1R)	109		Gov. Is., USSC-decis.
314.	May	*8*	1	*0*	1		
306.	Apr	20	3	*0*	*0*		
286.	Mar	21	7	2(1R)	11		Jdg Johnson's decis.
265.	Feb	19	8	1(R)	9		NCHR-rep 4
246.	Jan	20	10	1(R)	**1,354**		Clinton continues Bush-policy
	sum:	324	55	17(6)	2,404		
	=	100%	17%	(35%)	3.6%		
	of 1011	32.1%					

Article #	Month	Score	on: refugees	editorials (on refug.)	USCG interceptions		Major events during the Haitian crisis
1992							
226.	Dec	4	3	0	490		transition team neg.
222.	Nov	9	8	1(R)	1,016		Clinton's elect. vict.
213.	Oct	*4*	3	1(R)	737		
209.	Sep	10	*1*	1	*141*		NAACP/*TransAfrica*
199.	Aug	10	7	2(2R)	246		
189.	Jul	7	5	2(2R)	150		Democ. Convention
182.	Jun	12	4	1(R)	366		NCHR-rep 3
170.	May	23	**17**	2(1R)	**13,103**		Bush's exec. order
147.	Apr	8	*1*	*0*	6,158		
139.	Mar	11	3	*0*	1,141		
128.	Feb	**32**	20	5(2R)	1,223		House-vote, embargo, Washington accord
96.	Jan	14	2	2	6,663		
	sum:	144	74	17(10)	31,434		
	=	100%	51%	(59%)	46.8%		
	of 1011	14.2%					
1991							
82.	Dec	*24*	**18**	0	2,336		NCHR-rep 2
58.	Nov	25	12	1(R)	**6,023**		NCHR-rep 1, Guant.
33.	Oct	**33**	*0*	**2**	*68*		Haitian mass protests
-1.	Sep						Aritside's ouster
	sum:	82	30	3(1)	8,427	(yearly	total = 10,087)
	=	100%	37%	(33%)	12.5%		
	of 1011	8.1%			(84% of 91	-total)	
	totals:						
		1011	216	58(20)	67,198		
	=	100%	22 %	(35%)	100%		
					(68,984 from	91-94	[USCC/5-31-95])
					(-68,588 [USS	CR/95]	= 396 difference)

Haitian Refugees Crisis 1991-1994: Coverage by New York Times

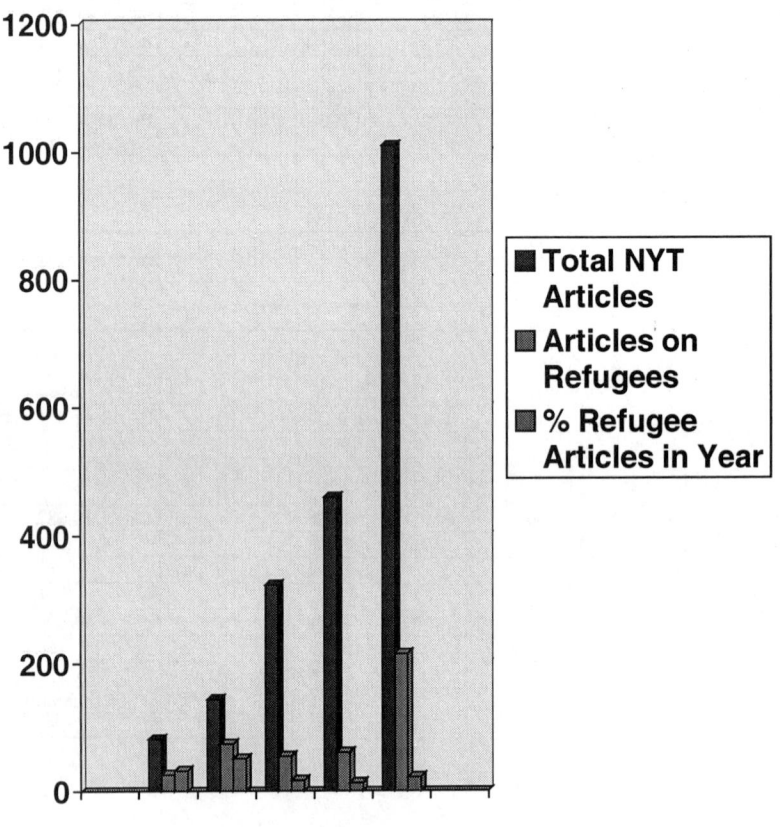

1991 | 1992 | 1993 | 1994 | 91-94

Statitsics of *Haiti Progrès*-Articles Included in the Pool as Basis for the Study
(320 of 331 articles including announcements in lits, articles on refugees in brackets)

Septembre 1991	9	(0)
Octobre 1991	23	(1)
Novembre 1991	22	(2)
Décembre 1991	8	(3)
	62	(6 = 9.7%)
Janvier 1992	8	(3)
Février 1992	16	(8)
Mars 1992	13	(5)
Avril 1992	13	(5)
Mai 1992	12	(4)
Juin 1992	5	(1)
Juillet 1992	5	(2)
Août 1992	2	(2)
Septembre 1992	12	(2)
Octobre 1992	4	(1)
Novembre 1992	7	(3)
Decembre 1992	8	(3)
	105	(39 = 37.1%)
Janvier 1993	9	(3)
Février 1993	8	(1)
Mars 1993	16	(8)
Avril 1993	9	(2)
Mai 1993	1	(0)
Juin 1993	0	
Juillet 1993	0	
Août 1993	0	
Septembre 1993	0	
Octobre 1993	0	
Novembre 1993	0	
Décembre 1993	6	(1)
	49	(15 = 30.6%)
Janvier 1994	10	(2)
Février 1994	5	(3)
Mars 1994	6	(0)
Avril 1994	10	(4)
Mai 1994	9	(4)
Juin 1994	16	(3)
Juillet 1994	14	(4)
Août 1994	17	(11)
Septembre 1994	16	(4)
Octobre 1994	1	(0)
	104	(35 = 33.7%)

1991: 62 + 1992: 105 + 1993: 49 + 1994: 104 = 320 (95) => 29.7%

Questionnaire for interview with Jocelyn McCalla/NCHR on February 15, 1995

Questions pertaining to particulars of person:

- How old are you?
- What is your nationality?
- When did you come to the U.S.?
- When and how did you get to work for NCHR?
- What is your professional background?
- What is a "normal" day as NCHR executive director like?

Questions pertaining to NCHR as an organization:

hitsory:
- Tell me a bit about the formation of NCHR
- When did the process start?
- Who initiated the formation?
- What were the immediate causes that triggered the formation?
- What is the hitsory of NCHR ever since?
- How would you characterize NCHR, what kind of an organization is NCHR, what are the "ditsinguishing marks" of NCHR?
  (Is it formal or informal, ad hoc or permanent, national or local, large or small?
- Would you consider NCHR to be effectively staffed, well-equipped, and ably led?
- Would you consider NCHR to be an authentic "Haitian" organization? What are the reasons for your answer?
- Where exactly would you place the location of NCHR on a vertical scale ranging from the individual to the government?

staff:
- How many staff members does NCHR have?
- What are their names and their various functions?
- What are their nationalities or ethnic origins?
- What age-group or generation do they belong to?
- How many staff members are employees and how many are volunteers?
- How many staff members work full-time and how many work part-time?
- What are their professional, educational and class backgrounds?
- Where has NCHR recruited its staff members from?
- Where do the staff members come from? Do they live in New York?

structure of NCHR:
- The NCHR human rights reports refer to 47 organizations as NCHR members, but the NCHR letter head litss only 28 groups. What are all the missing 19 groups?

- NCHR´s board of directors is composed of the executive committee and the members. What are the statutatory rights and duties of both the executive committee and the various members?

- Who are you as executive director accountable to? Who do you answer/report to?

- NCHR is a tax-exempt, non-profit organization which depends on private contributions. What are all the sources that provide funding for NCHR?

- Are their any other NCHR offices outside of New York or abroad, e.g. in Haiti?
- Who are the staff members that work in these offices?

Questions pertaining to relationship with Haitian community:

- How would you assess the degree of homogeneity of the Haitian community? Is there any evidence that Haiti's social duality Michel-Rolph Trouillot referred to (1990:60) is reproduced in the U.S.?

- Do you consider the Haitian community unified enough for NCHR to take advantage of its backing and its consensus? (intragroup unity)

- Has NCHR enjoyed rank-and-file support within the Haitian community, or was it not indispensable? What indicators do you have to measure this support?

- Is it your experience that foreign policy issues have been more inclined than most U.S. domestic issues to draw together diverse elements in the Haitian community?

- How wide has the range of efforts within the Haitian community been with regards to the Haitian refugee crisis? What are the most important organizations?

- What groups within the Haitian community would you designate as old institutions and what groups as newer organizations? Has the political crisis of Haiti triggerd the formation of new organizations?

- What were all the channels through which knowledge of governmental activities could be provided to the Haitian community? In other words, how did policymakers have their views become known, i.e. how did the Haitian community receive information on thoughts and activities of officials ?

- Do you think that NCHR also performs what has been called an "educative role" (Paul Y. Watanabe) vis-a-vis the Haitian community? How do you perform this role?

- In general, what ethnic groups and organizations would you categorize as opponents of NCHR and of the Haitian community?

- Have there been rivalries in foreign policy between the Haitian community and other ethnic groups (Cubans, other groups) which minimized the impact of NCHR?

Questions pertaining to lobbying:

- How has NCHR justified its lobbying activities in general, what are all the sources of legitimacy NCHR used in its organizing efforts?

- What are all the channels NCHR used to affect U.S. foreign policy? For example, who exactly has NCHR tried to reach by means of the 8 human rights reports published since the coup?

- Were among these
  - linkages to the general public within the U.S. (and indirectly to various governments),
  - linkages to the U.S. government (Congress, executive etc.),
  - linkages to the Aritside exile government (and indirectly to various governments),
  - linkages to the de facto regime in Haiti (and indirectly to various governments) ?
  - linkages to "foreign" groups, i.e. outside of US (in Haiti etc.)

- What are all the forms of group influence NCHR applied?

- Were among these
  - promoting or suppressing foreign events and problems (external environment)
  - serving as source of information (communication)
  - affecting the official definition of the problem (transforming final choice)
  - vetoing or supporting official choices
  - facilitating or obstructing the implementation of policies
  - promoting or modifying the intended effect of decisions

- It is said that ethnic American organizations have been regarded as little more than the extension of foreign governments (Watanabe, Paul Y. 1984:18): Has NCHR perceived itself as mere extension of the Aritside government? How would you characterize the relationship NCHR has had with President Aritside?

- Has NCHR only protested against and demonstrated mere opposition towards given policy measures or has it rather recommended alternative policies? In other words, was it more engaged in defensive lobbying or more in offensive lobbying?

- Has NCHR benefited from the ongoing struggle between the President and Congress over the ditsribution of power in the area of foreign policy? And if so, can you give me some examples?

- Which branch of government was better suited in concentrating NCHR´s lobbying efforts? What are the advantages of either one?

- What are the reasons for the fact that NCHR focused (primarily) on Congress? In other words, what are the characteritsics of Congress NCHR took advantage of? (representativeness and accessibility. receptivity, requirements of advocacy, disagreement with presidential policies, pronounced activits inclinations by key sectors of Congress etc.)

- Who are the members of Congress NCHR has primarily depended on for policy input? How did NCHR gain access to them?

- What do you think have the policymakers, you have been in touch with, been motivated by in cooperating with you?

- Do you think they were also motivated by a feeling of kinship and heightened ethnic or racial consciousness?

- Were the congressmen you have been in touch with moved by political calculations that suggest electoral support as a reward (i.e. by future assitsance at polls) for backing pieces of Haiti-related legislation?
(- What do you think were the results of the congressmen's assessment of potential loss and gain in terms of electoral support as lure or electoral punishment as threat)

- Did NCHR utilize money as political commodity in the form of campaign contributions as many Political Action Committees (PACs) do?

- Did NCHR utilize other resources such as professional staff or personpower, organizational expertise, and visibility or other tangible assitsance?

- Has NCHR's contact with Congress primarily been through the given members or through congressional personnel, and if yes why has this been so?

- How did NCHR perform what has been called the "intelligence function" (Paul Y. Watanabe) of ethnic groups? In other words, what were the major fields NCHR focused primarily on in its surveillance of developments?
(in the U.S. or abroad, in or outside of Washington, in or outside of the Haitian community)

- What were all the ways of communicating information, what were all the vehicles of conveying messages ?
(- Were among these also letters, telegrams, speeches, reports, documents, newsletters, hearing testimony, telephone calls, meetings, demonstrations, and personal visits?)

- How did NCHR perform what has been called the "educative role" (Paul Y. Watanabe), i.e. supplying documents, reports, speeches, and other kinds of information?

- Did this role result in the actual wording of resolutions and legislative proposals, and was it successful in countering the preponderance of executive branch information ?

- Did advocacy on behalf of the Haitian refugees require NCHR's organizing activities to be even more directly focused upon policymakers and officials rather than on intermediaries or on the shaping of broad public opinion ?

- Did these other resources compensate for some deficiencies in the Haitian community's inventory of resources?

- How important was what has been called "partial analysis" (Paul Y. Watanabe) to NCHR, i.e. the technique whereby to influence policymakers through persuasion ?

- How successful has NCHR been in demonstrating the compatibility of the various policymaker's perception of the national interest and the views of the Haitian community ?

- How important was the Congressional Black Caucus in NCHR's lobbying efforts? And how effective was the CBC in your view?

- What characteritsics of NCHR´s efforts enhanced its reputation and influenced policymakers´ assessments best ?
(- Was among these insightful, original, and credible information, accuracy, expertise, and political clout?)

- Have the activities of NCHR also been encouraged, to a certain extent, by policymakers in exchange for providing certain services such as information, political support, or support for legislative initiatives etc.?

- Is the span of influence of NCHR limited to the area of its special policy interest only, or does your organization have influence beyond this area ?

- Would you agree with the assertion that there is more evidence of the ineffectiveness of NCHR in the field of foreign policy than there are signs of direct or positive influence ?

- In hindsight, have you and NCHR been able to influence favorably officials´ perceptions of both the role of ethnic groups in the policymaking system and the substance of ethnic group communications as sound or legitimate or politically relevant ?

Questions pertaining to coalition-building:

- In general, how important was building support for NCHR?

- What are the most important nongovernmental groups and individuals NCHR has been allied with (business, trade, labor, public interest, and ethnic) ?

- What is the range of interest groups that performed as intermediaries (USCR, TransAfrica etc.)?

- How would you describe the forms of relationships among the organizations your organization cooperated with:
((Are they rather loose and collaborative arrangements (autonomy of various groups intact), are they rather formally structured arrangements of an umbrella-type institution ("organization of organizations"), or are they arrangements that combine the first two arrangements (formal structure, act in the name of individual groups))

- Has there been competition among NCHR and other organizations arising from opposing goals, opinions, and methods ?

- What are all the kinds of problems your organization encountered in building support? (problems of coordination, duplication, and competition, problems arising from those associations deemed outside the relative consensus ?)

- The NYT (2/20/95:A10) reported that the NAACP, "peppered with charges" of "financial mismanagement and sexual harassment and discrimination," "has spent a wrenching year fighting ideological wars over Mr. Chavis´s efforts to forge links with the Nation of Islam and its fiery leader, Louis Farrakhan."

- Has the condition of the NAACP, being a member of NCHR, had any effect on NCHR´s organizing efforts and its coalition composed of Jewish groups as well?

- How would you assess the effectiveness of Mr. Randall Robinson and TransAfrica in the organizing efforts of the Black community of the U.S. ?

- TransAfrica has been described as a type of organization which is supported by full-time, professional staffs, carrying the official status as lobbyitss, and maintaining offices in Washington, D.C.
    How does your organization compare to this type ?
    What has been NCHR´s relationship with TransAfrica like ?
    What other organizations come to your mind that fit this description ?

- Would you agree with what has been said by Herschelle Sullivan Challenor, namely that TransAfrica is clearly recognized as the key institutional voice in the black community on foreign affairs ?

- In which regard and to what extent did the interests of NCHR coincide with those of the groups you cooperated with? What were the common denominators?

- Was the purpose of a mutually advantageous combination of resources resulting in augmented power important in cooperating with the other groups ?

- Would you agree that your organization was most effective when maintaining and assitsing supporters and uncommitted policymakers rather than to wooing opponents ?

- Influence is said to be augmented, among other things, by concentration of ethnic group members in certain political jurisdictions. Do Haitians in the U.S. have influence in important sectors of the American society such as labor unions, church, media, intellectual or banking circles etc.? How important was this factor for NCHR?

- Has the "All American Council," which is the nationalities division of the Democratic National Committee (DNC), sought the support of Haitians and the NCHR in the U.S. during the Presidential campaign of 1992 ?

Questions pertaining to political issues:

- What has been the overall national interest of the U.S. in its foreign policy vis-á-vis Haiti, has it been economic, strategic, political etc. ?
- Has ethnic activism of Haitians living in the U.S. generally been an obstacle to pursuing this national interest ?

- Who was the first to react to the coup d´etat in Haiti? The Haitians in the United States, the OAS/UN, or the US-government? Was your organization among these Haitians ?

- Which nations, groups, or personalities, acting shortly before and after the coup d´etat, stired the indignation of NCHR in particular ?

Questions pertaining to nation, race, ethnicity etc.:

- Have you, NCHR or the Haitian community had any example or model you emulated when you started to organize in 1982 ? (African Americans, Jewish Americans or others)

- Interest groups have been divided into "tangible" interest groups, on the one hand, with interests and goals like economic or financial benefit or security of life and property and, on the other hand, "intangible" interest groups with interests in symbols, symbolic reassurance like ethnic unions etc. (Chiodzie F. Ogene 1983:224): Does this differentiation make sense with regards to NCHR ?

- In other words, have NCHR´s organizing activities been driven by common, primarily material, interests or by an affective tie springing from emotional needs ?

- How would you assess what has been called the "paradoxical ability" (Mohammed E. Ahrari): In other words, has the Haitian community and your organization been successful in assimilating into the U.S. culture while retaining enough ethnic identification to pursue foreign policy objectives affecting Haiti ?

- Or do the organizing efforts of the Haitian community more represent what has been called "rejection in participation" (Michael Parenti) ?

- Assuming that black Americans as "racial" hyphenates as opposed to "ethnic" hyphenates have low influence on U.S. foreign policy, what factors are in your mind responsible for that?
- Are among these   - the absence of black political power hitsorically,
                     - the low esteem accorded blacks,
                     - the official attempts to discourage close links between
                       Africans (and Caribbeans) and African Americans ?

- Do Haitians in the U.S. constitute an electoral voting bloc ? Who do they usually vote for and why ?

- Do you think that the Haitian refugee crisis would have unfolded in a different way had it not occured after the end of the Cold War, the issues of which tended to be universal and ideological rather than ethnic and racial ?

- How would you define "equality" ?
- Does it have primarily to do with material justice ?
- Does it also mean the right to be different in language, customs, and habits

- Do you agree with the assertion that the relative political and cultural clout of White Anglo-Saxon Protestants is and will further be diminished ?
- In other words, do you agree that the rise of ethnicity is in inverse proportion to the decline of white Anglo-Saxon Protestantism?

- Do you agree that Haiti had been anathema to most American black citizens because of its dictatorial regimes and despite its being a black republic ?

- Do you think that the overall political impact of the Haitian community tends to be weakened by the maintenance of dual cultures, that a large amount of ethnic politics is drained off in maintaining loyalties rather than extending to the policy-making arena ?

- How do you define a nation, what are all the components that constitute a nation ?
- Are among these language, territoriality, economic unity, and culture (Stalin) ?

- Do you think that ethnicity is a centripetal force forging an American consensus rather than a centrifugal force eroding that consensus ?

- How do you define an ethnic group, what are all the components that constitute an ethnic group ?
- Are among these language, territoriality, economic unity, and culture, i.e. the same components that constitute a nation ?

- What are all the elements that make Haitians in the United States different from other groups in this country?

- Do you think that the majority of Americans have shared a positive attitude to the activities of NCHR and other Haitians or have they been opposed to this activism ?

- Would you agree that your organization helped enhance both: ditsinctly ethnic aspects of Haitians in the U.S. on the one hand, and the realization of rights and performance of responsibilities that are theirs as Americans on the other hand ?

- Do you think that NCHR also serves the purpose of helping the Haitian community maintain identification and attachment with its homeland and ethnic heritage?

- Does your organization have more effect on foreign policy or on domestic policy ?

- Would you also view NCHR as an effective instrument for instructing about U.S. governmental processes and about the culture of the larger American society ?

Questionnaire for interview with Ronald Aubourg/HCC on September 19, 1996

1.) What do you think has been the overall national interest of the U.S. in its foreign policy vis-á-vis Haiti?

2.a) In general, how do you explain the fact that President Aritside could ultimately return to Haiti ? Whose success is this? What are all the factors that made it possible, and how would you put these factors into a hierarchical order ?

2.b) It is said that there have been two different strategies within the Haitian community with regard to the Haitian political and refugee crises: the one prioritized focusing on Pres. Aritside´s return, the other prioritized focusing on the refugees:

a) the majority is said to have tried to end both crises by winning the support of the U.S. government for the return of President Aritside while not focusing on the harsh refugee policy of the U.S. (emphasis on the return issue)

b) the minority is said to have tried to end the refugee crisis by exactly pressuring the U.S. government in face of its harsh refugee policy and thereby also winning its support for the ultimate return of President Aritside (emphasis of refugee issue)

Do you agree with this reading of reality? Which side were you personally on? Which side was NCHR on? Which side was the Haitian Centers Council on? Which side was the Emergency Coalition for Haitian Refugees (ECHR) on? What role did they play? Do you remember the names of the groups associated under ECHR?

3.) Do you agree with the assertion that there has been a lack of sympathy, of interest, and of support by the Haitian community in the U.S. toward Haitian refugees?

4.) It is said that there are certain reasons for this lack of sympathy, interest, and support toward Haitian refugees. About nine reasons were mentioned for that. Do you agree with the following lits of reasons? Which ones are right, which ones are wrong? Would you add other reasons? How would you put these into a hierarchical order?

a) the immense popularity of President Aritside with the majority of Haitians in the U.S., who follow him like "sheep," eclipsed the plight of the refugees because President Aritside himself prioritized the issue of his own return to Haiti

b) many Haitians in the U.S. buy into the negative perception of Haitian refugees in the general U.S. public (media image) as Black, poor, illiterate and disease-ridden

c) there is no disapproval of those prejudices in the U.S. as a racits society despite propagated ideals of equality; this even applied to African-Americans

d) the Haitian community did not want to be associated with Haitian refugees portrayed as HIV-carriers because of the AIDS-stigma inflicted on them (CDC, FDA)

e) Haitian socio-economic class differences alienated the political elite (middle and upper class professionals) from the refugees (uneducated Haitian-Creole speaking Haitians from lower social classes and rural backgrounds)

f) Haitians in the U.S. are so integrated into American society that Haitian refugees appear as strangers rather than co-nationals or peers

g) the legal aspects of the refugee issue (e.g. HCC vs. McNary) are so complicated for most Haitians that they shy away from the issue

h) Haitians in the U.S. don´t know how to lobby Congress, they can only take to the streets in great numbers, they cannot play "hard ball" nor "soft ball"

i) there is a lack of resources and man power within the Haitian community that hindered Haitians in the U.S. to assits Haitian refugees (resettlement)

5.) What are all the "push factors" that motivated Haitians to flee their country before and after the coup d´etat in 1991? How would you put these factors into a hierarchical order?

6.) What are all the "pull factors" that attract Haitian refugees to the U.S.? How would you put these factors into a hierarchical order?

7.) What factors explain the fact that the asylum approval rate for Haitian nationals has lagged far behind the world-wide average? Why are Haitian refugees not welcomed in the U.S.? How would you put these factors into a hierarchical order?

8.) What, in your opinion, is more important: Liberty or Equality? And how would you define both?

Lits of Members of National Coalition for Haitian Refugees´ Board of Directors
(based on a document given to author by Aphaly Coradin on February 9, 1995, * = supplemented by NCHR letter head of May 18, 1994)

Name: Position: Organization:
(44 in alphabetical order)

Executive Committee

Name	Position	Organization
Bevilacqua, Anthony Cardinal	Chairman	Archdiocese of Philadelphia
*Bellor, Kay		*Church World Service*, CWS
Chishti, Muzaffar Esq.	Secretary-Treasurer	*International Ladies Garment Workers Union*, ILGWU Immigration Project
Dewind, Josh Ph.D.		*Hunter College*
Ferris, Elizabeth G.		*Church World Service*, CWS
Gollobin, Ira Esq.	Acting Vice Chairman	*Nattional Emergency Civil Liberties Commission*, NECLC
Henderson, Wade	Vice Chairman	*National Association for the Advancement of Colored People*, NAACP (D.C. chapter)
Pillors, Brenda		aide to Hon. Edolphus Towns
Roth, Kenneth Esq.		*Human Rights Watch*, HRW
*Rubin, Gary		*American Jewish Committee*, AJC
Rev. Sansaricq, Guy		*Haitian Apostolate, St. Jerome Church*

Members

Name	Organization
*Rev. Adrien, Antoine	Haitian priest
*Cooley-Prost, Worth	*Washington Office on Haiti*, WOH
Deffenbaugh, Ralston H. Jr.	*Lutheran Immigration and Refugee Service*, LIRS

Demme, Jonathan	film director, *Clinica Estetico*
DeVecchi, Robert	*Int. Rescue Committee*, IRC
*Dorancy, Rolande	*Haitian Refugee Center*, HRC
Dorsinville, Paul	*Haitian Americans United for Progress*, HAUP
*Ferere, Gerard	*Coalition for Haitian Concerns*, CHC
Frank, Henri	*Haitian Centers Council*, HCC
*Guerrero, Reynaldo R.	*Center for Immigrants Rights*, CIR
Hill, Norman	*A. Phillip Randolph Institute*, APRI
*Hooks, Benjamin	*National Association for the Advancement of Colored People*, NAACP
Kirkland, Lane	*American Federation of Labor - Congress of Industrial Organizations*, AFL-CIO
*Klein, Wells	*American Council for Nattionalities Service*, ACNS
Kurzban, Ira Esq. Counsel	attorney of HRC
Mark, Deborah	*Hebrew Immigrant Aid Society*, HIAS
Mazur, Jay	*International Ladies Garment Workers Union*, ILGWU
*Most Rev. McCarthy, Edward A.	Archbishop of Miami
*Rabbi Michelman, Henri D.	*Synagogue Council of America*
Miller, Lenore	*Jewish Labor Committee*, JLC
*Rt. Rev. Moore Jr., Paul	(New York)
Munoz, Cecilia	*National Council of La Raza*, NCLR
*Neagle, Walter	*Bayard Rustin Fund*, BRF

* O'Neill, William	*Lawyers Committee for Human Rights*, LCHR
*Rev. Ryscavage, Richard	*United States Catholic Conference*, USCC
Saxon, Edward	film director
St. Cyr, Marie	*New York City Commission on Human Rights,* NCCCHR
Stepick, Alex Ph.D.	*Florida Internatonal University*
Tomasi, Lydio	*Center for Migration Studies*
Victor, Guy	*Haitian Refugee Center*, HRC
Rev. Wenski, Thomas	*Pierre Toussaint Catholic Center*, PTCC
Wilentz, Amy	author
Winter, Roger	*Immigration and Refugee Services of America*, IRSA

13 Communication Levels, on which NCHR Exerted Influence
(- in brackets = no communication found)

Level:

1. Channels to the public via the media

2. Channels to supranational organizations

3. Channels to international non-governmental organizations

4. Channels to the Aritside (exile) government

5. Channels to the Haitian *de facto* regime

6. Channels to "foreign" Haitian groups in Haiti

7. Channels to the executive branch of the US government (departments, agencies)

8. Channels to the US House of Representatives, legislative branch of government

9 Channels to the US Senate, legislative branch of government

10. Channels to the US judiciary system

(11. Channels to the State of New York)

12. Channels to the New York City Government

13. Channels to "domestic" groups within the US

14. Channels to Haitian "domestic" groups in the US

Haiti-Related OAS- and UN - Documents, 1991 - 1994 (chronological order)

OAS-General Assembly.
1991 "The Santiago Commitment to Democracy and the Renewal of the Inter-American System". Santiago, June 4.

AG/RES.1080: OAS-General Assembly.
1991 "Representative Democracy". AG/RES. 1080 (XXI-0/91). Santiago, June 5.

AG/RES.1103: OAS-General Assembly.
1991 "Legal Situation of Refugees, Repatriated, and Displaced Persons in the American Hemisphere". AG/RES. 1103 (XXI-0/91). Washington: June 7.

AG/RES.1117: OAS-General Assembly.
1991 "Support For the Democratic Process in the Republic of Haiti". AG/RES. 1117 (XXI-0/91). Santiago, June 8.

AG/RES.1126: OAS-General Assembly.
1991 "Cooperation Between the Organization of American States and the United Nations". AG/RES. 1126 (XXI-0/91). Santiago, June 8.

CP/RES.567: OAS-Permanent Council.
1991 "Support to the Democratic Government of Haiti". CP/RES. 567 (870/91). Washington: September 30.

MRE/RES.1/91: OAS-Minitsers of Foreign Affairs.
1991 "Support to the Democratic Government of Haiti". Resolution MRE/RES.1/91. Washington, October 3.

MRE/RES.2/91: OAS-Minitsers of Foreign Affairs.
1991 "Support For Democracy in Haiti". Resolution MRE/RES. 2/91. Washington, October 8.

CP/RES.575: OAS-Permanent Council.
1992 "Situation in Haiti: Monitoring the Trade Embargo". CP/RES.575 (885/92). Washington: January 22.

CP/DEC.1: OAS-Permanent Council.
1992 "Declaration on the Events in Haiti". CP/DEC. 1 (886/92). Washington: January 28.

CP/DEC.2: OAS-Permanent Council.
1992 "Declaration on the Situation in Haiti". CP/DEC.2 (896/92). Washington: April 1.

MRE/RES.3/92: OAS-Minitsers of Foreign Affairs.
1992 "Restoration of Democracy in Haiti". Resolution MRE/RES. 3/92. Washington, May 7.

CP/RES.594: OAS-Permanent Council.
1992 "Reestablishment of Democracy in Haiti". CP/RES.594 (923/92). Washington: November 10.

MRE/RES.4/92: OAS-Minitsers of Foreign Affairs.
1992 "Reinstatement of Democracy in Haiti". Resolution MRE/RES. 4/92. Washington, December 13.

CP/DEC.8: OAS-Permanent Council.
1993 "Declaration Concerning the Calling of Elections to the Senate Announced by the Defacto Government of Haiti". CP/DEC. 8 (927/93). Washington: January 13.

CP/DEC.9: OAS-Permanent Council.
1993 "Declaration in the Situation in Haiti". CP/DEC. 9 (931/93). Washington: February 11.

CP/DEC.10: OAS-Permanent Council.
1993 CP/DEC. 10 (934/93). Washington: March 5.

UN/OAS-Memorandum of Understanding between the Geneeral Secretariat of the Organiza-
1993 ation of American States and the United Nations for the International Civilian Mission to Haiti, May 6.

MRE/RES.5/93: OAS-Minitsers of Foreign Affairs.
1993 "Support For the Haitian People". Resolution MRE/RES. 5/93. Washington, June 6.

CP/DEC.14: OAS-Permanent Council.
1993 CP/DEC. 14 (960/93). Washington: September 8.

CP/DEC.15: OAS-Permanent Council.
1993 "Declaration on the Situation in Haiti". CP/DEC. 15 (967/93) corr.1. Washington: October 12.

MRE/RES.6/94: OAS-Minitsers of Foreign Affairs.
1994 "Support For the Haitian People". Resolution MRE/RES. 6/94. Washington, June 9.

CP/RES.610: OAS-Permanent Council.
1993 "Situation in Haiti". CP/RES. 610 (968/93). Washington: October 18.

CP/RES. 633: OAS-Permanent Council.
1994 „Situation of the OAS/UN International Civilian Mission". CP/RES. 633 (995/94). Washington: July 11.

ARES.45/2: UN General Assembly.
1990 "Electoral Assitsance to Haiti". Resolution 45/2. New York, October 10.

ARES.46/7: UN General Assembly.
1991 "The Situation of Democracy and Human Rights in Haiti". Resolution 46/7. New York, October 11.

ARES.46/138: UN General Assembly.
1991   "Human rights in Haiti". Resolution ARES.46/138. New York, December 17.

ARES.47/20A: UN General Assembly.
1992   "The Situation of Democracy and Human Rights in Haiti". Resolution 47/20A. New York, November 24.

ESC: Economic and Social Council.
1993   "Report on the Situation of Human Rights in Haiti Submitted by Mr. Marco Tulio Bruni Celli, Special Rapporteur, in   Accordance with Commission Resolution 1992/77". New York: United Nations, February 4. 44 p.

ARES.47/20B: UN General Assembly.
1993   "The Situation of Democracy and Human Rights in Haiti". Resolution 47/20B. New York, April 20.

S/RES.841: UN Security Council.
1993   "Resolution 841". New York, June 16.

OAS-Department of Public Information..
1993   "Haiti:The Governors Island Accord". Washington: July. 4 p.

UND: UN Department of Public Information.
1993   "Crisis in Haiti: Seeking a Political Solution". United Nations Focus: Haiti. New York: United Nations, August. 7p.

S/RES.861: UN Security Council.
1993   "Resolution 861". New York, August 27.

S/RES.862: UN Security Council.
1993   "Resolution 862". New York, August 31.

S/RES.867: UN Security Council.
1993   "Resolution 867". New York, September 23.

S/RES.873: UN Security Council.
1993   "Resolution 873". New York, October 13.

S/RES.875: UN Security Council.
1993   "Resolution 875". New York, October 16.

ARES.48/27A: UN General Assembly.
1993   "The Situation of Democracy and Human Rights in Haiti". Resolution ARES.48/27A. New York, December 6.

S/RES.905: UN Security Council.
1994   "Resolution 905". New York, March 23.

S/RES.917: UN Security Council.
1994   "Resolution 917". New York, May 6.

ARES.48/246: UN General Assembly.
1994 "Finanzing of the United Nations Mission in Haiti". Resolution ARES/48/246. New York, May 11.

S/RES.933: UN Security Council.
1994 "Resolution 933". New York, June 30.

S/RES.940: UN Security Council.
1994 "Resolution 940". New York, July 31.

S/RES.944: UN Security Council.
1994 "Resolution 944". New York, September 29.

S/RES.948: UN Security Council.
1994 "Resolution 948". New York, October 15.

ARES.49/27: UN General Assembly.
1994 "The situation of democracy and human rights in Haiti". Resolution ARES.49/27. New York, December 21.

Nordamerikastudien: Münchener Beiträge zur Kultur und Gesellschaft der USA, Kanadas und der Karibik

herausgegeben von Prof. Dr. Berndt Ostendorf (Universität München)

Angelica Schwab
Serienkiller in Wirklichkeit und Film
Störenfried oder Stabilisator? Eine sozioästhetische Untersuchung
Von Caligari bis Hannibal Lecter ...
Lange Zeit standen Serienkiller als tabuisiertes Sujet am Rande des Kulturbetriebes, heute haben die zugleich barbarischen und hochzivilisierten menschlichen Killermaschinen nicht nur im Kino Hochkonjunktur: Spätestens seit dem Erfolg von *Das Schweigen der Lämmer* sind die Bilder und Geschichten über das serielle Grauen salonfähig geworden, und der Massenmörder hat sich ganz unmerklich vom kritisch beäugten Störenfried in eine postmoderne Ikone der Beliebigkeit verwandelt.
Welche gesellschaftlichen, politischen und ästhetischen Entwicklungen stehen hinter dieser "Transformation des Bösen"? Wie und weshalb haben sich die medialen Repräsentationen des Serienmörders verändert? Und weshalb läßt sich inzwischen die furchterregende Schreckensfigur in gewisser Weise gar als stabilisierendes Element interpretieren?
Durch eine synthetische Verarbeitung verschiedener Theorieansätze – der Diskursanalyse, der Filmtheorie, Systemtheorie sowie der Psychoanalyse – zeigt Angelica Schwab auf, daß Serienkiller sowohl im Film wie auch in der Realität ihre Wirkung immer auf einer politischen und ästhetischen Ebene zugleich entfalten: Die Funktionalisierung des Schreckens zum Zwecke sozialer Kontrolle kommt hierbei genauso zur Sprache wie das cineastische Spiel mit den klassischen Normen der Wahrnehmung – wobei die Bandbreite der analysierten Filme von Fritz Langs Stummfilmklassiker *M – eine Stadt sucht einen Mörder* über Tobe Hoopers *The Texas Chainsaw Massacre* bis hin zu Jonathan Demmes Kultfilm *Das Schweigen der Lämmer* reicht.
Bd. 1, 2001, 384 S., 25,90 €, br., ISBN 3-8258-4542-7

Jahrbuch Tanzforschung

publiziert im Auftrag der Gesellschaft für Tanzforschung

Sabine Karoß; Leonore Welzin (Hg.)
Tanz Politik Identität
Bd. 11, 2001, 272 S., 20,90 €, br., ISBN 3-8258-5119-2

Gabriele Klein; Christa Zipprich (Hg.)
Tanz, Theorie, Text
Körper als Zeichen – Choreographie der Bilder – Choreographie der Worte – Doing Tango – Performing Gender – Tanzkultur paradox / Verschobene Körper – Groteske Körper / Das blaue Licht / Subjekte der Fremdheit – Die Entdeckung des Nicht-Choreographierbaren – Gedächtnisraum – Das Lächeln der Theorie – Experimentelle Tanzmedien – Flüchtige Schrift – Bleibende Erinnerung – Tanz-Fiktionen – Metanarrationen / Dancing is not writing – Körper als Zeichen – Choreographie der Bilder – Choreographie der Worte – Doing Tango – Performing Gender – Tanzkultur paradox / Verschobene Körper – Groteske Körper / Das blaue Licht / Subjekte der Fremdheit – Die Entdeckung des Nicht-Choreographierbaren – Gedächtnisraum – Das Lächeln der Theorie – Experimentelle Tanzmedien – Flüchtige Schrift – Bleibende Erinnerung – Tanz-Fiktionen – Metanarrationen / Dancing is not writing
Bd. 12, 2002, 644 S., 40,90 €, br., ISBN 3-8258-5901-0

Antje Klinge; Martina Leeker (Hg.)
Tanz Kommunikation Praxis
tanz . kommunikation . praxis | Hautsache Bewegung | Moving from the skin | Körperbewegung und Tanz | Projektbericht | Zur verschlüsselten Verständigung | Let's talk about ... | Gender - Körper - Kommunikation | In-Out-In. Körper, Tanz und Medien | Praxisbericht | Performing Arts als kulturelle Praxis | Rahmen - Bewegungen - Zwischenräume | Behinderung und Tanzsprache | Postkoloniale Kommunikation | Liveness und Medialität | Maya Deren | Zeittranszendenz und Tanzfilm | Bewegte Symmetrie | Connecting Differences | tanz . kommunikation . praxis | Hautsache Bewegung | Moving from the skin | Körperbewegung und Tanz | Projektbericht | Zur verschlüsselten Verständigung | Let's talk about ... | Gender - Körper - Kommunikation | In-Out- In. Körper, Tanz und Medien | Praxisbericht | Performing Arts als kulturelle Praxis | Rahmen - Bewegungen - Zwischenräume | Behinderung und Tanzsprache | Postkoloniale Kommunikation | Liveness und Medialität | Maya Deren | Zeittranszendenz und Tanzfilm | Bewegte Symmetrie | Connecting Differences |
Bd. 13, 2003, 224 S., 19,90 €, br., ISBN 3-8258-6903-2

LIT Verlag Münster – Hamburg – Berlin – London
Grevener Str./Fresnostr. 2 48159 Münster
Tel.: 0251 – 23 50 91 – Fax: 0251 – 23 19 72
e-Mail: vertrieb@lit-verlag.de – http://www.lit-verlag.de